D0327342

INTERNATIONAL BUSINESS MANAGEMENT

Readings and Cases

INTERNATIONAL BUSINESS MANAGEMENT

Readings and Cases

JOHN S. EWING
Stanford University

FRANK MEISSNER
San Francisco State College

WADSWORTH PUBLISHING COMPANY
Belmont, California

L.C. Cat. Card No.: 63-10637

Printed in the United States of America

Preface

That Americans are deeply involved in foreign trade and international business operations is obvious when we consider the following factors: we are the world's largest importer and exporter; American businessmen invest more capital abroad than entrepreneurs of any other country; the U.S. government pours great amounts of taxpayers' money into foreign countries to help friendly nations advance economically and socially, and to strengthen their defenses against the forces of Communism; and the U.S. dollar is a key international trade currency, and a leading monetary reserve.

No wonder that in recent years a tremendous demand has been generated for the study of international operations. The number of businessmen who want to explore opportunities abroad is growing steadily. So is the number of bright young men considering a career in international business.

Yet, both practicing businessmen and ambitious students are finding that global operations are immensely perplexing. Somehow "domestic" experience and training provide only a limited background for dealing effectively with the diverse problems encountered in running international business.

This book is intended for individuals who want to learn effective ways of approaching and solving some of the main problems encountered in world business.

The political and economic surroundings within which an international business executive reaches his decisions are in constant flux. The changes occur so fast that some conventional texts are out of date before they are published. In contrast, the materials presented in this book reflect major contemporary issues; both the readings and the cases can be readily updated through supplementary articles from current periodicals.

The content is divided into two parts, readings and cases. The interrelation of the readings and cases is shown by the list on page 331. The readings aim primarily at imparting broad knowledge about the new world of international commerce that is shaping up. They serve as a reservoir of facts and ideas on the social, economic, and political environment within which the international executive operates. They explore the implications of regional free-trade areas and common markets, and present some of the problems of trade with economically less-developed nations. A number of articles discuss the structure, organization, control, management, and financing of globally operating corporations, the sources of international intelligence, and problems involved in getting along with foreigners.

The readings are divided into four separate sections. Articles in the first part attempt to provide broad background on such topics as regional cooperation, economic development, and international trade; the second section concentrates on matters pertaining to management of international business; the third focuses on finance, while the fourth section explores sources of international intelligence.

Obvious duplications in readings have been avoided. Deletions are indicated, and our own comments are clearly identified. Typographical errors have been corrected. Lengthy footnotes have usually been left out. The original titles have generally been preserved. Annotated lists of selected references follow some of the articles.

We took the readings from a wide variety of sources: testimonies before congressional committees, government documents, public speeches, articles in the daily press as well as popular periodicals and scientific journals, published reports of management consultants, financial institutions, and research organizations. We have tried to show that there is considerable diversity of opinion, and that there is always more than one solution to every business problem.

Skills of administering a business cannot be learned by merely taking courses, attending seminars, participating in workshops, listening to lectures, watching TV, or even reading books and articles. In order to become a decision-maker, one simply has to practice decision-making. This practicing can be done with the cases, a collection of actual problems that have confronted practicing executives. The cases sample such diverse international business areas as market entry and expansion; export policies, procedures and problems; international human relations; development of marketing programs abroad, and establishment and operation of international companies.

The majority of cases included in this book have been developed at the Stanford University Graduate School of Business Administration. Choice of topics and problem formulations generally reflect an American point of view. Yet, the principles involved have general application. Most problems in the area of international business operations thus cut across several departments within an organization. This relationship holds true no matter to which country or which type of enterprise the case relates.

George Bernard Shaw once waspishly commented, "If all economists were laid end to end, they still would not reach a conclusion." In March 1963, President Kennedy, speaking before the Advertising Council, confessed that he was "more than ever convinced" of the truth in Shaw's insight. Today every economic problem still "has several alternative solutions, and every answer raises several questions."

And so it is with our case problems. There is no *one* correct solution. Yet, the task of data and idea gathering is universal. The decision-maker will have to consult different fellow executives, employees, owners, customers, suppliers, facilitating agencies, competitors, governments, and the general public both at home and abroad.

The over-all philosophy reflected in all the material in this book is exceedingly simple: we believe that free competition within the framework of private-enterprise capitalism—with all its real and imagined shortcomings—is ultimately most beneficial to our type of society as well as to our type of profit-seeking entrepreneurs. We do not feel apologetic about the private-profit incentive. We cannot think of a better way for furthering the public welfare.

Our strong preference for private-enterprise capitalism does not mean that all other systems can be ignored. On the contrary, an international executive—regardless of his nationality—will inevitably have to deal with "opposite numbers" in foreign countries that have different economic systems, different ways of doing business, and different ethical standards. In order to be able to accommodate himself to those differences, the skilled businessman needs to possess a great deal of sympathy and understanding. He has to develop a keen appreciation of such "fuzzy" socio-cultural variables as status, role, norms, values, customs, habits, education, kinship systems, religious practices, mythology, and language. In the area of politico-economic structure the businessman will have to be keenly aware of the importance of differences in form of government, judicial and legal procedures, taxation, social control, enterprise system, technology, and income distribution. These cultural differences are all in addition to the more readily ascertainable differences in physical characteristics—such as topography, climate, and resource endowments—due to geographic location.

To cope with his problems, the international executive will obviously have to introduce concepts from such a closely related field as the behavioral sciences. We heartily endorse interdisciplinary borrowings. Yet, we must raise at least one flag of caution. The borrower is an outsider looking in. Complications might arise where none are apparent. "Inheritable" generalizations and techniques were probably developed to answer other problems in other contexts. Many disciplines are evolving so rapidly that they are beset with internal disagreements. There is no general consensus. Moreover, ideas must be adapted and reforged before they can be fruitfully fitted into the conceptual home of international business operations. Even so, occasionally an integrator is liable to look for ideological and theoretical help where none is to be had. In short, interdisciplinary borrowing is potentially a tremendously rewarding activity. But, like most business activities, it is very much a calculated risk.

This broad approach to the subject has made the selection job more pleasant. We were able to include articles and cases that deal with fascinating people, lands, products, customs, and problems. The book can therefore be read for fun as well as studied for profit.

In addition to being a core for one-or-two-semester case-study courses in schools of business administration, this book can also be used as an up-to-date supplement to the many excellent standard texts that are already available in the field of international economics and trade. The material is suitable for many types of instruction at many levels of sophistication. Specifically, it can be used as a workbook for courses in managerial economics, sales management, insurance, marketing research, transportation, finance, personnel, and public relations. Parts of it can also be used for *supplementary reading* to courses in social and political science, sociology, anthropology, applied statistics, and history.

The book is particularly well suited for *in-service management training programs*. Many corporations are carrying on such programs aimed at grooming future executives for work abroad or in international operations. Colleges can organize seminars for local participants from firms unable to carry out intramural programs in such a specialized field.

Picking and choosing is, of course, an exciting job, but it also involves painful decision-making, particularly in a field as abundantly written about as World Business.

We are grateful for the many ideas and suggestions received from numerous students and colleagues, and other captive audiences on whom the readings and cases were tried out. Thanks are also due to our wives and children, without whom the book would presumably have been finished a long time ago, and now be quite dated. An unqualified appreciation goes to James McDaniel, Associate Editor of the Wadsworth Publishing Company. His enthusiastic and sustained encouragement was a source of constant inspiration to us. His patience with deadline-ignoring college professors has been most admirable.

John S. Ewing—Cases
Frank Meissner—Readings and Comments

Table of Contents

Preface v

1. Direction for the West, *Barbara Ward* 1

READINGS

SECTION ONE. International Trade, Regionalism, and Economic Development 7

2. The Common Market: Implications for the United States, *Robert H. Marshall* 9
3. The Trade Expansion Act—1962, *Harry G. Brainard* 24
4. Common Market and Commonwealth, *Drew Middleton* 37
5. Dangers of Regionalism, *Jean Royer* 43
6. European Integration and the Developing Countries, *Bela Balassa* 61
7. Commodity Agreements Are *Not* the Answer, *Karl Brandt* 67
8. The Regional Approach to Economic Development, *Walter Krause* 74
9. End of the Brussels Talks 87

SECTION TWO. Management of International Business 94

10. Government and Business in International Trade, *Heinrich Kronstein* 96
11. Conflicting Interests in International Business Investment, *Richard D. Robinson* 108
12. Creating a Strategy for International Growth, *John G. McDonald and Hugh Parker* 119
13. LRP for International Operations, *John Fayerweather* 130
14. Analyzing Foreign Opportunities, *Raphael W. Hodgson and Hugo E. R. Uyterhoeven* 146
15. New Patterns for Overseas Operations, *Gilbert H. Clee and Franklin A. Lindsay* 170
16. The Future Structure of International Companies, *John O. Tomb and Donald B. Shackelford* 184
17. Measuring Executive Performance in a World Enterprise, *C. Bruce McLagan and John D. Woodthorpe* 193

SECTION THREE. Financing of International Operations 201

18. The World Bank in a Changing World, *Raymond F. Mikesell* 203
19. Financing Foreign Operations 210
20. Helping U.S. Exports Meet Credit Competition 237

SECTION FOUR. International Intelligence 245

21. Looking Around Overseas Operations, *Seymour L. Linfield* 247
22. The World Customer, *Ernest Dichter* 257
23. The Honorable Picnic: Doing Business in Japan, *Dudley L. Miller* 268
24. From the Thoughtful Businessman, *Jiro Tokuyama* 279
25. The Japanese Worker, *Arthur M. Whitehall, Jr.* 282
26. Themes and Variations, *Igor Oganesoff* 290
27. Load Too Heavy, a Fragile Woman Breaks 291
28. The American Negro's Key Role in Africa, *Joseph C. Kennedy* 292
29. An African Student Studies Us, *Amos Kiriro* 298
30. International Intelligence for the International Enterprise, *John J. Beauvois* 302
31. Public Opinion—Achilles Heel of U.S. Business Overeas? *Charles E. Allen* 312
32. Information Sources on Foreign Marketing, *John C. Abbott* 322

CASES

Introduction 329
Cases and Related Readings 331

SECTION ONE. International Market Entry and Expansion 333

1. Clean-Away Corporation: *Factors Affecting the Decision to Enter World Business* 333
2. The Okinawa Campaign (I): *Consideration of Entry into a New Foreign Market* 335
3. Thornton Machine & Manufacturing, Inc.: *Consideration of Request for Foreign Licensing and World Sales Rights* 340

SECTION TWO. International Operating Policies, Procedures, and Problems 343

4. Wellbabe Products, Inc.: *Problems of Marketing Research in a Foreign Market* 343
5. Renown Products Company (I): *Organization for Export Marketing* 347

6. Renown Products Company (II): *Export Policies* 349
7. Renown Products Company (III): *Channels of Distribution Overseas: Combination Export Managers and Independent Exporters* 350
8. Reliance Hardware Manufacturing Company: *Appointment of Overseas Agents* 352
9. Smithers Paint Company (I): *A Foreign Distributor's Request for Representation* 354
10. Household Products, Inc. (I): *Selection of an Advertising Agency for Europe* 358
11. Household Products, Inc. (II): *Advertising, Sales Promotion, and Marketing Factors to Be Considered before Entering Europe* 363
12. Burroughes Welcome Daraprim: *Adapting Advertising Copy for an African Market* 369
13. The Okinawa Campaign (III): *Meeting Competition through Advertising and Sales Promotion* 370
14. Far East Representatives, Inc.: *Policy on Unprofitable Lines* 372
15. Smithers Paint Company (II): *Dealing with Foreign Salesmen's Reports and Requests* 376
16. Albert Edirsinghe & Co., Ltd.: *Difficulties over Agency Representation* 379
17. Federal Cash Registers: *Price Competition Overseas* 383
18. New Zealand Appliances, Ltd.: *Selection and Training of Personnel for Temporary Assignments Abroad* 385
19. Renown Products Company (IV): *Financial Arrangements in Export Marketing* 389
20. The Okinawa Campaign (II): *Export Financing and Shipping Arrangements* 391
21. Paragon Plumbing Equipment (I): *Decisions on Local Participation in a Manufacturing Subsidiary in Mexico* 393
22. Paragon Plumbing Equipment (II): *Policies to Minimize the Impact of Inflation Abroad* 399
23. Coproducts Corporation: *Problems of Securing Finance for an Overseas Investment* 400
24. Automotive Exports, Inc.: *Use of a Stand-by Letter of Credit to Acquire Overseas Equity* 413

SECTION THREE. International Human Relations 416

25. Stewart Sutherland: *Income Tax Avoidance by Officers of a Canadian Company* 416
26. Wilbur Armitage: *Request for a Bribe by a Customs Officer* 418
27. Swift Motors, S. A.: *Influence of Overseas Personnel on Public and Government Relations* 420
28. Foster Birkett: *American-National Relationships under Mutual-Assistance Contracts* 422

29. American Trading Corporation, Inc.: *The Conflict between Old and New Cultures* 425
30. Captain George Patrios: *Misunderstanding of Local Feelings in Turkey* 429
31. Richard Conklin: *Problems of Courtship and Chaperonage in Brazil* 430
32. Industrias Kaiser Argentina, S.A. (IV): *Compensation Policies for Expatriate Employees* 431
33. Packer, Inc.: *Personnel Policies for Japanese Employees* 447
34. The Ceylon Plywood Company: *Communication with Employees in a Developing Country* 452
35. Robert Thompson: *Inefficiency in Lebanon versus the American Way* 454
36. Holiday in Chittagong: *Lack of Appreciation of Pakistani Religious Customs* 455
37. Moosajees, Ltd.: *Motivating Workers for Greater Productivity in a Developing Country* 456

SECTION FOUR. The New World of International Business Management: Policies and Problems 459

38. Mr. Walter Murray: *Developing Suppliers in Italy for an American Variety Chain* 459
39. Francis X. O'Shea: *Violations of International Agreements by Non-U.S. Concerns* 461
40. Hewlett-Packard Company: *Considerations of Operation in the European Common Market* 463
Background Information on Guatemala 473
41. General Tire and Incatecu, S.A. (I): *Political Considerations Affecting the Sale of Common Stock in Guatemala* 478
42. General Tire and Incatecu, S.A. (II): *Foreign Antagonism toward U.S. Investment in Guatemala* 484
43. General Tire and Incatecu, S.A. (III): *Assessing Opportunities and Risks in the Central American Common Market* 494
44. Kaiser Motors Corporation: *Investigation of Investment Opportunities in Argentina* 498
45. Industrias Kaiser Argentina, S.A. (I): *Local Participation in a U.S. Overseas Operation* 504
46. Industrias Kaiser Argentina, S.A. (II): *Conflict in a Joint Venture over Capital Equipment Valuation* 527
47. Industrias Kaiser Argentina, S.A. (III): *Personnel Problems under Sensitive Political Conditions* 533
48. Industrias Kaiser Argentina, S.A. (V): *Relationships with a Foreign Government in Transition* 536
49. Esso Standard Eastern, Inc. (Ceylon): *Difficult Financial Relations with the Government of Ceylon* 541

50. Thomas Randall Knitting Mills: *An Australian Manufacturer Deliberates an American Offer to Franchise* 546

51. Sony Corporation: *Evaluation of the U.S. Market for a Transistorized Television Receiver* 550

INTERNATIONAL BUSINESS MANAGEMENT

Readings and Cases

1

DIRECTION FOR THE WEST *

Barbara Ward

During the early 1960's a strange new world of international commerce has started to shape up. The political and economic leadership of the United States is being challenged at every turn.

Successful participation in world business requires keen awareness of international power politics. The system is relatively simple. The world is split into three groups of countries: the West, the Sino-Soviet bloc, and the neutrals. Both the West and the Communists are trying to entice the neutrals into a commitment. Trade and aid are tangible and potent weapons in this struggle for power. The West can win. It has the political and economic institutions which can simultaneously create abundance, growth, more equal sharing of wealth, and freedom.

It is only natural that an exceptional woman charts the course for the male-dominated West. Barbara Ward, or Lady Jackson in her role of wife and mother, is a charming and brilliant human being. The quality of her accomplishment has been most eloquently expressed in the citation for an honorary degree of Doctor of Laws conferred upon her by Brandeis University in November 1961. "Author, editor, economic interpreter . . . as much at home on the faculties of distinguished universities as among the working groups of England . . . Demonstrating in her life and work the humane effectiveness of realism when it is ennobled by compassion and the religious spirit."

Barbara Ward combines the extraordinary analytic talent of an economist with a rare gift for clear and inspired exposition. Her exceptional ability to range broadly among the social sciences allows the bridging of many gaps that set off one special field from another.

Educated in France, Germany, and England, Miss Ward began her professional career as a lecturer at Cambridge University. In 1939 she joined the editorial staff of The London Economist. *Since then she has contributed some of that publication's most distinguished writing.*

During the past few years, Barbara Ward has devoted herself to the study of problems of underdeveloped countries. Her book The Rich Nations and Poor Nations *has been widely praised as a most penetrating and readable discussion of the contemporary problems of development.*

* From *General Electric Forum* (January-March 1962). Reprinted by permission.

Miss Ward is a resident of Ghana, where—appropriately enough—her husband, Sir Robert Jackson of the British Treasury, serves as Chairman of the Development Commission.

Editors

"If we could first know where we are and whither we are tending, we could then better judge what to do and how to do it." The words are Abraham Lincoln's, but the dilemma is our own. Over the last decade, we in the Western world have become more and more aware of being under steady, undermining attack. We have felt our institutions threatened, our aims thwarted, our pretensions mocked. After three hundred years of world-wide dominance, nothing in our experience prepares us for this sense of insecurity; our temptation is to lash out at it blindly and angrily. But there is no safety in such reactions. We must know "where we are and whither we are tending." Otherwise, we shall fight against symptoms, not causes, and battle with shadows whereas our real struggle is with the angel of history itself.

The point can be quickly illustrated. Just over a hundred years ago, Western power in the Far East began to seem virtually irresistible. The Western merchants with their new goods and vessels, the Western soldiers with their new weapons, moved inexorably in. It was the first rising—in the China Sea—of the great tide of modern science and technology. In China, the Westerners were dismissed as "barbarians" and blamed for all the disruption they brought with them. Their techniques were ignored while a passionate rearguard action was fought to keep old Mandarin society unaltered down to its last ceremonious particular. Within 50 years, Chinese society all but collapsed and then entered on another 50 years of anarchy.

In Japan, on the contrary, the West had been studied by leaders and soldiers long before Commodore Perry arrived to demand the opening of the Hermit Kingdom. Westerners were seen not as "barbarians" but as representatives of a new type of society which, to resist, Japan would need in some measure to assimilate. Heroic readjustments—including profound structural changes such as the abolition of feudal land tenure—were made and within 50 years, the West acknowledged Japan as an equal. In short, the Chinese suffered history, the Japanese controlled it. A similar choice confronts the West today.

COMMUNIST PRESSURE

Communist pressure on our contemporary society to some degree resembles Western pressure on the Far East a century ago. We can, like the Manchu dynasty in China, regard our adversaries as "red devils" and attribute all the disruption they cause to an immoral and violent conspiracy. Or we can, like the Japanese, look at the pressure not so much as a pressure exercised by malevolent enemies but rather as a deeper historical pressure of change and upheaval which they simply project and exploit.

Which of these interpretations should we choose? Let us look at three areas in which we are most keenly aware of Communist competition and challenge. They force us to confront the issue of a working world order for mankind, in part by their boasts that it will be Communist—"we will bury you"—in part by the frightful dangers of the arms race upon which both sides are engaged. Again, they compel us to consider the future allegiance of the "uncommitted" third of humanity by their claim that capitalism simply exploits the underdeveloped peoples whereas communism offers them the way to both equality and abundance. And this claim is in turn part of their more fundamental credo—that only communism has the secret of long term economic expansion and can confidently promise its people standards of living which, by 1980—so goes the boast—will be half as high again as those in stagnant, inhibited, self contradictory capitalist economies.

Clearly in this confrontation between communism and the West, none of the basic conditions has been created by the Communists. We need some form of coherent world order because science has annihilated space, opened up instant communication, and made the world a single neighborhood of potential destruction. Equally, the Communists did not create the desires and tensions of the emergent peoples. Modern industry and technology drew them into the web of world trade and set their feet on the first rung of the ladder of a modern economy. Communists or no Communists, they would try to climb the rest of the way.

MATERIALS FOR ABUNDANCE

As for the dream of abundance, science and technology are making it, not a dream, but a fact. In the developed world of the West, living standards are higher than ever before; yet some $60 billions are spent on arms each year. An American road program can swallow up as many billions in a few years. A space program will do the same. Yet men are unemployed, food is in surplus, oil is in surplus, aluminum threatens a surplus, steel capacity is not fully used, most colonial products are in surplus. In spite of the immensity of demand, science keeps supply ahead of it.

If, therefore, the Communists say they will increase their national income by five or six per cent a year, there is no reason to doubt their ability. They have been doing so for years. So have Italy and West Germany and—more recently—France. And the reason is the same. Science and technology have created the pre-conditions and the materials for abundance. All that is needed is the community's decision to mobilize them, by one means or another, to the full.

REVOLUTION OF SCIENTIFIC CHANGE

Nor is the picture any different in other areas of Communist challenge. We may become aware of the need for more widespread, vigorous, and scientific education as a result of Russia's Sputnik. But the need for such education is inherent in our growing technological sophistication. We may reach out into space to answer a Soviet challenge. But the decision to explore the upper air was in fact made when the new technology first took Orville Wright a few feet off the ground. Soviet competitiveness does no more than underline in more violent colors challenge and upheavals which are inherent in the fact that we are living through the greatest revolution humanity has ever known—the revolution of scientific change.

Nothing like it has ever happened before. When mankind moved from hunting and fishing to settled agriculture and the city state, the change stretched over millennia. Even so, it modified every human habit and institution. Today, changes of infinitely greater magnitude are occurring in decades, not even in centuries. Everything is exploding—population, knowledge, communication, resources, cities, space itself. These are the forces of change which we have to understand and master. Communism is in a sense, incidental. It exploits a revolution it did not create, and its pretension to produce satisfactory human solutions is answered by the wall across Berlin.

CHALLENGE TO THE WEST

Communist success or failure is not the point. The fundamental question is whether we in the West are able to confront the challenge of our times. And here we face the agonizing difficulty that some of the creative responses we need to make run deeply against the grain of our traditional thinking. The analogy from China and Japan is again relevant. China was so dedicated to the old rule of courtly Mandarin and country gentleman that it could not renew its leadership in terms of the new forces of industry and city, of entrepreneur and industrialist. But Japan did so, even at the cost of root and branch land reform, and then was able to counter the new pressures from the West.

Today, in each of the major areas of challenge—international order, the developing world, the use of our abundance—we are inhibited by attitudes inherited from our prescientific past. The attitudes are dear to us. We can modify them only with great distress and questioning. But these are precisely the pains of any great historical transformation. History does not offer men only the easy options. It tends to come up on their blind side and challenge them precisely where their interests and beliefs are most deeply engaged.

We instinctively distrust the idea of an organized international society because our emotional allegiance is still to our own isolated, independent, sovereign nation. We instinctively question the idea of a special effort or program to speed the development of the emergent peoples for we inherit the belief that "normal" trade and investment should govern the relations between sovereign states, developed or otherwise. And we tend to reject the idea of a sustained program of economic growth—by whatever percentage a year—because our instincts still regard "big government" as a menace and private activity as the really legitimate tool of economic expansion.

NO NATION CAN BE ISOLATED

Now, as we have seen, communism rejects all these reactions. What is more serious is that the facts of our scientific age belie them too. No nation can be isolated in the atomic age. Fall-out rains down on the committed and uncommitted alike. The underdeveloped areas cannot speed up their growth without special long term assistance since "normal" investment tends to go to wealthy countries, while in "normal" world commerce, the price of manufactured goods produced in developed countries goes up while the price of raw materials produced in emergent territories goes down. The national circuit is making the rich richer while the poor lag further behind.

PRIVATE DEMAND NOT ENOUGH

Above all, the experience of the last decades underlines the fact that private demand alone does not unlock the full range of modern scientific production. It took a vast arms effort to jerk American industry to double its size after 1940. It took the Marshall Plan to push Europe into the new pattern of the mass consumption economy. American food production, maintained by government aid, so far outstrips American—or Western—demand that the surpluses, grown on less and less land, could feed a hungry world. And Europe's farming now promises to show the same surge.

In short, the astonishing secret of the modern scientific economy is that, after a certain stage of development, we can have what, as a community, we decide to have. Imagination is not limited by scarce resources. On the contrary, resources are limited by scarce imagination. Yet it is broadly true to say that in the West today this freedom of imagination comes only when—as with arms or the space race—fear is involved. Even education has had to beg for funds under the guise of national security.

This, then, is the agonizing confrontation of needs and policies in the West today. It is possible to plan purposefully—through public agencies, through private agencies, through the cooperation of both—for an abundant world. But to many Western minds planning is seen as the abdication of freedom to total government. This is their core of orthodoxy. Here, as with the Manchus and their ancient traditions, they would, sooner than compromise, rather face defeat.

ABUNDANCE CAN BE ORGANIZED

Happily, however, the choice is not in fact so stark. To opt for purposive policies aimed at abundance does not involve slavery or totalitarianism or total government control. A profound inventiveness has marked much of Western policy since 1945 and on every side, there are now creative experiments to show how abundance can be organized in freedom.

The Common Market proves that free nations can concert their policies and achieve greater cooperation. France's Monnet Plan has shown how sensible governmental direction can stimulate free enterprise to new vigor while strengthening the country's social capital—Britain is tentatively adopting the same approach. The example of West Germany, Sweden, and Holland has shown how wise restraint by trade unions and careful consultation between government, labor and management can check potential inflation and allow rapid growth to be combined with stable prices.

CLOSER INTERNATIONAL COOPERATION

All these experiments point to the way the West must go—to closer international cooperation in the Atlantic area as the nucleus of world order; to Western support for quicker economic growth in new Common Markets in Latin America, in Africa, in Asia; to consistent Western programs for higher, steadier domestic expansion, for bolder aims in education, in culture, in better urban living, and for prosperous, free economies rolling forward on the two essential wheels of lively private expansion and vigorous public investment.

These are not pipe dreams. They have been partially achieved. What is needed now is that we should generalize them, weave them into an accepted grand strategy, and then challenge communism at its most vulnerable point, saying to the world: we can give you cooperation, abundance, growth, more equal sharing—and we can give you freedom too.

Readings

SECTION ONE

International Trade, Regionalism, and Economic Development

Articles in this section provide some broad background on such important topics as regional integration and cooperation and the role of international trade in economic development.[1]

Western Europe has traditionally been our most important overseas trading partner, and will remain so for many years to come. The lead-off article by Robert H. Marshall ably explores the implications of the European Common Market for the United States. Harry G. Brainard then shows why *The Trade Expansion Act—1962* should be considered a milestone in the commercial policy of this nation. There is considerable overlapping in these two articles—appropriately so, because the two topics go together like soup and a sandwich. Drew Middleton, in his *Common Market and Commonwealth,* shows how Britain's continuing ties with her former Empire may have to become looser and looser the more Europe-involved the mother country becomes. The entire discussion of the developments in Western Europe merely brings home the point that customs unions and common markets have a potential for great economic and political good. But if they follow a philosophy that is inward-looking and restrictive, such unions also carry within them the possibilities of much harm. Jean Royer

[1] For some quantitative magnitudes of our stake in world business, see Gerhard Colm and Theodore Geiger, *The Economy of the American People* (Washington, D.C.: National Planning Association, 1961), Chapter 12, pp. 130-160.

masterfully explores such *Dangers of Regionalism.*[2] Dr. Balassa's rigorous and imaginative analysis of *European Integration and the Developing Countries* dovetails smoothly with the other articles. Professor Brandt carries the discussion several steps further. He sees "widening scissors" between the prices of manufactured goods and primary products, and concludes, with a great deal of eloquence, that *Commodity Agreements Are Not the Answer* to the problem of unstable world agricultural prices.[3] Walter Krause continues the shock treatment in a stimulating piece in which he tries to reconcile the beneficial effects of the *Regional Approach to Economic Development* with the uncomfortable fact that it apparently runs contrary to the U.S. policy favoring multilateral trade relations.

The readings in this section merely "open up" the discussion of the economic and political setting within which a global business executive will have to operate. The instability of this setting became painfully clear to us when, in January 1963, President de Gaulle dropped a bombshell by vetoing Britain's application for entry into the Common Market. This blackballing of the United Kingdom was instantly followed by a collapse of negotiations in Brussels. Bitter recrimination sprang up within the EEC, across the Channel as well as in the United States. "The Five" became for the first time part of the Common Marketdom lingo, somehow suggesting the start of a countdown.

The storms of rhetoric soon calmed down, however. Staff members of the Chase-Manhattan Bank point out, in their level-headed appraisal of the *End of the Brussels Talks,* that the temporary breakdown of negotiations is unlikely to reverse the direction of trends in Europe. Economic integration among the Six will be slowed up slightly, particularly in agriculture. So will the speed by which reduction of trade barriers between Europe and America proceeds. Problems between France and the U.S. will add to the complications of harmonizing Western policies in the fields of foreign policy and defense.

But the interdependence of the European nations is a fact that is certain to ensure continuing interest in the Common Market by political leaders and businessmen everywhere. They are asking some basic questions. What

[2] For a summary of economic and political arguments for and against regional integration, see *Common Markets and Free Trade* (Menlo Park, Calif.: Stanford Research Institute, 1960).

[3] For an opposite viewpoint see William Butler's "Trade and the Less Developed Countries," *Foreign Affairs* (Jan. 1963). Butler regrets that the faulty "thesis of declining terms of trade dies hard." This in spite of the fact that "there is no evidence of a long-term deterioration in prices of primary products relative to those of manufacturers . . . [and] that export earnings from individual manufactured products have been just about as unstable as those from individual commodity exports." Dr. Butler argues vigorously that America has a huge stake in developing workable international commodity agreements. After all we are the world's biggest agricultural exporter and a major importer of commodities. In addition, we provide substantial amounts of economic aid to the developing nations. Because of the slump in prices of primary products, this aid has had to make up their losses in foreign exchange. As a result, the growth of the developing nations has lagged. Our exports to them have declined. Dr. Butler applauds the fact that the U.S. helped to establish the new coffee agreement. He suggests that we could go further, and call an international conference at which the possibility of setting up other effective agreements would be discussed.

will be the Common Market's ultimate political structure? Is full membership in the "club" limited to its six charter members? Will EEC become inward-looking and protectionist? How can a meaningful Atlantic partnership be constructed, particularly in the military area?

The breakdown of negotiations has, of course, provided no answers. But the questions are now phrased more clearly than at any time since the Common Market began.

Appropriately enough, this section therefore culminates with an illustration of one of the most basic managerial principles. To wit: A question properly asked is half the answer to a problem.[4]

[4] We have omitted articles on East-West trade for two reasons. First, the Communists conduct state trading as a phase of economic warfare rather than as a means of international cooperation and private profit seeking. An individual businessman is not equipped to deal effectively with this sort of situation. Second, the volume of Soviet exports is not high. Chinese exports are weaker still. Even within the Communist Bloc, international trade is not intensive. Until very recently planned development proceeded largely on the basis of local self-sufficiency rather than on the basis of international division of labor. About three-fourths of Soviet trade is within the Sino-Soviet block, 15 per cent is with the developed countries, and 10 per cent is with the newly developing noncommunist nations. Mainland China does less than 5 per cent of her trade with the underdeveloped countries, because she has little to offer in the way of capital equipment.

2

THE COMMON MARKET: IMPLICATIONS FOR THE UNITED STATES *

Robert H. Marshall

On September 17, 1787, in Philadelphia, there occurred a momentous occasion—an event that was to have great economic and political significance for the then infant republic of the United States of America and for the rest of the world. The occasion was the signing of the newly-drafted Constitution of the United States by the delegates to the Constitutional Convention. This instrument, which replaced the weak and ineffective Articles of Confederation, was to provide the basis for one of the strongest political and economic unions the world has ever seen.

One hundred and seventy years later, an equally momentous event occurred when six nations of Western Europe signed the Treaty of Rome on March 25, 1957, thus forming the basis for the establishment of the European Economic Community, popularly referred to as the Common Market or the "Inner Six."

* From *Business Topics* (Michigan State University, Winter 1963), pp. 33-47. Reprinted by permission.

Just as the United States Constitution had great economic and political significance for the United States and for the rest of the world, so too does the Treaty of Rome have great portent for the international community, and especially for the United States as the world's greatest economic and political power and the leader of the Western Community of nations.

The European Economic Community is more than a customs union. The Rome Treaty's 246 articles, plus protocols and annexes, envisage a broad, cooperative economic approach covering such important matters as the free movement of labor, free movement of money, the right to freedom of establishment for business and the professions, an antitrust policy, common rules of transport, common trade treaties and trade rules with outside nations, a joint economic stabilization policy, prohibitions against subsidies and the abuse of state monopolies, and (significantly) free trade in farm products and a commonly established agricultural policy.

Ultimately, the Treaty of Rome may possibly provide the basis for a political union—for something that heretofore has been considered impossible to achieve: a United States of Europe.

In the first four and one-half years of its operations, the Common Market has shown itself to be a challenge and an opportunity to the United States—both economically and politically. The challenge and opportunity are heightened by the application of Great Britain for admission to the Community, thus making the eventual joining of the Common Market by the other members of the European Free Trade Association (also called the "Outer Seven" nations)—either as full-fledged members or associate members—a virtual certainty. It is crucially important to assess the Common Market's immediate and long-run implications for the United States: these are both economic and military-political.

ECONOMIC IMPLICATIONS

The West European market is of great significance for the United States economy. An overwhelming barrage of statistics need not be used to drive home the essential fact of the economic relatedness of the European and American economies, but a few salient figures can be given.[1]

Pertinent Figures

In 1961, total United States merchandise exports to the Common Market were \$3.6 billion, while merchandise imports into this country from the Common Market totaled \$2.0 billion. In 1960, the Community imported about \$3.8 billion worth of goods from the United States, while selling about \$2.3 billion in merchandise to us. As of 1960, total U.S. private direct investments in EEC countries were \$2.6 billion; for the same

[1] The statistical data for this section are taken primarily from U.S. Congress, Joint Economic Committee, *The European Economic Community and the United States,* 87th Congress, 1st Session, Washington: U.S. Government Printing Office, 1961, pp. 23-25, 36, 37.

date, total EEC private direct investments in the United States were $1.4 billion.

Assuming the existence of an enlarged Common Market (that is, the Inner Six countries joined with the Outer Seven), under conditions existing as of year-end 1960, it would be sending a fifth of its total exports to the United States and would be getting a quarter of its total imports from us. In turn, some 30 percent of U.S. exports would go to the expanded Common Market, and such a market would be the source of 27 percent of total imports into the United States. As of the end of 1960, 20 percent of U.S. private long-term investment abroad was in this hypothetical Market, and over two-thirds of all private long-term foreign investment in the United States came from the thirteen nations of the enlarged Community.

Growth

As a group the six nations of the Common Market have been growing at a faster rate than the United States or the United Kingdom; the Six have been earning steady surpluses on external account; and the Common Market's share of world trade has been rising. More specifically, from 1950 to 1953, the real gross national product (GNP adjusted for price changes) of the Six rose by 18 percent; that of the United States by 16 percent; that of other European countries by 10 percent. For the period 1953 to 1960, the Common Market's real GNP increased 45 percent, while that of other European countries, including the United Kingdom, expanded by 26 percent, and the growth figure for the United States was only 15 percent.

In per capita terms, there is an even more striking contrast between the United States and the Common Market for the period 1953 to 1960: per capita output of goods and services spurted upward by 36 percent in the Common Market as compared with only 6 percent for the United States. It should be emphasized, of course, that it is impossible to determine precisely what role, if any, the formation of the European Economic Community has played in achieving this rate of economic growth.

In each year of the 11-year period 1951-1961 inclusive, the Common Market countries enjoyed a rising favorable balance of trade in shipments of goods and services abroad, so that today the Six constitute the region with the highest (net) gold and foreign exchange reserves relative to foreign trade volume.

Finally, the Common Market's share of total world trade also grew continuously during the decade of the Fifties. From 16 percent in 1950, the Market's share attained 26 percent in 1960, while the shares of the United States and the rest of Europe remained constant at 18 percent and 17 percent, respectively.

Imperatives of a New Trade Policy

The growth and development of the Common Market have made imperative a new trade policy for the United States. One of the most important and most publicized bills enacted in the second session of the 87th Congress was the Trade Expansion Act of 1962, a bill termed by President

Kennedy "a bold new instrument of American policy." This bill, which was signed into law on October 11, 1962, provides the President with two basic kinds of broad tariff-cutting power for use over the next five years:

> Overall authority to cut tariffs by one half for broad categories of commodities in exchange for concessions from other nations;
>
> Special authority to reduce or abolish all tariffs on those products where the United States and the Common Market account for more than 80 percent of free world trade.

The Trade Expansion Act is much more liberal in tariff-cutting power than was the Reciprocal Trade Agreements Act of 1934, the most recent extension of which expired on June 30, 1962. The new law, however, incorporates in modified form certain features of the Trade Agreements Act: the "most-favored-nation" principle, whereby tariff concessions negotiated with the Common Market would be extended to other nations of the Free World; the "peril point" provision, which provides for review by the Tariff Commission of proposed tariff reductions; the "escape clause" concept whereby the Tariff Commission may recommend relief for an entire industry that is adversely affected by a tariff cut (preferably such relief would usually be in the form of "trade adjustment" assistance rather than tariff hikes). Trade adjustment aid for firms would encompass tax relief, loans, and information for revamping production facilities for new products. Industrial workers idled by increased imports would be eligible for readjustment allowances, vocational retraining, and relocation assistance.

Passage of the Trade Expansion Act and the subsequent lowering of tariff walls between the United States and the Common Market should, on net balance, redound to the long-run benefit of American business, bringing increased sales, employment and income.

General Agreement

A recent case in point illustrating the favorable effects of negotiated tariff reductions for the United States was the agreement concluded March 7, 1962, between the United States, the Common Market, Great Britain, and 17 other countries to lower tariffs on many industrial products by as much as 20 percent over the next several years. The negotiations, which were conducted under the provisions of the General Agreement on Tariffs and Trade (GATT), provided for the United States to lower its import duty on automobiles, for example, from 8½ to 6½ percent in two equal steps. The European Common Market will reduce its proposed external automobile tariff from 29 to 22 percent, while Britain will cut its import levy on cars from 30 to 22 percent.[2]

Other important cuts in tariffs applied to electrical machinery and equipment, business machines and office equipment, machine tools, textile machinery, and materials handling equipment.

[2] Federal Reserve Bank of Chicago, "Trade Barriers Coming Down?" *Business Conditions,* May 1962, pp. 9f.

The chemicals industry was the only major industrial category for which no important concessions could be negotiated. The upshot of these agreements was that the United States received new concessions on about $1.1 billion of annual exports to the Common Market and Britain in return for lowering tariffs on some $900 million of imports from these latter countries. All told, foreign countries participating in the March agreement made concessions on $4.3 billion of United States exports in return for concessions by this country on $2.9 billion of imports into the United States—indeed, a concrete example of good old Yankee horse-trading.

The situation just described is but one illustration of the prospective benefits to be derived from intelligent tariff reductions mutually arrived at by the United States and the European Common Market.

Tariff Removal

In February of 1962, the U.S. Department of Commerce published a list of 26 commodity groupings on which the United States could conceivably bargain advantageously to remove all tariffs with the Common Market. In every case of these 26 groups, the United States and the Common Market (here broadened to include five other possible members: Great Britain, Denmark, Greece, Ireland, and Norway) account for 80 percent or more of free world exports. The list of 26 commodity groups comprised goods produced by modern highly-developed industries utilizing large-scale capital and having product demands which are expected to increase appreciably in the future. Some of the more important commodity groups included motor vehicles, industrial machinery, electrical machinery, aircraft, agricultural machinery, power-generating machinery, and office machinery.[3] The latter groups represent product lines where American industry has demonstrated repeatedly its ability to compete effectively in world markets, despite the fact that these industries pay some of the highest wages in the world. Significantly, in 1961 the combined United States and European exports to the free world of these 26 commodity groupings aggregated about $19.2 billion, with the United States accounting for some 45 percent of the amount.

This is no time for resting on past achievements, however. The dynamic and competitive growth of the Common Market emphasizes the need for United States business to expand and update its plant and equipment so as to compete more effectively in the burgeoning Common Market as well as in other areas of the free world economy. Of sobering significance here is the fact that the rate of investment in new productive capacity in the United States has been lagging behind Europe's pace. In 1961, for example, the United States invested 4.9 percent of its GNP in new plant and equipment—the lowest such rate since 1939. In this same period the average rate of new investment in West Europe was running at more than twice the United States rate. Changes in the tax law are aimed at improving the faltering rate of new investment in this country: a 7 percent tax credit

[3] See *ibid.*, p. 11f., for a brief summary of the major commodity groupings included in the list published by the U.S. Department of Commerce.

on new investment in machinery and equipment which should provide tax relief of almost $1 billion; administrative revision of Bulletin F of the Treasury Department governing the depreciation schedules for depreciable investment goods, with some $1 billion worth of tax benefits envisaged. Finally, a longer range measure is provided in the possible adoption in 1963 of across-the-board reductions in personal and corporate tax rates.

It should also be emphasized that tariff reductions negotiated with the Common Market will compel the reallocation of certain productive resources in the United States economy. As painful as such reallocation might be, the flexible adjustment of productive activity in response to shifting domestic and international demands is a vital feature of a competitive, free-enterprise economy. Unavoidably, the tariff reductions inherent within the Trade Expansion Act of 1962 will adversely affect a relatively small number of firms and workers in this country. The Department of Commerce estimates, for example, that some 700 to 800 firms would require "trade adjustment" assistance during the five-year life of the Trade Expansion Act. Such assistance would cover some $15 million in technical aid to these firms and about $120 million in loans. It is estimated also that annually some 18,000 workers would qualify for "trade adjustment" assistance of various types—all at a total cost of $50 million over the five-year period that the act will be in force.

AGRICULTURAL IMPLICATIONS

Having considered the general effects of the Common Market on United States trade in manufactured products, let us turn to an examination of the Market's impact on our agricultural trade and raw materials exports.

The Common Market countries and the United Kingdom together accounted for about one-third of all United States exports of agricultural products during 1960. If only commercial sales abroad of agricultural products are considered (that is, excluding the value of agricultural exports shipped under various United States government foreign aid programs), then these countries provided 45 percent of all the dollars received from agricultural exports in 1960. On the other hand, only a very small portion of United States agricultural imports comes from the Common Market and the United Kingdom. For the year 1960, these countries were *net* buyers of almost $1.3 billion worth of United States agricultural products.[4]

Common Market Policy

Recognizing the importance of the Common Market countries in United States agricultural trade, the common agricultural policy to be adopted by the Common Market will have significant implications for future sales of United States farm products abroad. In January 1962, the Com-

[4] Federal Reserve Bank of Cleveland, "U.S. Agricultural Trade and the Common Market," *Monthly Business Review,* April 1962, p. 14. The figures for this section are drawn mainly from this source.

mon Market countries established the following basic provisions governing general farm policy:

> The gradual removal of all intra-Market agricultural tariffs between 1962 and 1970;
>
> The ultimate establishment of uniform price supports in each of the member countries;
>
> The setting of variable import duties on imported farm products equal to the difference between the world price and the Common Market support price.

At this time it is uncertain what general level of price support the Six will ultimately adopt. If the price support level to be adopted is such that import levies offset any competitive advantage of external suppliers, then increased Common Market agricultural production would reduce the need for agricultural imports.

Following the announcement of the Common Market agreement on agricultural policy, the United States and the Common Market concluded major trade agreements involving such farm commodities as cotton, soybeans, tobacco, fruits, and vegetables. For the three year period 1958 to 1960, United States exports of these specific commodities to the Common Market accounted for over 45 percent of the total value of all United States agricultural products exported to the Common Market. It is expected that future United States exports of these specific products will be maintained and even increased as the standard of living rises in the Common Market countries. These commodities for which agreements have been reached are not produced on any large scale by domestic producers within the Common Market countries.

Feed grains are the major products for which trade agreements between the United States and the Common Market have not been concluded. Significantly, 39 percent of United States feed grain exports were sold to Common Market countries from 1958 through 1960. Dollar sales of these commodities averaged about $200 million during recent years. Maintenance of adequate export markets for feed grains is of great importance to the United States, particularly in light of our huge surpluses. As of January 31, 1962, three-fourths of the Commodity Credit Corporation's total investment of $7.9 billion in surplus crops was held in wheat, corn, and sorghum grain.

Currently, grain producers in the Common Market countries are protected from foreign competition by various governmental policies. Support prices in these countries are in excess of United States support price levels. Using wheat as an example, the French support price of $2.20 per bushel is the lowest of the Common Market countries, while the West German support price of $3.00 per bushel is the highest. It is thought that the uniform support price to be established for wheat some time before 1970 will be intermediate between the current French and West German levels. The current United States support price for wheat is $2.00 per bushel. According to the U.S. Department of Agriculture, studies made by the Common Market predict the attainment, by 1965, of such a level of self-sufficiency in feed grain and wheat production for the Common Market countries as will reduce their import requirements for feed grains by 10 to 15 percent and will reduce wheat imports to limited amounts for blending purposes. Note, however, that the previous projection does not apply to the United Kingdom, which will continue to be a large buyer of grain in the world market. The admission of Great Britain to the Common Market would make the enlarged Community more dependent on farm imports and thus force a reconsideration of the Market's common agricultural policy.

Criticism

The United States and other major agricultural exporting countries such as Canada, Australia, and New Zealand have sharply criticized the predominantly protectionist orientation of the Common Market's farm policy. More specifically, these critics contend that the Common Market's "variable import duties" on a large group of agricultural commodities inject too much uncertainty into the international marketing of agricultural products. Within the framework of GATT (General Agreement on Tariffs and Trade), tariff schedules established by participating nations are ordinarily "fixed" or "bound" against increases in the future. The variable import levies of the Common Market would not be so fixed or set against future increases. In effect, then, nations negotiating tariff concessions with the Common Market within the framework of GATT would be offering fixed tariff concessions in exchange for concessions subject to wide and uncertain variation.

Latin American nations are also extremely sensitive to the implications of the Common Market's agricultural policy. The Latin countries foresee their eventual displacement from the Western European market by the African countries which were formerly overseas territories of the Common Market countries. African shipments of nonferrous metals and tropical agricultural products would receive preferential treatment, while Latin American products would be subject both to the higher common tariff and quota restrictions.

The United States is currently exploring ways for easing the situation confronting the Latin American countries, many of which stake their livelihood on the exports of one or two commodities. The degree of success for these efforts should have great meaning for the effective working of the recently instituted Alliance for Progress.

Concessions

Worthy of note is the increased willingness on the part of the government of the United States to participate in international commodity agreements aimed at reducing price fluctuations for primary commodities traded in large volume in the world market. Heretofore, the United States has generally supported only international stabilization schemes involving products important to this country—wheat and sugar. In May 1961, our government informed the United Nations' Commission on International Commodity Trade of its willingness to consider "any reasonable proposal" for meeting the problems of international commodity markets. At the Inter-American Economic Conference in Uruguay, held in August of 1961, the United States agreed to join in a "workable international coffee agreement" and to use its influence to urge "participation by other coffee consuming countries." At this same time, our country promised to explore possible participation in the International Tin Agreement and to study problems associated with other important export commodities from Latin America.[5]

Then, too, in reporting out the Trade Expansion Bill in June of this year, the House Ways and Means Committee adopted provisions enabling the President to remove all tariffs on tropical agriculture or forestry commodities that are not produced in significant quantities in the United States. The President is to be advised by the Tariff Commission in his determinations for these products. His authority is conditional upon the existence of similar concessions by the European Economic Community—thus there would be equal access to the Common Market for such tropical agricultural or forestry commodities.

IMPACT

Now that we have examined the significance of the Common Market for United States manufacturing and agriculture, we can use this informational background to assess the impact of the Market on a current and pressing economic problem: the persistent deficit in the United States balance of payments, with our resulting losses of large amounts of gold.

The phenomenon of a deficit in our balance of international payments is not something new. With the exception of the year 1957, the United States has incurred a deficit every year since 1949. In fact for the twelve-year period 1950 to 1961 the total deficit (i. e., the excess of payments over receipts in international transactions of the United States) amounted to about $24 billion. Up until a few years ago, attention was directed to the so-called "dollar shortage" and to the need for the United States, as the world's largest creditor nation at that time, to aid in rebuilding the war-devastated countries of Western Europe and Japan and also to hammer out a common military and economic front against the encroachments of the Soviet Union. The annual deficit did not become large until 1958, when it soared to $3.5 billion, marking a great change from the previous year's small surplus, a reflection of the favorable impact of the Suez crisis. The annual deficit has averaged about $3.5 billion during the past four years. The 1961 deficit totaled $2.5 billion, but this figure included European debt prepayments of some $700 million.

It is difficult to determine precisely the causes of the persistent imbalance in our international payments position, but we can gain some general insight into the problem by examining the composition of our international transactions.

[5] Federal Reserve Bank of Chicago, "International Commodity Price Agreements," *Business Conditions,* February 1962, p. 15.

Our International Transactions

First of all, in goods and services (the so-called "current account" items), the United States has had a surplus for many years. In other words, inpayments from sales of merchandise, from services (such as tourism, transportation, and insurance), and from income earned on foreign investments have substantially exceeded outpayments abroad for these same purposes. Since 1949, the annual surplus on goods and services has ranged between $2 billion and $8 billion, with the surplus for 1961 being in excess of $7 billion. The larger part of this surplus is accounted for by merchandise sales. During the five year period 1957-1961, our merchandise exports have exceeded merchandise imports on the average of $4 billion annually. Major free world areas where we have sold more goods than we have bought during this period include Canada, Western Europe, Asia, and Africa.

Next, let us consider private capital flows. During the past five years, the net outflow of private long-term capital from the United States has averaged some $2 billion annually. Much of this outflow represents direct investments in plant and equipment abroad. Part of this outflow is portfolio investment: purchases of foreign securities. Although initially this net capital outflow results in outpayments to foreign countries, it ultimately provides a return flow of receipts in the form of interest, dividends, and debt repayments. Currently, United States direct investments abroad total about $35 billion, with much of this in such industrial lines as manufacturing, petroleum, and mining.

Finally, a large part of the payments deficit is related to the net outflow of United States government payments, which reflect military expenditures abroad as well as grants, loans and aid by our government. On a net basis, the outflow of government payments has averaged about $6 billion annually during the past five years with about half of this figure going for economic aid to foreign countries. Since World War II, the United States has provided about $85 billion in foreign aid of various types. Of this amount $56.5 billion were for purely economic aid, while the balance of $28.5 billion went for various military aid purposes. Almost half of the $85 billion in total aid has gone to Western Europe.[6]

Merchandise Trade

The immediate bearing of the Common Market upon the United States balance of payments will be reflected primarily in our merchandise exports and imports. An expansion of United States exports would, of course, be the most direct way for bringing our international payments into balance.

At this stage it is impossible to determine the precise impact that the Common Market will have on our merchandise trade abroad. Some observers estimate that an enlarged Common Market would cut United States exports by about $800 million a year. However, given the passage of the Trade Expansion Act and as much success in negotiating tariff concessions

[6] U.S. Congress, Joint Economic Committee, *The Task for 1962: A Free World Community,* 87th Congress, 1st Session, Washington: U.S. Government Printing Office, 1961, p. 6.

with the Common Market as was achieved in March of 1962, it is reasonable to conclude that the Market will have no significant adverse effect on our export trade.

In considering this conclusion, several *caveats* need be kept in mind: (1) the working out of the specific details of the common agricultural policy of the Common Market—especially as such policy would be complicated by the admission of the United Kingdom to the Common Market; (2) the extent of the ability of American producers to maintain competitive prices through judicious plant modernization and holding the line on production costs; (3) the extent of the probable inroads that the Common Market will make on third markets important to United States exporters, particularly Canada, Latin America, and Africa; (4) the increasing difficulties, as shown in the first session of the 1960-61 GATT tariff conference, in renegotiating compensatory tariff concessions to offset hikes associated with the establishment of the Common Market's external tariff.

Wage Costs

With regard to wage costs, it is generally believed that Common Market producers hold an important competitive advantage over their United States counterparts. It is difficult to make an accurate comparison of production costs in different countries. Nevertheless, the Joint Economic Committee of Congress has published data which suggest that United States exports are not necessarily handicapped by higher production costs as compared with the Common Market.[7] For the period 1953 to 1959, total wage costs in the United States increased 27 percent—a lower rate of increase than that recorded in four of the Common Market countries: West Germany, Belgium, the Netherlands, and Italy. During the same period relative increases in total labor costs in these four countries ran from a low of 37 percent for Belgium to a high of 55 percent for Germany. France's rate of increase was slightly below the United States figure, while no data were given for Luxembourg. In this same period, the United Kingdom registered an increase of 48 percent.

A more meaningful measure than proportionate changes in total labor costs is wage cost per unit of output. In the same period 1953 to 1959 wage costs per unit of output rose 12 percent in the United States as compared with increases of 20 percent in the United Kingdom, 18 percent in the Netherlands, and 7 percent in Germany. Due to large productivity gains, unit wage costs were reduced in Italy, France, and Belgium despite significant increases in their total wage bills. A recent survey by the National Industrial Conference Board of United States firms operating plants abroad showed that lower money wage rates in foreign countries are offset frequently by lower productivity and higher non-wage costs in these countries.[8]

[7] U.S. Congress, Joint Economic Committee, *Trade Restraints in the Western Community with Tariff Comparisons and Selected Statistical Tables Pertinent to Foreign Economic Policy,* 87th Congress, 1st Session, Washington: U.S. Government Printing Office, 1961, p. 58.

[8] Cf. National Industrial Conference Board, Studies in Business Economics, No. 73, *Costs and Competition: American Experience Abroad.*

Loss of Market

Taking a long-run view, the United States must be prepared to accept some erosion in certain of its exports to Europe as the Common Market removes internal tariffs and other trade barriers. For certain American manufacturers this erosion of European markets may be substantial: for example, chemicals, textiles, glass products, optical and photographic equipment, certain types of electronic equipment and electrical machinery, heavy engineering equipment, and general-purpose machine tools. The decidedly protectionist agricultural policy adopted by the Common Market may cut adversely such Community imports as wheat, fruits and vegetables, poultry, and certain dairy products. Future imports of these commodities may depend largely on the marginal requirements of the Common Market.

However, the loss of American export sales in these product lines may have a slight impact on our overall export position especially since shipments of finished manufactured goods to Western Europe have comprised no more than 7 percent of total United States merchandise exports in recent years. On the other hand, it is likely that loss of sales in finished manufactures may be more than offset by increased United States exports of such raw materials as cotton, coal, aluminum, copper alloys, and iron and steel scrap—all of which would feed the expanding needs of European industries. Many of these raw materials are in short supply in Western Europe and are admitted duty-free or at low rates.

In the latter connection it is worthwhile to reflect upon the view offered in a report to the Subcommittee on Foreign Economic Policy of the Joint Economic Committee of the Congress in late November of 1961:

> Quite apart from the effects of tariffs and other deliberate barriers, trade in manufactured goods between the Common Market and the United States is likely to change in character. Instead of representing an exchange of advanced U.S. products and labor-intensive European goods, it is more likely to consist of the exchange of specialties among partners more equally matched in technology and income. However, this need not mean a reduction in trade; on the contrary, as experience inside Europe itself has amply demonstrated, this closer matching of the economic characteristics of the advanced economies can actually provide a basis for considerable trade expansion. In addition, the probable continuation, and even acceleration, of the post-war rise in European living standards could well open up for U.S. exporters an expanding mass market for the wide variety of consumer durable and semidurable goods which U.S. industry produces so efficiently.[9]

Other Implications

In addition to the impact of the Common Market upon the merchandise accounts of our balance of payments, the Market also has important implications for the other two important components of our balance of

[9] U.S. Congress, Joint Economic Committee, *The European Economic Community and the United States,* p. 41.

payments: namely, private long-term capital movements and the United States government payments for military and economic aid.

The European Economic Community gives every indication of continued economic growth and expansion in the future. Such growth should make the Common Market countries even stronger, both economically and financially. As such, it is to be reasonably expected that the Common Market nations will come to play even bigger and more important roles in providing private long-term capital exports to the United States as well as to other parts of the international economy. Such an expansion in long-term capital exports should redound favorably upon the United States balance of payments, thus reducing the pressure of deficits in the international payments position of this country.

Commensurate with their strong international reserve and payments positions and their level of total production, the Common Market countries can be expected to shoulder a larger share of the economic and military aid burden of the West—a task which the United States has performed so well these many years since the end of World War II. In fact much of the present economic strength of the Common Market countries is attributable in large part to the economic aid provided by this country.

The United States contributes about $2.5 and $3 billion annually in net economic aid or, in other words, about six-tenths of one percent of its gross national product. The contribution of the United Kingdom is approximately in this same ratio. French participation is proportionately even greater; however, most of this aid has been directed to military expenditures in Algeria. Germany, Italy, and Japan contribute three-tenths of one percent or less of their respective gross national products to economic aid. Perhaps in the future these countries can be persuaded to increase their economic aid efforts. Discussions directed toward this end are currently underway in the Development Assistance Group of the Organization for Economic Cooperation and Development (OECD).

Monetary Cooperation

Still other developments promise to ease the pressure on the international position of gold losses facing the United States. These developments entail increasing cooperation between the United States and Western European monetary authorities aimed at meeting problems that arise from currency convertibility, including a defense against speculative runs on the key international reserve currencies—the dollar and the British pound sterling. These cooperative efforts utilize four different approaches:

The "Basel Agreement" was initiated in the spring of 1961; through this, Western European central banks that are members of the Bank for International Settlements have agreed to extend short-term credits to member countries experiencing short-run capital outflows. Although the United States is not a member of the Bank for International Settlements, senior representatives of our Federal Reserve System have attended regularly during the past two years the monthly meetings of the Bank held in Basel, Switzerland. It is likely that the United States would make use of the facilities of this group, should the occasion ever arise of this country being subject to intolerable short-term capital outflows. In March of 1961, for example, this Basel group extended $910 million of short-term credits to Britain in order to protect the pound against speculative pressures at that time. Had not such assistance been forthcoming, this situation also would have had adverse effects upon the international position of the dollar.

Efforts to offset speculative runs against the dollar have been undertaken by the United States Treasury in close collaboration with certain European central banks, particularly the German and Swiss central banks. Then, too, beginning in March of this year, the Federal Reserve has begun to acquire certain foreign currencies directly so as to facilitate official Federal Reserve intervention in the foreign exchange market should this action become advisable to protect the dollar against speculative attack. Dealing with foreign central banks, our Federal Reserve has acquired $50 million in each of the following currencies: the French franc, the British pound sterling, the Netherlands guilder, the Belgian franc, and the German mark. In addition, $250 million in Canadian dollars and $200 million in Swiss francs have been obtained through these reciprocal credit arrangements with other central banks and the Bank for International Settlements.[10]

Arrangements to provide the Fund with supplemental standby resources of $6 billion were recently negotiated between the International Monetary Fund and ten industrial nations (including the United States, the United Kingdom, the EEC countries, Japan, Canada, and Sweden). Of this amount, the United States' commitment is $2 billion, while the Common Market countries' share is $2.45 billion. This arrangement in effect establishes a pool of the world's leading currencies within the IMF, and would increase the drawing rights of the United States by $2 billion—the amount equal to this country's standby commitment.

The Organization for Economic Cooperation and Development—the OECD—provides the fourth avenue of international monetary cooperation. The members of the OECD are the United States, Canada, and the 18 nations of the old Organization for European Economic Cooperation. One of the most important "special working parties" within the OECD is that dealing with balance-of-payments problems of common interest. Membership in this special group is confined to those nine of the 20 members of the OECD who have the major responsibility and power to act in international monetary affairs: the United States, Great Britain, France, Western Germany, the Netherlands, Italy, Canada, Switzerland, and Sweden. This working party meets in closed session every four to six weeks in Paris. The main representative for the United States at these meetings is usually Robert V. Roosa, Undersecretary of the Treasury for Monetary Affairs, recognized as one of our leading experts on financial matters. In a recent address before

[10] "Treasury and Federal Reserve Foreign Exchange Operations," *Federal Reserve Bulletin,* September 1962, pp. 1146f.

the American Bankers Association, Mr. Roosa gave some overall insights concerning meetings of this important group:

> At these meetings, active financial officials from the capitals of ... participating countries are present, full of the current problems confronting them and eager to analyze together the financial forces at work which affect the balance of payments of any or all of the participating countries. Not much can or should be said, on a current basis, concerning the work of a committee of this kind. It is a pioneering experiment; it is being conducted with the flexibility and the uninhibited freedom of inquiry that is appropriate to such an experiment. The aim is understanding, not negotiation from prepared positions, and least of all the semantic exercise of prepared communiques. But the results of 1961—not only in terms of what has occurred at the meetings, or in the parallel discussions which the meetings make possible, but also in broadening our immediate awareness of what is going on abroad as we work out our own domestic financial programs—assure great potentialities for the future of this regular, frequent, face-to-face contact for international financial consultations.[11]

POLITICAL IMPLICATIONS

Any consideration of the overall implications of the Common Market for the United States must necessarily recognize its political impact upon us. Such an impact though difficult to determine precisely at this stage is highly significant in view of the United States' role as the leader of the Western Community of nations.

The driving political and economic forces behind the European integration movement have great future import for the United States in its long-drawn-out struggle—economic, political, ideological and military—with the Soviet Union. The major goals of the movement toward European unity, as most major observers view this phenomenon, include the following:

> To terminate the traditional rivalry and enmity between France and Germany by tying Germany closer to the affairs of Western Europe;
>
> To stimulate the economic growth of Western Europe—an economic region that traditionally had been burdened by lack of forceful drive and healthy economic competition;
>
> To mobilize and direct the political potential of Europe in a world significantly influenced and dominated by the existence of two major powers: the United States and the Soviet Union.

The successful achievement of these objectives has great meaning for the United States. Looking to the long-run political implications of a European Community enlarged to include the seven members of the EFTA, a

[11] Robert V. Roosa, "The Balance of Payments and International Financial Cooperation," *Monthly Review of the Federal Reserve Bank of New York,* March 1962, p. 50.

report specially prepared for the Subcommittee on Foreign Economic Policy of the Joint Economic Committee of the Congress states in forceful terms:

> If the European Community develops fast enough and well enough, the key industrial nations of Europe will form a new entity able to make common decisions, to mobilize its resources for common purposes, and to participate more actively in its own defense. As the members merge their economies and develop their capacity for acting as a unit, they will for the first time be able to play the role of an equal partner with the United States, sharing equitably in the responsibilities and burdens which have hitherto rested mainly upon this country.
>
> Thus the European Community should not endanger Atlantic cooperation but facilitate it. Only if the European nations are able to carry their share of the load to adopt common policies to influence the world, will there be the foundation for the kind of Atlantic relations which is required to face the challenge of the coming decades.
>
> The European Community therefore offers an effective means to enable the developed countries of the West to join together in discharging their common obligations and responsibilities. In tandem, the European Community and the United States can work for the creation of a more viable world order which can accommodate the needs and interests of the less developed countries as well. Together they can assure the growth of their own economies, provide their own people rising standards of life, and help the less developed nations in the gigantic effort to modernize. And finally they can concert more effectively for military defense against Communist aggression and for a common political approach designed to bring about ultimate changes in Soviet purposes and objectives.[12]

The Common Market has become a major force affecting political-military developments in the West—both today and in the future. It is unlikely that the signers of the Treaty of Rome envisaged the pace of political evolution during the first five years' operation of the European Economic Community.

[12] U.S. Congress, Joint Economic Committee, *The European Economic Community and the United States,* p. 12.

3

THE TRADE EXPANSION ACT—1962 *

Harry G. Brainard

On October 11, 1962 President Kennedy signed into law the Trade Expansion Act of 1962, which was hailed as a landmark in the foreign trade policy of this country. Whether or not this act ranks as a milestone

* From *Business Topics* (Michigan State University, Winter 1963), pp. 7-19. Reprinted by permission.

in the history of United States international commercial policy depends upon the answers to three major questions. If the evidence is in the affirmative, then the act is a significant break with the past; if not, then much of the publicity given this law as it passed through the legislative process was mere window dressing.

What are the questions to be raised and answered? First, does the Trade Expansion Act represent a new approach in philosophical terms to our tariff policy? In other words, is this nation now going to embark upon a distinctly new and different approach to the protection of American products from competition abroad? A second fundamental consideration relates to the objectives to be achieved. Are the provisions of the new law designed to meet objectives which are new and different from those sought by the Reciprocal Trade Agreements program initiated in 1934? And finally, even without reference to the two questions just posed, does the act provide new devices or techniques for implementing our commercial policies with other nations? The philosophy and the objectives may be basically the same as have existed for about three decades, but it may be that new and better tools of administration are provided by the Trade Expansion Act.

FOREIGN TRADE POLICY

The answer to the first question, namely, the basic philosophy of the Trade Expansion Act of 1962 in comparison with the Reciprocal Trade Agreements program, is neither yes nor no. It is, rather, that in certain important ways the new law represents a change in thinking on the part of the government; in other respects there is no change in the general approach to the foreign trade policy of this country. In order to give substance to this observation it is necessary to take a look at the tariff history of the United States during the past 30 years.

Hawley-Smoot Act

Congress in 1930 passed the Hawley-Smoot Act which established the highest tariff rates in the history of the nation. This action was taken in the sincere belief that it would contribute to a solution of the economic depression gripping the country. It was thought that the best way to save jobs for American labor and to provide orders for business was to drastically limit competition from foreign industry and agriculture. Imports of many commodities shared the market with domestic goods and hence added to the depressed economic conditions. Economic isolation contributed to domestic activity and was, therefore, not only good but desirable. This was a philosophy of economic self-containment.

Under the guidance of Secretary of State Cordell Hull, the Roosevelt administration promoted a foreign trade program which differed sharply from that embodied in the Hawley-Smoot Act. The new approach could not be characterized as "free-trade" in the literal sense, but it was based on a belief that a policy of economic isolation could not contribute to the creation of greater business activity. Reducing imports by the imposition of restrictive tariff rates would clearly leave a larger share of the home market to domestic producers. At the same time, however, markets for American products abroad could be expected to decline. Trade, it was argued, is a two-way street and a nation can export only if it also imports. The foreign trade policy of the Roosevelt administration was, therefore, to expand exports and in this way to raise the level of economic activity.

Reciprocal Trade Agreements Act

The Reciprocal Trade Agreements Act of 1934 implemented the basic philosophy of the Roosevelt administration and represented a milestone in United States tariff history. Henceforth tariff rates on selected commodities were to be reduced through bilateral negotiations with other nations in order to expand trade. This was a bold new program and a direct break with the philosophy of the Hoover administration expressed in the highly restrictive Hawley-Smoot Act of 1930. It is to be emphasized, however, that this was not a free trade program; instead it was a means to promote freer trade. This distinction is important because it puts into proper focus the nature of the policy inaugurated by Secretary Hull.

From 1934 to 1962 the Reciprocal Trade Agreements Act was renewed on 11 different occasions and typically for a period of three years. There were no significant changes in the legislation until 1948, although certain administrative procedures had been introduced to meet Congressional criticism. For example, while World War II was still going on, the Reciprocal Trade Agreements program was attacked with ever increasing intensity on the grounds that American producers were being injured or might be by tariff concessions granted to other nations. It was argued that a policy of reducing tariffs was acceptable so long as there was no injury to American industry and agriculture. Such a contention was, of course, without meaning for the simple reason that a tariff which was not sufficiently high to limit imports was not protective and hence of little use to those for whom it was intended. In practice the advocates of the no-injury concept did not push their argument this far, but were content to seek relief if a tariff concession threatened to cause a significant loss of market to the industry concerned. It was in response to this argument that an escape clause was included in the 1943 trade agreement with Mexico.

Peril-point and Escape Clauses. When the Reciprocal Trade Agreements Act was under consideration for renewal in 1948 the proponents of the no-injury philosophy of tariff negotiations were successful in including in the act of that year a peril-point provision and an escape clause. The law required a review by the Tariff Commission of each list of commodities proposed for tariff negotiation for the purpose of establishing the maximum concession that could be granted without inflicting injury on the industry concerned. A concession beyond this point could be negotiated but had to be justified in a report to the Congress. The escape clause established a procedure by which a tariff reduction already granted could be withdrawn on the Tariff Commission's finding an injury. If such action was not taken by the President an explanation had to be submitted to the Congress. Even though the no-injury provisions were withdrawn the following year, the protectionist philosophy had been accepted briefly as the prevailing sentiment of the Congress. It was again expressed in 1951 when peril-point and escape clauses were written into the law, where they have remained ever since.

A Shift in Attitude. The no-injury philosophy of the Trade Expansion Act of 1962 represents a sharp break with the past. The peril-point clause was dropped. In its place is a provision requiring the Tariff Commission to study carefully the probable economic effects of modifications of duties or other import restrictions on industries producing commodities appearing on the tariff bargaining list. The law does not require the determination of minimum duties essential to the protection of the industries concerned—the basic characteristic of the peril-point provision. An escape clause was retained but the newly enacted law recognizes that tariff concessions may be expected to cause a hardship on industries, firms, and workers. With few exceptions, the remedy provided is not to be found in an upward adjustment of rates but rather in helping those concerned to meet the new competition. In other words, it is assumed that in the administration of the Trade Expansion Act industries, firms, and workers can expect to be injured by tariff concessions. This is a reversal of the philosophy of tariff negotiations which has prevailed since 1948.

A comparison of the recently enacted tariff legislation with that which prevailed from 1934 to 1948 does not yield so precise a result with respect to the no-injury concept. Each time the Trade Agreements Act was up for renewal, the impact of increased imports upon domestic markets resulting from tariff concessions was dealt with at length in Congressional hearings. Moreover, attempts were made to include peril-point and escape clauses but they were rejected either by the Congressional Committee concerned or by the Congress itself. The inference that one may draw from a study of Congressional hearings is that the Roosevelt and Truman Administrations accepted as generally valid the no-injury concept but did not argue for it explicitly and were willing to compromise if necessary. Evidence of this is found by the inclusion of escape clause provisions in an agreement with Mexico negotiated in 1943, already noted above. These provisions were later written into other agreements by executive order and became a part of the General Agreement on Tariffs and Trade (GATT) concluded between 23 nations in 1947.

By way of summary it is fair to say that in writing the Trade Expansion Act the Congress recognized that tariff concessions can be expected to cause injury to certain industries and created machinery for dealing with the problem, relying on an escape clause as a measure of last resort. In adopting this philosophy of tariff negotiations the new law more nearly resembles the Trade Agreements Acts of 1934 through 1945 than those of the period from 1948 to 1958.

OBJECTIVES OF THE 1962 ACT

An appraisal of the Trade Expansion Act of 1962 must include a study of objectives to be attained by the legislation if one is to fairly evaluate the new program. When the Trade Agreements program was initiated in 1934 it was thought of as emergency legislation designed to deal with the foreign trade sector of the economy. The objectives to be attained by the new program were, therefore, geared to the recovery efforts of the Roosevelt administration. Secretary of State Cordell Hull, the architect of the program, looked beyond the economic situation then prevailing, however, and believed that as a long-run objective the best interests of the nation would be served over the years by gradually freeing trade from limitations imposed by high tariffs.

As the Reciprocal Trade Agreements Act was reviewed periodically, debate always centered around the contribution it could make to the solution of domestic and international problems then existing. The emergency character of the program as a device for dealing with a domestic depression was soon replaced by its usefulness in meeting the threat of war and of war itself.

In the postwar period and particularly in 1945, continuation of the Reciprocal Trade Agreements program was considered vital by the administration. One objective to be attained was to demonstrate to the world that this nation did not intend to turn isolationist as it had after World War I. More importantly the ability of the United States to continue tariff negotiations was deemed to be of great significance as this country moved into a position of leadership in world affairs.

Beginning in 1949 and continuing into the legislation being discussed, the Reciprocal Trade Agreements program has been supported as one method to combat the influence of Communism. The argument is that by prohibiting the extension of the benefits of tariff reductions to Communist-dominated nations, markets for their products are restricted, thereby limiting the effectiveness of economic penetration as a method for promoting their ideology. A negative action is taken, therefore, to attain a laudable objective.

By 1958 there were people in Congress, in the Eisenhower administration, and in the business community who believed the main objectives of the Reciprocal Trade Agreements program had been reached and, therefore, the act should not be renewed. The argument that was persuasive enough to lead to a continuation of the program was the need for our government to be in a position to deal with the problems of foreign commerce that would emerge as a consequence of the establishment of the European Economic Community, popularly known as the Common Market. Nations constituting the Community are The Netherlands, Belgium, Luxembourg, West Germany, France, and Italy. The Reciprocal Agreements Act of 1958 extending the life of the program for four years had as its main purpose the retention of a tool of foreign economic policy that might be useful in gaining the maximum access to the Common Market as a uniform external tariff wall came into existence. What the problem would be and how useful reciprocal tariff negotiations might be, it was thought, would become evident within the four-year period. Hence the program was kept alive until 1962.

Specific Ends

The language of the Trade Expansion Act of 1962 is clear and unequivocal in stating the purposes to be attained. There are two main objectives. The first is to achieve certain specific ends by lowering trade barriers through tariff negotiations. The resulting agreements will afford mutual benefits to such basic interests as the general welfare, foreign policy, and national security. In more precise terms these specific ends are:

> To benefit the economy of the United States;
>
> To strengthen economic and political relations between the United States and the other countries of the free world and in particular with the European Economic Community;
>
> To assist the economies of countries in the earlier stages of economic development;
>
> To counter penetration by international Communism.

New Methods

The second purpose of the act deals with new methods of meeting cases of actual or potential hardship arising out of trade negotiations. These adjustment provisions are in keeping with the new philosophy that the reduction of trade barriers can be expected to cause injury to industries, firms, and workers as foreign competition is intensified. In other words, a second purpose of the act is to expand the trade of the United States even though various segments of the business world may be subjected to loss of markets, profits, and even jobs. This objective is based on a rejection of the no-injury philosophy which had prevailed for more than a decade.

When the objectives of the Trade Expansion Act of 1962 are put alongside those of the Reciprocal Trade Agreements Act of 1934 as amended, it becomes clear that the new law represents a significant departure from the past. In the first place, the bargaining provisions are viewed as a tool to combat foreign trade barriers and thereby to expand the nation's exports. Secondly, it is proposed to expand commerce in specific areas as a consequence of trade negotiations. These are the Common Market and the nations that are developing economically, particularly those in South America. Finally, it is believed that an expansion of our foreign commerce will contribute substantially to overcoming balance of payments deficits experienced in recent years.

EXPANSION OF FOREIGN TRADE

A final area of investigation concerns the procedures by which the expansionist philosophy of the act is to be implemented. As with other aspects of the legislation, one finds here that improvements have been made on the former tariff negotiating procedures and new methods have been created.

Broadening of the Bargaining Unit

A feature of the Trade Expansion Act of 1962, which is new, although implicit in the 1958 Reciprocal Trade Agreements Act, relates to a broadening of the bargaining unit. Specifically, the new law recognizes the European Economic Community as an economic entity for trade negotiations as distinguished from its member nations (The Netherlands, Belgium, Luxembourg, West Germany, France, and Italy). The significance of this new arrangement cannot be fully appreciated until one understands earlier procedures. When the Reciprocal Trade Agreements program was first established, trade negotiations were conducted on a bilateral basis. Thus the United States government entered into separate bargaining sessions on a nation-by-nation basis and worked out a trade agreement containing tariff reductions on commodities of most importance to the country concerned. The lower rates thus negotiated were then extended to all other nations with which the United States maintained friendly trading relations. This was done in conformance with the most-favored-nation policy long accepted by our government. During the first 13 years of the program, 1934-1947, 29 reciprocal trade agreements were negotiated on a purely bilateral basis.

Beginning in 1947 the trade agreement negotiating process was modernized when the United States and 22 other nations met in Geneva, Switzerland, as a group to bargain collectively. There were altogether 123 sets of negotiations covering roughly 50,000 items. The end product of the conference was the adoption by the participating nations of the General Agreement on Tariffs and Trade (GATT). Since that first bargaining session four additional negotiating conferences have been held. The most recent was in late 1961. These conferences do not replace the conclusion of bilateral agreements as such but they greatly accelerate the process of negotiation. Only for individual nations that are not members of the GATT are bilateral sessions held.

What the new law does is to carry the trade negotiating process one step further by providing that tariff bargaining will henceforth be conducted between the United States and the European Economic Community instead of its member nations individually. This is a logical procedure because there will be coming into existence over a period of years a single uniform external tariff schedule applicable to all nations trading with Common Market countries. Hence it makes sense to deal with the European Economic Community as an entity in itself, and as the Common Market expands to include more nations, so will the importance of bargaining with it become more all-inclusive.

A Special Representative

As a corollary to the broadening of the bargaining unit Congress wrote into the Trade Expansion Act a section providing for the creation of a Special Representative for Trade Negotiations. The establishment of a new agency to conduct trade negotiations is also a natural extension of the former Reciprocal Trade Agreements program. It is designed to provide a more efficient administration of this country's foreign trade policy in an international climate different from that of the past few years. To fill this new position and to play the role of chief negotiator, the President recently appointed Christian Herter, Secretary of State in the Eisenhower administration. Mr. Herter has the rank of ambassador and is directly responsible to the President.

By establishing an agency for the expressed purpose of conducting trade negotiations, Congress departed sharply from previous procedures by removing responsibility for thc bargaining process from executive departments of the government. For nearly two decades the administration of the Reciprocal Trade Agreements program was centered in the Department of State. In the early years Secretary Hull took an active part in administering the program largely through an Interdepartmental Committee. Later an assistant secretary assumed responsibility for this nation's foreign trade policy. More recently the conduct of trade negotiations has been a function of the Department of Commerce with the interests of other departments represented by an Interdepartmental Committee. Throughout the years the Tariff Commission has served in an advisory capacity especially with respect to determining peril points below which rates could not be set without injury to the producers concerned.

In the administration of the Trade Expansion Act the Special Representative will have the assistance of certain executive departments and of committees of Congress. The President is required to establish a cabinet-level interagency organization as successor to the old Interdepartmental Committee. This organization, functioning through the Special Representative as an *ex-officio* member, will advise the President on trade agreement matters including tariff adjustment for seriously injured industries. It will also inform the Chief Executive of the impact of foreign import restrictions on the commerce of this country.

A new provision of the act relates to the role of Congress itself in trade negotiations. This clause stipulates that two members of the House Ways and Means Committee and two from the Senate Finance Committee shall participate in tariff bargaining sessions. This is the first time since the beginning of the Reciprocal Trade Agreements program that Congress has insisted upon taking part in trade negotiations. Previously it has been content to receive reports periodically on the conduct of trade negotiations. These reports will continue to be submitted and the Tariff Commission will provide the President and Congress with technical information and assistance as needed.

Greater Bargaining Authority

The heart of the Reciprocal Trade Agreements program has been the authority Congress has granted to the President to negotiate trade concessions and to enter into foreign trade agreements. This authority is continued in the Trade Expansion Act for five years, that is, to June 30, 1967 which, incidentally, is longer than any previous period. The ability to negotiate trade agreements has meaning, however, only to the extent that concessions can be granted and it is in this respect that the present act is of particular importance. The basic authority to modify import duties remains essentially unchanged from the Trade Agreements Act of 1958. Tariff rates may be reduced by 50 percent of those prevailing at a specified base period which in the new legislation is July 1, 1962. In addition, rates may be increased over the July 1, 1934 level (Hawley-Smoot Act rates) and additional import restrictions may be imposed.

It is in the authority to grant concessions beyond those indicated above when negotiating with the European Economic Community that the new law gains special significance. In the first place, the President is permitted to reduce *by more than 50 percent* or eliminate entirely duties on categories of articles instead of item by item when it can be established that the United States and Common Market countries together accounted for 80 percent or more of the free world trade in these groups of commodities in a representative base period. Secondly, similar duty reductions can be granted on certain agricultural goods when a determination is made that such reductions will tend to assure the maintenance or expansion of United States exports of similar articles. A final special negotiating authority is dependent upon similar action by the European Economic Community. Specifically, duties on tropical agricultural and forestry products may be reduced by more than 50 percent if it can be shown (1) that similar commodities are not produced in significant amounts domestically, and (2) that Common Market countries have agreed to give these products access to their market on equally favorable terms.

The law also permits the President to reduce duties in excess of 50 percent on those commodities subject to a rate of 5 percent or less on July 1, 1962. This authority is designed to facilitate administration of the law, since there is little likelihood that a duty of this magnitude would have economic significance.

Limitation on Use of Authority

In accordance with previous legislation, the new trade law places certain restrictions on the bargaining power of the President. These limitations are in all major respects the same as those of the Reciprocal Trade Agreements Act of 1958. First of all, duties on articles which have been the subject of escape-clause treatment cannot be changed for at least four years. The President is also restrained from negotiating reductions on certain commodities if a finding has been made by the Office of Emergency Planning that their importation may threaten the national security. And as a matter of fact, restrictions may be imposed to limit the flow of such products into the country to the point where they no longer constitute a national security risk.

A final limitation in the administration of the bargaining provisions of the act is concerned with the size of a duty reduction that can be granted at any one time. Thus, except in the case of the exercise of the tropical commodity authority, the law requires in general that reductions in duties are to be made in five annual stages. The purpose of this provision, of course, is to allow domestic producers time to adjust to foreign competition. Another restriction concerns trade with any area or country controlled or dominated by Communism. Under this provision no concessions granted through trade agreements with other nations can be extended to the Soviet Union or its satellites. During the debate on the Trade Expansion bill, an effort was made to exclude Poland and Yugoslavia from this restriction on the ground that economic penetration in these countries might be possible. The Senate bill had such an exception but House conferees refused to accept it; so these two nations were included with the other Communist countries.

Foreign Import Restrictions

A section of the present law which is a carry-over from preceding legislation allows the President to withhold tariff concessions from nations that impose import restrictions which discriminate against products from the United States. The purpose of this provision is to give greater bargaining power to the administration as it negotiates trade agreements. By threatening to cancel or suspend concessions that have already been granted, our government is in a strong position to compel the removal of barriers imposed discriminatively against our exports. The use of this authority is punitive, to be sure, but may be necessary under certain conditions.

A New Approach to Injury Cases

Earlier in this article it was suggested that in writing the Trade Expansion Act of 1962 Congress departed from its philosophy of "no injury" and accepted the idea that American industries might indeed suffer hardship as a consequence of tariff reductions. In accordance with this concept the new law contains special provisions in addition to the traditional escape clause for dealing with injury cases. This approach to hardship situations is a complete break with earlier legislation and, therefore, merits special attention.

Industry Adjustment. A petition for tariff adjustment may be filed with the Tariff Commission by a trade association, a firm, a trade union, or by an entire industry. When such action has been taken the Commission is then required to conduct an extensive investigation of the claim to determine if increased imports have caused or threaten to cause the injury alleged. When the Commission has completed its investigation, which must be done within six months, a report is made to the President and also to the public. In case of an affirmative finding, several types of action can be taken by the government. If it appears that an entire industry is adversely affected by a tariff concession, two kinds of relief are available. Under the terms of the escape clause carried over from the 1958 Act, the President may proclaim an increase in, or the imposition of a duty on, the article in question to the degree necessary to prevent serious injury to the industry. The word "may" is used advisedly since the Chief Executive is not required to take such action. In this instance he must report to Congress, which by a majority vote can override his decision and thereby compel action by the President.

Another kind of action that can be taken in industry hardship cases appears for the first time in the Trade Expansion Act. As an alternative to the escape-clause procedure, the government is authorized to negotiate international agreements with foreign countries designed to permit the orderly marketing of certain commodities exported to this country. Where this action is taken, tariff concessions are not affected but imports are limited by mutual agreement. For several years such arrangements have been in existence, having been negotiated under laws not directly concerned with trade policy. The most notable of these agreements is the one with Japan which limits the flow of a wide range of textile products to this country. In the future these agreements can be negotiated formally and directly between governments under this law which deals specifically with our foreign trade policy. It is to be emphasized that industry relief will be given as a last resort and only after it is certain that the various adjustment measures designed to assist firms and their workers to meet the new conditions are inappropriate.

Company Adjustment. An increase in imports arising out of reduced trade barriers may not affect an entire industry but rather be felt by certain firms only. It is quite possible for a high-cost domestic producer to be forced out of the market while other more efficient firms are able to meet foreign competition. To provide relief for adversely affected firms and their workers, Congress has written into the present law special adjustment provisions for individual companies and employees. The relief made possible by the act is not intended to shield the firms or workers from foreign competition; instead, it is designed to enable them to shift to the production of other kinds of commodities and employment. Since this kind of relief is new in tariff legislation and constitutes a rejection of the no-injury philosophy, a closer look at the adjustment procedure is warranted.

Once a company is certified by the Tariff Commission as eligible for relief, it may apply to the Secretary of Commerce who can provide assistance by one of three methods, singly or in combination. Assistance may take the form of technical aid which will be provided by a governmental agency or in unusual cases by outside firms or individuals. Appropriate technical assistance may include market and other economic research, managerial advice and counseling, training, and help in research and product development. A second kind of aid may take the form of financial help including guarantees of loans, agreements for deferred participation in loans, or outright loans. The extent of financial assistance is limited to the amount that will contribute to the firm's economic adjustment. Finally, a firm may be granted tax relief. Where this is done, a company is permitted a five-year loss carry-back as compared with a three-year period for taxpayers in general. This concession is allowed only on the condition that the company's losses were occasioned by increased imports resulting from a trade agreement concession.

The granting of assistance by any of the above methods is conditioned upon the acceptance by the government of a definite proposal of the firm applying for relief. A proposal will be approved if it can be expected (1) to contribute to the firm's economic adjustment, (2) to give adequate consideration to the interests of its workers, and (3) to require the company to make all reasonable efforts to use its own resources in the adjustment process. The requirement that a firm's proposal will meet such standards is intended to insure a systematic approach to the problems of economic adjustment, to increase the likelihood that the adjustment will be successful, and finally to restrict governmental aid to those firms prepared to help themselves to the maximum extent possible.

Assistance to Workers. Just as firms may be eligible for assistance due to injury caused by tariff concessions granted in a trade agreement, so also may workers in industries thus affected be given aid. If the Tariff Commission finds an injury, workers may apply to the Secretary of Labor for assistance. Eligible workers who meet minimum qualifications may receive unemployment compensation up to 65 percent of their average weekly wage instead of the current national average of about 35 percent. Moreover, payments may be extended beyond the normal 39 weeks to a full year. Older workers and those taking training may qualify for an even longer period of payments. This is the trade readjustment program and its cost is borne entirely by the federal government.

Of more importance are two other kinds of assistance. The first of these is the aid that can be given to train a worker for a different kind of employment. Governmental agencies can make available to these workers testing, counseling, training, and placement services to the greatest extent possible. Where the appropriate kind of training program is not available in his own community, the worker may be given financial aid to defray transportation costs and living expenses while away from home. For the worker who is totally separated from his job, who cannot find suitable employment locally, and who obtains a satisfactory position elsewhere, a relocation allowance may be granted. This allowance includes the reasonable and necessary expenses incurred by the worker in transporting his family and household effects to a new community. In addition, the worker is entitled to a lump sum payment equal to two and one-half times the average weekly manufacturing wage.

The training and relocation allowances are of special significance, since they are designed to do for labor what technical, financial, and tax relief programs do for injured firms, namely, to promote a shift of resources to more efficient uses. Worker training and relocation programs will reduce the number of persons eligible for trade adjustment allowances and thereby lessen the cost of this kind of assistance. But of more importance is the fact that through these programs workers can be removed from an over-supplied market and their talents directed to those areas where they are needed.

The law contains in addition to the general adjustment provisions outlined above clauses spelling out in detail technical aspects of the various programs. There are also throughout the act specific rules and regulations that have not been discussed in this article. This is because our interest has been centered on the philosophy, objectives, and methods of accomplishment of the Trade Expansion Act. With this analysis completed, a general appraisal of the law can be made.

CONCLUSIONS

In order to reach general conclusions concerning the Trade Expansion Act of 1962 it will help to suggest certain features which may limit its effectiveness and to indicate its strong aspects. The act retains in essentially the same language several restrictive provisions of the Reciprocal Trade Agreements Act of 1958. These are the escape clause, national security, and Communist area provisions. The use of the escape clause is actually made easier in the present law than in its predecessors in two ways. It now requires but a simple majority of both houses of Congress to override a negative decision by the President where formerly a two-thirds vote was needed.

Secondly, the profit criterion has been changed so that now one evidence of injury is the ability of an industry to demonstrate that it cannot operate at "a level of reasonable profit." Formerly, the profit criterion could not be used if the industry had any profits at all. By this change, injury due to increased imports resulting from a trade agreement concession can be more easily established.

The section in the law prohibiting the extension of tariff concessions to Communist-dominated nations cannot be criticized in strong terms. The fact that the Senate bill excluded Poland and Yugoslavia from this provision raises some doubt, however, about the action finally taken. It may well be that the use of tariff concessions would have made economic penetration possible in these two countries. In the long run, therefore, this limitation may prove to have been unwise, but there is no sure way to know.

A part of the new act which would appear to be a forward step may in the end turn out to be an empty gesture. Reference is made here to the authority granted to the President to reduce to zero duties on commodities exchanged between the European Economic Community and the United States provided 80 percent or more of such trade is between these two areas. Under the present definition of the Common Market (The Netherlands, Belgium, Luxembourg, West Germany, France, and Italy), the only commodity that can qualify is certain types of aircraft. The administration based its argument for the authority on the concept of a Common Market that would include the United Kingdom. If and when Great Britain becomes a member, a broader definition will have to be adopted by Congress to make the above bargaining authority meaningful. As of now, it is an authority without substance.

The insistence of Congress upon direct representation in trade negotiations must be considered as a weakness. This is so because it is a direct extension of Congressional power into the area of administration and hence is in contravention of the separation of powers inherent in our system of constitutional government. It may not be a significant intrusion but the fact that it exists at all is to be deplored. If the Congress lacks faith in the administrative ability of the executive branch, then it should require detailed reports and perhaps consultation, but to take part directly in tariff bargaining would seem to be undesirable.

Among the many virtues of the Trade Expansion Act three are deserving of special comment. The acceptance of the European Economic Community as an entity for bargaining purposes is important because it is a recognition of the trend throughout the world towards economic regionalism. Where a trading area with a common external tariff exists it makes sense to deal with it as a unit. Other trading areas are coming into existence, the most notable being the common market established by the nations of Central America.

The Interagency Trade Organization, as a replacement for the Interdepartmental Committee, will serve to strengthen considerably the administration of the act. The new organization is a creation of Congress with clearly specified duties and with responsibilities going well beyond tariff bargaining to include problems of injury adjustment. The administrative machinery is further strengthened by the establishment of the office of Special Representative for Trade Negotiations. This is an important change in administration because it centralizes in one person responsibility for carrying out the bargaining provisions of the law. This activity will constitute the Special Representative's sole responsibility where formerly it was but one of the many duties of first the Secretary of State and more recently the Secretary of Commerce. The appointment of Mr. Christian Herter as Special Representative is a happy choice since few if any men in public life are better qualified. It is because of these major improvements in the administrative machinery that one wonders why Congress has insisted upon direct participation in the negotiating process.

The strongest feature of the Trade Expansion Act is its rejection of the no-injury concept of tariff bargaining. By assuming that an expansion of trade will cause hardship to industries, firms, and workers, and by providing intelligent adjustment procedures, Congress in passing this act clearly set our foreign trade policy on a new and forward-looking course. In this sense the new law constitutes a milestone in the international commercial policy of the United States and gives this nation added stature as a leader in world affairs.

4

COMMON MARKET AND COMMONWEALTH *

Drew Middleton

Prime Minister Harold Macmillan has called it a family. Others have seen it as a club, as a dump for burned-out British politicos, as a sinister instrument of Western imperialism, and as a weapon for white supremacy in the non-Communist world.

* From *The New York Times Magazine* (February 18, 1962). Copyright by The New York Times. Reprinted by permission.

It is the British Commonwealth of Nations, whose members are the United Kingdom, Canada, Australia, New Zealand, India, Pakistan, Ceylon, Ghana, the Federation of Malaya, the Federation of Nigeria, the Republic of Cyprus, Sierra Leone and, provisionally, Tanganyika.

With Britain preparing to join West Europe in the Common Market and with Commonwealth members divided among themselves on such issues as the cold war, colonialism and the United Nations, this unique international organism faces extraordinary external and internal pressures in the coming months. Some, indeed, fear the strains will be so great that it may fall apart. Such forebodings discount the elasticity of the Commonwealth. It will be difficult to break up simply because there is so little tangible to smash.

The Commonwealth is difficult to define. Perhaps the best approach to understanding what it is is to begin with what it is *not*.

Clearly the Commonwealth is not an alliance, since its members take up opposing positions on some of the great issues of our time. It can scarcely be called an organization, since it has no written constitution, and depends for its day-to-day workings on the habit of consultation among its members. Except in the abstract sense that the idea of the Commonwealth originated in these islands, it is not British. Nor, finally, is it white, since the majority of its people nowadays are Asians and Africans.

What can be said accurately is that the Commonwealth is vast. Spread over North America, Europe, Africa, Asia, Australia and New Zealand, it has an area of about 9,500,000 square miles, compared with the Soviet Union's 8,600,000 and the United States' 3,600,000 square miles.

Its population is about 691,600,000, compared with 185,000,000 Americans and 218,000,000 Russians. Of this vast population, only 83,-400,000 live in the four "old members" of the Commonwealth: Britain, Canada, Australia and New Zealand.

What holds them together? Nothing more definite than a common pattern of government and institutions, an infinity of economic, political, diplomatic and social links—some official, many unofficial—and a symbol.

Queen Elizabeth II often is referred to as the Head of the Commonwealth. It would be more precise to say that she is the only symbol linking—to a greater or lesser degree—all its members.

The emotional depth of the ties with the Crown varies from country to country. The late John Lardner treasured the memory of a night in a bar in Darwin, Australia, when he mentioned amiably that King George VI stammered slightly.

"Wot if 'e does, mite?" asked a bosun of the Royal Australian Navy, clenching an enormous fist. " 'E's our King, eyn't 'e?"

In most member countries, the Queen is an essential element in Parliament, and all legislation requires the Royal Assent, usually given through a Governor General appointed by the Queen. This rule does not apply in India, Pakistan, Ghana, the Federation of Malaya and Cyprus—yet they remain members.

Government in all Commonwealth countries follows the pattern of British parliamentary democracy. Sometimes, as in Pakistan at present, the system is in abeyance. The important thing is that the current generation of Commonwealth leaders is accustomed only to this form of representative government.

In addition to a common system of representative government, the Commonwealth has a system of law founded, with one exception, upon the English common law. The exception is Ceylon, where the legal basis is Roman-Dutch law. The leading politicians of the new members are often lawyers. The fact that they learned their law by studying the great English masters has helped to hold the Commonwealth together.

Common systems of government and law would not have been such satisfactory solidifying agents without free cooperation among members. A Commonwealth Government is morally obligated either to inform or to consult all other members on any action that might affect their interests.

Normally, consultation is full and frank, whether it is written or oral. Problems that crop up from day to day are dealt with either through correspondence among Commonwealth Governments or through the High Commissioners whom each member maintains in the capitals of other Commonwealth countries. When questions of great importance arise, they are dealt with by meetings of Ministers in whose fields the issues lie. There also are yearly conferences of Commonwealth Prime Ministers.

These are the ties, as light as gossamer but, under stress, as strong as steel, that hold the Commonwealth together. They have been enough in the past. The immediate issue is whether they will be strong enough in the urgent present.

The basic effect of Britain's entry into Europe, no matter what arrangements are concluded for her overseas partners, will be a drastic change in the nature of the Commonwealth.

While Britain remained outside any great-power grouping in Europe, her political experience, economic situation and diplomatic prestige enabled successive British Governments to speak—and occasionally to act—for the Commonwealth.

In joining Europe, Britain will be abandoning a special position in the world. Whichever form, federation or confederation, the new Europe takes, membership will deprive Britain of her unique role as the center of a world-wide grouping of nations.

This role inevitably has been enhanced by Britain's trading position. But once Australian or Canadian or Indian products can no longer enter Britain free of duty, Commonwealth economic ties will be under strain. If they snap, then the plain good business sense of looking and listening to Britain will lose its rationale.

What will then remain in ten or fifteen years' time will be those cultural ties that affect Britain's relations with the older members of the Commonwealth; important, but not paramount, trading relations—the United Kingdom will always be a prime market for all producers of raw materials—and, in some cases, a shared political system.

The Commonwealth may exist in 1972, but it will take a great deal of political faith to recognize in it the same grouping that played so large a part in the world between 1945 and 1962. Indeed, the British, who believe they can at the same time enter Europe, maintain their political influence in the Commonwealth and retain their present intimate political and military partnership with the United States, are repeating the besetting error of all post-war London Governments: trying to do too much with too little.

The character and significance of the Commonwealth already are changing. To measure the change one has only to consider what this unique organism has meant to Britain in the past and what it means now.

The Commonwealth evolved from the British Empire. To Victorian and Edwardian Britons and their Governments, that Empire represented primarily a market for British manufactured goods and a source of raw materials. But since, the Marxists to the contrary, men are seldom moved by gain alone, Britons also saw the empire as a means of propagating various faiths, of introducing civilization to backward peoples—by "civilization" they usually meant law and order—and of ending recurrent threats to Britons in out-of-way places of the world.

The change from Empire to Commonwealth began in the last century when the older Dominions, as they were then called, began to establish self-government. The name dates back to a speech by the Earl of Rosebery in Adelaide in 1844 in which he said, "The Empire is a commonwealth of nations."

In the past twenty years, people, except for the troglodytes on the extreme Right, have increasingly described what was formerly known as the British Empire as the Commonwealth. This change in terminology has been an important psychological factor in British life.

To the great middle class that emerged in Victorian England the Empire meant much. They watered it with their blood from the Yukon to Jaipur. They were convinced, and with some reason, that Britain had brought peace, stability, law and the beginnings of modern technology to countries around the world.

The transfer of sovereignty to the new members of the Commonwealth after the Second World War enabled their descendants to believe that what had been done might endure in a changing world. The Commonwealth, to a large extent, but not entirely, became an emotional substitute for the Empire. Britain's position as leader of that Commonwealth also provided successive British Governments with additional reason for claiming great-power status for their sadly weakened country.

This emotional attachment has always been stronger on the Right. Yet the proposal to enter Europe has evoked sharp protests from the Labor party's left wing. The issue is splitting British parties. A section of Labor's moderate center advocates union with the Common Market, while much of the drive behind the Conservative party's policy is loyalty to the Commonwealth. Britain's attitude toward the Commonwealth over the last half-century thus is compounded of nationalism, a real (if indistinctly expressed) desire to continue service to underdeveloped peoples and, of course, pounds, shillings and pence. For the Commonwealth remains Britain's best customer, although no one member takes more of Britain's total exports than the United States: 9.2 per cent in 1960.

But in that year, 38.5 per cent of total British imports and 41.2 per cent of exports were accounted for by Commonwealth countries—including Canada, which is outside the sterling area. (Australia, Britain's best Commonwealth customer, took 7.1 per cent.) And Britain lives by exports.

The Commonwealth market is no figment of a politician's imagination. No prudent Government can enter Europe without attempting to safeguard it and the system of free entry for Commonwealth raw materials into Britain.

These are all aspects of what the Commonwealth has meant and now means to Britain. But what has Britain meant to the Commonwealth?

To begin with, a tremendous reservoir of friendship and loyalty has been created, especially among the older members. Australia, New Zealand and the Canadian West were settled largely by immigrants from Britain, tough-minded people who, although they wanted to rule themselves, also wanted to keep green thoughts of those mist-shrouded islands they still called "home."

The Commonwealth market is no figment of a politician's imagination.
and imperialist exploitation. How else can one explain why men from Brisbane and Calgary, Wellington and Pretoria found themselves in two world wars fighting at Britain's side on battlefields all over the world?

True, Britain at the height of her power had given them protection. But this does not fully explain why India, in the Second World War, raised the largest volunteer army recorded by history.

Of course, this sense of unity and loyalty has been adulterated since. American commercial and cultural influences have outstripped those of Britain in Canada. They have had their impact upon Australia as well, and even upon New Zealand, the most obstinately "British" of all Commonwealth countries.

New members in Africa and Asia rely largely on the shared system of law and government, plus constant consultation, to link them with Britain. Because they are mostly under-developed, they look first toward the United States for technical assistance and economic aid.

By far, Britain's most important exports to the Commonwealth have been men and women. People from the mining valleys of Wales, or the bleak dales of Yorkshire went out as immigrants and built careers and, incidentally, countries. The skilled technical manpower that built the Commonwealth came from Britain.

Nor is the heritage of this emigration restricted to the older members. In a cemetery near Kandy in Ceylon, for example, people come to put flowers on graves of Englishmen long dead. One had been a judge and, his epitaph indicated, a man of powerful convictions. Yet these shy, gentle people still honored his grave. Why? "You see, sir," an elderly Ceylonese lawyer explained, "he was a just judge, and a good man. When he died, many wept."

The builders of the Commonwealth are gone now, but the stream of emigrants continues. Month after month, ships sail from Southampton and Liverpool carrying young families headed for "young" countries.

But the economic ties are not what they were. Britain has to fight to hold its Commonwealth markets. Indeed, it often seems to the British that the Commonwealth means more to them than it does to any other member.

"Here are Canadians crying their eyes out about our going into Europe," said a young member of the present British Government. "But that doesn't stop them from raising the import duty on British cars."

With maturity, the Commonwealth has developed greater independence in international affairs. The division over India's invasion of Goa is the most recent example. Generally, the older members of the Commonwealth condemned the action, while the new Asian and African members applauded it. Six years ago, Suez split the Commonwealth, with India attacking Britain's "unprovoked aggression" and Australia and New Zealand supporting Britain.

Each country was constitutionally justified in taking an individual position, for the Commonwealth has no common foreign or defense policy. Canada has troops in Germany, and Australia and New Zealand contribute to the Commonwealth Brigade in Malaya. But India, Ceylon and Ghana are proudly non-aligned in the duel between East and West.

In many ways the Commonwealth seems like a great raft moving by fits and starts down the perilous river of time. Often it loses members of the crew, like Eire and Burma. Sometimes it forces others, like South Africa, to jump overboard. To an organizational eye, this ramshackle craft seems to stay afloat more by good luck than by good management. What would happen if it suddenly struck a rock and came apart?

The West would lose immediately its most proven instrument for contact and consultation between the Atlantic Community and four of the most important nations in Asia and Africa, India and Pakistan, Nigeria and Ghana. Britain, of course, speaks for herself to the Commonwealth, but she speaks from a position that, although far less than it once was, remains enviable. Respect for the fierce red-faced old men who, as John Betjeman wrote, "never cheated, never doubted" dies hard.

An incident this writer witnessed in Northern Rhodesia helps to explain why. A district commissioner had to stop his car to talk to a group of agitated Bembas. He listened, said a few words and we drove off. They seemed quieter.

"Someone or some group jumped one of the sub-chiefs," he explained. "Beat him up and burned his house. They wanted an assurance we'd catch them. We will. I told them so."

They caught them, all right.

But Britain also is a channel through which the strategy and policies of the West are explained repeatedly and in detail to Commonwealth members in Africa and Asia. It is the British, speaking in terms of familiarity and knowledge, who explain NATO or SEATO or Soviet duplicity to suspicious legislators in New Delhi or Colombo.

Even more important, the Commonwealth remains a unifying force among peoples as different as Canadians and Cypriotes. As a medium for exchange of ideas and techniques it has few rivals.

A world in which the walls of prejudice and intolerance grow higher every day can ill afford to lose any instrument that penetrates these walls. The Commonwealth is such an instrument. If a time comes when the last Commonwealth Parliament is dissolved and the last High Court of Justice with its bewigged judges gives way to a "people's court," then the West will have lost an invaluable means of binding the new and old together.

5

DANGERS OF REGIONALISM *

Jean Royer

The first fifteen years after the war saw a spectacular revival in the exchange of goods between all parts of the world. There can be no doubt that this great expansion of trade was fostered by the system which the trading nations had succeeded in establishing and which finds expression in the General Agreement on Tariffs and Trade (G.A.T.T.). It was a system based on the principles of multilateralism and non-discrimination. Equality of treatment was meted out to all exporting countries. The preferential arrangements which were a legacy of the pre-war confusion were frozen and condemned to slow decay. Trade ceased to be hampered by the paralysing effect of quotas and licensing regulations. Tariffs were negotiated downwards and—what may have been even more beneficial to trade—exporters were assured of stable conditions on most world markets, through the binding of import duties against increase.

Everything appeared to favour the perpetuation and development of such a successful pattern of trade when the Rome Treaty was signed and introduced a different concept of trading relations. When it became clear that the Six really meant business and were determined to overcome internal opposition—even when it was backed by powerful political forces—to carry out the grand design, the trading nations remaining outside the new Community began to take stock of the situation. They wondered whether the system of trading which had served them so well since the war could be maintained. Or would the future lie in the setting up of one or more regional blocs, trading between which might be governed by a new type of bilateralism?

This reappraisal is still in process and it would be somewhat presumptuous at the present juncture to try to predict what pattern of trade will emerge from the present negotiations and discussions. It may, however, be of some interest to analyse the main issues in the light of possible solutions and to assess the chances of solving the issues outstanding within the framework of the one or the other system.

* From *Lloyds Bank Review* (October 1962), pp. 1-22. Reprinted by permission.

Before discussing this, there is one point that deserves some comment. It is rather surprising that the setting up of the European Economic Community should have had such a devastating influence on the thinking of governments regarding the maintenance of a trading system which was so clearly successful and beneficial. It should be recognized that the challenge came at the wrong moment. The multilateral system which had worked wonders had just begun to operate with signal efficiency when the Rome Treaty was signed. Apart from officials and a handful of economists, however, few people had realized the contribution made by the multilateral system to the expansion of trade. Governments and public opinion had not accepted wholeheartedly the philosophy behind it and were often impatient with the apparent limitations on sovereignty which it implied.

Although the United States Administration had taken the lead in the elaboration of the new Code of International Trade which was embodied in the Havana Charter and implemented through the instrumentality of the G.A.T.T., it was unable to get Congressional approval for the scheme. The United States is a party to the General Agreement, but the U.S. Congress is not bound by it; it can—and it does—take decisions which may conflict with the commitments of the Executive, and the Administration has then to obtain from its trading partners some form of waiver of its obligations.

The Commonwealth countries, with a few exceptions, had some difficulty in accepting a system which was antagonistic to the philosophy of preferences. These misgivings were strengthened, in countries relying on the export of agricultural commodities, by the growing realization of the inability of the trading system to enforce the law as successfully in the agricultural as in the industrial sector.

The Western European countries for their part paid far more attention to discussions in the O.E.E.C. than to the operation of the G.A.T.T. and were prone to believe that the results obtained were due more to the regional techniques of the European organization than to the virtues of worldwide multilateralism. Although the objectives of the O.E.E.C. were the same as those of the G.A.T.T. the practical approach was different. Those who took part in O.E.E.C. discussions could not forget that they had spent much of their time in negotiating bilateral trade agreements, and they moved gradually from bilateralism to guarded regional multilateralism. Their confidence in the virtues of multilateralism was not unlimited and they preferred reliance on strict reciprocity.

Finally, the developing countries, which had feared that multilateralism would work in favour of industrial countries and hide a new form of economic domination, had only begun to understand that this system of trading was in fact helping them to promote their economic development—indeed, that the assistance of international bodies in the trade field was invaluable for the solution of the major difficulties hampering the expansion of their trade, and therefore, of their economies.

There is no doubt that the reaction of trading nations to the challenge of the Common Market would have been different if the multilateral system of trading had been able to consolidate its gains and if it had been given sufficient time to tackle the major outstanding problems, such as the setting up of an equitable organization for trade in temperate agricultural products, the overhaul of tariff negotiating techniques, and the consolidation of procedures to deal with market disruption. Governments would then have acquired a firmer confidence in the efficiency of the principles themselves. They would have been able to spread that confidence to their industry and their public opinion. They might have looked upon the Rome Treaty as an interesting venture which should be watched without undue anxiety. They might have realized that there was no need to change horses in midstream, since their horses were strong enough to bring them safely across to the other side.

CHOICE OF THREE APPROACHES

After this digression, it is time to get back to our main theme. The decision taken by six European countries to join forces and establish a Customs Union induced other countries to take stock of the situation, and to make a choice between three approaches:

a. to join the European Common Market, by accession or association;
b. to build up similar groups, strong enough to speak on equal terms with the E.E.C.;
c. to remain independent and make the fullest possible use of the protection afforded by the multilateral system.

For some countries, this was no more than Hobson's choice. Whether they liked it or not, they could rely only on the existing system. These countries had practically no chance of being accepted in the E.E.C. or of finding suitable partners in a regional group. This is more or less the position of Japan or Canada. For other countries, such as the United States, the price of accession to the E.E.C. was too high, at least for the time being. Public opinion in America, though enthusiastic about regional integration in Europe, was not prepared to accept the limitations of sovereignty that such accession would imply. As the setting up of a North American regional group would not significantly change the bargaining position of the United States, reliance on the present arrangements remained the only practical approach.

Other countries felt that the second approach would be fruitful. Many plans for regional integration have been put forward in America, Asia, Africa and the Middle East. Apart from the Latin American Free Trade Association—the conclusion of which was directly influenced by the desire to offset the impact of the E.E.C. on Latin American trade—nothing concrete has emerged so far from these discussions. Even in the case of the LAFTA (Latin American Free Trade Association), the governments concerned realize that this regional project does not provide a complete solution of their problem. As a result of the challenge of the E.E.C., the governments of that region have therefore become far more interested than before in the working of the multilateral system.

Finally, the Western European countries tried many methods. The first reaction, in conformity with the then prevailing O.E.E.C. spirit, was to pursue the so-called "European" approach. The ill-fated project for a free trade area open to all O.E.E.C. countries had, in the mind of many Western European countries, all the virtues of the customs union, without the drawbacks of a closely-knit community such as the E.E.C. Surprisingly, to most people, the E.E.C. did not feel able to accept a plan that appeared to them to dilute the integration process to such a degree that the association would have for them all the drawbacks of the union, without offering any real chance of securing the results which at least three of the E.E.C. members were seeking.

After this somewhat dramatic interlude, the O.E.E.C. countries other than the Common Market Six and the five "forgotten but unforgettable" ones (Greece, Turkey, Spain, Ireland and Iceland) decided to set up a free trade area along the lines of the original British project. E.F.T.A. came into being and followed the E.E.C. step by step in the process of tariff and quota elimination. This, again, did not provide a satisfactory answer. Soon after the entry into force of E.F.T.A. the United Kingdom, followed by other members of the Association, stated that it wished to join the E.E.C. All possible avenues have thus been explored, with the sole exception of the third one mentioned above: namely, reliance on the multilateral system.

Needless to say, the lack of co-ordination between the so-called "third countries"—i.e. those which are not members of the E.E.C.—and the reliance on different approaches did not make it easy for them to exert a constructive influence on the developments in the trade policy of the E.E.C.

FUTURE PATTERN OF TRADE

To a large extent, the future pattern of trade depends on the results of the negotiations between the United Kingdom and the Six. One thing, however, is certain: the trading world as a whole will cease to be governed by the same rules. One group, which will comprise a number of Western European countries as full members and a number of associated members, whose rights and obligations may vary, will trade among themselves in accordance with one set of rules. Trade among other countries, or between them and the regional group, will be subjected to other rules (which may be the present code of multilateral trade, or another code) or to no rules at all. As terms of competition will be different, whether a country belongs to a regional group or not, some trade flows will be sheltered and others unsheltered. This situation is bound to affect the aggregate level of world trade and to alter the specific channels of trade.

It may be argued that the very success of regionalism could, after a short while, restore a pattern which would be based on equality of terms as before. If, thanks to the skill of the British negotiators, the United Kingdom is able to open the doors of the European Community to its partners in E.F.T.A., and to bring in a large number of Commonwealth countries as associated members, the scope of the Community would be enlarged considerably. If, further, the United States and Canada are able to overcome their present misgivings and to see their way to accepting the severe limitations of sovereignty which would enable them to join the E.E.C. or become associated with it, the present system would be replaced by a new dispensation covering practically the bulk of world trade. The regional system would become more or less world-wide and its attraction would ensure its eventual universality. Through regionalism, multilateralism would thus have come back to the fore and the new rules would be far more liberal than could have been dreamt of a few years ago.

This happy ending may not be a pipe dream, but it would be safer to assume that a transitional period of some duration will in any event elapse before such an outcome is realized. The negotiations with the E.F.T.A. countries have not yet begun and they may prove difficult. The attraction of the E.E.C. for independent Commonwealth countries is not very apparent. Some time will be required before the deep-seated protectionism of North America melts away.

Moreover, there would, in any case, be a hard core of countries which may not be able or willing to join. Many unaligned countries may find it unacceptable to become closely linked with a group which will represent a particular political philosophy, whether the E.E.C. develops into a political federation or not. The Communist world will, in any case, remain outside the pale and will exert pressure on the neutrals. If a substantial number of countries are in that position, they will feel that discrimination is the harder to bear as the membership of the Community increases. The split between the Community and the rest of the world may become deeper and force the outside countries—the international proletariat of unprivileged nations—to close their ranks.

Another hope which is often expressed is that the entry into the E.E.C. of "liberal" countries would soften the inward-looking leanings of some of its present members. If trade discrimination becomes slight, outside countries would not suffer from the establishment of a European group, since the dynamic growth of the integrated economies would be more than sufficient to compensate for whatever disadvantages may result from inequalities in tariff treatment.

The preliminary results of the negotiations between the Six and the United Kingdom are encouraging in this respect. The Six have agreed to abandon duties on some goods, such as tea and sports goods, which are of particular interest to some Commonwealth producers. But one should not exaggerate either the protectionism of the present membership, or the scope of the reductions which the new acceders may be able to obtain. The E.E.C. external tariff, as a result of the Geneva negotiations, compares favourably with the tariffs of other industrial countries, and the attack by the United Kingdom on that tariff will not be on the whole front, but will probably be confined to key Commonwealth products. The results may not be very profitable to non-Commonwealth exporters. Moreover, the "liberal" countries will have to abandon their present policies and come closer to those of the E.E.C.

Whatever may be the results of the present negotiations in Brussels, the trading nations will have to consider as an urgent task the organization of the trade flows which will, at least for the time being, remain outside the E.E.C. ambit. In that connection, the first requirement would be to agree on a new round of tariff negotiations with the E.E.C., whether in its present or in a modified composition.

The prospects of such negotiations are different for *manufactured products,* on the one hand, and for *primary commodities* on the other. These two sectors of trade must therefore be considered separately.

TRADE IN MANUFACTURES

In trade in manufactured goods the markets of industrial countries with a few exceptions—some of which may be important—are protected only by customs tariffs. Quotas and licensing arrangements have been gradually dismantled and other forms of administrative protectionism have become less obnoxious. Tariffs have been brought down and bound against increase in many cases. But in spite of these reductions, tariffs are still high in many instances and their restrictive effect for certain suppliers is enhanced out of proportion when other suppliers can enjoy free or freer entry for their goods. In the context of a customs union or a free trade area, protection and discrimination are one and the same thing. In most cases, the present level of tariffs results from the tenacious efforts of industrialists in big countries to cling to a level of protection which was designed to shut off foreign competition from all sources. In smaller European countries, the position was different. Industries were more specialized; they had to compete on world markets and their main preoccupation was to bring down costs; a low-tariff policy was for them most appropriate.

Things have changed with the entry into force of integration agreements. In becoming a member of such a grouping, a country which was surrounded by tariff walls agrees to pull down part of the wall and to accept full competition from suppliers of some foreign countries, the other members of the group. Even if competition is not perfect, especially during the transitional period, the industrialist in such a country can no longer rely on government aids; he has to find the solution to his problems in rationalization and other industrial improvements. He may, however, ask his government to see to it that conditions of production are not too different in the other member countries of the group. Harmonization of conditions of production may be a prerequisite of free trade.

When conditions of production in countries outside the community are not different from those prevailing inside the community, the case for protection becomes much weaker and the tariff becomes, more or less, a bargaining counter in negotiations. It is only in cases where conditions of production are significantly different that industrialists in regional groups have some justification in asking for protection. This applies mainly to State-trading countries, to some Asian countries and to a few isolated cases where technological advances or other production factors may upset the usual terms of competition.

This change of situation has led the E.E.C. governments to accept new concepts of tariff negotiations among themselves, and also with other countries. Instead of negotiating, for instance, a concession on a particular textile product against a concession on bicycles, and balancing at the end of the negotiations a series of selective concessions on separate lists of products, the governments have agreed to lower the general incidence of their tariffs across the board. Strangely enough, industries much prefer this approach. They feel that it gives them a fair *quid pro quo*. With their new attitude towards protection, industrialists in the E.E.C. are prepared to meet competition on their home markets, provided that they can fight back and have the same opportunity to penetrate the home markets of their competitors. The new method of tariff reduction secures this kind of reciprocity. This explains why many industries find it easier to accept a complete elimination of duties within a customs union than to agree to a small reduction of duties in favour of a competitor in a country which is not prepared to do the same *in the same sector*.

In that situation, the old selective, product-by-product methods can no longer be applied. This is what the United States negotiators found out during the last Geneva Conference. The Ministers of Commerce assembled in Geneva in November, 1961, drew the necessary conclusions from this development: they instructed the G.A.T.T. to draw up new negotiating rules. The U.S. Administration introduced legislation designed to enable it to take part in tariff negotiations conducted along new lines.

NEW PRINCIPLE FOR TARIFF NEGOTIATIONS

Broadly speaking, the tendency is now to adopt the so-called "linear approach." Instead of assessing reciprocity by a subjective appraisal of the value of the sum of individual concessions granted and received, the negotiating countries would accept a simple formula along the following lines. Country A will reduce its tariffs by x per cent. if the other participating countries are prepared to reduce *their* tariffs by x per cent. This equation is the ideal one, but in practice it may be more complex. The adoption of such a principle would have enormous advantages. Negotiations would not drag on for months as they have often done hitherto. Governments would be in a much stronger position *vis-à-vis* protectionist forces, and the results of the negotiations would be far more substantial.

The United Kingdom has been converted to this new approach during the last tariff conference; but even if the U.S. Administration is empowered to negotiate along these lines, it is doubtful that American industries would accept readily the new attitude which is becoming popular in Europe. Agriculture and allied industries would not take part in this exercise and there is a risk that even the entire industrial sector would not be covered by the new technique. Even in the negotiations which took place at Geneva between the United Kingdom and the Six, the linear cut did not affect some reserved sectors on both sides. There would be a tendency to exclude from the cut a series of "sensitive" industries.

This is undoubtedly a serious complication, because exclusion of one sector by one country may lead to the same exclusion by the other negotiating countries. If all the "sensitive" sectors were thus added in a common list, the scope of the negotiation would become hopelessly narrow. The preliminary negotiation regarding the area to be covered by negotiations and acceptance of the exclusions might retard the opening of substantive discussions and jeopardize the success of a future tariff conference.

In spite of these difficulties, it is reasonable to expect that governments will not be hampered by opposition to the new methods of negotiation, and that the United States Administration will be in a position to take a leading part in a new round of negotiations. If that is the case, countries with diversified export interests will find that the external tariff of the E.E.C. is no longer a serious obstacle to their exports of manufactured goods.

TARIFF LEVELS AND TRADE

Apart from the prospects of such negotiations, the accession of the United Kingdom and of other European countries to the E.E.C. would have an influence on the tariff level of the Six and of the acceding countries. It would seem that any idea of averaging tariffs has been abandoned, and that acceding countries will have to accept the E.E.C. common tariff, without many changes. For certain items of interest to Commonwealth countries some reductions will be made; but, by and large, the common tariff will stand.

This means that the tariffs of the United Kingdom, in the industrial sector, would be reduced, sometimes substantially, for consumers' goods and be raised on capital goods. If Austria joins, its duties will undergo a significant reduction. On the other hand, the tariffs of Switzerland and of the Scandinavian countries would have to be raised for most items.

Such tariff adjustments would have the effect of stimulating trade diversion in exports to the low-tariff countries and of limiting such diversion in the case of high-tariff countries; as, in the latter case, tariff differentiation would be compensated to a certain extent by tariff reductions. This is the reverse of what happens in the case of a free trade area, where trade diversion is more pronounced in the case of exports to high-tariff members.

The trade of acceding countries with the Six will be stimulated by accession or association, both on the import and on the export side. It is impossible to guess how this upsurge of trade will affect the trade balance of these countries with the E.E.C., on the basis of past performances. The change in the pattern of trade may be more abrupt than was the case with the formation of the E.E.C. or the E.F.T.A., since the initial cuts in the tariffs will be larger. It may, however, be safely assumed that, from a strictly trade point of view, accession would not bring about a dramatic change in the position of the acceding countries, compared with what would happen if these countries remained outside the Community and took an active part in a determined effort to bring down the E.E.C. external tariff by means of a new-styled tariff conference fully backed by the United States.

So far, the establishment of the European Economic Community has not brought about any significant alteration in the export trade of countries which have a diversified range of industrial exports. The E.E.C. market plays about the some rôle in the total exports of these countries as before the Rome Treaty was concluded, as can be seen from the following table:

SHARE OF EXPORTS TO THE E.E.C. IN THE TOTAL EXPORTS OF INDUSTRIAL COUNTRIES

Exporting Countries	Share of exports going to the E.E.C. (%)	
	1957	1961
Austria	49.3	49.6
Sweden	33.0	33.0
Switzerland	38.4	41.5
United Kingdom	13.8	16.7
United States	16.9	18.6
Canada	8.3	8.4
Japan	4.9	5.0

Apart from Switzerland, the United Kingdom and the United States, whose exports to the E.E.C. have increased more than their total exports, there is a complete lack of evidence that the E.E.C. has had any effect, favourable or adverse, on the export trade of industrial countries outside the Community. Of course, these countries did not enjoy the spectacular increases which were recorded in intra-Community trade. This is only natural, since these countries had not accepted the commitments of the E.E.C. Although the evidence may be considered as incomplete, since the integration process has not come to an end, it would seem reasonable to conclude that, so far, the expansion of intra-Community trade has not been at the expense of outsiders and that third countries which export mainly industrial products are not worse off now than if the E.E.C. had not been set up.

EFFECTS ON PRODUCTION

If accession to the E.E.C. does not, after all, make such a tremendous difference, why should countries such as the United Kingdom and other European countries be so anxious to join the Six? It would seem that the main benefits these countries hope to derive from such action lie more in the field of production than in the field of trade.

Industry in the United Kingdom needs some reorganization, which would hardly be attempted so long as producers can rely on tight protection against foreign suppliers. The cold wind of Community competition may be a prerequisite to such overdue transformation of the structure of production. The example of France is a clear evidence of the salutary effects which sharp competition may exert on pampered industries. Accession to the E.E.C. may not be essential to protect export markets in Continental Europe, but may be indispensable to enable European countries to compete successfully in world markets in face of the increased aggressiveness on the part of Common Market exporters and of the advantages enjoyed by the extremely modern and closely-knit producers in North America.

European industry may not be as backward as is sometimes stated and not a few industries in the United States have found that competition from Europe may be severe, not so much due to labour costs as because of advanced technology. When United States firms enter into agreements with their opposite numbers in Europe for the exchange of patents, they often stand on the receiving end. But the fact remains that, apart from the smaller European countries that have specialized in certain lines in which they are remarkably efficient, most of the European industries are still relying to an excessive degree on their home markets and are not equipped to enter into fully-fledged competition with the new industrial giants. Accession to the E.E.C. may be more important for its influence on the structure of production than for its effects on the flows of trade with the E.E.C.

POLITICAL CONSIDERATIONS

Political considerations also play an important part. The E.E.C. is becoming a new world power; this infant giant might have had feet of clay, but this has not been the case. The severe test of the common agricultural policy showed that the Six are able to overcome serious internal difficulties to maintain their cohesion. By its sheer weight, the E.E.C. is bound to influence the course of events. A great power like the United Kingdom cannot run the risk of being squeezed between Continental Europe and the United States, the more so as public opinion in the U.S. is very much attracted by the political advantages of European integration.

Some people fear—or hope—that the entry of the United Kingdom into the E.E.C. would slow down the drive towards political federation or, at least, lead to a dilution of the political aspirations of the European Community. This may be the case, but the reverse may also be true. Neither the United States nor the major partners in the Community would be prepared to turn their backs on political objectives. It may well be that the United Kingdom would give a renewed stimulus to the negotiations on the political *rapprochement* in Europe.

The world is groping for new forms for collaboration among the industrial States in the free world, and between them and the developing countries. The British Commonwealth may not be the most appropriate machinery for linking together countries at various stages of development and the United Nations is hamstrung by its unmanageable proportions.

The French government attempted to use the E.E.C. as the means of keeping Europe and Africa together. This attempt could not be successful so long as part of Africa was associated to the new organization and part of it kept aloof. The division of Europe weakened the chances of a genuine reconciliation between Africa and its former masters. By broadening the scope of the experiment, something more constructive might be worked out. An enlarged E.E.C. might be the most appropriate forum in which a sensible collaboration between the various groups in the free world could be worked out.

TRADE IN TEMPERATE AGRICULTURAL PRODUCTS

So much for trade in industrial products. Whether the negotiations between the United Kingdom and the Six succeed or not, the prospects are fairly encouraging. If they succeed, the United Kingdom and other European countries would enjoy the stimulus of economic integration and their trade with other European countries would develop, at the price of widespread adjustments in the structure of production. If they do not succeed, but the United States accepts new methods of tariff negotiations, the general lowering of tariff barriers which would come about would make it comparatively easy to absorb the European group in the multilateral context. There would not seem to be any excuse for abandoning the present system in trade relations and reverting to the bilateral jungle.

The picture is more gloomy when one looks at the agricultural sector. The problems here were not created by the trend towards regionalism; but that development has no doubt crystallized them and deepened the divergences between exporting and importing countries. Whereas the code of multilateral trading introduced in 1947 was surprisingly successful with respect to trade in manufactures, it was simply inoperative in the agricultural sector. While paying lip service to the ban on restrictions, most governments pursued domestic agricultural policies which made it practically impossible for them to live up to their obligations. If the United States had given the lead, there might have been some chance of enforcing the rules of the game. But it rapidly became clear that any undertaking assumed by the U.S. Executive would be of doubtful efficacy, so long as the U.S. Congress was determined to treat agriculture as an exclusively domestic matter which should not be affected by foreign trade considerations.

The latest version of the Sugar Act as approved in 1962 by the U.S. Congress shows the type of arrangement which can result from excessive preoccupation with domestic interests. It contains all the practices which successive U.S. delegations have tried to ban as detrimental to trade and in conflict with the code of international trade: import quotas; variable levies over and above an import duty bound against increase; preferential arrangements allowing certain suppliers to pay only a fraction of the levy for certain quantities; distribution of the quotas in accordance with criteria difficult to reconcile with the principle of non-discrimination (as a preference is given for the allocation of the "Cuban quota" to suppliers of the Western Hemisphere and also to those countries which are prepared to purchase additional quantities of surplus agricultural products from the United States).

Bilateralism, with a slight flavour of barter, is thus a feature of this Act. It is argued that sugar is a special case and that this arrangement is the best that all concerned can hope for. That may be the case, but from the point of view of the organization of international trade that is neither here nor there.

Either this type of arrangement makes economic sense or it does not. If it does, there is no justification for preventing *any* country from having recourse to similar arrangements. Consequently, the ban on quotas, discrimination, the raising of import charges without previous renegotiation, preferences and the like should be removed in so far as agriculture is concerned. Or this does not make sense, and there is not the slightest hope of enforcing the rules of the game if one of the major trading nations is unwilling to accept them. It would be far better to admit frankly that the present efforts to organize agricultural trade in accordance with accepted legal commitments have failed and to start again from scratch.

In this new attempt, will regionalism be more successful than multilateralism?

FARM PRICES AND SUPPLIES IN E.E.C.

It should first be noted that, because practically all industrial countries maintain agricultural support prices which are above world prices, regional integration has a different impact on agricultural trade than on trade in manufactures. The "third country" supplier of manufactures has only to overcome the tariff differential, which can be achieved by price reduction. On the other hand, the "third country" supplier of agricultural products can enter the market only when all the suppliers in the common market have disposed of their supplies; price reductions would be of no avail.

Before the establishment of the Common Market, no imports could take place until the *domestic* producers of a particular country, say Germany, had sold their crop. But then the "third country" supplier would have a chance to compete with French or Dutch exports. Now that the Common Market is operating, that supplier has to wait, not only until the German suppliers have sold their crop, but also until all the *Common Market* suppliers having export surpluses have disposed of them. Only then can they hope to sell anything—provided, of course, that there remains some residual demand for their products.

The extension of the domestic support price system to the whole of the Community makes the position of "third country" suppliers very precarious indeed. But this is not the whole story. Support prices have a tendency to generate production and surpluses, which are then dumped abroad at world prices or even below world prices, thanks to export subsidies or other forms of compensation. The setting up of a powerful financial unit such as the E.E.C. may encourage an expansion of subsidized exports of agricultural products, and the traditional exporting countries may find their markets shrink as a result of these sales at commercial or concessionary prices.

In this respect, the accession of the United Kingdom would make things even worse for traditional exporters, whether they belong to the Commonwealth or not. The United Kingdom has followed an agricultural policy which, outwardly at least, does not interfere with imports. The deficiency payment system has the advantage of keeping consumers' prices at a lower level than is the case on the Continent; it does not depress consumption of products like butter which have a fairly high price elasticity. But it affords to the British farmers a protection no less effective than the Continental system: overseas exporters have to wait until the entire domestic crops have been disposed of before entering the British market. In that respect, the adoption by the United Kingdom of the Continental system of protection will not affect outside suppliers.

On the other hand, the United Kingdom is still a major market for exporting countries. Whereas the Continental European countries continue to keep a large proportion of their active population on the land, the United Kingdom, thanks to its liberal policies in the 19th century, has had a comparatively small farming population since before the second world war. Agricultural protection is powerful enough to keep the farmers on the land or to slow down the natural migration from the land to the towns, but it can hardly induce people in the towns to move back to the farms. In this respect there is not the same danger in the United Kingdom as on the Continent of excessive stimulation of agricultural production through price support, and there is a better chance of maintaining a substantial market for outsiders.

The accession of the United Kingdom to the E.E.C. would, however, lead to a significant change in the sources of supply to Britain. The British market would be part of the Common Market and governed by a common policy. Supplies from other E.E.C. countries would enter free of charge, whereas supplies from elsewhere would be subjected to a variable levy; and, with the operation of the "Community preference," the prices of those supplies would be higher than those of Common Market products. Outside suppliers would enter the British market only when the surpluses of Common Market producers had been disposed of. For many products, this change in the terms of competition could lead to significant trade diversion.

In the course of the Brussels negotiations, the British negotiators were trying to obtain a waiver of these obligations in order to keep as large a flow as possible of Commonwealth supplies. It seems probable that some transitional arrangements will be feasible, but it is open to doubt whether the United Kingdom could indefinitely escape the logic of the agricultural common policy. This would leave many questions unsettled and the problem of trade in agricultural products would have to be tackled somewhere else. Recourse to the multilateral technique would be unavoidable. This is clearly recognized in the reference to a world-wide solution contained in the statements issued concerning the Brussels negotiations. Many agricultural supplying countries being in any case outside the Commonwealth, it was difficult to imagine that such a problem could be settled through regional methods.

RAISE WORLD PRICES?

What are the prospects of such a world-wide solution and what kind of solution can be contemplated? The only concrete proposal which has been put forward so far is the idea developed by M. Baumgartner, then French Minister of Finance, at the last Ministerial meeting of the G.A.T.T. In his opinion, it is politically impossible to bring the domestic prices ruling in many countries to the level of world prices, which, by the way, are often artificial. To close the gap between the two price levels, the only practical method is to bring world prices up to the level of domestic prices, such as those of the E.E.C.

As an element in a global solution of the agricultural problem, this suggestion has some merit. It would do away with the artificialities of present world markets and give some compensation to the exporters who may lose part of their traditional markets, mainly the British market. It has met with support from certain producing countries, although their acceptance would depend on additional guarantees concerning access to import markets. It has been coolly received by countries such as the United Kingdom and Japan, which benefit from the low level of world prices and for which the adoption of such a formula would involve a substantial increase in their food bill, in sterling or foreign exchange.

In any case, the common policy of the E.E.C. would require all importing countries in the Community to levy a special tax on imports from third countries (including in principle Commonwealth supplies) in order to bring their prices up to the Community level. Consumers' prices will then be the same for home supplies and imports. The revenue derived from such levies would go to a Community Fund, which would serve various purposes, including the subsidization of exports of agricultural surpluses. The United Kingdom would be a contributor to that Fund.

If the Baumgartner suggestion is accepted, prices paid by the importer would be the same as Community prices and the levy would be nil. The exporting countries would get a better price, and the Community Fund would have less money with which to subsidize exports. This solution has no doubt some attraction for exporting countries. It is doubtful, however, that the new deal on agriculture could be hammered out in a purely trade context. It will have to be dealt with in a broader context in which political considerations bearing on the relations between industrialized and developing countries will be a determining factor.

It is usually assumed that this vexed problem of agricultural protection, although important, has not the same political undertones as other trade problems, because it does not affect really poor undeveloped countries. It is true that the main agricultural exporting countries are fairly rich countries—such as the United States, Canada, Denmark, the Netherlands, Australia and New Zealand—for which a loss of market is less serious than it would be for a very poor country. It should not be forgotten, however, that there are poor, under-developed countries in the temperate zone, such as Spain, Portugal, Greece or Turkey. Moreover, countries like Argentina and Uruguay, even Australia and New Zealand, if they are better off than many developing countries, are still dependent on the export of a few agricultural products. Price fluctuations may not have the same influence as before on their national incomes, but their balance of payments situation is still determined by the trend of their agricultural exports.

Another factor which is sometimes overlooked is that some of the so-called "temperate products," such as sugar or tobacco, can be produced both in temperate and tropical climates. Sugar protection is affecting Cuba or Brazil to the same extent as Belgium or Czechoslovakia; tobacco regulations are of interest to Greece, Turkey, the Federation of Rhodesia and Nyasaland or Indonesia as well as to the United States. When the trading relations between industrial and developing countries are considered, agriculture should not be ignored.

The Brussels negotiations will have an important bearing on the problem of agricultural trade, in so far as it affects imports from Commonwealth countries and indirectly those of non-Commonwealth suppliers, who may be left without any real advocate in these talks. It is to be expected that some temporary arrangements will emerge from these discussions. But no real solution can be worked out on a purely regional basis, because of the world-wide nature of the problem. A new multilateral approach remains indispensable. Some preliminary contacts have taken place within the framework of G.A.T.T. regarding wheat and meat. It is too early to assess the chances of success of these discussions. Public opinion is not yet alive to the seriousness of the problem of agricultural trade and some delay may occur. It is, however, to be hoped that a rapid solution is devised before the situation becomes worse.

EXPORTS OF DEVELOPING COUNTRIES

Apart from agricultural exports, which have been considered above, most developing countries face two main trade problems:

a. the need for more stable prices for their traditional exports; and
b. increased markets for their exports of semi-manufactures and manufactured goods.

Stabilization of commodity prices is a major trade problem; it has, however, proved impossible to have this problem considered alongside other commercial policy problems. Strong theoretical opposition from many industrial countries has weakened international collaboration in this field. That attitude has been somewhat modified recently by the realization of the importance of stable prices for the political stability of producing countries. It has, moreover, become clear that consumer countries also have an interest in keeping commodity prices as stable as possible, since severe fluctuations force developing countries to cancel orders and reduce import programmes. Whatever may have been gained in the form of reduced prices is lost by a slump in the export trade.

Developing countries spend all the exchange they receive from their exports on purchases, mainly in the industrial countries. If industrial countries wish to maintain the level of their exports, they have to buy more from developing countries (or pay a higher price for these supplies) or give their exports away, in the form of grants, soft loans or similar devices. It was recognized years ago that high wages may be a prerequisite for developing sales in the home market. It may be worth considering whether a similar policy would not be profitable on an international basis. Industrialists who deliberately offered wages above the rates which would result from the free play of demand and supply of labour have contributed to the prosperity of their industries and of their country. Is it a fallacy to believe that the optimum price for primary commodities may not necessarily be the ruling market price?

This is a delicate subject which must be tackled with caution. High prices may be in fact unremunerative if they encourage substitution or speculation; on the other hand, low prices may discourage production and prevent reasonable development. There are examples of support price programmes that have had beneficial effects on production and development.

In Senegal, for example, the maintenance of a stable price to producers of groundnuts contributed to a remarkable improvement in production techniques; practically all farmers now use selected, improved seeds and are prepared to buy adequate quantities of fertilizers. If the price paid had fluctuated as often as world prices and remained often at low levels, there would have been no incentive for the Senegalese farmer to change his traditional, inefficient methods of cultivation. Importing countries may have paid slightly more for their groundnuts or groundnut oil, but they have exported more to Senegal, as the farmer has spent his additional income on food, consumer goods, farming implements and fertilizers.

Although bilateral and regional arrangements may have their usefulness they are not satisfactory, as they create two classes of producers, some privileged and some not. The general feeling seems to be that these arrangements should be replaced as soon as practicable by wider agreements, placing all suppliers on the same footing. The idea of an international price parity system which would freeze the terms of trade between primary products and manufactures has been abandoned and the commodity-by-commodity approach remains the only practical one. Single-commodity agreements of the usual type have their limitations; they can only reduce the magnitude of fluctuations, without being able to stabilize the level of earnings of exporting countries. Their technique might be improved; their Councils could get more power of decision and take a more active part in the co-ordination of production plans or other aspects of commodity policy. But commodity agreements could never fulfil the exaggerated hopes placed in them by producing countries some ten years ago.

Another technique which has evolved lately is compensatory financing. If there is no practical way of maintaining stability of export earnings for exporting countries when demand fluctuates, there would be a substantial advantage in putting at the disposal of these countries some foreign exchange to enable them to maintain the level of their essential imports. The rate of their economic development would not be affected by price fluctuations and the exports of the industrial countries would not suffer either. On the face of it, there would seem to be good prospects of reaching some useful agreement in that direction. Detailed plans are under consideration in the U.N. and in the Organization of American States.

NEW EXPORTS

Development of traditional exports and improvement of the earnings derived from that trade are a major preoccupation of developing countries. But it has become apparent during the last few years that this would not suffice to enable them, taken as a group, to maintain their imports at a level commensurate with the minimum requirements of economic development. According to a recent analysis made by the G.A.T.T. secretariat, developing countries would have to increase their present trade deficit by $15 billions by 1975 if they were to reach the target of an annual increase of their national income by 5 per cent., which was considered by the U.N. Assembly in 1961 as a "minimum desirable rate." The only region of the world which is likely to reach this target without too much difficulty seems to be Latin America.

There is no hope of filling the gap by financial aid. To expect governmental grants to increase by $15 billions a year by 1975 is out of the question. To rely on loans, either private or public, would prove illusory, since these loans would burden the future balance of payments of developing countries in a hopeless manner. The only practical remedy lies in the development of new exports by developing countries and in the acceptance of such exports by industrial countries.

With a few exceptions, these new exports should take the form of semi-manufactured goods or of consumer goods. Some developing countries have already been able to produce consumer goods for world markets. This is true of textiles, where the Japanese, followed by India, Pakistan, Hong Kong, Egypt, Spain and Portugal, have secured a substantial share of world markets. Other consumer goods from these and other countries are coming on to the market. There is no doubt that at least part of the expected trade deficit of developing countries could be covered by exports of this kind. Production facilities exist or are readily available. The only real obstacle lies in the severity of protection in most import markets. Apart from the United Kingdom, which for political reasons had to take the matter seriously, most industrial governments have listened to the complaints of their industries and have shut off what was considered as unfair competition.

The problem is not confined to cotton textiles or to supplies from a few Commonwealth countries. It is becoming a world-wide issue of the first magnitude. Governments will have to consider whether they are prepared to encourage production to shift from the consumer goods sector to the more elaborate products, such as consumer durables and capital goods. In view of the unlimited demand for import goods in developing countries, this structural reform would increase the total production and exports of industrial countries and would lead to a more than proportional raising of national income. This would not be a sacrifice but a boon to industrial countries, although it would raise a number of awkward short-term adjustment problems.

One may believe that, even if the 5 per cent. rate of increase in the national income of developing countries fails to materialize, nothing serious would happen and that the world would continue as before. This is not absolutely certain. Too much emphasis has been laid in developing countries on economic development; frustration may prove fatal to present governments and lead to political confusion or worse. Moreover, Communist countries are in a position to absorb ever increasing quantities of traditional exports as well as of manufactures from developing countries; recent experience has shown that they are also able to provide these countries with the capital equipment which they purchase now in Western Europe or America. If the industrial countries in the free world are not prepared to accept a change in the present structure of international trade, there is an alternative solution, which may be fraught with political drawbacks for the free world.

Is there any hope that regionalism could solve this problem? In the course of the Brussels negotiations, it has been considered in connection with exports from India, Pakistan and Hong Kong. Some compromise will be reached on some specific problems, but it is doubtful that much progress could be made so long as the discussion is limited to a few European countries. British influence inside an enlarged Community might remove some of the rigid opposition of producers on the Continent; on the other hand, the industrial opposition in the United Kingdom to a liberal policy may be strengthened by support from Continental industries. In the discussions which led to the conclusion of an agreement on cotton textiles from developing countries one fact emerged: no industrialist is ready to accept competition from developing countries unless his opposite numbers in the other industrial countries are prepared to share the sacrifices required. For this reason alone, the multilateral technique appears more conducive to concrete results than a regional one.

CONCLUSION

Perforce, many of the conclusions reached in the preceding paragraphs are tentative, even speculative. Much will depend on the issue of the Brussels negotiations. Much will depend also on the time required by public opinion in North America to accept the implications of an Atlantic Economic Union. There is, however, some reason to believe that although multilateralism will lose some ground, since any accessions to a regional group means a loss to multilateral trade, many of the major issues in the trade field will not be amenable to regional techniques.

If the Brussels negotiations fail, that failure may be remedied, from a trade point of view, by recourse to the technique of tariff negotiations, provided that the United States Administration has the necessary power and determination to act. Even if the negotiations succeed, they will not set up the machinery which is urgently required to solve the agricultural problem and the problems of developing countries. A more active use of the multilateral machinery would be required in either case.

Governments will therefore have to continue to give attention to the possibilities offered by the multilateral approach. As regionalism becomes fashionable, there is a danger that European governments, at least, would spend so much time in their regional discussions that they would be unable to give the required attention to world-wide issues. This would be serious indeed, because these trade problems can no longer be left to the discretion of technicians, especially those problems which raise the question of how to work out a reasonable *modus vivendi* with developing countries. Public opinion is dimly aware of the fact that these issues are of direct interest to the man in the street, but is not yet able to understand their political implications.

Governments will probably have to redefine their commercial policy in terms of their over-all basic objectives. Once this is done and duly explained to the peoples some agreement should be reached concerning the respective roles of regional and wider bodies, on the basis of the respective qualifications and performances of the organizations concerned.

6

EUROPEAN INTEGRATION AND THE DEVELOPING COUNTRIES *

Bela Balassa

The main purpose of economic integration in Europe is to accelerate the growth of the participating economies. The creation of the European Economic Community was geared to this objective; it was not intended to facilitate (or hinder) economic development in nonindustrial countries, though special provisions were made for associated overseas countries and territories (colonies and former colonies of EEC countries). Still, integration in Europe cannot fail to cause repercussions in other areas of the world, including the less developed countries.

These repercussions can be classified as "preference effects" and "growth effects." Trade diversion (the substitution of commodities produced in member countries for the products of nonparticipating nations) falls in the first category. The "growth effects" refer to the increase in imports resulting from the accelerated growth of Common Market countries.

Some trade diversion will no doubt occur after the removal of tariff barriers within the Common Market. For example, while Belgium used to import most of her oranges from Spain (the cheapest source), she will, in the future, increase her imports from Italy, a fellow member of EEC. Should production costs be 15 per cent higher in Italy than in Spain, Italian oranges will still be able to undersell oranges from Spain, since the Common Market tariff has been set at 15 to 20 per cent.

Thus, it is clear that the "preference effect" leads to a reduction of exports to the Common Market on the part of nonparticipating countries. These countries will, however, benefit from the "growth effect," for, as integration accelerates economic growth in the Community member countries will spend more on goods from abroad. It is difficult to tell in advance which of the two effects will be stronger. Still, a discussion of expected changes in regard to various commodities can indicate the possible lines of future development. In the following, we will examine the prospects in tropical agricultural products, in Temperate Zone agricultural products, in minerals and in industrial products.

* From *Challenge, The Magazine of Economic Affairs* (May 1962). Reprinted by permission.

Tariff preferences granted by the industrial countries of the Temperate Zone to each other have no effect whatsoever on imports of tropical agricultural products. (Sugar and tobacco, which can grow in temperate climates, are exceptions.) Trade in tropical crops is affected, however, as a result of the preferential treatment accorded to the Common Market's associated overseas countries and territories.

At the insistence of the French negotiators, special provisions on the status of the overseas territories of the member countries were included in the treaty establishing the EEC. The treaty and the implementing convention did not spell out what should happen once a dependent territory achieved independence. But, in the absence of a stipulation to the contrary, EEC authorities have taken the position that these territories can maintain their status in the Community, even after their political ties with member nations are loosened or cut off entirely. As a result, all former French colonies—including Mali, Senegal, Upper Volta, Gabon and Guinea—as well as the former Belgian Congo, still enjoy preferential treatment.

But what does preferential treatment amount to? First, development assistance; second, free entry to the market of the Community; and, third, the privilege of retaining or establishing tariffs on the imports of industrial products from the Common Market.

Development assistance is handled through a development fund provided for in the treaty. But, so far, the fund's impact has not been great. If we consider that the U.S. alone gave Ghana $133 million for purposes of the Volta Dam project, the $100 million per year the development fund allocates among the Common Market's overseas territories looks small by comparison.

It appears, therefore, that the main benefit these countries derive from association with the Community is the duty-free entry of their exports to the markets of the European members. This privilege not only gives them an important advantage in selling traditional export products, but can also stimulate their industrialization since they will find market outlets in the Common Market countries for processed food and light industrial products manufactured with cheap labor.

After the completion of the transitional period, the associated countries will enjoy a margin of preference equal to the tariff paid by outsiders. Nonassociated producers of bananas, for example, will have to pay a 20 per cent tariff on exports to the Common Market. Therefore, their competitors in associated countries will have a 20 per cent advantage over them. In the case of sugar, an associated producer will have an 80 per cent advantage, in the case of tea, 18 per cent, etc. But in a number of instances the commodities produced by the two groups of countries are not identical. Coffee, bananas and tobacco are examples.

Coffee, the most important tropical import, appears in two main varieties on the European market: arabica and robusta coffee. The former, though more expensive, is more popular in Europe (with the exception of France). Hence, though several robusta-producing countries will have tariff preference in the Common Market, they are not likely to make significant inroads into arabica sales there.

Since climatic and geographical conditions in the associated areas are not favorable to the production of arabica, the coffee producers of Latin America, Kenya, Ethiopia and Tanganyika stand to lose very little of their trade with Common Market countries. But imports of robusta coffee from African countries not associated with EEC are expected to decline.

Quality differences are of importance in the case of bananas, too. In Germany and the Benelux countries the predominant variety consumed is the more expensive Gros Michel, which is grown chiefly in Latin America and the Canary Islands. On the other hand, the African Cavendish banana is imported to France and Italy from their respective overseas territories. But the Gros Michel has been grown successfully in the Belgian Congo, and British consumption has recently shifted to a variety of the Cavendish banana. And although Germany's traditional sources of supply still have the benefit of a duty-free quota, this quota will be progressively reduced. Consequently, we can expect the "preference effect" to reduce not only the banana exports of the nonassociated African countries, but also those of Latin America.

In the case of tobacco, since the common tariff of EEC is calculated as a percentage of the value of imports rather than as a flat rate, the greatest burden falls on high-quality products. As a result, dark tobacco produced in the former Belgian Congo, the Malagasy Republic and the French Cameroons will replace some imports from Nyasaland and Rhodesia.

Similar consequences are expected to follow as a result of the preferences accorded to Greek tobacco and the possibility of the expansion of tobacco production in the Common Market countries themselves. On the other hand, the cigar leaf exporters of Indonesia, Brazil, the Dominican Republic and Cuba have little to fear from direct competition. Substitution may take place on the consumption side, however, if cigarettes replace cigars to a greater extent.

Quality differences are less important in the case of cocoa; hence the Common Market tariff is bound to affect the patterns of cocoa trade. Before the Common Market was established, about half of the cocoa imports of member countries came from the French, Belgian and Dutch overseas territories. Now this share is expected to increase, while the share of Ghana, Nigeria and Brazil will fall proportionately.

The situation in sugar is akin to that in cocoa, since it makes little difference to the consumer whether he uses beet or cane sugar. But in the case of sugar, the Common Market countries themselves, rather than the overseas territories, are the most dangerous competitors to outside countries. Behind the high-tariff wall, domestic sugar producers (especially Italian) will be able to expand their production at the expense of producers in Haiti, Brazil, the Dominican Republic and Cuba.

To what extent are the preferential advantages accorded to producers in associated countries greater than those enjoyed before integration took place? In the case of the former Belgian Congo and Ruanda-Urundi, tariff preferences under Belgian rule did not amount to much; affecting only banana imports. Since the Common Market tariff on bananas is 5 per cent above the old Belgian tariff, the position of producers in the Congo and Ruanda-Urundi will improve. The new tariffs on other commodities, such as tobacco and tropical timbers will also serve as an advantage to these areas. On the other hand, the former Italian Somaliland will actually suffer, since its bananas will no longer be sheltered by the higher Italian tariffs and by the Italian state monopoly.

The position of the former French colonies is more complicated. The exports of these countries to France are exempt from customs duties. In addition, they have received preferential treatment in the form of special marketing arrangements. These arrangements have often brought producers in these areas prices considerably above the world market figures. In recent years, coffee, oilseeds, vegetable oils and bananas from French territories have sold in the French market at prices about one-third above the world market price.

The treaty does not expressly state that France should do away with her special marketing arrangements, but they are clearly incompatible with the spirit of the treaty. Assuming that these special arrangements will be discontinued, the preferential treatment many producers in these countries will receive in EEC, may actually be less advantageous to them than their privileged position in the French market. This will be true for the producers of coffee, bananas, sugar and groundnuts, but not for producers of cocoa, tea and tropical wood. Consequently, coffee and banana production in the former Belgian colonies will benefit and the losses suffered by the nonparticipating countries will be reduced.

Given the fact that producers in the associated territories will receive higher prices than other producers, we must consider the extent to which these territories are likely to expand production. In the short run, the prospects for expansion are limited. Most tropical products are yearly crops and many require a number of years from planting to harvesting. Output can be increased to some extent through more careful harvesting, better care of crops during the growing season and the use of fertilizers. But such measures can only have a limited impact.

The short-run impact of the Common Market in the case of most tropical commodities will be to promote a shift in trade patterns. The associated territories will sell more to the Common Market countries and less to outsiders, while other African as well as Latin American countries will redirect part of their exports from the Community to, say, the United States. Still, the producers of nonassociated countries will suffer a loss since they will now receive lower prices and hence their export earnings will decline. In addition, there will be a decline, in absolute terms, in their exports of commodities such as coffee and sugar, which are in over supply on the world market.

The possibilities of expanding the production of tropical commodities are greater over the long run. But even then expansion is restricted by the availability of land, labor and capital. A significant increase in the production of any one commodity will necessarily entail a smaller rise in the output of another; at the same time, moves toward industrialization will draw labor and capital away from tropical agriculture. Still, on the basis of available evidence, we may expect that the output of tropical products will double over a 15 to 20 year period. Expansion at this rate would not reduce Common Market imports from nonassociated countries in absolute terms, but it would reduce them in relative terms. Also, the growth of the exports of these areas would likely be inhibited.

Some modifications of these conclusions will be required if European integration accelerates the economic growth of member countries as it is expected to do. At a higher level of GNP, these countries would import more tropical foodstuffs, for consumption of these products increases considerably in response to increases in income. Thus, EEC's effect on growth should roughly compensate nonassociated producers of tropical products for the losses suffered because of tariff discrimination.

This conclusion, however, does not hold for all commodities. Sugar consumption, for example, increases but little as income rises, and, furthermore, a large expansion of sugar production is expected to take place within the European Common Market countries. Some of the rise in the consumption of tobacco will also be taken up by the expansion of domestic production.

The example of sugar and tobacco indicates the problems faced in the case of Temperate Zone products. The recently adopted common agricultural policy of EEC appears to be directed toward self-sufficiency. Although the new support prices have not yet been established, it is expected that they will be low enough to freeze out inefficient, marginal farmers, but high enough to give a stimulus to the expansion of agricultural production, especially in France and Italy: The goal of self-sufficiency will be furthered by the establishment of an agricultural fund designed to assist farmers in buying modern equipment and to subsidize exports of excess agricultural products.

Cotton and soybeans will be the only nontropical agricultural products to enter the Common Market duty-free. Other commodities will have to pay tariffs equaling the difference between the world market price and EEC support price. This regulation ensures that no imports will be admitted as long as home output, produced at costs equal to or lower than the support price, can satisfy the demand. The new agricultural policy of the Common Market will affect primarily the producers of cereals, beef and poultry, and it is also likely to have some effect on trade in hides, skins and wool.

There will be no increase in the Common Market's demand for bread grains as incomes go up. In fact, human consumption of bread grains may actually fall. And, though a larger proportion of grain will be fed to cattle, the anticipated expansion in domestic production is likely to take care of this need. As EEC attains self-sufficiency in grain production, some grain-exporting areas will suffer—primarily Argentina, and, to a lesser extent, Australia and the Middle East.

Somewhat better are the prospects for the outside producers of rice, since Italy presently does not grow the preferred long-grain variety. But plans for a shift toward the production of long-grained rice in Italy, if realized, would adversely affect the position of Thailand and Burma. Italy will also be the chief beneficiary of increases in the consumption of citrus fruits, although outside producers may maintain their relative share in the market by reason of a growth in consumption.

Under the new agricultural policy, France is making strong efforts to increase beef production and some expansion is expected also in Germany and in Italy. As a result, imports of beef are bound to fall, despite the fact that the consumption of beef increases as incomes rise. Argentina, New Zealand and Uruguay are likely to be hit hardest by these developments.

The picture is quite different in respect to minerals and fuels. The accelerated growth of incomes in the Community will benefit producers of these commodities, for minerals and fuels are not subject to duty in the Common Market with the exception of low duties on lead, zinc, aluminum and manganese. And the anticipated increase in manufacturing will lead to a rising demand for them.

What about the ability of developing countries to bring manufactured goods—especially processed food and light industrial products—into the European Community? The establishment of EEC will have a two-fold effect in this regard, first, trade among the Common Market countries themselves will increase at the expense of their trade with the outside. In addition, assistance given to the associated territories in their efforts to establish light industry and food-processing plants will be prejudicial to similar efforts made by the nonmember countries. A good example is the manufacturing of cocoa powder and butter. The Common Market duty of about 25 per cent will benefit the former French and Belgian colonies at the expense of Ghana and Nigeria.

It appears, then, that the establishment of the European Economic Community will have wide-ranging repercussions on the developing countries. Exporters of minerals, fuels and some tropical products will certainly benefit. But a number of nonparticipating countries are likely to be adversely affected. In Africa, the cocoa and coffee producers of Ghana, Kenya, Uganda and Tanganyika appear to be in a vulnerable position. For Latin America, competition from the European members of the Common Market in products grown under temperate climate presents the greatest danger. Finally, in Asia, the exporters of tea, rubber, hides and skins will see their earnings decline while there will be few changes in exports of cotton and jute.

This picture will be modified if the United Kingdom and Denmark join the Community. Denmark's participation would further dim the export prospects of countries in Latin America's Temperate Zone. In addition, preferences given to the Commonwealth countries could be prejudicial to the interest of outside producers in both the Temperate and Tropical Zones. For example, there are strong possibilities that coffee production will be expanded in Kenya—a development which would threaten the coffee industry in Brazil and other Latin American countries. Finally, the outsiders would suffer further if some kind of preferential agreement should be reached between the United States and the Common Market.

These considerations clearly bring into focus an important economic and political problem the industrial countries of the West will have to face. Their self-interest dictates that they should reduce tariff barriers that presently interfere with economic intercourse among them. But every reduction of tariffs unaccompanied by concessions to the developing countries amounts to discrimination against the latter. Thus, the establishment of an Atlantic Community can easily have the side-effect of endangering Temperate Zone agriculture in the nonparticipating countries and obstructing their plans for industrialization.

Furthermore, there is no reason why some developing countries should receive preferential treatment while others are discriminated against merely on the basis of their former relationships with Europe. Preferential treatment of the Congo over Ghana, of Somaliland over Ethiopia, or of Upper Volta over Liberia, is not likely to contribute to harmonious relationships between an Atlantic Community and the nations of Africa. And if most of Africa received advantages in one form or the other, can we expect Latin America to approve?

These are matters which the industrial countries of the West—both inside and outside EEC—cannot afford to ignore.

7

COMMODITY AGREEMENTS ARE *NOT* THE ANSWER *

Karl Brandt

Some 50 years ago Leon Trotsky used the term "open scissors" to describe the differential between the prices of various commodities. Today the scissors concept still lies at the heart of Soviet economic strategy. It requires deliberate policies that worsen the terms of trade for agricultural products vis-à-vis manufactured goods. The purpose is to prohibit or reduce capital formation in agriculture and thus accelerate industrialization by investing the state's farm profit in new industrial capacity. This inequity for the collectivized rural proletariat is still the outstanding social and economic feature of the Sino-Soviet empire.

But the non-Communist world, too, is faced with an open-scissors situation. It is not, however, the consequence of any preconceived plan. On the contrary, it emerges from a variety of heterogeneous, partly independent, causes, some of which are rooted in the domestic economic policies and politics of the industrially advanced countries; others stem from many understandable but very costly and imprudent policies of the less developed countries.

The balance sheet of the free world's heartland—the United States, Canada and Japan on one flank of the Sino-Soviet bloc, and the United Kingdom and Western Europe on the other—shows enormous economic strength. Economic growth in the war-damaged parts of Europe and Japan has been particularly brisk since the end of the Korean war. The amazing rate of expansion of industrial production is apparent from the following seasonally adjusted index figures (1953=100) for the second quarter of

* From *Challenge, the Magazine of Economic Affairs,* XI (February 1963), 33-36. Reprinted by permission.

1962: the United States, 129; the seven British-led countries of the European Free Trade Association, 136; Canada, 144; the six European Economic Community countries, 193; Japan, 350.

As a natural corollary of this tremendous economic expansion, trade among the industrial countries and with the nonindustrial countries increased materially. Thus the total value of the entire world's international trade increased from $78 billion in 1953 to $131 billion in 1961, or an average annual rate of nearly six per cent. To this total the Sino-Soviet bloc contributed less than 12 per cent.

Since the end of World War II enormous political and social changes have occurred in the underdeveloped countries. Some 850 million people have gone through the transition from colonial administration to independence. In the process they received sizable economic, technical and military aid from the United States, from former colonial powers and from various independent international agencies of the Western world. In addition, they were assisted by hundreds of private, industrial, commercial and educational enterprises as well as by charitable organizations. A major part of the Marshall Plan funds found its way to investment in those former dependencies of European powers and contributed a great deal to the acceleration of activity there while simultaneously advancing the boom in Western Europe and Japan. This holds particularly for formerly French, Belgian and British Africa as well as Kenya and Burma.

In many parts of the nonindustrial world political sovereignty and economic progress, coupled with their first experience with democratic government, have raised expectations that far exceed any reasonable prospect of realization. In spite of the conspicuous evidence of progress, there is the ominous shadow of a wide-open pair of scissors rising over the horizon of the free world. It is a warning signal that augurs considerable hardship and many difficult adjustments in the years ahead.

The index figures for prices of primary materials (food, feed, fibers, wood, rubber, beverages, minerals) have declined from 100 to 90 during the last nine years. The index figures for prices of industrial manufactures, on the other hand, have increased from 100 to 109 during the same period. The ratio of index figures of both types of commodities has declined from 100 in 1953 to 83 in 1962. The scissors are thus open at a span of 17 per cent and are likely to open further because industrial prices will undoubtedly continue to rise.

The terms of trade have become more and more favorable for the industrial exporting nations, and less and less favorable for the developing raw material exporting countries, of which quite a few are already exporting semifinished products and light industry consumer goods such as textile fabrics.

The fact that primary materials prices declined at a time of rapid expansion and prosperity adds particular weight to the assumption that there is a serious maladjustment in the world's economy. This maladjustment originates partly in governmental market interventions designed to help agriculture and the extractive industries. In most industrial countries such intervention occurred in the midst of highly dynamic economic changes.

Research and innovation have changed the mix of inputs, increased productivity and decreased production costs in basic industries.

At the same time, two global shifts have occurred with almost geological force. The overabundance of oil and gas, combined with a sharp decline in transportation costs, provides energy for the mechanization of farms, for irrigation projects and for transportation facilities at costs much lower than ever before. This overwhelming wealth of hydrocarbons is also the cause of other shifts. The petrochemicals industries provide highly effective marginal products to increase yields at declining prices, and at the same time furnish substitutes for farm products and raw materials, also at declining prices. This applies to agricultural production in tropical as well as Temperate zones.

Labor-saving machinery and other capital equipment, energy-bearing materials, irrigation water, improved varieties of plants and animals, fertilizer and pesticides have increased, beyond all expectations, the potential productivity per man-hour, per plant and per animal. These productivity-increasing and cost-reducing factors were most effectively utilized in the industrially advanced countries and on large, commercial farm enterprises. Yet the large number of small, high-cost producers continue to derive income from farming because leaving the farm would be difficult or, at best, uncomfortable.

As a result, instead of a world-wide shortage of food, feed and fibers, the effective capacity, actual output and available supply are substantially larger in their aggregate than the markets of booming industrial economies can absorb, even at price levels that prevailed five or 10 years ago. This price decline is particularly hard on the masses of small marginal producers. In the underdeveloped countries the rise in industrial prices (their chief imports), coupled with the decline in farm prices (their chief exports), results in a serious foreign exchange crisis.

A problem that goes hand in hand with the open scissors in the international exchange of goods and services is the deterioration of the financial situation in a large number of underdeveloped countries. Some of them are precariously close to insolvency, and their currencies are deteriorating through rampant inflation. Excluding export surpluses of the oil-exporting countries, the underdeveloped countries incurred foreign trade deficits amounting to $5.8 billion in the first quarter of 1962. This deficit resulted neither from a stagnation of exports nor from a lack of economic development in the nonindustrial areas but, rather, from the underdeveloped nations' desire for imports which they cannot pay for.

The value of exports from the nonindustrial countries to all areas increased from $24 billion in 1953 to $32 billion in 1961. The latter figure included $8.2 billion in exports of oil and gas from only a few countries. Foreign trade (excluding fuels) between industrial and nonindustrial free world areas showed a $6.4 billion deficit for the nonindustrial countries in the latter part of 1961. It is obvious that these deficits cannot continue indefinitely.

If the scissors remain as wide open as they are now—to say nothing of the possibility of opening wider—the primary materials-exporting countries will be compelled to buy less from countries exporting industrial goods, unless, of course, the industrial countries are willing to finance their exports on a long-term basis. This, in turn, foretells potentially serious interruptions in economic development and subsequent unrest, devaluation of currencies or reintroduction of some of the worst of all trade obstacles: quantitative import restrictions, licenses and foreign exchange controls.

Industrial exporting countries are continuing to shift to more regional preferential trade systems, such as the European Common Market. If they insist on protecting their internal markets for primary products, the subsequent tendency to attain greater self-sufficiency in these products makes the development of nonindustrial countries even more difficult. The repercussion may lead to a serious and prolonged recession in industrial countries. These difficulties will inevitably become more serious if the industrial countries in their new regionalism refuse to accept semiprocessed raw materials and products of light industries from underdeveloped countries. Industrial exporters thereby reduce opportunities for selling machinery and other producer goods to developing countries. This creates unemployment and rising costs in the affected export industries.

If we were only concerned with short cyclical price drops in individual commodities, the tenor of anxiety which pervades this article would be groundless. Many signs indicate, however, that there is far more cause for worry. The Western world may be faced with a serious setback to economic activity and development though a continued downward trend in foreign exchange earnings.

During the last nine years the industrial areas have expanded their exports from $45 billion to $85 billion, or by 89 per cent, while the nonindustrial areas expanded their trade from $24 billion to $32 billion, or by only 33 per cent. As a result of this sharp difference in the rate of growth, the share of the industrial areas in the non-Soviet world's trade increased from 65 to 73 per cent, while the nonindustrial area's share declined from 35 to 27 per cent.

What can be done to improve the trade position of the nonindustrial countries?

The most frequently suggested remedy for improving the open-scissors situation is the so-called "stabilization" of prices of primary products through international commodity agreements. This would result in the establishment of the same sort of intervention in the world agricultural market that has been used since World War I in domestic markets, namely compulsory commodity cartels which fix prices, operate stockpiles, and buy or sell.

Such price fixing would create a structural change in the entire global market economy for the commodity in question. Hence, while it might mitigate the violence of short-term price fluctuations, it inevitably causes profound and serious dislocations for production, processing, stockholding and consumption. This is not a theoretical speculation, but a matter of historical record. The "stabilization" of cotton prices in the U.S. has not only frozen production in high price locations, but it has spurred and accelerated cotton production in other countries. And 60 years of efforts to stabilize coffee prices have led to such extreme methods as destroying within a period of 12 years a quantity equivalent to three years' total world coffee consumption. This did not appreciably help Brazil or Colombia, but instead spurred competitive production in other parts of the world, primarily in Africa.

None of the primary commodities have such a safe and unassailable monopoly position that a cartel-manipulated pegged price could avoid a consumer response of partial substitution and reduced demand or prevent producers of competitive commodities from taking advantage of the artificially created price edge for their products.

It has been demonstrated in recent years that even a commodity like steel faces tough and effective competition from organic materials like lumber, and inorganic compounds and commodities like concrete, aluminum, magnesium and formica. The same is true of all agricultural commodities, irrespective of whether they are food, animal feed or industrial raw materials. Wherever substitution is feasible, cartel-manipulated high prices usually result in a net gain for the substitute commodity.

What, then, is the potential effect of closing the scissors by adjusting raw materials prices through international commodity agreements? Such agreements necessitate diplomatic machinery, institutional arrangements and the adoption of elaborate administrative procedures for each individual commodity. All producing and exporting countries, and preferably all importing countries, have to be persuaded to participate. If the time-consuming preliminaries do not founder on the noncooperation or the hostility of some countries with a strong comparative advantage, then efforts can be made to "stabilize" prices by reducing export quotas and, consequently, production quotas. But reduced exports at somewhat higher prices may yield no actual improvement in the balance of trade.

The worst feature of this sort of planned economic intervention is the confinement of measures to prices, trade and production of one single commodity, which distorts the relation to prices of all other goods and services. Within an environment of dynamic change, such static and isolated single commodity measures create more maladjustments within a few years than improvements. One of these maladjustments is the higher real estate values accruing to efficient producers. In a short while these values become higher costs in the fixed cost structure. This is one reason why the U.S. government finds it politically impossible to extricate itself from the price-support program.

There are some commodities for which price fixing by international agreement would be disastrous: natural rubber, for example, with its sharp competition from a whole range of synthetic materials; or such fibers as jute, Manila hemp, silk or wool, for which substitute materials are competing effectively. If, on the other hand, international cartels just go through monopoly motions to perform what the market would do anyway, their work would be a costly waste.

This leads to the conclusion that international commodity agreements, at best, do not offer more than a temporary sedative that may give the political sensation of relief. Any attempt to ameliorate the problems of the raw materials-exporting nations requires a different approach.

It must be recognized that agricultural protection in highly industrialized countries creates export surpluses which seriously impede the necessary exchange of goods, services and capital with underdeveloped countries. The same applies to the unwillingness of industrial countries to accept an increasing amount of semimanufactured and consumer goods from the underdeveloped countries without duties, excise taxes, import quotas and other restraints. The opening of borders to such imports would increase the purchasing power of underdeveloped countries which, in turn, would be used for imports of industrial producer goods.

The correction of the open-scissors situation could, of course, also proceed via a moratorium on price increases for industrial goods. Indeed, there is a fair prospect that more competition among industrial exporting countries and the loss of markets in overseas areas could do exactly that. However, keeping price inflation in industrial countries in check is largely a question of relieving the cost-price squeeze in industries which have a reduced profit margin. Here a thorough revision of corporate income taxes in several leading industrial countries would be extremely helpful.

The main assistance government can give to industrial expansion without inflation begins with appropriate policies which serve to strengthen the currency and keep it hard, i.e., freely convertible. Recurrent anxiety about the strength of the world's leading currency is certainly no help in the trade difficulties between developed and underdeveloped nations. Strengthening the currency requires the creation of a business climate in which the expansion of exports can proceed without rising costs. Since wages make up the lion's share of costs in industry, and since competition is the only force that can effectively stimulate the private actions that increase productivity, free competition must be the rule for all the parties involved—unions, farmers and cooperatives, as well as business enterprises.

This leads to one major issue of Western strategy concerning the underdeveloped parts of the world. These countries need a heavy capital import for many years to come to enable them to develop faster than their population increases. But the imported capital must lay the groundwork for its amortization. If this capital comes chiefly through grants and loans from foreign governments or international agencies, it goes into the hands of the government of the recipient country.

It will then be subject to often overambitious central planning with no assurance of prudent investment or competent execution of projects. Moreover, transfer of capital from government to government does not provide the decentralized probing necessary to decide which projects should have priority. This delicate matter of judgment requires experienced and skeptical specialists, and they are not normally at the disposal of the government. They are usually employed by private companies and are available only when their company is interested in investing in a foreign country. The argument that such alien capital investment causes resentment seems very shallow. Foreign-owned and operated enterprises can make a large part of their stock available to citizens of the host country and thus establish a true partnership.

It is obvious that the acceptance of the unrealistic and defeatist idea that capital for the development of nonindustrial countries can and must be contributed only by government-to-government grants and loans will prove to be the greatest disservice to the countries in need of such capital. It is up to developing nations to create conditions and a legal environment which attracts private foreign capital.

If the governments of the industrial countries want to assist their capital owners and corporations in foreign investment, they can do so by the way they tax income earned from such investment. In addition, they can underwrite a certain part of the purely political risk involved in such ventures. Indeed, multilateral arrangements—say, the Organization for European Cooperation and Development—to insure a part of the political risk of private foreign investment in nonindustrial countries would seem a much more legitimate aid to the nonindustrial parts of the free world than international commodity agreements. This would establish the possibility of excluding from insurance and thereby from foreign investment countries which only are luring private foreign capital into a trap which closes by "nationalization" with only partial and inadequate payment.

Even if all these lines of strategy should be followed in the majority of underdeveloped countries, it is still likely that such countries will not develop as fast as they would like to grow. What the industrial countries should try to avoid, by all means possible, is a deterioration of the process of economic advancement of the nonindustrial areas, partly because those areas are needed as a source of raw materials and as markets for industrial exports, but partly also because stagnation leads to unrest which can only benefit the Communists.

It is high time that the Western industrial powers close ranks and coordinate their policies.

ADDITIONAL REFERENCES

Blau, Gerda (FAO—UN, Rome, Italy), "International Commodity Arrangements," International Economic Association Vienna Congress, September 1962.

Caine, Sydney, "Commodity Agreements—A New Look," *Lloyds Bank Review,* January 1963.

Morgan, D. J., "International Commodity Problems . . . ," Rome: *Banca Nazionale del Lavoro Quarterly Review,* December 1962.

Swerling, Boris C., "Current Commodity Policy," *Essays in International Finance* (Princeton University), June 1962.

Swerling, Boris C., "Problems of International Commodity Stabilization," *American Economic Review,* May 1963.

8

THE REGIONAL APPROACH TO ECONOMIC DEVELOPMENT *

Walter Krause

The years since World War II have witnessed the generation of much interest in the status of the underdeveloped countries of the world. These countries, historically subject to extreme poverty and near stagnation, began to strive with a new found energy for an improvement in prevailing economic circumstances. Concurrently, the developed countries—and especially the United States—exhibited a new degree of concern as to the well-being of peoples within regions as yet underdeveloped, ostensibly in great measure because of profound implications posed by the "revolution of rising expectations" within the overall context of global affairs.

As interest in "economic development" reached intensified levels, public officials and academic economists—in both underdeveloped and developed countries—found themselves confronted not only with a need to isolate the reasons for the poor economic performance of particular economies, but also, as a logical follow-up, with the public policies and specific actions needed to implement a program designed to yield economic improvement. To say the least, much controversy was thereby engendered, and it has continued in light of the fact, especially, that sufficient time has not yet elapsed to provide positive proof as to the superiority of given strategies and tactics over others.

In course of the controversy, one idea put forth, and to which much attention has come to be directed in recent periods, was that of a *regional approach* to the task of economic development. Reference to remedial action in the underdeveloped countries along lines of a regional approach was perhaps inevitable, considering that regionalism at the international level had experienced popularity earlier in other quarters of the world. Specifically, operations under the Marshall Plan had served to give a great impetus to the approach in Western Europe. There a whole series of regional arrangements made their appearance, both during the recovery phase associated directly with the Marshall Plan and during the longer-run growth phase which followed: the European Payments Union, the Coal and Steel Community, and—most important of all—the Common Market and its counterpart, the Outer Seven market area. As some beneficial impact came generally to be ascribed to arrangements of this form (with pronounced further beneficial impact envisaged), a firm basis was established in terms of which to argue for the forthright application of the regional approach within the

* From *Iowa Business Digest* (Spring 1961), pp. 29-37. Reprinted by permission.

underdeveloped sector of the world, the peculiar plight of which had become the object of widespread concern at this juncture.

Evidence of a rising interest in the potentialities of an attack upon the special problems of the underdeveloped world along regional lines abounds on all sides. Within the underdeveloped world, talk is heard as to the merits of common-market arrangements—especially in Latin America, but also in Southeast Asia and elsewhere. Within this country's foreign-aid agency (ICA), regional projects—which link the resources, as well as specific problems, of two or more contiguous countries—are receiving growing attention. Concern is exhibited in major countries as to whether the newly emerging countries of Africa can prove viable as distinct economic entities. Important policy documents arising in major countries, both officially and non-officially, are found to make reference to the applicability of greater economic cooperation among similarly situated countries. And one American political party is on record, by virtue of its most recent political platform, as sanctioning a movement toward "regional economic confederations."

Coexistent to an important extent, then, are the desire for economic development and the hope that measures of a regional nature can prove meaningful for its attainment. This presentation is concerned with the second of the facets cited: the applicability of the regional approach as a means for the effective promotion of economic development. Primarily attention is directed to two main matters: (1) a survey of the major measures which might be framed along regional lines, and (2) an examination of the extent to which accelerated development might reasonably derive from resort to these measures.

THE RATIONALE

First, however, what is there about a regional approach that serves to recommend it to some people as a means for the promotion of development? The basic answer is found in the fact that the political boundaries of countries frequently do not circumscribe the particular geographic areas which, taken as distinct entities, can offer a good environment for well-ordered economic activity. The system of national states, as it exists today, in important measure represents the outgrowth of a series of political decisions, not of decisions made in terms of economic considerations. If individual countries are then to experience economic gains, and are to do so effectively and efficiently, they are obliged—so the argument evolves—to create an environment more conducive for well-ordered economic activity. Since a wholesale re-drawing of political boundaries is not a practical suggestion, the remaining alternative which comes to mind is to de-emphasize the significance of political boundaries in their bearing upon the pace and direction of economic activity.

If it is agreed that a de-emphasis of national boundaries makes good economic sense, one could next argue that the liberalization movement should be global in scope. Seemingly, if any liberalization of this type is good, then nothing short of the maximum is ideal. There are obstacles, however, to the pursuit of such an all-out goal. Not all countries are equally ready to proceed—and understandably so, given the degree of diversity in situations and responses to be found within a complex of roughly a hundred countries, all nominally sovereign and ever concerned with their own special national well-being. The result, as envisaged by many persons, is that effort aimed to achieve the ultimate in short order is doomed to failure as individual impediments act and interact to form an end situation which is insurmountable generally. It is more hopeful, these people argue, to proceed piecemeal—with specific action undertaken at any point where and as it is readily possible. In short, the governing philosophy is that "half a loaf is better than no loaf." Translated into an implementation framework, closer economic contact is sought—at least as a first step—*within regions* and in *particular connections,* rather than universally and indiscriminately.

FORMS OF REGIONALISM

Basically, economic action at the regional level can proceed in either of three main veins: projects, trade, and payments. Each of these possibilities is examined below.

Projects

Some projects are possible, in a physical sense, only if undertaken on a regional basis, involving activity in two or more countries, or become possible on a more efficient basis, in an economic sense, if undertaken regionally rather than nationally. This situation is observable in three distinct types of cases.

First, some basic facilities can be created and managed more readily on a regional basis than separately by each country concerned. To illustrate, assume a river which crosses or borders on two or more countries. Development of hydroelectric, irrigation, and transport facilities can then probably occur to better advantage if all countries act in unison rather than independently—in which case one country might choose not to act at all, and thereby hamper even that activity contemplated by others. Specific instances in which a regional approach seems apropos include the finalization (in 1960) of the Indus Waters Treaty, involving the development and utilization by India and Pakistan of the water resources of the Indus River basin, and the possible future development along TVA-lines of the Mekong River basin in Southeast Asia (embracing no less than four countries: Thailand, Laos, Cambodia, and South Viet-Nam—and possibly also Mainland China).

Second, the areal distribution of resources frequently makes their pooling necessary, as between two or more countries, if effective utilization is to follow. To illustrate, assume a case in which one country has iron ore but no coal, while an adjacent country has coal but no iron ore. A steel mill might be possible if the iron ore and coal can be linked. Theoretically, trade makes such a linkage possible; however, a formal arrangement covering the steel mill itself may prove necessary, as a first step, in order to set in motion those market forces which can result in the actual bringing together of the resources. A conceivable case in point involves Philippine iron ore and Taiwan coal.

Third, individual national markets may prove too limited to permit an economic scale of operations on the part of given productive units. In contrast, however, the same productive units, if situated in each instance in only one country among a grouping of two or more countries, while given untrammeled access to the domestic markets of each of these countries for any output accruing, may succeed in reaching a scale of operations which can prove economic. To illustrate, assume again the previous case involving iron ore in one country and coal in another country. The normal process of trade would then, of course, make possible a linkage of these resources, eventuating in the establishment of a joint processing facility; however, it is possible that each country, when left to act unilaterally, would instead strive for a steel mill of its own, with a resultant scale of operations in each country perhaps incapable of yielding efficiency in output. Therefore, a basis arises for a formal inter-country arrangement to cover the pooling of effort in resource utilization on behalf of a single enterprise, and the subsequent disposal of this enterprise's output within a shared market.

Notwithstanding its economic plausibility as respects particular projects, the regional approach often is difficult to implement—largely because of frictions stemming from the matters of cost-sharing and location. Thus, there is a tendency for individual countries to underestimate the amount reflective of their legitimate share of the cost of a joint undertaking. Again, when an end facility has to be situated in its entirety in one country, but is destined to service a regional grouping of countries, the typical participant tends to begrudge location anywhere outside itself. It is significant, however, that such impediments ordinarily can be substantially lessened if outside financing is capable of being drawn upon—and is available, specifically, in terms of use in conformity with the basic pattern of a regional approach previously agreed upon in principle. It is in this vein that this country's foreign-aid agency (ICA) introduced the Asian Economic Development Fund in 1956, under terms of which $300 million was earmarked for use in support of qualifying regional-development projects arising in Asia. And, the previously cited Indus Waters Treaty, which followed a dispute in existence between India and Pakistan since partition, is backed by an Indus Basin Development Fund of almost $900 million, capitalized largely with funds derived from external sources.

Trade

Examination of flows of global trade reveals that, characteristically, only relatively little exchange occurs among underdeveloped countries situated within the same general region; instead, individual underdeveloped countries tend to trade largely with industrial countries, generally located at some distance (while, further, the larger proportion of inter-country trade occurs within the complex of developed countries). Some persons feel that underdeveloped countries within the same general region ought to do more trading with one another. If more trade occurred regionally, so it is argued, added gain as a by-product of greater specialization might accrue to the participating countries. Accordingly, a frequent suggestion is that *particular* barriers to trade between countries within the *same general region* be eliminated or lessened, in the hope that greater intra-regional trade might result. Generally a customs-union arrangement of some sort comes to be proposed, the usual term invoked in such references being that of "common market."

Why do underdeveloped countries within the same general region currently trade so little with one another? The answer is found, basically, in the type of production prevailing within a given region in which all countries are underdeveloped. As matters stand, these countries are committed to raw-materials production—in fact, most are non-diversified raw materials producers, with output concentrated in relatively few major commodities (and with high similarity in the array of commodities characteristic among the several countries within a particular geographic region). Under these circumstances, the end output of each of the countries tends to be competitive, not complementary, with that of the others within the region. The exportable portion of each country's output is obliged to find its market outlet largely in advanced industrial countries located outside the immediate region; concurrently, many commodities—especially industrial-type items—not produced within the region but desired by the individual countries must derive from sources entirely outside the region, or be done without. As one sees in practice, the individual countries of Southeast Asia, all engaged in roughly similar types of raw-materials production, are not favorably geared for large-scale trade with one another, but do find a firm basis for trade with Japan, Western Europe, and the United States, all of which have an interest in the region's raw materials and in its demands for industrial-type goods; or, to cite another case, the countries of Latin America trade only little with one another, but are heavily dependent upon the exchange of local raw materials for a variety of imports, especially of industrial-type goods, originating in Western Europe and the United States.

In short, little economic complementarity prevails within a region comprised entirely of underdeveloped countries; and, to the extent that economic complementarity does not prevail, the basis for mutually advantageous trade tends to be weak. Interestingly enough, however, this lack of economic complementarity within a region of underdevelopment stands in sharp contrast to the situation evident in regions already developed. To illustrate, most of the countries of Western Europe are heavily industrial—but despite the fact that an industrial emphasis is the general rule, the flow of trade between the countries of the region is great. The essential point is that the industrial process tends to yield a diversity in end output which conforms with the principles of economic complementarity, and which can then serve to sustain a substantial exchange of goods between countries within the same region. Thus, French luxury goods, German heavy machinery, and Italian light machinery can be expected to fit reasonably well into a regional trade framework—even while it is unreasonable to expect Honduras and Nicaragua to carry on a thriving interchange in bananas, or Burma and Thailand to carry on a thriving interchange in rice. It is perhaps not surprising, therefore, that regional market arrangements of a formal nature should be suggested within locales such as Western Europe, and should come into being with minimum transitional difficulty and over only little opposition (considering that immediate benefits of a mutual order are widely regarded as likely); indeed, it is against this background that the early histories of the European Common Market (linking Belgium, France, West Germany, Italy, Luxembourg, and the Netherlands) and of the Outer Seven trade pact (linking Austria, Denmark, Norway, Portugal, Sweden, Switzerland, and Great Britain) appear to take on special significance within the context of issues raised here.

Notwithstanding the current lack of economic complementarity between countries within regions of underdevelopment (which situation then hampers large-scale intra-regional trade), a regional-type trade arrangement may nevertheless hold plausibility in the case of these countries. Just because complementarity is not currently present does not mean that it cannot become a fact at some future date. Indeed, should the possibility exist that the presence of a regional-type trade arrangement can help to *create* greater complementarity within a given region, such an arrangement quickly acquires a special attraction. Thus, the introduction in individual countries within a region of underdevelopment of some industrial-type enterprises may have the direct effect of generating greater complementarity between these countries, which—if realized—would make greater intra-regional trade possible. But, the introduction of these new enterprises may be long delayed, or indeed prove entirely impossible, in the absence of an ability for the end output to reach an area-wide market. Accordingly, a case arises for the establishment of regional-type trade arrangements—not as a means to yield participating countries immediate gains from an interchange of goods arising under the prevailing economic order of things, but rather as a means to promote economic development itself. Then, as economic development proceeds, individual countries come to enjoy a new and higher level of economic activity generally, and as a companion feature, find themselves engaged in a new and higher volume of intra-regional trade. Significantly, it is in this manner that the introduction of regional-type trade arrangements (e.g., "common market" arrangements) is especially meaningful for underdeveloped countries desirous of economic development; put simply, a common market arrangement, in making intra-regional trade *possible,* may help to bring about the introduction of some new enterprises.

Payments

Some persons regard regional currency-clearing arrangements to be of help in the promotion of regional trade. As matters stand, many underdeveloped countries continue to rely upon exchange controls (unlike Western Europe, where convertibility was restored as the problem of the dollar shortage faded in severity for the individual countries of the region during the latter 1950's). The common situation in the underdeveloped world, as a consequence of the environment of underdevelopment, is one of heavy demand and low supply-potential as respects foreign exchange, so that a rational pattern of utilization of whatever foreign exchange is available appears dependent upon governmental intervention. But if upgraded foreign-exchange usage derives from such intervention, it is true also that a free market in goods is thereby ruled out. All the while, of course, more trade seems needed, not less trade or constant trade. Accordingly, the hope is readily fostered that somehow means can be found which might allow the volume of trade to be expanded *despite* the persistence of payments obstacles. Perhaps, to cite a seemingly reasonable ambition, some trade can be fostered outside and beyond customary foreign-exchange channels. Unfortunately, an attempt to proceed in this vein on a global basis is subject to many complications, particularly as each country and region adds further variables to what is a complex undertaking even under minimal circumstances. More hopeful, many feel, is an attempt geared to more limited arrangements. Perhaps a regional currency-clearing arrangement offers a practical course for gain, even if world-wide multilateralism appears beyond immediate grasp.

The idea of a regional currency arrangement as a means to foster intra-regional trade received a great boost through initiation of the European Payments Union (EPU) in Western Europe roughly a decade ago. The countries of Western Europe at the time were much subject to the dollar shortage, one effect of which was to undermine the process of settling international accounts as related to even purely intra-regional trade. The hope was that payments impediments to trade might be lessened through resort to a currency-clearing arrangement of regional scope, and that a growing volume of intra-regional trade might thereby result, notwithstanding the persistence of payments impediments between the region and the rest of the world. Significantly, the EPU proved successful, at least to a point, in the promotion of intra-European trade—indeed, in strengthening the economic capacity of the region in its trade relations with the rest of the world. In view of the general success experienced in this instance, it was perhaps only to be expected that thought should be given to the applicability of this means in efforts to promote intra-regional trade elsewhere, including regions of underdevelopment whose past records showed a low volume of intra-regional trade activity.

An important point, however, is that a currency arrangement can be expected merely to *accommodate* a trading arrangement economically justifiable on real grounds (i.e., on grounds other than pure currency considerations). Applied to regions of underdevelopment, it is well to recall that the basic reason for a low volume of intra-regional trade is found in the characteristic feature of a current lack of economic complementarity in the production patterns of the countries concerned; and, as long as there is no firm commodity basis for intra-regional trade, the case for a special currency-clearing arrangement as a means of easing the movement intra-regionally of present goods is undermined at the very outset. Thus it is that a currency-clearing arrangement can offer hope for beneficial impact upon current trade between countries within developed regions, such as Western Europe, even while the prospect for like benefit for countries within underdeveloped regions remains gloomy; it is simply that economic complementarity is present to substantial extent in the first instance, but is essentially absent in the case of the second.

Nevertheless, even if the magnitude of intra-regional trade in underdeveloped regions appears uncertain of marked increase during the near-term future as a consequence of the introduction of currency-clearing arrangements, there is good reason to believe that longer-run economic growth —and the trade pattern dependent upon this growth—is capable of being much influenced by the presence of such arrangements. Granted that a currency arrangement tends to yield little trade impact as long as underdevelopment is characteristic, the fact still remains that considerable meaning would attach if a regional production pattern were to evolve under which economic complementarity did prevail. Of significance in this connection, it is possible that the adoption within a region as yet underdeveloped of an appropriate currency arrangement might foster the introduction there of the very enterprises which, once they were part of the scene, could assure that region of the measure of economic complementarity essential for the support of a thriving intra-regional trade. In short, a currency arrangement, even if it does not result in a rapid rise in intra-regional trade, may have major impact in terms of *speeding economic development*—with this stimulation of economic development attributable, basically, to the salutary effect of the special arrangement in terms of curbing the deterring doubts of prospective entrepreneurs as to how and where disposal of future output is to occur.

An Overall View

As one surveys the potentialities of a regional approach as a means to foster economic development, several points seem to stand out:

1. Economic development calls for greater output. Such added output requires the introduction of various new projects. Some of these projects can be handled in more economic fashion on a regional basis than if left for unilateral action by single countries.
2. Important advantages are to be had from foreign trade. Efforts to promote such trade can take many forms—but one approach, the regional one, is to cultivate closer economic links among countries situated near one another.
3. Implementation of a regional approach to trade, in the case of underdeveloped countries, is hampered by two main obstacles: noncomplementarity in trade items and weaknesses in the payments mechanism.
4. When all is said and done, growth in intra-regional trade remains fundamentally dependent upon the evolution of *both* a) an appropriate production pattern and b) an appropriate currency mechanism —and in this sequence *the production pattern is basic.*

THE CASE OF LATIN AMERICA

The particular regional approach which carries greatest popular appeal as a means for the promotion of developmental progress in underdeveloped countries unquestionably is the one directly related to trade. As intimated earlier, regional-type trade arrangements are capturing much interest in several major underdeveloped regions, and in one of them, Latin America, the "common market movement" is far advanced. Given this state of affairs, some merit attaches to a brief further examination here of the particular approach—using Latin America, where the approach has proceeded farther than elsewhere in the underdeveloped world, as the special case in point.

While much discussion had occurred in Latin America over the years concerning the pros and cons of intra-regional trade agreements, it was not until 1958 that formal action was actually taken to put such an arrangement into effect. In that year the Central American Free Trade Area was established, with membership scheduled for five small countries: Guatemala, Honduras, El Salvador, Costa Rica, and Nicaragua. Thereafter, in early 1960, formal status was given a second and more ambitious arrangement, the Latin American Free Trade Area (LAFTA), with initial membership scheduled for seven countries, several of them being major countries of the region: Argentina, Brazil, Chile, Mexico, Paraguay, Peru, and Uruguay.

Of the two arrangements, LAFTA is clearly the more important. Not only is it scheduled to embrace the larger countries of Latin America from the very outset, but its governing Treaty was formulated in a manner intended to invite additional countries in Latin America to join—offering as a goal a single trade unit encompassing all Latin America. With this complexion on matters, the following comments on the formal aspects of the movement for greater intra-regional trade in Latin America are framed in terms of LAFTA.

Plan

Countries accepting membership in LAFTA agree to a program for the gradual removal of trade barriers between one another. Specifically, trade barriers are to be lowered at three-year intervals, until at the end of 12 years there is "free trade." Alongside this lessening in trade barriers within the region, individual member countries remain free to place restrictions of whatever form they wish upon imports arising outside the region. In short, LAFTA is intended to lead to a "free trade zone"—meaning no barriers to trade within the region, but unilateral determination by member countries of restrictions to be placed upon imports from countries outside the region; this is to be contrasted with the European Common Market, where recourse to the "common market" principle calls not only for the removal of trade barriers within the region, but also for the erection of a single uniform tariff structure upon imports entering any member country from outside the Common Market area.

Rationale

The basic rationale behind LAFTA relates to the promotion of economic development. But what should suggest a connection between a regional trade arrangement and economic development?

As matters stand, the countries of Latin America are heavily committed to raw-materials production, and all of the countries—despite wide variations among them—are subject to low per capita income (as compared with the United States and some other developed countries). Viewed from the standpoint of this environment, higher income requires greater output. Greater output (on a sustained basis), however, is dependent not only upon acceleration of effort, but also upon an ability to dispose of end products to good advantage. Significantly, raw materials are obliged to enter export channels to considerable extent, and there come up against a market situation averse to expansion (e.g., face conditions of inelastic demand). The result is that if greater output, and higher per capita income (under circumstances of a rapidly rising population), is truly desired, raw-materials production needs to be supplemented in important measure by output stemming from a new and growing industrial sector.

New industrial enterprises, if they are to arise, can be geared to cater to either a foreign market or the domestic market. In either case, efficiency in output is a desired, and needed, attribute. Of utmost importance, this efficiency is intimately tied to scale of operations. An economic scale of operations in export-type enterprises is a practical possibility, of course, even in the absence of a regional trade arrangement (since sales are tied to the foreign market, not restricted to a more limited market near at hand); in the case of enterprises producing import-substitutes, however, it is the home market which is crucial—and here a regional market offers more potential for an economic scale of operations than does dependence upon single country markets. If, further, it can be shown that export-type enterprises do not offer adequate scope for yielding those income gains believed needed (because of, say, complications posed by the entrenchment of old-line suppliers in markets outside the region), then the focal point is quickly shifted to enterprises of the import-substitution variety. Indeed, as variously argued (for example, by Raul Prebisch, the eminent Argentine economist who is, above all others, the guiding force behind the "common market movement" in Latin America), it is these enterprises which hold the key to the situation in regions of underdevelopment. Unless considerable success is had in the introduction of import-substitute-type enterprises, which can then spearhead the movement to continuing economic growth, progress in economic development can only be moderate. And to make possible substantial growth in such enterprises, a regional-type trade arrangement, assuring a market area going well beyond the confines of a single country, is an absolute prerequisite.

Thus, to generalize this argument in its applicability to the underdeveloped world, the first basic step toward pronounced economic development is that of expansion in enterprises yielding import-substitutes. These enterprises, however, need assurance of a wide market if an economic scale of operations is to prevail. This necessary market ordinarily can be had only within a multi-country area—hence the case for the creation of a regional "free trade zone."

Problems

The introduction of a regional trade arrangement does not proceed without difficulties. This fact, however much demonstrated in earlier experiences in developed regions, is being driven home anew in the case of LAFTA. The central problem is one of compliance. Member countries need to conduct themselves in accordance with the "rules of the game." Not only must members be willing to accept trade liberalization per plan (and to make such internal adjustments as then come to be required of them), but they must be willing to pursue basic public policies of a type conducive to application of the program of trade liberalization. Above all, the monetary and fiscal policies of member countries need to be coordinated to an extent which can yield compatibility between the economies for application of a unified program geared to invite economic expansion.

In practice, the basic "rule of the game" is that member countries subordinate independent economic decision-making (in the public-policy realm) in order better to accommodate group (regional) decision-making, from which greater benefits for all are expected to accrue. Such reorientation in thinking and action is sought through, basically, a two-fold approach: (1) stress upon good faith, with members being encouraged to live up to the commitments assumed with acceptance of membership, and (2) the extension of help when and as economic troubles arise to make compliance difficult, so that it is possible for members to live up to their commitments. By way of generalization, the central control authority which supervises the introduction and operations of a regional trade arrangement needs to possess two things: power and money—power to command respect, and money to facilitate action.

Objective

As intimated earlier, the hope is that LAFTA will help promote economic development. Indeed, help in speeding development takes precedence over maximization of trade in the current period. To elaborate, under 15 per cent of the total current foreign trade of all Latin America is intra-regional in nature. Further, continuation of the prevailing production pattern, with its bias toward non-complementarity in goods within the region, is likely to result in a relatively low volume of intra-regional trade in future years—whether or not a special regional trade arrangement exists. Therefore, if a markedly greater volume of intra-regional trade is desired, the production pattern within the region must undergo significant change, a change which augments complementarity. Such a change may prove possible, indeed be encouraged, if a workable regional trade arrangement is in being—at least, this is how the basic argument for LAFTA proceeds.

In short, both the success and meaningfulness of a regional trade arrangement are tied to economic development. Its success is dependent upon the achievement of economic development, which can augment complementarity and provide an improved basis for trade. Its meaningfulness is dependent upon the realization of economic development, since only in terms of how it helps bring about a changed production pattern can it register real impact.

Size Limits of the Trade Unit

LAFTA was scheduled to have an initial membership of seven countries. The hope, however, was that all countries in Latin America would eventually acquire membership. But, at the same time, the hope was to restrict membership to Latin American countries. Specifically, membership by the United States was ruled out—so that the idea of a Western Hemisphere Common Market is not at issue.

The aim of an all-Latin trade unit is to promote the interests of Latin America as an economic entity. Indeed, much of the attendant effort is in terms of strengthening Latin America *in the face of* the economic strength already existent outside the region, as in the United States. As a matter of fact, were the United States to be part of the same trade unit along with Latin America, the presence of this country, with its advanced status (which, among other things, places it in a complementary position, tradewise, with Latin America), would have the effect of freezing the economic status quo of Latin America, rather than of helping to change it. Given this essential fact of life, it is not surprising to find the Latin view to be one favoring a new trade arrangement *exclusive* to Latin America.

IMPLICATIONS FOR THE UNITED STATES

What are the implications for the United States of a movement in the underdeveloped world to proceed along regional lines in grappling with pressing economic problems? A reasonable general answer seems to be that action there which serves to improve economic conditions for the countries concerned, and for the world at large, is of benefit to the United States. Specifically, improved economic conditions in underdeveloped regions stand to help this country by easing world tensions and by rendering beneficial impact upon foreign trade generally. Therefore, if a regional approach can be helpful in the promotion of economic development (as is argued here), the United States should normally feel kindly disposed toward it.

The foregoing may suffice as a general answer, but what is to be said on more particularized scores? For example, there is the question of how the United States Government might reconcile a pro-attitude toward "regional economic confederations" with its long-standing position that the proper goal is all-out multilateralism. And, there is the question of how American business should choose to react, given its particular set of interests. These two questions seem sufficiently important to merit special comment.

Multilateralism Versus Regionalism

Historically, the United States Government has adhered to the policy position that multilateralism should be the goal of this and other countries. The particular position undoubtedly was grounded in this country's appraisal of its own self-interest—specifically, the need for added export markets and investment outlets. Actually, of course, this country has not always practiced what it has preached in this respect (witness, for example, repeated resort to various protectionist actions: "escape clauses" in tariff concessions, tying provisions in loan agreements, etc.). Notwithstanding such apparent deviations from avowed policy, however, considerable progress toward liberalization has been recorded by this country since, say, the days of the Great Depression.

Once the idea spread that particular problems should be attacked along regional lines (as in the realms of trade promotion and payments accommodation), the question arose as to how this country should react. Should it sanction the new approach, and at the same time forego the goal of multilateralism? Or, should it endorse the new approach, at least in instances, while clinging to the hope that specific action along regional lines might somehow prove compatible with attainment of the dominant goal of multilateralism? Following a period which clearly reflects indecision, the country began to give selective endorsement—first in Western Europe in terms of some measures inspired by the Marshall Plan, and then in a sequence of measures applicable within the underdeveloped world.

How was the United States to rationalize even limited endorsement of such regional measures? Basically, the sustaining logic was premised on three main considerations: a conviction that the presence of formidable obstacles made impractical an all-out movement to multilateralism in the here and now; a belief that some specific problems merited immediate attention, and that the regional approach held potential in their case; and a hope that current actions along regional lines would not hamper attainment of the greater goal, world-wide multilateralism, at that future time when environmental factors are more favorable. Thus, the regional approach found favor (say, in trade and payments) in terms of what it might offer during the near-term future—even as multilateralism continued as the long-run goal of foreign economic policy. Besides all this, of course, it was possible that some regional-type actions would have occurred anyway, even in the absence of this country's sanction—in which case nominal sanction, and a continuation of rapport with those who guide action, may well represent the course of wisdom.

In principle, therefore, the United States remains committed to multilateralism. But with an environment in the world today that is not conducive to all-out multilateralism, the United States feels obliged to settle for something less for now—even while it clings to the hope that *greater* multilateralism will prove to be the case over time. It is in this way that sanction and support can be given regional arrangements in the present. While regional arrangements are thus not beyond endorsement by the United States, this country is interested in assuring itself that its own economic position within an international context is not thereby specifically injured. For example, the United States commonly insists that the practices initiated under new intra-regional trade arrangements do not violate the code of conduct set forth by the General Agreement on Tariffs and Trade (GATT). In practical terms, this means that the United States tries to prevent market intervention of a type which would eventuate in particularized discrimination in international markets against American exports.

Markets and Competition

Common markets and free trade zones in essence comprise trade blocs. As these trade blocs arise, how is American business affected? And what should it choose to do about what it finds?

As intimated earlier, the fundamental purpose of a regional-type trade arrangement (and of a supporting payments arrangement) in an underdeveloped area is to promote intra-regional trade, the accomplishment of which is sought through the evolution of added economic complementarity within the particular trade region. The counterpart of greater economic unification by such a region, however, is an alteration in the status of the region vis-à-vis already developed regions. Economists in the foreign trade field commonly argue that a changing economic environment of the type cited need not prove injurious to any country; specifically, it is argued that development within regions of underdevelopment need not injure a developed economy, provided there is a willingness there to undergo adjustment (i.e., all countries can be better off as a greater volume of output and trade, albeit of changed composition, becomes characteristic).

Even if it is admitted that no advanced economy is made to suffer as long as it is willing to adjust to the new situation, the fact remains, however, that the adjustment process at issue involves *specific* firms. Some firms experience gain in the adjustment process, while others face retrenchment—quite apart from the matter of overall impact upon the total economy. Thus, individual firms are obliged to weigh their own status against the environment which is evolving.

Significantly, some firms heavily dependent upon exportation to a region undergoing economic unification may find it advantageous, as they attempt to maximize individual well-being, to contemplate a shift in production-locale to the foreign region. To elaborate, if development within a common market area or free trade zone threatens the market of a firm based in an already developed country outside the immediate region, the firm may find that self-protection requires entry into production *within* the foreign area. It is in this way that a regional-type trade arrangement can have the effect of attracting foreign investment. Indeed, foreign investment in a magnitude perhaps never attainable through simple exhortation may prove forthcoming in response to the subtle coercive pressures of a new type of trade barrier.

9

END OF THE BRUSSELS TALKS *

The breakdown of negotiations between Britain and the European Economic Community has some economic causes and many economic implications—for Britain, for the EEC, and for the United States. But the main causes and some of the most important implications lie in the realm of politics.

* From *Report on Western Europe* (Chase-Manhattan Bank, February-March 1963).

THE BRUSSELS TALKS

For fifteen months, negotiators of Britain and the Six had sought a formula for British entry into the Common Market on terms acceptable to all. The British had agreed to accept most of the provisions of the Rome Treaty as written, but continued to seek certain concessions which the Six found difficult to grant. The most important of these were:

> 1. Transitional arrangements for some Commonwealth products which would cushion the shock of shutting off their British markets. An example is New Zealand dairy products, whose sale to Britain now accounts for about 20% of New Zealand's total exports.
>
> 2. Transitional arrangements for British agriculture. Britain's present farm policy is based on subsidies and low prices, while the EEC system calls for high guaranteed prices and no subsidies. An abrupt switch would pose problems of adjustment for British farmers and consumers.
>
> 3. A guarantee that other members of the European Free Trade Association (Austria, Switzerland, Portugal, and the Scandinavian countries) would get an opportunity to join the Common Market or negotiate association with it on acceptable terms.

The Six had made a number of concessions—including elimination of the common external tariff on tea as well as commitments to negotiate later agreements covering important Commonwealth commodities. They were reluctant to make any changes in the Treaty, however, and particularly fearful of tinkering with their common agricultural policy, which was already under stress from conflicting interests inside the Six. France had put up the stiffest opposition to granting concessions—particularly those involving agriculture—but the other five member countries and the EEC Commission agreed with the French concern for the Treaty and the agricultural policy.

Not only in France, but throughout the Common Market, there were some fears that if Britain were followed by Denmark, Norway, and Ireland, plus association for the three neutral countries (Austria, Sweden, and Switzerland), then the Common Market would have grown too large too quickly and its momentum would have been slowed.

THE TALKS END

The first move toward the breakdown of negotiations came at President de Gaulle's press conference on January 14, when de Gaulle implied that Britain was not yet ready to become a full member of the Common Market.

Four days later the French delegate at Brussels called for the negotiations to be broken off. The other five EEC members objected strongly, but the French insisted, and the talks ended January 29.

Reactions from the Five at the French stand were sharp and regretful. The EEC Commission noted that the Common Market "is not an enterprise in the service of selfish interests of its members, but that it has responsibilities toward others, whose fate is affected by its actions and its omissions."

The fact remains, however, that France has power under the Rome Treaty to block British membership indefinitely, since any application for membership must be approved by the Six unanimously. Short of breaking up the EEC and working out a new arrangement with Britain, the Five have no sure way to take Britain in. And the benefits of EEC to each of them are so evident that such an extreme course is most unlikely.

POLITICAL BACKGROUND

French objections to British membership in the Common Market go far beyond the issues that were being negotiated in Brussels. Since the Common Market began, France has held a position of leadership. Britain as a full member would provide another source of leadership and make it impossible for any one nation to shape Common Market policies.

Some of these policies will be decided soon, under provisions of the Rome Treaty. For example, the Six have not yet decided how high to fix the Common Market's guaranteed price for butter. If Britain had a hand in making this decision, its weight would go on the side of a relatively low price level, while France would prefer a higher price.

Other policies to be decided are not so imminent, but probably more important. The Common Market countries are moving slowly but perceptibly toward closer coordination of their policies in areas only dimly sketched out by the Rome Treaty—such as monetary affairs—or not covered by the Treaty at all—such as foreign policy and defense.

The EEC Commission has proposed closer coordination of monetary policies among the Six and is studying a proposal by Jean Monnet for a European Reserve Union, in which the Six would pool part of their gold and foreign exchange reserves.

Plans for political integration also have been put forward. De Gaulle's plan for a "political community" envisages periodic meetings among heads of state and more frequent meetings of ministers and sub-cabinet officials to coordinate cultural affairs, defense policy, and foreign policy. This plan is actually incorporated in a French-German Treaty signed late in January.

If Britain were in a position to influence any of the common policies that may grow from these beginnings, France might find herself outvoted and unable to get the policies she wants. This would be particularly true if other EFTA countries followed Britain into the Common Market.

De Gaulle's basic objections to British membership go still deeper. Expansion of the Common Market would, he feels, make it more difficult for Europe to follow policies independent of the United States. De Gaulle summed it up at his press conference:

"It is conceivable that the cohesion of all (the Common Market's) members, who would be very numerous and very diverse, would not hold for long and that in the end there would appear a colossal Atlantic Community under American dependence and leadership which would soon swallow up the European Community.

"This is an assumption that can be perfectly justified in the eyes of some, but it is not at all what France wanted to do and what France is doing, which is a strictly European construction."

THE NATO PROBLEM

There is good reason to believe that the French decision to end the talks was influenced by de Gaulle's quest for an independent nuclear deterrent.

Shortly before the sudden breakdown of negotiations, the United States had cancelled the Skybolt missile project, which had promised the means for Britain to maintain an independent nuclear deterrent. President Kennedy met Prime Minister Macmillan at Nassau in December and offered Britain the opportunity to buy Polaris missiles, capable of carrying British thermonuclear warheads, which could be launched from nuclear-powered submarines built with U.S. technical assistance. These weapons would be placed under NATO command along with part of the U.S. Polaris force. Britain accepted the offer.

Kennedy also offered to sell Polaris to France, although there is doubt that U.S. law would permit nuclear technology to be transferred to France to the same degree. In any event, France refused the offer.

De Gaulle explained his refusal at the same January 14 press conference. His argument ran that missiles under NATO control would be under U.S. control, and therefore would not necessarily serve French or European defense under all conditions. He said that a U.S. deterrent had been a good defense for Europe only so long as the Soviet Union was unable to strike the U.S. with nuclear weapons. Once the Soviets were able to strike the U.S. heartland, Europe could not always depend on the U.S. taking decisions with Europe's own interest as the main consideration.

By giving up nuclear independence—however slight—rather than adding to Europe's nuclear position, Britain took a step away from de Gaulle's conception of an independent Europe.

THE TWO DESIGNS

The abrupt cancellation of the Brussels talks thus brought into the open a conflict between two broad designs for the development of the Western Alliance—the French "grand design" of European independence and the U.S. "grand design" of Atlantic interdependence and partnership.

Like all slogans, these terms exaggerate the difference between the ideas behind them. Both designs recognize—and welcome—Europe's return to prosperity and strength. Both envision a united Europe working with America to hold the line against further expansion of Sino-Soviet power and to enhance the prosperity of the free world.

The conflict is mainly one of emphasis. While the present French design seeks first to harness European nationalism to a close continental alliance, the U.S. stresses the need for ties between this European group and America. Our own design recognizes that Europe, because of geography as well as history, should be able to come much closer to unity than an Atlantic Community can. But it does visualize coordination of many European and American policies. These include policies to promote world trade—to the mutual advantage of Europe, America, and the rest of the free world. They also include coordination of aid to the developing countries and coordinated efforts to strengthen the monetary system on which the free world depends.

The French design recognizes the need for such coordination, but gives a higher priority to Continental ties—particularly those between France and West Germany. It also stresses the need for a nuclear deterrent which could be employed independently of the United States.

STRESS AMONG THE SIX

The other five members of the Common Market do not now share the French view about an independent nuclear force, nor do they feel that Atlantic partnership is incompatible with European unity. Further, most groups within the "Five" would welcome Britain into the Common Market for both economic and political reasons.

The unilateral French stand against Britain's entry, therefore, touched off the first serious political crisis in the Common Market's five-year history. The Italian and Dutch governments reacted strongly against de Gaulle's conception of Europe, and some West German leaders threatened to decline parliamentary ratification of the new French-German treaty. Overtures have been made to revive the Western European Union, whose members are the EEC countries and Britain. Yet French cooperation is necessary to implement any common policy, and no real solution can be reached as long as the Six are divided.

IMPLICATIONS FOR EEC

One probable consequence of the crisis will be a slowdown in the EEC's own timetable. During the first five years the Six moved ahead on an accelerated schedule and twice speeded up the original 12-15 year transition period. More recently, the "Action Program" of the EEC Commission called for full implementation of the Rome Treaty by 1968. Now it seems likely that the other Five will drag their feet on some programs of great interest to France.

Three programs in particular were slated for 1963:

1. A new treaty of association between the Six and 18 African states, mostly former French territories.

2. Implementation of the common agricultural policy, to the benefit of France's farm exports.

3. French-style planning on the Community level, particularly in regard to U.S. investment in Europe.

Although some progress will be made on these programs, it seems very unlikely that the other Five will back them as quickly and as enthusiastically as before. And beyond such deliberate reprisals, other common policies will be harder to achieve in an atmosphere of discord.

The program of internal tariff cuts and adjustments toward a common external tariff is not likely to be affected, however. The Six already have decided to cut internal tariffs another 10% (bringing them down to 40% of their pre-EEC levels) on July 1, 1963 and to make the second 30% adjustment toward the common external tariff on the same date.

Another effect may be to focus the EEC's attention on its internal problems, rather than on its relationship with the outside world. De Gaulle's emphasis on "a strictly European construction" is at odds with U.S. efforts to insure that Europe would look outward, reducing its external tariff and working cooperatively with the rest of the free world. British membership would have helped to insure an "outward looking" Europe.

IMPLICATIONS FOR BRITAIN

British entry into EEC over the longer run, or association with an eye to eventual membership, is still a possibility, since both trade and political interest incline Britain toward the Continent. The long negotiations in Brussels, which clarified many issues, may yet provide the basis for future agreement, although there is no certainty of this.

At any rate, negotiations are not likely to reopen soon. The breakdown probably has postponed British entry at least until 1965, and possibly longer. Meantime, Britain's problems remain.

Britain's main economic problem in recent years has been a slow rate of growth accompanied by recurring exchange crises. Unemployment has been rising lately and some plant capacity has been idle. Britain had expected that entry into EEC would force her economy to adjust to competition—shifting resources into the strongest industries and modernizing plant and equipment. Now this competition will not automatically appear.

One alternative for Britain is to work hard for further tariff reductions, in order to stimulate her exports and force her industry to modernize. This implies an effort to strengthen the seven-member European Free Trade Association and strong support for global tariff cuts in the next round of negotiations under the General Agreement on Tariffs and Trade (GATT) due to get underway next year.

Another likely move will be to stimulate the British economy through expansionary policies at home, even at the expense of the short-run balance of payments. The government already has indicated that this April's budget will emphasize growth; while Britain's drawing rights on the International Monetary Fund and other multilateral currency arrangements should suffice to counter short-run speculation against sterling.

IMPLICATIONS FOR THE U.S.

The United States and Britain still have close links with Western Europe, through NATO, OECD (Organization for Economic Cooperation and Development) and GATT. The U.S. undoubtedly will press for continuing close cooperation with the Common Market through these agencies.

President Kennedy's authority to bargain tariffs down in exchange for reductions by EEC has been reduced by Britain's exclusion from the Common Market, but it remains substantial. De Gaulle's attitude may hinder negotiations, however, since access for U.S. farm goods is one of our main objectives and France stands to gain most from European agricultural protectionism. At the same time, U.S. exporters—particularly of farm products—will gain from Britain's not being included inside EEC trade barriers.

For U.S. firms, the exclusion of Britain probably will mean some diversion of new investment to the Continent. Existing operations in Britain are not likely to be transplanted, however, since few if any were established primarily to serve the Common Market.

At the same time, some recent U.S. investments in France have run into opposition—largely unrelated to the breakdown in Brussels or the Nassau Agreement. The French government has expressed concern over investments in industries where a relatively large share of French production is controlled by foreigners (e.g. food processing, automobiles) and has withheld approval in some cases. Other U.S. investments which dovetail with the French economic plan have been approved.

The other five EEC members have given no sign that they intend to follow France's lead. But Community-wide planning, if it is adopted, might give rise to a more selective approach to foreign investment throughout EEC.

The breakdown of negotiations in Brussels seems unlikely to reverse the direction of trends in Europe, but it has certainly slowed them up. Economic integration among the Six probably will be slowed up slightly, particularly in agriculture. Adherence of Britain and other EFTA countries to the Common Market has been slowed up appreciably, if not entirely blocked. Reduction of trade barriers between Europe and America probably also has been slowed, and current problems between France and the United States add to the complications of harmonizing Western policies in the fields of foreign policy and defense.

But the interdependence of the European nations and, to a lesser degree, of the Atlantic nations is still a fact; and this is certain to assure continuing interest in the Common Market by political leaders and businessmen of Britain and the United States.

Although it has settled nothing, the breakdown in Brussels has posed some hard basic questions which must be pondered on both sides of the Atlantic: What will be the Common Market's ultimate political structure? Is full membership in the Club limited to its six charter members? Will EEC become inward-looking and protectionist? How can a meaningful Atlantic partnership be constructed, particularly in the military area?

The breakdown of negotiations has provided no answers, but the questions are now clearer than at any time since the Common Market began.

SECTION TWO

Management of International Business

The previous section provided a picture of the overall politico-economic forces at work both in the U.S. and abroad. Management has little or no control over them. Yet, those external forces help to shape the environment within which the business executive has to make his decisions.

The objective of this section is to take a closer look at the "internal" forces that affect the decision-making of individual businesses.

In the early 1960's U.S. industrial companies were adding $2 to $3 billion annually to capital investment in foreign countries; they were exporting in excess of $20 billion of goods; and production of U.S. subsidiaries abroad grew at more than twice the rate of the annual increase of the Gross National Product within the United States. Many businessmen—stay-at-homes as well as veteran "internationalists"—have ambitious plans for further profitable expansion outside the United States.

In his home market, the executive moves with ease and confidence. He knows the ground rules. Distribution patterns, trade terms, nuances of consumer tastes and preferences, and competitors' strengths and weaknesses are second nature to him. Not so abroad; there many of the comfortable assumptions that the executive uses at home may not hold true. In some ways, this is to the good. It permits a fresh viewpoint and thus enables the American businessman to grasp opportunities that others do not see. Drawing from domestic experience, the creative executive may spot the early signs of a trend for convenience items, packaged foods, or new appliances. Or he may see the chance to apply a proven technique in a new situation. Yet he may also stub his toe. He may erroneously assume that foreign consumers react in the same way as Americans do; he may think that practices that were successful at home will work equally well abroad. They may, or they may not. Thus, both the risks and opportunities resulting from executive action abroad are often greater than they would be at home.

Risk comes in many guises: political situations, governmental controls, or markets unready for a product may be all-important. . . .

American businessmen generally find government interference in foreign operations more objectionable than its tendency to do so at home. Professor Kronstein's think-piece on *Government and Business in International Trade* shows possible ways out of the dilemma. It is required reading for anybody concerned with matters of international trade. The same goes for R. D. Robinson's absorbing discussion of *Conflicting Interests in International Business Investment.*

The broad philosophical strokes of Kronstein's and Robinson's writings become more and more "applied" once the basic decision to spread wings abroad is made. Now a concrete means of implementation has to be devised. John McDonald and Hugh Parker take the reader through the successive stages of *Creating a Strategy for International Growth.* They start with export-import activity that requires very little change in management outlook, company organization or product line; and culminate with emergence of a "global approach" that encompasses both domestic and overseas operations. These ideas are further elaborated in *LRP for International Operations* by John Fayerweather.

Hodgson and Uyterhoeven point out, in their path-breaking article, that the conventional pro-forma profit and loss statements are an inadequate basis for *Analyzing Foreign Opportunities.* They therefore proceed with the development of a new management tool called "operating margin analysis," or OMA for short. OMA helps to avoid the inherent dangers of making false analogies by transferring industry reasoning from one country to another. It also allows construction of an analytical framework within which various foreign opportunities can be compared with those at home.

Lindsay and Clee, in their *New Patterns for Overseas Operations,* show how systems management—a variation on the theme of the primary contractor used in U.S. military procurement—can be applied while spreading risk among several participating entrepreneurs. Finally, Tomb and Shackelford do some exciting crystal gazing about the *Future Structure of International Companies.* They explore the rationale behind the creation of organizational forms that are tailor-made for the needs of global enterprises. They also suggest criteria that can be used in deciding when a more advanced management structure is needed.

Organization charts have to be filled with performing men. The chains of command are only as strong as their weakest links. Specifically, the success of foreign operations depends on the performance of men who have responsibilities for local decision-making. Outstanding performance, determined by a sound system of measurement and appraisal, must be tangibly rewarded if top management expects superior efforts from its managers. Similarly, failure to meet established goals must be followed by penalties. This is particularly so under a bonus system. Otherwise the performance-appraisal process will not make the contribution to management development of which it is capable. McLagan and Woodthorpe, in *Measuring Executive Performance in a World Enterprise,* show alternative ways of relating compensation to results actually achieved.

10

GOVERNMENT AND BUSINESS IN INTERNATIONAL TRADE *

Heinrich Kronstein

In examining the relationship between political government and private power (private corporations or trade unions), it seems to be agreed that an order should be re-established which would assure the domination of political power in the field of government, while maintaining the autonomy of private organization in trade and industry. In this new order private power should be brought into line with the "public interest."

This all sounds very well, but experience has shown that without the aid of *workable standards* government cannot effectively promote an alleged public interest, nor can corporations be blamed if they should happen to violate that interest. In the anti-trust field, for example, there is continued conflict between the approach of the government to international trade and that of private corporations.

Corporation lawyers would like to see their clients and their clients' subsidiaries free from any legal action restraining them from joining an international or foreign cartel or combine. The anti-trust agencies of the federal government, however, consider that such international practice will often be inconsistent with the Sherman Act, since its effect may be to hinder the foreign trade of the United States as a whole.

Behind this controversy there is a basic question: Is there an existing American order into which American corporations have to be integrated? Without such an order, and with only the Sherman Act for guidance, it is questionable which acts of American corporations abroad are outlawed and which are not. Unless we have a clear guide defining the aim of American trade policy, we risk prohibiting advantageous enterprises while permitting undesirable ones. The problem, of course, is a part of the fundamental issue of what the proper relationship is not only between government and corporations in foreign trade but between government and corporations in general.

The issue arose in an intense form at the time of Theodore Roosevelt and continued until the Federal Trade Commission was established in 1914. There were three main groups engaged in the dispute, representing the interests of Theodore Roosevelt, of Woodrow Wilson, and of "business." Roosevelt, together with his adviser, Harry Augustus Garfield, the first Corporation Commissioner and son of the President, envisaged a state

* From *Occasional Papers* (Center for the Study of Democratic Institutions, Santa Barbara, Calif., September 1961). Reprinted by permission.

powerful enough to regulate decisively in the governmental interest. They saw public investigation of corporations and publication of their activities as means of promoting public information and bringing corporations into line with the public interest. They expected, further, to see a development in the United States similar to the trend in Germany, where, in their opinion, government by its very status in society was truly in a commanding position over business enterprise and other private institutions. The Wilson group agreed as to the need for publicity, but for quite another reason. Their aim was to force corporations to behave according to fixed rules of competition which alone, they felt, would keep the corporations within the boundaries required by the public interest. The third group resisted all demands for public inspection or information, and in effect favored the *laissez faire* principle of using private power wherever the corporation might see fit.

The dispute remains unresolved. Although the Federal Trade Commission, with substantial visitorial power over corporations, was authorized to publish reports on corporations and to issue cease and desist orders, the legislature left undetermined to what end these powers should be used. The controversy was obscured behind the words "fair" and "unfair" practices. Twice since 1914 the gap in the law was temporarily bridged, first during the early period of the New Deal in the direction proposed by Theodore Roosevelt, and then during the second period of the New Deal when Thurman Arnold was in charge of the Anti-Trust Division, this time in the direction desired by Wilson. Today we are again faced with the same uncertainties.

It is frequently suggested that it should be the responsibility of the government or of governmental agencies to determine the public interest and to instruct corporations how best to serve this interest. The notes by W. H. Ferry in the Center's pamphlet, "The Corporation and the Economy," refer to "the fragmentation of foreign aid activities and their ambiguous relations to one another and to private enterprise." Ferry refers to the recommendation of a Presidential Commission that "all foreign economic programs be brought under a single agency" which "would also be 'concerned with assuring that private enterprise is used as fully as possible.'" He would entrust the over-all problem to some type of planning agency.

I should like to expand and elaborate upon these suggestions. To this purpose I will offer some observations on the present international trade situation. I hope my examples will indicate to what extent both government and corporations today fail to serve those functions in society which have been entrusted to them and how, as a result, the balance of our social forces is fast disappearing. Perhaps these examples may show what can be done to re-establish the balance between corporations and government and to clarify the functions of each. For without some such clarification it is impossible to define the "public interest" that is to be assured by "some type of planning agency" of government.

The following three propositions, which are examples of the complete dichotomy between American private and public power in the area of international trade, will serve as materials for discussion of the question of how public and private interests can be reconciled under a common denominator. From this it will then be possible to proceed into the larger issue of the present relations between corporations and government in the United States.

Proposition one: The American private corporation, the powerhouse of American technology and economic experience, is being deterred from the mainstream of activity in new underdeveloped countries.

During recent years the United States developed, or at least accepted, a fresh approach to American activity in the new countries. The government has conducted economic relations through its different agencies, or jointly with other governments, usually through the United Nations or an institution established under the auspices of the United Nations. In turn, the recently sovereign nations have entered into economic relations through *their* governments. As a result, private enterprise has to a large extent lost its role as instigator, planner, and executer of development in these new lands. Adaptation of private policy to the needs of the countries or to American needs in foreign markets has declined. Many governments not in the Communist bloc have excluded private enterprise as a participant in important industrial fields or have created difficulties that amount to practical exclusion.

A number of more or less settled practices has developed, such as making outright gifts of military and other technical materials, offering governmental long-term loans, and guaranteeing through governmental agencies credit which is made available as corporate loans.

The combination of military and economic aid by the same organization, the United States government, is a clear example of the confusion of social functions. The Executive and the Congress, formulating one budget, make basic decisions on military, technical, and economic aid, even though these are administered by different agencies. Compare for a moment the coincidence between the development of military dictatorships in new underdeveloped countries and the concentration of aid in their centralized governmental agencies.

Corporations have more or less accepted this policy. Today they are active in the new countries only insofar as the government will assume the risk. One reason for this is undoubtedly the rule of international law that local governments may nationalize commercial enterprises and other forms of foreign investment at any time. The expropriations in Cuba are recent examples, as is the expropriation of the Belgian-owned street-car system in Cairo, which was carried out without any previous conflict or warning. Since even old underdeveloped countries may behave in this way, the governments of new countries may be expected to follow suit as soon as enough private investment has accumulated to make so-called nationalization attractive.

American corporations do not really fight this situation. They are satisfied with receiving guarantees by the government through the channel of a semi-governmental bank which amount to 90 per cent of the possible losses provided the contemplated transaction conforms to the rules and limitations established by the American government. This means that the transaction must be acceptable to and supported by the friendly sovereign government of the other country. Therefore, there is no room for any careful autonomous planning by American experts with a view toward a long-term program. As a result, the initiative is left in the hands of the new nations and their governments.

American government personnel engaged in this work are often as over-zealous and idealistic as they are naïve. They expect a very speedy growth of technical and administrative skill in the new nations. They believe that the colonial powers could have educated a sufficient number of experts at any time. It is true that much more could and should have been done, but the evidence indicates a need for caution on this point. Only research twenty years from now will show whether and to what extent naïveté led to the pressure on Belgium to leave the Congo on such short notice. Our governmental agencies entrusted with the foreign aid program have had little or no chance to find staffs of technicians and experts prepared to operate successfully. Instead, a bureaucracy smothered by red tape has been built up almost unobserved.

The observation is often made that whenever governments in an otherwise non-socialized economy "take over," corporations stay out, even if large business opportunities remain. A business organization of the nineteenth century would certainly not have overlooked the opportunities available in the following situation: The last GATT report for 1959 indicates a considerable step-up of imports into developing countries from the present $35 to $40 billion to $50 or $55 billion in 1969. The report estimates that these countries during the same period will have developed industries in the manufacture of bicycles, kitchen tools, diesel motors, and textiles. The report assumes that this development will require for the entire group of underdeveloped old and new countries an annual capital contribution of between $12 and $13 billion, compared with $7.5 billion in 1960.

Perhaps a nineteenth century company would have concentrated on only one particular country or one particular line of business, but it would have involved itself in some way in this potential development in spite of risks. For the contemporary American corporation, however, the philosophy of safety has taken over and deprived management of business initiative.

Systematic planning of foreign development operations is a job ideally suited to the industrial experts in our corporations. Perhaps some corporations are engaged in this work, but I doubt that their part is substantial. The advisory services of industrial planners or economists not connected with industry may be helpful, but these people are not occupied with the actual job.

It is interesting to see what great success a relative newcomer, Italy, has had in industrial planning. Fiat, Montecatini, Italian Edison, Innocento, and Pirelli established a joint agency to prepare a plan for underdeveloped territories. The Iranian government employed it to outline the development of the southeast part of Iran. Argentina, Egypt, Tunisia, and Togo soon followed. Negotiations with Central African states are now pending. This systematic inclusion of a private agency in the planning job is an important step. The Federal Republic of Germany is considering setting up a mixed agency composed of government and private groups to serve the same purpose. But this is still not enough. Private experts continue to be needed after the plan has begun to operate, as is evident in the recent efforts of the Argentine government to bring American and European technicians there to run industrial plants erected with government aid. In spite of the fact that the number of industrial plants in Argentina set up with government aid had increased substantially by 1960, the total industrial production has decreased because of the lack of qualified people to run the plants.

Proposition two: The American corporation, which has invested substantial funds, especially in the old underdeveloped countries, is not treated as a part of the economy when American trade policy is being formulated.

Among the American enterprises most active in foreign countries, irrespective of government guarantees, are the omni-present oil companies. Like other corporations, they have not always put the interests of their own country first, but recently their actions have begun to show an intention to help the United States and the local countries.

Our special problem can be best illustrated in the transformation of Venezuela by the American oil companies from a poor agricultural economy into a country with a mixed economy, to a certain extent modern and effective, in other respects still at the economic level of the fourteenth century. Then, a few years ago, the American steel industry, having acquired highly valuable iron ore deposits in Venezuela, became the second great United States investor there. This further revolutionized life in Venezuela. Only the lethargic remained unmoved, and no one's aspirations stayed the same. A modern industrial life, a modern capitalistic spirit, was forced on the nation.

No one can be surprised that investments of this scope should lead to social upheaval. The farming population, living at the lowest possible level, met American luxury and a standard of living they had never even imagined. Many people left their farms and tried to get jobs in the oil and steel industries. Some of them succeeded. Those who did not, and who are now living in the cities under conditions worse than those they had left, threaten the public order in Venezuela.

Now if relatively open market conditions had been maintained within the United States, the ups and downs of business cycles would not have brought about the dangers of a revolt in Venezuela. Iron ore deposits developed by American enterprise would have led the country further away from its undesirable monolithic economy. But at a time when Venezuela had a weekly income of about $25 million from oil, and could expect and hope for development of its large resources of minerals and cheap power, the United States government, led by the Congress, accepted a new type of isolationist policy. The American oil industry had gone to Venezuela in the light of forecasts that the end of our own oil supply was imminent. But our statisticians and planners proved to be wrong. The United States did not enter a period of shortage of energy. Local coal interests and independent oil producers persuaded Congress and the Executive to act in their sole interest. The Johnson Oil Import Bill authorized the President to establish quotas on oil imports into the United States.

American politicians did not consider what would happen to Venezuela and to the American investor there. Not only did Venezuela suffer from the new legislation; the American consumer, especially in New England, was forced to pay higher gasoline prices. Venezuelan oil was forced to look for substitute markets, and turned to Western Europe. Near East oil, which to a large extent is under the control of American firms, had its principal markets there. United States coal also had an important market in Europe, at least for a time. Now we find the American coal corporations attempting to persuade Europe to keep out Venezuelan oil by fixing import quotas. Such attempts show our lack of a clear trade policy. We deal with expediencies, ignoring the interdependencies of corporate and public interests.

Other cases point up the degree of confusion existing in our international economic relations. For example, in the same week the American government was making a drastic demand in Bonn for foreign aid not tied in any way to the buying of German goods, the president of the United Mine Workers submitted a paper to a committee of the House of Representatives strongly recommending that foreign aid be given only to those nations purchasing their coal supply in the United States. This proposal was supposed to be a remedy for unemployment in the American coal industry. We may well ask whether it would not be cheaper to grant temporary unemployment benefits in the coal industry than to enact an import quota of this kind.

Proposition three: The United States government has no influence on investments made by American private corporations in other industrial countries, such as England, Australia, Western Europe, or Japan.

The American public has suddenly found itself confronted with a crisis in the balance of payments. For years it was common to speak of the dollar gap of the industrial European nations. Recently, however, the newspapers reported on the same day a request for German aid to the United States, and a new dollar investment by Ford in shares of its English subsidiary. The American government appeared to be without any controlling influence over investment in Western Europe. Besides the undesirable results that this could have for the United States, the European governments themselves are unhappy with the extent of present investment in Europe by American firms and private individuals. These investments have an inflationary effect and constitute an element of insecurity, especially in dangerous political and social situations. They have now destroyed the balance between the currencies that existed for about twenty years, a balance that was always rightly considered one of the proud accomplishments of American post-war policy. The German revaluation is only the beginning of many new currency ventures unless the United States, Europe, and Japan, the industrial nations of the world, come to a clear agreement on economic policy that will obviate currency fluctuation resulting from speculation. Currency measures can be justified only if they are part of a combined new economic plan.

American corporations defend their investment policy in Europe in varying terms. For one thing, the United States has proved unable to avoid a price level that is non-competitive with other industrial nations. I agree with those who consider it at least superficial to assume that this price level is an effect of trade union policies. Wages are just another element of costs, whatever trade unionists or economists may say. In modern industry labor cost is usually such a small percentage of total cost that it is not the major factor responsible for the present price differentials. Is it not possible to find a workable base for comparing labor costs, taking into consideration housing aid, unemployment and sickness insurance, and other indirect wage support? It is my impression that labor unions are not much interested in learning the facts because they would like to preserve the argument that management prefers foreign operation with its cheap labor. On the other hand, management uses the allegation of cheap foreign labor as a basis for seeking such governmental support as satisfactory tariff laws.

The rift between European and American prices is the product of many elements, more or less historical in nature. American corporations that have invested in Europe apparently expect this price gap to continue. In fact, they are interested in maintaining it since otherwise one of the immediate reasons for their policy of investment would be proved incorrect.

A thorough study of the elements that have determined the international price level would be helpful in trying to answer such questions as:

1. To what extent are foreign imports excluded from the United States, especially by public trade devices other than actual tariffs; and, conversely, to what extent are American products excluded from or handicapped in importation into other countries? Is the result of these practices that price determines success in competition?

2. To what extent is the United States foremost in price leadership in the international field, and what part do American subsidiaries in foreign countries play in regard to that leadership?

3. By what method in the United States and other countries is the top price of a given product maintained?

In the opinion of American corporations investing abroad, the European governments are in favor of high tariffs. For this reason American merchants and exporters consider it good policy to set up their own strong and independent position behind the tariff wall of the Common Market and of the EFTA. They have good reason for wanting Europe to continue this type of high tariff policy, for, once their investments are made, they do not wish to see an open market policy which might permit other American corporations that have not made large investments to compete in the European market or in other parts of the world through European companies. The United States government has just the opposite interest, from both a political and an over-all economic point of view. Its interest is in a low tariff policy in Europe and in a slowly developing but planned common market consisting of Europe and the United States.

American industry, whether admitting it or not, is vitally interested in collecting and using all modern technology. Obviously, one of the most effective ways to maintain a continuous access to new technology is to keep a strong financial interest in European corporations that are themselves doing research.

Up to now European trade with new or old underdeveloped territories has been easier and more profitable than American trade, partly because of the different price level, partly because there are fewer bureaucratic entanglements. How do we define the governmental or public interest with respect to this fact? Has the public enough material to reach a considered judgment? The fact is that misinformation is especially rampant about American interests in foreign technology. Just as he did in the Twenties, the man in the street believes that the United States is technologically self-sufficient and that a corporation making investments in other industrial countries is a kind of traitor to America.

I hope that these brief references show the lack of any fixed policy into which the acts of our government and our corporations may be integrated. How can we find a clear line of policy? Before we approach this question, let us pose another and ask how we appear in the light of Communist propaganda. Where do our three "propositions" put us in the dialectical game with our adversaries?

I am not saying anything new when I refer to the allegation of Communist propagandists that our corporations are penetrating underdeveloped territories in the service of the capitalistic system and are exploiting these nations; that government is nothing but an executive instrument of the monopolistic capitalists; and that the corporations are bound to cooperate with the new capitalist groups in the young nations and extend capitalism throughout the world. The most articulate formulation of these allegations is to be found in *Political Economy—A Textbook,* published by the Academy of Science of the U.S.S.R., which is required reading in Russia and all satellite countries.

The conditions exemplified by our three "propositions" appear to be answers to these allegations. Certainly Americans are pragmatists. During the last fifty years American policies have happened; they have never been planned or formulated on a long-term basis. It is consistent, therefore, that no group of American political or economic leaders has planned our present conditions as answers in the dialectic game. But it is also true that no one is more susceptible to the dialectical trap than the pragmatic politician or economist who permits himself to be driven from decision to decision.

It happens that in our system economic and technological wealth is concentrated in the hands of corporations. The only area in which our system is necessarily inferior to that of the Russian is the utilization of government as a power group in technological and economic organization. And by excluding or deterring our system's economic counterpart, the American corporation, from active participation in underdeveloped territories, we put ourselves in a weak position by assigning to the government that function which has in American history been reserved to private enterprise.

European sources allege that in 1960 the entire Russian bloc spent $700 million for economic and military aid to underdeveloped territories while the West spent $4 billion, not including strictly military aid. Compare the results. By disregarding the interests of American capitalism in underdeveloped territories, our government has to that extent contradicted Communist propaganda. But in the world dispute there is no distinction between the corporate and governmental elements of American society. The more our legislature insists on satisfying the parochial interests of U.S. workers or producers, the more it sacrifices American interests abroad, and the more harm it brings indirectly to every American. This point is demonstrated in the oil and coal problems resulting from the protectionist policies set up against Venezuelan oil.

It is understandable that some people want to overcome these difficulties by setting up a public planning group of one or another kind. Indeed, something like this is necessary. But how would such an agency determine what is actually in the public interest? And could such an agency operate in a democratic society?

The economic order functions only as long as all participants, public and private, preserve an order within the social order. This is equally true for the special order of international trade. Under the nineteenth century European idea of social order, the state, whether organized on a democratic or an autocratic order, had the exclusive legal and sociological role in setting up the principles of the social order. Today in Europe, whatever pluralistic tendencies may exist, the concept of the state as standing over society in each of its elements remains the prevailing idea. This distinction is felt especially in the relations between government and corporations. But whatever the present character of society in the United States may be in practice, the original concept of a pluralistic society remains the controlling force in America. The social groups composing American society are not coordinated, but each of them—labor, farmers, industrialists—must be directed to a set of unified goals. It should be the special function of the President of the United States by his moral force to set the pattern of American society.

The origin of the American corporation differs from that of the European mercantilistic corporation, which was operated by the government. After the American Revolution the road was open in all parts of the country for business to step in, and the American corporation became an institution built into the American pluralistic system. In this system, government was never considered a superior group able to dictate to other groups. James Madison, for example, described the government as a kind of presiding judge and the other social forces as co-judges. In his time, and for a hundred years thereafter, the American society was a force integrated by the enthusiastic will to build up a nation of free individuals covering the entire continent. It was not until the time of Theodore Roosevelt, Brandeis, Wilson, and LaFollette that any question ever arose of how the social organizations can be maintained in the face of corporate power.

This brings us back to the original questions. What are the standards by which an agency should determine what is and what is not in the public interest? And what is the most efficient procedure for reaching such a determination?

A solution of the second problem is impossible unless a satisfactory solution can be found to the first. Almost any reorganization of the federal administrative agencies will bring some good, but the basic deficiency will remain—that they have no criterion by which to decide cases. No truly judicial proceedings, no rational determination by an "outsider" of any contested issue, are possible unless one has a principle or purpose to which the proceedings or the determination can be related.

By now it should be clear that the needs of American trade in the international field are sufficient to form the basis for national policy. Such a policy would assure the use of our advanced technology in building up that of our neighbors and a movement toward a balanced market which would insure an open exchange of opportunities for individual industries to exploit their talents. Under the conditions of the American system, standards cannot be established by mere legislation but must be the natural product of cooperation among the various social forces, especially those of government and corporations. Although under the Constitution the formulation of "law" is up to Congress, Congress can only enact statutes. The actual meaning of each piece of legislation has to be interpreted according to its control over the social order. The more ambiguous and indefinite this interpretation of legislation or of judicial and executive decrees is, the less effective will be the law. Within the social order there are also rules set up by corporations, which, if established by oligopolistic or monopolistic corporations, have the effective power of law. Public law and these private rules should not remain unrelated. Even private tribunals, such as those of organized arbitration, have done their part in the disintegration of the social order. They too have to be assimilated into a new concept of order.

Corporations engaged in the foreign trade of the United States can only be coordinated with the public interest after some basic decisions have been made. We have to resolve whether we want to see a new mercantilistic trade policy in which the test of any decision is its effect on the public and private treasury of the United States, or an open market within the family of industrial nations. Once this determination is made, it will be possible for a public agency to decide whether or not specified acts of corporations in foreign trade are in the public interest. And it will be possible for our corporations to determine what is in the public interest.

We must also decide whether we would like to retain, or, better yet, to rebuild a free enterprise economy in which corporations and other private business organizations have control of technology and of commercial and economic machinery. There are not enough people to do both—to develop and administer this technology in all fields on both a governmental and a private basis. Nor do we have enough capital for such duplication of work. Furthermore, experience shows that this type of mixed economy will not work in our system. We must give corporations both the power and the responsibility to make a large part of the American contribution to the development of new countries. Governmental coordination should consist of devices for public support such as tax exemptions, tax credits, and investment insurance.

I realize that this calls for something foreign to the American scene—a decision to establish a long-term political international trade program. Congress does not like the President to bind himself and the country to a long-term program, because to do so may make it difficult to adopt restrictive measures in favor of special groups when politically expedient. Obviously this opportunism does not allow an order to develop into which

American corporations can integrate themselves, and so they have had no choice but to lead a kind of double life—as American and as non-American.

It is not the purpose of this paper to present such a long-term program, but it is important to realize the following: The assumption that our case-by-case method of deciding problems does not set a policy is deceiving. Whether the pragmatists realize it or not, some day so many obstacles will have been placed in the way of free international trade that the United States will no longer be able to pursue the ideal of its post-World War II programs. Furthermore, foreign countries following the steps of the United States—as they may do under the rules of GATT—will be placing similar barricades in the same road. We may soon find ourselves in a mercantilistic system made up of groups of nations held together by some open or secret, public or private, cartel.

A long-term program would be able to fix workable rules governing the behavior of American corporations abroad, which would be in line with our general standards of ethics and of economic policy. In the cases dealing with American participation in foreign cartels, the courts have set up principles that may be helpful in this new work. Even now an American corporation operating in a foreign country in a manner inconsistent with defined American interests is subject to the control of our courts and eventually of our administrative agencies.

In implementing the new policy we could bring to bear the full weight of our influence to change the international law regarding expropriation of American or other foreign assets by countries in our own sphere of interest. And I suggest the establishment of a tribunal that would have jurisdiction over any dispute arising out of agreements between U.S. corporations on the one hand and governments or individuals in underdeveloped territories on the other.

We should be interested in what the Communists are thinking about this situation. They are convinced that the economic interests of the free nations will finally lead to conflicts and open the road to Communist take-over. But I daresay that the establishment of an Atlantic Common Market, in which after one or two decades public and private restraint could be abolished, would guarantee the fullest possible access to technological development and would eventually lead to a uniform price and wage level. The standards of living of Western Europe and the United States, which even now are not as disparate as commonly thought, would then become more uniform. Corporations would find their place wherever the market position is best. They would behave in the Atlantic Common Market as they are behaving in the American market. The most effective device in the economic recovery of Western Europe was the combination of government and corporations together directing all their efforts toward building up a European Common Market. This success supplies the Atlantic Community with a model and a direction.

American labor and Americans in general have only one thing to fear: that they may remain isolated from the technological and economic dynamics that are gathering momentum around the world. A country of the power and imagination of the United States can only gain from being a member of a large family of industrial nations.

To summarize:

1. Modern business corporations can only be brought effectively in line with the public interest if the government (agencies and legislature) operates under a clear definition of "public interest." In the field of corporate activities abroad the President of the United States and the Congress should define that public interest as quickly as possible. Each agency involved in the control of corporations must base its decisions on this statement of policy. The Congress should exercise the greatest self-restraint in enacting any statute, bill, or regulation inconsistent with the policy. It should not interfere in the general principles of international trade any time it thinks certain domestic interests are jeopardized, but if interference inconsistent with the welfare of underdeveloped nations becomes truly necessary, the Congress should compensate these countries for losses of trade resulting from our interference.

2. The international trade activities of corporations and of government should be completely separated so that business enterprises may have the opportunity to act in accordance with their business interests as well as with the public interest. Present governmental activities in underdeveloped territories (outside of military aid) should be curtailed as quickly as possible, and new devices should be found for governmental guarantees. A ratio of governmental guarantees to private risk in these territories should be fixed in such a way as to further the aim of relegating all governmental action to the field of military and other non-economic help.

3. American corporations doing business abroad, directly or indirectly, are bound to obey principles of American law wherever they are. Administrative agencies and eventually courts should be given the power to force any corporation to remain in line with the announced policies. As a beginning, the Federal Trade Commission should be authorized to investigate the current business methods of American corporations in the different foreign countries, and on the basis of this investigation corporations should be ordered to cease and desist from any practices that might occasion future complaints in Latin America or other countries.

4. The government should be asked to re-examine its official attitude on the rules of international law concerning the legality of nationalization of foreign enterprises. The possibility of a rule that would give assurances sufficient both to American corporations and to underdeveloped countries should be explored. There should be an international tribunal to examine the fairness of agreements between American and foreign corporations or governments. It should be considered unfair if local interests are not permitted to take over a foreign enterprise after a certain period of years provided fair compensation is guaranteed.

5. We should examine how far American and foreign (especially Western European and Japanese) corporations might be able to go in building up joint programs for underdeveloped territories, provided that the programs stay within the limits of American anti-trust legislation and conform to the policy set by the President. Private bond issues should again become an important device for financing long-term investments in new countries.

6. American and European governmental and private institutions should study jointly the channels between the United States and Europe that now exist, the effect of the present trend of investment between the United States and Europe, and the prospects for the development of an American-European Common Market. Those who have envisaged the Common European Market have set clear goals for it. Each European corporation and each governmental agency know what the aim is and what the end should be; they know by what standards each act has to be evaluated. Even if Europe never accomplishes political unification, the trend started by the Common Market has been most effective in the dynamic development of Europe. Although the immediate development of the Common Market may be slow, the trend remains potent.

The United States has no such trend. Until it does, it will have no chance of setting up an effective policy of cooperation between government and corporations.

11

CONFLICTING INTERESTS IN INTERNATIONAL BUSINESS INVESTMENT *

Richard D. Robinson

There is much talk these days of vast business opportunities awaiting us within the emerging markets of Asia, Africa, and Latin America and of the compelling need for promoting an ever higher level of private American investment in those areas. Although admitting the validity of both points, we should be aware that much present overseas investment carries with it massive potential conflict of interest between U.S. investors, their foreign associates, and the governments of some of the host countries.

It is recorded that in the early 1840's "at least one American of irreproachable antecedents was barred admission to a London club, specifically because he belonged to a republic which did not fulfill its financial engagements." [1] As 19th-Century America defaulted on many foreign investment obligations, so likewise, one may reasonably anticipate, will many of the presently emerging nations. Frankly, it may be in their long run interest to do so, given the present structure of international business and an intensely nationalistic world characterized by vastly disparate national economic levels.

But surely we do not need to continue duplicating past errors, thereby rendering insecure our foreign investment and building an antagonistic,

* From *Business Review* (Boston University, Spring 1960), pp. 3-13. Reprinted by permission.

[1] Leland, Hamilton Jenks, *The Migration of British Capital to 1875* (Alfred A. Knopf, New York and London, 1927), pp. 104-106.

compartmentalized world rather than an integrated one. If we consciously and skillfully structured our overseas enterprises to fit the long-run interests of the host countries, we could build true mutuality of interest between the rich and the poor nations within the context of international business. Only when those responsible for making international business decisions become sensitive to this need will there be any real hope of creating an internationally viable private enterprise system, and by so doing, of gaining security for our overseas property rights. In other words, we ignore the interests of others at the peril of our foreign business assets.

MANAGEMENT INDIFFERENCE

In a three-year study of the management practices and attitudes of over 200 U.S. firms vis-a-vis foreign investment,[2] the Harvard Business School's Division of Research found little awareness of the long-run implications of what was happening, though some of the more thoughtful executives expressed vague fears and misgivings. Unilateral breach of international business agreements—or violation of property rights—could occur at any moment, and often there was no remedy. Sometimes an executive wondered out loud whether his company's operation in Country A really contributed more than it extracted, and how long would it be before the local citizenry began having similar doubts. But it was a rare management which had measured the long-run impact of its local enterprise on Country A. Perhaps the local resources consumed by that enterprise—including skills, capital and foreign exchange—could be better used in other activities ("better," as related to the long-run interests of the host country). Very few executives, we found, had pondered such questions. Their lack of concern is likely to prove very expensive indeed.

DIFFERENT INVESTMENT CRITERIA

The recipe for a decision relating to investment in Asia, Latin America and Africa *should* differ significantly from that for domestic and European commitments. In the emerging nations, in many of which accelerated and sustained development is now irrepressible, measures other than projected return on investment, anticipated growth, and relations with the parent company structure become critical. Most important among these new measures are the impact of a given project on public revenues, on the national balance of payments, and on the national product—with due regard in all cases for external economies and diseconomies induced by the proposed enterprise, such as short-term impact on employment, housing, and urban services. At least two further measures should be added: the degree of product essentiality as measured against the long-run interests and aspirations of the foreign society, and the extent to which a given enterprise or industry is politically vulnerable.

[2] By the term "investment" we include commitments of skills and know-how as well as cash and hardware.

Even these measures should not be used as absolute ones; they are really meaningful only if employed to measure the desirability of a given enterprise to Country A as compared with other possible projects in Country A within the foreseeable future. That is, does the enterprise deserve high priority rating by responsible authorities of Country A given Country A's short supply of developed resources (raw materials, skills, capital, labor), inadequate public revenues, subsistence-level per capita income, and chronic balance-of-payments problem? Because a foreign investment always means the commitment of some of Country A's resources as well as those of the foreign investor, the government of Country A has the undoubted right to determine the desirability of foreign-sponsored projects and to exclude those felt to be of low priority. Not being fully cognizant of all possible projects at any given time, the Government of Country A may later realize that an earlier commitment of resources to a foreign investor was not of the highest priority in terms of the national interests. Also, the degree to which local resources (particularly manpower) are developed will change with time, thereby possibly altering the relative value of the foreign contribution. A shrewd foreign investor should therefore try to anticipate what development and reallocation of resources is likely to occur within the foreseeable life of his investment in Country A and to evaluate his opportunity—and security—accordingly. Such a decision calls for a high order of knowledge about, and understanding of, Country A. In few managements does this kind of country or regional expertise exist. Indeed, few executives even realized the need for highly-trained experts in this area. "The important thing is to know the business," we were told repeatedly. But is it?

We may look at the problem in a slightly different way. It is not enough to prove that Country A profits by reason of a company's operation there. Given the enormous pressure for capital and production in the underdeveloped countries, the question is rather: how may Country A gain *maximum* benefit from the operation? If there were any reason for believing that the enterprise could be run under national ownership just as well as foreign, the foreign owners might soon be in trouble. Nationalistic sentiments then become effective. (The Egyptian take-over of the Suez Canal is a case in point. The Nasser-led nationalists might have been somewhat less extreme had they known that they were unable to keep the canal in operation. Twenty years before, they would not have been able to do so.) Or, if another foreign firm appears willing to operate a given enterprise in a manner to generate greater return to the host country, such as employment of a greater amount of local labor in a more integrated operation, property rights may be threatened or lost. A recent dispute over the construction of petroleum refineries in Turkey is an example. Cases of outright expropriation have been surprisingly rare, but instances of subsidized or politically supported competition are not. Permission to repatriate profits or to export may become difficult to secure for the unfavored, low-priority enterprise, and leases or concessions may be terminated. These practices do not constitute unfair treatment; a nation struggling up out of the mud must be sensitive to its own highest interests. Sometimes the judgment of the leaders is wrong or influenced by considerations other than national interest, as sometimes we err and make self-seeking judgments. But one suspects that many charges of corruption and stupidity voiced by American businessmen against foreign regimes stem from a misunderstanding of the very real problems besetting the emerging societies. These countries feel compelled to utilize their resources so as to maximize return to themselves; their primary concern is their own national interests, not those of the foreign investor. Nor do they subscribe to an economic philosophy that endows private property with unalienable rights. Therefore, there is little hesitation to harass a foreign firm if it appears to suit local interests.

SOURCES OF CONFLICT

For a variety of reasons, the bulk of our foreign enterprises probably make a larger contribution *initially* to the national product of the host countries than is withdrawn in fees, dividends, royalties, services, and products. But what about twenty years later when the locals realize that there is no earthly reason why profits should accrue to foreigners, that the foreigners are contributing nothing *new* that could not be found locally? For example, as the Indian motor vehicle market and industry grow, an increasing percentage of the necessary skills and parts will be produced wholly within India. Eventually, the percentage will approach 100% on both counts. Long before, the value of the contribution made by foreign automobile firms to their Indian enterprises will have dropped. If the foreign "owners" nonetheless continue to expect the same level of earnings as before, they may well be disappointed. Some businessmen observed that the potential conflict of interest in the long-run was so great as to render impossible—or at least highly insecure—any profit seeking investment in the underdeveloped countries, for conflict of interest foretold insecurity and eventual loss of control—and profits.

Take the usual United States parent-foreign subsidiary relationship as an example, assuming for the moment 100% American ownership. In many cases, such subsidiaries either utilize intermediate products supplied by the American parent or supply the parent with goods produced abroad for sale in the United States or elsewhere. Where profits are taken is a matter of some importance to the tax collecting authorities in the host country. The decision is also relevant to the troublesome matter of maintaining a healthy balance of payments position. The pricing of materials between a subsidiary and its parent is nearly always based on a number of arbitrary allocations of cost, some of which stem from the impact of the tax law of the state or country of parental incorporation. Cost allocations may also simply be a carry-over of domestic United States practices. Basis for conflict is inherent in this relationship. And when conflict of interest spans an international frontier, property rights are imperiled.

For a United States company faced with unending restrictions in Asia, Africa and Latin America in respect to repatriation of profits in dollars, there is a natural inclination to take a maximum profit in the United States (or in its tax haven subsidiary). Many firms charge their foreign subsidiaries top prices for intermediates and parts purchased from their subsidiaries at abnormally low prices. The host country correspondingly loses, but not—one suspects—for long.

Many United States firms maximize export sales and minimize local manufacturing abroad. There is always pressure, it seems, to undertake as little overseas processing or manufacturing as possible. The interests of the country involved are rarely given consideration; only short-term profit-and-loss is believed relevant. Some firms deliberately set up their foreign subsidiaries in such a way as to make them wholly dependent upon products or materials of a semi-processed or intermediate nature that can be supplied only by the parent. Such dependence, it is believed, builds security of control over one's foreign enterprise by making it a "captive buyer." But does it?

Firm M refuses to construct a plant in Chile for the processing of a mineral it is extracting there. The reason, very bluntly stated, is that the company does not wish to be "at the mercy" of the Chilean government. So long as the mineral must be shipped out for processing elsewhere, management feels that it has leverage against the local government. One might well anticipate cancellation of M's mining leases if and when another firm moves in with a domestic processing plant. Firm M is living dangerously. Even such an enlightened government as the Canadian has some legal prohibitions against the export of unprocessed raw materials. Quite naturally, it wishes to have Canadian labor employed in the processing of Canadian material and to export the product of both, thereby increasing national product and tax revenues.

One foresighted American firm has adopted the deliberate policy of steering clear of all foreign enterprises that can be undertaken just as well by local nationals. Non-availability of local capital alone is not considered enough to warrant involvement in a foreign project unless it be of a short-term pilot type. In such cases, the capital supplied by the firm might be debt rather than equity, possibly accompanied by a short-term management contract, technical assistance agreement, and/or license. The need for special skills, the results of continuing research, global integration of production, international market organization—unless some need of this nature is fulfilled by foreign ownership the firm does not come in. But how many American managements see foreign projects in this light? Virtually none, we concluded.

Nationalism—including the American variety—is such in many places as to react against foreign ownership of significant sectors of a nation's economy unless it be clearly in the national interest. Special sensitivity to foreign ownership can be anticipated in respect to public utilities, transport, communications, national defense industry, production of basic consumer goods (salt, sugar, matches, etc.) and agriculture. Lest we become too critical of the national sensitivities of others, let us assume for the moment foreign infiltration in a significant way into the ownership of *our* oil industry, *our* shipbuilding industry, *our* steel industry, *our* dairy industry. Indeed, by law we prohibit foreign ownership in some areas of transport and communications.

Hence, the nature and the importance of the industry in a national economy should have much to do with channeling investment and in shaping the form that it takes. This is not to say that American firms should stay out of large, important projects abroad. Far from it. But it is to say that such projects should be structured so as to minimize offense to nationalistic sentiments. Perhaps the capital should be of a debt nature. Perhaps the foreign equity should be held to a minority. Perhaps the return should come through a license or other contractual relationship rather than ownership. One large American firm long active in the production of certain agricultural products abroad is considering complete withdrawal from the ownership of foreign farmland in favor of limiting itself to the sale of research results (i.e., technical assistance) to local independent farmers, the purchase of the crop and its distribution within the United States and elsewhere. By so doing the firm would be in a very much less vulnerable position politically, and it need not identify itself with those interests blocking land reform. Production methods might still be controlled via the providing or withholding of improved seed, insecticides, fertilizers and farm credit. In other words, the firm is considering changing its foreign investment from an equity to a debt basis, but a debt capital that would be serviced constantly by continuing research and an integrated distribution system.

American managements rarely look at what they are proposing to do abroad from the point of view of foreign national interests. Hence, much direct investment overseas has been flowing into types of products in which the only unique contribution made by the foreign firm in the long-run lies in the capital itself, and often these projects are sufficiently large as to constitute a very conspicuous portion of the total foreign economy. One can anticipate heavy-handed regulation or "unfair local competition," perhaps the investment equivalent of the "Buy American" Act.

DIVERGENT MANAGERIAL INTERESTS

The interests of a foreign economy and of an American firm operating an enterprise within that economy may be quite different in respect to the plow-back of earnings. Increasingly, governments in the underdeveloped nations are refusing to agree to the repatriation of profits and capital unless the foreign firm first agrees not to attempt repatriation for a period of years —often five or ten—meanwhile re-investing all in the local enterprise. Within the overall operation of the American parent, such a fixed policy may not be in the firm's best short-run interest. Indeed, in one case in which a U.S. firm held a foreign license and received a given percentage of sales as income, the host government declared at the end of ten years that inasmuch as the U.S. company had made no significant contribution of skill and know-how since the initial deal, no further dollars would be made available for the repatriation of earnings.

Unless an investment—whether of a tangible or intangible nature—continues to be serviced in some way (i.e., continuing research, promotion, marketing service, managerial skills, plow-back of earnings or addition of new capital) the host government may very well, after a period of time, reappraise the property rights held by the foreign firm. The principle of time-limited property rights—even with continuing service—is recognized in law now by at least India and Indonesia.[3] One suspects that a trend will develop in the direction of periodic reappraisal of foreign property rights by host governments, such reappraisals being based on a judgment as to the value and uniqueness of the continuing foreign contribution and of the net contribution made by the enterprise to national growth as measured against alternative uses of resources.

Whatever dividends or fees a U.S. firm receives from a foreign subsidiary or associate, the firm will often be required to justify the payment in terms of net contribution to the gross national production of the host country generated by the U.S. firm's *continuing* ownership or association. If the *continuing* relationship cannot be so justified, if the net *annual* addition to national product is less than that subtracted in profits and fees, the time has come for either withdrawal, a joint venture with local capital, or some form of contractual relationship. Otherwise, the business may be lost entirely.

Although a joint venture obviously has many advantages—and is required in a number of countries (i.e., India, Mexico, Spain, and Japan)—in some respects it tends to make even more real and immediate the conflict of interest we have been discussing. The local partner participates in profits only on the foreign enterprise. Hence, the pricing of parts and intermediates by the parent is a matter of very real concern. So, likewise, is the plow-back of earnings for a period of time to grow with the foreign market. The American firm may maintain its profit level from enterprises elsewhere. For the foreign partner, this may be his single large investment, from which he must have immediate income.

The reverse may also constitute a problem. In a very rapidly developing foreign market, the United States firm may face real difficulty in maintaining its equity position. Examples of such pressure are found in the chemical industry in Italy and Japan. The American firm may not wish to commit more capital and hence, if in control, may hold back expansion, thereby acting contrary to the interests of both the local investors and the host government. Nor do local investors (and their governments, such as the Japanese) wish American companies to control sales of associated local firms, perhaps for the purpose of avoiding competition with the American parent in third markets or possibly within the American market itself. The American parent derives a profit on sales to such excluded areas, but not its foreign subsidiary and local stockholders.

All the problems of majority-minority interests are compounded many times over when the majority is held by Americans and the minority by

[3] Note the twenty-year limitation on the guarantee against expropriation of industrial enterprises and thirty-year limitation in the case of plantations stipulated in Indonesia's 1948 law on foreign investment. The implication is that after the twenty- or thirty-year period, alien-held investment should be subject to nationalization. The Indian government seems to have used a similar time limitation in agreements with certain foreign investors and, significantly, the Indian Government has not, until very recently (February, 1960), been willing to participate in the ICA Investment Guaranties program in respect to expropriation, only nonconvertibility of profits.

citizens of an underdeveloped country. Business is then laid on top of possible national economic and political differences, plus a long-standing prejudice against Christian, Caucasian capitalism.

The nature of a product obviously relates to the desirability of that product within a given market. Some goods, given the limited resources of many nations, should perhaps not be produced at all. How far should a government go in permitting the stimulation of hitherto non-existent demands for new products and services? Many governments are caught in a frightening squeeze between investment and consumption. Should new consumer goods production be allowed, thereby diverting funds from investment in the tools of future production? Yet, the local mass production of an *already popular* consumer good might do much to contain inflation. The production of Coca-Cola in Egypt, where it had been long known, was perhaps quite different from a Coca-Cola enterprise in Turkey, where the drink had never appeared before.

When a product is of such an essential nature as to be subjected to state control, such as certain pharmaceuticals, the host government may well demand some degree of public participation in a proposed manufacturing venture. Witness the experience of Merck & Company, Inc., in India. Most American managements seem to take a doctrinaire position against such mixed enterprises, and refuse them serious consideration. This position is rationalized in terms of inherent conflict between public and private interests. "Who ever heard of a state enterprise boasting of its profits?" one executive asked rhetorically. We could make a twofold reply: (1) "We have, and (2) if public and private interests are at such variance, the private group had better stay out anyway; something is wrong." For a variety of reasons, the government of an underdeveloped country probably must play a more direct role in economic life than that assigned the United States Government, and the mixed venture is perhaps an important contribution to the merging of capitalistic and socialistic concepts.

Surely these potential conflicts of interest might be reduced substantially by acting only on those projects furthering the interests of the host country and justified convincingly in those terms. One large American corporation has gone so far as to devise a screening test through which suggested projects must pass before given serious consideration by management. The screen consists of a set of criteria which relate to the process of accelerated economic development.

Some foreign governmental agencies (e.g., the Central Bank of the Philippines and the Industrial Development Bank of Turkey) have set up formulae for evaluating present and prospective foreign investment projects. These formulae attempt to measure the net long-run impact of a given investment on the national product. Admittedly no formulae of this nature can rest entirely on objective, statistical measures. Such factors as the creation of new skills, stimulation of local entrepreneurship, foreign exchange earning potential, and external economies do not lend themselves to easy measure. But still, by limiting himself to projects that could be convincingly stated in terms of the long-run interest of the host nation, one could surely contribute much to the security—and hence, profitability—of an enterprise.

Some executives suggested going even further.

A retired vice-president of one of our largest corporations wrote to his successors as follows:

> "If we are to succeed in our efforts to attain a better balance in world economy and standards of living for all people, which is almost our only defense against the spread of communism, we must find a way for all debtor nations to pay their debts, to acquire ownership in international trade and industry in accordance with their participation in same, and to enjoy the profits therefrom."

He went on to point out that the organization of foreign subsidiaries with a degree of local ownership was not a real solution because "it introduced the problem of 'minority stockholders' whose rights must always be considered, [a condition] which almost inevitably results [sic] to reduce flexibility of operation." The simple solution, he concluded, was "worldwide ownership of parent companies in industry or trade by citizens of all countries in the approximate proportion that each nation contributed to the profits of production or distribution." He observed that there was a small amount of investment along these lines today, but that it was "hampered in many cases and in no measure encouraged by international politics." For example, such an arrangement would have to rest on an agreement among the participating nations "that profits generated within any country may be distributed to stockholders who are nationals of that country without withholding taxes of any kind or amount by any other nation and with no higher taxes than are applicable to a domestic company."

The organizational structure shown on page 117 was considered by an American firm planning to invest in an Iraqi oil concession, as diagrammed. (Negotiations were not undertaken; Soviet drillers were invited in before the Americans moved.) This manner of association offered a number of advantages, not the least of which was the area of mutual interest it would have created. Everyone, Iraqi and American, would have been in the same boat.

Even so, we suggest, there remains an important obstacle to achieving genuine mutuality of interest and economic integration within the context of international business organizations; the corporate parent must have a national identity. An American-chartered corporation is controlled by U.S. law. Like it or not, in time of crisis a United States corporation, however organized, cannot be divorced from American foreign policy. Would many Arabs or Indians invest in an American corporation? One doubts it. But what if it were possible to denationalize business by creating an international corporation chartered by an international agency and controlled by some sort of international S.E.C.?

CREEPING EXPROPRIATION

Stated very bluntly, the essence of our thesis is simply that if international business is not restructured, future years will see an expropriation of Western business properties on a hitherto unheard-of scale in the now-underdeveloped, poor countries. The expropriation may not generally come

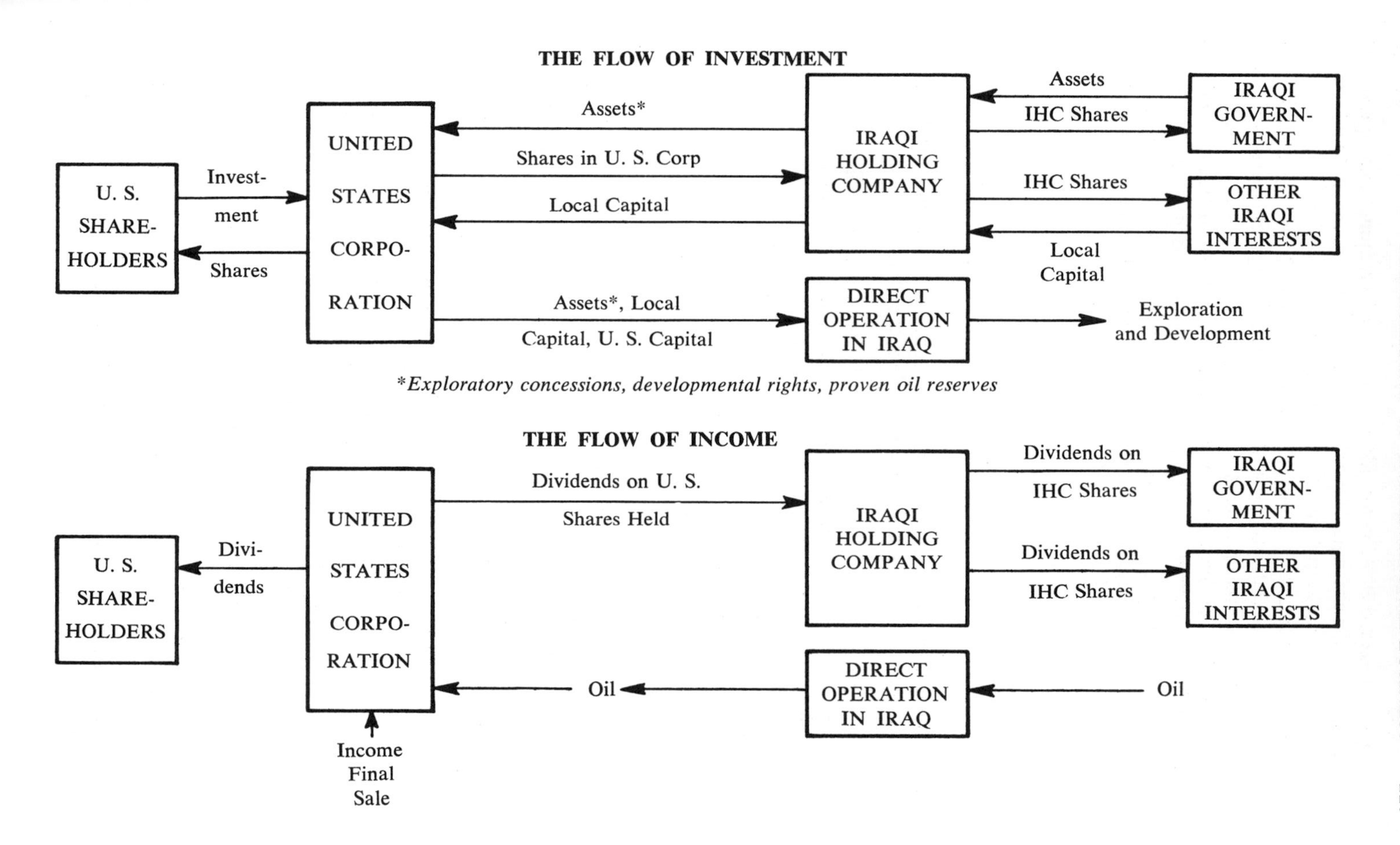
THE FLOW OF INVESTMENT
U. S. SHARE-HOLDERS
Invest-ment
Shares
UNITED STATES CORPO-RATION
Assets*
Shares in U. S. Corp
Local Capital
Assets*, Local Capital, U. S. Capital
IRAQI HOLDING COMPANY
DIRECT OPERATION IN IRAQ
Assets
IHC Shares
IHC Shares
Local Capital
Exploration and Development
IRAQI GOVERN-MENT
OTHER IRAQI INTERESTS
*Exploratory concessions, developmental rights, proven oil reserves
THE FLOW OF INCOME
U. S. SHARE-HOLDERS
Divi-dends
UNITED STATES CORPO-RATION
Income Final Sale
Dividends on U. S. Shares Held
Oil
IRAQI HOLDING COMPANY
DIRECT OPERATION IN IRAQ
Dividends on IHC Shares
Dividends on IHC Shares
Oil
IRAQI GOVERN-MENT
OTHER IRAQI INTERESTS

as outright seizure; it is more likely to be a "creeping expropriation" through a gradual tightening of public regulation to a point at which effective control by a Western firm of its overseas business is lost.

The only insurance against this loss of control, we suggest, lies in structuring *present* relationships with associated foreign enterprises in such a way as to build common interest.

By way of summary, Appendix A lists a series of questions, answers to which will serve to shed light on the more general query: *Are you on the way toward losing control of your overseas enterprises?* If no one in your firm can answer these questions convincingly, your international operations are a poorly-calculated risk, if not an outright gamble.

APPENDIX

Questions relevant to establishment of a community of interest between foreign countries and U.S. enterprises resident therein.

1. What is the return to the host country by reason of your firm's activity there? Now? Ten years from now? Twenty years from now?

   As measured by net annual impact on public revenues?

   As measured by net annual impact on national balance of payments?

   As measured by net annual impact on national product?

2. What is your firm's presence costing the host country?

   In reference to relocation of people?

   In reference to housing and urban services?

   In opportunity cost of the skilled labor and other scarce resources (including foreign exchange) that you use?

   In reference to the creation of new demands (including education)?

3. What is the net annual contribution of your firm's enterprise in these several respects (above) to the host country as compared to the potential net annual contribution of other possible enterprises? Now? Ten years from now? Twenty years from now?

4. Is there any conceivable way in which you could restructure your enterprise so as to make a larger net contribution to the host country and still maintain a feasible profit margin for yourself?

   Is a greater degree of local manufacturing and/or processing possible?

   Are you servicing the local domestic market to the fullest extent possible?

   Can more local labor be employed?

   Can more management responsibility be turned over to local nationals?

   Can more services and/or supplies be purchased on the local market?

Can you educate and train your own labor?

Is the production mix the most appropriate one or is it simply a carryover from domestic American practices?

Is your product design and quality really the best for the market or does it simply represent an American spillover?

What of your competitors in these respects?

5. Is your firm making continuing contribution to the host country (skills, know-how, research, new capital, market organization, etc.) which cannot be obtained locally? What of ten or twenty years from now?
6. What is the net contribution (see question #1) your firm would make to the host country if its participation in the enterprise were:
   - On a joint venture basis?
   - On a minority equity basis?
   - On a debt basis, rather than equity participation?
   - On a contractual basis (managerial, license, technical assistance)?
   - A combination of these?
7. Where is your firm really taking its profits on its overseas business? Would you be willing to be completely frank in this regard with the host government?
8. Does your firm structure and finance politically vulnerable enterprises in a manner different from those less vulnerable?

12

CREATING A STRATEGY FOR INTERNATIONAL GROWTH *

John G. McDonald and Hugh Parker

Growing numbers of American companies are spreading their wings abroad. The roster includes not just small- and medium-size manufacturing companies, but some of the largest and most powerful firms in the country. "By 1970, some 50 percent of our profit will come from overseas operations," predicts the chief of a large diversified company. Du Pont, which once restricted production to this continent, is now producing in Holland, Belgium, and Northern Ireland. The Campbell Soup Company has launched a $30 million assault aimed at capturing a major share of the growing European food market, and I. B. M. World Trade is growing even faster than its ebullient U.S. parent.

The blue-ribbon list goes on and on. Some one thousand American companies have established postwar operations in Europe, most within the

* From *International Enterprise* (McKinsey and Co., Inc., Management Consultants, 1962).

past four years. A recent McGraw-Hill survey indicates that the investment plans of American companies called for a $1.7 billion addition to plant and equipment overseas in 1961, 25 percent more than in 1960. The census of private U.S. investments abroad, recently released by the Department of Commerce, shows that during the year of the census (1957) U.S. firms abroad paid wages and salaries of nearly $7 billion, employed about 3 million people, and spent about $17 billion for materials and services. This international flow of funds and goods is becoming one of the most important economic forces in the world today.

Companies set up manufacturing facilities abroad for a variety of reasons. Some want to enjoy the rapid growth offered by expanding foreign markets. Others seek to reduce their production costs with an eye to worldwide exports—including exports to the United States.

Not long ago, the stay-at-home competitors of these "internationalists" would have been unconcerned with these moves, but things have changed. Today many stay-at-homes see a threat to their home market position and the possibility of being blocked out of increasingly interesting foreign markets. Some companies are already being harassed in their domestic markets by low-cost goods produced abroad by their U.S. rivals (the 1957 census showed imports of $1 billion from overseas enterprises of U.S. companies). And there is now the prospect of tax and tariff changes that may further cloud their futures.

As a reaction to these threats, actual or potential, many companies are establishing beachheads of their own abroad. Thus for many reasons, some offensive, others defensive, the flood of American companies overseas continues to grow.

Here, based on our own experience and the experience of others, is a report on what these companies find in the way of risks and opportunities, and how they create strategies to minimize these risks.

SPECIAL PROBLEMS IN MOVING ABROAD

Setting up a new production base and marketing organization abroad is far more risky than establishing a new business at home. Manufacture abroad means that large sums of money are invested in plant and equipment for a long period of time in an alien, often changing environment. Management effort and personnel problems take on new dimensions, and profits can sometimes have a long lead time in a new land.

In his home market, the executive moves with ease and confidence; he knows the ground rules. Distribution patterns, trade terms, nuances of consumer tastes and preferences, and competitors' strengths and weaknesses are second nature to him; his judgment in this familiar environment is usually sound, since he operates under a set of fairly stable economic and political conditions. But many of the comfortable assumptions that the executive uses at home may not hold true overseas. In some ways, this is to the good. It permits him to view situations with different eyes and thus grasp opportunities that others do not see. Drawing from domestic experience, he may spot the early signs of a trend for convenience items, packaged foods, or new appliances; or he may see the chance to apply a proven technique in a new situation. But he may also stub his toe. He may assume that foreign consumers react in the American pattern, or he may assume that practices that were successful at home will work equally well abroad. As a result, both the risks and opportunities resulting from executive action abroad are often greater than they would be at home. (See special section, *Keys to Marketing Success Abroad,* at end of article.)

Risk comes in many guises and varies from country to country. The political situation, governmental control, or a market unready for a product may be all-important. Several years ago, General Motors, whose European and Australian subsidiaries are currently booming, shut down an expensive assembly plant in India. A prime factor in this painful decision was the unforeseen political climate and the effect of governmental control. In another instance, an American consumer-goods producer moved too soon; after establishing a plant in Belgium, he then found the market was not ready for its product. As a result, he has been conducting an expensive holding operation for the past three years.

Most companies have moved abroad too recently to know how well they will do in the long run, but reports are beginning to filter back. Some companies have been eminently successful, others have run into trouble, and still others have had both successes and failures in different countries. Clearly, long-term success or failure depends on the way a company moves into its overseas adventure. Once a company decides to move and invest abroad, it faces a basic problem: How does it plan its moves to take advantage of obvious opportunities at minimum risk?

STAGES OF FOREIGN INVOLVEMENT

The evolution of a domestic company into a functioning world enterprise normally follows four distinct but overlapping stages.

> *Stage one:* Export-import activity with a minimum of change in management outlook, company organization, or product line.
>
> *Stage two:* Foreign licensing and the international movement of technical know-how, still with little impact on domestic operations or management outlook.
>
> *Stage three:* Establishment of overseas operations. At this point the company makes substantial international investments in funds and management time, and begins to develop special international skills. But still the domestic operations remain essentially unaffected.
>
> *Stage four:* Emergence as a world enterprise with an integrated global approach encompassing both domestic and overseas operations.

These stages may be passed through one at a time, or any one can be bypassed. It is even possible to find a company with its various parts involved in all four at once. But as a rule, the take-off point for moving abroad occurs when a company makes the decision to risk large investments on the prospects of becoming a world enterprise.

It is important that a company re-examine its position at take-off, for it may well have some built-in obstacles to a successful launching of an overseas manufacturing operation. One company, about to enter stage three, fortunately identified such an obstacle in its organizational pattern in time to avoid any delays in achieving its goal. At the take-off point, the company had a group of "international" specialists organized in two departments—exporting and licensing—under one international executive. Ironically, the project team responsible for studying the feasibility of moving abroad found most resistance from the place it expected most support, the export and licensing departments. With the export department already feeling the squeeze from competition built up by the license department, it naturally resisted schemes to squeeze its profits further. Similarly, the licensing department was not cooperating since it foresaw some adverse effects on its profits if single subsidiaries were to replace its numerous licenses in various countries. To surmount this obstacle, changes had to be made in organization and profit responsibility.

Earlier licensing agreements or exclusive distribution rights can also cripple moves overseas. One manufacturer of marine equipment is doing fairly well in Europe, but is encountering tough competition from a German company, which was "educated" with patent exchanges and a licensing agreement several years ago. Many companies that would now like to move abroad are locked out of certain countries by exclusive licensing agreements that seemed wise, low-risk, profitable decisions just a few years ago.

When top management is alert to some of these environmental and strategic problems, it can develop sound organizational plans and safeguards in advance of a move abroad. Step-by-step international experience can become a major asset if it gives a company this foresight. But if top management does not plan its business ahead, existing international activities and agreements can be a major obstacle.

HOW COMPANIES MAKE THEIR MOVES ABROAD

Some companies have been content to move abroad without much planning and have done well; some have been disappointed. Other companies have evolved standard and, in some cases, fairly sophisticated approaches.

The Unplanned Approach

The decision to move into a given country at any time may be based almost entirely on chance. Perhaps the company president has been to the country and likes it, or he may know businessmen there. Many such moves are made in response to an invitation. One successful electronic relay company, with little interest in foreign adventures, was recently approached by a European company about setting up a joint venture. Intrigued by the possibility, the American company joined the enterprise and decided other moves would be made "after we've experimented a bit." A company with a patented line was recently approached by a Wall Street finance group with this suggestion: "We have been contacted by a company that is convinced there's a real opportunity for your product in Europe. If you are ever interested in moving, let us know."

An increasing number of companies have gone abroad recently in response to just such random opportunities. Reasons given include: "Our competitors have done so," or "our suppliers are moving," or "we've been offered an interesting opportunity, but it won't be available for long."

Sometimes this random and essentially "one shot" approach works quite well. Dozens of companies that are now successfully established overseas virtually tumbled into their present spots. But, as the following examples show, the inherent risks are numerous.

Some companies have experimented with moving idle production equipment and setting up shop in another country. Certainly there is a worldwide market for much secondhand U.S. manufacturing equipment, but setting up a subsidiary with an obsolete plant can backfire. Local companies are equipping themselves with the latest devices and can sometimes outproduce and outprice a U.S. subsidiary saddled with old machinery. This is happening in electronics, where rising European manufacturers are using the latest automated equipment.

One Midwestern heavy equipment manufacturer, spotting what looked like a fine opportunity to enter the European market, bought up a good-sized French company in the same field. The French concern looked good on paper, but it was actually a high-cost operation on the verge of losing important markets. The Americans apparently looked at past performance, not at future trends. They took over just as the new property started down the roller coaster and have poured in over a million dollars trying to salvage it.

An American hospital equipment firm without experience in Europe was approached by a small Dutch manufacturer. By bidding for U.S. military supply contracts, the Dutch company had obtained plans and specifications for special equipment identical to that made by the American company, and was producing this equipment—with improvements. The Dutch owner asked the Americans whether they were interested in a joint venture in Europe. The Americans were impressed by the man; they were not only interested in the idea of growth abroad, but were anxious to avoid further competition in a saturated home market. They took a minority interest in the Dutch venture—and watched their cash investment sink out of sight. It turned out that the European company, which had been a very low-cost producer before the U.S. investment, used the added capital to convert from a "garage operation" to a plant operation. The company thereby became a high-cost producer in a beautiful home, but found it could not break even on its low sales volume. With little likelihood of gaining more volume in a hurry, the joint venture developed an insatiable demand for dollars. In addition, the joint venture agreement prevented the American company, now wiser, from tackling the European market on its own.

Country-by-Country Analysis

Unplanned approaches have sometimes paid off, but their often fatal drawback is the absence of any analysis of alternatives. As companies realize this, a number who have already made some moves overseas have evolved a more systematic approach.

An overseas veteran has a standard approach for analyzing the feasibility of manufacturing in a specified country. Basically, this involves three steps taken in the order listed:

> The home office conducts desk research on the market, briefly reviewing reference material available in the U.S., plus its own past international experience and intelligence. This step gives top management a quick reading on the investment required and the possible financial returns. (It also gives management an estimate of the budget, in terms of time, men, and money, required to complete the investigation.)
>
> If the investment looks profitable, a marketing man makes an on-the-spot investigation. In addition to studying the market, he obtains answers to questionnaires supplied by the manufacturing and financial people. This results in a "first approximation," or feasibility, report.
>
> An on-the-spot confirmation study by a small task force (including a senior member of management) results in the "second and final approximation" report and, later, actual investment, postponement, or rejection of a project.

This type of approach—a study of key information at home followed by on-the-spot investigation of special factors in the target country—is becoming common. It is a useful, and almost textbook-perfect approach. Unfortunately, it can yield critically misleading results. The reason is that no country is so self-sufficient that it is not affected by trends in world trade; therefore, the optimum decision for a single country might be fatal in view of capabilities and economic trends in other countries. If one looks at each country individually, for example, it may seem perfectly sensible to establish manufacturing plants in Italy, Germany, and France. In view of the increasing integration of European economies, a better solution might be to build one large plant.

A NEW APPROACH—GLOBAL PLANNING

A few companies, some American and some European, are building new approaches that minimize the risks of moving abroad. Generally, these approaches begin with one of the fundamentals of good planning—understanding the ultimate goal—and come under the term "global planning."

Global planning assumes that the ultimate objective of any company taking the first move overseas is to expand later without encountering any obstacles created by its first move. It also assumes that the chief executive is willing to extend the scope of his responsibility. Before making any move, he will ask: Where in the world should I invest my company's time, manpower, and funds for the best long-term interests of our stockholders?

A Case Example

Here is a step-by-step account of how one major company went about global planning.

Phase one. The company appointed a select executive committee to formulate the company's worldwide policies and strategic plans. This global planning committee began by making decisions to:

1. Familiarize all members of corporate management with the principles of a world enterprise so that they would all know the company's ultimate international goals.

2. Concentrate the company's initial expansion in countries that were already developed industrially.

3. Consider the world as four basic areas: North America, South America, Europe (and Africa), and the Far East.

4. Assign priority to study of the whole European area—since Europe represents the bulk of the industrial free world outside the U.S. —to identify opportunities and ways of capitalizing on them.

5. Place a moratorium on all foreign licensing and joint-venture opportunities throughout the world until this study was complete.

Then, one of the senior executives from the global planning committee was named vice president for European operations and was assigned the task of developing a strategy for the company's entry into Europe. After getting approval of a set of ground rules (the amount of money the company was willing to invest, a policy on bringing European products into the U.S., and so forth), he then appointed a task force to lay out a plan of action and prepare a budget.

Phase two. The task force laid out the plan of action for the next three phases. During *phase two* the committee examined the export and licensing agreements to see if any exclusive selling or manufacturing rights had been granted that would prevent the company from operating in certain European countries. Also, from data available in the U.S., the committee identified countries with potential markets and laid its plans for European field work. This preparatory work included developing interview guides (standardized to facilitate later consolidation of individual interviewers' results) based on the market indicators used in the U.S.; studying the history of the industry in the U.S. in order to identify the stage of maturity that the industry had reached in Europe; determining the factors governing the success of various products in the U.S., in preparation for checking to see whether the same factors applied in Europe; and, finally, working out a detailed schedule of fact-finding.

Phase three. Next came fact-finding in Europe. The objectives were to review general economic and political conditions in Europe as a whole and then in each major country; to perform an economic study of the company's industry in Europe as a whole, and then a more detailed study of the countries identified with major investments in this industry; and to analyze how well the company's strengths and position had already been established in the area through previous export and licensing activities.

The economic analysis of the firm's industry in Europe showed that the countries producing this equipment could be divided into those of major importance and those of minor importance. The major producers—England, West Germany, France, and Italy—had large local markets. The major producers were also the major suppliers for the minor producers and the nonproducing countries. The industry in each of the four major-producer countries was then studied in depth, and two representative countries in the minor-producer group were examined to see what factors were essential for success in such a market.

The economic analysis of the industry in each of the four major-producer countries included growth trends and potential markets for local production, exports, and imports, plus the structure, relative importance, and trends of the major sectors. It also included the relative importance and trends in product groups in each sector and in their end-user industries, as well as key factors for success—importance of local service and installation facilities, and the need for a corporate image as an indigenous company. The study looked at any obstacles to entry and the general requirements of the field—large investment, unique patented product, and long established engineering reputation.

Phase four. The stage was now set for *phase four,* the development of a long-term operational strategy for capitalizing on the opportunities defined in the fact-finding phase and for sidestepping any adverse effects of economic interaction between the countries. Separate strategies were developed for the major-producer countries and minor-producer countries. Major-producer countries, where local production was likely to offer serious competition, demanded strategy involving the establishment or acquisition of local production facilities. The strategy for the minor and nonproducer countries, which offered no sizable local markets, was to rely on imports from the U.S. or from European sources.

Another part of phase four was development of a statutory plan, once the operational strategy and organization had been defined. The operational strategy defined what had to be done, where companies had to be set up, and where distribution or licensing had to be performed. With the operational organization defined, it was possible to mold a statutory organization—that is, a system of ownership links—that would provide the most effective cash flow. In this case, the statutory organization consisted of a headquarters in Switzerland, with the ownership of various subsidiaries linked so that the company could capitalize on tax and other statutory advantages. Since tax laws and regulations are subject to constant change, the statutory plans were recognized as temporary; actions that could endanger flexibility were avoided.

Plans for establishing the European operations also involved companywide changes. Organization patterns, management information and control systems, and procedures for evaluating new investment proposals had to be reoriented so that, in major company deliberations, Europe was always considered as a possible alternative. Once these changes were agreed upon —and only then—positive moves were made to establish new activities abroad.

Major Advantages

Some of the major advantages of global planning are these:

> Setting long-range objectives and developing a long-term strategy before moving abroad enables a company to coordinate all the interim moves so that they do not cancel each other.
>
> Investigating a whole area in depth enables a company to take action in as many countries as desired, so that later integration can be achieved with a minimum of expensive overlapping and duplication.
>
> Developing statutory plans ahead of time gives a company a framework for making country-by-country decisions that will permit later shifts in cash flow without serious consequences (for example, capital gains tax on transfer of appreciated equity ownership).

In effect, the global approach has provided the essential key to long-range planning in the internationalization of American business.

Pitfalls in Global Planning

Like any technique, global planning has its dangers; these stem mainly from some form of misapplication.

One case of superficial application occurred when a billion-dollar corporation, with a few haphazardly placed overseas activities, decided to use the global planning technique to assess the feasibility of its conversion to a world enterprise. Its international division in New York was very powerful politically and, as a peace offering, was allowed to retain all existing remote control powers over foreign subsidiaries. In other words, the company went through the motions of appointing area managers for the various regions of the world, but they were virtually powerless since every decision still had to be referred back to corporate executives in New York.

The new area manager for Europe was not given a budget to perform a fact-finding study that would enable him to reappraise and coordinate the company's existing activities, which were spread thinly across Europe. As a result, it was not long before he found that many of the company's subsidiaries were launching new products just because "New York had advised them to do so" and not because they were appropriate for Europe. In effect, therefore, the company had remained domestically oriented while giving lip service to global planning.

Another company ostensibly adopted global planning but continued to allow its domestic divisions to encourage visits from foreign buyers of their products. As a result, the man assigned to set up operations in the European area was constantly being sidetracked in order to chase down special situations for the strong domestic divisions.

Cases of misapplication of global planning also result when a company succumbs to "international fever." This reportedly happened in one Midwestern consumer company. Shortly after a special team had been selected to set up operations in Europe, the team's attractive itinerary caught the eyes of other firm members. Soon letters from hitherto unknown distributors began reaching the company from Asia and South America—each letter suggesting that the company send a man to look over the "fabulous" opportunities in the writer's country. As it turned out, random opportunities did exist in Hong Kong and Brazil. In effect, the global planning technique had been applied partially—that is, in Europe—while plans for the rest of the world resulted from the old unplanned approach. This led to a conflict of interest. One of the European companies that had been selected for acquisition had subsidiaries in the Far East that competed with a property the international division was negotiating for in Hong Kong.

In summary, too often corporate moves overseas are motivated more than a little by the fad to go abroad. Admittedly, real pressures to move overseas are mounting, but the consequences of poor analysis and false moves in this rapidly changing world can be painful. Approaches based on short-term thinking are not sufficient. Any move overseas must be looked upon as an integral part of a clearly defined long-range goal.

There is no magic formula for successful global planning, but companies that do it well do possess and make use of one open secret. This is the understanding that only the company president or chief executive officer can successfully implement a series of moves abroad. Only a company president can effectively persuade a board of directors of the value of a move abroad. Only a company president can effectively control and channel the inevitable rivalries and seeming contradictions in policy that simultaneous operation in several countries creates. Only a company president can successfully create the new marketing and financial controls needed for the new kind of company he will head if he creates a world enterprise.

KEYS TO MARKETING SUCCESS ABROAD

Adapting Domestic Skills to Foreign Markets

Leadership in American marketing is no guarantee of leadership in marketing abroad. Some outstandingly successful American firms have been able to duplicate in foreign markets their domestic success with ease and speed. For others success has come slowly and expensively. And for others not at all.

An analysis of the experience of leading American firms in major markets of the world has identified four characteristics of the outstanding marketer. These characteristics describe his fundamental approach to marketing decision-making, which, even in the short run, appears far more important than advantages in price or product.

1. The outstanding marketer exports his approaching marketing decision-making rather than his domestic practices. Foreign competitors are often alert, tough, and aggressive; but many are relatively inexperienced in analyzing marketing techniques. This experience—the ability to diagnose the problem, identify the best alternatives, and choose wisely among them —is the American competitor's real advantage. The marketing practices

he now employs in the U.S. may be totally inappropriate in the rest of the world: but his technique for developing these practices has application everywhere.

2. The outstanding marketer is keenly aware of the variation from one market to another. He never thinks solely in terms of "the European market," "the Latin American market," or even "the Common Market." He knows that countries, and even sections of countries, differ enormously in almost every factor critical to his market planning:

> Distribution Channels: In Italy and France, chain stores are in the ascendant. In Germany, wholesaler groups are growing rapidly. Distribution practices in the north of the United Kingdom are very different from those in the south.

> Consumer Attitudes: In Germany, utility may be more important than style; in France, advertising and brand name may play larger roles. Hence product design and promotion have to be tailored to individual markets.

> Competitive Environment: In one country, the market for a product may be dominated by a single company; in a neighboring country many firms scramble for their shares.

> Market Size, Maturity, and Rate of Growth: An American power tool manufacturer found only replacement opportunities in one market but a completely untapped potential in a country nearby. Within the Common Market, per capita sales of widely used products vary enormously, and rates of growth for the same product differ by as much as 100 percent.

3. The outstanding marketer is sensitive to differences in his competitive position. American companies heavily committed to foreign markets are often industry leaders at home. In the U.S., they have become accustomed to the privileges and responsibilities of leadership. They may have a powerful influence on the industry pricing practices. They may be able to avoid discounts and deals. They can limit their distribution to carefully selected outlets. But their domestic position does not travel with them like a passport. The competitive structure of an industry varies widely from one economy to another and so does the industry position of a corporation that competes in several markets around the world. A company that has 30 percent of the American market may have to fight for 3 percent of a foreign market. And the company that gets 3 percent and more does so with a strategy appropriate for its position in that market.

4. The outstanding marketer combines policy-making at home with tactical decision-making abroad. Only corporate management is in a position to make broad policy decisions and to integrate local plans into a company-wide program. Without this kind of leadership, the most knowledgeable and skilled local marketing people can be only partly effective. But broad policies and plans are implemented best when the tactical decisions are made by local people in each market. There are three reasons for this:

> Referral of every problem to the U.S. invites poor decisions and involves unavoidable delay.

Policy-level executives in the U.S. cannot know enough about foreign markets to make every detailed decision.

Information required for operating decisions is often almost impossible to transmit.

A short time ago American corporations found things easier and more profitable abroad than at home; but today margins are shrinking, rates of return are declining, and competition is everywhere more intense. How American companies will fare depends greatly on the way they approach the new problems of international marketing.[1]

[1] Parts of this article are from "Minimizing risks of moving abroad," by John G. McDonald, *Business Horizons* (Spring 1961), Indiana University, Bloomington, Indiana.

13

LRP FOR INTERNATIONAL OPERATIONS *

John Fayerweather

"What will be the key policy questions for international managements in the next five to ten years?"

In the past 15 years U.S. business has "gone international" on a truly extraordinary scale. Our overseas investments in manufacturing operations have more than tripled. Whereas foreign operations were essentially the province of a few hundred major concerns before World War II, today an estimated 3,000 U.S. companies of all sizes and descriptions have some interest in overseas production—either through their own investments or licensing agreements. Thus in a multitude of companies one basic policy decision is an accomplished fact—the commitment to move outward from purely domestic business and become an international enterprise. In retrospect, with foreign markets expanding explosively and import controls forcing local production, that decision was an obvious and easy one.

Now come the more difficult problems. The task of shaping the character and policies of a far-flung organization into a unit which can meet effectively the challenges of increasingly tough competition and evolving political and social forces. The major aspects of these problems are already apparent and with the knowledge gained from experience and research in the past few years we may outline the thinking which can lead to their effective solution.

At the risk of oversimplification, I will single out three areas which I

* From the *California Management Review*, III (Fall 1960), 23-35.

believe present the critical problems which must be resolved in every company which hopes to have an effective international operation five to ten years hence. A few companies have already gone a long way in the direction of solving these problems but for most international managements these will be major preoccupations for the next few years. The three are:

1. Establishment of operations which are viable in highly nationalistic environments with particular attention to the ownership question and joint ventures.

2. Development of local national executives for senior posts in overseas managements.

3. Welding and molding world-wide operations into an integrated unit.

THE THREAT OF NATIONALISM

Through much of the world, especially in the less developed areas, the environment for U.S. business is dominated by two forces:

1. The powerful emotion of nationalism combining patriotic pride and a thrust for independence with negative reactions against racism, colonialism, economic dependence and in general to being "second-class" citizens of the world society;

2. A substantial measure of dependence for rapid economic progress upon the capital and industrial know-how of the economically more advanced nations, especially the United States.

These forces are fundamentally in opposition and it has only been the overriding political and economic importance of the second which has held the first in check. But the balance between the two is by no means static, it is in every sense dynamic and one of the major keys to future planning is recognition that the second, dependence on what U.S. business has to offer, is declining steadily while nationalism shows little signs of abating.

What this means for U.S. business has been spelled out recently from two quite different viewpoints with conclusions, which though different in fact are very similar in implication. Speaking from the perspective of their global study of industrial conditions Professors Harbison and Myers observe:

"Eventually the firm is forced to recognize that, in the opinion of the effective political leaders, foreign management and foreign financial control are only temporary instruments for industrial development. In a very real sense, therefore, expatriate managers are expendable, and their power and influence in any rapidly industrializing country will inevitably shrink. Like patrimonial management in the advanced countries, expatriate management too will become an anachronism in modern society. . . . We feel that the wholly owned foreign firm has a limited role to play in the industrializing countries. The future is likely to see an expansion of locally controlled companies which have an affiliation, through licensing, marketing, or consulting arrangements, with large business organizations in the United States, England, and Europe." [1]

Approaching the situation with the eyes of a practicing executive, Harold Solmssen of Schering Corporation perceives the same sort of trend.

"As far as we can remember, ours was the most progressive economy and, as a result, we are the leading economic power today. The rest of the world had to adapt itself to our methods if they wanted our money and our products. But this may not always be so and we should guard against considering our views right and those of the others 'unfair' or 'wrong.' " [2]

Thus there is a pressing need for U.S. international operations to set their policies so that they will be welcome in countries abroad when the need for our capital and know-how has largely passed. What does this require?

The answer lies essentially in policies that satisfy the major aspirations in the host country falling within the province of the U.S. operations. While the importance of these will vary among countries we may define at least four such aspirations:

1. The quest of individuals, especially at the managerial level for personal opportunity and advancement;

2. The urge of the individual with entrepreneurial instincts to realize them in the creative and financial satisfactions of developing a business venture;

3. The desire of local government and financial circles to retain within their borders a full share of the financial returns of industrial operations; and

4. The drive of governments for economic progress directed in large measure by their plans and conceptions of what is in the best national interest.

That the policies of U.S. business may frustrate or at least threaten realization of these aspirations is all too easily documented. A recent study of U.S. subsidiaries in Brazil and Mexico by John Shearer showed that U.S. personnel "dominate most of the top posts. . . . The general manager, and key executives at the second level are non-nationals—usually Americans." [3] Under these circumstances hundreds of foreign executives can only be promoted as U.S. nationals above them are moved and this movement to date has not been notably rapid.

The reactions of local entrepreneurs to U.S. operations are strikingly illustrated in Sanford Mosk's description of the "New Group" of small Mexican manufacturers who gained a foothold during World War II and were the focal point of protective and restrictive policies as they sought

[1] Frederick Harbison and Charles A. Myers, *Management in the Industrial World* (McGraw-Hill Book Company, New York, 1959), p. 391.

[2] "Organization Planning for International Operations," *The International Executive* (Winter 1960), p. 5, summarized from a paper delivered at the American Management Association.

[3] "Overseas American Managers—Necessities or Luxuries?", *Management in the Industrial World: An International Analysis,* Princeton University, Industrial Relations Section, p. 17.

shelter from the incursions of bigger, more efficient U.S. companies who they felt, probably correctly, could wipe them out if given free rein.[4] More recently concerted drives among organized commercial interests have threatened Sears, Roebuck and Woolworth as numerous small Mexican merchants have seen a threat to their future in new, mass merchandising methods.[5] They have attempted to curb expansion of such chain firms in various ways.

The classic case of dispute over financial returns from a venture is that of General Motors in Australia. The profits from GM's fully owned Holden operation are running over 30% on its investment, a return in which local investors would like a share and the allocation for GM dividends of $16.8 million of foreign exchange out of total Australian dollar earnings of $173 million in 1959 is a hard fact for the government to swallow. This situation is extreme but in lesser degree the feelings it involves apply to every successful overseas venture making profits and seeking to repatriate them.

Finally, conflicts with government economic planning are found in limitless variety, ranging from major disagreements such as the reluctance of U.S. automobile companies to accelerate manufacture of parts in Brazil a few years ago because they felt it was uneconomic to many lesser problems such as the Indian government's criticism of the "wasteful" expenditures on selling efforts by U.S. tire companies.[6]

"Yankee Firm, Go Home!"

So there is a solid nucleus in frustration of objectives around which the forces of nationalism may be aroused against U.S. foreign operations. One solution of course is to accept the eventual withdrawal of U.S. companies from abroad. Rejecting this as a defeatist approach, the challenge lies in the conception of policies which give sufficient scope to national aspirations so that U.S. business remains, if not loved, at least accepted as a useful industrial citizen abroad.

Much of the thinking of affected national groups on this subject has coalesced around the concept of the "joint venture." The jointly financed enterprise, especially one in which U.S. interests have a minority position, is seen by government officials, local industrialists and others as the ideal for utilizing United States capital and especially a continuing flow of know-how while still giving full scope to national aspirations. In some instances by legal requirements, but more commonly by administrative pressure and persuasion, new United States ventures are encouraged to move in this direction in many countries.

Reflecting this influence, a research project on joint ventures directed by Professor Wolfgang Friedman at Columbia University, to be published later this year, reveals that there has been a significant increase in interest in joint ventures in the post World War II era. As a percentage of new in-

[4] *Industrial Revolution in Mexico* (University of California Press, Berkeley and Los Angeles, 1950), pp. 32-52.

[5] John Fayerweather, *Management of International Operations* (McGraw-Hill Book Co., N.Y., 1960), pp. 222-232.

[6] J. Fayerweather (see note 5), pp. 247-248.

vestments, however, joint ventures still remain a minority and few established investments have been changed from 100% United States ownership to a joint ownership status.

According to the latest census of overseas investments only 26% of subsidiaries had as much as 5% ownership by local capital.[7] United States international managements have not as yet therefore, made any broad shift in policies in the direction of joint venturing. Should they? Or can the pressures of national aspirations be contained without such a policy shift?

Guide to Basic Policy

In answer to these questions I propose three basic guides in policy making. Individual situations will vary greatly from company to company and country to country defying universal recommendations. But a general adherence to these guide lines will, I believe, result in enduring policy decisions.

> 1. A joint venture which contemplates a substantial sharing of management control is fundamentally undesirable and to be avoided except in unusual circumstances.
>
> 2. A major portion of foreign national aspirations can and should be met by statesmanlike management policies independent of the ownership question.
>
> 3. Some sharing with local nationals of financial participation in foreign ventures without relinquishing of management control is desirable.

The first point is the most important for it strikes to the heart of joint venturing as many people conceive it. Their idea is that an existing or budding local entrepreneur joins forces with the management of a U.S. firm and, pooling their assets, they form a far stronger enterprise than either could present alone. The local entrepreneur knows his country, he has government contacts and, by giving the venture a strong local flavor, he contributes to the morale of the personnel and the public image of the company. The United States management brings its skills in management and technology and a continuing flow of new know-how from research.

Competent analysts of this subject like Professor Emile Benoit emphasize the necessity that the partners be compatible.

"Finding the right partner is nine-tenths of the problem. . . . As in marriage, there is nothing so important as mutual confidence, and basic agreement on values." [8] With this proviso the theory of the marriage of foreign and U.S. managements appears sound and demonstrated successes among the many case studies collected in the Columbia University research indicate that it is feasible.

However, there is clearly another side to the question sharply defined

[7] U.S. Department of Commerce, *Foreign Investment of the United States* (Washington, 1953), p. 23.

[8] "When Businesses Marry," *International Management Digest* (October 1958), p. 20.

in the difficulties encountered in a number of joint ventures and the ultimate failure of others such as Sears, Roebuck's union with Waltons, Ltd. in Australia which was severed in late 1959 because of disagreement over financial and expansion policies.[9] The significance of these difficulties can be summed up in the question of whether it is reasonable to expect continuing sound and dynamic management to result from a marriage of the entrepreneurial drives and ideas of two managements. This question admits no simple answer and this paper is no place to attempt a full exposition of the subject.

I submit, however, as a general thesis that where success has come out of mergers and other marriages in industry, it has largely come through an unusual coincidence of managerial outlooks or more commonly through the submersion or ultimate elimination of the viewpoints of individuals on one side or the other resulting in dominance of a single partner.

Those who disagree with this thesis should have no difficulty in accepting joint international ventures as a general policy. But, if the thesis is acceptable, it casts grave doubts on joining forces with local national entrepreneurs as a means for satisfying national aspirations. It is important in evaluating this thesis to look more towards the future than the present.

It can be shown quite readily that in the early stages of a joint venture the marriage of assets is of great value. The United States company new to a foreign country profits greatly from the local know-how of its partner and the local partner derives great benefits from American products and technology not otherwise available to him. But these immediate benefits diminish in importance fairly rapidly and then the strengths of the joint venture as with any enterprise begin to depend upon the ability of its management to conceive and execute policies with a unified and persevering direction.

Joint Ventures

If the marriage has in fact been between two competent entrepreneurial managements (and that is assumed to be one of the key objectives of joint ventures) then, as market conditions change, political forces shift, product changes evolve, etc., it is almost certain that there will be significant differences of opinion between the management groups. It is possible that they may work them out and the advantages of the marriage will support effective union. It seems more likely, however, that the venture will either suffer from vacillation and inability to develop effective unified policy or that out of conflict will emerge one dominant management, so that the other loses an effective vehicle for achieving its objectives in the union. Either the entrepreneurial aspirations of the local national are frustrated or the United States company loses effective control over the policies of its foreign unit.

This negative conclusion leads to reexamination of the proposition put forward by many local nationals that joint ventures should be adopted as a means of satisfying the varied national aspirations listed on page 132.

[9] *Business Week* (November 7, 1959), p. 60.

The position of the local nationals is justified today, but primarily for one major reason which need not exist.

If a major share of ownership were in local hands, they could readily force changes in those policies of many United States subsidiaries which currently frustrate national aspirations. For example, they could require the removal of U.S. executives and promotion of local personnel to top positions. However, it is certainly not essential that ownership be shared for such a change to be made.

The success of our most enlightened United States international companies in utilizing local executives, in blending company policies with those of government economic plans, in developing local suppliers, etc., is ample proof that a large portion of the local aspirations can be met without sharing management control.

The critical significance of the strong support of joint venturing from overseas, therefore, lies not so much in a yes or no response as in imaginative and persevering execution of policies which relieve the pressures for sharing management control by undertaking independently those actions which local nationals would foster if they gained control. This objective, we must grant, cannot be fully achieved for much the same reasons that even the most enlightened paternalism is never fully successful. There will always be a residual desire for full control which United States ownership frustrates. But, given a continuance of respect for private property, there seems every reason to assume that United States companies which make a concerted effort to give scope for national aspirations will be able to continue overseas operations indefinitely.

Profit Sharing

The third suggested guideline, sharing financial participation with foreign nationals, is essentially part of this approach but it is treated separately because it is a more difficult area of execution than, for example, promotion of local executives. The rates of return on investment earned by American overseas operations are generally no greater than those of local capitalists and the dollars allocated for remission of profits can almost always be justified on sound economic grounds as less than would be required for importation of products made locally as a result of the investment or gains from exports of the products of the U.S. operations. Yet the furor surrounding the Australian General Motors situation cited above is only the most notable expression of a widespread desire by local investors to "have a piece" of the earnings of U.S. companies and dissatisfaction of government authorities at the allocation of dollars for remission of earnings which might otherwise be used for importing machinery, raw materials, etc.

Stock Sale in Host Country

Rejecting the concept of shared management in joint ventures, I feel United States managements must still give full consideration to the possibility of limited joint venturing by allowing local capital to invest directly in their operations. A number of companies have already taken steps in this direction by selling common or preferred stock to local investors.

A few are moving in the opposite direction—one major company, for example, recently bought up outstanding common stock rather than face further displeasure from local investors who were dissatisfied with the low dividend payout of the company. Experiences such as this underscore the fact that sharing financial participation is not without significant disadvantages. However, as compared with disputes where management control is shared these disadvantages do not appear to endanger operating success and some concession to the financially oriented nationalistic aspirations seems essential for the continuance of integrated international enterprises.

Mutual Stock Exchange

One approach suggested by *Business International* is the union of companies through mutual exchanges of stock. BI feels such a step "would remove conflicts of interest between majority and minority shareholders. It would create an internationally owned firm that, as it expands and acquires owners of parent stock of an increasing variety of nationalities, can give the only final answer to nationalistic hostilities and the problem of being labeled 'foreign.' "[10]

This solution of course has limited application in that it would involve the marriage of a number of managements but the idea behind it of overcoming hostilities by spreading ownership of the international company all over the world is open to very general application. General Motors stock, for example, could be (and to some degree already is) owned by investors in every continent and in that way they could share in such profits as GM made in their own countries. In fact, however, this solution is currently so impeded by exchange controls and the end result is so far detached from the individual foreign operations that it is less promising as an immediate solution and more likely as BI suggests to be the "final answer" many years hence.

Must Retain Operating Control

Of more immediate promise is the sale of a part of the stock of subsidiaries to the general investing public in individual countries. With such broad sharing of ownership, the U.S. management, even if only retaining a minority interest, can retain operating control. It is by no means essential to sell majority ownership, however, to accomplish the essential objective of giving local capital a chance to share in the venture and to satisfy the desires of local governments. More practical are such efforts as Kaiser Industries' sale of 42% of the equity in its Argentine venture to the public.[11] As a broader investing public emerges through the growth of the middle class and the evolution of security markets in country after country this practice should become increasingly common.

[10] *Business International* (October 23, 1959), p. 2.
[11] *Business International* (May 23, 1958), p. 6.

To summarize then, in this first area of policy planning we are confronted with the necessity of satisfying the aspirations which underlie nationalistic drives. Despite pressures to resolve all of these through acceptance of minority positions in joint ventures, United States managements will be wise to adhere to full operating control of overseas ventures seeking to satisfy local national aspirations through statesmanlike operating policies including sharing of some degree of financial ownership through broad sale of company stock.

DEVELOPMENT OF LOCAL NATIONAL EXECUTIVES

Today, as Dr. Shearer's study has noted, most of the key executive assignments in the overseas units of most companies are handled by United States executives. But the forces of economics and politics are set against this practice and in favor of the eventual transfer of all management jobs abroad to local nationals. The relatively higher salaries paid to United States executives and the travel and living allowances they require make it appreciably less expensive to employ local nationals in virtually any situation.

Equally important are the pressures of government officials and public opinion in favor of turning management over to local nationals. In some countries these pressures are felt tangibly in the form of laws requiring employment of nationals or refusing entry papers for American executives on the grounds that local personnel are adequate for the work. Such restrictions are not common in the case of senior executives, United States companies generally being legally allowed today to bring in men for top positions.

However, there is strong pressure from government and national opinion directed against those companies which are slow in turning over management to nationals and, conversely, in favor of those who do give responsibility to local executives. These pressures may be expected to grow as the number and capabilities of local executives increase.

Thus a sensible management must adopt a policy of turning over progressively greater management responsibility to local nationals and it must prepare for the day when the senior position in one country after another will be entrusted to a local executive. This thought may be disturbing to some, but it need not be. Some companies have already gone a long way down this road—National Cash Register, for example, has only some half dozen U.S. executives throughout its large and highly effective international organization. But the transition will be effective only if the national executives have been adequately prepared. There have been in recent years cases where management of a foreign unit was turned over to local executives who were not ready and who had subsequently to be replaced by U.S. executives with most unfortunate public relations and organizational repercussions. Thus, it is imperative that a thoughtful plan be evolved for the development of overseas executives.

What are the requisites of such a plan? First, it must be directed to the levels of managerial characteristics at which development is needed. Second, it must foster specific qualities essential for men in senior positions. And third, it must provide experiences which will have a permanent developmental effect. These are fundamentals applicable to all executive development. Our concern here is with the special considerations which enter into their application to overseas executives.

"Conditioning" Executives

A basic, if usually unstated, assumption of United States executive development plans is that the executives' attitudes are essentially in accord with the codes and objectives expected of men in top management. We assume that they will regard cooperation with other executives as desirable; that they will favor thorough analysis in the formulation of policies, and so on. This is realistic. Individuals to varying degrees may be deficient in attitudes of this sort. But, by and large, they are an integral part of the personalities of managerial candidates, impressed upon them by a variety of experiences from childhood to maturity.

They are by definition part of our modern managerial culture and, since so many phases of a man's life work toward their development, little explicit attention need be given to them in executive development plans. Accordingly most attention is directed at two less basic phases of men's qualities—technical skills (budgeting, labor negotiations, etc.) and administrative behavior (skill in managerial coordination, approaches to analysis of policy problems, etc.).

In overseas executive development such assumptions about the attitudes of men are not so broadly justified. Research into managerial organizations abroad emphasizes the prevalence of administrative attitudes which are substantially different from those of the U.S. managerial culture. Harbison and Myers, after extensive surveys of management organizations abroad, report:

> In each of the countries . . . the conditions generated by the process of industrialization have required increasing attention to managerial organization, attitudes, policies, and development. There are, however, significant differences among countries both in the problems faced and in the types of reactions; these differences reflect various cultural patterns as well as variation in the stage and pace of economic development.[12]

The main theme emerging from my intensive research with management organizations in Mexico was that "the significant difficulties in relations between United States and foreign executives are due to the differences in their national cultures." [13] The codes which govern men's relations with others, the way they approach their work, their motivations, and other attitudes are in many societies significantly different from our own and strongly influence executive performance.

These differences force us to approach overseas executive development

[12] F. Harbison and C. A. Myers (see note 1), p. 123.

[13] John Fayerweather, *The Executive Overseas* (Syracuse University Press, Syracuse, New York, 1959), p. 6.

at the attitudinal level which is unnecessary in domestic programs. Philosophically one may say that the cultural attitudes of others should be respected and foreign executives should be allowed to evolve administrative patterns consistent with their own culture.

This point of view is however impractical on two counts. First, both research and the practical experience of United States executives confirm that United States managerial attitudes, when applied intelligently, result in more effective management than adoption of local attitudes. The effectiveness of U.S. subsidiaries abroad is based as much on the efficiency and drive generated by United States administrative attitudes as it is on superior technology and capital.

The American Pattern

Second, there are strong indications that the evolution of the general administrative attitudes in other countries is in the direction of our own pattern. For all its shortcomings, the United States is the leader among the nations of the world in the evolution of a highly efficient managerial society and the administrative attitudes of our executives are an integral part of that efficiency.

As other nations progress toward a comparable type of society it appears inevitable that they will experience problems similar to ours, and evolve somewhat the same type of culture. Indeed, one finds strong evidence of this trend in the fact that the able and alert managers of Europe, Latin America and Asia have more in common with Americans than do the general run of managers in their societies. Thus it appears that the effectiveness of United States subsidiaries applying United States managerial attitudes is simply evidence that their approaches place them in the lead in a general cultural revolution which will in time envelop the whole society.

While the specific attitudes toward which executive development efforts should be directed will depend upon the nature of each individual, two broad categories emerged from the research reported in *The Executive Overseas* as of widespread importance: attitudes toward interpersonal relations and approaches to work assignments.[14] The attitudes of businessmen in much of the world, especially the less industrialized areas, are strongly influenced (1) by the merchant-trader attitudes characteristic of commercial (as distinguished from industrial) life and (2) by authoritarian social institutions (family, church, schools, etc.).

Foster Group Attitudes

Both of these influences foster individualistic personality characteristics and produce the sort of man who looks on those around him as antagonists and operates as a lone wolf, "dealing-with" and maneuvering around others as best he can. Though such attitudes are highly effective in the bazaar, they are incompatible with the requirements of an integrated management team. There is a common need therefore to foster the group-

[14] John Fayerweather (see note 13).

oriented attitudes which are emerging as the small, one-man or family concern gives way to larger, professionally managed industrial units.

The approach of U.S. management to individual work assignments is a lineal descendent of two major forces which spread out of Western Europe in the 16th century: the scientific revolution and the Calvinist "Protestant Ethic." They account in cultural terms for the analytical, disciplined attitude toward managerial responsibilities which is the norm of our industrial society. For the most part these forces scarcely touched the cultures of vast areas of Asia, Africa, the Middle East and Latin America. As a result there is a substantial need in overseas executive development to build disciplined, scientific attitudes.

In considering the development of such attitudes in senior overseas executives it is important to appreciate the need for a real "take" in the personality of the individual and not a superficial acceptance at the behavior level. The latter may result in acceptable performance among junior executives if they work under the strong leadership of an able executive whose own standards set the basic tone of management action. However, when we are considering men to whom the senior leadership position is to be entrusted it is essential that the acceptance of effective management methods be deeply rooted in personal conviction.

Thorough Involvement a "Must"

What type experiences are required to achieve this sort of development? The answer lies in two words: *involvement* and *thorough*. The executives must be given experiences in which they become deeply involved personally and which are sustained to the point of thorough absorption.

We must accept as a starting point that changing attitudes is an extremely difficult process and that radical changes are not generally feasible, thus our concern is with gradual changes and in large measure with fostering the development of pre-existing potentials, not injecting new ideas. But even this limited objective can be accomplished only by experiences which have a penetrating and enduring effect on the personality of the individual.

The implications of these generalizations for actual executive development plans are fairly clear. First, because the greater part of a man's experience will come on the job in his own country, it is essential that senior supervising U.S. executives understand the importance of attitudinal development and foster it by their own actions.

Second, extended periods of work experience in the United States should be scheduled at key stages of the development process. Actually living and feeling the various components of the U.S. managerial system has an impact which can never be achieved in a U.S. subsidiary set in the midst of another culture.

American companies have found from experience that local nationals who have gone to college in the United States or worked here for substantial periods often have acquired attitudes which make them good executives. Extended assignments for executives at the formative stage of development can accomplish the same degree of involvement. It is important to emphasize, however, that the visits must be long enough and must immerse the individual deeply in the real functioning of an organization. Companies which have used development of this type effectively have found that periods of several months to a year are the minimum requirement.

A survey by the Institute of International Education indicates that some 5,000 foreign nationals were given training experience in the United States in 1959 but that only 10 percent of these were here for over six months.[15] Doubtless those who were here for brief visits acquired useful technical training but it is only the visits of several months which can be regarded as effective executive development experiences.

A more intensive study of the development practices of 150 U.S. companies by the Council for International Progress in Management to be published soon shows that some companies have given careful thought to design such experiences so that they include extended periods of formal training and working assignments. Taking their policies as harbingers of the future, we may predict that in the next few years other alert managements will develop plans for intensive development experiences in the United States for local national executives.

INTERNATIONALIZING MANAGEMENT

There is little doubt that the international operations of most companies will grow in coming years both in absolute terms and in proportion to domestic business. This has been generally true for the past decade and the higher rates of growth of foreign economies suggest a continuation of the trend. Inevitably the pattern of management will shift to accommodate this change in the nature of corporate business but the manner in which the pattern evolves will require careful thought based on a realistic view of each company's situation.

The general thrust of the change of corporate management has been described in essentially similar terms by several authors in the past year.[16] It starts from the traditionally segregated status of export departments and international divisions which operate with a large measure of autonomy, too often accompanied by ignorance and lack of interest on the part of senior company management and domestic associates. The international side of business draws products, know-how and capital from the rest of the company but structurally its operations are largely independent of the main body of domestic parent company functions. By contrast the emerging new patterns of management involve a high degree of integration between international activities and the rest of the company.

As a general trend this thesis is incontrovertible. It can readily be observed in various stages in many companies today and the growing importance of international business argues for its continuation. The problem

[15] *Open Doors* (Institute of International Education, New York, 1960), p. 14.

[16] For example, John J. Beauvois, "Internationalism: A New Concept for U.S. Business," *California Management Review* (Winter, 1960), pp. 28-37; and Gilbert H. Clee and Alfred di Scipio, "Creating a World Enterprise," *Harvard Business Review* (November-December, 1959), pp. 77-89.

of planning lies not, therefore, in establishing the basic direction of change but rather in determining the character it should assume for a specific company. In all probability the result both in operating policies and organizational structure will show many characteristics of the ideal integrated world enterprise, but will retain some of the features of the segregated organizations which are still the dominant pattern today.

Operating Policies

In the development of *operating policies,* the integration ideal stresses a pattern of activities which renders the optimum economic return. Manufacturing plants are established in countries with low costs, research activities are distributed according to costs and the scientific resources of various areas, financial assets are moved about to maximize return, and so forth. That substantial progress in this direction has already been made is observable on many fronts; for example, in the rapid increase in foreign "sourcing" to supply U.S. markets with goods made in company plants abroad,[17] and in the growth of research facilities in Europe.

The fact that a significant degree of change has occurred does not mean that the process will be carried through to the ideal of the economic optimum concept. Its limitations can be best understood by visualizing an extreme, yet not illogical case. It is quite conceivable that, on an economic basis, the most profitable structure for a small electronics company would consist of a single large production unit in Japan, a research organization in Europe, and a sales organization spread around the world.

Such a structure immediately gives one pause. Would any management wish to commit itself so heavily in single separated political areas? In fact, of course, even the economic optimum would rarely call for such an extreme, but the limitations, highlighted by the extreme case, will always be present. Even at the expense of some cost economies a responsible management must plan its operating structure so that it is reasonably secure.

Political Factors

Planning the extent and character of the integration of international and domestic operations becomes therefore a complex problem in which many economic and non-economic factors must be weighed.[18] Most important undoubtedly are the political forces. The hazards of a global war may be given some weight, though the broader implications of such an eventuality are so catastrophic that probably no plan could really take them into account.

More realistically therefore our concern should be with minimizing the risks from single upheavals and with the evolution of integrated economic areas such as the European and Central American common markets. The former militates against placing a substantial portion of company activities

[17] "Americans Speed Up Foreign Sourcing," *Business Week* (January 2, 1960), pp. 66-68.

[18] For a fuller discussion see John Fayerweather, "Logistic Planning" (see note 5), pp. 506-512.

in any but the most stable countries. The latter calls for a substantial segregation of activities on a regional basis.

Indications are, for example, that the European common market will maintain a substantial protective wall which will perpetuate present restrictions on imports from countries like Japan. Projecting this characteristic, we may reasonably assume in our plans that a Latin American common market would be equally, if not more, protective and that current manufacturing plans, to the extent that they attempt to anticipate the development of the Latin American area, will be based on that assumption.

Besides the political factor must be added consideration of the more complex and difficult-to-discern trends of currency restrictions, exchange rates and antitrust laws. When all of these elements are weighed in the balance most companies will find that a significant shift toward the international economic optimum will be in order but that it will also be judicious to hedge their position by a good deal of "uneconomic" dispersion and including retention of a large portion of their activities within the boundaries of the United States.

Standard Oil Pattern

So far as *organization* is concerned, the ideal of the new concepts calls typically for a world headquarters with globally oriented top executives, a line organization divided by areas (North America, Europe, etc.), and staff divisions which serve the whole world in their speciality. Structures along these lines have been characteristic for some time of major international operations like Standard Oil Company (N.J.) and other petroleum companies and of manufacturing companies with large international interests such as National Cash Register, whose Chairman Stanley Allyn is as well known on international rostrums as any international division manager. There is no reason to doubt that, as the international interests of other companies expand, they also will shift their organizations to give greater emphasis and better management attention to overseas operations.

There is another side to this coin, however, which leads me to doubt whether the days of the segregated "international division" are really numbered. It seems more probable that the typical organization a few years hence will be a hybrid, with a substantial degree of internationalization, especially at the very top, but also a good deal of clustering and segregating of international as distinguished from domestic activities in both line and staff personnel.

The essential objective in developing any organization is, of course, to deal effectively with management problems and not to conform to an ideal. The new concept of international organization is an approach to dealing with the problems of an integrated world enterprise. It must be modified, however, to fit those aspects of the enterprise which remain substantially unintegrated or segregated and further to conform to the capacities of individuals.

For the predictable future there will be many aspects of a business for which there is a practical division of approaches between international and domestic, and effectiveness in the management of each will call for specialized skills of individuals. For example, consider the financial and tax situation. Whether it be through a foreign based tax-haven corporation or a U.S. based international business corporation (the so-called Boggs Bill proposal) it is going to be financially desirable to manage the financing of overseas units so far as possible as a unit independent of the domestic activities.

International Specialists

Thus, regardless of the character of the over-all organization chart, there seems sure to be an executive who has some over-all supervisory responsibility for international financial activities. Furthermore, in the nature of performance of their work it seems quite certain that the men responsible for operations in areas outside the United States will spend a good deal of their time with this international financial supervisor working out the allocation of the international financial resources and that someone will be designated to coordinate and facilitate the efforts of these men as they work as a group. This coordinator may be called, for example, "chairman of the investment committee" but it takes little perception to visualize that such a man will have already assumed much of the role of a "vice president for international operations."

This same line of reasoning may be pursued for personnel, advertising and other aspects of operations. It does not in any way conflict with the basic thesis that organizations must move away from segregation toward integration of international, parent and domestic personnel. It does, however, indicate that the organizational planners have a very difficult task in discerning the exact form that integration should take for any one company at a given stage of its evolution.

The prospect therefore is for steady progress in the evolution of the integrated world enterprise, modified to fit realistically the prospects and requirements of each company situation.

This article has outlined three major areas in which major policy and organization changes are required for satisfactory international operations in the next few years: (1) meeting the threat of nationalism, (2) developing local national executives, and (3) internationalizing management. In each, the general direction of the future is quite clear. The problems lie therefore in the formulation of realistic and effective plans. This will be no small task.

In each area there are conflicting factors to consider and there are, as always, elements of inertia and ignorance to overcome. The hard facts of the tremendous potential of expanding world markets and the increasing competition to capture them should, however, provide ample incentive for U.S. managements to tackle the task realistically and energetically.

14

ANALYZING FOREIGN OPPORTUNITIES *

Raphael W. Hodgson and Hugo E. R. Uyterhoeven

One of the most significant business trends of our time is the entry of many United States manufacturing companies into foreign markets. How should the managements of these companies size up their opportunities abroad? The approach commonly followed is to analyze present market potentials and assess the prospects of future growth. On the face of it, this approach may seem rational—and certainly it provides *part* of the data top executives need. By itself, however, it is inadequate. As a basis for decision making it may even lead to more wrong answers than right ones. Here are just a few illustrations to make our point:

The European market for an important line of electronics systems was growing rapidly, and firms participating in this market were enjoying large profits. A U.S. company contemplating entry into this business possessed the skills and resources necessary to gain a competitive market position. At first glance, the company's prospects for doing well looked excellent according to conventional criteria.

Yet closer examination showed that high levels of demand relieved firms of the need to offer a considerable amount of customer service and special systems work normally required in more competitive situations. Given the absence of these sales expenses, profit margins were not as high as one would expect in this industry. Also, product shortages greatly reduced the levels of finished goods and work-in-process inventories, thus requiring less debt and equity capital. Profitability in this business could therefore be expected to decline rapidly as maturing conditions imposed increased sales expenses and capital requirements.

In the late 1950's in Europe, a capacity shortage prevailed in an important plastic. In addition, consumption appeared to be increasing at over 20% per year, and prices were very high relative to entry expenses and plant investments. Most firms felt that the problems of raw material supply and "coproduct" disposal, which are normal to a chemical business, were surmountable in that the huge demand and high prices for the plastic relieved management of having to secure either the most economical source of raw materials or the most appropriate distribution for the coproducts. Consequently, the requirements for entry appeared less forbidding than in most other chemical product areas.

It was not surprising, therefore, that the field was entered by almost

* From *Harvard Business Review,* XL (March-April 1962), 60-79. Reprinted by permission.

every candidate capable of doing so, and that capacity mushroomed all over Europe. Worse was to happen. The marginal cost of this product was low, yet capital investment was very high; with a considerable surplus for export already available in the United States, and with low European tariffs, dumping by U.S. producers occurred on a large scale. Today, the compounded effect of dumping by American producers and of large additions to capacity in Europe has collapsed prices to such an extent that a large number of the new business operations will probably become questionable ventures, if they have not already.

Profits were low among many European manufacturers of an important class of electric components, even though the market was a dynamic one. Most firms were under price pressure from two major producers. Investigation revealed that both producers had standardized their production around three basic types of products, thereby achieving higher scales of production resulting in much lower costs. This enabled them to enjoy considerable profits, while keeping prices low. Their low prices even enabled them to extend their market into areas where their products appeared overengineered or extravagant.

Competitors, although still holding the major market share, were making their profits largely on special items which were job-shop runs, while incurring losses on their standard offerings. There was clearly an opportunity for entry by developing a product policy similar to that of the industry leaders and sustaining the necessary production and distribution system. However, this opportunity would not have been suggested by a conventional market analysis.

In 1959 many firms entered the rapidly growing British refrigerator industry on a small scale. At that time, typical high profitability conditions prevailed in the refrigerator business along with a considerable amount of resale price maintenance. Plants of small scale were common, even among the leaders. Since then, however, imports, over-capacity arising from other new entrants, a break in consumer demand, and a break in price maintenance have brought prices down considerably. This trend eluded forecasters using the standard tools.

In short, management's investigation of foreign business opportunities should go beyond judgments of market growth if it is to recognize the opportunities before they become obvious to the world at large, and is to spot dangerous situations before investments are unwisely committed. Special reliance will have to be placed on a financial, economic, and operational analysis of competing companies as well as on the technical and economic development of the field itself. We call this broader type of evaluation *opportunity analysis.*

PURPOSES AND USES

Opportunity analysis provides data and ways of looking at data that help top management with its most important decisions regarding foreign operations. More specifically, opportunity analysis helps executives to recognize:

1. *The limits within which a firm must operate abroad and plan its foreign strategy*—These quantitative limits are essential guideposts in defining the tightness or looseness of competition, which is the principal criterion of whether there is a margin (a) for the expense of getting a business started and of sustaining the running expenses, and (b) for profits.

To recognize and analyze these limits for any given industry is especially important in international operations for two reasons. First, the limits often differ markedly among countries. Failing to appreciate this, companies often look at Europe or another region "as a whole" and thereby draw false analogies. Secondly, these limits change over time. Management often ignores such changes, particularly when planning foreign ventures under currently prevailing high profitability conditions. In many European industries, tighter competitive conditions appear inevitable; in fact, this change has already occurred for some products and has caught several producers off guard. Opportunity analysis assists in determining *when* and *to what extent* the limits are likely to change.

2. *The means of competition in a foreign country*—Only by analyzing how local participants compete is it possible to determine how a foreign entrant can most successfully participate regardless of whether or not he produces locally or exports. Opportunity analysis ensures identification and evaluation of alternatives and avenues which may lead to success. Even within the same industry, competitive methods vary significantly among countries. Therefore, the recognition of their impact on capacity planning, pricing policy, distribution strategy, financial planning, and so on, is vital before clear entry and participation requirements for a foreign venture can be formulated.

3. *The critical elements of the industry*—We use the phrase "critical elements" to refer to important factors in operations that vary, not only from industry to industry, but also within the same industry from country to country. For example, variations in depreciation policies, working-capital requirements, utilization of debt, capacity building, operating control, inventory control, product policy, and distribution requirements may be significant.

Opportunity analysis is a valuable tool in appraising the foreign ventures of both established companies and newcomers. It helps the established firm reappraise its operations and judge the merits of expansion or diversification opportunities, and it serves the firm seeking foreign entry for the first time, whether by way of a foreign distributor, licensee, manufacturing partner, suitable acquisition, or an entirely new operation. Opportunity analysis aids, not only in judging the value of the products or technology one has to offer (thus possibly increasing one's bargaining power in negotiation with potential foreign associates), but also in judging the competitive standing of potential associates and evaluating the capabilities of foreign competitors. It is, furthermore, of value to security analysts and underwriters in appraising foreign industry conditions as well as the relative strengths of competing participants.

Actually, opportunity analysis would be worth following here in the United States if businessmen were more dependent on formal analysis. At home, however, they can blend investigation, analysis, and judgment with an acute, fine, and, at times, intuitive sense—often the result of many years of experience. Abroad, the American businessman is without this guide; considerable and vigorous analysis, therefore, must take its place.

Coping with Change

Opportunity analysis is most vital in industrialized areas (a) if economic and competitive conditions are expected to change markedly, and (b) if these changes are likely to occur very quickly. Both the amount and the rapidity of economic change magnify the danger of missing opportunities and making unsound investments. This is the situation in European industry today for the following reasons:

Extraordinary growth rates (often as high as 30% per year) enable large-scale production in several consumer and industrial sectors, thus reducing manufacturing costs significantly. Firms lagging behind in market share may find themselves priced out of the market.

High growth rates severely tax a firm's financial ability. Yet if it fails to concentrate its resources on keeping up with the growth requirements of its industry, it may sacrifice its future profitability.

Financial burdens will be augmented by the merging of hitherto separate national markets. Until now, industries in each nation have usually been dominated by that nation's own companies, and the narrowness of national markets has frequently limited participation to very few firms. But in the years ahead economic unification will greatly widen the market size while simultaneously exposing predominantly national companies to competition from their foreign neighbors. The impact will be felt both in production and in marketing. For example—

> The European chemical industry has hitherto constructed its productive capacity in relatively small steps (in contrast to the large capacity additions common in the U.S. chemical industry). A major reason for this difference is that in Europe, with participation in each country limited to a few firms, the risk of forfeiture of opportunity by not engaging in a capacity race has not been too great. This risk, however, will become more acute after the merging of national markets. That it will increase financial burdens, create unused capacity, and aggravate price instability seems all too evident from the U.S. experience.

The task of dislodging national companies from their dominant marketing positions (which is particularly difficult because of structural distribution differences and varying national characteristics) may impose even more severe financial burdens on outsiders. We have already noted that under high growth rates it is a major achievement. This strain will be greatly compounded if a rapid exploration of continental opportunities requires a firm to multiply its position in as many markets as there are nations. In fact, the magnitude of such a task appears to exceed the financial and management resources of a great many European firms.

The need for large-scale plants, the search for low-cost production sites, and the difficulty of breaking into national distribution structures may lead to a considerable number of mergers and acquisitions, thus creating truly continental firms. As a result, companies which continue to limit their activities to their own national market may find themselves at a cost disadvantage. Their local distribution strength will have to be immense to withstand price competition by foreign entrants. However, these high-cost producers may find themselves becoming desirable objects of acquisition by more efficient outside concerns seeking distribution outlets.

Because of differences in product concentration, market sizes, vertical integration, and so on, considerable variations in the costs of materials and parts prevail from country to country. Thus:

> The French washing machine industry pays a higher price for its components than does the Italian washing machine industry, which in turn pays more than the German and British industries do.
>
> British and French refrigerator manufacturers as a whole pay high prices for their compressors, largely because too many of them make their own compressors in small volumes instead of purchasing the very low-cost units made in Denmark and Italy.
>
> The French cathode ray tubes are more expensive than elsewhere because of the lack of price competition among the two big domestic producers, both of whom have important captive television manufacturing outlets.

These differences, which have hitherto been buttressed by national tariffs, are bound to disappear with the progressive reduction of tariff barriers, for purchasers will be able to select the lowest cost suppliers more freely.

The application of technology has been accelerated by international interchange. Thus, a receiving country may go through a technological evolution in five years which took twenty or so years in the country which pioneered in the development. The compression of a long history of U.S. technological change into a short time period in Europe stimulates the already rapid economic growth but also compounds it by creating considerable flux in the product lines of many companies and markets.

Ill-conceived Ventures

The conditions of change just described allow sizable profits to many corporations today. However, at the same time they invite many new entrants. The additions to capacity may create surpluses of major proportions which, coupled with the coming adjustments required to survive in large unified markets, spell a tightening of competitive conditions. Indeed, the danger signals are already apparent in two of Europe's most dynamic industries—plastics and domestic appliances.

Many a participant will be incapable of withstanding the impact of the new competition. Unfortunately, this does not seem to be appreciated. Current profitable conditions hide crucial weaknesses; they invite complacency in that, because ventures are still so profitable, managements are not disposed to take steps to ensure their future. Conventional methods of analysis do not sufficiently focus on the danger signals or spot the real opportunities.

Errors in judgment are aggravated by the currently fashionable trend to establish operations in Europe. Often a businessman sees a market for his product and is impressed by its growth rate. However, he is pressed for time as he hears competition announcing new ventures; and since he feels he cannot afford to wait, he directs that an arrangement be made right away. Perhaps the contemplated operation is not the best one, but he hopes this can be adjusted afterward; the important thing, it seems to him, is to be in the market on time. He typically assesses the profitability of his contemplated operation by making cost analogies with his existing American operation, allowing for European plant scales and labor rates. The difference between his cost forecast and prevailing price levels usually appears to justify the investment.

Our businessman will, to be sure, ask whether this difference can be maintained in years to come. He expects his future costs to decline with increasing scale of operations. As for future prices, a look at the industry price trend seems to provide him with as good a guess as any. By using this highly respectable approach, he concludes, in most cases, that his costs will decline faster than the industry price trend. The resultant ever-expanding profit margin (how common a phenomenon in company forecasts!) augurs very healthy black figures for the years ahead. Such unrealistic optimism is the cause of many ill-conceived foreign ventures.

At the other extreme, and equally dangerous for sound international business planning, some managements are inclined to exaggerate foreign difficulties and dangers, especially by ascribing inordinately severe price declines to the economic integration process. Opportunity analysis, by *identifying* and *quantifying* the crucial competitive conditions abroad, enables the businessman to put a ceiling on unrealistic optimism and a floor under exaggerated pessimism.

OPERATING MARGINS

A vital tool in opportunity analysis is *operating margin analysis.* The "operating margin" in a business is defined for the purposes of the following discussion as the difference between the sales price and the cost of materials purchased. (For example, in January 1960 a French manufacturer paid the equivalent of $66 for materials that went into a refrigerator which he sold for the equivalent of $101. His operating margin thus amounted to $35.) It is the margin within which a firm will have to operate, i.e., manufacture, sell, pay for research, conduct all other corporate activities, and make a profit.

In planning foreign ventures, operating margin analysis enables management to reconcile its basic manufacturing, marketing, and growth plan within the price-materials cost limits imposed by foreign competitive environments. It ensures that a venture meet the basic conditions of viability, that the operation of a business be carried out, and that the prevailing prices be met.

We have found it convenient to express the operating margin as a percentage of the cost of materials purchased. Thus, the operating margin for the French refrigerator just mentioned would be (sales price − materials cost) ÷ materials cost = $35 ÷ $66 = 53%.

Clearly, the operating margin concept is not new. It is often referred to as "value added." It should not be confused with a common accounting usage, according to which operating margin constitutes the difference between sales price and cost of goods sold. This accounting definition has its usefulness in financial statements but is only of limited value for planning management strategy.

Framework of Use

What is novel about our concept is the framework in which we suggest that it be used. Simple in principle, operating margin analysis is complex in its application and interpretation. But in practice we have found the resulting conclusions to be straightforward and revealing.

What makes the approach so useful is that it defines the condition of an *industry* and not just of an individual firm. The margin limits are almost identical for all competing participants in a given country because each sells his products competitively and buys his materials at approximately the same price. Variations in margin within the same product line do not hinder the approach, but invite investigation as to the reasons for the difference. Likewise, different degrees of integration among companies can be reduced to a common denominator by using one of the least-integrated firms as a base and segregating the additional activities of the other participants as separate "businesses."

The operating margin concept is also helpful because it keeps management from placing excessive emphasis on the accounting statements of established firms. Accounting principles leave companies great flexibility, especially in allocating expenses, even in the United States, thus making "true" profit a rather elastic notion. The correct profit figure becomes even more elusive in foreign countries with their different accounting practices, tax laws, disclosure regulations, and so on.

In short, the operating margin as we conceive it is an essential and highly exact element in corporate planning. It is highly exact because its two base points always remain unobscured and untouched by either accounting convention or company practices. Both the selling price and the cost of materials purchased can be determined objectively. In most cases they are common knowledge. If not, they can be readily determined either through trade channels or with the help of an engineer familiar with the product requirements.

Treatment of Costs

The operating margin becomes particularly useful when its two totally different components, involuntary costs and discretionary expenses, are analyzed.

Involuntary expenses arise from the nature of the firm's business, its scale of manufacturing, the types of processes used, and the degree of product specialization or standardization that has been achieved. They consist mainly of minimum manufacturing costs; they cannot be eliminated unless a firm cuts production. Therefore, they have to be incurred by everyone in the industry. Their level can be recognized by an engineer who is experienced in the product line and manufacturing processes. He also can develop, through careful product appraisal, a schedule of costs for various volumes of production and various manufacturing methods. Thus, relative changes in involuntary costs resulting from volume increases can be predicted with reasonable accuracy.

While involuntary expenses normally constitute the difference between cost of goods sold and cost of materials purchased, there are exceptions. For example:

> Tooling expenses, though usually included in the cost of goods sold, are really discretionary expenses.
>
> Manufacturing costs which are not absolutely necessary but which may add desirable features to the product line are also discretionary expenses, even though included by accountants in the costs of goods sold.

Discretionary expenses allow a foreign venture to fulfill its marketing and development objectives. Within the framework of competitive conditions, a firm has a certain latitude in determining which and how many discretionary expenses it wants to incur. Corporate strategies among firms vary chiefly because managements put their discretionary money to different uses. One firm may wish to make large profits for distribution to the stockholders or for retention to finance further expansion or diversification. Another firm may direct discretionary expenses toward product development, upgrading of quality, and tooling arising from frequent model changes, or it may incur discretionary expenses to strengthen its marketing position by establishing distribution outlets, creating brand loyalty, improving service to customers, and so forth. Still another firm may surrender discretionary money to reduce its prices.

Discretionary expenses are the lifeblood of a business. They often qualify as true economic investments and should be considered as such even though they are entered into accounting statements as expenses and not as assets. In terms of a company's long-term competitive strength, money invested in building up the distribution position or in creating product differentiation may be no less important than money invested in fixed plant and machinery. During periods of rapid growth, management often emphasizes increases in productive capacity while ignoring discretionary expenses of an investment nature. With the maturity of the industry, however, the emphasis usually shifts from the "capacity to make" to the "ability to sell," thus penalizing companies which in earlier years ignored discretionary expenses for marketing.

Because discretionary expenses of an investment nature in a firm's income statement (in contrast to fixed-asset investment) reduce current profits substantially, a careful analysis of these costs is needed if low profits (or even accounting losses) in growth industries are to be interpreted correctly.

Actually, profits are considered to be part of a firm's discretionary area in our analysis. This is because profit levels are so highly dependent on the types and amounts of other discretionary costs which management needs or wants to incur. In fact, retained profits to be used for further expansion are quite similar to discretionary expenses of an investment nature. On the other hand, rigid profit levels imposed by the need to maintain or increase dividends may reduce other discretionary uses of the money, possibly with perilous consequences.

APPRAISING COMPETITION

Ordinarily, management wants to be sure that a new venture will generate adequate resources for growth and be able to sustain itself for a period of years. The enterprise must, therefore, be able to live within the prices imposed by competition and still generate a sufficiently wide operating margin to achieve growth. For this reason, in determining entry and participation requirements of a foreign venture it is vital to analyze its position relative to the industry leaders. By considering the involuntary costs and discretionary expenses of the leaders, management can predict future price trends. Turning then to the new venture, it can assess its relative capacity to compete and estimate its ability to pay for the necessary discretionary expenses of an investment nature that will be needed to achieve a viable position in the industry.

Analysis of involuntary and discretionary expenses thus enables a firm to plan for possible contingencies by estimating the extent to which industry leaders may be able to lower prices. These reductions will primarily hinge on (a) the lowering of their involuntary costs; and (b), as an industry moves to maturity, the extent to which achievement of product and marketing objectives allows the leaders to lower their discretionary expenses. Even though industry leaders will not in all cases exploit these advantages fully, it is necessary in planning a foreign venture to determine whether it will be able to survive under the most adverse eventuality.

Lowering Involuntary Costs

In a dynamic industry, characteristic of so many in Europe today, volume is the prime determinant of the operating margin. Larger scales of production reduce involuntary costs, enabling industry leaders to lower prices. Here is a case in point:

> In France, the largest firms in the refrigerator industry make 150,000 units a year and operate within a margin of 50%, while in Germany the leading manufacturers have achieved a volume of 400,000 units per year and are able to operate more profitably within a margin of only about 35%. A manufacturer in Germany making only 150,000 refrigerators a year would clearly be the victim of a price-cost squeeze; indeed, precisely this condition led to the recent withdrawal of a major German electrical manufacturer and of one of the largest U.S. firms.

The extent as well as the timing of price reductions can be fairly accurately predicted by analyzing the leader's involuntary costs and by establishing a schedule of his costs for various increases in volume that can be anticipated with market growth. Price declines will often depend not only on increases in the scale of manufacture of a single product, but also on increased production volumes of similar products. In such cases an appraisal should encompass those products as well as the one of main concern.

When these assessments of future price declines, and hence of lower operating margins, are in hand, management is likely to have some interesting questions of strategy to consider. For one thing, a manufacturer contemplating entry into a business in a less mature stage of development must anticipate the conditions under which he could be the victim of a price-cost squeeze. This contingency will occur if prices drop faster than a company's ability to lower costs, which could happen if the industry leaders grow faster than anyone else. Should a price-cost squeeze develop, management may have to incur losses and match the price reductions in order to maintain its relative market share. Otherwise, it may not achieve sales levels which justify increasing its plant scale, to the point where this would ultimately bring the venture's costs in line with the costs of industry leaders.

If no such sacrifice is made, the decline in sales volume will result in even higher involuntary costs. These in turn will reduce the margin available for discretionary expenses and will push management into a vicious circle of still further concessions in the market. The venture will soon have to surrender its growth objectives. Next it will have to abandon its marketing objectives—and from that point on the downward cycle will be repeated, culminating in the loss of the business.

It is therefore essential to establish entry goals, such as market-share objectives, and to decide what production and sales efforts are necessary to achieve them. This will help to ensure that the venture will generate adequate resources at least to sustain its position relative to the industry leaders.

Cuts in Discretionary Expenses

During rapid growth periods, companies are likely to make substantial discretionary expenses of an investment nature—e.g., outlays to establish the product, to strengthen distribution, and to finance expansion. As the growth slackens or as objectives are achieved, however, fewer discretionary expenses of this type will be required, thus freeing the money for price reductions. The magnitude of this drop can also be predicted through operating margin analysis, although it is more difficult to foresee its timing.

High discretionary margins are also vulnerable when competitors lower their profit margins or undertake less expensive marketing methods and resort to price cutting in order to gain a larger market share. Analysis of discretionary expenses will reveal the magnitude of such potential price reductions.

During periods of substantial excess capacity, the temptation may develop to make sales so long as this will cover out-of-pocket costs, resulting in a major price break. Such conditions, however, cannot last indefinitely. As demand catches up with capacity, prices will usually return to a level at which the most efficient industry leaders can still make a reasonable return on their investment.

Conditions of Entry

Often overlooked is the fact that a high rate of growth does not necessarily make for profitable business opportunities. Indeed, dramatic foreign growth rates have often obscured the dangers of low profitability and the difficulty of entry. What is more, even conditions of high profitability may obscure formidable obstacles to foreign entry.

A look at the operating margin provides a first indication. A company experienced in its industry, and thus knowing how much it requires to manufacture, pay for research, sell, and so forth, is able to judge fairly easily whether the operating margin in a foreign industry is either "narrow" or "wide." Such an evaluation is often facilitated—as will be explained later in this article—by using an analytical grid which compares operating margins of the same industry in different countries.

A wide operating margin indicates that a new venture can incur high levels of involuntary and discretionary costs. As would be expected, a margin tends to be wide when:

> Even the industry leaders have a comparatively low scale of output.
>
> The industry leaders have high discretionary expenses or cash requirements for marketing, product development, construction of new capacity, or diversification programs.
>
> There is insufficient competition.
>
> The industry leaders have priced their products to maximize their profits even though this induces smaller competitors to use minor price reductions as a competitive weapon in furthering sales.
>
> The leaders are inefficient manufacturers or marketers.

Narrow operating margins, on the other hand, reduce a company's flexibility and are significant hurdles for foreign entry, regardless of whether "tight" or "loose" competitive conditions prevail. A tight industry will be characterized by relatively low profits for the industry leader, while loose competitive conditions permit satisfactory profits to both leaders and followers. It is important to recognize, however, that both loose and tight conditions are possible under a wide as well as under a narrow operating margin.

Combinations of Conditions

1. A *narrow* operating margin in an industry usually results in *tight* conditions, allowing only few discretionary expenses (including profits) after involuntary costs have been incurred. To illustrate:

> The German refrigerator industry has margins only 30% to 40% above materials costs. Two giant firms are dominating the field. The product lines of both firms consist of stripped-down models. Manufacturers engage in little merchandising, maintain minimal sales forces,

offer only limited service, and allow low distribution discounts based on the quantity shipped. The overriding emphasis is on price, effectively forestalling entry by newcomers and threatening the profitability of small followers.

2. Narrow operating margins also permit loose competitive conditions. For instance:

The German radio and television industry operated in 1959 within a narrow operating margin, but because of plants of large scale most participants experienced generous profits. In spite of this high profitability, the narrow margin imposed formidable entry goals for a new venture in terms of production volume and of market-share objectives. Last year, the industry moved to tight competitive conditions as participants used part of their discretionary profit money to cut prices.

3. An industry enjoying a *wide* operating margin may nevertheless experience fierce competition, resulting in *tight* conditions. Given the levels of involuntary costs as well as the discretionary expenses required to compete effectively, profitability may be low. To illustrate again:

The French refrigerator industry is, in spite of its higher operating margin, almost as competitive as its German counterpart. The difference in margin is almost entirely absorbed by higher involuntary costs (due to smaller plant scales) and higher discretionary expenses (in view of limited distribution channels). One large firm selling stripped-down products at a low price (much as German firms are doing) is competing with other firms selling better made models at a premium through their own captive distribution channels and engaging heavily in retail promotions.

4. On the other hand, in Europe there are still many industries with *wide* operating margins and loose competitive conditions—what might be called immature industries—in which entry is not only relatively easy to achieve but may also prove highly profitable. However, timing is most important because an immature, loose industry may rapidly move to highly competitive, tight conditions. For example:

In 1960 the washing machine industry in both Britain and Germany experienced wide operating margins under loose competitive conditions. Each market was dominated by one large company which had achieved maximum economies of scale in production. However, in both cases the leading company was not seriously challenged; and, therefore, it was able to maintain relatively high price levels. Because of low involuntary costs the leader in each market clearly was able to retaliate quickly and effectively against challengers, thus changing the competitive conditions from loose to tight.

In sum, experience shows that opportunities and difficulties in *entering* a foreign industry are more a function of the magnitude of the operating margin than of the profitability of industry members. A wide operating margin can provide a better opportunity for entry than a narrow operating margin *whether the industry leaders are profitable or not*. For instance, the French refrigerator industry, despite its lack of profitability, probably provided an easier entry opportunity than did the German television industry.

On the other hand, a profitable industry with narrow operating margins may be very difficult to enter.

Choosing a Battleground

The most important condition of entry is that the company's initial marketing objectives create discretionary margins which are large enough to sustain its growth objectives. Recognizing the importance of maintaining the venture's position relative to industry leaders, management may see that it is not sufficient merely to match their discretionary expenses; it may be necessary to exceed the other firms' expenses substantially. For example, if there is a shortage of distribution channels, the capture of which is critical to achieve success, management may have to spend more than competitors on the product lines, services, or promotion needed to secure these channels.

However, the wisest strategy may be to undertake efforts that do *not* duplicate the programs of industry leaders. The chances to achieve success are often enhanced if management selects its own battleground instead of imitating what the established firms are doing. If so, the important thing still is to make sure that the new approach is consistent with the discretionary margin it will provide.

One area where a new venture may have considerably more flexibility than industry leaders is pricing. Often, industry leaders wish to maximize their profits by holding the line on prices. This will often be done at a price level that gives considerable discretion even to followers with higher involuntary costs. As a result they can use small price decreases as a competitive weapon to increase their market share and thereby their total profits. In the end, their constant nibbling at the leader's position results in a loss of his market share. For example:

> In 1960, competitive conditions in the German and the British washing machine industries were very loose largely because each field was dominated by one firm which was not seriously challenged and because washing machines, unlike refrigerators, justified considerable discretionary expenditures in service, quality manufacture, and demonstration at retail. Instead of matching the leader's heavy discretionary marketing expenses, an entrant might have been able to use price reductions effectively.

Emphasis on price under conditions like these can save many discretionary expenses which, if incurred, would have little impact anyway. To illustrate again:

> A German subsidiary determined its advertising budget by using the same percentage of sales as its U.S. parent. The subsidiary spent the budget in approximately the same way. Indeed, its whole marketing approach was a mirror of the U.S. parent's program. In the United States, the parent company was one of the leaders in its industry and was, therefore, reluctant to use price concessions. The subsidiary was equally reluctant to use pricing and relied almost exclusively on advertising, even though its market share was only 5% compared with 45%

for the German industry leader. It is hardly surprising that top company executives did not consider the subsidiary's operation entirely successful.

Analysis of the discretionary expense span of industry leaders will also show if a new venture can maintain or improve its relative position by incurring fewer discretionary costs. For example, it is not unusual to see leaders dissipate their resources through unwise diversification, excessive component manufacture, and so forth. These wastes need not be duplicated. Also, a venture may be able to save on discretionary expenses if it is a subsidiary. It may be able to cut down on such items as research and development costs, tooling costs, and design and engineering expenses if the parent corporation has done the needed work in these areas.

CRITICAL CONDITIONS

While fitting the manufacturing, marketing, and growth plan of a business in the limits established by the competitive environment is important, it is not the only task that demands top-management attention. A foreign venture may be unsuccessful if other critical elements are not given equal consideration. We refer to a series of conditions that not only differ markedly among industries, as is well known, but also vary greatly within the same industry from country to country. At the outset of a foreign venture, therefore, it is imperative that management (1) recognize these essential industry conditions and (2) analyze the relevant differences between the United States and the host country. Failure to do so may lead to incorrect assumptions as to a venture's future discretionary margin, resulting in turn in an insecure "plan" or design that is often beyond correction later on by managers in trouble spots. Five industry conditions deserve particular attention.

Impact of Financial Charges

Financial conditions often vary remarkably among countries because of major differences in (1) depreciation policy, (2) working-capital requirements, and (3) utilization of debt leverage.

A recent study provides a case in point. We observed that three companies, one in the United States, one in France, and the other in Germany, were operating under almost identical conditions in the same growth industry. Even though all three were generating approximately the same cash per dollar of gross plant, they were earning 13%, 23%, and 35% respectively on their equity investment. The following points are especially noteworthy:

> In France, and particularly in Germany, rapid depreciation provisions provide growth industries with sizable tax-free funds for reinvestment.
>
> In Germany, product shortages enable manufacturers to operate with almost no finished-goods inventories, thus cutting down the working-capital charges.

In France, banks lend as much on reputation as on financial analysis, resulting in considerably higher debt-equity ratios than banks would permit in the United States. Consequently, companies in France with a high capital turnover and a good "reputation" benefit from a degree of leverage which is unusual by our standards in the United States.

The utilization of debt leverage hinges partly on the availability of investment opportunities, which in turn depends on the relative maturity of an industry. For example:

In the United States during the early 1950's, the cash generated per dollar of gross investment was significantly higher for producers of finished chemicals than for the basic chemical companies. Nevertheless, companies in both ends of the chemical business were earning approximately the same return on their equity, because basic chemical companies were able to offset their disadvantage through greater debt leverage.

Recently, the basic producers have experienced a decrease in profitability. However, this is caused less by a decrease in the cash generated per dollar of gross investment than by the fact that the industry's financial resources available for investment have increased faster than have the available investment opportunities, which in turn has reduced the need for debt and thus cut down the use of leverage.

Burden of Overcapacity

Differences in requirements as to when and how much capacity has to be constructed are vital. To illustrate, compare the household appliance industry with the chemical industry:

In the household appliance industry, the ratio of sales to gross plant investment is very high, while profit margins are rather low. The latter element makes low costs imperative, while the high capital turnover requires tight control of capital. The vital implication is that one has to be very careful about building too much in excess of current demand; large plants are vital to mass-production economies, but if constructed too far ahead of the time that demand materializes, the resulting drain on profits can be disastrous.

In spite of these basic truths, several household appliance companies in Europe have succumbed to the temptation of building—far in excess of their market share—huge modern plants which they felt were vital in their type of mass-production industry. U.S. companies in particular—influenced, perhaps, by the fact that overcapacity is common at home—seem to have lost sight of the heavy burden which surplus capacity imposes if competitors are operating at near capacity and setting their prices on that basis. Their large, not fully utilized, plants in Europe have constituted a severe drain on profits and have become especially burdensome when financed by bank debts.

The profitability conditions of the chemical industry are very different. The emphasis is on process economies and chemical routes with ancillary problems of location, raw materials supply, plant scale, and outlets to the market for several coproducts. New processes, based perhaps on new materials and having different scale economies, may change the competitive position of a particular project markedly, as may new developments in the market. The industry thus experiences a high degree of flux and change.

With most chemicals requiring a large investment in plant for each sales dollar, high profit margins are necessary to justify the investment. Usually, price levels decline with time, while costs mostly depend on scale of operations. Hence, there is a considerable premium on "getting in early" on a new development when profits are large. Early starters, if they succeed in maintaining their initial market position in subsequent periods of maturity for the field, will also be enjoying the cost advantages of large plant scale supported by market leadership. Thus, "thinking early" and "thinking big" are both necessary ingredients in a successful chemical venture.

Specialization and Concentration

Another critical factor to watch is the need for specialization and concentration rather than diversification. Not always are the former important, but in industries where they are crucial, a great deal may hinge on top management's sensitivity to them. As illustrations we can again look at the chemical and household appliance industries:

> Thinking big in the chemical industry requires a certain concentration of investment funds. Concentration, however, necessitates a high degree of confidence. Lack of sufficient confidence may lead to several small projects to hedge against the failure of any one project. This is undesirable because, while hedging in small ventures to spread risks may ensure survival, it does so only at a subsistence level; it is the bold large-scale operation that makes the money in this industry.
>
> At the same time, specialization and concentration are complicated by what might be called *structural* requirements. Entry usually is not possible without the satisfaction of a wide range of such conditions as having a low-cost and secure source of raw materials and marketing or disposition arrangements for the several coproducts which are simultaneously manufactured in a variety of chemical processes. Also, a successful marketing program may require several complementary products, thus further extending the scope of a chemical operation abroad. It is inability to satisfy these structural requirements completely which inhibits foreign entry by chemical companies in a major way. Thus, even large American chemical firms have experienced major difficulties in entering the European market.
>
> Specialization in the household appliance business is crucial for different reasons. Because of its narrow margin, price and cost control must be very tight, with the result that top management must place a great deal of reliance on the ability of the manager in immediate charge of operations. However, price concessions will always be required to move inventories that inevitably pile up because even the best forecasting cannot fully anticipate all variations in consumer demand. Hence, considerable attention must be given to systems which keep inventories low as well as to the skill of merchandising. The latter, in fact, can be de-

fined in the appliance industry as the ability to move inventories with the minimum concession in price.

Therefore, the type of management necessary is one that combines promotional skill with a fine sense of control. Close familiarity with the appliance business has shown that management will work best when both these qualities can be found in one man. And because so much sensitivity is required in the merchandising job, it is best performed when only one major product is handled. Consequently, there are convincing arguments for specialization in the appliance business.

Product Policy

Different income levels in foreign countries often demand different product lines from those offered in the United States.[1] Nevertheless, the major European operations of some U.S. firms are exclusively devoted to manufacturing the U.S. product. Because of size, versatility, quality, or price, American-type products usually occupy a place only at the top of the effective European product line. With most of Europe's current market growth occurring not in these products but in the *basic* models, the result is that the firms mentioned are losing their market shares. This leads to under-capacity operations of plants that are already relatively small, thereby increasing costs. Indeed, the U.S.-type products can usually be supplied more economically from American plants than from European sources.

Distribution Requirements

As was mentioned earlier, distribution can be one of the critical obstacles to successful entry into international business. It is therefore vital to analyze the particular distribution requirements for an industry as well as the prevailing conditions in the foreign country. Differences among countries can be most significant, requiring great flexibility and varying policies on the part of international businesses. *Even in the same industry* the distribution setup can favor the entrant in one country, while constituting a major hurdle for him in another country. To illustrate:

> In the German consumer-goods industries, wholesalers are by tradition nonexclusive, making it difficult for leading manufacturers to control distribution. The alternative, direct selling, may increase costs more than prices can support. Hence, an opportunity exists for the smaller manufacturer to an extent precluded in countries where there are distribution bottlenecks. However, the situation puts greater emphasis on other marketing elements, such as price and reputation. For instance, it may increase the importance of advertising. This provides an opportunity for the importer who can advertise, who can be expected to meet prices, but who usually has difficulty in controlling distribution in a foreign country.
>
> In France, the actual shortage of distribution (a large city such as Lyons has only two really capable appliance wholesalers) puts an ex-

[1] See Raphael Hodgson and Michael Michaelis, "Planning for Profits in World Business," *Harvard Business Review* (November-December 1960), p. 135.

traordinary burden on newcomers in the industry. They normally must sell direct, and in France—with its widely dispersed population—this is a very expensive proposition. Also, distributors who are available insist on a full line of white goods (i.e., refrigerators and washing machines), a condition which can tempt manufacturers into a full-line operation that (as we have indicated) is difficult to manage.

In Britain, distribution is similar to what it is in the United States with a relatively large number of exclusive wholesalers. Some manufacturers have begun to sell direct, a condition which has left their former wholesalers available to importers who wish to use them.

INTERNATIONAL COMPARISONS

By comparing the operating margins of companies in different countries, management can easily recognize the opportunities for entry. The question that executives may face now is: Can the policies and practices which permit a profitable operation at home under a lower operating margin also prove successful abroad? As our earlier discussion of industry conditions has shown, there are inherent dangers in transferring the reasoning that works in an industry from one country to another. Operating margin analysis checks false analogies by providing a useful framework for evaluating them. For example:

> Most electrical components in Europe are sold at a price several times the cost of materials, compared with an operating margin of only 80% in the United States. This points to sizable opportunities. But before any action can be taken, it is necessary to ask why operating margins are so much larger in Europe, and whether it is appropriate to analogize American involuntary and discretionary costs in determining how a U.S. entrant should behave in this industry in Europe.
>
> *Involuntary* costs appear excessively high in Europe because of lack of standardization and because a large number of companies have relatively small scales of manufacture. On the basis of American experience, it would appear desirable to standardize the product line around a few basic types, impose it on the industry at a low price, manufacture in great quantities, and "shake the business down." One manufacturer is doing precisely this. At present, this firm cannot meet demand; delivery times are up to 15 months! It has become an outstandingly profitable operation and has not yet been seriously challenged.
>
> In the case of *discretionary* expenses, however, an analogy with U.S. experience does not appear relevant. For instance, discretionary expenses in one U.S. electronic systems industry have become truly defensive; it has become a competitive necessity here to spend between 15% and 20% of sales in providing custom-tailored systems engineering to industrial customers. Without this provision, a company's market share would suffer seriously. In Europe, on the other hand, not nearly as much systems work is required. Also, current growth requirements lead to long deliveries, resulting in minimal sales expenses or direct sales of components to large users.

Thus, while U.S. experience in the involuntary cost area appears to be a promising guide, the opposite is true in the case of discretionary expenses.

Threats & Opportunities

International comparisons of operating margins are helpful in still another way. Foreign import threats or export opportunities can be spotted by comparing the domestic operating margin in a given country with importers' operating margins. The operating margin of an importer indicates the degree by which the selling price in the importing country less import duties and freight exceeds the materials cost in the exporting country. It thus expresses for the firm selling abroad the margin within which both the domestic manufacturing and the foreign sales effort must be conducted.

By calculating the operating margin for various exporting nations and using the domestic operating margins, management can construct a grid of opportunity which compares the foreign opportunity with that at home. An example is shown in Table 1. Such a grid also shows the discretionary cash available for any volume of goods to be moved abroad.

TABLE 1

RELATIVE OPERATING MARGINS OF INTRA-EUROPEAN SALES OF 150-LITRE REFRIGERATORS, 1959-1960

(Margins existing in each country are circled)

EXPORTING COUNTRY (DOMESTIC SALES ↘)	IMPORTING COUNTRY France	Germany	Italy	Britain
France	(50) circled	8	(6)	56
Germany	61	(40) circled	6	68
Italy	81	37	(45) circled	81
Britain	47	10	(2½)	(75) circled

Note: The operating margin is calculated as follows: (1) from the sales price in the country of destination subtract (a) the tariffs, taxes, and freight costs to ship the goods there, and (b) the materials cost in the country of origin; (2) divide the figure thus obtained by the materials cost in the country of origin. (Figures in parentheses indicate negative margins.)

Knowing its position relative to that of foreign competitors, a firm can decide whether and how to enter international markets. This analysis will take into account both the industry conditions and the nature of competition in the foreign country (which implies analyzing the discretionary expenses of the established firms). To illustrate the total approach:

> The opportunity grid in Table 1 shows that in 1959-1960 a German refrigerator manufacturer could expect a 61% and 68% operating margin in France and Britain respectively, compared with 40% in his own market. However, analysis of industry conditions as well as discretionary expenses in France and Britain during that period showed significant

differences. In view of France's acute shortage of distribution, it was necessary to spend a significant portion of one's discretionary money on distribution, especially on direct selling. This aspect, combined with lower plant scales, required higher margins in France than in Germany, while still making for very low profits. In Britain, on the other hand, distribution was less tight and, in spite of high involuntary costs, the industry was enjoying high profits.

As a result, even though German producers could count on almost equal operating margins in both France and Britain, entry into the British market was more profitable and could be more easily achieved. In Britain, price reductions alone proved highly effective; while in France, the situation would also have required a distribution investment (e.g., a full product line or company-sponsored outlets).

Check Points

In evaluating foreign opportunities, three elements are often of crucial importance: *product line, pricing,* and *distribution:*

1. In the preceding example, German refrigerator manufacturers had little difficulty of a *product-line* nature because their product was very similar to British refrigerators. Also, commodities such as chemicals, aluminum, steel, paper, or glass are fairly identical among countries, thus not only saving trouble for the producer but also enabling buyers to switch more easily to foreign sources of supply. However, in many instances product lines will differ in composition from country to country, sometimes requiring expensive adjustments. The cost of these adjustments should be taken into account in drawing up the opportunity grid.

2. Opportunity grids for commodities normally show wide operating margins because a significant portion of a firm's discretionary money is required to meet fixed plant costs. In commodities, as a result, the foreign entrant enjoys wide discretion, giving him greater *pricing* flexibility than that enjoyed by an exporter of differentiated products with their lower operating margins. In short, price cutting is most likely to be effective where there is a wide operating margin, a minimum of product differentiation, and a marked tendency on the part of customers to shop around for low-price suppliers.

3. The *distribution* bottleneck is normally less critical for commodities than it is for differentiated products. Although a domestic commodity manufacturer may have established a firm hold on local distribution, it does not take much foreign competition, even through irregular channels, to put severe strains on the local pricing structure. On the other hand, the earlier examples from the household appliance industry show how distribution may constitute a serious hurdle to the exporter of differentiated products.

In view of these three elements, the level of tariffs that will inhibit trade must be considerably higher for commodities than for differentiated products such as appliances; the former are more sensitive to changes at the top of the "wall" than the latter are. Therefore, the impact of economic integration in Europe with its gradual abolition of tariff levels will most probably be felt more quickly and more strongly by commodity producers. This may force them to become continental in scope more rapidly than manufacturers of appliances and other differentiated products.

CONCLUSION

Opportunity analysis imposes a strong discipline on business planning by ensuring that both the immediate and the ultimate goals of management are consistent with the industry's current and future competitive conditions. Such goals, in turn, can be translated into clear entry and participation requirements for a foreign venture. These requirements have to be consistent with the firm's capabilities and willingness to commit the necessary resources. It is the reconciliation of these interrelated objectives which makes the application of operating margins so useful. For example:

> Suppose that a venture has a 50% operating margin and that management's target is a volume of X dollars. Estimating the involuntary costs at this volume plus the discretionary expenses required to achieve it, executives can determine whether the needed outlays can be covered by the 50% margin while leaving an adequate profit. If not, either the venture should be abandoned or the sales objectives must be raised. Perhaps a larger marketing investment would produce sales levels of a magnitude large enough to lower involuntary costs to the point where an adequate profit could be made within the 50% operating margin.

Opportunity analysis enables management to cut through the confusion of current fluctuations and erratic circumstances to the conditions of ultimate success. It will not exaggerate these conditions nor lead to the extraordinary pessimism that, say, a run on prices may otherwise induce. Also, it helps executives to foresee any important differences between the venture under their consideration and the industry leaders'. The very discipline of this exercise may reveal errors in the initial project—for example, by demonstrating that instead of spreading resources over several projects it might be better to concentrate on one, or that the contemplated program is too large for the resources a company is able or willing to commit. Thus, opportunity analysis leads to consistency in planning in terms of:

> The immediate goals of a venture.
>
> The ultimate goals of a venture.
>
> The parent company's capabilities.

Let us consider each of these elements in turn.

Immediate Goals

In terms of the discretionary margin, a project should be designed to avoid starting at too great a disadvantage with direct competitors. Thus, the test of viability of a new venture will be whether it starts in a sufficiently advanced form to assure progress as well as profits, considering the leaders' position, their probable rate of growth, and the corresponding decline of their involuntary costs. Consequently, if competition in the field chosen is already established at a certain scale and cost level, supported by certain distribution outlets and promotional resources, it is absurd to try to enter the business with a higher cost and a smaller distribution investment.

These statements may seem evident enough, but some highly sophisticated American companies have recently undertaken ventures in Europe that are laboring precisely under this type of disadvantage—all the result of an inadequate initial plan. If it is the scale of a chemical plant or the type of process that is at fault, the error cannot be rectified without a major new investment. If a consumer products business ignores a virtual distribution monopoly of its competitors, it cannot rectify the situation without a major investment in direct distribution. Recognition of these additional investment requirements at the outset might have changed management's thinking about the initial venture.

Selection of immediate goals should be based on recognition of the rate of growth of the market, and the objective should be at least to maintain the firm's relative position with the leader's. The route to this objective may lie either in direct competition with industry leaders or in avoiding the field of direct competition altogether. There is no better way to recognize the costs of various strategies than to catalogue the marketing mix of every competitor and to determine, by analysis of discretionary expenses, what each method costs and what sales volume is supporting it. With these data should be included the "defensive" costs of many types of business—e.g., the very high systems expense that is characteristic of the American process control industry, or the high level of research expenditure imposed on the pharmaceutical industry by rapid product obsolescence and product insecurity.

An analysis of this type can be invaluable in helping management to recognize:

1. The margins that must be provided for various channels of distribution, which in turn helps with the selection of those channels that would be within a venture's resources and objectives.

2. The cost of developing direct distribution, if satisfactory distribution is no longer available, or of challenging manufacturers in existing channels.

3. The size of the service organization and the level of promotional effort (e.g., advertising expense and point-of-sale effort) required to sustain a business.

4. Whether complementary product lines are necessary to sustain the distribution system and, if so, what the cost of purchasing or manufacturing such lines is.

5. The needs for new capacity and product-development programs to maintain a profitable position.

6. The discretionary savings that might be achieved if different competitive methods are chosen, thus making a contribution to profit or providing a price wedge.

All this means that management can define the entry and participation requirements which will prove effective under given conditions. For example:

> If the competitive route requires control of distribution, the system created for that purpose must be maintained through tight inventory policies and satisfactory discounts. Or complementary product lines may have to be carried. It may also be necessary to maintain an adequate market share even though this may involve a declining price policy.
>
> If the competitive route is through price competition, such tactics as frequent model changes or large promotional campaigns may have to be dropped. More attention will have to be paid to the lowest cost distribution through such outlets as mail order or discount houses. It will also be imperative to have an efficient manufacturing plant.
>
> If product features are a vital selling argument, it will be necessary to back them up with outlays of the discretionary type, e.g., advertising and demonstration.
>
> If manufacturing opportunities in a standardized line of products are going to be exploited in an unstandardized market, initial promotion and distribution channels should be consistent with manufacturing plans.
>
> If a small venture is contemplated, management should not select a market or a product that is big but a segment that is within its concentrated capabilities and that can be served independently. A segment of this size may be a source of dissipation or an unimportant sideline for the bigger firms.
>
> If only a small venture with a relatively poor discretionary margin is possible, then management should abandon the project unless it can offset the disadvantage with some special advantage such as U.S. technology, depreciated tooling, or a more complete product line supplied partially by U.S. imports.

Ultimate Conditions

In almost every product field comes a time of maturity. This period is not necessarily an unprofitable one. Market leaders are usually able to stay profitable, as evidenced by the experience of many American businesses. Nevertheless, these periods can be characterized as highly competitive, with operating margins very low because of high volumes of production by the leaders, which enables them to enforce severe price pressures to reduce participation in the industry. The leaders of the German refrigerator and the British television industries have pursued such a program to the extent that only two profitable and dominant manufacturers remain in each field.

The foregoing analysis of operating margins and involuntary and discretionary costs provides some yardsticks of the ultimate conditions within which a venture may be required to operate. For example:

> In the case of the refrigerator industry in Europe, discussed earlier, we doubt whether in the long run operating margins can get much

> below 35% despite the volume levels or degree of competition that may ensue. This is the margin which would provide a satisfactory investment return to a manufacturer who has achieved his distribution objectives and who is manufacturing at a scale of about 300,000 units a year. A participant who achieves this level of production and marketing and who does not dissipate his management talent should have a permanently profitable condition. Unless management is prepared to operate under ground rules such as these, it would be unwise to enter this business.

The implications of such an analysis depend completely on management objectives. For example, a company might decide not to stay in a business for a long period but enter only for early profits and sell out before competition gets tough. Some chemical ventures are launched on this basis. With innovation providing an early lead, prices are set to maximize profits regardless of the competition that is invited. A rapid payback makes the operation worthwhile, regardless of the ultimate consequences.

Extent of Commitment

A foreign venture's goals and the resulting entry and participation requirements must also be consistent with the parent company's capabilities, resources, and willingness. It is perhaps the *unwillingness* to commit physical resources and management rather than the *incapability* to do so that creates the real deficiency of so many foreign ventures. Easy profits in an immature, loose industry entice companies to risk the luxury of limited operations. At times, in fact, the limited foreign operations of American firms appear to be the consequence of attempts by operational managers to gamble with time in order to have at least some foreign program; if they were to place heavy demands on corporate purse strings, they might kill the contemplated foreign program altogether. Perhaps the weakness of several American foreign operations may be traced to this problem more than to any other.

If foreign operations are limited at first in order to conserve corporate funds, is the company willing to pitch in with more capital later on during the "shakedown"? It requires an unusually determined and confident management to increase investments in a losing business in order to secure a competitive position. Therefore, if a firm is incapable or unwilling to commit sufficient resources, it may be preferable to forget about a limited operation in a large field. On the other hand, it *may* still be profitable to select a *narrow* field in which a full-scale operation can be conducted. Companies with limited resources might, therefore, do well to reverse the usual process of analysis. Instead of choosing the field first and the cost of entry afterward, they might first determine the cost of entry they are willing to pay and then select projects accordingly. Rather than match the firm to the field, in other words, it would be better to match the field to the firm.

In this endeavor opportunity analysis once again becomes a valuable tool for decision makers by pointing up the possibilities of using resources in the most economical way. Four of these possibilities stand out and, because of their pertinence to management's final decision, make a fitting close to our discussion—

1. *Better timing*—Even though the risks of a venture may be greater, an early start makes it much easier to achieve a viable position by building up quickly to a competitive scale of manufacture or to an adequate market share. Furthermore, poor starts can be rescued more easily.

This possibility of reducing costs is important in Europe today because there are many areas of considerable immaturity there comprising industries that, in the United States, rank high in maturity. For instance, a large part of the electrical manufacturing industry in Europe still enjoys a great deal of looseness, lack of production standardization, and continuing market growth.

2. *Acquisition*—This is often a very inexpensive method of entry into mature businesses, especially when an unprofitable firm is acquired which fills top management's structural objectives either as a source of supply or as a means of distribution. (The latter is particularly important during the maturity of a field, when a slackening rate of growth makes entry difficult for outsiders.)

3. *Specialization*—This approach enables a company to make limited resources go further and achieve a strong relative position in the field in which it concentrates, without compromising its product line or distribution requirements.

4. *Exploitation of special skills*—This kind of effort may significantly reduce the demands on a foreign venture, especially in relation to its competitors. For instance, research and technical know-how developed in the United States may give the venture an obvious edge in competing for sales. Similar results may be achieved by supplying parts of the product line or certain components from the United States, by using idle or obsolete machinery and tooling from American plants, by utilizing the parent corporation's design and engineering staffs, and so forth. Such backing by the parent company may also enable a significant reduction of a foreign venture's discretionary expenses.

15

NEW PATTERNS FOR OVERSEAS OPERATIONS *

Gilbert H. Clee and Franklin A. Lindsay

The historians of the future may record the decade of the 1960's as the period during which United States industry led in building the economies of underdeveloped nations as integral parts of the Free World. Or, on the other hand, historians may record this as the decade during which the communist leaders laid the base for world economic domination. What

* From *Harvard Business Review,* XXXIX (January-February 1961), 65-73. Reprinted by permission.

they record will, in large measure, depend on how fast and in what direction industry in the United States moves during the next few years.

The current movement of United States companies into the Common Market, the United Kingdom, and a few of the economically less developed countries gives promise that U.S. industry is using its managerial and investment resources constructively in the creation of great international enterprises. This movement has sound economic reasons for developing and, in some areas, is taking place with almost explosive speed.[1] Its future course and potential, especially in Africa, Asia, and South America, will depend largely on management's success in applying new forms of organization and new approaches. The concept of systems management as applied to international economic development, which will be analyzed in this article, is in our opinion an especially useful approach.

DANGERS AND OPPORTUNITIES

Industrial expansion abroad is necessarily creating additional headaches for U.S. industry. To the already knotty problems of running large-scale enterprises at home are now being added the much more complex problems of managing world enterprises. Executives ponder such questions as:

> How should we organize world-wide research and development programs to take advantage of special opportunities and conditions wherever they are found?
>
> How can we penetrate the most profitable and rapidly growing markets?
>
> How can we assure that products will be turned out in locations which will give the company the greatest possible competitive advantage in all markets?
>
> How should the activities of the entire corporate enterprise be pulled together so as to give the greatest strength to the "corporate system" as a whole?

In addition, management faces difficult political and economic problems that lie largely beyond the control of any individual firm. As a company's operations and investment spread from area to area, they become more vulnerable to political and economic forces, some of which can be influenced by groups that are basically opposed to the philosophy of a free competitive society. Such conditions tend to destroy the environment necessary to the success of private enterprise.

Although these political and economic risks are present everywhere, most of the countries which are economically highly developed have created business climates within which risks can be measured and taken. For example, the countries of Western Europe have developed through the cen-

[1] See Gilbert H. Clee and Alfred di Scipio, "Creating a *World* Enterprise," *Harvard Business Review* (November-December 1959), p. 77.

turies an inherent respect for law, a tradition of national integrity, and good commercial judgment that make it possible to assess the uncertainties and take the risks if business opportunities are present. Partly because of this, a large share of the recent attention of U.S. industry (except for extractive industries) is being centered in the more "developed" areas of Western Europe and the Americas.

Cold-War Battleground

But it is in the *less* well-developed countries that the greatest long-term opportunity exists for both private enterprise and the Free World. These areas in Latin America, Africa, and Asia account for 67% of the world's population, but for only 12% of the world's industrial production. They may well provide the greatest *ultimate* markets and resources in the century ahead.

Why is U.S. industry not moving forcefully into them? From a business point of view, the answer is understandable. At present some of these countries provide only limited markets because of the low purchasing power of the population. Also, there is the political and economic environment. For instance, major private investments in some of the newly formed African nations and certain areas of the Far East are not realistic at this time; either the risks are too great or private investment is not welcomed.

Yet these are the very regions where the great economic struggle between communism and the Free World may be waged and won—or lost. If their peoples and resources are absorbed and become an economic and political part of the Communist World, the power and opportunities of the Free World will be seriously eroded, if not ultimately destroyed. These conditions are evident to both sides.

Our problem lies not in recognizing the danger, but in developing a program to do something about it. The less developed areas are determined to advance themselves economically, and the pressures for development cannot and should not be dampened. What we need to do is establish a combined business-government approach capable of doing what neither private nor public leaders can do alone.[2] Today, in the United States economy there exists no single responsible authority that has as its mission the catalytic job of putting government and business together to formulate and carry out economic development programs abroad. What is especially needed are new and imaginative ways of providing incentives for private participation in areas where political and economic instability are too great to attract private capital in the usual way.

Russia's Weapons

Russia has announced her intention of becoming economically supreme and of penetrating the Free World with her economic and industrial strength. Russia's and Red China's world-wide economic penetration is

[2] See "A Plan for Waging the Economic War," an address by Donald K. David, Chairman, Committee for Economic Development, before the Business Advisory Council, Hot Springs, Virginia, October 17, 1958.

not, to be sure, along the lines of the classic methods of industrial penetration. The communist economic system permits them to disregard price or profit in their effort to capture markets and thereby to control governments and economies. Similarly, they effectively employ political and psychological weapons, such as their present anticolonial propaganda, to gain their objectives. An added Soviet advantage is the example of its own very rapid rise to become one of the leading industrial and scientific countries of the world. Because of this example, underdeveloped nations, faced with almost impossible internal pressures, often find persuasive the argument that the only road to rapid industrial growth is the communist way. Some are convinced that the road to free enterprise is a luxury which they cannot afford because, so they reason, it does not guarantee the essential elements of industrialization as rapidly as they must have them.

One of the greatest strengths of the Soviet Union is its ability to mobilize into an integrated program its total political, economic, and industrial might for the economic capture of a geographic segment of the globe. Before the end of this decade Soviet economic power may have grown to the point where the Kremlin can move into an area with a total economic program that supports a country's balance of payments, purchases the products of the country, supplies heavy equipment and consumer products, provides managerial and technical assistance, and supports the entire effort by an integrated political strategy that provides reasonable assurance of success. This capability for a fully integrated program sufficiently large to make a real impact on the development of a country may be Russia's greatest weapon.

American Problems

The United States competitive position *under our existing policies* does not seem to be as strong as that of the U.S.S.R., for neither private enterprise nor government in our country is fully geared to meet the need. Here are our major problem areas:

> A single individual company operating within a free enterprise system cannot be, nor should it be expected to be, fully effective in developing a total economy abroad. The impact that any one firm can make on the economy of a country is seldom sufficient to do the job. It is true that the oil companies in Venezuela have had a great impact on the economic well-being of that country. Companies like Cerro de Pasco Corporation, W. R. Grace & Co., and International Petroleum Company, Ltd. have given Peru the economic base to help the country create a higher degree of prosperity and financial stability than would have been the case if those companies had not grown and prospered to the degree that they have. But the situations where individual companies have had a far-reaching effect on the economy of a country are the exception rather than the rule.
>
> Private enterprise, collectively, can significantly help the development of a country's economy *if* the investment climate is favorable. Wherever private enterprise exists and has flourished, the standards of living and individual freedom have flourished. The demonstration of the

power of a free economy given to the world during World War II by the United States is further evidence of the force and capacity of private enterprise harnessed to achieve a common objective. So the door is still open.

The unique strengths of the United States lie primarily in private industry. Yet, as of now, this strength has not been brought fully to bear on the solution of the problems of the less developed areas. How are we to harness the power of private enterprise and provide incentive for it to operate in areas where investment risks are high?

Neither the government of the United States nor that of other countries in the Free World can, under present policies, do the job of economic development alone. The experiments tried so far have often had a constructive effect but have been inadequate to accomplish the desired results. For example, the U.S. government's program of sending individual technicians to underdeveloped areas has undoubtedly had some beneficial effect. The training of villagers to use steel plows instead of wooden ones and the creation of cottage industries may have helped a relatively small percentage of the population. But in each instance the effort has often been lost in the total economic needs of the countries.

A principal shortcoming of the foreign economic programs of the United States has been their failure in many cases to stimulate a balanced development of agriculture, industry, manpower, and capital. Instead of providing for a combination of public services (roads, power, and so on), basic industry, consumer industry, and distribution and marketing services, we have more often financed isolated projects, such as dams (sometimes in areas that lack the supporting facilities to use either electric power or water for irrigation). We have also, perforce, found it necessary to use our limited funds to finance deficits in balance of payments; and we have supplied consumer goods as an antidote to inflation, but without curing the source of the problem.

Another difficulty has been that technical and managerial assistance has not always been provided in a way that makes the greatest contribution to the long-range upgrading of the skills of local manpower. Too often, technical people have been sent into underdeveloped countries for short periods only, and have been withdrawn before they had a chance to pass their skills on to local personnel. The practice by the government of borrowing individuals from corporations for this purpose fails to take advantage of one of the corporation's major strengths—an organization of highly skilled individuals who are accustomed to working together effectively as a team. Working alone, in an alien atmosphere, the individual is likely to be much less effective than when he is part of a team with which he has learned to work.

The creation of permanent economic institutions capable of making continuing contributions to economic development has not always been a primary objective of our government and consequently has not had adequate emphasis in development programs. Nor have the government programs always recognized the importance of continuity of management. Industrial construction projects, for example, financed by government but carried out by private contractors, often do not provide for a single management organization to direct both the planning and construction phases and the operating and marketing phases.

International organizations like the International Bank for Reconstruction and Development have been excellently managed, and they have provided means of stimulating a balanced development and financing of individual projects. But here again the effort, while helpful, has not met the full need.

A final weakness of our approach to economic development is that we have not done enough in foreign countries to help develop a philosophy and atmosphere tolerant of private enterprise and in which both local and international private enterprise can make their full contribution. Indeed, we have not been able to explain adequately the reasons why we believe in the effectiveness of private enterprise.

Because of the high risks in many areas, a private company may be forced to require both an unusually high return on investment and special guarantees and concessions from the government concerned. Even then, it may not be able to contribute a great deal quickly because of the lack of a balanced economic structure—such as a well-equipped transportation system, a farm credit system, or a broadly established retail distribution system.

These difficulties can place a private company, as well as private enterprise generally, in the most unfavorable light in the eyes of the leaders of a new country. To them private enterprise appears to be demanding unusually high and immediate returns on investment, special guarantees, government financing, and special operating privileges. Americans (and would-be local entrepreneurs) are thus placed in the position of trying to demonstrate the superiority of free enterprise under the least favorable circumstances.

SYSTEMS CONCEPT

The moral of all this is that we have to do better. And we *can* do better. We "have the horses"; the task is to get them to pull together. With teamwork between government *and* industry, we can do everything that Russia can do—but with greater effectiveness and lasting benefit both to the countries involved and to ourselves. One key to success lies in what might be called the *systems management concept of economic development.*

The concept of systems management is not new. It has been successfully used for years by the Air Force and the other services as a means of producing a completed weapon system ready for operational use. Thus:

> In a typical case the Air Force asks a single contractor, the systems manager, to assume over-all responsibility for the development and production of a missile system, including the engines, the fuels, electronics guidance system, nose cone, and launching equipment.
>
> The Air Force has thereby delegated the responsibility to a skilled and reputable contractor to see to it that all of the components are compatible, that they will fit together and function perfectly, that they will be produced in balanced numbers and at the right times. In carrying out this over-all responsibility the systems manager is free to mobilize every needed skill and capability by employing specially skilled subcontractors —but he remains responsible to the government for the delivery of a completed weapon system, on schedule, that will perform the job expected of it.

The problems of economic development in many parts of the world show marked parallels to the problems of producing a complex weapon system. The components are different—but the problem is similar. In underdeveloped areas a successful program might, for example, require the balanced development of raw material resources, power supplies, transportation, management institutions, trained manpower, financial institutions, and marketing organizations. The economic development "system" may not be as clear and tangible as a military system, but it will exhibit many of the same basic characteristics.

To make another comparison, the military system provides for the production of component parts in balanced quantities and on a balanced time schedule for assembly, while the economic development system provides for the development of productive facilities in balanced capacities in time-phased stages. Both provide for the training of operators, technicians, and managers in phase with physical facilities.

Planning and Programming

The systems management concept of economic development can be illustrated by a hypothetical case example:

> A South American government has concluded, either by independent study or in cooperation with the U.S. government or an international institution, that a major agricultural development program in a fertile river valley could provide an important foundation for the country's economic development. The program might raise significantly the standards of living of the people in the area; provide more employment; provide products that could be exported and improve the foreign exchange position of the country; and provide products that could be used internally and thus avoid imports that currently are creating a foreign exchange drain.
>
> The country has approached the U.S. government for assistance. Our government suggests that the Latin American government ask a broad segment of U.S. industry to submit proposals for a "feasibility" study. The feasibility study, undertaken by a company or the joint effort of several companies, would have as its objective (1) the blocking out of a program of individual but interrelated projects that would provide balanced development of the area, and (2) an estimate of the economic contribution of the total program to domestic growth and to the country's foreign exchange position. The study would also include—
>
> A *financial plan* showing the approximate costs and the potential public and private sources of capital, the requirements for foreign exchange as well as the anticipated foreign exchange earnings, and a scheme for reinvestment of earnings and for the payment of reasonable dividends when justified by earnings of the projects financed with foreign equity capital. The financial plan might identify those parts of the program that would require government financing and those parts, such as a fertilizer plant, that might attract private capital.
>
> A *marketing plan* showing the size and nature of foreign and local markets, the type of marketing organizations and physical distribution systems needed, and possibly the credit structure needed to finance sales.

A *manpower plan* showing numbers and types of managers, technicians, and workers needed—outlining a program for supplying these needs from foreign and domestic manpower sources, and including specific steps to develop local manpower into successively higher managerial levels that are tied in with the country's basic educational system.

The program might also recommend any *government policies and regulations* that should be instituted or modified to make the plan both economically sound and attractive to foreign public and private capital. Finally, the program might provide for *public information activities* that would explain the purposes of the program as well as remove misconceptions, such as the idea that the program is simply a disguise for a new form of cartel.

Outlining the Advantages

The feasibility study should provide sound evidence to the local country that:

Its real needs would be met.

Its industrialization could proceed faster.

Its own manpower would be brought into senior management positions as rapidly as possible.

A balanced development program plus sound government economic policies could attract public and private capital on terms favorable to both the country and the investor.

The foreign exchange earnings under the plan would be adequate to support continued industrial expansion and still permit repayment of foreign loans and the transfer of reasonable earnings out of the country for those parts of the program which might be privately financed.

Private enterprise in the country will have real opportunities both for profitable investment and for profitable management contracts.

The systems concept should not, however, be extended to the point of giving any component enterprise a monopoly position. Nor should it include centralized government control of prices or production schedules. The essential competitive elements of pricing and marketing should be preserved and strengthened as the agricultural or industrial complex grows stronger. The systems need only be large enough to provide for the balanced development of a single region or a single industrial grouping. It thus might be possible to have several systems and systems managers operating within a single country.

Getting the Job Done

When the feasibility study is completed and accepted by the Latin American country, a systems management contract might then be let, either to the company that has made the study or to another qualified firm through competitive bidding. The systems manager would then have the responsibility to "manage" the program as an agent of the government or of its development bank.

Some of the component projects might initially be financed and managed by private companies using their own funds if the risks appear acceptable. If the risks are initially too great, they might be reduced to acceptable levels by guarantees or by government participation in either equity or loan financing.

Those parts of the program that do not lend themselves to private investment might be owned by a national development bank or development corporation. Their financing might be provided through any combination of a large number of possible alternate sources, including the International Bank for Reconstruction and Development, the U.S. government, European governments, local currency funds that have accumulated as the "counterparts" of United States aid previously provided, and local taxation.

After an activity is well started, the development bank might arrange to sell to private companies any projects that constitute potentially profitable businesses. As economic growth and stability occur in response to operation of the development plan, the risks to private investors might decrease accordingly and projects that initially were too risky might find ready buyers. These buyers could be domestic companies, foreign companies, or a combination of both.

In some cases the systems manager might subcontract with an American firm to construct the facility and to train local management in its operation. In other cases he might assist in arranging financing directly between the local government or a local private company, on one hand, and the U.S. government or one of the international financial institutions, on the other. The systems manager might also arrange for design and managerial services to be provided by direct contract with an American company. In still other situations he might bring about the establishment of new companies financed and owned jointly by the local government or bank and a private American firm. Finally, he or any foreign company might provide the capital and management for a component enterprise.

In every case, however, the systems manager would be responsible to see to it that the most suitable financing and ownership are arranged, that the individual project fits into the over-all system, and that sound engineering, managerial, and marketing skills are provided.

No matter what the form of ownership or financing, the systems manager might employ the skills of several U.S. or European firms on individual parts of the system. In the foregoing example, he might employ the resources of:

> An engineering firm for the building of a power supply, an irrigation system, and farm-to-market roads.
>
> An agricultural chemical company for the development of a source of supply for fertilizers, fungicides, and insecticides.
>
> An agricultural machinery company for the creation and operation of strategically located pools of agricultural implements.

A food-processing company for the establishment of facilities to process agricultural products.

A marketing agency to place products of the area in the hands of the customer at home and abroad.

The systems manager and the subcontractors would obtain reasonable profits from the contracts, and be provided an opportunity to make private investments in the projects if they wish.

Heading Off Communism

A second hypothetical example illustrates a somewhat different way in which a private American company might provide the initiative:

> The management of an oil company with long experience in the international field has become increasingly concerned about a steady trend toward government ownership and away from free enterprise in a key country of the world. The government of this nation contends that Western private enterprise is no longer investing in the country and, in effect, is dragging its feet in the creation of a fully integrated domestic oil industry. As a result, the government is about to start construction of a government-owned oil industry, and is contemplating a request to the Soviet Union for financial and technical assistance.
>
> In order to counter this threat, the company develops a comprehensive program designed to supply a large part of the needs of the country and to fit the firm's own development plans. Thus—
>
> Its program provides for creation of an integrated industrial system based on petroleum. Its component projects include a refinery, a drilling program, a pipeline and port facilities, a small tanker fleet capable of delivering oil via the country's main rivers to deep inland points, a petrochemical plant, a chemical fertilizer plant, and a lubricating oil plant.
>
> In addition, the company proposes a substantial training program designed to bring local employees into successively higher technical and managerial levels, and to develop a comprehensive marketing system.
>
> For some of the facilities the company is prepared to invest its own capital, for others it is prepared to go 50–50 with government, and for still others it will suggest that the U.S. government and World Bank funds might be obtained.
>
> Management will also suggest that local private investors share in the equity ownership of some of the facilities.

From the standpoint of the local government this proposal could have important advantages. It would provide for many large amounts of dollar capital that otherwise would have to come from the country's grossly inadequate current dollar earnings. It would provide a means of bringing a broad range of technical assistance to the country. Finally, it would provide a responsible management to assume full responsibility for bringing into being a vital part of the country's development program.

PROGRAMS IN ACTION

There are good reasons for believing that systems management will work as well in overseas economic development as in military weapons development. And, like military advances, it has great potential for heading off the communist threat. This potential has not been realized yet, but we are convinced that it exists.

The difficulties of working out this type of "system" will naturally be great. There will be problems of obtaining the concurrence and cooperation of the foreign government. Delays in getting approval for the project from everyone concerned will be great. Frustrations and some failures due to the difficulty of private enterprise working closely with a government development agency can also be expected. However, these are problems that intelligent management and men of good will should be able to solve through experience.

Corfo Projects

The experience of the Chilean Development Corporation, known as Corfo, is a case in point. Its history provides an illustration of at least some elements of the systems management concept, but under government control:

> Corfo was established in 1939 as an autonomous public corporation to manage the economic development of Chile. As the "systems manager" it has developed over-all plans for economic growth, provided initiative and financing to launch new enterprises, operated individual enterprise through subsidiaries, and developed both technical and managerial talent.
>
> It has been active in industry, agriculture, construction, transportation, electric power, and petroleum. It has organized new public ventures and in some cases has supported the expansion of private ventures. On occasion, Corfo has sold its subsidiaries to private investors once they were firmly established and had become profitable operations.
>
> Corfo has financed private enterprise both by loan and by equity investment, and it has financed joint ventures with other private and public organizations as well. Thus the Chilean Steel Corporation, Compania de Acero de Pacifico, was established in 1946 with 53% of the stock owned by private investors and the balance by Corfo and other government agencies. As a result of subsequent sales of stock, the Corfo and government equity is now below 25%.
>
> Corfo's total investment averages $100 million annually, or approximately one third of Chile's total gross investment.
>
> Corfo also serves as a central financial institution for obtaining funds from a variety of sources. Its sources of funds include the Chilean government, the World Bank, the Export–Import Bank, and private foreign companies, as well as local capital. Its credit is such that it can draw on sources of funds that would be unavailable to many of its individual enterprises.
>
> In those activities where Corfo has been successful as the systems manager for Chile's economic development, four factors can be cited:

1. It can provide a flexible blending of government and private activities. It has much of the operating flexibility and autonomy of private enterprise, and at the same time it is able to concentrate its investments to provide for balanced long-range growth of the economy.

2. Because of the breadth of its scope and its size, it can undertake large and complementary development activities and thus avoid a piecemeal and unbalanced hit-or-miss investment in small, unrelated activities.

3. Corfo can be flexible in its financing patterns. It can participate with others or go it alone, and is not committed to exclusive support either of public or private activities.

4. Corfo incorporates within itself the functions essential to successful systems management of economic development. It makes over-all plans, obtains and invests funds, and supervises execution of programs. Further, it is concerned with developing manpower and management as well as with physical plant and equipment.

Although some of Corfo's projects have not fully achieved the hoped-for objectives, it is generally credited with making a substantial contribution to Chile's economic growth. It is now being called on to manage the reconstruction of the Chilean economy after the disastrous earthquake.

Further Successes

Two other examples of partial application of the systems concept, quite different from the cases which were described previously, deserve attention:

> In Iran, public and private institutions have come together to establish "The Industrial and Mining Development Bank of Iran." Its ownership includes Lazard Freres & Co., the Chase International Investment Corporation of New York, other financial institutions in the United States and in several Western European countries, private Iranian investors, and the government of Iran. Both the IBRD and the U.S. government's Development Loan Fund are investors or creditors. The professional staff of the bank is able to draw on the combined skills of its owners in providing sound and professional systems management of the economic development of Iran.
>
> In Peru, the private firm of W. R. Grace & Co. has operated for over 100 years. Hence a systems concept has not been consciously applied but has evolved over the years as Grace developed first one element, then the next, into what is now a system of closely related activities in many fields including sugar, textiles, paper, boxes, bags, industrial chemicals, paints, food, ores and ore concentrates, air, truck, and sea transport, and marketing of industrial and consumer products.
>
> The special contributions of Grace to the concept of systems management of economic development have been two—
>
> 1. Grace management took the initiative in developing needed new industries and integrating them into the economy of Peru.
>
> 2. The firm has shown the sensitivity and understanding of human attitudes and social forces to be able to integrate itself, as a private

international company operating key segments of the economy, into the Peruvian social structure. It has done this by requiring all of its foreign employees to speak Spanish, and by consistently encouraging and developing its Peruvian employees so that by now they occupy positions at all levels within the company. Only 1% of the employees in Peru are not Peruvian.

In addition to the work of private companies, both our government and various foundations have taken steps toward the systems concept. The International Cooperation Administration, for example, is prepared to finance feasibility studies, done by private companies, for the economic development of specific problem areas. The Rockefeller Brothers Fund is financing private corporate feasibility studies for development programs in two of the Central African countries. And the World Bank is working continuously with countries to develop practical over-all programs and specific economic plans that can be reasonably financed through both equity and loan capital.

CONCLUSION

What are the essential characteristics of the systems management approach to economic development? They appear to be:

1. The encompassing within a single system of the responsibility for a sufficiently large sector of the economic activities of a country to permit the balanced development of all of the key elements.

2. The provision of technical and managerial manpower, facilities, and capital in balance and in phase.

3. The flexible interweaving of public and private activities in the planning, operating, and financing phases according to (a) the best capabilities of each to contribute to the over-all system, and (b) any economic and social conditions which often set limits on the forms that economic enterprise takes.

Great Progress Attainable

When, through trial and error, the systems management concept proves out in an area (and this should generally be the case, we believe), it should lead to important gains and advantages for both the underdeveloped nation and the Free World:

1. It could provide the means of mobilizing the forces of both free enterprise and free government to develop and execute fully integrated economic programs that will make major economic advances possible.

2. It could provide effective means of combining all potential sources of capital in the most effective manner—such sources as private equity capital, private loans, local equity and loan funds, U.S. and other government loans, IBRD loans, Export–Import Bank loans, International Finance Corporation financing, guarantees, counterpart loans, and capital internally generated by the program itself.

3. It could provide a method of building permanent management institutions staffed by skilled professional personnel of private foreign companies and, increasingly, by citizens of the developing country. It would offer on-the-job training and provide for the rapid development of local managerial capabilities.

4. It could assist in providing permanent institutions for continuing capital formation through reinvested earnings. This is especially important in countries in which the population pressures for consumption make it extremely difficult to generate enough capital, either from private savings or through government taxation.

5. The systems management contract should make it possible for private enterprise to participate in economic development at a reasonable profit in areas where the high political and economic risks would otherwise make private investment unattractive. Private firms should then find it possible to give development programs a call on some of their best managerial talent and resources.

Further, management contracts can provide the added incentive of permitting the systems managers to be "on the ground floor" in the event that attractive long-range investment opportunities develop. The opportunity for the managers and subcontractors to sell their products as a part of the development program can also be an incentive to take a systems contract.

Also, unless some form of effective public-private approach is developed, private firms are simply not going to have the opportunities to operate at all in many underdeveloped areas of the world.

6. The systems management concept may provide a device whereby the United States and other countries of the Free World can jointly maintain a perpetual state of alert to meet threats of communist economic penetration in developing countries with programs as completely integrated as those of Russia or Red China. It also provides the flexibility to return to a more normal state of doing business, whenever local tensions ease.

7. The systems approach can assist in the creation of both political and economic conditions in which private enterprise can take root and progressively make greater and greater contributions to economic development.

Leading from Strength

The systems management concept is certainly not the *only* answer to the economic development of developing countries. It may not even be the best answer. It is submitted here as an illustration of a way in which free enterprise might be molded to meet the challenge of this coming decade—without losing the strengths and capacities that it took centuries to create.

ADDITIONAL REFERENCES

Harvard Business Review has published a series of articles on different aspects of planning and operating a successful world business:

Gilbert H. Clee and Alfred di Scipio, *Creating a World Enterprise* (November-December 1959).

Peter F. Drucker, *Realities of Our World Position* (May-June 1959).

John Fayerweather, *Foreign Operations: A Guide for Top Management* (January-February 1957).

Lincoln Gordon, *Private Enterprise & International Development* (July-August 1960).

James A. Hagler, *How Are Marketers Meeting the Import Challenge?* (September-October 1960).

Edward T. Hall, *The Silent Language in Overseas Business* (May-June 1960).

Raphael Hodgson and Michael Michaelis, *Planning for Profits in World Business* (November-December 1960).

Charles Henry Lee, *How to Reach the Overseas Market by Licensing* (January-February 1958).

Franz M. Oppenheimer, *Notes on Podsnappery* (July-August 1954).

Clifton R. Wharton, Jr., *Aiding the Community: A New Philosophy for Foreign Operations* (March-April 1954).

16

THE FUTURE STRUCTURE OF INTERNATIONAL COMPANIES *

John O. Tomb and Donald B. Shackelford

Many American executives are taking a hard second look at the organization of their international activities. Their companies—like most American concerns with substantial foreign business—traditionally have grouped overseas operations into international divisions. But with increasing frequency, executives in some industries are questioning whether an international division is the best form of organization for future overseas management.

> At a recent conference on international operations, top executives from business machine, heavy machinery, and ferrous metal companies said that the major roadblock to continued overseas growth was their present international division form of organization.

* From *International Enterprise* (McKinsey and Co., Inc., Management Consultants, 1962).

> A large metals producer which set up an international division only two years ago has spent the past five months trying to develop a better way to organize for overseas activities.
>
> An executive who recently has been promoted to head the international division of a large packaging business disputes the whole organizational concept on which his job is based.

The executives who question the future usefulness of an international division are not challenging this form of organization in principle. What they are doing is to recognize that their own particular pattern of worldwide activities may be evolving beyond the stage where an international division can be fully effective. They point out that this form of organization was created by companies basically concerned with exporting from a North American base. Now that operating at multiple points around the world has become more important than exporting for many companies, these executives contend that a different organizational structure may be needed. One man put it this way: "We think our international division is obsolete; we've simply outgrown it."

The fact that some executives have reached such a conclusion does not, of course, mean that an international division never should be used by companies with worldwide activities. The success achieved overseas by such companies as Colgate, Heinz, and National Cash Register is, in itself, good evidence that this form of organization can be effective when international activities command the attention of top corporate levels.

The key question is: When does a company reach the stage where the international division form of organization no longer meets its operating needs? If executives understand the factors that may limit the usefulness of an international division, they can make intelligent decisions on the adoption of alternative approaches to organizing their own worldwide activities.

PROBLEMS OF AN INTERNATIONAL DIVISION

Executives who ask if their companies have already outgrown the usefulness of an international division trace their concern to one fundamental characteristic of this form of organization. The very existence of an international division tends to isolate corporate management from overseas operations. Faced with language barriers, differing business practices, and complex governmental regulations, most corporate headquarters executives are glad to delegate all aspects of overseas operations to an international division. Ironically, the more successful the international division is in coping with its overseas assignment, the more it becomes a filtering device that effectively separates corporate management from overseas problems and opportunities. Thus, the corporate headquarters team tends to focus its attention on the domestic scene while the international division deals with foreign operations. Out of this separation may flow three consequences that greatly hamper the profitable growth of many worldwide enterprises.

> When domestic and foreign operations are artificially segregated, neither corporate management nor the international division can make

decisions in terms of worldwide opportunities, because neither is in a position to be fully informed about global operations. For example, corporate management may make decisions to keep or to replace domestic equipment without knowledge of the equipment needs of its foreign operations. At the same time, the international division may be making its own commitments without an awareness of the planned changes in domestic facilities and products that may have a profound effect on international operations. The separation of domestic and foreign operations can be particularly frustrating to the international executive, for he must often rely on the support and approval of his colleagues, who are not responsible for overseas operations, or who assign second priority to overseas ventures. Several heads of international divisions cite instances of having their plans outvoted by their domestic associates, who obtained incomplete or erroneous impressions of conditions abroad from a short trip or a magazine article.

Setting up separate organizational compartments for domestic and international operations adds rigidity rather than flexibility to the corporate structure. The worldwide enterprise must be capable of fast response to rapid change. National and multinational trade policies are being altered at an accelerated rate. Two outstanding examples are the contemplated expansion of the European Common Market and the recent proposals to step up the rate of tariff reductions within it. And there is the prospect of further changes in the American tariff structure as well.

As a result of these trends, the past strategy of establishing overseas operations, in order to get behind restrictive tariff walls and quotas set up by nations suffering dollar shortages, has become outdated. That strategy called for highly self-sufficient overseas operations within each major country or trade block. But now, executives who are alert to current trends are learning that they must be in a flexible position to serve key markets from the most advantageous source and that this source may change from year to year. Thus, a company's assembly plant will be served this year with some parts made in Germany and others made in the United Kingdom. In the plans for next year, however, forecasted changes in demand or costs or tariffs or design may call for shipping the German parts to the U.S. A company that has organizationally segregated the U.S. from international operations usually is at a disadvantage in reacting swiftly.

An international division may present obstacles to the flow of technical information between domestic and foreign operations. This problem is particularly acute in companies where research and development are important or where the product is highly engineered. It is also a major source of difficulty for companies that are in the early stages of international expansion. The overseas plants or licensees typically have not developed to the point where they are technologically self-sufficient; they may still rely heavily on their North American parent for technical assistance. Instead of flowing from one technical specialist to another, information is filtered through the intermediary of an international division. The usual result is delay, misinformation, misunderstanding, and friction.

The manager of a British plant of an appliance manufacturer summed up his experience with the caustic comment: "International is

> just a paper-massaging operation; they can't contribute anything except delay to solving our problems. The closer we can get to the factory in North America the better."

These problems, stemming from the separation of domestic and foreign operations, are leading many executives to conclude that use of an international division conflicts with the current and future needs of their companies. Such executives recognize that they cannot be successful in an increasingly competitive world economy if they retain an organizational structure that artificially separates domestic operations from overseas activity.

In some cases, the difficulty is not with the divisional form of organization as such. Instead, the problems may arise from the failure of top corporate management to adopt a worldwide point of view; they may come from the inability of most members of corporate management to deal effectively with the complexities of international operation; or they may be the result of serious inadequacies in the information system for planning and control.

In other cases, however, the problems are so deep-rooted that something more acute than "cleaning up" the present situation is needed. Some executives will find themselves thinking in terms of a single, integrated organization to manage all operations on a worldwide basis. They will explore the desirability of transforming the entire corporation into a world-encompassing international division. This is the concept of the world enterprise.[1]

NEW DIMENSIONS OF A WORLD ENTERPRISE

Adoption of a world enterprise organization structure adds several new dimensions to the management of a company with global operations.

First, such a move indicates that corporate management is expected to give equal attention to equal profit opportunities throughout the world. A company that decides to manage itself as a world enterprise no longer can appraise proposed uses of corporate resources on a country-by-country basis; each opportunity needs to be related to other opportunities available throughout the operating complex. This is the way corporate management will decide which countries are the lowest net cost locations for production (taking into account such factors as accessibility to key markets, transportation, tariffs, taxes, or political stability). Instead of thinking and planning separately for U.S. and overseas operations, the chief executive and his staff would ask:

> Where in the world can we market our products to assure ourselves of the most rapid and profitable sales growth?
>
> Where in the world should we do research and development to capitalize, at optimum cost, on the technical capabilities that exist in the world?

[1] "Creating a World Enterprise," by Gilbert H. Clee and Alfred di Scipio, *Harvard Business Review* (November-December, 1959), pp. 77-89.

> Where in the world should we make our products so that we will be competitive in all major markets, including the U.S.?

Second, this move indicates that the company intends to function as a single operating complex. Transactions among operating units (involving, for example, research, components, or finished goods) will be encouraged wherever such action improves global profits. Conversely, the company will discourage self-contained, autonomous units—if they generate costly duplications in product design, facilities, and overhead expense.

Third, the role of logistic decision-making becomes of paramount importance. The logistic decision-making process includes a continuing reexamination of the relationships among key markets and alternative sources of supply. For example, political or economic developments might make it more profitable to serve a Canadian assembly plant with component parts made in the U.S. instead of parts manufactured in Britain. Or, it might be more profitable to shift research efforts in Germany to development of products that have a limited German demand but a substantially larger market potential in Latin America and Africa.

This concept of the world enterprise is relatively new to the U.S. business scene. However, Unilever, Philips Lamps, and Royal Dutch Shell have operated for years under a world enterprise organization structure. In 1955, Massey-Ferguson, the Canadian-based producer of farm equipment, reorganized as a world enterprise in response to its growing profit potential in Europe and other areas.

MOVING TO A WORLD ENTERPRISE

Moving to a world enterprise form of organization usually involves three major steps:

> Regrouping worldwide activities into logical operating units with coequal organizational status.
>
> Developing a corporate staff with worldwide scope and responsibility.
>
> Assigning responsibility for worldwide logistic decisions to top line management.

Regrouping Operating Units

A worldwide structure consists of operating units around the world that enjoy coequal organizational status. It eliminates the typical organizational separation between U.S. and foreign operations.

Some companies relate their operating units to major production facilities. Others take a key market as the basis for organizing geographical operating units.

Each such operating unit in the new organization—North America, Europe, Latin America, Africa, or Asia—reports directly to top management. And each unit has complete responsibility for conducting the company's operations within the area assigned to it—operating, of course, within a framework of overall corporate strategy laid down by corporate headquarters. For example, a machinery company which considers consistency of product performance to be of critical importance requires centralized approval of all changes in basic machine design.

Developing New Roles for Staff

The second major step in implementing the world enterprise structure is to make the corporate staff truly responsible for the performance of its functions on a worldwide scale. This step is a critical prerequisite to establishing a team that can assist the president to review such management questions as investing the corporation's assets, utilizing research and production facilities, deploying key personnel, and developing short- and long-range marketing strategies, all in the light of alternative opportunities available to the company in any part of the world.

Deep personal knowledge of international operations and personnel is an important ingredient in the discharge of this corporate headquarters team's responsibility. The top executives of a European-based electronics company cover the world three or four times a year. Much of the success of ITT has been attributed to the on-the-spot inspection of operations by Colonel Sosthenes Behn and his successors. Unilever emphasizes the importance of two-way executive movement this way: ". . . . Directors of the parent company and the top people in the Advisory Services must visit the units on the circumference, and the top men from the units must visit the centre. It is only by personal contact that mutual confidence can be built up." [2]

Creating a corporate headquarters team that functions on a worldwide basis often is a difficult step. Executives who have tended to concentrate attention on the domestic scene (because the international division had previously handled overseas activities) need to learn about a wide range of business practices and governmental regulations. They may even need to become acquainted for the first time with executives in operating units around the world. Corporate management may find that some executives who have been successful in the U.S. lack adaptability to other cultures and ways of doing business.

Making Logistic Decisions

Given a number of coequal geographical operating units reporting directly to top management, and a headquarters team with truly worldwide responsibilities, the third major step in organizing a world enterprise is to provide for logistic decision-making. As previously suggested, this is a function that cannot be delegated to the operating units; its effectiveness depends on a global perspective.

[2] Comments in speech by Mr. Paul Rykens, formerly the Chairman of Unilever N.V., at the International Industrial Conference, San Francisco, September 1961.

In Massey-Ferguson, the president has ultimate responsibility for logistic decision-making. In long-term decisions—such as the introduction of major products, construction of new facilities, or raising of funds—he relies heavily on advice from corporate marketing, manufacturing, and finance executives. For shorter term decisions involving changes in the relationships between markets and sources of supply, he relies primarily on his corporate director of planning and procurement. These logistic decisions are never made in terms of the problems or needs of a single area. They are made after considering the situation in relation to the company's global operations.

The organizational structures of world enterprises like Massey-Ferguson (see page 191) have these distinguishing characteristics:

Direct reporting relationships between operating units around the world and the chief executive.

A corporate staff that has responsibility for world-wide operations.

An organization designed to make logistic decisions on a worldwide basis.

WHO SHOULD ORGANIZE AS A WORLD ENTERPRISE

Only a relatively few companies may now have the characteristics that place them in the category of a world enterprise. In general, the world enterprise form of organization is most appropriate to businesses that meet the following five criteria:

Heavy commitment to direct participation outside the U.S.

High manufacturing costs.

Alternative markets.

Alternative sources of supply.

Geographical separation of raw materials sources, raw materials processing, and major markets.

Heavy commitment. As soon as a company commits itself to substantial investments in direct participation abroad, it begins to establish the need for adopting the world enterprise concept. The very existence of partly or wholly owned facilities in several foreign countries makes it important for corporate management to think in worldwide rather than domestic terms. And, if some of the characteristics discussed below also are present, there can be a major need for logistic decision-making on a global basis. A rule of thumb measure is that companies whose future plans call for less than 20 percent of their business outside the U.S. do not benefit substantially from a full-fledged world enterprise organization.

High manufacturing costs. Companies with manufacturing costs substantially above marketing costs are strong candidates for a world enterprise structure. This is because the economies of worldwide logistic and

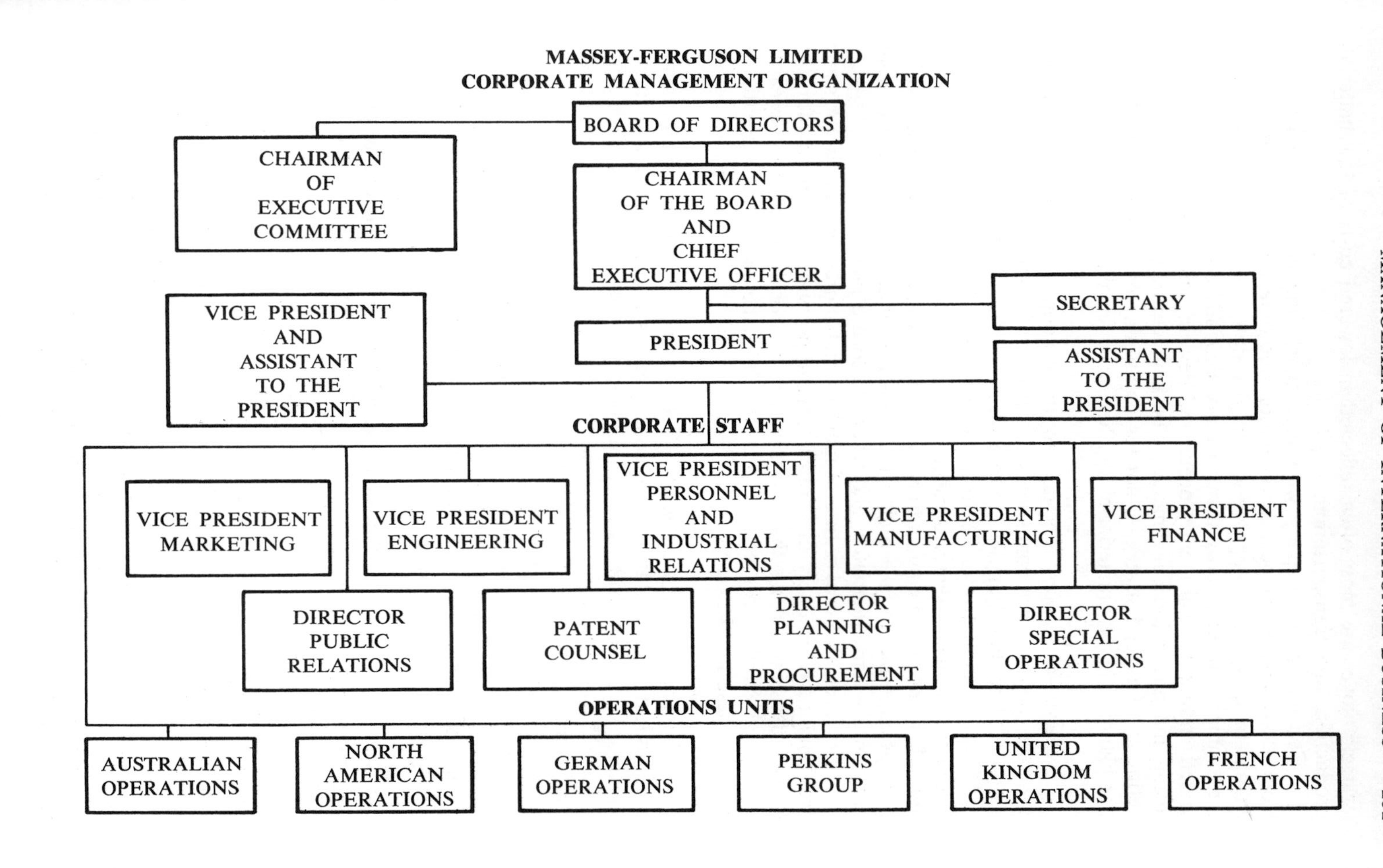
MASSEY-FERGUSON LIMITED
CORPORATE MANAGEMENT ORGANIZATION
BOARD OF DIRECTORS
CHAIRMAN OF EXECUTIVE COMMITTEE
CHAIRMAN OF THE BOARD AND CHIEF EXECUTIVE OFFICER
SECRETARY
VICE PRESIDENT AND ASSISTANT TO THE PRESIDENT
PRESIDENT
ASSISTANT TO THE PRESIDENT
CORPORATE STAFF
VICE PRESIDENT MARKETING
VICE PRESIDENT ENGINEERING
VICE PRESIDENT PERSONNEL AND INDUSTRIAL RELATIONS
VICE PRESIDENT MANUFACTURING
VICE PRESIDENT FINANCE
DIRECTOR PUBLIC RELATIONS
PATENT COUNSEL
DIRECTOR PLANNING AND PROCUREMENT
DIRECTOR SPECIAL OPERATIONS
OPERATIONS UNITS
AUSTRALIAN OPERATIONS
NORTH AMERICAN OPERATIONS
GERMAN OPERATIONS
PERKINS GROUP
UNITED KINGDOM OPERATIONS
FRENCH OPERATIONS

strategic moves are most often reflected in lowered costs of raw material, production, and transportation.

Conversely, a company with high marketing costs may gain more from a worldwide perspective on major one-time decisions than from a change in structure to improve logistic decisions. In a cosmetic company, for example, profit improvement usually depends on developing a better understanding of local market needs and devising more effective merchandising and promotional techniques. The key requirement here is for marketing and financial strategies, not for day-to-day or month-to-month central planning of raw material or finished product allocation.

Alternative markets. The desirability of adopting the world enterprise structure increases if a company with substantial commitments abroad has a product line that is applicable to a number of markets.

In the automotive or electronic equipment industries, the world enterprise concept makes sense. Because the same basic product can be used in multiple markets, a manufacturer who wants to establish a dominant worldwide position has to take a global approach in determining where to concentrate his marketing effort and where to locate facilities.

However, the local nature of markets and sources of supply for some drug and food products may offer little opportunity—or need—for the logistic decision-making that characterizes a world enterprise. Research may be about the only activity that can be handled on an international basis in these industries.

Alternative sources of supply. When extensive overseas commitments and product applicability in numerous markets are combined with interchangeable products from several production points, the case for adopting the world enterprise concept becomes hard to resist. Companies with these characteristics can shift the source of supply for a given market from one country to another. In this way, they can take maximum advantage of changes in political, economic, and industry conditions. To make changes that best serve corporate interests, however, requires an approach to decision-making that overrides local unit interests and considers worldwide alternatives.

Geographical separation. The world enterprise structure is particularly applicable to industries with geographically separated steps in the manufacturing process. Two of the best examples are petroleum and soap. These are industries with multiple sources of crude or vegetable oils. These are usually located at some distance from refineries or processing plants. The latter may or may not coincide with location of markets. Thus, there is a wide range of opportunities for shifting the source of supply of raw materials in relation to markets. It would be extremely difficult to optimize profits with this pattern of geographical separation unless management was able to make basic decisions in terms of worldwide operations.

If North American companies expect to maintain or expand their position in world markets, many of them need to examine the future usefulness of their present international division. In many instances it may have become an obsolete organizational device, better for yesterday's emphasis on exporting than for today's growing emphasis on operating.

The world enterprise structure is an alternative that some companies are finding to be a good substitute for the international division. This structure forces the use of a worldwide viewpoint in running a company. It eliminates the traditional distinction between domestic and foreign operations. It focuses attention on the importance of logistic decision-making.

Five questions can help determine whether a company is ready to adopt this approach to organizing and operating its activities:

> Does the company have a significant commitment in overseas operations?
>
> Do manufacturing costs outweigh marketing and promotional expenses?
>
> Can the company's major products be sold in a number of markets?
>
> Do these products have a high degree of interchangeability, whatever their source?
>
> Are raw material sources, processing facilities, or markets widely separated?

If the answer to each question is "yes," the company may have reached the stage where it should become a world enterprise in form as well as in fact.

17

MEASURING EXECUTIVE PERFORMANCE IN A WORLD ENTERPRISE *

C. Bruce McLagan and John D. Woodthorpe

Ineffective and inadequate appraisals of executive performance are the direct cause of one of the greatest economic wastes that management incurs—both in America and abroad.

Even in the U.S., where there are no language barriers to complicate appraisal, where managers can be evaluated against a background of commonly understood economic and political conditions, and where a wealth of material has been written on the subject, most companies still have difficulties in measuring, objectively and factually, the performance of their managers. Many companies, as a result, pay the penalty year after year of unsatisfactory performance in key positions. Other companies suffer the sometimes greater loss of unrealized potential in many of their executives.

But it is in the worldwide enterprise that this failing occurs most fre-

* From *International Enterprise* (McKinsey and Co., Inc., Management Consultants, 1962).

quently and most acutely. Indeed, it is one of the major factors contributing to today's shortage of competent, well-trained international executives.

COMMON APPRAISAL PRACTICES

It would be reasonable to expect that worldwide companies might have already solved the problem of measuring their executives' performance. These companies have enormous stakes abroad and their investment continues to grow at a rate higher than the rate of increase in their domestic assets. The intricacies of successful operation in foreign environments make corporate management peculiarly dependent on its managers overseas and thus especially in need of accurate indications of the extent to which each of these managers is serving the corporate interest. But the fact is that worldwide enterprises do little more in trying to measure foreign performance than they do in their domestic operations. Almost without exception, they follow one of three courses of action—none of which begins to meet the real need.

No Performance Appraisal

One approach is to remove performance altogether as an element in compensation, promotion, and transfer decisions. These decisions are reached automatically, on the basis of tenure, location, and other considerations that are not related to accomplishment.

There is considerable evidence that this approach is far more common than companies are prepared to acknowledge or one might expect. Recently, McKinsey & Company completed a survey of executive compensation in Europe and Latin America. An important aspect of the survey was to determine relationships between compensation and individual performance. The findings show that salary and bonus decisions—major elements in executive personnel administration—are only rarely influenced by individual performance. As the survey report observes: "Salary adjustments are generally perfunctory. The executive has little hope that outstanding performance will be rewarded by a larger than normal increase. The practice of one large company, which guarantees automatic salary increases up to the maximum of the salary range within five years, is not unusual. Profit-sharing bonus awards are rarely based on individual performance."

Reliance on Personal Impressions

A second approach is to gauge accomplishments by subjective impressions. In such instances, top management appraises performance in terms of intangible executive qualities—aggressiveness, creativity, maturity, tact—but without a tangible measure of performance to which these personal judgments can be anchored, such ratings can easily vary by how well the rater likes or gets along with the individual manager being rated, by the day of the week, or even by the time of the day.

This second approach is illustrated by an international drug company which recently changed its executive bonus plan from one based on a "formula approach" to a strictly judgmental one based on an annual performance review. Country managers raised hue and cry. One complained vigorously: "At least I used to have something I could rely on—now head office is just going to peg my bonus by the seat of its pants. It has no idea of the problems I face out here or any way of knowing whether I'm doing a good job in overcoming them."

The faults of a nonquantitative appraisal system are not unique with worldwide companies, but they are greatly aggravated. How is it possible for the president of an American company that is rapidly expanding into world markets to judge the aggressiveness or creativity of a newly appointed Middle Eastern regional manager? How can he evaluate the political judgment of his manager in Venezuela? Should he try to conduct the appraisal interview with his French manager in his own poor French or the latter's inadequate English? Clearly, management in a worldwide enterprise must come up with more reliable techniques for measuring performance.

Acceptance of Operating Results

The third approach is to take reported operating results at face value, ignoring the fact that they very often do not reflect the contribution of local management. Thus, for example, a capital goods producer continued to award salary increases and large bonuses to a British management group because overall results looked good. But when corporate management took a careful look at the report, it quickly recognized that the favorable results stemmed entirely from shipments to another part of the world. In fact, the performance in the local market had declined to such an extent that almost the entire management had to be replaced.

What are the causes of this failure to carry out properly one of the key responsibilities assigned to the management of a worldwide enterprise? A recent review of practices in a number of such companies suggests two primary causes:

> The inherent inability of existing reporting systems to measure performance.
>
> The failure to establish new systems that can appraise accomplishments tangibly and accurately.

WEAKNESSES OF PROFIT MEASURE

In domestic companies that are organized into separate operating units, divisional profit is the cornerstone of programs that measure executive performance. And since most of these divisions are relatively self-contained, the profits they report can serve as reasonable measures of managerial ingenuity and effectiveness. It is true that the performance of a division manager cannot be properly evaluated on the basis of profits alone;

other factors also must be considered. Yet few chief executives would dispute profits as the critical measure of managerial performance.

But how does divisional profit hold up as a measurement in the worldwide company? It might be well to examine its usefulness in two companies with interdivisional transactions.

> Company A operates in 45 separate countries. A typical management report treats each country as a separate "division." Eleven divisions show a loss; seven of those losing money are in South America. The question to ask, of course, is: Are the company's South American managers weak? A closer look reveals that the largest single profit is reported for the United Kingdom; furthermore, this profit is larger than the total South American loss. What is the connection here? The United Kingdom manufactures all South American requirements and takes an unusually full manufacturing profit. As a result, the South American units are left with only a minimum margin in which to absorb their marketing costs and little opportunity to produce "profits" in the conventional accounting sense.
>
> Company B has several statutory operations in the Bahamas. One is a Bahamian corporation through which it markets products. This corporation is a subsidiary of a tax-haven corporation in Canada. A second Bahamian corporation is itself a tax-haven corporation and re-exports products to other countries. All products are imported by the first Bahamian corporation from the parent, a Massachusetts corporation. Finally, there is a third Bahamian corporation which handles the self-insurance of the group. It is a direct subsidiary of the parent. Reports of these three statutory entities obviously give no measure of the profitability of the Bahamian market. Certainly the nominal operating results do not provide a reliable indication of the Bahamian manager's actual contribution to overall company profit.[1]

These two situations clearly point up the difference between the usefulness of divisional profits in a domestic enterprise and in an international one. Profits of an individual operating unit in a worldwide company may only rarely reflect the performance of the unit's management. There are two primary reasons for this situation. First, logistic decisions made centrally to expand worldwide profits very often reduce the profits of one or more individual country units and increase the profits of others. And second, financial, tax, and other legal considerations may lead to the accumulation of profits in low-tax units rather than in operating units.[2]

Impact of Logistic Decisions

A worldwide enterprise tends to look upon itself as a complex of closely integrated operating units to be used in whatever combination will increase overall profits. Raw materials, components, and semi- or com-

[1] "Tracing Profits Overseas," by John D. Woodthorpe, *The Controller*, March, 1961, Controllers Institute of America, New York.

[2] Monetary and political instability in some countries may make reported profits even less reliable. What appear to be high profits can, in fact, be altogether unsatisfactory when inflationary trends or political risks are considered.

pletely-finished products frequently are produced in the lowest cost operating units and sold throughout the world in whatever markets will generate the most revenue. But the use of such "operating complexes" creates havoc with divisional profits as a measure of performance and raises some unresolved questions.

As a case in point, there is the example of a world-wide machinery manufacturer which supplies its North American factories with major components produced in England. The decisions concerning what components are to be produced in England—some are more profitable than others—are made by a logistics planning unit at corporate headquarters. The actual quantity produced in England, which, of course, dramatically affects profit, is dependent upon North American sales efforts. Who should receive credit for the "profit" on such components? Should it be the English producing unit? The assembling and marketing unit in North America? Or the logistics planning unit at corporate headquarters?

Another kind of logistic decision is illustrated by the experience of an international company which manufactures and sells the same product in two countries in Western Europe. Markets in both countries are expanding and both country managers are requesting additional funds. Country X has a higher price structure; but because Country Y has lower manufacturing costs, its margins are greater. Top management decides at corporate headquarters to invest in Country Y's low-cost manufacturing facilities but to market the additional product in Country X at more attractive prices. These intercountry transactions will heavily influence future reported profits for each country and will make profits, taken at face value, meaningless as a measure of performance for either of the country managers.

In both cases the critical profit-influencing factors of volume and product mix are controlled centrally for individual countries. And so, even though a country manager supervises a fully integrated operation, he does not control its profits. If a decision, for example, is reached by a corporate logistics planning unit to move production of certain component parts for use worldwide from France to Germany, the French manager in all probability has no opportunity to maintain previous profit levels by stepping up sales efforts in France. His reported profits offer no real help in measuring his performance.

Effect of Legal Factors

Financial complexity has long been the hallmark of international business. Exchange rates, currency conversion restrictions, amortization and depreciation regulations, and a host of other legal considerations continually influence the pattern of operation and investment. And, in addition, there are many special arrangements and transactions to increase profits—using tax-haven companies in Nassau, Liberia or Liechtenstein; taking markups on products transferred on paper through Switzerland; participating in the ownership of overseas subsidiaries with local investors.

It is natural, then, that all the moves taken in response to these factors make reported profit a poor indicator of local accomplishment. The following two cases show what can happen:

In the earlier example of production in Country Y for sale in Country X, the transfer prices were established to accumulate most of the profit in Country Y because of its more liberal attitude toward profit repatriation. As a result, Y's profits were "inflated" by sales efforts for which X received little profit credit. Plainly, the country manager's performance in either instance could not be measured on the basis of profits.

A capital goods producer chose to expand its facilities in the United Kingdom rather than in the U.S. mainly because of the former's rapid amortization and depreciation regulations. And this in spite of the fact that North America represented the major market for plant output. The reduction in U.K. per unit manufacturing costs resulting from this expansion obviously had no relation at all to the performance of the manager of the U.K. operating unit.

Effective performance appraisal is possible only when the operating manager and his superiors know how well he is doing the things he is supposed to do. Ordinary reporting systems fail because they do not distinguish between the manager's actual accomplishment and all the other influences on local operations. Instead, they indiscriminately combine results of local action and the effects of logistic and financial decisions beyond the manager's control. Even were this not the case, ordinary systems would still fall short because they measure only current profit or loss, not the activities that determine future success or failure.

PERFORMANCE CAN BE MEASURED

A sound system of executive appraisal based on tangible elements of accomplishment in a manager's job can be developed for any worldwide enterprise. There are two requirements. First, non-accounting measures of performance must be used in addition to conventional reports. Second, operating unit profits must be analyzed to identify the major influences on local operating results.

Non-Accounting Measures

Measuring concrete elements of performance—other than profits—is little more complicated for each operating unit of a worldwide business than for many domestic divisions. Reliable indicators already exist or can be developed for critical factors.

Market share of a manager's home market (the only one he can control) can be measured according to established techniques. Although basic market data in some countries are not as readily available as in the U.S., executives are often surprised at how much information can be obtained with a little "digging."

Distribution can be accurately determined in any part of the world. The number and quality of retailers, wholesalers, or agents are tangible evidences of accomplishment or failure to perform in this often vital aspect of marketing.

New product development in overseas units is as easily measured as in domestic divisions and can often result in measurable profits to other units in a worldwide complex.

Improvements in productivity can be measured in the plants supervised by a country manager with the same methods and degree of accuracy as in a domestic unit.

Quality and delivery performance is readily measurable if care is taken to identify those influences over which the country manager has no control.

Analysis of Operating Unit Profits

With the application of some managerial ingenuity and a little extra effort, even *profit performance* of individual operating units can be measured. The steps that must be taken are fairly simple in principle. And if they are carried out with reasonable attention to the objective sought—performance appraisal and not accounting precision—they can be accomplished without undue cost or excessive complication.

The basic step in obtaining a meaningful picture of profit performance in the individual operating units of a worldwide company is to identify the results for which local management can be held accountable and to segregate those results that are governed by decisions made outside the operating unit. Four factors affect the profit results of an operating unit:

Decisions of the individual operating unit.

Decisions of other units with which the operating unit does business.

Corporate logistic decisions.

Corporate financial decisions.

With reliable cost data available (including appropriate distinctions between fixed and variable items), the profit results of each operating unit can be analyzed in terms of these four factors. In this way, attention can be focused on the performance of the management of each particular operating unit.

Two important guides should be followed in segregating local and remote influences on reported profits. First, the analysis should be considered only a memorandum adjustment of profits. The results of the analysis should not be entered into the company's accounting records. Second, identification of responsibility for profit variations outside an individual operating unit should be restricted to major items large enough to change its relative profit results.

Although further steps are possible to refine the way results are analyzed and reported, the approach proposed here will provide top management with a basic measure of the profit performance of each country manager. With such a measure of tangible accomplishment, plus the others already mentioned, top management will be prepared to appraise managers in all operating units on the basis of what they have done, not merely on the basis of personal impressions.

To make its executive performance pay off, however, top management must tie compensation to results actually achieved. Outstanding performance, determined by a sound system of measurement and appraisal, must be tangibly rewarded if top management expects superior efforts in the future from its managers. Similarly, failure to meet established goals must be followed by penalties, particularly under a bonus system, if the performance appraisal process is to justify the time involved and to make the contribution to management development of which it is capable.

Once individuals learn that superior performance pays off and that inferior performance brings a penalty, worldwide companies will begin to get their money's worth, as indeed leading domestic companies have done, from their executive appraisal program and from their managers.

SECTION THREE

Financing of International Operations

It takes money to make money. This truism applies in domestic as well as in international business relations.

It is the objective of this section to (1) acquaint the reader with sources of funds and (2) equip the decision-maker with some of the tools needed in developing strategy for financing international trade and operations both on the private enterprise and governmental levels. Also outlined are major problem areas in international finance.

All material is analytical. It explains how and why the different financing organizations have developed and what purposes they serve. Advantages and shortcomings of the major institutions are critically evaluated.

Professor Mikesell starts out with an analysis of the *World Bank in a Changing World*. He points out that in the first decade following World War II international lending agencies tended to focus attention on restoration of productive capacity in developed countries with similar economic structures. A relatively standardized lending approach was therefore possible.

In the latter part of the 1950's the emphasis started to shift from reconstruction to aiding countries in all sorts of stages of economic development and cultural evolution. To meet the broad spectrum of these new financial requirements, international lending institutions have increased not only in number but in scope of activity as well.

Dr. Mikesell makes a case study of the metamorphosis from reconstruction to development financing. He shows how the World Bank used its existing framework in adapting operation to new needs. The job, which is far from finished, called for skilled exercise of the "art of development diplomacy."

The hopeful tenor of Dr. Mikesell's contribution ties in nicely with extensive excerpts from *Financing Foreign Operations*. The original opus magnum—113 oversized, double-column pages—was prepared and published in 1961 by Business International, a leading consulting firm (200

Park Avenue South, New York 3, New York). The book contains detailed examples of how individual entrepreneurs can skilfully tap alternative sources of private as well as public capital available for investment and operation in seventeen different countries.

The reader will be impressed with the great diversity of international financial institutions. Yet, he might be surprised to note the predominance of U.S. interests in most of these organizations. It is caused more by default than by design. In spite of its economic health, postwar Western Europe has failed to generate enough investment capital either to meet its own needs or to become more prominent in world finance.

In fact, European capital markets are so inadequate that Wall Street remains a crucially important source of funds. This is embarrassing to us because American lending abroad contributes to the U.S. balance-of-payments deficit. For instance, in 1962 foreign governments and companies borrowed a record $1.2 billion in New York, of which about $300 million went directly to Europe. Furthermore, much of the money borrowed from the U.S. by developing countries could have come from "affluent Europe" if their capital markets were more effectively organized. This difficulty is so common that in most of Europe investment capital has traditionally been a major business problem. Britain, the most highly developed capital market in Europe, effectively limits most of its loans to the Commonwealth and the Sterling Area. France imposes such heavy restrictions on capital that in recent years only 15% of the investment of its own businessmen came from the capital market. The Dutch and the Swiss both clamp ceilings on what they will lend. German interest rates are so high—and bankers demand so much control over companies they lend to—that even prosperous businesses seek loans outside to keep out of the bankers' clutches.

With the exception of Britain, Europe has no tradition of a free capital market. Its many family-held enterprises have long preferred to finance expansion out of profits rather than to float stock issues that might bring in outsiders. Many of today's rigid controls are a heritage of the desperate need of postwar European governments to ration every asset. Now that more capital is available, much of it is soaked up by expensive government welfare programs. Little risk capital comes from wage earners because they are still wary of risking savings on the Continental stock exchanges.

In the meantime, as European economies grow stronger their demands on the U.S. capital market mount. There is, however, some hope on the horizon. The Common Market has ambitious plans for freeing internal capital movements by 1967. In the meantime the OECD is urging liberalization within each country. Early in 1963 a French study commission has gone on record supporting the OECD recommendation. Furthermore, Italy has passed regulations forcing banks to put more funds into long-term loans.

However, Europe is ahead of the U.S. in intermediate-term loans with one to five year maturities. This is because of the well developed international credit insurance facilities which help European (and Japanese) exporters carry the risks of selling abroad. In 1963 more than 20 nations provided export credit insurance for their exporters. In each case the government participated in the programs.

The relative unimportance of foreign trade in relationship to the total U.S. economic activity is one of the reasons for our tardiness in providing adequate export credit insurance. For instance, in 1962 our exports amounted to $21 billion, or only about 4% of the Gross National Product. In contrast, exports of Benelux countries represented one-third of the GNP. In the other important trading nations this proportion varied from one-tenth (Japan) to one-fourth (Switzerland).

Persisting deficits in the balance of international payments of the United States since 1958, with accompanying gold losses, have prompted Federal remedial action along several lines. One course of such action occurred in 1961 when the Ex-Im Bank was able to persuade over 70 insurance companies to join the Foreign Credit Insurance Association, which writes comprehensive insurance against credit and political risks. Fittingly enough this section therefore concludes with a piece in which editors of the Morgan Guaranty Trust Survey analyze the significance of the new FCIA in *Helping U.S. Exports Meet Credit Competition.*

18

THE WORLD BANK IN A CHANGING WORLD *

Raymond F. Mikesell

The retirement of Eugene R. Black, after 12 years of service, from the presidency of the World Bank (officially the International Bank for Reconstruction and Development) provides an opportune time to assess the changes which have taken place in the Bank's policies and operations since it opened its doors in 1946.

The World Bank's charter, which was formulated at the Bretton Woods Conference in 1944, and the early operations of the Bank itself were reflections of the prevailing attitudes toward international finance in the mid-1940s. Private international capital had virtually dried up in the 1930s. Thus it was not expected to play its predepression role either for postwar reconstruction or as a source of development capital. It was believed, therefore, that loan financing for the reconstruction of war-torn economies and for assisting economic growth in the poorer areas of the world would have to be provided mainly through public financing, either in the form of direct loans or as a guarantor of private loans.

At its inception, the most urgent task facing the World Bank was the restoration of war-torn economies. In fact, during its first two years virtually all of the Bank's loans were for European reconstruction. But even

* From *Challenge, The Magazine of Economic Affairs,* XI (February 1963), 14-17. Reprinted by permission.

before the Bank opened, it became clear that its resources would not be sufficient for the job. Consequently, the United States made available additional resources from the Export-Import Bank and granted a large loan to Britain. But even these and other sources of funds proved to be inadequate for financing European recovery, and in 1948 the bulk of the job was taken over by the Marshall Plan.

The Bank then began to turn its attention to development loans. By the end of 1949 only seven loans had been committed to developing countries outside of Europe, and only a small portion of these loans had actually been disbursed. By the end of 1953 the Bank had made only 65 loans outside of Europe and Japan, aggregating about $1 billion.

By mid-1962, however, the aggregate value of loans outside of Europe and Japan was in excess of $5.5 billion. Moreover, during the year ended June, 1962, the World Bank made 29 loans to 19 countries and territories totaling $882 million, all but $45 million of which went to countries outside of Western Europe and Japan.

In addition, the World Bank's two subsidiaries, the International Development Association (IDA) and the International Finance Corporation (IFC), extended credits during the fiscal year ended June, 1962 totaling more than $150 million, so that aggregate lending to less developed countries by the World Bank and its affiliates during the past fiscal year exceeded $1 billion.

The IBRD was established as an international bank to be operated in accordance with "sound" principles of international finance and not as a development agency. In both its charter and the statements of its officials, one finds numerous references to the soundness and "bankability" of loans and the employment of loan criteria which will protect the interests of the Bank and its creditors, since most of its loan funds must be obtained from the international capital markets.

The Bank, for its part, has felt that emphasizing the economic soundness of the projects which it finances and their contribution to the productivity of the borrowing country, together with its concern with the over-all economic and financial policies of its borrowers, are in the interest of both the borrowing country and the Bank. It has maintained the "project" approach to development lending on the ground that only by financing soundly conceived projects will its funds contribute to an increase in productive capital. The Bank has continually argued against the idea of "general purpose" or "balance of payments" loans.

More than two-thirds of the Bank's development loans have gone for projects in the fields of power and transportation and less than 20 per cent for the financing of industry and mining. The reason for this emphasis on infrastructure financing stems, in part, from the requirement in the Bank's charter that loans must be made either to member governments or be guaranteed by a member government. As a rule, private industrial firms are either unable to obtain government guarantees or do not welcome the governmental involvement which such guarantees may entail.

But even without this requirement, it is unlikely that the distribution of the Bank's development loans would have been much different. In fact, other international public lending institutions, such as the Inter-American

Development Bank and the Export-Import Bank, have also tended to concentrate on loans to governments for infrastructure projects, even though their charters do not require them to obtain a governmental guarantee. The reason for this is that, outside of a few industries such as iron and steel, most industrial firms in less developed countries tend to be small, and international lending agencies are not equipped to handle applications for thousands of small loans.

In addition, the World Bank, along with other international lending agencies, has tended to limit its loans to the foreign exchange components of projects. But for small industrial firms and farms, the principal need is for local currency rather than for foreign exchange loans tied directly to imports. Moreover, foreign exchange loans involve an exchange risk which in most less developed countries is substantial.

Less than eight per cent of the development loans of the World Bank have gone for agricultural and forestry projects, and these have been mainly for government-sponsored irrigation and flood control projects. Virtually none of the Bank's loans have been for so-called social impact projects such as housing, hospitals, rural improvement and educational facilities. The Bank prefers to confine its financing to projects making a more or less direct contribution to the physical output and productivity of the borrowing country, partly because such projects are consistent with its "public image" in the financial markets of the world. Social project loans, such as those for slum clearance, hospitals and schools, do not fit the concept of "bankability" and "soundness" in international finance. Moreover, they present difficult problems in the application of the economic and engineering standards which the Bank has evolved in judging projects.

In its early days, the Bank viewed its job as mainly limited to reviewing applications for loans for soundly conceived projects with little responsibility for actively involving itself in the development process. Its attitude was akin to that of a commercial bank whose loan officers sit behind their desks and politely receive customers who come in with loan applications. This approach might be contrasted with that of an investment bank which has provided much of the financing for an industrial firm, maintains a senior officer on the firm's board of directors, and is constantly reviewing and taking responsibility for financing expansion.

The changing role of the World Bank from that of an almost purely financial institution to that of a development agency which sees its role in considerably broader terms has been a gradual one. It has taken place both as a consequence of the Bank's involvement as a project lender in member countries and of a general change in attitudes toward the development process and the role of external assistance in that process.

During much of the 1950s the Bank was subject to continual criticism on the part of its developing members, as well as by many social scientists in the free world generally. The critics charged that it had the financial capability of providing a larger flow of funds. Various United Nations and other reports calculated the external capital requirements for minimum rates of growth in the underdeveloped world on the basis of assumed capital-output ratios and argued for new sources of external financing. These new sources would be able to pour capital funds into the less developed countries in sufficient volume to achieve these rates of growth.

The Bank's officials have rejected any mechanical relationship between external capital inflow and rates of growth. Until recently, they took the position that the major deterrent to both greater capital inflow and growth was the failure of developing countries to prepare projects suitable for external financing, and to provide a political, economic and financial climate conducive to both foreign and domestic private enterprise.

The Bank has gradually come to realize that it is not enough to stand ready to provide financing for projects, but that it must, in cooperation with other agencies, assist countries in their development planning, in the preparation of projects and in the training of development administrators and other specialists. However, the Bank has tended to be somewhat skeptical of over-all development plans based on long-run projections and highly sophisticated programming techniques of the type engaged in by the U.N. Economic Commission for Latin America. Its officials feel that more attention should be given to the concrete content of an economic program in terms of specific projects and economic activities. On the other hand, the Bank has been sending economic survey missions to member countries with a view to surveying their resources and potentialities and providing a broad framework for the determination of investment priorities.

In recent years the IBRD has increased its activities in the field of technical assistance, including project preparation, help in development programming, and advice on economic and financial policies. This work has taken a variety of forms, including survey missions, resident representatives and advisers, training programs and the fostering of development banks. In cooperation with the United Nations Special Fund and other organizations, the Bank has also undertaken detailed studies of specific economic sectors such as transportation, power and agriculture.

In 1956 the Bank established the Economic Development Institute, which provides six months' training for senior development officials from less developed countries. The importance of these advisory, training and technical activities was dramatized in November, 1961 by the establishment of the Development Services Department to administer the Bank's technical assistance work, and by the creation of a Development Advisory Service designed to provide a corps of experts to render economic and financial advice. The latter was set up in response to the growing demands for such services from member governments.

By 1958 the Bank's loan disbursements had risen to over a half billion dollars per year, and it became clear that its borrowing power, governed mainly by the subscribed capital of the industrialized countries of the world, would soon be inadequate. In addition, the Bank's membership has grown from 51 countries in 1952 to some 80 countries at the end of 1962 largely as a consequence of the creation of new nations, all of them in need of development financing. Hence, in 1959 the authorized capital stock of the Bank was increased from $10 billion to $21 billion. The subscribed capital of the United States and most of the industrial countries of the world was doubled; in some cases, notably Canada, Germany and Japan, it was more than doubled. Except for a few cases, however, the amount of the paid-in capital of the Bank was not changed. The object was, basically, to increase the amount of uncalled capital that was needed as security for the sale of the Bank's obligations in the world capital markets.

The increase in the Bank's pace of lending has occurred as a result of a number of factors both within and outside of the institution itself; but most of its basic policies, such as those with respect to project loans and the limitation of financing to the external exchange requirements, have remained the same. It might be said, however, that the Bank's policies with respect to the relationship between a potential borrower's public debt burden and its foreign exchange receipts have been liberalized, and that it has perhaps become more lenient in making loans to countries whose internal financial policies have not measured up to IBRD standards.

With the growing concern over the economic development of its members, the Bank has become more and more conscious of certain limitations to be found in its charter and the sources of its own financing. The Bank is a "hard loan" institution in the sense that it must make loans repayable in convertible currencies on terms which bear a close relationship to the cost and conditions of its own borrowing in world capital markets. In recent years it has become increasingly evident that the major limitation on the Bank's loans to many countries has not been the lack of good projects suitable for financing, but rather the long-run debt servicing capacity of the borrowing countries.

There had long been a demand on the part of less developed countries for an additional source of international public financing which would provide grants or soft loans. The idea of a United Nations loan or grant fund was long rejected by the United States and other Western industrial countries. But in the late 1950s an idea for a soft loan institution, to be called the International Development Association, was developed in the Congress of the United States under the sponsorship of Sen. Mike Monroney (D.-Okla.).

While there were many shortcomings in the Monroney proposal, officials of the World Bank prepared a revised plan for an IDA which would operate as a subsidiary of the Bank and constitute a source of loan funds on terms far more liberal than the Bank itself could provide. The IBRD played a leading role in promoting acceptance of IDA, and the new agency was established in September, 1960.

Financing for IDA came mainly in the form of subscriptions by the industrialized countries of the West. Credits from IDA, which totaled $235 million on June 30, 1962, are repayable in foreign exchange, but on very lenient terms. The credits have called for repayment over a 50-year period, with a 10-year period of grace, and are free of interest except for a three-quarters of one per cent annual service charge. These terms are similar to those established by the United States Agency for International Development (AID) on its loans.

Although IDA is a separate legal entity, it has the same executive directors, management and staff as the World Bank. They operate in close cooperation with one another, constituting, in effect, hard and soft sides of the same organization. In many respects, IDA has followed policies similar to those of the World Bank, such as the emphasis on project loans and the policy of providing, with few exceptions, only the foreign exchange requirements for the projects. Although IDA's loans are mainly to government entities and frequently for the same types of projects, such as power and transportation, which are financed by the World Bank on a hard loan basis, there is a tendency for IDA to finance projects which are more in the nature of social impact investments than has been the case with the World Bank.

For example, IDA has made loans for the improvement of urban water supply facilities, a field which the Bank has generally avoided. Also, a considerably larger proportion of IDA's loans have been for the agricultural sector of the developing economies, particularly for irrigation and transportation in rural areas. IDA's funds have been committed rapidly, and by the end of 1963 its modest resources are very likely to be entirely committed. At the September, 1962 conference of the Boards of Governors of the World Bank and IDA, Eugene Black, president of both, called for an increase in the subscriptions to IDA and emphasized the desirability of a shift on the part of free world countries from bilateral to multilateral assistance for economic development.

The World Bank has sought to deal with its limitations on making loans to private enterprise in two ways. First, the Bank's staff prepared the charter for the International Finance Corporation (IFC) which came into being in July, 1956. The first public suggestion for an IFC was made by the U.S. International Development Advisory Board in 1951, and in the following year the Bank published a "Report on the Proposal for an International Finance Corporation," and in subsequent years helped to develop governmental support for the idea in the United Nations and among the members of the Bank.

The subscribed capital of the IFC on June 30, 1962 was $96.5 million, the amounts coming mainly from the developed countries; its total commitments up to that time were $62.5 million. The IFC is empowered to make both loans and (since 1961) equity investments, and to participate in the underwriting of common shares. Its investments range in amount from $200,000 to $5 million, and the use of its funds is not restricted to the financing of the foreign exchange component of specific projects, as is generally the case with World Bank loans. A considerable portion of the IFC's financing has been for joint ventures involving both foreign and local interests.

Although the IFC has made some contribution to the problem of channeling foreign public funds into the private sectors of developing economies, it has severe limitations for meeting the enormous development financing needs of private enterprise in most of these countries.

These limitations are much the same for all international public lending agencies: namely (a) they are not equipped to handle many thousands of applications for small loans and to provide the technical assistance services required in small loan operations; and (b) many small firms require local currency rather than foreign exchange financing. (Even though the small firms need imported goods, they may buy from local importers rather than directly from abroad.)

Because of these limitations, the World Bank and its subsidiaries have assisted developing countries to establish development banks to provide various types of financing, including equity financing, not otherwise available on reasonable terms to small and medium-size firms.

Since responsibility for providing development financing for the countries of the free world is divided among more than a score of international, regional and national agencies, the efforts of these various agencies must be coordinated to carry out the long-range development plans of individual countries. Thus, in recent years the World Bank has been active in the creation of so-called consortia of national and international sources of aid, such as the "India Club" and the Pakistan consortium, as a means of obtaining advance commitments for carrying out long-range development programs. This approach, while especially important in the case of countries like India which have formulated comprehensive development plans, is still a long way from fruition.

It is perhaps because of his appreciation of the need for achieving this kind of coordination that Eugene Black, in his final address to the Bank's Board of Governors in 1962, emphasized the desirability of the multilateral approach to foreign aid and recommended an expansion of the resources of IDA as an alternative to large bilateral assistance.

In recent years the World Bank has been increasingly cognizant of the political dimensions of external development assistance and of the political problems which inevitably arise from the involvement of external assistance agencies in the social and economic life of host countries. The IBRD has had its share of disappointments and mistakes in this area, as evidenced, for example, by acrimonious relations with the Turkish government some years ago and by harsh official criticisms of the Bank and its policies by several Latin American nations.

While continuing to exert pressure for internal financial reforms on the part of borrowing countries, the Bank has learned a great deal about how to make its influence felt without becoming involved in serious political controversies.

The Bank's consciousness of such problems was reflected in a series of lectures by Eugene Black and published in a book entitled, *The Diplomacy of Economic Development* (Harvard University Press, 1960), in which he analyzed in an incisive fashion what he called the "art of development diplomacy."

The Bank's most dramatic achievement in applying this art was perhaps the successful culmination of the long negotiations between India and Pakistan over the division of the waters of the Indus River basin.

The fact that the Bank's image in developing countries has become increasingly more favorable in recent years, except, of course, with the extreme left, is testimony to its greater mastery of the "art of development diplomacy."

In conclusion, we can perhaps do no better than quote from an address of Richard H. Deumth, Director of the Development Services Department of the World Bank, before the Economic and Social Council of the United Nations, July 11, 1962, in which he said:

"Thus the Bank, which began as a purely financial institution concerned initially with postwar reconstruction needs, is today the keystone of an integrated complex of development assistance agencies, able to offer to their members financial and technical help over a broad front."

19

FINANCING FOREIGN OPERATIONS *

I. U.S. PRIVATE SOURCES

This section provides a detailed analysis of the variegated private sources of loan and equity capital within the U.S. which may be approached by a company seeking financing for its overseas operations. The most active organizations in this field are Edge Act corporations and investment companies. Commercial banks, insurance funds and the securities markets, for reasons explained below, are of little importance in financing foreign investments—though even they can be of help under the proper circumstances.

When contacting these sources of loan or equity financing, the potential borrower or investment partner must present a wealth of information pertaining to the project before the negotiations even begin. A checklist of information required by financing banks will usually be attached to the loan-application form.

Most of the funds are concentrated in the east, almost entirely in New York City, though Boston, Philadelphia, Chicago and San Francisco have gained some importance. Of these extensive sources, only a modest portion is available for medium and long-term financing of foreign operations. Even New York lacks the long and intimate experience of other traditional international financial centers such as London or Zurich, and this plus burdensome laws and regulations (federal, state and Federal Reserve Bank) hamper the expansion and flexibility of U.S. international financial institutions. Progress is being made, however, and the U.S. capital market remains the most important one for U.S. companies.

Capital-seeking firms must remember that no bank, Edge Act corporation or private financing company is interested in granting a medium or long-term loan just for the going interest rate. There are plenty of domestic lending opportunities at current interest rates without the inherent risks of foreign financing or the need of tying up funds for long periods. The

* From *Financing Foreign Operations,* prepared and published by Business International, 757 Third Avenue, New York 17, N.Y., pp. 6-31. Copyright 1961. Reprinted by permission.

financier wants an additional compensation or incentive such as a share in the profits of the financial enterprise and/or inclusion of an "equity feature" in the financing contract that will enable the lender to participate in the company's success through capital gains. Such a feature may take the form of:

1. Convertibility of part of the loan, debentures or other instruments of debt into stock of the foreign enterprise (a percentage is usually fixed) at maturity of the loan or sometime before;
2. An option to purchase capital stock at par or some other agreed-upon price. The option may be exercised before maturity of the loan, or sometimes even later;
3. Stock-purchase warrants attached to the debentures;
4. A bonus in the form of capital stock or gratis shares.

One or the other of these features may also be demanded if the investor provides equity financing; the financing company wants a higher return on its investment, commensurate with the risks involved, not investment for investment's sake. Therefore, equity taken over by the financier will more often than not be sold after satisfactory appreciation has been achieved; the seller usually gives to his partners (or the majority owner) the right of first refusal. (More details on the varying practices will be found below.)

Many U.S. companies supplement their funds by utilizing or extending their line of credit with their U.S. bank (or by obtaining a loan in their own name) and using the proceeds for foreign financing. They find this the least costly method of financing foreign operations. Others prefer to have the foreign subsidiary obtain the money, often in foreign currencies and from local banks and other lenders. Here, the parent company can enter the picture by giving a guarantee which usually results in a lower interest rate.

But reluctance to give such guarantees is increasing. If a company has a separately incorporated international subsidiary or foreign base company, a guarantee by these affiliates is often offered—but frequently not accepted. A company can sometimes overcome the necessity of issuing a parent company guarantee by giving the lender a "letter of intent" or "letter of approval" covering the loans to be made to a base company or operating subsidiary. Many lenders, among them foreign banks and U.S. financing companies, are satisfied with such an instrument. Its advantage to the parent company is that it is not considered a liability to be shown on the balance sheet.

In a consolidated balance sheet the subsidiary's debt appears as a liability of the parent company, just as do its liabilities. Companies that do not consolidate would have to show a guarantee, usually in the form of a footnote.

Another valid reason for a parent's refusal to guarantee a subsidiary's liability is a reluctance to add the additional risk (in the respective country) of losing more than the subsidiary's assets, should the venture fail.

The letter of approval or intent must be carefully worded to avoid its being construed as a guarantee and yet satisfy the lender of the funds. A simple statement that the management of the parent company has knowledge of the financing transaction and approves of it is likely to be considered adequate by all parties.

It may also declare that the parent will make sure the lender does not lose on the loan, or even guarantee repayment of the loan at the time it comes due (which promise, made by a firm that cannot sign a guarantee because of a U.S. insurance company loan provision, simply means that the parent will buy the paper from the bank if its sub cannot pay at maturity).

Finally, an outright promise to buy the loan note at maturity if the sub cannot repay is often used. (This approach is preferred by banks, since it is a simple, airtight declaration by the parent; yet accountants say that even this pledge need not be carried on the books or even footnoted.)

Commercial Banks

Commercial banks are a huge source of capital—but only rarely for a manufacturer that seeks long-term or medium-term venture capital. They are hemmed in by laws, regulations and, last but not least, sound banking policy. A bank is supposed to lend out money for about the same term it receives deposits—no longer than 12 months. Actually, most of a bank's foreign credits are granted for not longer than six months and are usually concerned with export financing. Federal Reserve Act rules provide that banks shall not accept commercial drafts or bills with terms longer than six months; drafts or notes running for more than six months are not "bankable," i.e., the bank that financed them could not refinance with the Federal Reserve Bank. An exception to the general rule is the new Eximbank set-up which permits the commercial bank to participate with Eximbank and extend credit on medium term. Despite official authorization, however, some banks seem not overly eager to take advantage of this provision; it is too much against tradition.

Companies trying to get medium-term money from a bank for venture financing have often been disappointed. While not all banks refuse medium and long-term credits, the exceptions are rare. As one corporate executive said: "Only if the bank cannot say 'no' to a big client will it grant such a loan, and then only to the parent company." Another said: "We are only borrowing our own money"—meaning that the firm's average balance on deposit with the bank is much higher than the credit asked for.

Too often, a bank will make the decision not on the merits of the proposed transaction but in consideration of other benefits and profits the bank derives from its client. This attitude has found much criticism among companies, and the banks know it. They have, therefore, tried to find ways to accommodate capital-seeking clients hoping to set up new foreign operations or expand existing ones. One way is to finance on medium term, by way of export financing with or without Eximbank participation or guarantees, that part of the manufacturer's investment that is represented by equipment (and sometimes supplies) shipped abroad. For the additional capital needed by the subsidiary abroad, the bank refers the potential borrower to its foreign branch or affiliate for credits in local currencies to provide working capital. The influence of the New York bank is usually enough to induce the foreign affiliate to extend the credit and, more important, to arrange for renewal after the initial period. This method has worked well in many instances.

Table 1 shows the 11 Edge Act corporations, all of them owned by U.S. banks, which were operating in 1961.

TABLE 1

EDGE ACT CORPORATIONS, 1961

Name	Address	Capital (in $ million)
Financing Corporations		
Bankers International Financing Co., Inc.	16 Wall Street, New York, N.Y.	2.0
Chase International Investment Corp.	1 Chase Manhattan Plaza New York, N.Y.	5.0
Chemical International Finance, Ltd.	165 Broadway, New York, N.Y.	5.0
Morgan Guaranty International Finance Corp.	23 Wall Street, New York, N.Y.	2.0
Philadelphia International Investment Corp.	421 Chestnut Street Philadelphia, Pa.	3.5
The Boston Overseas Financial Corp.	67 Milk Street, Boston, Mass.	2.0
Banking Corporations		
Bank of America (International)	41 Broad Street New York, N.Y.	34.0
Bankers International Corp.	16 Wall Street, New York, N.Y.	2.0
Chemical International Banking Corp.	165 Broadway, New York, N.Y.	2.0
First Bank of Boston (International)	2 Wall Street, New York, N.Y.	2.0
Guaranty International Banking Corp.	Wall Street, New York, N.Y.	2.0

The outstanding sources for venture capital are the financing corporations. The objectives of all these institutions are substantially the same, though there are differences in emphasis. Some are highly flexible and active, others are conservative to the point of merely furthering the parent bank's domestic business. Resources of the Edge Act corporations, though large, are limited by the regulations preventing a parent bank from investing more than 10% of its capital and surplus in all of its Edge Act subsidiaries; and the subsidiary may not loan to or invest in any single firm more than 50% of its capital and surplus, with a limit on equity participation of 10% of its capital and surplus. On the other hand, an Edge Act financing corporation may borrow 10 times its capital and reserves. Their available funds are also augmented by repayments.

All transactions are medium term (the short-term business is taken care of by the parent bank) with five to seven years as the norm, though extended terms to 10 years are gaining in frequency. The more aggressive managements of Edge Act corporations are trying to get away from the concept (originally widespread) that foreign financing should be limited to parent company customers or firms expected to channel their domestic business through the bank. This change of attitude, however, is not yet universal.

The pattern that has evolved also shows an ever-increasing readiness to give prospective customers advice and guidance on investment opportunities, incentives, tax laws and regulations abroad. The investment bank does not strive to be the only capital source for a given project; it likes to spread and limit the risk, and the cooperation and participation of several financiers and public institutions such as IFC and DLF are becoming more and more familiar. The finance corporation will often arrange for group financing or the formation of a consortium for the capital-seeking company. Finance corporations, as distinguished from banking corporations, are not much interested in medium-term export financing or in granting simple loans or guarantees. They are moving rapidly toward investment and equity financing, and the development loans they negotiate almost invariably have an equity feature (see above) as a condition. They never seek voting control, though occasionally they may obtain a majority of the stock.

Edge Act Corporations

A way around the strict limitations imposed on commercial banks engaged in international business and financing was paved by the Edge Act, effective since January 1919, which amended the Federal Reserve Act by new Section 25(a). The Act creates two types of corporations:

A. Banking corporations
B. Financing corporations

A third type, *agreement banks,* was authorized to fill a gap in the regulations by permitting U.S. banks to invest in institutions engaged in foreign banking in countries where branch offices of U.S. banks are not permitted; the minimum capital of $2 million is not required. Operation of such banking corporations requires a prior agreement with the Federal Reserve Board.

The Edge Act was implemented by Regulation K of the Federal Reserve Board, amended Jan. 15, 1957. Under Regulation K, *banking corporations* may engage in commercial banking, accept foreign deposits or domestic deposits that are incidental to foreign business transactions, accept drafts or bills of exchange and make loans related to foreign business, but they may not make equity investments abroad, except in stock of other corporations engaged in foreign banking activities.

Financing corporations may not engage in commercial banking (receive deposits and accept drafts and bills) but may engage in equity financing and make investments in foreign enterprises not engaged in the banking business. Activities in the U.S. are also limited to those incidental to their foreign activities. This non-banking type is important as a capital source for financing the international business of U.S. companies. The financing corporations must have a minimum capital of $2 million, but as subsidiaries of U.S. banks their actual capital resources are vastly greater than the authorized capital. The term "Edge Act corporations" usually refers to the financing corporations.

Investment Companies

A new type of merchant and investment banker, specializing in equity financing of foreign ventures and in development loans, has emerged in recent years. Still growing in numbers and activity, these organizations have become a large and satisfactory private source of capital. (Table 2 lists ten companies that are outstanding in the field.)

TABLE 2

U.S. FINANCE FIRMS PROVIDING CAPITAL FOR FOREIGN VENTURES, 1961

Name	Address	Capital (in $ million)
International Basic Economy Corp.	30 Rockefeller Plaza, New York	21.3*
Deltec Corp.	72 Wall Street, New York	4.25
Transoceanic AOFC Ltd.	630 Fifth Avenue, New York	14.8*
American Express Co.	65 Broadway, New York	22.3
American & Foreign Power Co., Inc.	100 Church Street, New York	187.7
N. A. Bogdan & Co., Inc.	63 Wall Street, New York	(not available)
Financial & Development Fund	230 Park Avenue, New York	2.0
Overseas Investors Inc.	500 Fifth Avenue, New York	(not available)
Pan American Capital Corp.	535 Fifth Avenue, New York	1.3
American International Investment Corp.	400 Montgomery Street, San Francisco	1.0

* includes retained earnings

Insurance Funds

Large accumulations of funds that have always attracted the eye of the capital-hungry manufacturer are the *insurance companies* union pension funds and similar organizations. Unhappily, they are not a source of venture capital or even long-term loans to subsidiaries abroad; laws and conservative investment policies prevent such activity. To be sure, insurance companies do make long-term investments, but the investments open to them in the foreign field clearly violate their policy and the regulations under which they operate. A plan has been worked out by the Chase Manhattan Bank to establish a new finance company specializing in export financing. The new company would sell seven-year to 10-year debentures to insurance companies; the debentures would be backed by export paper—but the whole plan hinges on establishment of an export credit insurance facility to guarantee these drafts.

Securities Market

Underwriting houses, old established investment banks and brokerage firms (members of the New York Stock Exchange) are not playing the role in providing venture capital to U.S. industry that is generally assumed by the public. Their interest is centered in the floating of new issues —capital stock or debentures—of U.S.-based companies. Only in rare cases can a U.S. company seek to issue stock of a foreign subsidiary in the U.S.; only very sizable issues could be so offered, and high costs plus the strict regulations of the SEC make it unprofitable to tap the securities market for such financing. Private placement of the debentures or notes of a foreign corporation maturing within five or 10 years has occasionally been negotiated, but this type of financing has not reached any appreciable volume.

Stock issued by a foreign subsidiary abroad, however, may be traded on the New York financial market. The shares of a few large foreign corporations whose majority (or a substantial minority) is owned by a U.S. company, such as various Ford subsidiaries (Belgian, Dutch) and Kaiser Industries in Argentina, are traded freely. SEC rules provide that foreign shares can be offered to the public only if they have been traded on a foreign stock exchange for a minimum period of time (usually 40 days). If not, the shares must be registered with SEC first. Registration with SEC, however, is not only time-consuming but generally difficult to obtain.

Foreign Trade Financing

An increasing number of private U.S. commercial financing companies and factoring firms are engaging in foreign financing. When a satisfactory system of export credit insurance (now under discussion at Eximbank in Washington) is established, their number will shoot up even faster and the cost of financing through them will decline. These firms are not a source of medium or long-term venture capital. Their field is mainly foreign trade financing, but they can be very useful to U.S. companies with foreign operations if the relatively high cost can be borne by a particular transaction.

A U.S. exporter, wishing to shorten the period between shipment of and payment for goods or wishing to discount his foreign accounts receivable or foreign paper without recourse to him, may reap advantages from utilizing the facilities of "foreign factors." These firms stress export financing which is not available from Eximbank or commercial banks, offering non-recourse financing (which a commercial bank will not do) and granting terms up to two years on export credits. U.S. manufacturers have tended to shun them because of the high cost of this type of financing, which generally ranges from 8% to 14% per annum, depending on the nature of the goods financed, the country of destination and the services rendered by the financier. Part of the extra cost is offset by the non-recourse clause, the quick collection of the export proceeds from the finance firm and savings of time and effort in collecting outstanding bills from the foreign importer. In view of mounting credit competition abroad, U.S. exporters may find it increasingly worth their while to use the services of these private export financiers.

Far from handling only the scraps of business not good enough for a bank (or transactions with an undue credit risk), these firms apply strict and conservative standards with regard to the debtor's credit rating and countries of destination, though they are more flexible in individual situations than are commercial banks.

Private financing firms are especially well equipped to smooth relations between a U.S. manufacturer and its franchised distributor abroad. A typical example of distributor financing is provided by one of the leading firms in this field, *Intercontinental Credit Corp.* ICC concludes a draft purchase agreement with the manufacturer for those countries and distributors found acceptable. ICC then establishes revolving credit lines for the distributors in agreement with the manufacturer. Within the limits of these lines, the manufacturer presents his export drafts (with terms usually 180 days) to ICC for payment (accompanied by shipping documents). As an alternative, ICC makes its own credit arrangements with individual distributors, again setting up revolving credit lines, and confirming payment for the distributors' orders to the manufacturers. In both cases, ICC pays the manufacturer the full value of his export documents without recourse to the manufacturer for credit, exchange and political risks. The distributor does not tie up his working capital or local bank credit at the supplier's end, but can use his own sources of capital for the financing of his inventory and sales.

A manufacturer planning to obtain financing from a private company should ascertain its cost before quoting prices to the foreign importer, in order to include it (wholly or partly) in the export price.

Among the firms active in financing foreign trade are some with very substantial financial resources, and with branches and correspondents in the important foreign markets. Leading firms in this highly specialized field (all located in New York) are:

A. J. Armstrong & Co., 60 East 42 Street, resources $60 million;
American Swiss Credit Co., 37 Wall Street, resources $2 million;
N. A. Bogdan & Co., 63 Wall Street, resources in excess of $1 million;
Continental Commerce Corporation, 30 Broad Street;
Feuchtwanger Corporation, 60 East 42 Street, affiliated with Feuchtwanger (London) Ltd.; Feuchtwanger Bank, Tel Aviv; Feuchtwanger Bank, Munich;
Inland Credit Corp., 11 West 42 Street, resources over $15 million;
Intercontinental Credit Corp., 2 Park Avenue, resources in excess of $15 million; subsidiary of Pan American Trade Development Corp.;
NYHACO Credit Corp., 120 Broadway, affiliate of New York Hanseatic Corp;
Park Bridge Corp., 52 Wall Street;
The Slavenburg Corp., 62 William Street; resources $4 million; wholly owned by NV Slavenburg's Bank, Rotterdam;
James Talcott Inc., 221 Park Avenue South; predominantly engaged in domestic factoring but expanding foreign financing; very substantial resources;

Trumann & Co., 70 Pine Street; resources about $1 million;
Zilkha & Sons, 120 Broadway.

Amstel Club. A welcome source of medium and short-term capital, mainly to finance exports and imports, is an association of international finance companies known as the "Amstel Club." Finance companies in 12 European countries and the U.S. (see list below) cooperate closely in arranging financing for practically all transactions related to export and import, granting credit to the importer, the exporter or the seller of goods on an installment plan. Coverage is extended by the Club even beyond the borders of the respective European countries and the U.S. by including most (but not all) overseas possessions and Canada, the latter being served by the U.S. and UK members of the group.

The technique is as follows: The manufacturer that wants to export to one of the countries represented by a member approaches that member which, in turn, refers the proposal to the member in the importing country. The decision to provide financing is always made by the member in the buyer's country, and all negotiations must be carried on there; the role of the finance house in the exporter's country is limited to referring the case to the foreign member. If a contract is closed, the financier in the importer's country pays direct to the exporter, recovering the funds from the importer according to contract. In some cases, financing is without recourse to the exporter, but this question is also decided by the foreign financier.

AMSTEL CLUB MEMBERS

Austria: Ava (Automobil-und Warenkredit Verkehrs-Anstalt GmbH (Subsidiary of Creditanstalt-Bankverein), Hanuschgasse 1, Vienna 1.

Belgium: Banque de Bruxelles, 2, rue de la Regence, Brussels.

Denmark: Diskonto-Selskabet A/S (Subsidiary of Kobenhavns Handelsbank), Vingardstraede 3, Copenhagen.

France: Credit Mobilier Industriel (SOVAC) (Subsidiary of Lazard Freres), 18, avenue Matignon, Paris 8c.

Germany: Kundrenkreditbank, KGaA, Kasernenstrasse 8, Duesseldorf.

Italy: Compass SpA. (Subsidiary of Banco di Credito Finanziario SpA.), Via Filadrammatici 8, Milan.

Netherlands: Industrieele Disc. Maatschappij, NV (Subsidiary of Twentsche Bank), Keizersgracht 119-121, Amsterdam C.

Norway: A/S Norsk Handelskreditt, Kogensgate 33, Oslo.

Portugal: Fincol-Sociedade de Financiamentos Limitada, 12-1 Rua dos Remolares, Lisbon 2.

Sweden: Finansieringsaktiebolaget Vendor (Associated with Stockholms Enskilda Bank), Wahrendorffsgatan 1, Stockholm 16.

Switzerland: AKO Bank Anspar-und Kredit-Organisations A.G. City-Hochhaus, Talacker 50, Zurich 1.

UK: United Dominions Trust Ltd., United Dominions House, Eastcheap, London E-C. 3.

US: Commercial Credit Co., 300 St. Paul Place, Baltimore 2, Md.

The advantages of using the Club are the greatly simplified procedures and the lower interest rates that may prevail. Cost of financing depends largely on interest rates prevailing in the importer's country. On the average it has been 5% or roughly 2% above the discount rate or the "prime rate." Duration of the credits is two to five years, depending on the life of the product financed. Typical rates in Germany and Austria are 5.5%, in Holland 5%.

Subsidiaries of U.S. companies in Europe, selling on credit to wholesalers, retailers or direct to consumers, may utilize the factoring facilities of the member finance firms, which will finance accounts receivable as well as inventories (in local currencies). Shipments on consignment are also eligible for financing.

"Swap" Transactions

If a foreign subsidiary or branch cannot or does not want to add to its existing local debts, or if local interest rates are excessive, the U.S. parent may be called upon to provide needed local-currency funds. In these circumstances the U.S. company may want to protect itself against exchange-rate depreciation. Therefore, instead of simply buying foreign currency with dollars and lending to the sub (or lending dollars for repayment in dollars, which would expose the sub to the exchange risk), the firm follows one of two alternatives:

1. *Conclusion of a "foreign currency swap."* The parent company buys the required amount of foreign currency on the market for immediate delivery at the "spot rate" and simultaneously re-purchases the dollar amount on the forward exchange market, i.e., for delivery at the time when the local currency funds are expected to be returned by the subsidiary. Forward delivery of dollars in countries with a depreciating currency obviously requires a premium for the dollar. Such currency swap transactions are possible only in countries with a free exchange market, and are usually limited to periods of up to 12 months except in countries with convertible currencies, where longer periods are possible.

2. A more satisfactory alternative is to *swap a dollar credit for a foreign currency credit.* This is a credit transaction that is not to be confused with a foreign currency swap as mentioned above. It is feasible in countries suffering from a dollar shortage, and is the cheapest way to obtain local funds for a limited period of time, particularly in a country with tight money conditions and high local interest rates. The usual technique is this:

The U.S. company opens a dollar credit in the U.S. to a foreign bank (central bank or private bank) and the foreign bank lends the countervalue in local currency at an agreed upon rate of exchange to the subsidiary for a specified period of time. The dollar funds will be returned at maturity of the swap and simultaneously with repayment of the local currency loan. The parties to the deal agree on:

1. a fixed rate of exchange applied to both phases of the transaction;

2. a fixed period of time;

3. an interest rate for the local currency credit, which is usually below the current rate of interest and certainly much lower than the total cost of credit in tight-money markets (no interest is paid for the dollar credit opened by the U.S. company).

The advantage to the U.S. parent is full protection against the foreign exchange risk, and to the subsidiary a (sometimes considerably) lower rate of interest for the local funds borrowed. The foreign bank carries the exchange risk but has the benefit of the free use of the dollar funds—a very important factor in dollar-poor countries.

The cost factors are the interest rate charged to the borrower of the local funds, and the loss of interest on the tied up U.S. dollars.

An additional factor to be considered is the mutually agreed upon exchange rate at which the dollar funds are converted into and out of the foreign currency. This usually requires the U.S. company to make more dollars available for a given amount of local currency than if it were to buy this amount on the free market. But this is offset by the fact that the foreign bank absorbs the entire exchange depreciation risk during the life of the swap. In private swaps, i.e., those concluded with a private bank or firm abroad, the exchange rate is usually closer to the free market rate than in swaps with official bodies. If the swap is with a central bank, as has been the case for very large amounts with the Banco do Brasil, conversion and interest rates may be fixed very much below current free rates.

For example, the Brazilian central bank converted at rates down to about 58 cruzeiros per dollar and charged interest for cruzeiros as low as 1% per annum at a time when the free market rate was double and treble this fictitious rate. Swaps with the Banco do Brasil attained such volume (at times it had more than $200 million outstanding) because the desire of the Brazilian Government for dollar credits was matched by the desire of U.S. companies to furnish large funds to their Brazilian investments at a time of a sharply depreciating cruzeiro.

Before closing a swap deal the U.S. company should carefully calculate the actual costs of a swap and compare them with the estimated exchange loss that would be suffered if, instead of closing a swap, it bought foreign currency at the current free-market rate. It should also calculate the cost of an ordinary credit obtainable locally in the foreign currency.

II. U.S. PUBLIC SOURCES

The single largest source of direct financing for U.S. private international traders and investors is the U.S. Government. Through the $7 billion Export-Import Bank of Washington (Eximbank), it:

Lends to industrial projects and to U.S. businesses in developing lands;

Extends credit to exporters;

Is broadening its guarantees and insurance of credits against political and commercial risks in export.

Beginning this year, a new unified foreign aid agency—Agency for International Development (AID)—will consolidate and broaden the functions of the State Department's Development Loan Fund (DLF) and the International Cooperation Administration (ICA), plus some of the foreign financial operations connected with domestic surplus crop disposal. As an improved source of private international finance, AID will:

> Make direct loans to U.S. private development ventures abroad for project feasibility surveys and initial capital costs;
>
> "Tie" U.S. aid funds closer to subcontracting through U.S. private suppliers of goods and services;
>
> Improve private foreign investment guarantees generally, and, in special high-priority cases involving "must" projects in less-developed areas, "experimentally" cover at least a portion of U.S. investors' stakes in such projects against virtually all risks.

All these are *direct* ways in which the U.S. Government can provide dollars, and in some instances foreign currencies, to finance and guarantee an almost unlimited range of private exports and investments overseas.

There are also *indirect* ways in which Washington can help finance and insure U.S. private trade and investment. Three examples: massive contributions of public funds to international financial institutions (whose roles as capital sources for U.S. private foreign business are discussed in subsequent sections); participation in joint international public-private ventures where public underwriting of basic "infrastructure" costs paves the way for private trade and investment; and U.S. foreign military aid, which helps finance exports of a broad segment of U.S. industry, including makers of metalworking machinery, vehicles, chemicals, and electronic products. . . .

The Administration in Washington is following the growing trend toward priority emphasis on the underdeveloped areas of the world. U.S. Government financing and credit guarantees for exports will be continued, and even expanded, without specific regard for their final destination. But federal financing and guarantees for U.S. private foreign investment will be limited strictly to investment in the emerging lands.

Export-Import Bank of Washington (Eximbank)

Eximbank is by far U.S. private investors' and traders' largest, most direct, and oldest official source of capital for financing exports and overseas plants. The 27-year-old, $7 billion agency, set up as an independent organization answerable directly to Congress as well as to the White House, serves U.S. international business in three main ways:

> It makes long-term dollar loans—which must be spent for purchases in the U.S.—to economic development projects in less-developed areas (more than half of all Exim loans have gone to Latin America);
>
> It extends medium-term (six months to five years) credits to U.S. exporters to help finance shipments of U.S. goods and services throughout the free world;

It guarantees private short-term export credits (30-180 days) against political risks, and is now committed to provide partial backing for private short-term credit commercial risk insurance. It guarantees medium-term credits against political and commercial risks, or political only.

Twice in the past 18 months, Eximbank has liberalized its financing and guarantee policies substantially, and at this printing of Business International's special report, is planning further benefits to U.S. exporters. All three rounds of liberalization stem, at least in part, from the considerable criticism that Eximbank policies have been too conservative. How far the comparatively new policies will go toward answering this criticism must remain an open question until their practical effects can be measured. But clearly Eximbank's role in promoting U.S. private foreign trade has been considerably broadened.

Briefly, Eximbank policy changes include:

1. Extension of guarantees against both political and commercial risk to short-term export credits and extension of political only, as well as comprehensive coverage, to medium-term credits. Eximbank will attempt as far as possible to "farm out" the writing of short-term commercial risk insurance to a pool of private banks and insurance companies. Previously, Eximbank guaranteed only medium and long-term credits and financing against all risks.

2. Broadening of the kinds of exports for which Eximbank will finance and guarantee medium-term credit to cover semi-finished manufactures and consumer durables (autos, refrigerators, radios, TV). Eximbank also now includes oil field equipment and will finance and guarantee sales of such equipment to state-owned or controlled foreign enterprises. (Previously, Eximbank would not lend or guarantee exports to a Latin American government oil monopoly or mining company.)

3. Abandonment of Eximbank's traditional role as "economic doctor" in financing or guaranteeing export credits. (Previously, the Bank extended credit or guarantees only to those export sales its economists felt would contribute to the productive development of a host country.)

4. Establishment of a new method (currently under study) of insuring individual export shipments or charging varying rates for political and commercial risk coverage for different destinations—or some combination of the two. There is, however, some doubt that Exim will actually come through with such a change.

5. Speed-up of paperwork on export credits and guarantees, which will involve advance Eximbank commitments on all operations other than long-range project development loans, and greater Bank reliance on private exporters' credit standing with commercial banks in place of exhaustive Bank investigations. (Here, too, there remains some skepticism as to the Bank's success in eliminating delays.)

The main Eximbank innovation (still under study) is how to inspire more private commercial bank and insurance company handling of both short-term and medium-term export credit financing and guarantees. Eximbank thinking is that such a program will involve a pool of private companies and banks which will write most, if not all, the commercial risk coverage for the U.S. Government, backed by at least a partial Eximbank guarantee. For example, Eximbank would guarantee all the political risk, and perhaps 50% or less of the commercial risk in a given export credit, with the pool of private companies underwriting half or more of the commercial risk.

The Bank expects to apply its new system to medium-term deals as well as short term. However, the problem of directly financing medium-term export credits remains to be ironed out. Eximbank has announced plans to work through exporter associations formed under the Webb-Pomerene Act (exempting such export consortia from certain provisions of anti-trust laws) in conjunction with Edge Act companies to provide medium-term financing. The trouble is that most Edge Act companies require 6-7.5% interest rates on such financing, substantially higher than Eximbank's average 5.75% interest charge for direct financing. Since Eximbank, like other U.S. Government institutions, is theoretically precluded from competing with private financing, it is under some pressure to either raise interest rates for medium-term credit financing or else turn over such operations to private companies. Bank officials are currently looking for some less drastic compromise.

It should be noted that Eximbank's recent and contemplated policy liberalizations apply to its function of financing and guaranteeing medium-term exporter credits and guaranteeing short-term credits. Aside from these most direct forms of financial assistance to U.S. exporters, the Bank serves numerous other related functions in the field of financing U.S. foreign trade and investment. It:

> Commits roughly $500 million a year to project development loans, compared to a current rate of less than $100 million for exporter credits and guarantees;
>
> Makes balance-of-payments loans to foreign governments;
>
> Acts as fiscal agent for other U.S. Government agencies, administering ICA grants and Defense Department loans overseas, administering ICA private investment guarantees and collecting U.S. World War II claims against Germany and repayments of foreign loans authorized under the old Reconstruction Finance Corp. (RFC);
>
> Administers Cooley fund foreign-currency loans of proceeds from U.S. foreign agricultural surplus disposal programs to U.S. private companies abroad for expansion and improvement (but not for long; this function will now be taken over by AID—see below).

Eximbank's long-term project development loans go primarily to "friendly" foreign governments (it pioneered in U.S. Government foreign-aid lending to Yugoslavia and Indonesia, and is deeply involved in the new Ghana hydro-electric-aluminum project), although private U.S. and foreign enterprises are eligible to receive these loans directly (when the host government guarantees the loans, a precaution also required by the World Bank). Like the World Bank, Eximbank concentrates in this phase of its lending on basic industrial projects: power facilities, transportation, ore mining and milling, fertilizer and cement plants.

Also like other international financiers, Eximbank of late has emphasized loans to foreign national and private development banks and credit institutions, for relending to private enterprise—U.S. and local. Eximbank's "Buy-American" loan-tying policy applies in these cases as well as in government-to-government loans.

Eximbank project lending also can include balance-of-payments loans and commodity import loans to foreign governments for purchase of U.S. goods. Project loans are repayable in dollars, and must contribute to the economic productivity of the host country. They run up to 20 years. Again, like other international capital sources, Eximbank is currently stressing joint participation in these projects with U.S. and foreign private capital as well as with other public financial institutions, domestic and foreign. Interest rates average 5.75%.

Eximbank medium-term exporter credits, which carry a similar interest rate, are extended to a wide range of U.S. capital goods exports—aircraft and raw cotton providing the outstanding examples to date. These, too, are made and repayable in dollars, and run up to seven years (most run for five years, except for aircraft). Eximbank finances up to 85% of the export credit—after a 20% cash payment by the buyer—with the exporter financing the remaining 15%. This means that of the transaction's total face value, the buyer puts up 20%, Eximbank 68%, the exporter 12%. If a private commercial bank participates, the exporter may not be required to do so. U.S. exporters may establish lines of credit with Eximbank, but this device so far has been rarely used.

The guarantee programs carry these approximate charges: comprehensive political and commercial risk coverage on medium-term credits—1.5% per year on the declining balance guaranteed; medium-term political risk coverage only—0.75% per year on the outstanding credit balances; short-term political risk coverage—1% per year; short-term commercial or comprehensive risk coverage—not yet determined, but Eximbank officials feel rates should not exceed comparable rates for medium-term credit, because the risk, contrary to appearances, is actually the same or less.

Exporter credits and guarantees are generally "non-recourse"—that is, the exporter is not held legally liable in case of default.

Eximbank adheres to the international ground rules established for export credit by the Berne Union—a clearing agency for information whose main task is to avert cut-throat competition among exporting countries in the credit and credit insurance field. The basic rule is that credits (or credit insurance) must be limited to five years following delivery of the goods to the foreign purchaser. This limit, however, is quite elastic in practice:

> The limit is measured after delivery (or even installation) of the *last* component of the export order; thus, if deliveries under a single order are spread over, say, three years, the actual credit insurance can run eight years.
>
> Any bank (and both public and private banks in most industrial countries in the world adhere—in theory—to the rules) can violate the limit, when there is some reason for doing so (e.g., shipment of an electric power plant), but they must notify the Union—and other members then have a right to do likewise.

A bank or group of banks can arrange supplemental financing beyond the insured five-year portion, and this need not be reported to the Union. (Only blue-chip exporters could get such treatment, of course.)

Jet aircraft are allowed seven years.

No limit exists on government-to-government development or project loans—with the result that much equipment that would be limited to five-year financing under simple exporter credits receives much longer financing via this route. In addition, the dividing line between exporter credits and development loans can be fuzzy.

Agency for International Development (AID)

Next to Eximbank, AID will be U.S. private foreign traders' and investors' second most important source of capital.

It supersedes the two U.S. agencies hitherto operating in this field—State Department's Development Loan Fund (DLF) and the semi-independent International Cooperation Administration (ICA). It will take over from Eximbank the administration of foreign currency loans to U.S. private enterprises in less-developed areas under the so-called Cooley Amendment to PL480—involving money earned from sale abroad of domestic crop surpluses.

As a capital source, AID's benefits to U.S. private business abroad fall into three main categories: development financing, other financial assistance, and investment guarantees.

I. Development Financing

AID has a proposed five-year capitalization of $8.8 billion, to be borrowed from the U.S. Treasury within annual limits, earmarked for economic and social development *loans*. Loans planned for FY 1962 total close to $1.2 billion, an estimate that will rise in the four succeeding fiscal years. This compares to a total DLF commitment of $1.8 billion (328 loans) from its inception in 1957 through calendar 1960.

In addition . . . AID has scheduled $20 million this year for *development research* which includes both academic and field work on long-range "country planning" and a special $5 million fund set aside for *industrial project feasibility studies and surveys.*

Development financing is by far AID's most important contribution to capital sources—and the area in which it will work most closely with private enterprise. This is the function which will absorb most of the current lending operations of the DLF, plus some of ICA's grants.

1. *Loans*—Who Gets Them. AID will lend a substantial proportion of its available loan funds to foreign governments, foreign private enterprises, and foreign institutions such as national development banks and private credit agencies—as has DLF. The important innovation here is that AID plans to make direct loans to private U.S. investors, companies, and foreign affiliates. . . .

AID, like DLF, will favor as borrowers foreign private enterprises over state-owned ventures, wherever possible. Often, this depends on the type of project involved. Of DLF's $1.8 million, one third went to foreign private enterprise.

2. *Types of Projects.* DLF concentrated on basic industrial infrastructure: power facilities, railways, highways, telecommunications, airports, harbors—and raw material mines, mills, and processing plants. Recently, DLF also stepped up loans for "social" public works projects—health, housing, agriculture, and education—and for relending to local private enterprises through development banks and credit institutions. One of DLF's requirements was that the project contribute to the productive capacity of the receiving country.

AID's lending policies will be more flexible. The basic aim is the same—to promote sound economic development and, wherever possible, free enterprise. But AID plans loans to a much wider spectrum of projects, within its prime framework of carefully planned long-range country development programs. This means that AID probably will lend more money than has DLF both to public-owned foreign social and basic industrial projects *and* to private productive, processing, and manufacturing facilities, and will not be as rigid in determining what is or is not a "productive" venture.

3. *What Countries Qualify.* DLF, limited by law to ill-defined "friendly, less-developed areas," concentrated on Southeast Asia and the Far East, partly because Eximbank and World Bank financing in other areas has been relatively heavy. AID will not consciously favor any one of its four regional administrative distribution areas—Africa and Europe, Far East, Latin America, and Near East and South Asia—although it inherits DLF's limitation to "less-developed" areas. However, AID planning officials point out that the bulk of its proposed $1.2 billion development loan fund for FY 1962 is already committed as part of overall U.S. foreign aid pledges to three individual nations—India, Pakistan and Brazil. Whatever the U.S. Congress and those three nations leave untouched will be allocated without geographical prejudice. But it should be noted that U.S. commitments to India, Pakistan and Brazil underscore a tendency to select "pilot" areas for U.S. aid, where officials have reason to believe it can produce the best economic results. Other candidates for "pilot" aid projects include Nigeria, Tunisia and Bolivia. Then there are the politically "must" countries—South Vietnam, Ghana, Argentina and Venezuela, to cite but a few examples, not to mention the military "musts"—such as South Korea, Formosa, Turkey and Iran.

4. *Terms and Conditions.* AID's lending terms will be significantly different from DLF's. It will lend dollars, as has DLF, but will generally require repayment in dollars, whereas DLF has received some repayments in local currencies.

AID will have an almost open-end interest rate schedule. DLF rates averaged about 3.5% for basic public projects, and 5.75% on loans to private, profit-seeking enterprises. AID will charge nominal interest—say, 2%—or no interest on some of its social development loans, up to prevailing international institution rates (approximately 5.75%) on other basic infrastructure loans, and up to prevailing local foreign private interest rates on its loans to private ventures. In unusual cases, where AID may lend at low rates to U.S. private investors to get a top-priority plant built, it plans to control or participate in the profits of the enterprise through convertible debentures or profit-sharing securities. Also, in such cases, AID may require local private investment participation. Where it makes direct loans to U.S. private investors, it will select the country, industry, and company to be financed.

Whereas DLF was specifically banned from competing with private capital sources, and was required to "take into account" whether financing could be obtained from other free-world sources such as Eximbank or international institutions on reasonable terms, AID is bound only by the latter caveat. AID will step up DLF's limited moves toward joint participation with other U.S. and international capital sources, public and private. Like DLF, it will have to consider the economic soundness and feasibility of a project loan—but under a broader frame of reference on how well a project fits into the overall social and economic development plan of a given country or region. Again like DLF, AID will expect "reasonable prospects of repayment," and—now more than ever—will require recipients to demonstrate willingness to take local "self-help" measures.

AID loans may run up to as long as 50 years before they mature, with an added 10-year grace period granted. Payments may be set lower in the first few years, sometimes with no repayment of principal. DLF loans averaged 15 years, could be stretched to 30. AID loans to U.S. and foreign private investors generally will fall due faster—say, in 10 years, if the project appears profitable by then.

AID will inherit DLF's authority to guarantee private commercial loans (it exercised this authority only twice), and will continue DLF's general requirement that supplies be shipped at least 50% in U.S. bottoms. Like DLF, AID loans and loan guarantees will not require "clearing" with host governments, but will be subject to host government "veto." In line with its local self-help and country-planning requirement policies AID will concentrate on projects favored by host governments.

5. *Procurement Policy.* AID will maintain DLF's requirement that loan money be used to "buy American" wherever possible.

6. *Grants.* AID's development grants, which private firms can benefit from through subcontracting, will take over similar government-to-government assistance now handled through ICA. Of the $390 million planned for FY 1962, all but $125 million will go for existing programs. The priorities are: education and technical training, including construction of buildings and provision of supplies; agricultural, rural and community housing projects; health and sanitation projects; surveys of natural resources and industrial project feasibility studies; and in some instances basic industrial infrastructure projects such as roads, dams, waterworks and communications facilities.

Africa, particularly the tropical parts, and other especially needy areas unable to afford or absorb loans will continue to be the primary beneficiaries of this type of aid.

Grant funds also will be used to finance U.S.-sponsored schools abroad, and the Atoms-for-Peace research project.

7. *Research.* AID's low-budget ($20 million for FY 1962) development research program includes a $5 million fund for another form of direct financial aid to U.S. private investors. This is the "Investment Survey

Program" under which AID will pay up to 50% of the costs of private feasibility studies of investment opportunities in underdeveloped areas.

Previously, under ICA, Government financial participation in these studies was limited to contracts with private companies which would *not* benefit directly from the project under consideration, thus excluding potential investors. Now, AID will specifically invite companies that are prospective investors to participate in the program. AID will either contract with the private firm to conduct the study, or where prospective investors "cannot justify financing the needed investigation," underwrite as much as half the cost. In such cases, the prospective investor cannot recover his portion of the costs from the Government, regardless of whether he follows up with an actual investment.

II. Other Financial Assistance

Apart from development financing, AID is scheduled to assume the administration of various other foreign aid programs which directly or indirectly finance U.S. private international trade and investment.

Cooley Loans. The most direct and probably most important program in this category is the so-called Cooley Fund, which reserves "up to 25%" of foreign-currency proceeds from the sale of U.S. agricultural surpluses overseas for loans to private U.S. companies and their foreign affiliates abroad to cover local costs of expansion and improvement, and to private U.S. and foreign companies for expanding normal commercial markets for U.S. agricultural exports. . . .

There are few restrictions on these unguaranteed loans, other than that they be used to promote economic development overseas. They run up to 10 years, and can be used only in the country in which they are lent. They are not convertible to dollars. Interest charges are "related" to prevailing local rates. These loans are not taken into account with respect to any other form of U.S. or international agency financing. Like AID development loans, they may be vetoed by host governments.

AID, which inherits the handling of this program from Eximbank, will "re-examine" both the usual rates and length of maturity requirements, with an eye toward liberalizing them. Eximbank officials will, albeit reluctantly, approve Cooley loans to be used for working capital, the only U.S. or international agency funds eligible for such use other than investments of IFC. However, they point out two major limitations: foreign governments, which have a veto power over Cooley Fund loans, often take a dim view of working capital loans in competition with loans used to finance plant and equipment, and Eximbank itself will okay working capital loans only when there is a plentiful supply of the foreign currency in question. In other words, working capital loan applications get a low priority both from foreign and U.S. officials. However, officials who will man the private enterprise offices of AID do not share the Eximbank view and say they are working on a plan to broaden AID's authority to approve Cooley Fund loans for working capital purposes.

Supporting Assistance and Contingency Fund. AID will take over "supporting assistance" (formerly known as "defense support") from

ICA, and the President's emergency contingency fund from the White House.

Supporting assistance—$610 million earmarked for FY 1962, largely in grants to foreign governments—is to be gradually replaced by development loans. Two thirds of this year's total will go to friendly and often militarily allied nations on the borders of the Sino-Soviet Bloc, most of it to finance needed imports. Other uses include aiding overstrained government budgets and maintaining U.S. and local military forces.

About 10% of it this year will go for economic projects—those "highly visible roads and factories" to which host governments are "particularly attached," and which Communist Russia or China have offered to finance. Part of this money also will be used to help finance sound economic development programs in these countries.

This year's contingency fund of $500 million is to be held in reserve for a wide variety of emergency grant uses such as meeting Congo-type social as well as military crises, disaster and other relief needs, and in some cases to contribute to emergency economic programs similar to the one recently adopted by Bolivia.

III. Investment Guarantees

Apart from its role as direct and indirect financier of U.S. private trade and investment overseas, one of AID's most significant contributions in this field promises to be its expanded and improved private investment guarantee program.

This function, too, was inherited from ICA and DLF. Present guarantees, largely under ICA, are severely limited, little used, and much criticized by private investors. DLF has broader guarantee authority, but has never used it.

Assuming Congressional approval this year, AID will offer:

> Some $400 million worth of investment and loan guarantees against the "political" risks of inconvertibility, expropriation and war—left over from ICA's $1 billion authority—which it will broaden to cover "insurrection, rebellion, civil strife, governmental breach of agreement, arbitrary acts of government which materially and purposely adversely affect an enterprise, acts of provincial and municipal governments as well as national governments in the country where the project is located, and economic sanctions by other governments (including the U.S.)";
>
> Coverage of the above risks for reinvestments of loans and equity, as well as new investments covered under the present ICA program;
>
> Coverage for U.S.-controlled (majority-owned) foreign subsidiaries and other foreign-chartered companies as well as U.S.-chartered enterprises covered under ICA's program;
>
> $100 million worth of "experimental all-risk guarantees" (carried over from DLF authority), covering normal commercial business risks and all losses except those due to gross negligence, fraud, malfeasance or misfeasance on the part of the private investor.

The dollar limits on the guarantee program are *not* significant. AID planners say they will request Congressional authority to write more guarantees, if, as and when present dollar limits are used up.

The experimental all-risk guarantees will be limited to no more than 75% of the total loan or equity investment for which coverage is requested. In actual practice, AID hopes to guarantee part of the investment under its larger general political guarantee program and part under the experimental all-risk coverage. One AID planner put it this way: "Instead of covering all of part of the risks, we hope to cover part of all of the risks."

Political risk coverage can be written up to 100%. Under the limited ICA program, inconvertibility coverage could be written up to 200%, but this option never has been exercised.

Guarantee rates will remain the same as under ICA and DLF—roughly 0.5% of the guarantee's total face value for each risk covered.

AID will extend its expanded political risk coverage to the $600 million worth of guarantees already in existence.

Like ICA and DLF, AID will limit new guarantees to investments in less-developed areas. Guarantees will run for 20 years, as under the old program.

Another important proposed innovation is that guarantees need not be approved by host governments under international bilateral treaty—a process that has delayed coverage in some countries for years. Instead, the President will have the authority to "make other suitable arrangements for the protection of U.S. interests."

IV. Summary

In sum, AID offers three important new opportunities for financial assistance to U.S. private overseas investment: direct loans for selected projects; more help in financing feasibility studies; and vastly improved investment guarantees. To U.S. exporters, AID offers a new emphasis on subcontracting of federal aid funds, and a continued tying of U.S. aid to purchases of U.S. goods and services.

III. INTERNATIONAL SOURCES

There are four international institutions directly engaged in financing international trade and investment: the International Bank for Reconstruction and Development (IBRD, better known as the World Bank); two agencies affiliated with the World Bank—The International Finance Corporation (IFC), and the International Development Association (IDA); and the Inter-American Development Bank (IDB). Of these, the World Bank is the most important capital source, if only because it is worldwide in scope, the oldest institution in the field (1944) and the biggest (capitalization: $20 billion). IFC, on the other hand, is the most direct capital source for private enterprises, U.S. and foreign, which it was specifically created to promote. IDA is devoted entirely to so-called soft loans in local foreign currencies. IDB, devoted exclusively to Latin American economic and social development, has been operative only since the first of this year, yet already is bidding strongly to replace the World Bank, if not Eximbank, as the most powerful and influential financial institution in the area.

Each of these institutions has its own purpose and, indeed, each is precluded by charter or policy from competing with either private capital sources or another international institution. Nevertheless, there are clear similarities among them:

> All four, like the U.S. Government, are required to concentrate on the less-developed areas of the world.
>
> World Bank, IDB and IDA are limited to financing basic industrial projects of the infrastructure type (aside from IDB's social projects, it should be noted that IDB has wide flexibility in its selection of projects to finance). Therefore, except through IFC, the great bulk of international financing goes for government projects.
>
> All four generally follow worldwide procurement policies on their hard loans, though IDB requires purchases to be concentrated in Latin America or the U.S.; local currency loans are, of course, spent primarily in the host country.

In addition to these four (described in detail below), a fifth international agency, the International Monetary Fund (IMF), functions primarily as an economic and currency stabilizer, a clearing house whose job is to "promote international monetary (policy) cooperation and encourage stability by providing resources to meet short-term balance of payments problems."

With a capitalization of nearly $15 billion (U.S. subscription: more than $4 billion), IMF lends gold and "hard" convertible currencies such as dollars, pounds and marks to its 66 member governments to smooth out payments imbalances, stabilize foreign currencies and promote efforts toward freer exchange and convertibility. It also finances and encourages economic, monetary and budgetary reforms. Through these means, the financing of expanded world trade is very much IMF's business. More directly, IMF quite often joins with one of the international or U.S. trade and investment financing agencies in a "package" bail-out loan, such as its recent contribution to the joint U.S.-European-international institution financial rescue operations in India, Pakistan and Brazil. In these cases, IMF participation for balance-of-payments reasons was deemed vital to programs of trade and industrial development directly financed by the World Bank, Eximbank, DLF and others.

In other cases, particularly in Latin America, IMF serves as a sort of economic doctor, prescribing monetary, budgetary, and exchange policy reforms to which a beneficiary nation's government *must* adhere in order to qualify for loans from other financial sources.

IMF, however, is not a direct capital source for U.S. private trade or investment.

One highly significant trend in the international financing of private trade and investment—whether by public or private sources—should be emphasized. The order of the day is for projects to be joint ventures—

that is, mixes of both public and private money, and combinations of local and foreign private capital (including U.S. and other Western Allies).

This is now the goal toward which the U.S. Government—through Eximbank and AID—and the various international finance agencies are pressing. This approach is notable even in predominantly private undertakings—the Eregli steel mill in Turkey and the Volta River hydro-electric-aluminum project in Ghana, to name but two significant precedent-setters.

International Bank for Reconstruction and Development (IBRD or World Bank)

By sheer size and volume, the World Bank (established by the Bretton Woods international financial agreements in 1944) has become the most influential international financier of investment and trade in the free world. While its charter permits loans to private enterprise, the World Bank has never directly lent to a U.S. company. It has, however, made numerous loans to foreign private investments, several of which have included U.S. private interests.

Its loans, which have been averaging close to $700 million annually for the past several years, are over 90% for basic industrial development projects—transportation (including roads, railways, port facilities, pipelines), power (dams, hydroelectric plants, transmission grids and networks), and basic industries such as ore mining and milling, primarily of iron and steel.

It has lent to projects in every major industrialized nation of the free world except the U.S. and U.K., but now—like other international financial institutions—puts primary emphasis on the underdeveloped areas of its 69 member nations, particularly India, Pakistan, Africa and Latin America.

The bulk of its loans goes to member governments. However, two recent trends should be noted in World Bank financing as in other similar international financing:

> The growth of lending to national or private development banks, proceeds of which are re-lent (often *required* to be lent) to private enterprise.
>
> Participation in multilateral public-private projects, often along with other capital sources, again both public and private.

The best example of joint financing is the $500 million hydroelectric power-aluminum smelter project on Ghana's Volta River. In this deal, the World Bank joined with the Governments of Ghana, the U.K. and U.S. (Eximbank and DLF) in financing (and guaranteeing) both the public power plant and a private consortium of aluminum producers headed by Kaiser Industries Corp.

World Bank officials do not consider private consortia the only method, or even always the best, to get an economic development project under way. But the Bank *does* favor the trend toward spreading financial risks (and therefore political risks) as broadly as possible among all interested parties.

Perhaps the World Bank's most important direct contribution to U.S. private international business lies in the export markets it helps to generate. The Bank, of course, follows a worldwide competitive bidding procurement procedure. But of the close to $6 billion it has lent since its founding, about 40% has been spent in the U.S. The proportionate share of U.S. purchasing has, however, been declining in recent years, as Western Europe and Japan have become more competitive.

World Bank loans generally run 15-25 years at a 5.75% interest rate plus 1% commission and expense charges. They are disbursed in hard currencies, principally dollars. Repayments are in both hard and soft money, and an interesting note here is that World Bank stocks of inconvertible soft currencies have been rising of late. Like other capital sources, the Bank may not compete with private financing. Another recent trend has been for private U.S. and foreign commercial banks to join in World Bank projects —for example, 14 private banks (including seven U.S.) took over half of a recent World Bank loan of $8.4 million to the Belgian African protectorate of Uganda for electric power development.

The World Bank requires host-government guarantees of loans to private enterprises, and has the authority (so far unused) to re-guarantee such loans on its own.

Perhaps the most conservative of all capital sources, the World Bank insists that projects contribute to the productivity of the host-country economy and demands high standards of credit-worthiness on the part of the borrower.

International Finance Corporation (IFC)

The International Finance Corporation, established in 1956 as an adjunct to the World Bank, is unique among international institutions which finance trade and investment. IFC is:

> The smallest, with a capitalization of only $96 million, subscribed by its 58 member governments (U.S. share: $35.2 million);
>
> The only public capital source devoted exclusively to financing private enterprise;
>
> The only institution that invests in the enterprises it helps finance (although the new U.S. AID agency may soon follow suit under certain unusual circumstances involving direct loans to U.S. private investments).

IFC finances productive industrial projects that contribute to economic development in the less-developed countries that are members of IFC and in the underdeveloped overseas territories of members. Its unique function is to act as a catalyst, sowing "seed capital" in areas where private investments are lacking and serving as a "finder" of capital for such projects in the wealthier money markets of the industrialized free world.

IFC participation in its investment ventures varies widely, and is "tailored" by the agency to suit what it judges to be the needs and profit potential of each investment. Mostly, it takes a percentage share of the profits (terms in this regard are not disclosed but may run as high as 10% in some cases), or an option on stock shares which, under present rules, it may only hold and broker, not own, but which it may own under the proposed rules-change, or convertible debentures, or "payments related to dividends" (actually in lieu of dividends), or "payments contingent upon profits" (instead of an actual percentage of the profits), or some combination of these arrangements. IFC's profit-sharing starts after the first 10% return on capital.

International Development Association (IDA)

The International Development Association, set up last year as another adjunct of the World Bank, is the most indirect capital source of all, as far as U.S. private investment and trade are concerned. It is designed to contribute to the economic development of less-developed countries through the lending of the free world's immense stocks of "soft" currencies —local, usually inconvertible exchange.

The agency's capitalization is $1 billion (U.S. share: $320 million) from 46 member countries. Its loans, which are repayable in soft currency (either that lent or the currency of the host country), go to local governments or local private enterprise at no interest rate other than a 0.75% "service charge" and run up to 50 years, plus a 10-year grace period. U.S. affiliates are free to borrow, but, like locally owned firms, will probably have to approach local development banks through which IDA will make most of its industrial loans.

Projects are a mix of both social public works (education, health facilities, and the like) and basic industrial infrastructure (roads, dams, basic plants) for which World Bank terms cannot be met. Between the two, the emphasis is likely to be on the latter.

Like other international agencies, IDA insists on a world-wide purchasing policy, though the bulk of its loans will cover local costs rather than imports.

Inter-American Development Bank (IDB)

Although its interests lie heavily in the area of basic economic and social development (schools, housing, transportation, communication, etc.), IDB has already shown itself to be an agency to which private industrial firms can turn—including those with majority U.S. control. For private loans the Bank does not require government guarantees (as does the World Bank). At least three of the local development banks that have borrowed from IDB for re-lending to local borrowers (including private industry) have promised non-discrimination between local and foreign-owned enterprises. To some extent, IDB can insure equitable treatment since it will sit in on loan decisions by the development banks when more than $250,000 is involved. However, in a showdown the local government could use its veto.

To be sure, IDB has to date shown a preference for lending to governments; though three fourths of all applications so far have come from private firms, the bulk of the funds actually lent has gone to governments. . . .

IDB wants to boost the proportion of its loans to private industry—both directly and through local banks—though only for fixed capital.

IDB has the power to guarantee repayment of loans made by private lenders to private investors in Latin America. But to avoid tying down any more funds than necessary, it will not use this authority.

European Investment Bank (EIB)

The $1 billion European Bank, created by the Rome Treaty as an autonomous agency of the European Economic Community, may develop into an important capital source for large firms entering or expanding in the Common Market. It is now stepping up its lending activity after rather sleepy beginnings, establishing itself as a promoter of projects in the less-developed regions of EEC, and as a lender of "big" money. . . .

The resources of EIB are ample and will be expanded. It already has $250 million paid in by member states (out of the $1 billion authorized)—one quarter in gold and the rest in national currencies. . . .

In lending, EIB does not discriminate against subsidiaries of U.S. corporations. While a number of its loans in the past have been for industrial projects, it is now entering a new phase in lending, in which communications and agriculture will be first served (these sectors have more difficulty than does industry in borrowing from conventional sources, and their needs are great). . . .

Nearly all borrowers so far have chosen loans at 5.62% interest under EIB's first "monetary clause," whereby they accept whatever currencies the Bank offers (any of the Six's, or dollars) and repay in the same currencies. Loans can be obtained more cheaply, at 5.25%, under the second monetary clause: the borrower can designate the currency of his choice, but the Bank is entitled to do the same for repayment, so that the borrower takes the exchange risk.

Loan amortization is "harmonized" with equipment amortization—for example, 12 years for chemical manufacturing equipment, 20 years for an electric power project. A two to four-year construction period is allowed before first payments are made on the principal. In granting loans, EIB does not always require guarantees from governments as does the World Bank. Ordinary bank guarantees may suffice.

Since EIB is designed to further the growth of the entire Community rather than any single member, its loans are not tied to use within any specific member state (they may be tied to EEC producers as a whole, or opened to international bidding).

Under its implementing statutes, EIB is empowered to grant loans or guarantees (so far it has confined itself to loans) for three general types of projects: 1) investments in underdeveloped areas, 2) modernizing or converting enterprises or creating new activities that are called for by the progressive establishment of the Common Market, and 3) investments of interest to several member countries. Among the "underdeveloped areas" are the Borinage in Belgium; northeast and southwest Holland; Brittany in France; Southern Italy, Sicily and Sardinia; and the German areas along the frontier with the East Zone, Schleswig-Holstein and Bayerische Wald.

EIB can lend outside the EEC if the project is approved by its Board of Governors.

Private firms interested in EIB financing may apply through the EEC Commission, or through the member state concerned (both must approve the application), or directly to the Bank itself. Loans are usually made through existing national development agencies. The firm should be able to demonstrate that the investment is in a region considered by the Community (not simply by the individual country) to be underdeveloped; or that, under the EEC's plans for developing transport, communications, irrigation, etc., the project will contribute to the development of the Community; or that the project is of direct interest to several member states.

EIB is required to "subordinate" its own loans to other sources of financing—either the intended borrower's own or a third party's. In effect, this means that it is the bank of last resort; it will not compete with ordinary commercial banks in financing projects, and in processing applications it asks what other capital sources have been approached. Nonetheless, there is in EIB a strong temptation to sponsor worthy projects, despite the availability of alternate capital. The Bank is also prohibited from acquiring any "interest" in, or undertaking any responsibility for management of, projects it sponsors except to protect its own rights as creditors (e.g., requiring a debtor enterprise to issue bonds or other securities to retire its EIB debt).

Cie. Financière de Suez (CFS)

One enormous accumulation of investable funds in France is the *Cie. Financière de Suez* (CFS), which took over the assets of the Suez Canal Co. after its expropriation by Nasser in 1956. Under the 1958 compensation agreement, the United Arab Republic undertook to pay CFS the equivalent of $79 million in sterling or francs between July 1958 and January 1963. CFS is now mainly concerned with 1) managing liquid assets and short-term funds, 2) managing a portfolio of worldwide investments, and 3) promoting and developing industrial, commercial and property undertakings in which it acquires an interest. It carries out financial transactions both directly and through the subsidiaries described below.

CFS does most of its business through the *Société d'Investissements Mobiliers* (SIM) and the *Banque de la Cie. Financière de Suez* (BCFS), both headquartered at 1, rue d'Astorg in Paris. SIM, formed in 1955, is now the largest privately-owned investment trust in France, with total assets of $32 million at the end of 1960. It is controlled and managed by CFS, which holds 30-40% of its share capital. SIM's portfolio includes some 250 securities of the most important companies quoted on the Paris Bourse and foreign stock exchanges. BCFS, a merchant and investment bank founded in 1959 with total assets of *Nfr* 94 million ($19 million) at the end of 1960, is more than 99% owned by CFS. Its primary role is as banker to the Suez Group, but it also makes its own and the Group's resources available to an increasing number of carefully selected French and foreign clients, both through short and medium-term credit facilities and in stock market and foreign exchange transactions.

Other important CFS financial affiliates are:

The *French American Banking Corp.* (New York City), a commercial bank with capital and reserves of over $25 million and specializing in foreign business, ownership of which is equally distributed between CFS, Comptoir National d'Escompte and the Banque de l'Indochine.

The *Suez Finance Co. (London) Ltd.*, capitalized at £50,000 and owned almost entirely by CFS. This company provides advisory and executive services for all CFS's dealings in the Sterling Area.

20

HELPING U.S. EXPORTS MEET CREDIT COMPETITION *

The Export-Import Bank of Washington, established in 1934 with the chief aim of stimulating trade with the newly recognized Soviet Union, is still at the business of promoting United States sales abroad. Significant recent broadening of the Bank's role reflects government's concern with increasing the exports of U.S. industry—not, as in 1934, in order to relieve a deep depression, but rather to reduce the balance-of-payments deficit that presses on the dollar in world exchange markets and inhibits economic growth at home.

Russia, of course, is excluded from the list of countries covered by Eximbank's present programs. In fact, the depression-born idea of financing shipments to the Soviet never really got under way. When the U.S. government couldn't negotiate a satisfactory settlement of Russia's prerevolutionary obligations to U.S. creditors, the extension of further loans lost its appeal. The Bank, however, early struck up a business with other countries; for a brief while, in fact, a Second Export-Import Bank of Washington existed to provide credits for trade with Cuba, also excluded from today's list of eligible countries. The tendency to create a separate institution to deal with each country was arrested, and Eximbank II was dissolved in 1936, its loans and commitments assumed by the original agency. Since then, the Bank's evolving franchise has taken it into a number of innovations in government-sponsored finance, including loans for economic development, but probably into none more loaded with potential meaning for America's place in world trade than the program of export promotion it has fashioned in the fall of 1961.

What the Bank now has, if it uses them boldly and imaginatively enough, should be a set of tools adequate to repair a long-standing defect in America's export machinery—the inability of exporters to extend credit facilities competitive with those offered with government support by sellers in other major industrial countries. In a world long on aspirations and short of capital, the seller who gives the most generous terms of credit often gets

* From *The Morgan Guaranty Survey* (August 1962), published by Morgan Guaranty Trust Company of New York. Reprinted by permission.

the order. This is true especially in selling to the less-developed countries, which must figure heavily in any long-range plans for substantially expanded foreign sales.

FILLING A VACUUM

The idea of a government bank to finance trade was attractive in the 1930's because of the general drying up of private international credit that followed the world-wide economic collapse. With defaults piled high and faith in currencies shattered by the wave of devaluations, neither manufacturers nor banks in the U.S. were inclined to be particularly venturesome in extending credit to new foreign buyers of goods. Yet the cultivation of new export markets offered hope of helping to unstall the domestic economy. Eximbank, backed by the massed resources of the taxpaying public, was supposed to give a push by making some of the loans that private lenders adhering to traditional standards couldn't make.

Essentially the same philosophy underlies the Bank's expanded operations today. With the national interest calling for an increase in exports, one of the most promising ways to achieve such growth is by making it easier for prospective foreign buyers to pay for the goods. More sales can be made, for instance, if the U.S. manufacturer is willing to ship goods on credit even though he may have some fear that the country to which they are going may impose new exchange controls before payment is received. Selling likewise is easier if the payment period can be stretched out—say to five years in the case of capital goods. This normally means that the exporter must find a bank willing to hold the notes of an importer on whom credit information of the thoroughness customary in domestic banking is not obtainable. Exporters and their banks, as individual enterprises, can't assume the risks such loosening of ordinary credit practices would involve.

In a strict commercial sense, it could be argued that business which must be done on such concessive terms should not be done at all since commercial considerations cannot support it. Two realities, however, make the strictly commercial standard academic under present circumstances. In the first place, countries no longer are willing to go through the traditional long process of development. They haven't the patience to build their capital plant by gradual saving out of current product. They are eager to get their plant now, and pay for it later out of the product it then will yield.

The second reality is that a number of the industrial exporting nations have for some time been accommodating these pressing aspirations. The governments of a score of countries have promoted exports by making liberal credit facilities available. The United Kingdom and West Germany, in particular, have regarded this kind of export stimulus as a form of foreign aid. Under balance-of-payments pressure, the U.S. government in recent years wisely has made the bulk of its foreign loans an automatic source of exports by "tying" them to the purchase of U.S. goods. In the realm of purchases not financed through government loans, however—which constitute much of the buying being done by nongovernment customers abroad—American exporters have been at a considerable disadvantage because of the generous credit extended by their government-aided foreign competitors.

When the decision was made to do something about the disparity, the Export-Import Bank became the chosen instrument of equalization. This assignment has been in addition to the Bank's chief role in recent years—that of making loans for development projects to foreign governments and corporations. Two years ago Exim stepped up somewhat its direct participation in export finance. It had sporadically purchased promissory notes of foreign buyers issued to U.S. sellers. It undertook to do more of this kind of lending in cases where a commercial bank would extend a portion of the credit with no call on the exporter in case of nonpayment.

This approach proved to be a highly limited remedy. On the funds they advanced, the banks were exposed not only to the credit uncertainties involved in lending to distant parties of whom they had only scanty knowledge but also to the even less calculable political risks that could interfere with completion of the transaction—e.g., war or revolution, confiscation of property, cancellation of import permits, blockage of payment in dollars. It was difficult for commercial banks to stretch lending standards to meet such conditions, and consequently the volume of business done under the program was disappointing.

Last October (1961) Eximbank moved to make its export promotion more realistic by offering commercial banks, for a fee, a guarantee against a substantial part of the hazards they assume in taking on the nonrecourse financing of foreign buyers' promissory notes. This plan provides, under specified conditions, that the lending bank can purchase a full guarantee against political risks throughout the entire period of the financing and against credit risk—i.e., the possibility of default by the borrower—on payments maturing after eighteen months. The exporter is required to extend, without guarantee, at least 15% of the total credit given the purchaser. Thus both the exporter and the commercial bank have ample incentive for satisfying themselves as to the importer's creditworthiness.

Early this year (1962) the Bank launched an even more significant innovation, calling on the nation's insurance industry for help in underwriting the risks involved in export credit. It persuaded 71 insurance companies to join the newly established Foreign Credit Insurance Association, which writes comprehensive insurance against credit and political risks. FCIA and the Bank—on a half-and-half basis—insure exporters against 85% of any loss they may suffer from the credit risk while Eximbank alone, as part of the same package, insures the political risks—to the extent of 95% in the case of short-term financing, 85% for medium-term. The importer can be required to make a down payment of as much as 20% of the purchase price.

A JOB FOR PRIVATE ENTERPRISE

The implications of the creation of FCIA are far-reaching. It taps the resources and know-how of another segment of the private economy for a role in export promotion. This is important philosophically: the very nature of the export credit problem requires that government play a part, and this fact makes it especially urgent that private enterprise broaden its own participation in every way possible.

FCIA, by applying insurance principles of risk-spreading and averaging, can give Eximbank's program a flexibility not possible under the banking dictum that every transaction must stand on its own credit merits. It is not yet clear that the Exim administration, which holds veto power over FCIA's writing of coverage contracts, has fully adopted this underwriting viewpoint; it will have to do so if the program is to realize its full potential.

Entry of the insurance companies also means that an energetic sales force will be at work all over the country, seeking out prospective users of the offered service and thus, hopefully, spurring interest in exporting on the part of manufacturers who hitherto have not exploited that source of business. Alert to the prospect of commissions, agents and brokers of the participating underwriting companies have been busy familiarizing themselves with the new item in their line.

The item comes in two styles, tailored according to the maturity of the financing to be insured. For an exporter's short-term credits, meaning those of six months or less, FCIA insists on a blanket policy covering the insured's total volume of foreign shipments except those to Canada and those made under irrevocable bank letters of credit. This "whole-turnover" requirement is imposed to assure the underwriters a diversification of risk, both as to quality and as to location. In some cases, and with a compensating adjustment in fee, waivers to the requirement can be negotiated, provided there is a "representative spread" of risk. Each exporter's policy is an individually tailored contract.

The exporter wishing to insure medium term credits, running from six months to five years, can deal with FCIA on an individual-case basis rather than having to buy coverage for his entire volume. This phase of the program, inaugurated only last month (July 1962) is certain to draw a greater concentration of poorer risks than the short-term plan with its compulsory inclusion of the exporter's whole volume. The shading of quality will be offset in part by limiting to 85% the share of loss from political risks that will be covered (compared with 95% on short-term credits) and by a higher scale of charges. Coverage of losses from credit risk is 85%, the same as in the short-term policies.

For guidance in fixing charges, and also in determining adequacy of risk diversification, Eximbank has drawn up a credit-rating list of the 164 countries and territories to which exports may be sent under insured credits. For reasons of international delicacy, the Bank hopes to keep the ratings confidential, but a country curious as to its standing hardly could have much trouble in finding it out.

FINDING THE FUNDS

The gist of the Export-Import Bank's recent innovations has been a shift of emphasis in its program from the granting of credit directly to foreign importers through development loans, and toward the assumption of a large part of the risks incurred by those who grant the credit—through FCIA insurance in the case of loans made by exporters themselves, through Exim guarantees where the loan is made by a commercial bank. Ideally, the shift can have the effect of maximizing the participation of private funds and initiative in export lending while government confines its role largely to assuming those hazards which are beyond the capacity of private risk-takers.

The ability of the FCIA program to draw funds into export finance stems not only from the security it gives exporters in their extensions of credit but also from the fact that FCIA policies are assignable to banks or other financial institutions. This should enable the exporter to sell some of his paper to secondary lenders. Or, if he prefers to carry the paper, its insured status should strengthen his position when he seeks a bank loan for working funds.

For the longer range, looking to a time when commercial-bank portfolios may be saturated with export paper, there remains the problem of tapping totally new sources of credit. A hopeful prospect is the institutional field—trusts, savings banks, insurance companies. These investors generally prefer commitments of longer term than the five years which normally is the maximum maturity in export financing. There is good hope, nevertheless, that an instrument properly designed can find a market in the institutional community, and bankers have already begun to explore the possibilities.

SNAGS AND SHORTCOMINGS

As might be expected, some rough spots are showing up as Eximbank's new program goes through the early stages of application. Some exporters have lined up sales in the expectation of having payment insured, only to learn belatedly that their transactions did not square in all details with administrative rules that Eximbank had imposed—sometimes without notice. Sudden changes in rulings—with respect to such matters as cost, foreign bank guarantees, amount of credit, or eligibility of certain goods for shipment to specific countries—can only discourage the exporter in the sales effort he is urged, by other agencies of government, to make. If he is to undertake the arduous business of increasing sales to foreign markets, he wants to do so from the firm base of fixed rules.

Streamlining of administration can remedy some of the defects that so far have reduced the effectiveness of the program. But there are deeper problems, notably a need for greater flexibility in the tailoring of the program. As things now stand, in order to buy any insurance the exporter frequently must buy a great deal more than he needs or wants. For instance, he must take both credit and political coverage, even though he may be so confident of the creditworthiness of his customers that he not only is unworried about the possibility of default, but would grant larger credits than FCIA may be willing to insure. Eximbank used to issue political-risk insurance separately but discontinued the practice when it instituted the present arrangements.

The compulsory buying of both coverages, together with the all-or-nothing requirement so far as short-term credits are concerned, could easily dissuade an exporter who already does a large volume of relatively riskless business from venturing into some of the more chancy kinds, since in order to insure the doubtful credits he would have to pay premiums on all. The added sales of established exporters, obviously, are one of the chief potential sources of improvement to the balance of payments; any provision that tends to deter them should be subjected to the closest scrutiny.

Eximbank has explained its insistence on combining credit and political coverage on two principal grounds: that most other countries insuring export credits observe the same coupling, and that separate coverage would produce disputes over the nature of a given loss. As to the first, conformity with the practice of other countries is not in this case demonstrably a virtue: in fact, some aspects of the program represent definite improvement on what others are doing. As to the second, although it represents a more tangible difficulty, careful definition in the contract and a provision for arbitration where needed ought to offer adequate remedy.

Giving the exporter a wider choice of facilities would, of course, work against the underwriters' objective of getting the widest possible spread of risks. This fact is the rationale especially of the whole-turnover requirement applying to short-term credits. In the much more risky medium-term field, however, the requirement does not apply; a higher scale of charges compensates for the sacrifice of risk-spread. It would seem that the same approach could be applied to make possible a greater diversity of coverage throughout the program. Higher fees would have to be charged for the more specialized and risky protections, but this is not likely to be objectionable to exporters who would be better accommodated. And the over-all result would be more effective promotion of exports.

IF THE SPIRIT IS WILLING

The ultimate success of the insurance and guarantee program will not depend only on smoothing out procedures and designing a more flexible structure. It will require also the continued enthusiastic participation of banks and insurance companies, and a real conviction on the part of the Export-Import Bank management that export credit through private channels has a place in national policy along with governmental development loans.

As to the response of banks and insurance companies, the score thus far is promising. Some 60 banks have signed agreements with Eximbank enabling them to submit medium-term paper for guarantee. The volume of loans made thus far has been small, especially in relation to the number of applications processed. But this can be explained, to some extent at least, as an inevitable part of the starting-up process. Encouragingly, the banks report that a number of the promissory notes they have bought are those of importers to whom their exporting customers had not previously sold. This suggests that new business is being generated. So does the experience of FCIA. Of thc 800 or so policics issued since short-term insurance became available in February, about 100 have been issued to firms which had not previously competed in export markets. FCIA estimates that during its first year it will write short-term insurance alone aggregating nearly $1 billion.

As to Eximbank's basic attitude, there may be some question. The program the Bank has conceived for stimulating exports is, despite defects, a bold and imaginative one. It preserves broad scope for participation by the private sector of the economy, including a share in the risks. A general stickiness in working out practical applications, however, suggests that the break-through may not have the Bank's full enthusiasm. If such is the case, the program's effectiveness could suffer severely, perhaps fatally.

Lurking in the whole business of government backing for export finance is the danger of an unsound international credit scramble. With a number of the world's richest and most productive nations competing aggressively for export business, there may be temptation to push terms beyond the outer limits of reason. In self-defense, eighteen exporting nations, constituting a group called the Berne Union, have an understanding designed to impose restraint. The Export-Import Bank represents the United States in the group.

The principal precept of Berne is that insured transactions, other than those properly characterized as economic aid, should not extend in terms beyond five years. Length of maturity, of course, is not the only relevant test of credit soundness; indeed, loans for some kinds of capital goods might be sounder on a longer payout. The danger of an international credit race lies more in considerations of quality than in length of term. Whether Berne or any other panel can promulgate serviceable criteria of creditworthiness is open to question. More likely, reliance will have to rest on each nation's good sense and good faith.

Reckless extensions of credit would pose a threat to the borrower nations as well as to those lending. The countries whose importers typically receive extraordinary credit terms are those suffering shortages of foreign exchange and needing to screen their imports carefully for essentiality. It is the business of the developing nations to determine what their exchange resources, present and future, shall be used to pay for, and it is far preferable that they regulate imports than that agencies in the exporting countries —Eximbank, for instance—undertake to make those decisions for them as part of the administration of export credit programs. The capital-rich nations, bent on increasing their foreign sales, will do the less affluent ones better service simply by following sound rules of credit extension. Overease in lending would mean not only losses to the lenders but also possibly irresistible temptations to unsound purchases by the borrowers.

ADDITIONAL REFERENCES

For current regulations on foreign credit insurance contact: your banker; the Bureau of International Commerce, U.S. Department of Commerce; the Office of Development Finance and Private Enterprise, Agency for Economic Development, U.S. Department of State;[1] or the Foreign Credit Insurance Association (110 William Street, New York 38). Critical essays on FCI appear periodically in leading trade publications. Information on cargo insurance can be obtained from local representatives of the American Institute of Marine Underwriters.[2]

[1] See: U.S. Government Memorandum: *Aids to Business,* Agency for International Development (Washington, D.C.: U.S. Department of State, January 1963), pp. 46.

This attractively arranged bulletin shows how our government is trying to encourage and facilitate the participation of private enterprise in investment in underdeveloped countries. Four major AID programs are comprehensively reviewed: sharing the cost of conducting investment surveys undertaken by U.S.-owned business firms; authorization of dollar development loans to private borrowers; administration of the PL 480 local currency (Cooley) loan program formerly handled by the Export-Import Bank; and administration of the broadened investment-guaranty program.

Also discussed are functions of the newly created Office of Development Finance and Private Enterprise, the initial point of contact within AID for private businessmen interested in overseas investment.

[2] See: *Exporter's Guide to Cargo Insurance* (New York: American Society of Marine Underwriters, 99 John Street, 1962), pp. 16.

New exporters can pick up the rudiments of cargo insurance from this booklet. The following subjects are covered: arranging ocean marine insurance coverage; how "C. I. F." helps exporters sell; open-cargo policy provisions; valuation of goods; cost of insurance; factors in underwriting; payment of claims and foreign credit insurance.

SECTION FOUR

International Intelligence

Knowledge is power, ignorance destruction. This maxim follows man from womb to tomb.

Technical knowledge can be mastered relatively readily. "Mekura boeki"—a condensed Japanese expression for "blind foreign trade, or engaging in selling or trying to sell a foreign market without knowing anything about that market"—is no longer excusable in an age of rapid communications.

We can use many media to transmit the fact that only one out of three Frenchmen brush their teeth, or that cars are status symbols, or that only one out of five Germans change their shirts more often than once a week, or that in many countries bribes are considered essential lubricants which make the wheel of business go around. What do these scattered facts mean to management of enterprises with the foresight to capitalize on international opportunities? Nothing, really. To be useful, the meaning of those facts has to be creatively interpreted and made to bear on the solution of specific problems.

Few executives are skilled in this sort of interpretative activity. In fact, Margaret Mead—the anthrolopologists' anthropologist—fears that:

> Businessmen, both as citizens and as international merchants, suffer from the accumulation of overwhelming quantities of data . . . each administrator knows too much about his competitors—what their market is, what changes they are making, how they are diversifying, retrenching, and expanding. When knowledge of a field was very limited, the imaginative man made an informed guess and forged ahead. His success or failure—in actual profit—gave him a measure of his achievement. But today, when every field is researched, we have the spectacle of each company copying its competitors and, in so doing, limiting the profits of all of them.[1]

It is the objective of this section to explore some much-neglected informational nooks and crannies, and show how they can be put to use.

[1] Margaret Mead, "Must Capitalism Crawl?" *Harvard Business Review* (November-December 1962), pages 8 and 10.

The above quotation has been intentionally taken from an eminent anthropologist. It discloses our bias, which reappears in the choice of cases. To wit: surprisingly often it is lack of awareness of human relations that leads to trouble even though the financial, organizational, and physical relationships all appear to be perfectly well arranged.

Authors of most of the readings readily acknowledge the truism that human desires are by and large pretty much alike everywhere. But they emphasize that the most successful among managers of global enterprises are skilled students of basic differences, as well as of basic similarities. They know the relatively cut-and-dried subjects of political economics, statistics, finance, cost accounting, production management, marketing. But they also know how to effectively merge some of the more "fuzzy" sociocultural variables such as status, role, norms, values, customs, habits, education, kinship systems, religious practice, mythology, language. . . .

Seymour Linfield leads off by *Looking Around* the literature dealing with different aspects of *Overseas Operations.* He also delineates "areas of darkness" that ought to be illuminated in future writings.

Ernest Dichter examines one of these areas. He shows how the successful global marketer of the future will have to think not of a U.S. customer, nor even of a Western European or Atlantic Community customer, but of *The World Customer.* Following Dr. Dichter's admonition we take the reader into non-European societies. Some heartwarming rewards for honest attempts at understanding are well brought to the fore in the sequence on Japan. It starts with Dudley Miller's *The Honorable Picnic,* and is followed by Jiro Tokuyama's letter to the editor of the *Harvard Business Review.* Arthur Whitehall's essay on *The Japanese Worker* points out that labor is not the same the world over. Automobile assemblers and steel mill workers in Osaka and Tokyo do not work for the same reasons as their opposite numbers in Pittsburgh and Detroit. Cultural values are a key force which can integrate a group and increase the productivity and job satisfaction of its members.

Igor Oganesoff's delightful *Themes and Variations* give us some insights into the mystery of semantics. There follows, in an Associated Press release, a tragic side to the Japanese picture as well. Mrs. Chieko Takenaka kills her children and commits suicide. Reason: inability to cope with western ways that defy her understanding, a load of anxiety too heavy to bear.

These explorations into human ecology are carried into the Dark Continent by Joseph C. Kennedy, who takes a look at *The American Negro's Key Role in Africa.* Amos Kiriro then shows how *An African Student Studies Us.* These are must readings for any U.S. citizen concerned with the impact abroad of our domestic racial conflicts.

Yet, out of the apparent confusion come John Beauvois' convincing arguments that proper *International Intelligence* is no cloak and dagger affair. He insists that companies operating abroad need an intelligence officer to keep them posted on developments. He is, or should be, one of the smoothest members of the firm. Beauvois shows how to pick, train, and use this executive diplomat. He warns that penalties for inaccuracy or misevaluation can be grave in these days of seething nationalism and expropriation. Charles Allen translates these socio-psychological bits and pieces into practical suggestions for hard-headed *Public Opinion* programs that should help remedy the *Achilles Heel of U.S. Business Overseas*. Specifically he explores the following five questions:

1. Is Castroism an isolated development, or is it symptomatic of public opinion problems affecting American business abroad?

2. What are the major international public relations problems faced by U.S. business?

3. Is American business dealing effectively with these problems?

4. How does public opinion affect a company's profitability abroad?

5. How can a company develop an effective public relations program abroad?

It is only natural that the section on international intelligence concludes with an essay about *Information Sources on Foreign Marketing*. In it John C. Abbott, an international civil servant (chief of the Marketing Branch of the Food and Agriculture Organization, United Nations), reviews the main marketing references and points up the need for a new bibliographical service. His criterion for selection of titles is usefulness to readers in countries other than those of publication. Dr. Abbott would like to see a chain of correspondents "with common standards, who would 'feed' the international service and at the same time draw upon it for dissemination of marketing information." That makes eminently good sense. Any volunteers among our readers?

21

LOOKING AROUND OVERSEAS OPERATIONS *

Seymour L. Linfield

To date, Osborn Elliott's "men at the top,"[1] and their responsible associates, have been reticent to examine *publicly* certain *long-range policy* questions related to private United States international operations. Basic questions for U.S. industrial and financial leadership are here involved:

A philosophy of overseas operations.

An organizational structure to maximize international profit potential.

The operational controls (policy and personnel) to effectuate realization of corporate overseas goals.

* From *Harvard Business Review,* XXXVIII (September-October 1960), 41-50. Reprinted by permission.

[1] *Men at the Top* (New York: Harper & Brothers, 1959).

This review will examine how each of these fundamental aspects of overseas operations is treated in recent books—or could well be considered in new volumes—devoted to international management, operations, and trade.

A Philosophy of Overseas Operations. In this section, it will be necessary to "review" a book which still remains to be written. For the sorry fact is that there is no volume which deals with a philosophy of overseas operations for U.S. corporations. This fact precisely reflects the tacit assumption made by so many companies—that they can operate overseas without a specially defined philosophy of operations, that private international operations merely require a geographic transfer of corporate philosophy applicable to domestic operations.

This assumption is fostered by the absence of an *integrated* U.S. foreign economic policy which would here officially mark the substance and limits of national interest. This assumption is also frequently punctured, at high cost to U.S. enterprise, by a world market in growth and ferment—politically, economically, and socially—to which proper accommodation has not been made.

Whatever the peculiarities which may characterize the approach of any particular company to overseas operations, it seems to me that the first book which develops a philosophy for *successful, long-range* overseas activity by United States business will have to base itself on the following *minimum* postulates:

1. *When a U.S. company goes into a foreign country, it must go in "for keeps."* It cannot safely enter to make the biggest possible profit, as quickly as possible, letting the chips fall where they may.

National Cash Register has underlined the requirement that, in this respect, foreign operations be placed at least on a level of equality with domestic operations, when it publicly stated that "regardless of wars, revolutions, depressions, we have never voluntarily withdrawn." [2] It may be added that major, national industrial powers (other than the United States) view overseas operations as a necessity—not a convenience, or even a special opportunity—assign to it a preferred position in public and private economic policy, and expect even a lower rate of return from it than from domestic operations.

2. *No country will long permit its economic institutions to be in the control of foreigners.* This applies to ownership, control, and employees. This is clearly expressed in the industrialized countries of Western Europe —where, in the event of choice, national capital is increasingly preferred to foreign capital, or where a government will nationalize industry which it considers essential.

In the long run, it applies even more forcefully to the less developed countries—whether in Asia, Africa, or, more particularly, Latin America —and is not necessarily related to the extent of direct government participation in the economic life of the country. It may be added that this

[2] Address by Stanley C. Allyn, Chairman of the Board, at the 45th National Foreign Trade Convention, New York, November 15, 1958.

"long run" is frequently shorter than anticipated, and, in truth, may be expected to become increasingly so.

3. *No U.S. company may, except at great risk, intervene in the political life of a foreign country.* This applies to developed countries, but especially to the less developed countries of the world, where colonial empires are politically dying with a bang, and will be stone dead within the next decade. Great new countries and political federations are emerging, or are about to emerge, and the governments and peoples of these countries, as they increasingly play independent roles in world affairs, will not permit political participation by foreigners.

4. *A U.S. company overseas must participate in the economic and social life of the foreign country.* More and more, this is *not* measured in the host country by the additional resources brought into use by the United States company, by its contributions to local living standards, or by resulting, local institutional benefits. Increasingly, all these are being primarily viewed as by-products of business ventures profitable to foreigners, rather than as strong social reflexes of U.S. industry.

For the long run, the crux for the growth and survival of private U.S. enterprise overseas is becoming the voluntary, increasing reinvestment of profits in the country where earned—with control of the country's economic institutions either remaining or increasingly coming within control of the country's nationals. It should be noted that, in 1957 and 1958, foreign subsidiaries of U.S. manufacturing companies retained about 50% of their earnings abroad. Such reinvestment helped pay for new manufacturing plants, sales and service facilities, as well as contributing to the economy of the country or region.

5. *A U.S. company overseas must honor its contracts, and its local conduct must be grounded on equality.* Such contractual fulfillment must be in spirit as well as in letter, with relations between the U.S. company and the local nationals and government conducted on both a businesslike and a fair basis. In the long run, contracts which express the duress of superior economic strength, or which express ideas of U.S. superiority, only breed suspicion, enmity, and invite serious efforts to vitiate or cancel them.

Each of these *minimum* ground rules—detailed and expanded—could easily comprise a section of our hypothetical book. When such a volume is finally written, we will all certainly be wiser—especially if the extensive experience of U.S. companies with respect to those matters is carefully analyzed and synthesized.

Organization for Overseas Operations. The only book devoted to a consideration of this problem is a recent study published by the American Management Association. Alexander O. Stanley's *Organizing for International Operations,*[3] is a research study in depth of the overseas organizational structure of 30 major American corporations (the majority identified by name). Included are profile charts of 20 international divisions and 10 international companies, job descriptions of 104 executives who direct international work, and, expressed in general terms, typical management patterns of organizational control employed in overseas operations.

[3] New York: American Management Association, 1960.

No quantitative statistical generalizations have been made with respect to these data, the author wisely recognizing that wide variations of organizational structure would have rendered any averages meaningless. Rather, a detailed picture is presented of the organizational structure of each of the selected companies. In so doing, the author accomplishes his stated purpose, the filling of the gap in information (which has persisted until now) concerning existing overseas organizational structures. It may be seriously questioned, however, whether it meets the claim of its publisher that "it should be extremely useful to anyone who is engaged in setting up a new overseas structure or interested in finding ways to improve an existing organization."

In designing a structure of international operation, one must maintain a distinction between corporate organization and administrative organization. The rationale is obvious: legal, tax, and financial considerations are the major determinants of statutory structure; the most effective operating performance of the overseas units (with emphasis on an effective system of communication and flexibility) should be the major determinants of administrative structure. At times, the two types of organization may be identical; more usually, as would be expected, they differ sharply.

Organizing for International Operations completely blurs this necessary distinction. It is true that no single volume exists which comprehensively examines the organizational forms for transacting foreign business and the legal, tax, and financial considerations applicable to each. But there are many volumes to which we can turn for help on legal and tax matters connected with overseas operations—and the best of these are listed in Exhibit 1. Stanley's volume, however, falls short of joining this list of volumes which valuably consider the major factors determining statutory structures of overseas operations.

Exhibit I. Books on Law and Taxation in Overseas Operations

LAW

1. Kingman Brewster, Jr., *Anti-Trust and American Business Abroad* (New York: McGraw-Hill Book Company, Inc., 1958), exhaustively examines the policy and problems involved in the origins and application of antitrust laws to foreign commerce, and the impact on specific arrangements (exports, licensing, and ownership of private enterprises). Included is a list of applicable statutes, cases, complaints, and consent decrees.

2. Wolfgang Friedmann and Richard C. Pugh, editors, *Legal Aspects of Foreign Investments* (Boston: Little, Brown and Company, 1959). This symposium volume of the Columbia University International Legal Studies Program authoritatively examines the administrative and public law factors affecting foreign investments, foreign company law, and the problems of legal security in 39 major non-Communist countries of the world.

In view of the increasing consideration of the merits of single ventures as compared with joint ventures, mention should here be made of the extremely valuable "Joint International Business Ventures," now in the process of being edited for book publication by Professor Friedmann. It will include authoritative studies, describing the role of joint ventures —historically, legally, and tax-wise—in 12 selected countries, which have been prepared and mimeographed under the auspices of the Columbia University Projects on International Business Ventures.

3. Rita E. Hauser and Gustav M. Hauser, *A Guide to Doing Business in the European Common Market* (New York: Oceana Publications, 1960). Volume I presents a good consideration of the key aspects of French and Belgian private and public law affecting business operations in those countries, with Volumes II and III of the projected series intended to do the same for Germany and Luxemburg, and Italy and the Netherlands, respectively.

TAXATION

1. E. R. Barlow and Ira T. Wender, *Foreign Investment and Taxation* (Englewood Cliffs: Prentice-Hall, Inc., 1955). This volume, prepared by the Harvard Law School International Program in Taxation, examines in Chapter 14 the rules of taxation for corporate foreign income.

Mention should be made of the *World Tax Series,* also prepared pursuant to the same Harvard Law School Program, in consultation with the United Nations Secretariat, each volume of which gives a full and authoritative description of the tax system of the foreign country discussed.

At the same time, the tables of organization and job descriptions in Stanley's book, while of some utility, do not reveal the mechanisms and experiences of international administrative functioning. These experiences alone can serve as guideposts for the designing or modification of administrative structures.

Thus, Stanley's tables of organization do not answer some important questions that occur to the careful reader of his book. For example:

What administrative advantages, if any, accrue in organizing along geo-economic lines, as a number of companies are already doing?

What considerations should determine the administrative relationships between the line and staff of overseas units and the line and staff of the parent organization?

How have special problems—in overseas manufacturing operations, including quality control; in overseas marketing, including international market research; or in overseas R & D—been reflected in the international administrative structure of United States corporations?

Finally, while it is true that the volume would have benefited from the grouping of the various types of structures—as done, for example, by John Fayerweather with respect to overseas administrative structures in his ably prepared college textbook, *Management of International Operations* [4]—its major practical limitation inheres in the original limits of the study. It describes, within the indicated limits, what *is;* it does not describe *why.*

[4] New York: McGraw-Hill Book Company, Inc., 1960.

Organizing for International Operations has value, but it does not tap the extensive and available administrative experience of United States companies in organizing their international operations. That job, like others in the field, still remains to be done. Our author has helped us on the first step of the road, which is long, complex, and constantly changing.

Operational Controls of Overseas Business. We have observed that the *posture* of overseas operations is limited by its corporate philosophy, the *corporate structure* by statutory considerations, and the *administrative structure* by functional considerations. We now briefly turn to basic *operational controls*—which, of course, are integrally related to organizational structure, although separate from it. They seek to assure that the structure is most effectively utilized to effectuate the philosophy so as to maximize corporate profit from overseas operations.

There is no usual pattern of operational control of overseas business. However, it may be said that two *minimum* areas of such operational control are to be sought in corporate determination of basic policy, and in the choice of personnel to effectuate it.

These are also key areas of operational control of domestic activities. Therefore, some observations with respect to the *long-range* policy considerations involved in overseas operations are in order.

Policy controls—Of course, for the particular company the specifics are decisive; but basic to such specifics, regardless of the company involved, is recognition that any long-range policy decision must comport with—not oppose or resist—the basic trends and developments in international operations. The compass and logic of the problem may be simply stated in this way:

Under the pressure of heightened international competition, the increasing international division of labor, and loyalty to the flag of its corporate interests, no U.S. corporation will have any alternative, subject to existing law, but to:

> Invest wherever in the world it can get the best return.
>
> Purchase its raw materials, or partially processed or manufactured items to become components of finished articles, wherever in the world it can do so most cheaply.
>
> Manufacture either the finished product, or a component, wherever in the non-Communist world it can do so most productively.
>
> Market these manufactured products wherever in the world (including the United States) it can do so most profitably.
>
> Recruit its personnel wherever in the non-Communist world it can do so best.
>
> Conduct its nonmilitary R & D wherever in the non-Communist world it can do so most effectively.

Unless the present trend is reversed—and everything indicates its most rapid acceleration—U.S. industry, especially big industry, will have no alternative but to shape its policy, organize itself, and conduct its operations as a world company. This is the shape of things as they are now in the process of becoming.

The implication of viewing overseas operations from a world geographical viewpoint was publicly and valuably considered for the first time in "Creating a World Enterprise," by Gilbert H. Clee and Alfred di Scipio.[5]

The importance of their article does not lie in whether the proposed organizational structure is properly applicable to major United States corporations. Rather it lies in its projection of the necessity for top management to orient its corporate thinking to encompass this entire planet as the geographic limits of its international operations. These considerations, without much public discussion, are in the process of being applied by major U.S. corporations (although not necessarily as part of an integrated plan). In so doing, U.S. corporations will rapidly join the ranks of outstanding world organizations such as Unilever, Phillips Lamps, and Royal Dutch Shell.

Of course, determining basic policy in long-range terms from this vantage, and with this guide, means that the world becomes the oyster for aggressive exploration of possibilities for investment and export. Products will be specially designed and manufactured for world sales and adapted to the market being entered. All plans and operations, furthermore, because a world strategy is involved, would be regularly reappraised and readjusted, and could be done so quickly.

Within this framework would be determined the manner of corporate participation overseas, the identification of critical organizational needs, the creation of new concepts of planning and control, and the host of other decisions which shape the character of corporate overseas relationships with financial partners, foreign governments and local nationals.

Thus, operational control of overseas units, by such determination of basic corporate policy, becomes similar to or indentical with operational control of domestic units. In philosophy and in operation, no foreign unit need be any longer a step child, no corporate unit any longer "foreign."

Personnel controls—We have observed that determination of corporate policy is one basic area of control of overseas operations. The choice of personnel to implement these policies is another.

The *policy* considerations involved in the choice of personnel for overseas operations are often blurred. Basically, there are two, not necessarily interrelated, considerations:

1. As a matter of long-range policy, should United States or local nationals be employed in overseas operations?
2. If United States nationals are employed, what special qualities, if any, should determine their choice, beyond the requirements of the same position in domestic operations?

Both of these questions involve long-range policy considerations for top management and not mere techniques of personnel selection.

Their resolution and implementation vitally affect overseas operations.

To answer these questions, managerial requirements outside the

[5] *Harvard Business Review* (November-December 1959), p. 77.

United States should be considered. For this purpose, we are indebted to Frederick C. Harbison and Charles E. Myers' *Management in the Industrial World,*[6] which offers the first comparative analysis of management in the international industrial world. A joint project of the Industrial Relations Section of Princeton University and the Massachusetts Institute of Technology, this book carefully traces the logic of management development as it is related to the processes of growth in 23 countries. Authorities discuss with respect to each country: the nature and extent of industrialization; the national context of industrial management; and management as a resource, as a system of authority, and as a class. In each instance there is also a concluding evaluation of national management.

(Readers of Harbison and Myers' book may want to compare the Dutch, Belgian, and French managerial experience in less developed countries in a carefully prepared report by the Foundation for Economic Research of the University of Amsterdam for the International Bank for Reconstruction and Development, *Management of Direct Investments in Less Developed Countries*;[7] and the revealing study of British managerial experience, particularly in Asia, in J. S. Fforde's *International Trade in Managerial Skills.*[8])

Management in the Industrial World is well organized, clearly written, and maturely edited. The sound conclusion is drawn that the general direction of management development in all advancing industrializing countries is importantly similar. There are, however, significant differences with respect to the problems faced and to the types of reactions which reflect cultural patterns.

Within this context, consciously or not, U.S. corporations state their acceptance of a policy of placing local nationals in management positions overseas. This is stated to be a matter of sound overseas business operations. Nevertheless, as of 1957, more than 25,000 U.S. nationals were working for U.S. corporations overseas,[9] and the estimate has been made that today the total is over 50,000.[10]

The expressed recognition of the need for local nationals in management positions overseas is usually qualified only to the extent of excluding top management. Three observations, therefore, seem to be in order:

> 1. These estimated 50,000 positions obviously were not primarily "top management." For example, of 48,000 supervisors, professionals, and technicians working for U.S. companies in Latin America, one out of six is a U.S. national. This suggests that the commitment to employ local nationals is often honored more in the breach than in the observance.
>
> 2. Local nationals in overseas management frequently are in a position of second-class citizenship; their abilities are inadequately utilized, and their opportunities for advancement are limited within the U.S. company.

[6] New York: McGraw-Hill Book Company, Inc., 1959.
[7] Leiden, Holland, Stenfert Kroese, N.V., 1957.
[8] Oxford, England, Basil Blackwood & Mott, Ltd., 1957.
[9] Harlan Cleveland and Gerard J. Mangone, *The Art of Overseasmanship* (Syracuse: Syracuse University Press, 1957), p. 20.
[10] *Wall Street Journal* (May 26, 1960).

3. While an integration of U.S. nationals and local nationals seeks to establish a middle ground, the policy problem is thereby, at the best, only temporarily deferred.

There can be only one permanent and stable resolution of a condition whereby local nationals are not available for an important responsibility, including a top position. It lies in a decision to eliminate this condition, firmly taken and resolutely implemented, so that a definite answer, with timetable, is given to the question: How soon will a particular local national be trained to replace a particular U.S. national in a specified job? This is costly and time-consuming, often involving overseas higher education, but the alternative is to maintain a slowly maturing time bomb within the overseas operation.

However, even an affirmative decision will not result in quick replacement of the estimated 50,000 employees. We still need to know, with respect to the selection of U.S. nationals, what special quality (or qualities) is the secret of success, without which a U.S. national working abroad cannot succeed.

This question threads a recent volume, John Fayerweather's *The Executive Overseas,*[11] which merits consideration. This book explores administrative attitudes and relationships in a foreign culture, specifically the U.S. executive in the culture of Mexico. It examines executive relations and patterns of administrative action; individual work with respect to innovation, analysis, and action; problems and possibilities of learning; motivations; and patterns of action by U.S. executives. Its essential conclusion: the major problems in relations between U.S. executives and those of other nations develop from differences in cultural attitudes which change but slowly.

Certain important qualities of overseas executives emerge as essential: an objectivity and openmindedness (to make possible an understanding of the nature of the differences in the value systems), tolerance of these differences, and a knowledge of the history and life of the country. The author concludes that the most productive U.S. executives overseas are those who have discovered the ways of operating profitably within management methods that are consistent with the attitudes of local national executives.

The major limitation of Fayerweather's book stems from the fact that it posits a *toleration* of the alien culture rather than stressing the need for its *affirmative acceptance* as different but equal. Consequently the book views the learning process as involving essentially the local national, rather than stressing the necessity for basic relearning on the part of the United States executive overseas.

These are major limitations. Inasmuch as they directly relate not only to a philosophy of overseas operations, which opened the discussion of this article, but also vitally to its success, a few words may perhaps be properly added here.

Basically, a U.S. national working overseas is a guest of a foreign country, its government, and its people. He should act as a gracious guest. The guest learns his host's language, expectations, and business etiquette, not only his laws, but also his traditions, national traits, and customs—and

[11] Syracuse: Syracuse University Press, 1959.

respects them fully. This involves a long process of learning, or more aptly, relearning, painful as the case may sometimes be.

This point was ably made in a recent revealing article by Edward T. Hall, "The Silent Language in Overseas Business," which explores cultural differences in the language of time, space, material possessions, friendship patterns, and agreements in overseas business operations.[12]

The essence of this learning (or relearning) is a respect based on recognition that the local national is different but, as a person, equal; that his culture is different from ours but equally worthy. One, therefore, should not merely tolerate him, or express a tolerance of his culture but, being his guest, affirmatively understand, accept, and adapt to it.

This is not a matter of semantics. The U.S. national overseas must puncture by his conduct an unwanted image of "superiority." His acts will be weighed as genuine or token—with the latter exposing the democratic *poseur,* the patronizer pretending an acceptance of equality.

There is indeed no place for zealous attempts to convert local nationals to our culture and its multiform attributes. Unless a U.S. national overseas understands that "there is no part of the earth to which we, as a people, can say: 'We, the Americans, are flawless models for your future destiny,' "[13] then he cannot successfully fulfill his overseas responsibility.

This is the essence without which no U.S. national can successfully function in an alien culture as a foreigner, especially among the three fourths of the world's population which is of brown, yellow, or black skin pigmentation.

These, then, are the major elements involved in the *long-range policy* consideration of personnel control of overseas operations. They remain for conscious exploration and decision, and successful application by top echelons in U.S. industry.

This review, and its subject matter, calls for fresh consideration of long-range policy with respect to private United States operations overseas. Its public examination by leaders of United States industry and finance—and discussion of its integral relation to United States foreign economic policy—is long overdue.

[12] *Harvard Business Review* (May-June 1960), p. 87.

[13] Address by Nelson A. Rockefeller at University of Chicago Law School, May 2, 1960.

22

THE WORLD CUSTOMER *

Ernest Dichter

Only one Frenchman out of three brushes his teeth.

Automobiles have become a must for the self-esteem of even the lowliest postal clerk in Naples or the Bantu street cleaner in Durban.

There is a supermarket in Apia, the capital of Western Samoa (which received its independence in January of this year). I found can openers and the cans to go with them in a remote village on the island of Upolu.

Four out of five Germans change their shirts but once a week.

Amazon Indians use outboard motors in deep green water alleyways.

What do these facts, and many others like them, portend for the future marketing manager? For top management in companies with foresight to capitalize on international opportunities? They mean that an understanding of cultural anthropology will be an important tool of competitive marketing. They mean that knowledge of the basic differences, as well as basic similarities, among consumers in different parts of the world will be essential. They mean that the successful marketer of the future will have to think not of a United States customer, nor even of a Western European or Atlantic community customer, but of *a world customer.*

For Western European countries, it is specific marketing facts and consumer purchasing behavior patterns which are of moment to today's businessman seeking new customers. At present, these countries comprise the biggest potential overseas market for most products. They are also the countries about whose consumers the most research information has been gathered. However, as some of the above examples illustrate, other parts of the world too are becoming potential markets, as human desires break the barricades of centuries in South America, Africa, and Asia.

Emergence of the European Common Market has forced businessmen and philosophers alike to take a look at the European as a distinct species. We now see the European as more than a Frenchman or an Austrian. The Atlantic community market and the world market may make us yet take a fresh look at what is alike and what is really different in humans, their desires, hopes, fears—in short, their motivations. Close observation of customers, and potential customers, all over the world reveals that there *are* some striking similarities, yet at the same time a considerable degree of permanent difference. From objective examination of these basic cultural similarities and differences, one may discern clues for serving the World Customer today.

* From *Harvard Business Review,* XL (July-August 1962), 113-122. Reprinted by permission.

In this article, I shall first point to a number of consumer behavior patterns relevant to international marketing, particularly within the Western European market but also in some of the less developed areas. Then I shall examine the differential role of national pride, which obviously affects and will affect the success of American-made products in Western European and other countries in the Atlantic market. Finally, in an effort to define and interpret the economic and psychological differences among world customers, I shall postulate six world market groups of nations, measured by the yardstick of middle class development.

THE DISTINCTIVE EUROPEAN

The U.S. company going into Europe has to study the culture and the psychology of the people of the country, not just its manufacturing facilities and markets in the technological sense. The advertising and sales managers have to learn that reaching customers in a given country involves a real understanding of the basic motivations which operate within that country.

In dealing with various European markets, the American businessman must open his eyes to certain paradoxes, stereotypes, and hidden competitors.

Apparent Paradoxes

There are paradoxes between the way in which American products are perceived and the way they are used. Thus, anti-Americanism is strongly coupled with a desire for many U.S. products, often out of pure snobbery, often because they are symbols of an affluent society. The Italian housewife considers her American sister a poor cook and a lady of leisure, but dreams day and night of owning a Hollywood kitchen.

A similar paradox is that of the West German businessman who scoffs at American know-how, pointing out the technical superiority of many of his national products, but proudly puts his elegantly uniformed chauffeur in a Ford, polished up to the last fold of its lacquered steel hull tuxedo.

Ingrained Stereotypes

The American businessman must cast off deeply ingrained stereotypes in analyzing the purchasing behavior of European consumers, in reference to product meaning, "purchasing morality," and quality consciousness.

We all "know" that French women are very fashion conscious. Yet a study recently showed that this was exactly one of those glib stereotypes that have little if any basis in reality. The purchase of a dress or coat is much more of an investment for the Frenchwoman than for the American woman. This results from differences both in income and in prices of fashion products. It is not enough, therefore, to tell a French shopper that a garment is fashionable. She also wants to know, in a way, the "trade-in value" of the dress or blouse. How long will the fabric last? How many years will she be able to wear it? These are promises and appeals which have to a very large extent lost their attraction to the American woman.

The European is very conscious of preservation. He collects and retains things. The only parallel that we have had in this country was during the period of World War II, when we developed a new kind of pride, a pride in doing without, a pride in not having bought a new car for several years, for example. This pride did not last very long. Just as soon as cars became available again, we reverted to our somewhat affluent American habit of replacing models quite rapidly. Yet this concept of "purchasing morality" still exerts influence in the United States for some products. For example, the average male still hesitates to buy two or three suits at one time because he feels that suits, together with many other articles of clothing, are highly overvalued, and therefore it is extravagant to buy more than one at the same time. On the other hand, most of us have learned that it no longer pays to resole shoes more than twice.

As for quality consciousness, as well as confidence in the trustworthiness of the manufacturer, this is quite different in different countries. In Australia or South Africa—and for that matter in England—you find on most toilet tissues the reassuring message that the manufacturer guarantees that the paper was not made out of secondhand rags, but only new rags and new raw materials.

Such a promise has become completely unnecessary in North America. Whatever advertising may be accused of, in many areas it provides the consumer, particularly in branded merchandise, with an assurance that he will not be cheated as long as he buys a well-known brand. It is true today that whether we buy a Westinghouse, a General Electric, or a Kelvinator refrigerator, we get more or less equal values as long as we pay about the same amount of money. What we have learned to buy is the freedom of individual choice. We buy images; we buy the sizzle because we have been reassured that the steak itself is of generally good quality. *In many European countries this confidence,* this almost blind reliance on the promise of the manufacturer, *has not yet been established.* Therefore, advertising approaches have to be based much more on definite proofs of quality.

Hidden Competitors

Another problem facing Atlantic marketers is that in many areas they are still dealing with hidden competitors, lurking in places unfamiliar in domestic marketing. Taking toilet tissue again, in some recent motivational research done in West Germany I found it was much too premature to promise the German consumer luxury softness or colors compatible with the bathroom fixtures. Instead, the hidden but real competitor with which the toilet tissue manufacturer has to contend is the newspaper and the old standby of the German equivalent of the Sears, Roebuck catalog. The West German family feels that toilet tissue, particularly the American luxury type, is wasteful and unnecessary. The advertising approach, then, has to deal much more with providing absolution and selling the concept that good quality toilet tissue is a part of modern life.

ETHOS OF NATIONALISM

Nationalism obviously plays a major role in determining consumer acceptance of nondomestically made products. Understanding its manifold aspects is a *sine qua non* for U.S. businessmen operating overseas.

National feeling manifests itself in many ways. Some of these have already been touched on briefly before. In this section, I shall show in greater detail how: (1) national pride can be a motivating sales factor employable by the astute overseas marketer as an asset; (2) long-standing cultural traditions in one nation can dictate the *discard* of advertising approaches proven successful in another nation; (3) stereotyped national *self*-illusions can alter the direction of marketing strategy.

National Pride

Admiration of foreign products often goes together with *hidden inferiority feelings* which are overcompensated by tearing the foreigner down. These products are the tangible symbols of foreign superiority. For example:

> In Venezuela, despite various forms of anti-Yankee sentiment, it is considered chic to smoke U.S. cigarettes. Even when the American brand name is used and the Venezuelan smoker can discover the little phrase "Hecho en Venezuela" on his package, the almost completely identical cigarette suffers at least a 50% prestige loss. A successful approach used in overcoming this problem was to convince Venezuelans that the people they secretly admired in a form of love-hatred—the Americans—indeed liked Venezuelan tobacco, used it for their own cigarettes, and had no negative feeling toward Venezuelan cigarettes.
>
> A similar solution was found in connection with Venezuelan rum by serving this rum in hotels in Caracas frequented by U.S. businessmen and tourists. The Venezuelan could be convinced that if it was good enough for the supposed foreign connoisseur, then it certainly ought to be good enough for him.
>
> The French gasoline, *Total,* had a domestic marketing problem arising from a national inferiority complex. Gasoline, to the Frenchman, was for a long time represented by American and British companies. Gasoline and oil (to a lesser extent) are symbols of power. The Frenchman was not convinced that his own gasoline would have the same power as the foreign brands. The approach calculated to overcome this sentiment was to present *Total* as an international brand that happened to originate in France and the Sahara, but was accepted and well-liked in many other countries.
>
> In Morocco, sales of French pasteurized milk had dropped considerably with the advent of Morocco's independence. This stemmed partly from the exodus of the French army with its families, and also from Moroccan unfamiliarity with drinking pasteurized milk.
>
> But the drop in milk sales was also due to other factors, psychological in nature. One was the lack of confidence in the quality of pasteurized milk—Moroccan women were accustomed to buying from

street vendors who milked the cows in front of their own eyes and then ladled the milk out of the pail. The soulless, odorless, clean pasteurized milk in bottles was simply too far removed from the original natural source of milk for the women to realize that they were still receiving the same quality of product.

But even more interesting was a factor dealing again with the phenomenon of national pride. The company had changed the lettering on its milk bottles and milk cartons from French to Arabic. The purpose was to please the newly independent consumers. Research showed, however, that instead of being pleased, consumers reacted negatively to this attempt at flattery. They stated it in the following way: "What is good enough for the French people is good enough for us. We don't want Arab milk. We want good French milk that the Frenchmen drink themselves."

For *marketing purposes* it thus was necessary to re-establish confidence in the naturalness of pasteurized bottled milk by showing cows and having street vendors also peddle pasteurized milk. A second measure was to change the lettering on the milk bottles back to French. Both steps resulted in increased sales.

The little phrase "Made in ——" can have a tremendous influence on the acceptance and success of products over and above the specific advertising techniques used by themselves.

In a recent study in West Germany, this query was posed as part of a projective test: "An important discovery has been made in the technical field which has a great influence on our daily life. Which country has made this discovery?" As many as 78% answered: "Germany." (The study is being repeated in other countries. It will be interesting to examine the answers.) We also asked the Germans to think of a new product which through an error in production caused the death of several hundred people. The task of the respondents was to indicate which country would be most likely to manufacture such a product. We found that Germans considered this most likely to happen in the East zone, Russia, or the satellite countries, and then up to 30% in Italy or France.

The strong positive attitude evidenced by Germans toward their own technical product influenced an advertising approach developed for Ford in Germany. Research showed that the name Ford had a strong American association. The reaction of Germans was: "Americans drive our cars, Volkswagen and Mercedes; therefore they must be convinced that German cars are better than their own; so why should we buy their cars?" When the German Ford was presented as an example of cooperation between American ingenuity and know-how and German thoroughness and efficiency, considerable sales success was achieved.

"Inverted Morality"

The influence of cultural traditions permeates a host of consumer behavior patterns.

The fact that 64% of Frenchmen don't brush their teeth is in part caused by the lack of running water in many communities. But a far more interesting aspect of this behavior could be explained on the basis of what I call "inverted morality." Here is an illustration of what can happen:

> In Puritanical cultures it is customary to think of cleanliness as being next to godliness. The body and its functions are covered up as much as possible.
>
> But, in Catholic and Latin countries, to fool too much with one's body, to overindulge in bathing or toiletries, has the opposite meaning. It is *that* type of behavior which is considered immoral and improper. Accordingly, an advertising approach based on Puritanical principles, threatening Frenchmen that if they didn't brush their teeth regularly, they would develop cavities or would not find a lover, failed to impress.
>
> To fit the accepted concept of morality, the French advertising agency changed this approach to a permissive one. The new approach presented the brushing of teeth as modern and chic but not as an absolute necessity which when neglected would result in dire consequences.

In line with the "inverted morality" notion is the fact that deodorant sales in France are lower than in most other countries. The majority, up to 80% of French housewives, use laundry soap instead of toilet soap. Only 20% of them have discovered perfumed, feminine soap which in the United States is frequently referred to as a "French type" of soap.

Self-Illusions

Often nationals of a particular country are completely mistaken themselves about their own main characteristics. Successful marketers must be as cognizant of these national self-illusions as they must be aware of the mistaken stereotypes noted earlier. For example:

> Germans still refer to themselves as a nation of poets and thinkers; yet the largest selling newspaper, *The Bildzeitung,* has a circulation of 2½ million based largely on sensationalism and tabloid treatment of news. Even German *advertisers* had to be shown that this circulation, although proven by audits, was indeed psychologically possible. The only way this could be done was to force the German advertiser to look at his own people, including himself, without hypocrisy and in the harsh light of reality.
>
> All references to economy, comfort, and warmth had only a minimal effect in getting Englishmen to install central heating. They all ran up against a barrier of traditional self-illusion that Englishmen are of a hardy race that does not need the softening and effeminate effect of central heating. Inroads could be made only when the health of babies was used as a rationalization and after reassurance was given to the English "he-man" that to feel comfortably warm would not be detrimental to his self-image of virility.
>
> Most Europeans are convinced that they are individualists and nonconformists. Studies have shown that this is to a very large extent an illusion. There is a widely expressed fear of losing individuality, but right now it is the European who is becoming the representative of the mass market while it is the American market which in turn relies more and more on psychological segmentations. U.S. manufacturers may pro-

> duce individuality on a mass scale, but individuality has become the decisive appeal in many products and services.

National self-illusions are hardly restricted to other nations. In the United States, as in quite a few other countries, many of our ethical principles are still based on the concept that we have to work by the sweat of our brow. In Germany, this is even more so. *The more you work, the more moral you feel.* Yet at the same time our modern psychological development and automation have resulted in a situation where fewer and fewer people work with their hands. Service fields are increasing, and we have more and more leisure time. The recent victory of the electricians' union in New York introducing a five-hour day aroused the nation for many reasons. Particularly pertinent here is that it clashed with most of our cherished beliefs of the importance of achieving happiness through work.

We are now confronted with increasing leisure time. Our discomfort results to a large extent from a lack of hedonistic morality such as prevailed among the Greeks for whom life was here to be enjoyed by a few people who did not have to work and did not have to feel guilty about it.

Leisure pursuits are spreading rapidly. Labor-saving devices are multiplying, and they are being adopted all over the world. The major difference lies in the degree of manifest or latent guilt feelings which are aroused:

> Instant coffee is used by the Dutch housewife accompanied by the verbal protest that she only uses it in an emergency. What happens, however, is that the number of emergencies has increased amazingly.
>
> French farmwives are inclined to say that they need large kitchen stoves in order to do the cooking for their large farm families. Young farmwives, however, have begun to admire and gradually buy the smaller units used by their city sisters. They have discovered that they do not have to stay as long behind the stove, and so are finding interests in other roles than that of a kitchen slave.

BREAKING BOUNDARIES

Politically, in recent years we have watched a host of new nations emerge from erstwhile colonial status. It may be argued that many colonies would have been better off staying under the protection of enlightened colonial powers. Yet their desire for independence, no matter how premature we consider it to be, is so impulsive, explosive, and uncontrollable that no other solution remains than to satisfy this emotionally, humanly understandable hunger.

More important to the marketer is the fact that the same desire which spurred these political events has another dimension—viz., *in terms of consumption, whole centuries are being skipped in a world revolution of human expectations.*

Thus, from the viewpoint of the international psychologist's concern with the people still living in national units, we see the gradual development of the World Customer who breaks all boundaries:

When a South African clothing manufacturer asks how to sell more long pants to previously half-naked Bantus, he is the first one to smash the barrier of apartheid, no matter how segregationistic his views may be. The moment one starts thinking of 10 million natives as consumers, one has to concern himself with their emotions and motivations.

Research revealed a greater psychological parallel between the emancipated Zulu and the emancipated white worker than between the nonemancipated Zulu and his emancipated tribal brother. The latter is ashamed when visited by his former ethnic peers. He has learned to speak English Afrikaans, has started to wear long pants, and often owns a car—a secondhand, dilapidated car, but nevertheless a car. He represents in many ways the same emotional conflict as that which existed between the first- and second-generation immigrants during the period of heavy immigration in the United States.

In Australia until a few years ago 10% of the population was represented each year by newcomers, migrants, or—more euphemistically—"new Australians." These new Australians will change the basic Australian character in unrecognizable fashion within another ten years or so. As consumers, on the one hand, they want to eat, drink, and use the same products as the established Australians; on the other hand, they bring in their own customs and often superimpose Italian, German, or Spanish culture on the Australians.

Six Market Groups

How can we locate the World Customer at various stages of development? How can we measure nations?

The "consumer revolution" which we are witnessing is basically not a proletarian one, but is *a revolution of the middle class*. It is the degree of development of a large middle class which makes the difference between a backward and a modern country both economically and psychologically. That is the clue for appraising and interpreting different cultures, for measuring their achievement.

The most important symbol of middle class development in the world today is the automobile. It is the automobile which represents achievement and personal freedom for the middle class. And this restless middle class is the most important factor in the constructive discontent which motivates people's desires and truly moves them forward. In some countries, like the United States, West Germany, Switzerland, Sweden, and Norway, most people have enough to eat and are reasonably well housed. Having achieved this thousand-year-old dream of humanity, they now reach out for further satisfactions. They want to travel, discover, be at least physically independent. The automobile is the symbol of mobility; the auto-mobile has become the self-mobile!

Using middle class development as a measure of achievement, if we were to visualize the social composition of each country in terms of a scale showing the size of its middle class, upper class, and lower class, we could probably define some six groups.

Group One: The Almost Classless Society, Contented Countries. In this group we would include primarily the Scandinavian countries. The middle class takes up almost all of the scale, with very few people left who could be considered really poor and few who are really rich. We are dealing with a socialistic security and equalization which sounds like paradise, but often leads to loss of incentives.

In these countries, products are viewed in a rather sober fashion. The car, for instance, is strictly utilitarian, and showing off with one's auto is not considered correct.

Studies have shown that reliability and economy are very important. Attitudes toward products are rational: they do not represent a special status value. There is generally a conservative attitude toward new gadgets and styles. Second cars are practically nonexistent.

Group Two: The Affluent Countries. This group includes the United States, West Germany, Switzerland, Holland, and Canada. Few people starve, and there is still some room at the top. The top of the middle class itself, however, often is high and desirable enough so that there is no need to break through and trespass into the unpopular and threatened class of financial aristocracy.

Among these countries the most advanced is the United States. What happens in many areas in the United States represents the latest and leading trends and permits us to predict what will happen in the next few years in the other affluent countries. People in affluent countries want greater individuality in their products. They dream of high-quality, repair-proof, almost custom-tailored articles.

While the German still uses his car for prestige purposes, in the United States the status value of cars has substantially diminished and has been shifted to other products and services such as swimming pools, travel, and education. The average American considers his car more like an appliance than a status symbol. Conspicuous cars like the Cadillac or the Lincoln try to emphasize their quiet elegance to avoid being considered cars for show-offs. There is increased attention to functional values and integration in car designs. Cars are not pampered; they are expected to do their job.

Group Three: Countries in Transition. In this group we may place England, France, Italy, Australia, South Africa, and Japan. These countries still have a working class in the nineteenth century sense. But this class is trying to break out of its bondage and join the comfortable middle class. The upper classes still have privileges and can afford maids, Rolls-Royces, and castles; but their privileges are being rapidly whittled away. These countries have not had complete social revolutions. (The Labor government in England represented such an attempt but failed.) Servants are still cheap but rapidly getting more expensive and less easily available. Many wage-earning groups suffer from low wages. Living standards are behind those of the United States and West Germany. The white-collar worker often makes less money than the factory worker, but he has not integrated yet with the developing labor-based middle class. Prestige still plays an important role.

Cars are pampered in these countries. They are an extension of one's personality. They are given pet names. They represent major investments. Cars are outward symbols of success. There are still many first-car people, who have only now bought their first proof of "having arrived." Price plays an important role as an invitation to enter the automobile world—upgrading the buyer from bicycles and motorcycles. For top classes, some very expensive cars are available. Style plays a role with certain groups; there is much experimentation, curiosity, and desire for product adventure. Markets are still fluid, have not stabilized yet. There is resistance in all these countries against planned obsolescence. A lot of people hold onto their cars for six to ten years or more. American cars are considered to be too flashy and also too expensive.

Group Four: Revolutionary Countries. Venezuela, Mexico, Argentina, Brazil, Spain, India, China, and the Philippines are in this group. In these areas large groups of people are just emerging from near-starvation and are discovering industrialization. Relatively speaking, there are more extremely rich people, a small but expanding middle class, and a very large body of depressed economic groups that are beginning to discover the possibilities of enjoying life through the revolution in industry.

In these countries large sections of the population have not even reached the level of being consumers. These are the Indians living in many South American countries, the people living in villages in India and Indonesia, and so on.

Automobiles are available only to a relatively small group. They are expensive and considered a luxury. They are taxed so highly that they are beyond the reach of most people. American cars are considered the ideal. People want to show off. Small cars are bought as a way to get started. As the middle class develops, there should be an even further increase in the sale of small and compact cars, with the really rich people preferring big American cars.

Group Five: Primitive Countries. The newly liberated countries of Africa and the remaining colonies comprise the fifth group. In these countries there exists only a very small group of wealthy indigenous and foreign businessmen, new political leaders, and foreign advisers. The rest of the population is most often illiterate and ignorant and exists in a preconsumer stage, characterized either by barter or by almost complete primitive "self-sufficiency." The few cars that are sold are primarily for the government bureaucracy. There is no real car market as yet.

Group Six: The New Class Society. In Russia and its satellite countries, there is emerging a class of bureaucrats who represent a new form of aristocracy, while everybody else represents a slowly improving, low middle class. True, in these countries the extremely low income and the starving proletarians have disappeared.

The automobile, the modern home with its mechanized kitchen and mass-produced food items, and supermarket distribution represent the symbols of a new industrial society. By understanding the basic position of a country on this scale of development one can understand the role of products at present and one can also predict their future possibilities.

There is an interest in prestige cars. All the bourgeois symbols of capitalist countries are being copied—particularly those of the United States.

Our Greatest Opportunity

Many recent stories in the press—most of them picked up in foreign countries—make it appear that we ought to be ashamed of the good life we are leading. This recanting has its origin in a deep-seated guilt feeling which is unhealthy and dangerous. Some of the recanting is directed against a number of specific products, such as electrical gadgets, big cars, luxury and leisure time, and merchandise.

The real measuring rod of the success of one system over another should be based on the happiness of the citizens, their creativeness, and their constructive discontent. The desire to grow, to improve oneself, and to enjoy life to the fullest is at least equal, if not decidedly superior, to the goal of being ahead in a missile or a satellite program.

Our present life, therefore, should be presented as a challenge to the outside world—not in a boastful way, but as a life attainable by everyone through democratic and peaceful pursuits.

CONCLUSION

In most countries I have visited, I find that human desires are pretty much alike. The big difference lies in the level of achievement, in its many different forms.

In Iquitos, on the Amazon River, I recently visited an Indian tribe. They live in blissful fashion, hunting and planting bananas and yuccas. Who is smarter—we, the hard-working "civilized people"—or the contented Indians? Part of the answer was provided by the fact that our guide complained that there were fewer and fewer Indians for tourists to see. They were becoming "too civilized." In other words, these primitive people who were supposed to be happy are caught in the inevitable maelstrom of development. They smoke cigarettes and are beginning to wear jeans and shirts.

Growth and progress are the only possible goals of life. I believe that the clue to man's destiny lies in his relentless training toward independence, not only politically, but also in the psychological sense. We are beset by fears, by inhibitions, by narrow-minded routine thinking. Step by step, year by year, we free ourselves more and more. Jets reduce physical distances; international trade and mass communications break down barriers. The world is opening up. The Common Market will broaden into an Atlantic Market and finally into a World Market. In order to participate effectively in this progressive development of mankind, it is essential to have a creative awareness of human desire and its strategy throughout the world—to understand and prepare to serve the new World Customer.

23

THE HONORABLE PICNIC: DOING BUSINESS IN JAPAN *

Dudley L. Miller

In 1924 there was published a short satirical novel by Thomas Rauçat, entitled *The Honorable Picnic,*[1] in which a French businessman in Japan, bent on man's primeval chase, invited a charming Japanese young lady for a week-end outing at Enoshima, a seaside resort near Tokyo. Although the game was suggested by the Westerner, it was played, in the last analysis, under Eastern rules. The forces which he set in motion produced a resultant directed only in part by his desires and in the main by the Japanese.

So it remains today. The foreigner who wishes to do business in Japan usually makes the first move, but he is thereafter only one of the factors in a complex and perplexing economic, cultural, and legal continuum. To the uninitiated, the ample supply of cheap labor and the manifold manufacturing talents of the Japanese promise a sumptuous picnic which may be freely partaken, but those who have been there know that the Japanese, in their own intricate and interesting manner, have made the party an "honorable picnic," to be enjoyed only in the Oriental style.

It is the purpose of this article to explore some of the legal and cultural problems which Westerners encounter in seeking to do business in Japan. Many Americans have been impressed with the tremendous industrial progress made in that country; the gross national product nearly doubled between 1952 and 1959,[2] and Premier Hayato Ikeda has announced that the economic goal for 1970 is to double the gross national product of 1960. Japan and the United States share many important values and in a number of ways, industrially and ideologically, have been moving together. However, Americans should also be impressed with the fact that their business techniques are unavailing unless drastically modified in the light of the unique, delightful, and often puzzling Japanese culture.

Just as one looks about the business lunch clubs of lower Manhattan and sees numerous Japanese businessmen investigating and negotiating here, so one may look around in Tokyo and see equal numbers of Ameri-

* From *Harvard Business Review,* XXXIX (November-December 1961), 79-86. Reprinted by permission.

Editors' (HBR) note: Before deciding to publish this article we consulted a number of Japanese authorities; they all approved its factual content and particularly its spirit.

[1] New York: The Viking Press, Inc. The novel was reprinted in 1955.

[2] See *The Japanese Economy,* Bulletin No. 9, New York University Graduate School of Business Administration, 1960, pp. 3, 5.

can businessmen on missions there. This article seeks to help the latter gain a keener appreciation of the psychological and cultural influences that they will experience in Japan—and even more broadly to make the point that, in dealing with *any* foreign people, businessmen should place themselves within the foreign culture, both for the sake of successfully doing business and also for the sake of enriching their own insights. Japan offers a striking case study for the American preparing himself for international trade and industry.

JAPANESE ATTRACTIONS

Preceding any business trip to Japan, corporate management will have studied and been attracted by the human and material resources available there. Plentiful and cheap labor, ranging across the board of manufacturing skills, constitutes the foundation of Japanese industrial power, and any management which has not considered the tide changes engendered by this power may well find its sand castle surrounded by competitive waters in due course. The International Labor Organization has estimated hourly wages in manufacturing industries for 1957 as being $2.07 for the United States, $0.65 for the United Kingdom, $0.51 for West Germany, $0.33 for Italy, and $0.26 for Japan.[3] This means that the Japanese cash wages in 1957 were about one eighth of wages in the United States and about one half of British and German wages.

Counterdefensive

The Japanese government has attempted to forestall the defensive maneuvers which other countries (and industrial units within them), mindful of the prewar dumping of Japanese goods and the spectacular postwar recovery of the Japanese economy, are naturally tempted to adopt in the way of boycotts, tariff barriers, or others. For example, the Amalgamated Clothing Workers Union announced that after May 31, 1961, its members would refuse to process Japanese textiles in the United States. Only at the urging of the President himself was this drastic threat rescinded.

The government takes the position that a simple comparison of cash wages is misleading, because "real" income is not represented by the numerical figure, which would presumably be more comparable (i.e., higher) if based on equal units of purchasing power, and also because there are a number of what Americans would call "fringe" benefits furnished by the Japanese companies in addition to cash wages. The Ministry of Foreign Affairs gives the example of A, "a male worker who is employed in a fairly representative company in Tokyo":

> "To begin with, A lives in a house provided by his company, and the rent he pays is amazingly low when compared with average city rents. His daily trips between home and factory are paid by the company. A's

[3] Cited in *Exports and Wages—The Case of Japan* (Japan, Ministry of Foreign Affairs, 1960), p. 2.

working hours are from 9 A.M. to 5 P.M. with a break for lunch which he usually takes in the company restaurant at a very cheap price. He often brings back to his wife food, clothing, and other miscellaneous articles that he buys at the company store at a discount ranging from 10% to 30% below city prices. The company store even supplies furniture, refrigerators, and television sets on an installment basis, for which, if necessary, A can obtain a loan from the company almost free of interest.

"In case of illness, A is given free medical treatment in the company hospital, and if his indisposition extends over a number of years, the company will continue paying almost his full salary. The company maintains lodges at seaside or mountain resorts, where A can spend the holidays or an occasional week end with the family at moderate prices. . . . It must also be remembered that when A reaches retirement age [usually 55] he will receive a lump sum retirement allowance or a pension, either of which will assure him a relatively stable living for the rest of his life." [4]

Realistic Appraisal

Those familiar with Japan will recognize in the above description the situation of employees in some large corporations of Tokyo and other cities, and James G. Abegglen's study of *The Japanese Factory* reveals that paternalism is known in smaller firms, too.[5]

On the other hand, while labor and the unions established and fostered by the Allied Occupation Force are making fair progress, the employees' utopia put forth by the Ministry of Foreign Affairs remains relatively rare. The Japanese family requires by Western standards little in the way of housing, heating, furniture, clothing, and food, and consequently demands far less return for the labor of its members. An astoundingly large percentage of Japanese enterprises are so tiny that they are operated on a psychologically familial basis where a paternalistic politeness often substitutes for pay increases and other benefits.[6] Over 50% of all industrial companies in Japan employ from one to three persons, a little over 25% have between four and nine employees, and another 15% employ between ten and nineteen persons.[7]

Thus, in spite of the Japanese government's counterarguments, which will probably increase in cogency as the passage of time, the pressures of collective bargaining, and the influence of Western labor standards accomplish their changes, alert American managements have appraised the Japanese industrial phoenix as a competitive threat. They have become sensitive to the Japanese presence in their domestic and international futures. They are impressed with the desirability of having a facility in Japan so as to be able to take advantage of the favorable labor market and secure a comparably favorable base of operations if the competitive going gets too rough.

[4] Ibid., pp. 2-3.
[5] Glencoe, Illinois: The Free Press, 1958.
[6] Boye De Mente, *Japanese Ethics & Manners in Business* (Tokyo: East Asia Publishing Co., Ltd., 1960), p. 24.
[7] Ibid., p. 106.

FIRST IMPRESSIONS

Upon arrival in Tokyo at the Haneda International Airport, the expeditionary force of Western businessmen sent by the home office to explore the possibilities of a Japanese license arrangement, a joint venture, or even a wholly owned subsidiary operation will be greeted by possibly the entire staff of officers and directors of the Japanese company or companies with whom they have previously been in contact by correspondence. Sometimes rival groups of greeters meet the visitors, resulting in ill-concealed Japanese embarrassment.

Operation "Smother"

In the absence of any such embarrassment, and assuming a Japanese corporate host of some size, the Westerners are smoothly and enthusiastically welcomed. Thus starts the process known variously as the "clobber" or "smother" technique. After Customs have been cleared, suitcases are shepherded to waiting taxis, pictures of all are taken, and the group proceeds to the visitors' hotel, for which the Japanese have long previously arranged. Over the next several weeks, during which the talks progress slowly but carefully, the Westerners are not permitted out of sight. Their schedule is carefully filled with a succession of luncheons and dinners planned and paid for by the Japanese.

This steady entertainment covers the week ends as well, for the Japanese husband may, and frequently does, absent himself for long periods from his home without apparently offending his wife. In fact, the Japanese ladies are carefully kept out of sight and are seldom even mentioned. Excursionary trips to the places of historical interest such as Nikko, Nara, and Kyoto are often planned, and the arrangements are invariably expertly handled by the hosts.

All of this is, of course, both beneficial and impressive to the visitors. Tokyo, especially that part known as the Ginza, is a nighttime town that is filled with thousands of bars, cabarets, and night clubs. To be exposed to the beautiful, intricate colored neon displays in the many streets and alleys of the Ginza district, to enter through an unpretentious dark doorway into a brightly lit and luxurious cabaret, and then to be attended by a dozen attractive young Japanese girls—hired to dance with and make the customers comfortable in their surroundings—has been known to affect the business judgment of many an otherwise steady Westerner. By thus incapsulating and relaxing the visitors, the Japanese leave little time for independent study and other considerations—including contact with competitors.

Caveat Visitor

The motives of the Japanese are not, of course, wholly cynical, for they delight in showing off their country and its customs to interested visitors. The hosts explain and demonstrate at great length and seem indefatigable in teaching their guests the rituals of Japanese culture. Nothing pleases them more than to find that some prior study of Japan has been made by the foreigners. They laugh delightedly if a few words of Japanese are spoken or reference to one of their customs is made.

Foreknowledge of this self-consciousness (and of the fear of inferiority or dislike underlying it) can be used, in fact, to major advantage by the foreign negotiator, who otherwise may be irritated and thrown off stride by its unconscious emotional effects on him. Indeed, to *orient* himself, and the word is used advisedly, the visitor who does not have a mental outline of Japan's history, and some reading knowledge of the origins and practice of its culture, will find himself bewildered and ill-equipped to represent his company.[8] Without flexibility in his own attitudes in accepting or at least tolerating differences in such matters as ways of bathing, flavors of food, modes of dress, and in basic patterns of thinking, the visiting businessman will seldom be able to negotiate to a satisfactory conclusion.

Some wary Westerners, warned in advance of the "smother" technique, do not inform their Japanese counterparts of the exact time they intend to arrive and so are astonished to find the Japanese reception committee on hand at Haneda or at their hotel. This is because amateur but skillful detective work has been done with the airlines and Western hotels in Tokyo to determine the foreigners' plans. The solution to this problem, if the visitors wish to avoid commitment of their time so early in the game, would seem to be an extremely ambiguous advance notice of arrival, but even this may be only partially successful.

SECOND THOUGHTS

As the negotiations wear on, one realizes that apparently the Japanese have suspended all or nearly all their business to be with the visitors. Time seems unimportant; they appear quite content and interested to be talking exclusively and at length with their guests. The Westerners are, in fact, frequently asked to express their views on many relevant business matters —much after the manner of a management seminar—without discussion or commitment from the other side, but obviously with much educational benefit to it.

This use of time is at once a philosophical matter and a negotiating weapon of the Japanese. Shintoism, Confucianism, and Buddhism—Japan's main religions—all reflect the "natural" flow of time, and the American precept that "time is money" has not been adopted as an effective motivation. (The parable of the talents, whereby a vengeful god punishes for failure to grasp an opportunity for self-improvement, has no counterpart in the Japanese culture.) It is well understood, however, that Westerners are

[8] The classic reference is Ruth Benedict, *The Chrysanthemum and the Sword* (Boston: Houghton Mifflin Company, 1946). An excellent cultural history is *Japan, Past and Present* (New York: Alfred A. Knopf, Inc., 1952) by Edwin O. Reischauer, United States Ambassador to Japan. See also *Japan Today* (Tokyo: Ministry of Foreign Affairs, 1956); Reischauer, "The Broken Dialogue With Japan," *Foreign Affairs* (October 1960), p. 11.

greatly affected by "loss" of time, and one candid Japanese has been quoted as saying, in effect, "If we make you [Americans] wait long enough, you will agree to anything." [9] It appears clear that the visitors should allow as much time for their task as is practicable (and then some) and, above all, should avoid any appearance of discomfiture at the slowness of progress.

In most cases, the Westerners are unable to speak or understand the Japanese language, and the Easterners will frequently converse for long periods of time among themselves during the negotiating sessions without in some cases indicating the outcome of their deliberations. It is possible for a pointed Western question to be asked, much Japanese deliberation to follow, and then absolutely no answer to be forthcoming; the question is apparently thoroughly treated and then simply ignored. This ordinarily means that the Japanese group is in disagreement within itself, and no action is then taken until all its members either agree or are at least willing "to go along."

Usually the Western side is invited to put forth its proposal. Psychologically, this is probably a desirable thing for both sides, since the Japanese are historically accustomed to listening to the outsider, and the outsider is usually anxious to get to the picnic. On the other hand, if it is practicable to obtain the first offer from the Japanese (generally thought in the West to be a desirable ploy of negotiation), the outsider's cause is likely to be advanced.

All this is conducted in an atmosphere of utmost cordiality; Japanese green tea is served every hour or so, together with *o-shobori* (hot damp towels for the face and hands). Small jokes and laughter by both sides induce an atmosphere of good humor, which is charming, but may also be disarming. It is nonetheless a pleasant way to negotiate.

Dealing with MITI

From time to time, the Japanese may say to a foreigner's offer that "the government won't allow it"; or if export to the markets of other countries is mentioned, that "the government will approve of your proposal." It is thus that, little by little, the Westerner recognizes the invisible presence at the bargaining table of a third party—the Japanese MITI, or Ministry of International Trade and Industry.

Immediately after the war, Japan and the Allied Occupation Force welcomed the entry or re-entry of foreign companies, especially those which had done business in Japan prior to Pearl Harbor, and frequently permitted remittance of profits and capital to the home country on a temporary or permanent basis without much delay or red tape. As Japan has grown economically stronger, however, the MITI has progressively increased its restrictions to a point where "validation" of capital investments and royalty or license agreements, under which profits and capital would be returned to the parent country, have been either impossible to achieve in some cases

[9] Edward T. Hall, "The Silent Language in Overseas Business," *Harvard Business Review* (May-June 1960), p. 89; see also *The Silent Language* (New York: Doubleday & Company, Inc., 1959), pp. 23-41.

or, if granted, have been obtained only after many months or even years of extensive negotiation in Tokyo.

In recent years this has discouraged or delayed a number of foreign companies from entering Japan, and the frequent criticism of Japanese policies has recently led to a well-advertised "liberalization," which is probably more apparent than real. Nevertheless, the incredible economic recovery of Japan has led many knowledgeable Japanese and foreigners alike to believe that in due course the yen will be made freely convertible and remittable. Anticipating this, a number of Western businesses have created unvalidated Japanese "yen corporations" with the intention of either ploughing back their profits into the enterprise in Japan or permitting the profits to remain there in yen until the MITI authorizes general remittance.

WHAT MAKES SAMA RUN?

It is a familiar sight, even in the cosmopolitan city of Tokyo, the most heavily populated city in the world, to see two Japanese meet and follow the ancient behavior pattern of "status-seeking." To an American, this phrase means self-betterment, but to the Japanese it means determining the other person's status so as to know how to act toward him. When a Japanese *sensei,* or teacher, meets a former student, the two bow in the traditional manner with the student making sure that he bobs up and down longer than the teacher. The student uses the honorific words and polite verb endings to which every *sensei*—stupid or intelligent, effective lecturer or artless pedant—is entitled, while the teacher uses the more condescending forms of speech.

If strangers meet, both bow while keeping an eye cocked to watch the other's depth and number of bows, and in the meantime they determine their relative status by indirect questions in the polite forms. Suddenly, the one found to have higher status lapses into condescension, while the other continues as before, taking care that he remains in his bows deeper and longer than the other. There is no competition about this, for the process is simply one of ascertaining where the duties lie for each. Nor is there any bluffing, as might well occur in the United States, with the person of lesser status assuming a superior role and seeking to better himself.

Origins of Discomfort

The origins of this rigid social behavior lie in the psychological conditioning of an isolated people for a period in excess of 1,200 years. The undeviating acceptance by the Japanese of their hierarchical classes, from the *Mikado* (emperor) at the very top down to the *eta* (slaughterers and tanners) considered next to the animals, is sometimes thought to be the work of the Tokugawa *Shogun,* or supreme generals. This is the clan that controlled Japan, including the *Mikado,* with an absoluteness unbelievable today, from 1603 until 1854—the date of Commodore Perry's treaty and the end of Japan's isolation.

Apparently, however, the Tokugawa merely built upon the Confucian and other Chinese concepts of familial organization, introduced to Japan as governmental models during the Sui and T'ang dynasties prior to 907 A.D.[10] Shinto, with its simple reverence for places and trees of unusual beauty and majesty, as well as Buddhism with its teachings of submission to life, helped the Japanese to feel that their "natural" places were the ones assigned to them in the family structure and also in the national structure, which was modeled upon the family. To vie with one's fellows of the same class so as to rise above them was "unnatural" and therefore unthinkable.

The Tokugawa merely made sure that such rivalry remained unthinkable. The *samurai* warriors were entitled to execute on the spot anyone found deviating from the patterns of life which the Japanese came wholeheartedly to believe produced harmony rather than tyranny. The lower classes in the hierarchy acted in terms of their obligations to those above and not in terms of personal liberty or rights.

The closing of Japan to foreigners occurred early in the 1600's, and the only contacts with the outside world thereafter came through the Dutch traders who were restricted to a small island in Nagasaki harbor. In its capsule the civilization of the Japanese developed to individual perfection, while the remainder of the world progressed until it was almost too late for Japan. It is interesting to speculate on what might have happened to the Japanese if their isolation had been permitted to continue until 1900, when one of this century's aggressive nations surely would have undertaken to enlighten them in a style different from Commodore Perry's.

Nevertheless, in this background can be seen the origins of the Japanese discomfort in the presence of foreigners and their difficulty in coming to terms with us. We do not fit into the scheme of their hierarchy, which is still unconsciously the foundation of Japanese daily thoughts and actions, because its formulation left no place for outsiders. Here also is the reason why Nisei, or Americans of Japanese blood born in the United States, are not favorably received in Japan. Theoretically, being "Japanese," they should be in the hierarchy some place, but they are not bound by the traditional thought and behavior patterns and are therefore the objects of native suspicion.

Obligation and Competition

In addition, there are two crucial aspects of the Japanese psychology of which the visiting businessman should be constantly aware. The first relates to that complicated and well-advertised phenomenon known as "keeping face," and the second concerns their innate reluctance to compete among themselves and consequent lack of aptitude for salesmanship. Both characteristics are apparently derived from the hierarchial thinking at the base of the Japanese approach to living.

Unlike our own culture—based on psychological guilt and punishment—the Japanese way of life is based on a system of obligations and shame for failure to perform them. Thus, when a Japanese does not know

[10] G. B. Sansom, *A History of Japan to 1334* (Stanford, California: Stanford University Press, 1958), pp. 74-76, 129.

the answer to a question asked by a foreigner, he experiences a strong sense of shame. In his view he has failed to discharge an obligation which he believes is "naturally" his in the situational context. It is indeed a Westernized Japanese who says, "I don't know," or, "We cannot manufacture that product"; and even then, if one observes closely, he will find a trace of discomfort registered by the Japanese admitting such "failure."

Similarly, competitors in Japan are loath to outdo each other. For centuries members of the same class were trained not to excel each other, for to do so would disturb the peace—harmony being the product of uniformity and aggression the product of competition. It should be noted, however, that while many other national characteristics of the Japanese, such as the need to preserve "face," apply to situations involving foreigners as well as their own people, the reluctance to compete does *not* apply vis-à-vis outsiders. Indeed, since foreigners are not in the hierarchy, competition with them not only is possible but even desirable in view of the centuries of Japanese preparations against threats of foreign invasion.

Sense of Beauty

A word should be said about the extraordinarily well-developed admiration of the Japanese for simple beauty. The manifestations of their appreciation are multitudinous, but those best known to foreigners include their gardens, poetry, wood-block prints, and wood sculpture.[11] In each of these art forms lies a sensitivity to the natural state (or order) of things. The gardens, for example, are composed of carefully positioned stones of unusual size or shape, artfully pruned shrubs and trees, and intricately formed ponds, all man-placed, but so contrived as to enhance nature and not replace it.[12] An interesting contrast can be made with the triumphs *over* nature represented by the Italian gardens with geometric patterns and marble statues, the French gardens also showing geometry and *grandes allées,* and the English gardens with vast sweeps of carefully cropped lawns.

While some have puzzled over the seemingly contradictory Japanese traits of sensitivity to beauty and warlike aloofness, the contradiction readily disappears upon analysis in terms of a psychological system based on a hierarchy related to, and consistent with, the phenomena of nature. It is entirely "natural" for them to appreciate the beauties of the mountains, lakes, and waterfalls of the Japanese islands and, at the same time, to stand constantly ready to repel the foreign invaders who have threatened from time to time. While the translation of this unconscious national psychology into terms of daily behavior sometimes renders its origins difficult or impossible to discern, the foreign businessman is well-advised to keep in mind the underlying structure of Japanese thinking.

[11] A careful analysis of the art form of prints is contained in James A. Michener, *Japanese Prints from the Early Masters to the Moderns* (Rutland, Vermont: Charles E. Tuttle Co., 1959).

[12] For a most helpful book on the art of Japanese gardens, see David H. Engel, *Japanese Gardens for Today* (Rutland, Vermont: Charles E. Tuttle Co., 1959).

ADVICE OF COUNSEL

One method of "repelling the invader" in the present day is the legal system for regulating foreign business in Japan adopted by the MITI.[13] I shall mention just a few salient features:

Licensing—License agreements are scrutinized to determine whether the know-how involved will benefit Japan as a whole, and governmental validation is required even if the royalties are to remain in yen on deposit there. Agreements covering periods of more than five years, or for royalties in excess of 5% of sales, will not be validated except in unique circumstances. Even so, by word and deed, the Japanese government is now approving tie-ups which directly, *or indirectly,* improve the country's foreign exchange position and the development of its industry, so long as there will be no "unfair" competition for small Japanese companies or "serious" disturbance to its industrial order.

Ownership—In addition to licensing, foreigners may consider a joint venture with Japanese partners or a wholly owned subsidiary. While the Japanese corporation law contains no restrictions against the nationality of shareholders, except for a few classes of corporations of a highly public nature, there are many restrictions on share acquisition contained in the drafting and application of the Foreign Investment and Foreign Exchange Control Laws. These involve criteria such as the nationality of the purchaser; whether the shares are "new" (bought from the issuing company) or "old" (bought from a previous owner); whether or not the yen paid for the shares were obtained through conversion of foreign exchange; the nature of the corporation; and whether or not remittance of principal and dividends to the home country is sought.

Convertibility—If the foreign investor seeks free convertibility, the Japanese government must validate the purchase of shares, regardless of other factors. To obtain such validation the shares must be purchased through foreign exchange or the contribution in kind of imported material, the value of which is fixed on application to a Japanese court. Once validated, the foreign investment carries with it the right to remit principal and interest in a designated foreign currency; the investment usually continues to be convertible after subsequent assignments, subject to required formalities of reporting to the Japanese government.

Acquisition—If, however, convertibility is not sought, "new" shares may be acquired by a foreign investor either through payment of yen or by foreign exchange without validation. An information report to the government is required under most circumstances, but is not necessary if the investor is a national of the United States, Germany, Great Britain, the Republic of China, France, and certain other countries, and if the issuing company is not of a public nature. "Old" shares may be acquired by nationals of these countries, through payment in yen currency not obtained by conversion of foreign exchange, except that validation is required when the issuer serves a public function. If the yen used for

[13] For a short comparative study, see Robert Braucher, "Commercial Law in Japan and America," *American Bar Association Journal* (February 1961), p. 150.

the purchase have been converted from foreign exchange, foreign investors may also acquire "old" shares without validation if the issuer is not public and the investor is a national of the designated countries. Such acquisition of "old shares" does not carry rights of remittance.

Branch offices—A final possibility is the establishment of a branch office of a foreign corporation in Japan. For purposes of both foreign exchange and taxes, all debits, credits, and transfers between the nonresident home office and Japanese branch office are subject to approval under the Foreign Exchange Control Law.

SAYONARA

The departure from Haneda may be depressed or elevated for the foreigners depending on the success or failure of their negotiations. In any event, it will be accomplished with a farewell from the same group that greeted their arrival. This is part of the discharge by the Japanese of their obligation to the visitors, especially felt if the foreigners have been formally invited to Japan. It illustrates, upon occasion, the remarkable ability of the Japanese to maintain on the surface, at least, good personal relations despite any underlying feelings of disagreement or resentment that developed during the talks.

In one case, negotiations in Tokyo between visiting Americans and a large Japanese firm were terminated after three weeks of daily discussions, and the Americans then successfully negotiated a joint venture with a competing firm during the next two weeks. Nevertheless, the original group of Japanese insisted that the Americans attend a *sayonara* dinner, at which the Japanese presented gifts of unusual beauty and value to each of the Americans, and then showed up at Haneda to say good-by in an atmosphere of utmost joviality and good will. While the particular American group was unusually attuned to the Japanese culture and thus had made a greater impact on their hosts than is usual, the necessity for discharge of the burden assumed by the Japanese in their invitation appeared to be the principal motivating factor.

Unless the negotiated arrangement has been reduced to writing and signed before departure, it is likely that months will pass before concrete results can be reached by correspondence, even though the sides seemed entirely in agreement when the foreign businessmen left. This is caused by the vicissitudes of dealing at long distance and perhaps more fundamentally to the unwillingness of the Japanese to commit themselves to an unwitting obligation through letters in the English language, which they all have studied but in which only a very few are truly conversant. However, the Japanese language, which is an ambiguous tongue of broad words and many expressions of mood and feeling, should be avoided in the ultimate legal documents, and the Japanese, aware of the lack of specification in their language, are usually agreeable to this.[14]

Therefore, when the time for *sayonara* has come, most foreign busi-

[14] See Fosco Maraini, *Meeting with Japan* (New York: The Viking Press, Inc., 1959), pp. 246-257.

nessmen will have spent more time and will have learned more by experience than they ever anticipated. Of course, if agreement in writing *has* been reached, they will have avoided the frustrations of months of attempting to reduce things to paper by letter. Otherwise, they may have to return to Japan for further discussions—and that is probably all to the good.

24

FROM THE THOUGHTFUL BUSINESSMAN *

Jiro Tokuyama

FROM:

Jiro Tokuyama
Director of Public Affairs
Japan Trade Center

RE:

"The Honorable Picnic: Doing Business in Japan," by Dudley L. Miller, *Harvard Business Review* (November-December 1961).

It was with great interest that I read Mr. Miller's comprehensive, well-balanced article. The author has obviously grounded himself well in Japanese lore and Japanese history.

The Editors state in a note that they have had several Japanese authorities read the article to substantiate its tone and its data. The opinion of these authorities is to be respected. However, as the author himself points out, Japan is a land of many postures, so, "with my eye cocked to watch the others' depth and number of bows," I should like to present mine.

I most wholeheartedly concur with Miller's purpose, "to explore some of the legal and cultural problems which Westerners encounter in seeking to do business in Japan," and his point "that, in dealing with *any* foreign people, businessmen should place themselves within the foreign culture." Understanding always prevents tensions and ill will—emotions which neither of our countries can afford at present. It is with Miller's appraisal of the current Japanese economy and his analysis of the Japanese culture that I have some disagreement.

Miller points out the attraction of the cheap and plentiful Japanese labor supply for the U.S. businessman. He warns the businessman not to be fooled by the Japanese government's claim that the many fringe benefits given to Japanese employees must be added to the base pay rate to give a fair approximation of the "real" income since this is primarily to protect Japan from boycotts and protective tariffs by importing countries. He states

* From *Harvard Business Review,* XL (March-April 1962), 24-26. Reprinted by permission.

that although these benefits do exist in large firms, they do not in the smaller ones, and cites statistics to show the large proportion of small business and the relatively small percentage of large business. (I was unable to check these statistics. Miller cites Boye De Mente's book, *Japanese Manners & Ethics in Business,*[1] as the source of his statistics on the size of Japanese business, but De Mente did not indicate his source.)

Laws have been enacted by the Japanese government that protect the employees of small businesses as well as those of large companies. Japan has a minimum wage law. Industrial firms are required by law to provide social security benefits. Furthermore, it must be noted that small firms in Japan are operated as family enterprises. Even if an employee is not a member of his employer's immediate family, the boss will take care of health and other fringe benefits through long-established Japanese custom —this is one of the advantages of our so-called industrial paternalism.

It is still true, nevertheless, that the wages in the small firms are less than those in the large ones. But this fact does not necessarily benefit the foreign businessman. The Ministry of Foreign Affairs of Japan reveals that the output of the large enterprises (500 or more employees) accounts for nearly 70% of Japanese exports:

> Generally speaking, wages in the small enterprises are about one-third of those paid by the larger enterprises, while productivity in these small enterprises is only one-sixth of that in the latter. Therefore, the smaller concerns are considerably weaker in competitive power. And when one considers the tremendous difference in capital equipment, one can readily appreciate that, in a comparison of two companies engaging in the same field of production, the larger company is usually the stronger in competition.
>
> ... Since the wage level in these large enterprises is above the average wage level, in some cases as much as 1.5 times that of the average, we can conclude that, for most of the export industries, the Japanese wage level is equivalent to that of the countries of Western Europe.[2]

The figures for a few of the industries most often discussed are presented in Exhibit 1.

American readers must constantly keep in mind the difference between the basic cost of living in the United States and in Japan. In Washington, D.C., the other day, a bus ride cost me a quarter. My friends in Tokyo can use public transportation for a nickel's worth of yen.

In preparing his article, Miller read the famous book by Ruth Benedict, *The Chrysanthemum and the Sword.*[3] Miss Benedict's socioanthropological study of Japan during World War II saw many Japanese business customs stemming from a society based on "obligation and shame."

[1] Tokyo: East Asia Publishing Co., Ltd., 1960, p. 24.

[2] *Exports and Wages, The Case of Japan* (Tokyo: Ministry of Foreign Affairs, Japan, 1960), p. 14. It is to be noted that the wage rates and productivity of small enterprises are increasing rapidly in our expanding economy. The recently published 1961 Labor White Paper shows this change: wages in small enterprises are about one-half of those paid by the larger enterprises and productivity 3.5 of that of the latter.

[3] Boston: Houghton Mifflin Company, 1946.

EXHIBIT 1. SCALE OF ENTERPRISE FROM WHICH PRINCIPAL JAPANESE EXPORTS ORIGINATE, FOR 1957

	NUMBER OF EMPLOYEES				
Classification	1-9	10-29	30-99	100-499	500 or more
Foodstuffs	3%	5%	7%	23%	62%
Textile goods	1	6	12	18	63
Steel and nonferrous metals	0	1	4	12	83

Source: *Exports and Wages, The Case of Japan* (Tokyo: Ministry of Foreign Affairs, Japan, 1960), p. 15.

It is true that many of them do originate within such a framework, but it is equally important that the reasons for such behavior be adequately explained.

The Japanese businessman has a real respect and admiration for the acumen and technical virtuosity of his U.S. counterparts. He is also a very hospitable, well-mannered person. So, when his guests' plane taxies in at Haneda Airport in Tokyo, the Japanese businessman is on hand to greet them. He will also see his guests off when they leave.

In Japan, business and personal life are mixed to a degree rarely found in the United States. The Japanese must choose his business for life, and it then becomes an integral part of living. Japanese business paternalism is basic to this consideration. There is every effort to make each group in society a part of the functioning whole. Thus elaborate manners infuse business as well as personal life in Japan.

From a sociological point of view, the Japanese businessman must be seen against an island background where survival has long been difficult. Every possible advantage in the direction of future prosperity must be gained.

Traditionally, the Japanese is in a weak position. When he conducts business with another firm, he feels that he must leave that source of business with as pleasant a feeling as possible. Though the customer may not have bought this time, maybe he will the next.

Miller makes some very cogent observations concerning the discomfort felt by the Japanese in the presence of foreigners. I would like to point out some additional reasons for this discomfort:

> Japan's economic situation was unstable for so long, and each individual had so little economic leverage, that groups tended to coalesce for purposes of self-protection. This is the traditional technique leading toward harmony in a small country. Within the group the individual tends toward the average in order not to interrupt the harmony of the whole.
>
> Japan has succeeded in maintaining a competitive society, but only by introducing some unique Japanese devices. When one of the Japanese discovers he has tremendous stamina and talent, he will often employ his considerable energies to keep some of his abilities under wraps, thereby

maintaining a social balance within the small circle which radiates upward and outward until it reaches the national level.

The system of free enterprise and freewheeling competition that exists in the United States would wreak havoc in Japan because of its limited natural resources. The unlimited raw materials and elbow room that exist in the United States do not exist in Japan. Consequently, Japan's group-mindedness often leaves the outsider somewhat isolated when he visits that country. He has no group to associate with and occasionally feels alone and unwanted.

Miller's article was most interesting and very well written. But we must admit that it is truly difficult to generalize about any society. Japan is particularly resistant to classification.

However, as the author himself discovered, this much is true of Japan: there are distinct differences of philosophy, dress, attitude, and habit between the younger generation and the older one. We can easily, and I believe successfully, attribute this difference to the changes brought about in the economy, education, and social system of Japan after the war. For a good deal of this, Japan is sincerely grateful to the United States.

25

THE JAPANESE WORKER *

Arthur M. Whitehall, Jr.

Greater understanding of worker motivation—of why men work—lies about as close to the roots of good human relations as any problem faced by administrators today. And in the human aspects of administration lies the greatest hope for increased productive efficiency so critically needed in the years ahead.

In a world increasingly occupied with a re-examination of basic values, it seems useful and timely to explore the relationship of cultural values to man's willingness to work. As Everett E. Hagan, director of the Motivations Project at Massachusetts Institute of Technology, has stated so well: "Principles of business administration are not absolute; they are relative to the culture of the society." [1]

The study outlined in this article suggests a little-explored approach to motivation research which shows promise of adding to our knowledge of this most important problem. Results thus far indicate that cultural values may be the force which integrates other elements already proved significant

* From the *California Management Review,* III (Winter 1961), 32-38. Copyright 1961 by the Regents of the University of California. Reprinted by permission of the Regents.

[1] In the Foreword to James C. Abegglen, *The Japanese Factory* (Glencoe, Ill.: The Free Press, 1958), p. vii.

to the effectiveness of a group and the individual productivity and satisfaction of its members.

Some of these elements are (1) technical organization and social structure of the group, (2) individual task motivation, (3) rewards and penalties received on the job, and (4) individual satisfaction from being a member of the group.[2] There is no need to question the demonstrated significance of these forces in explaining human motivation. We have turned up some compelling evidence, however, which indicates that cultural values may have a great deal to do with the way these elements are thought about, talked about, and acted upon in concrete work situations.

To test this line of thinking, we chose for our initial laboratory the culture of Japan. In association with Professor Shin-ichi Takezawa of the Industrial Relations Center, College of Social Relations, Rikkyo University, Tokyo, the author studied and interviewed workers in five Japanese companies in an effort to determine the influence of cultural factors on their motivation and morale as workers. The research was financed jointly by grants from the Johnson Fund of the American Philosophical Society and the University of North Carolina through the Business Foundation and Research Council.

There were several reasons for our choice of Japan as our first testing ground. To begin with, we were familiar with the proved efficiency of Japanese workers in factories characterized by working conditions and social relationships quite different from those in the United States. Furthermore, there is little doubt that Japan stands today as the most highly industrialized nation in Asia. Comparison of value judgments which have motivating force for workers in two such different cultures could, we felt, tell us whether our proposition was fairly substantial or too slippery to do much with.

This article presents the results of a modest, first step on a long-range research program. The findings, therefore, are partial findings and should be considered tentative in nature. A comparable study will be conducted in selected U.S. firms for purposes of comparison and control. Also, we intend to extend the investigation of cultural values to the management level, with particular reference to the influence of such values upon decision making.

CULTURE AND BEHAVIOR

Behind this investigation is the basic conviction that how a man thinks and acts in a given situation will be significantly influenced by what he thinks is appropriate, proper, and expected of him. However, whether or not his attitudes and actions coincide with this role expectation will depend to a considerable extent upon how faithfully those with whom he interacts fulfill his conception of their proper role—that is, how "fair" their behavior seems to him.

In short, we all make decisions concerning behavior at least partially

[2] A. Zaleznik, C. R. Christensen, F. J. Roethlisberger, *The Motivation, Productivity, and Satisfaction of Workers* (Boston: Harvard University, Division of Research, 1958), p. 35.

on the basis of what we feel is expected of us—and how well others are fulfilling our expectations of them. These concepts of *role expectation and role fulfillment* seem to provide a vital connecting link between culture and human behavior. How they work out in practice will vary markedly from one culture to another.

"PROPER" BEHAVIOR

Transferred to the work place, these phenomena play an important part in shaping men's motivation, or will to work. The notion of proper behavior, in this context, may be thought of as behavior expected of "good workers." And the extent to which workers decide to follow this pattern of behavior will be considerably influenced by how faithfully management (either at the supervisory or at the company level) fulfills the workers' notion of "good management." There is a complex network of shared obligations which, when disregarded or even slighted, can seriously jeopardize the motivation and morale of industrial workers.

GIMU

The culture of Japan puts great stress upon such feelings of obligation. Early conferences with business and labor leaders, plus a number of intensive interviews with bench-level workers, convinced us that worker perception of shared obligations between labor and management provided the key to exploration of the unique cultural values which today contribute to motivation in Japanese factories.

A special study indicated that of several traditional obligation systems which Japanese workers recognize and can talk about (*on, gimu,* and *giri*), the concept of *gimu* proved to be the most meaningful and compelling. Our problem, then, was to devise a procedure for identifying and evaluating the forces of *gimu* as they affect behavior of present-day Japanese workers.

CULTURAL CONTINUUM CHECKLIST

It did not take long to discover that this would require a new research tool—a special sort of questionnaire. After a good bit of intercultural anguish, we devised a unique device called "The Cultural Continuum Checklist."

The C.C.C. sets forth forty realistic, down-to-earth choice situations in terms which are meaningful to respondents. In other words, the participant is placed smack in the middle of a series of dilemmas and then required to work his way out. The decisions he makes provide a wealth of insight concerning the values which to him are most attractive and compelling.

The four alternatives available to respondents on each C.C.C. question were designed to provide a continuum of behavior patterns ranging from an extremely traditional, or highly indigenous, choice within the culture of Japan to a comparably extreme position in the substantially different culture of the United States. In this study, therefore, the alternatives were courses of action which we believed reflected Extreme Eastern, Moderate Eastern, Moderate Western, and Extreme Western value concepts respectively.

THE PEOPLE INVOLVED

Before describing some of the things we discovered, a word should be added about the participants in this pilot study. Limited time required that the sample be realistically selected. First, we decided to restrict it to male, production-level workers. Furthermore, we chose only permanent workers (*Honko*) rather than including the substantial floating reserve of temporary workers (*Rinjiko*). Of all the industrial workers in the world—including the United States—those of Japan who are employed as *Honko* enjoy the greatest job security available within a private enterprise system. Therefore, the impact which even latent fear of job loss can have upon motivation was minimized.

Only five companies were studied. However, these ranged from one of Japan's largest steel companies down to a small firm of thirty employees making *shoji,* or sliding doors. Two of the participating companies were unionized. In every instance, management allowed the survey to be conducted during work hours and on company time.

Worker participants typically gathered in a sufficiently large room, often the company cafeteria, for a period of 1½ to 2 hours. As they entered the room, each respondent was presented a copy of the checklist, a pencil, and a gift of a small cotton towel (*tenugui*). That this modest gift was accepted with appreciation by all workers impressed us as one of several instances in which the study itself was being affected by certain unique culture-based practices.

Just a few highlights of the study can be reported in this article, but these may be sufficient to point up the need for further exploration of this approach to motivation research. At least one question from several of the major C.C.C. categories will be described in an attempt to convey some of the flavor of this initial investigation.

LIFETIME JOBS ARE EXPECTED

Career Employment: One of the most important areas of difference when comparing human relations in Japanese and Western companies is the degree to which both workers and management recognize an obligation to continue the employment of all permanent employees until retirement or death. In our study we found it useful to make a distinction between (1) worker expectations and (2) worker commitments.

Worker Expectations: What does a production worker expect of "good management" when, because of automation or other reasons, he is no longer needed on the job for which he was hired?

In the United States most rank-and-file workers feel they are employed to perform a particular job rather than to join the compay for life. Job analysis first points up job requirements, and effective placement then matches men to the job. Management obligation, for example, to find work in a white-collar office position for a displaced drill-press operator goes beyond the role of "good management" as perceived within a Western cultural context.

We found worker expectations in this situation to be quite different in the Japanese culture as opposed to that of the West. Japanese workers voted an impressive 84 per cent for the Extreme Eastern response which said management should find such employees different work, wherever available in the company, since they had been hired for the company rather than for a particular job.

WORKERS MUST REMAIN "LOYAL"

Worker Commitments: If the company must keep workers on the payroll even when their jobs disappear, what sort of return commitment are these workers willing to make to management? What does the role of a "good worker" demand in return for this sort of plush security?

To get a reaction to this situation, we asked participants what a man should do if another equally desirable company offers him a similar job at 20 per cent higher pay. We expected that at a time of high-level economic conditions—such as 1959 when the questionnaire was administered—many workers would show real "Western-style" independence and just walk out if faced with such a substantial increase in pay.

About one-fifth of the respondents fulfilled our expectation and said they would accept the offer and quit. An additional 42 per cent were tempted, but wanted to hedge a bit by talking it over with their foreman before making such a decision. However, the remaining one-third of participants displayed the persistent force of *gimu* to the company in saying they would "show loyalty and patience" by staying with their present employer. It should be recognized, of course, that some of this willingness to accept such an extreme degree of commitment may reflect, particularly among older workers, a desire to protect their right to receive full severance allowance upon normal retirement.

WORKER IDENTIFICATION WITH COMPANY

The basic proposition behind C.C.C. questions in this category is that the extent to which workers recognize an obligation to identify with their company, and to subordinate individualism to groupism, will influence management's ability to stimulate willingness to work. More specifically, we propose that close personal identification with the company is a positive force in worker motivation!

A question posed in this connection asked what sort of company environment workers expected "good management" to create. It seems reasonable to assume that most Western workers believe a company should be a business-like place for workers and management to accomplish mutual goals—not a replica of family-type organization and relationships. And almost 30 per cent of Japanese respondents selected this "business-like" notion as best describing the sort of job environment they thought most desirable.

But cultural forces exert a strong pull and, as William F. Whyte has observed, "The impact of cultural differences does not seem to pass away before advancing industrialization." [3] This generalization becomes quite clear in the situational context posed by the C.C.C. question just described. About one-third of our respondents believed management should create an environment "very much like a big family" to which workers may belong until retirement. Another 32 per cent agreed that the company should be a part of their lives "at least equal in importance" to their personal lives.

WAGES BASED ON NEED

Culture factors also contribute to each employee's notion of what company policy should be in the critical matter of wage payment if the "good management" role is to be fulfilled.

In the United States there is little real disagreement with a "contribution basis" for determining individual pay rates within the range established by collective bargaining and prevailing practices. It seems "fair" to Western workers that they should be paid more on the basis of their skill, care, and effort on the job than on the basis of their special personal needs. Individual need, for example, is reflected in U.S. wage rates only indirectly—and modestly—through exemptions for dependents under federal and state income tax laws.

Just how differently our Japanese respondents saw this problem can be demonstrated by their reactions to a question concerning payment of a "family allowance." A vast majority (77 per cent) believed their take-home pay should include a family allowance with extra compensation preferably for all, but at least for a limited number, of family members.

PATERNALISM EXPECTED

Cultural differences seem largely behind the relatively greater dependence of Japanese workers, in contrast to their counterparts in the United States, concerning management responsibility for the personal welfare of the individual. Company policy covering sick leave is a case at point. Western workers expect some help from management when illness strikes. But few employees of U.S. companies would seriously propose that the com-

[3] William F. Whyte, *Man and Organization* (Homewood, Ill.: Richard D. Irwin, Inc., 1959), p. 10.

pany continue his pay, or even hold his job, in cases of prolonged illnesses —say those lasting more than a year.

We asked Japanese workers what they thought "good management" should do when an employee becomes seriously ill. Thirty-six per cent thought the company should continue a sick worker's pay until he recovers no matter how long that may be! A more "moderate" 51 per cent believed that his wage should be continued only for about two years, but then insisted that his job should be held until recovery.

PERSPECTIVE FOR THE FUTURE

Many other examples could be cited of the effect in specific situations of indigenous cultural factors upon employee perception of his own role as a "good worker," and of company policies and actions he sees as necessary to fulfill the role of "good management." The extent to which these roles are satisfied in the day-by-day experiences of workers both inside and outside the plant appears to significantly influence motivation.

But not all the questions on the Cultural Continuum resulted in Japanese responses which were so radically different from those which we would expect of U.S. workers. Answers to some items revealed quite clearly the fact that more than five years of military occupation, plus almost ten years of close civilian cooperation, have had their influence.

GIMU IN TRANSITION

The plain fact is that cultural values in Japan, and more specifically the concept of *gimu* with which we are most concerned, is in a critical state of transition. Generalizations are risky; situation-by-situation analysis, slow and costly though it may be, seems to be the more useful approach to greater understanding of the culture-based forces behind employee behavior.

At this point in the discussion, business executives well may be thinking, "Interesting—but what has all this got to do with me?" Evidence is accumulating which makes the only sensible answer "Plenty!"

CULTURE DETERMINES ATTITUDES

First, it is important to recognize that in each culture with its special set of needs, business management is challenged to recognize—and to satisfy within the dictates of sound management—those values which have meaning and importance to employees. It is pretty clear that cultural values do influence the way workers size up their own role, and that of management, in their total work environment.

This is difficult enough in our own culture; much more research and continuing study is needed to identify and evaluate the impact of "the American way of life" upon employee behavior in the United States. But when extended to radically different foreign cultures about which we know so little, the plot really thickens.

WANTED: EXECUTIVE AWARENESS

Difficult though the problems may be, administration in business no longer can be pursued within relatively comfortable and familiar national boundaries. Competing in world markets—either directly or indirectly—demands that executives have an awareness and understanding of cultural differences that mold and shape the motivation, and hence the efficiency, of workers throughout the industrialized world.

COMPANIES CAN CREATE VALUES [4]

Second, there is another, and perhaps even more vital, concern of executive leadership with the influence of culture factors upon man's will to work. Cultural values are not static—they are highly dynamic! Quite clearly they are subject to the stress and strain—the push and pull—of economic, social and political events which communication media have made increasingly available to workers for their consideration.

It is difficult to escape the conviction that a sober obligation of administrators in the world of today is to create or restore through company and community leadership an acceptance of new or previously rejected values, the achievement of which can contribute to both individual satisfactions and organizational goals.

FUTURE PROJECTS

Finally, we suspect that further exploration of the role of cultural values will be of vital interest not only to business administrators, but to scholars, diplomatic personnel, technical specialists, and others who must relate themselves effectively to individuals and groups in a complex culture quite different from their own.

Without attempting to push an analogy too far, it might be said that we have selected a large canvas, sketched in the broad outline, devised a new brush for our special purposes, and dabbed a little paint in one corner. We are quite aware that much remains to be done before the day arrives, if ever, when the canvas will be complete.

[4] Boye De Mente, *Japanese Manners & Ethics in Business* (Tokyo: East Asia Publishing Co., Ltd., 1960), p. 168.

26

THEMES AND VARIATIONS *

Igor Oganesoff

"Kono dark red one-piece dress wa charming, des' ne?"

An American hardly needs to know that in Japanese "kono" means this, that "wa" follows the subject of the sentence and that "des' ne" means isn't it, to get the gist of this question. But what may astonish an American—and chagrins most Japanese educators—is that a Tokyo lady who utters these words, with a slight shift of pronunciation, is speaking acceptable modern Japanese.

Or switch on a television set here and listen to an announcer bark out a commercial as the screen shows a Japanese auto cruising down a seashore highway: "Number one popular car. Instant start. High speed thrill." And this without resort to a single syllable of true Japanese.

These linguistic acrobatics illustrate a mass invasion of English words and phrases into the Japanese tongue, on a scale that no language in modern times has probably suffered. Because of some radical twists in pronunciation and even usage, the trend has not meant that more Japanese can actually speak English. On the contrary, compared with a decade ago when the American occupation of Japan ended, probably fewer local citizens can now handle an ordinary conversation with an American.

Nevertheless, hardly a Japanese would be caught saying "atatakai gyunyuu o hitotsu" when he can simply ask the waitress for "one hot milk." And a Japanese motorist pulling up to a filling station almost invariably calls a breezy "oil check," instead of "abura shirabete." This is pretty comforting to a foreigner who finds real Japanese both unreadable and lacking the slightest verbal link to his own tongue.

It isn't enough for the American tourist merely to pronounce these adopted words in his usual manner. A Japanese inflection must be given before any listener here will understand. For instance, the television announcer's spiel on motoring thrills is almost unrecognizable to the untutored foreign ear. The nearest that Japan's inflexible phonetic script can come to the word thrill is "s'riru." And because Japanese has no "l" and nearly every consonant is followed by a vowel, milk comes out "miruku."

Japanese find such words as grotesque, unique, shocking and naive more precise and shorter in their English forms and constantly use them.

Many of the English words, of course, are straight out of the 20th century machine age. Because true Japanese is a pretty static language, many modern terms have no Japanese equivalent at all. A recent issue of the ladies' magazine, *Fujin Gaho,* contains an article about automobiles which

* From the *Wall Street Journal* (Jan. 29, 1963). Copyright by the *Wall Street Journal.* Reprinted by permission.

is illustrated with an explanatory diagram of a car's main parts. Of 34 such labels, only four are in pure Japanese, the rest in phoneticized English.

In the course of Japanization, many an English word comes out slightly mangled in meaning. There is no Japanese word for steering wheel, so back some years ago somebody decided to call it a handle and the label sticks today.

Attempt to explain the correct English usage of such words to a Japanese and you'll be rewarded with a blank stare; he's dumbfounded by your temerity in correcting his Japanese. So thorough is the process of assimilation that few Japanese consciously think of the English words as having foreign derivation, however recently imported. "Are they doing the twist in your country?" inquires a Tokyo bar maid of her American customer.

Japanese manufacturers, moreover, are endowing their products with English brand names, printed in English letters. And, curiously, the more difficult the word for Japanese tongues, the more acceptable it is, possibly for reasons of snob appeal. A popular midget auto here is labeled the Colt. In the phonetic Japanese equivalent, the pronunciation travels some distance to become Coruto.

Often, the process results in some unwitting goofs. A prominent cosmetic maker recently unveiled a new cold cream which he brand-named "Peculiar," apparently hoping to suggest its unique properties.

To those who regard the Japanese language with its 2,000 multi-stroke Chinese characters and difficult usage an educational millstone, the import of English words is a welcome trend. Some sort of reform, many educators agree, is highly desirable. And the 47-character phonetic alphabet of angular strokes is easy to learn, though it lacks the literary economy of the Chinese character, which carries a large meaning in a small space.

And though the Japanese scholar may rail against the wholesale corruption of his mother tongue, he'll still probably enter a restaurant and call for "one hot milk" for the same reason everyone else does—it's easier.

27

LOAD TOO HEAVY, A FRAGILE WOMAN BREAKS *

She was only one of 8 million people in New York, a tiny fragile woman of 33, unable to adjust to western ways after three months in America. She pined for her native Japan. Even her two small children could not fill the aching void in her heart.

She was Mrs. Chieko Takenaka, who lived in a well-furnished sixth floor, 4½ room apartment in Forest Hills.

* Associated Press release of January 29, 1963. Reprinted by permission.

When she encountered neighbors, she bowed, the only gesture of friendship she could manage, since she spoke no English. But they indicated to her that her oriental obeisance was alien to them, that in this country the handshake or the spoken greeting takes the place of the bow.

Mrs. Takenaka disliked being alone when her husband, Tokutaro, 36, was at work for a Manhattan export house. Last night she found herself without her husband again.

Shortly after midnight Mrs. Takenaka telephoned the manager of her husband's firm. She pleaded with him to arrange for the family's transfer back to Japan. She told him of her loneliness in a strange country. He could do nothing.

After she hung up the phone, Mrs. Takenaka drew her children into her arms. There was a boy, Jung, 6, and a daughter, Setsuko, 2.

With the dawn, a first floor neighbor looked out and saw Mrs. Takenaka's body crumpled on the front lawn of the apartment building. In her arms was the body of Setsuko.

Police entered the apartment and found the body of Jung. His mother had strangled him with a towel before she gathered her daughter into her arms for a six-story leap into oblivion.

There was no suicide note.

But the small faces of both children bore a profusion of lipstick kiss marks—left by Mrs. Takenaka before she took them with her forever out of the strange western world that defied her understanding.

28

THE AMERICAN NEGRO'S KEY ROLE IN AFRICA *

Joseph C. Kennedy

One of the first questions asked of an American Negro returning from Africa these days is: "As a Negro, how were you treated by the Africans?" Should the American Negro going to Africa for the first time expect to be treated better—or worse—than any other group going there? Is there some special relationship between the African and the nearly 19 million Americans of African descent?

Recently I spent a year in West Africa—in Ghana, Nigeria and Liberia—traveling more than 30,000 miles into large cities with recently constructed modern buildings, and into tiny villages which could be reached only after walking miles through thick forest. I talked to hundreds of literate

* From *The New York Times Magazine* (February 4, 1962). Copyright by The New York Times. Reprinted by permission.

and illiterate Africans. I went into schools and colleges and talked to students.

From my experiences I am convinced that a very special relationship exists between the African and the American Negro, that there is a skin-color affinity which creates an unusual bond of warmth and draws the two together.

This is not to say that this bond is immediately apparent, that the African immediately reaches out to embrace the American Negro. Indeed, the first reaction on the part of the American Negro to being in Africa is one of mixed and confused feelings—so much so that the Negro who spends only a short time in Africa is bound to return home just as uncertain of his relationship with Africa as when he went.

Any American Negro going to Africa for the first time must arrive with an uncertain image of Africa and of what to expect. In America he has long heard Africa described as the "dark continent"—a land of tribal dances and mud huts and filled with primitive, black people. In America, he has known black skin to be associated with inferiority, and he has been penalized for his own dark skin color. Adding to this uncertainty, he has heard and read of Negroes who have gone to Africa with great expectations of warmth and brotherhood, but who have met instead with frustrations and disappointments.

At the national airport in Accra, Ghana, this image of the "dark continent" is immediately disturbed. The airport is a mixture of African and Western cultures: Ghana Airways' Bristol Britannias and Russian Ilyushins with their neatly uniformed African air hostesses; women dressed in brightly colored cloth with small trays on their heads and children on their backs; African men in either European dress or *kente* cloth; magazines from various parts of the world.

And there are many other contrasts. While there are the small, nearly impassable dirt roads, and houses with thatched roofs and mud-brick walls, while at night the drumming from a near-by village can be heard in Accra, there are at the same time, in the heart of the city, modern office buildings and a supermarket where nearly anything can be purchased—from a suit of European clothing and Elvis Presley records to Maxwell House instant coffee and frozen foods. There are a modern museum, hundreds of horn-blowing taxicabs, four-lane streets with white-gloved African policemen, and a smart 100-room hotel where tea is served in the afternoon and an orchestra plays for dinner.

Although the preconception of Africa is affected immediately, the expression of the bond between the African and the American Negro may not come so quickly. I had been in Ghana for several weeks before I had my first encounter with any special relationship. I had been preparing a questionnaire which I would use in my research and had gone to a small village about thirty miles out of Accra for pre-testing. I was accompanied by a Ghanaian interpreter, my wife and 6-year-old son.

As I was talking to an elderly African woman, she held out her hand to my son, took him on her lap and smiled as she whispered, "My grandson." Here was an old African woman we had never seen before, who had never been out of Africa, but who spoke of kinship with a 6-year-old American boy.

Shortly after this encounter, another incident took place which was both puzzling and confusing. Driving with my interpreter along a narrow dusty road which cut through dried, sunburnt fields, past village after village, frequently we would see small clusters of children walking along the road to the village school. Sometimes there would be long, straggling lines of women and children returning from the river with gourds of water on their heads, or there would be people moving about in the village. As we passed along the way, the children would wave and smile, and call out "Hi, father!" or "Hi, *oburoni!*"

When I asked the interpreter what this meant, he laughed and said, "Well, *oburoni* is Twi [one of many Ghanaian languages] for 'white man,' and I guess they are calling you 'father' because the only *oburoni* they have seen has been a Catholic priest."

I learned later that the word *oburoni* has gone through interesting mutations to acquire its present meaning. Originally and literally it meant "people from the corn land" or "those who brought the corn." Of course, the people who introduced corn to Africa were European or American missionaries and they were white. So, today, *oburoni* means both "European" —or non-African—and "white."

As I moved around the country I realized that the people who perceived me as "white" were the uneducated people and children. Also, that "white man" or "European" often was used to describe people who wore European or "different" dress, who had a certain kind of job, and so on. Thus, a very dark-skinned American Negro could be called "white man" because he did not speak an African language.

However, this "white man" description actually has greater dimension than simply dress, job, language and so on. At the completion of each interview with an illiterate person, through my interpreter I would say, "Now, tell me, what kind of person am I?" Usually the answer would be, "You are a white man," or "European," or sometimes, "You are a red man"—a skin-color description sometimes used in place of "white."

On one occasion though, I had been talking to a Ghanaian man about 50 years old who happened to have skin color identical with mine. This man spoke halting English. I had asked him, "What kind of person am I?" He had said he didn't know. Then I said, "Well, do I come from Ghana, am I Ghanaian?" His reply was, "No, you are not Ghanaian." "Why not?" I asked. "Because we Ghanaians are black." Placing my bare arm beside his I said, "But what color am I?" "You," he said, "are white."

While contributing to a puzzling problem, perhaps this uneducated Ghanaian man, through his skin-color confusion, had a lesson to teach which all America could learn—if black can become white and white become black, depending upon the situation, how valid is a social system which places merit in the color of a man's skin?

While many illiterates had this perception of "white man," often there were mixed perceptions. In one especially beautiful village, which stood along a lagoon among coconut trees and sand, I had been taken to meet the chief before interviewing. After the chief and elders had been seated, and some of the young men had entered the house, the chief sent for the person to be interviewed, "the first educated man in this village," a man of about 45.

As the educated man began to answer questions, a few women entered and sat, and others peered through the windows. Children looked in from the door. Only the educated man and some of the young men spoke English. Occasionally the educated man would laugh and say, "That's a hard one." The interpreter would translate for the audience and they would laugh.

For forty minutes they all sat, listening but not understanding a single question or word. Finally, on completion of the interview, I asked the teacher who was acting as interpreter to ask the elders what kind of person I was.

As he went around, they all replied, "You are white," until he came to the chief. The chief replied, "From America, you come from America, because of your hair. You are a black man. You are one of us." The elders, the women, and the children in the door smiled. Here was another seeming contradiction. But actually the chief appeared to use the word American only to mean American Negro (identified by curly hair as well as skin color); if he had been dealing with an American white he probably would have said *oburoni* or "European."

Later, outside under the shade of the coconut trees, men and women walked over to gaze at me from time to time, then exchange a few words among themselves. When I looked at them, they would move behind the trees. About twelve children stood around looking and smiling. I was told the people and children had never seen a "European" before. The chief came out and gave me a pan filled with coconuts and two bottles of warm beer. Finally, when the interviews were finished and I was leaving, all of the young educated men asked for my address and requested that I write to them.

The association between being black (or American Negro) and "one of us" was the predominate association among the educated population, whether in the schools or in the villages. It was here at this educated level that a pronounced skin-color affinity was found, that the bond of warmth was most evident. So many times in so many places, Africans would say to me: "You are Negro, aren't you?" or "Why has it taken you so long to come back?" or "Why don't more American Negroes come here to help us, to teach us?"—and "Welcome, brother."

Social scientists have often said it is impossible to go "cold" into a village and gather information, that a period of time must transpire in which rapport is established. Yet the success of my work depended on the ability to arrive at a village early in the morning, establish contact, interview people and leave late in the evening.

In Ghana, Nigeria, Liberia—wherever I went—I met with cooperation and warmth. During the day, and at the end of the day, I was always offered food, and at night a place to sleep. After hours of talking to people, they would shower me with gifts of bananas, pineapples, kola nuts, live chickens. Wherever I went, I entered the village an unannounced stranger but left as a friend.

This acceptance in the village was possible because, on entering a village, I first made contact with an educated person—the headmaster of the school, a teacher, a local council member and so on. These persons recognized me either as an American Negro, or at least as a "non-white," and accepted me. One of these persons then took me to the chief who accepted me, and then the people would accept me, too. Without this initial acceptance from the educated person, I undoubtedly could not have so readily gained entrée in the villages.

Within the secondary schools this bond of warmth was quite evident. On numerous occasions, after interviewing, I would address the student body. Often the headmaster would introduce me by saying, "He is an American Negro; do you know what that means?" The students would reply, "His parents came from Africa; he is one of us."

In the universities or technical colleges or teacher-training colleges, invariably the students would ask about segregation in the United States—how could it exist, how bad was it, what was being done about it? Often they would say: "We believe you because you are Negro" or "You have given us honest answers" or "This is the first time we have been able to ask a Negro about this." Just as invariably, these students would ask about African-American Negro relationships, saying, "Will more Negroes come back to Africa?", "Why don't they come here to work with us?"

Many Americans have said that these demonstrations of African-American Negro ties among the educated are political, that it is politically expedient to profess such a relationship, that if there is preachment of "pan-Africanism," there certainly should be this kind of verbal service to the concept. Yet, many of the people I met were not politicians. They were school teachers, or farmers, or *kente* cloth weavers, or fishermen, or clerks, or taxi drivers—just people who seemed truly moved and happy at seeing their brothers from America.

Once, while visiting the University of Nigeria at Nsukka, I was returning from a village with three professors from the university—one American Negro and two American whites. As we stood on the manually operated ferry boat which was large enough to carry just one car across the stream, two young Nigerians came over to me.

They began to talk, "You are Negro, aren't you? He is too, isn't he?" —pointing to the other American Negro. "We can talk freely with you, but can't with those other Americans." "What other Americans do you mean?" I asked. "Those white Americans," was the reply.

Later, one of these boys—they were students in a teacher-training college—wrote to me. "On that day you met us on the river bank," he said, "you know that we did not hesitate in coming to meet you, for we immediately knew that this must be one of our brothers from the U.S.A."

Other people whom I met at social affairs, or gave rides to along the road, or passed on the street, often asked for my address and wrote to me. A Ghanaian said in a letter: "I was even considering that you might have been a distant relative of mine." And a Nigerian wrote: "We did [studied] a lot about our African brothers in the U.S.A. How they were treated in olden days and all other stories about them. But now we learnt some of them are high government officials and lecturers in the universities. In fact, people in Africa admire the great progress that our African brothers are making in the U.S.A. I hope that you people will create such tendency in us. . . ."

Again from Ghana: "We wish that the Negroes all come back to Africa. Will it be possible?" From Nigeria: "I will visit you . . . I want to have an American friend through you, preferably a Negro. . . . I hope we will be good friends." And from Togoland: "I pray God that everywhere you will go, you may be successful by the Grace of God. Now I want you to know well that we are brothers."

Whether written or spoken, whether in the home, over an African dinner or on the road, whether in the movies where the audience gave a tremendous cheer every time a giant like American Negro William Marshall appeared in an old American film or while watching an old TV rerun of "Harlem Review," whether in the village or in the college, whether in the words of an American Negro in Africa who says, "This isn't new, this reminds me of Harlem" or of an African who says, "When I was in the United States and went into Harlem it reminded me of home," or whether in response to a direct question, "should the American Negro be treated more like a brother by the African than the white man is treated like a brother" (and seven out of ten say "Yes")—wherever it is, this expression of a very special relationship between the African and the American Negro is real.

That this relationship is found predominantly among educated Africans, and to a lesser degree among the illiterates, is as it should be, for it indicates that this relationship, as with all relationships among people, is learned—born out of the knowledge of the common suffering of all black men who originated in Africa. It is this knowledge which creates the skin-color affinity and bond of warmth that draws the African and the American Negro together.

That this skin-color affinity exists should not be confused with "reverse racism." It is not, for the white visitor is treated well in Africa also. Nor should it be thought that a special relationship based on skin-color identity is a desirable and final one. Someday the color of a man's skin will not matter.

Because this affinity exists, however, the American Negro has a particular role in Africa, a role which only he can fill for all America and which America cannot afford to deny him. Sensitive, honest, understanding relationships are essential to building goodwill between America and emerging Africa, and in this America's greatest asset is the American Negro.

One result of the skin-color identity is that the American Negro and the African can move together in an easy, relaxed way. Every American Negro, regardless of his own skin color, has long associated with dark-skinned peoples and can be at ease with other black men, while many white

Americans, no matter how "unprejudiced," can never be at ease with Negroes—can never relax and forget that they are whites and blacks together.

When any two people first come together, there is a subtle but sure awareness of uneasiness, of being uncomfortable, whether in sharing a dinner or a conversation. But where there is lack of tension, there can be acceptance and brotherhood. That is why the American Negro and the African can say, "Welcome, brother" and be sincere. That is why perhaps, as several Africans and American Negroes have remarked, "Slavery was evil, but now maybe good will come out of it. Now maybe American Negroes who have become highly educated and developed will come back and help lift their brothers."

This is the role the American Negro can take in Africa. Perhaps, too, this was meant to be his destiny.

29

AN AFRICAN STUDENT STUDIES US *

Amos Kiriro

Early this fall three planes from Kenya landed at New York's Idlewild Airport. On board were over 200 African students who had made arrangements through the State Department, the Institute of International Education and the American African Students Foundation to study at American universities and colleges. Within a few weeks we were scattered all over the country.

Some of us are here to study engineering and medicine, others to study economics and government, and some like myself to complete a basic education. We are all here with a purpose. We are part of a crash program designed to provide Kenya with a large number of educated Africans who will be responsible for the country's future once she receives her independence and becomes a free member of the British Commonwealth. It is with great insight that the African leaders and the Government of Kenya have made this program possible, with the cooperation of the State Department, for we all realize the folly of handing the Government of Kenya over to an illiterate people.

Our stay in the States will not be a sort of holiday. We have a lot to learn of American "know-how." The American system of education is my main concern: how you manage, how you grade, and how you teach, and how you train your teachers, and how you pay your teachers—these are the things I want to know, for I am a school teacher; in fact, before I came to study at the Suffolk County branch of Adelphi College I was the headmaster of a school of 450 pupils in Kenya.

* From *The New York Times Magazine* (December 10, 1961). Copyright by The New York Times. Reprinted by permission.

Because I am a teacher, there are a few things that I knew about the United States before I came. I must admit that what I knew was rather vague and a little disjointed. In high school we studied the American Revolution and were familiar with such things as the Boston Tea Party, the Navigation Acts, the bitterness of the American colonists and some of the basic causes of the American struggle for independence. In my classroom at the Nessuit Intermediate School I placed a large wall map of the United States and with this map I could show my pupils the routes of the westward expansion of America as well as point to the place where Comdr. Alan B. Shepard Jr. was launched into outer space. It is no secret that I also knew the location of American cities like Little Rock and Jackson.

I have been asked so many times since I have come here, "What do you think of America?" Before I came I had some ideas about America. I had seen a few American movies—mostly what you call Westerns; I had met a few American missionaries and remember them for their American cars and their strictness on trivial details. (Smoking is looked upon as black sin and drinking as running away from God. I was severely criticized by an American missionary because I walked across the mission area with my girl friend. My answer was that many were called but few were chosen.)

American novels and love stories are widely read in Kenya. But English teachers keep warning their students to avoid the use of American slang phrases in their compositions, because the Cambridge University English examiner would not accept them. Many schools in Kenya have received gifts of books, tape recorders and laboratory equipment from the American consulate in Nairobi, for which we are thankful. In addition we received from the B.B.C. very brief summaries of news about America.

However, there was nothing into which to fit all these little facts. No one can claim to know another country from isolated facts, for there is no background for these scattered bits to make sense.

Africans therefore, tend to see America as a kind of blurred image. We knew that this was a wealthy country, but I must admit that I didn't know what that word really meant until I came here to live. When an African reads or hears about your wealth, he is inclined to take it for granted that your wealth is a gift from nature. It didn't take me long to realize that what you have has been earned and worked out through years of tremendous and well-directed exertion.

Many countries have ample natural resources but nevertheless remain poor. It takes something else and the first indication I received of this special "something" was to meet owners of local businesses here in Sayville working with their hands, with their sleeves rolled up and their aprons on.

I do not envy your wealth because from what little I have seen, I realize you have worked for it. But I must say that your concern about wealth and material things may be out of control. Whenever I have been given a ride to the college by my fellow students I am asked, "Do you like cars?" or "Do you have many cars in Kenya?" or "What type of houses do you live in?" or "Do you like TV?" To me there is nothing wrong in asking these questions except that they reveal the kind of things you live for. Nobody has yet asked me how we are trying to develop Kenya or what Kenya's real needs are as she approaches the day of her independence.

I have learned a new American expression, "Keeping up with the Joneses." This particular phrase is very interesting, because among Africans there is no such thing as keeping up with the people next door. Each individual is satisfied with what he has, and if he can get more, well and good; if not, he keeps up with what he has. We do not see things in terms of wealth being that important.

In wonder if the wealth of America distorts your vision. From conversations with American students I feel that your fear of communism is largely a fear that communism will take away your wealth and your possessions. The face of the world is changing and the disparity between the rich and the poor will not last long. The world cannot survive half rich and half poor. If a nation is to be a great nation, she must measure her greatness in something besides things and possessions.

One of the really great things about America that I have been discovering since my arrival is your public school system. I think I have an advantage here over many of my fellow students from Kenya because I am living with an American family which has children in the local public schools. Being a school teacher, I am amazed at what I have seen.

Your public schools are tax-supported and everybody who is a property owner pays school taxes. This is not so in Kenya where only the parents of children who go to school pay school fees. I am sure there are many Americans who do not like to pay these taxes, but it does show the kind of concern that you have for education. But I see some disadvantages to this system, too.

Kenya is now in a transitional period from colonial rule to full independence. Education with books and schools is only sixty years old in Kenya; it is something very new and still for a very few. To the African today, education is the key to everything and because of this we are very conscious of the value of an education. Our young people will travel long distances every day to go to school; they will go without lunch or even leave home to get an education. Parents are willing to make real sacrifices to see that at least one of their children receives an education.

Our schools operate under great hardships. There is a shortage of textbooks, pencils and basic teaching materials. In the Nessuit Intermediate School there was only one dictionary for the whole school. Despite shortages, leaking roofs and all sorts of discomforts, our children are learning to read and write because they want to learn. Education in Kenya is a privilege; our children know it and I believe they work very hard at it.

In America the picture is different. You have magnificent buildings, the kind of materials and textbooks that are a joy to see, and yet something is lacking. The price of an educational system that takes in all children is that you are bound to have some who come only because they are made to, rather than because they want to. You have so much to work with and so much to be proud of, and yet I cannot escape the feeling that many of your children take their public schools for granted, and do not appreciate the gift that is theirs to take.

College work in America is demanding; at least I have found it so here in Sayville. One real difference that I have noticed is that any really intensive specialization in a particular field comes much later in the American colleges. Perhaps this is due to the fact that your pre-college education is not so rigorous as the English system. The students that I have met here are rather serious about their work but occasionally they seem to try to get through by doing as little as possible.

One of the most difficult questions that have been asked of me is the question of race relations and segregation in America. I find this very hard to talk about because I have not encountered any problems along these lines since my arrival in America. I know they exist; I was well aware of the racial tensions in America from what I could read in the newspapers of East Africa. I am also aware that your Constitution and your Bill of Rights say one thing about the equality of all men and yet all men do not practice the high ideals of your country. Please remember that I have come from a country that has had its full share of racial tensions and that the causes of these tensions will not simply go away just because laws are passed in legislatures. Laws can solve some of the outward signs of segregation of men from men and protect the rights of individuals under the law, but law alone cannot do the whole job. The basic causes of racial tension and segregation will be done away with only when free men understand one another's needs and are willing to accept each other as children of God.

When it comes to the question of American understanding of Africa there are some things I would like to say. First of all, I have discovered that Africans who have received only a little education know more about America than Americans know about Africa. And what you do know about Africa is distorted.

Ask an American about Africa and he usually thinks in terms of the Congo or South Africa or jungles or poverty. This is understandable because these are the things you tend to read about in your newspapers. It would help if your newspapers and magazines would tell you about the whole of Africa rather than just its troubles.

Africa is an enormous complexity of all kinds of people and all kinds of nations and races and religions and climates. Americans would say, "You name it and we have it"; the same is true of us. And we are proud of what we have. It is important to realize that Africans have a growing consciousness of themselves, a sense of identity. We are neither East nor West. We are learning to look at things in terms of Africa.

I was recently asked at a Rotary Club meeting here in Sayville what Americans could do for Africa. I don't know if my reply was appreciated, but I stated that, first of all, we need your moral support. Where things are wrong America should stand up and say so, and I feel that this is needed particularly in view of what has been happening in Angola and South Africa.

Secondly, we do need your material help, not in terms of money so much as practical assistance in learning how to develop and use the resources that we have. Despite the misgivings of many Americans, I feel that your Peace Corps idea may produce better and longer-lasting results than you can dream of. If Americans are going to come to Africa to help, they must be free from racial feelings about us and also willing to let us develop our own culture in our own way.

Lastly, allow me to write something about the community where I now live. I and seven other students from Africa are all staying in the homes of Americans here in Sayville. It is a warm and friendly community. The trees, the quiet and the general atmosphere remind me of my home. I have an impression that this community has a "good neighbor policy"; it is a policy deeply rooted in our African society. We came as strangers from a land 7,000 miles away and they have taken us in. We have eaten at their tables, shared their family life, and have come to know our hosts as generous, warm people who are really concerned about our future and the future of Africa.

My immediate acquaintances are the members of St. Ann's Episcopal Church, a church that is friendly and full of vigor. After the morning service, everyone wants to shake hands with me. I like their smiling faces. I am with a band of men and women whose hearts God has touched. The young people of St. Ann's are full of energy, and I feel at home with them when they come around to ask me questions about Africa. (Every child I meet is eager to see my teeth because they hear that I can crack chicken bones.)

Not only do I want to find out about the American school system, but also more about the churches here. Under conditions as they are in Kenya today, many of our customs and laws of behavior are breaking down, and many of our churches have condemned them as un-Christian—and yet they have failed to give us substitutes. This is leading to an alarming situation, especially among youth. I want to find out and know how the American Christian churches are dealing with their youth.

With this in mind, I feel a strong obligation to take home some benefits from the education I am going to get here.

30

INTERNATIONAL INTELLIGENCE FOR THE INTERNATIONAL ENTERPRISE *

John J. Beauvois

Every morning the President reads through a thick sheaf of secret-situation reports prepared by specialists in the State Department, the C.I.A., and other government agencies that give him a summary of the latest politi-

* From the *California Management Review,* III (Winter 1961), 39-46. Copyright 1961 by the Regents of the University of California. Reprinted by permission of the Regents.

cal and economic developments the world over. Every morning at Number 10 Downing Street, Prime Minister Macmillan and his top aides go over similar reports made by British agencies. In Paris, President de Gaulle also gets a political and economic pulse reading from key points around the world. These reports are vital in keeping top political leaders informed of trends and developments affecting their countries.

While the President and his counterparts in London and Paris are studying intelligence reports, the heads of large international corporations like Unilever or Shell are also studying political, economic, and business information that affects their world operations. Today international intelligence is as essential to international businesses as it is to governments.

As an increasing number of American companies become international enterprises in the 1960's, international intelligence will become equally vital to them. It is my purpose to review here why information is necessary, what information is necessary, and how it can be obtained.

WHY INTELLIGENCE IS NECESSARY

The impact of international developments on business is not new. Throughout history economic and political events have affected business in many ways. In the fifteenth century, Venice's commercial supremacy was struck a fatal blow when the Portuguese discovered the Cape route to India. In recent times, American companies have been seriously affected, favorably or unfavorably, by international developments. One has only to think of the expropriation of foreign oil companies in Mexico in 1938, or the implications of the Cuban revolution.

But, if business has always been sensitive to international developments, it now operates in a world increasingly ruled by shifting and complex trends. Industrialization, recent independence, and the emergence of new economic units are forces causing rapid change in many countries. In addition, in several parts of the world political pressures and ideological conflicts deeply affect the business climate. India, for example, has been oscillating for some time between state capitalism and the need for foreign private investment. And in the Middle East frequent political upheavals compel the foreign investor to maneuver continually in order to protect his investment.

Furthermore, never before have economic and political forces been interwoven so closely in determining business conditions. Today, governmental intervention can be felt at all levels of economic activity, and this trend will most likely continue. Economic unions, like the Common Market, are decided, planned, and enforced by governments. In most underdeveloped countries the urgency of industrialization has resulted in economies that are closely controlled by the state. As a result, the international manager must work increasingly with governments. And he must be increasingly alert to any evolution in their thinking or philosophy.

AMERICA'S ROLE

As these complex forces shape the business world of the 1960's, they will affect the growing number of domestic enterprises that will be moving into the international field. Whether it is in response to opportunities abroad or to the threat of foreign competition in the United States, the trend is towards internationalization of American business. In 1961, for instance, total private United States investments overseas are expected to reach $45 billion, a 25 percent increase over 1957.

Internationalization of American business itself would justify the need for international intelligence. But this need is underscored by the role of American business in the economic war with Russia. As the struggle for survival gains momentum, ignorance or misinterpretation of Soviet economic strategies could be fatal. At the same time, American business's responsibility for the development of underindustrialized countries demands that local needs and aspirations be recognized. Only in such a way can this responsibility be discharged in the Free World's best interest.

DUAL RESPONSIBILITY

As a result, the international manager of the 1960's will bear dual responsibilities. One will be to his stockholders for the results of his worldwide operations, the other to the United States and the Free World for playing his part as effectively as possible in the economic struggle against the Communist bloc. In order to discharge these two basic responsibilities, the international manager, like the political leader, must keep informed of world developments and trends.

Thus, companies operating in an international environment must develop an intelligence system alerting them to any short or long-term trends affecting their businesses. As a matter of fact, international intelligence is so vital and sensitive an area that many large international companies are reluctant to divulge, even privately, their approaches to this problem.

DANGER OF MISINFORMED DECISIONS

The chances of making misinformed decisions are greater in an international enterprise than in a domestic one. The international manager works in a more complex environment than his domestic counterpart. At the same time, he is in many ways less well prepared to cope with it.

The domestic executive can follow current developments in the United States and evaluate their significance to his business with reasonable accuracy. Because he works in a familiar environment his chances of erring are greatly reduced. Furthermore, he has many ways of testing his own judgment against sources such as newspapers, trade publications, government reports, and the like.

By comparison, the international manager often lacks familiarity with foreign markets. He must perceive and interpret international developments with a much scanter knowledge of their context and with little, if any, first-hand experience of their environment. As a result, he is sometimes prone to use United States criteria too freely in appraising overseas trends.

Here are two examples of environments that must be understood.

> The social climate in many underdeveloped countries hampers the training of local management. For centuries economic life in these countries has been based on the family, the tribe, or the village—a self-governed unit. At the same time, local religions, Hinduism for example, often emphasize spiritual values to the detriment of material accomplishments. As a result, the concept of corporate management is unknown, and business is not always enticing to the local elite.
>
> Labor relations in most foreign countries are guided to a large extent by ideological considerations. Typically, local unions follow the Marxist line. As a result, collective bargaining must be carried out in a completely different perspective than in the United States.

Thus, the chances for making misinformed decisions are great in an international enterprise. In addition, the penalties for making them can be extremely high. This is true today and it will be even truer in the greatly competitive world economy of the future. Then, more than ever, well-informed management will be a critical factor for success in the world markets.

PENALTY FOR WRONG DECISIONS

There are numerous examples of the penalties paid by American business for misjudging foreign conditions. Here are two significant cases.

> Long-range planning cannot be carried out in the best corporate interest unless foreign trends are recognized. For instance, during World War II, an American company established a leading position in a highly specialized field of military equipment. After the war, peace-time applications began to develop in many foreign countries. The Company's failure to realize the implications of such trends and to move quickly into product modification and world-wide servicing facilities resulted in a sudden and substantial loss of position. In an effort to recoup, a licensing arrangement was worked out with a European manufacturer. Extensive know-how provisions were incorporated in the agreement. Today, substantial opportunities exist for an American manufacturer to produce similar products in Europe. However, this company is effectively excluded from participation by its agreement, which requires that it share design and product development with its licensee, who would then become its European competitor. Thus, by failing to recognize and appraise market trends, this company finds itself out of a profitable market.
>
> Management decisions affecting personnel require recognition of local business practices and ethics. For instance, a large American corporation operating in a Western European country was about to embark on a cost-reduction program. This program would have resulted in substantial savings, but a significant number of employees would have been laid off at its main plant. Besides the fact that firing employees on such

grounds is not an accepted practice in that country, it would have created unemployment in the area. It so happened that a large percentage of this company's business was with governmental agencies. Had this project been seen through, political pressure would most likely have been put on those agencies to place their businesses with some other suppliers. Thus, the savings expected would have been offset by losses in sales, not to mention the ill effect on the company's reputation.

Because intelligence is so vital to the international enterprise, its collection and interpretation must be systematically planned rather than left to chance. The remainder of this article is devoted to an analysis of the kinds of information companies need and the way in which it can be collected and interpreted.

WHAT INTELLIGENCE IS NECESSARY?

The scope of an international intelligence service will of course vary with the nature of the business. Companies with worldwide operations require more information than enterprises that are geographically more limited. Similarly, some companies are more sensitive to specific economic or political trends than others. (For instance, utility companies have historically been concerned with foreign trends toward the nationalization of sources of power.) Nevertheless, every international intelligence service should provide two kinds of information: general background studies, and reports on current developments.

BACKGROUND STUDIES

Most American companies long established in overseas markets have accumulated a sound knowledge of local economic and political conditions over the years. Companies with a shorter international history and companies that are entering overseas markets also need this type of information. Current events can be fully understood only in their historical and cultural context. Likewise, the anticipation of future developments hinges on an accurate evaluation of present conditions.

General background studies should cover two major areas, economic intelligence and political social intelligence. A checklist of points to be covered and questions to be raised and answered follows:

ECONOMIC INTELLIGENCE CHECKLIST

In the area of economic intelligence, material collected should aim primarily at providing management with a general picture of a country's economy, emphasizing its major strengths and weaknesses; an analysis of its investment climate; an analysis of the main factors affecting business operation.

Information should be given about the basic strengths and weaknesses of a country's economy. For instance:

Population growth and its effect on unemployment.

Sensitivity of the economy to depressions.

Sufficiency of basic raw materials or deficiency of food supply.

Projection of growth and description of factors that may accelerate or slow down economic development.

Foreign trade and payments situation.

It should also provide an interpretive analysis of the local business framework. For instance:

Degree of state ownership of or participation in the economy.

Industrial concentration and climate of competition.

Transportation facilities and standards of service.

Price level and price-fixing mechanisms.

In addition, this general study should analyze the investment climate of the country, interpreting current legislation and drawing if possible on practical experiences. It should cover:

Incentives to attract foreign investors.

Limitations to foreign investments or investment conditions.

Corporate structures available to United States companies.

Ownership requirements.

Exchange control and transfer of profits, royalties, interests.

Fiscal discriminations against foreign companies.

Licensing opportunities and history of litigation between American licensor and local licensees and/or local governments.

Finally, this general study should analyze the main factors affecting business operations. For instance:

Availability and cost of energy.

Availability and quality of local labor.

Availability of raw materials.

Size of markets.

POLITICAL AND SOCIAL INTELLIGENCE

As essential as economic information is a sound intelligence of political and social conditions abroad. Here, three major areas should be covered—the local political and social climate; the government's policies; the administrative structure of the country. In providing an interpretive analysis of the local political and social climate, this study should treat, for instance, the following areas:

The present political system.

The political parties, their importance in vote and representation at national and local levels; their attitude toward foreign investments.

Nonpolitical influential groups and their role, for example the Army or the Church.

The social climate and the state of labor-management relations.

The local unions, their strength and influence on the life of the country.

In addition, a general study should describe the current government's policies and their significance for business. For example:

Local government's stability, past history, and outlook for the future.

Monetary and credit policies.

Attitude toward free trade.

State controls over economy, e.g., control of sources of energy.

Economic and political affiliations (alignments).

Finally, this study should provide an analysis of the administrative structure of the country, such as:

Number and policies of governmental agencies concerned with economic affairs and business.

Local standards of administration, for instance, the speed with which decisions on investment and licensing are made.

Government practices against existing regulations.

CURRENT SITUATION

Background information would be misleading if it were not brought up to date regularly by reports of current developments. In a dynamic world new trends can rapidly modify investment or business climates. They can affect the attractiveness of one or more markets to the international enterprise. They can also present it with problems with new dimensions in its current markets. Here are two illustrations:

> Economic conditions in foreign markets may change rapidly. For instance, the ranges of alternatives open to an important segment of the electrical industries changed dramatically from July 1958 to January 1959. Two things happened during the six-month interval. Some companies that had not been very active abroad had reached decisions about timing, markets, product research, and methods of operations. Other companies already abroad had responded to sudden changes at home and overseas by reappraising their current ability to face growing competition and opportunities ahead.
>
> New plants were started, going concerns purchased, licenses granted, and research contracts signed. Any major manufacturer in this industrial group still worrying at the beginning of 1959 about problems and choices six months old ran a real risk of wrestling with phantoms.

Also, political developments may dramatically change the local business climate. In 1958, for instance, a large United States chemical company, Olin Mathieson, joined French, Swiss, and British interests in a $135 million project to exploit bauxite deposits in French Guinea. Long-term agreements were signed with the local administration.

A few months later, President Charles de Gaulle offered independence to the member states of the French Union. Guinea became independent and severed its links with France. As a result, the United States management and its partners were faced with completely new political conditions. And the success of the initial project depended heavily on the ability to deal with the new government.

Current reports cannot reasonably cover every economic and political development abroad. The cost of providing such service would be excessive. Furthermore, much of the speed with which current developments must be brought to management's attention would be lost and corrective decisions might come too late.

Thus, in determining the scope of such reports their true significance to corporate activity must be the measure. This is a decision in which individual judgment must be exercised. In fact, it raises the basic question of how to organize for effective intelligence.

CREATING INTERNATIONAL INTELLIGENCE

The purpose of international intelligence is to enable the international manager to make well-informed decisions and thus to discharge his basic responsibilities more effectively. Because it reflects the needs of a particular business, an effective intelligence service can obviously assume many different forms. However, its basic objective is always the same.

International intelligence is particularly important in the following areas:

Planning the long-range development of the business on a worldwide basis.

Mapping out global strategies for the corporation in order to ensure the highest return on investment.

Coordinating the execution of these strategies in order to strengthen the company's competitive position on a worldwide basis.

Reappraising original programs of action and making corrective decisions as needed.

Controlling and evaluating the performance of local operations.

THE INTELLIGENCE COORDINATOR

The intelligence function must be centrally coordinated. This can be done in many different ways. In some large international companies, the intelligence function is centralized in an economics department. In smaller concerns that have a more limited geographical scope, intelligence is under the supervision of the administrative manager.

Whatever the solution adopted, the basic functions of the intelligence coordinator remain the same. He should be responsible for:

Planning the collection of information and ensuring that it is accurate and significant to the company's business.

Deciding on the choice of intelligence sources. (For instance, the corporation may want to rely on its overseas managers for that purpose or it may prefer to use outside agents.)

Testing the validity and credibility of information when necessary.

Supervising the interpretation of the information received in the light of the corporate objectives and policies.

Preparing and supervising the circulation of information throughout the corporate headquarters and the overseas operations as needed.

THE EXECUTIVE DIPLOMAT

In addition to the intelligence coordinator, international companies require executives with a new kind of skill and their need is reflected in the development of a new type of executive, the "executive diplomat."

Large international companies find themselves competing with increasingly extensive and powerful international concerns. At the same time, they also find that they are affected more and more by the rulings of local authorities. In fact, the future success of American business in many world markets will depend less and less on technological advantages and more and more on the ability of the international manager to deal with foreign authorities.

To cope with this increasingly important aspect of international business, many international corporations are evolving a special staff of "executive diplomats." This staff makes up what amounts to a corporate state department. Oil companies, of course, have for a long time recognized this need and most of them possess just such a staff. But a growing number of companies in diverse industries may also require this new type of executive soon.

The basic responsibility of these executives is twofold. On the one hand, they are responsible for establishing and maintaining close relationships with local governments and other influential groups. On the other hand, they must keep corporate headquarters informed of all economic and political developments of any significance. In addition, they must be able, as much as possible, to anticipate future developments and their possible impacts on business.

Executive diplomats are essential to a large international enterprise. Besides their "government relations" role, or because of it, they can obtain for corporate management information that will either not be made public or, if it is, will be known too late for action. With such information corporate strategies can be quickly adjusted to current developments, thus giving the company a significant competitive advantage.

THE OUTSIDE SOURCE

Many companies find it necessary to supplement their own intelligence service with the services of outside agents. In addition, companies new in the international field often find it impossible to set up their own intelligence departments in the time and at a cost they can afford. As a result, in the last few years the number of international-research specialists has grown. The service of these specialists can be of great value to business. For example, a large steel manufacturer decided to improve its competitive position domestically by affiliating with similar firms in one or several of the major steel-producing countries. This company had had little experience in foreign business. Furthermore, the affiliation was a rush project and there was no time to organize for international intelligence. Yet the investment decision required considering economic and political factors in six countries, so the company retained a specialized intelligence service in London that prepared intelligence reports on the countries considered.

This is a typical example of a rush, one-time project that can be better and more economically handled by an outside agent. In addition, many outside agencies will provide a continuous service of current intelligence reports.

SELECTING AN AGENT

However, the large number of international-intelligence agencies in existence as well as the absolute necessity of obtaining sound intelligence, underscores the importance of selecting the "right" agent. Here are a few questions that the international manager should ask himself before making this selection.

> Does this intelligence agency have its own network of agents in major foreign countries? This is important, for the same standards of accuracy must be used in the collection and interpretation of all data.
>
> How long has this agency been operating in this field? This is equally important. The local contacts that are essential to effective intelligence are made over a period of time. Firms newly arrived in the field cannot expect to have as easy access to non-public information as older firms.
>
> Does this agency have an American business outlook? Of primary importance is the ability of the intelligence agent to understand the basic problems of the American-based international enterprise. If he does, he can interpret the information collected more usefully, and he will be alert to specific data that may have particular significance for his client.
>
> Has this agency had previous experience with our type of problem? Political intelligence in particular requires special skills and contacts that often cannot be improvised.
>
> What are the standards of service provided by this agency? This can be appraised in many cases by looking over some sample intelligence

reports. For instance, one of the most common faults in intelligence reports is an emphasis on a purely historical approach at the expense of an interpretation of the current facts.

DEVELOPING "CONTACTS"

Besides specialized intelligence agencies, some companies use individual contacts in foreign countries. University professors abroad are a valuable source of information, particularly in the field of political intelligence. Few people are in a better position to interpret local political developments than some educational leaders, especially those in the fields of economics and political sciences. Moreover, in many countries, they are well versed in local politics. And they usually occupy pre-eminent positions in influential local circles. As an illustration, a large pharmaceutical company maintains close contacts with medical-school professors in several foreign countries. This practice has proved extremely valuable in keeping both the United States and overseas management informed of current and future legislation in the fields of social medicine and drug regulations. It also has proved useful in seeking government authorization for the local manufacture of various drugs.

Thus, the relative success or failure of many American companies in the 1960's can depend in part on the intelligence of international developments that is available to them. Whether they succeed or fail will in turn affect the outcome of the Free World's economic war with the Communist bloc.

Napoleon is reported to have said that the issue of every battle, no matter how long, was actually decided within a fifteen-minute span. The development of international intelligence may be just that fifteen-minute span.

31

PUBLIC OPINION—ACHILLES HEEL OF U.S. BUSINESS OVERSEAS? *

Charles E. Allen

Fidel Castro is a painful reminder of the power of public opinion to damage U.S. business interests abroad. The Castro regime has used "Yankee imperialism" as a popular devil to strengthen its support among the Cuban people. And the Cuban public, showing little understanding or

* From a speech given before the American University Training Program for International Business Executives, June 1960. Published by Hill and Knowlton (150 E. 42d St., New York 17, N.Y.). Reprinted by permission.

appreciation of American business, has largely applauded the government's actions in taking over U.S. enterprises.

It might be comforting to chalk off the Cuban situation as an isolated development, an unavoidable revolutionary explosion. But there are abundant signs of incipient Castroism elsewhere in Latin America and in other underdeveloped areas of Asia and Africa where U.S. business has substantial investment. Moreover, there is disturbing evidence that American business has real public opinion problems even in highly industrialized countries which have close political, economic and cultural ties with the United States.

The tremendous influx of U.S. business into the European Common Market, for example, is generating serious concern among European public opinion. A survey of public attitudes toward American business in France and Germany, completed last year by Opinion Research Corporation, disclosed the following:

That 58 percent of the French opposed encouraging U.S. companies to locate plants in France; only 24 percent favored it. In Germany such American investment was opposed by 49 percent and only 19 percent supported it.

This surprisingly strong public opposition contrasts sharply with the official policies of the French and German governments which, along with other European governments, are actively encouraging further American investment.

But it is not difficult to understand the reasons expressed in the survey by those opposing the entry of more U.S. business. Both French and Germans emphasized the fear that increasing foreign competition would hurt their domestic industries in home markets, and that foreign capital might ultimately control important sectors of their national economies.

HOW STRONG IS PROTECTIONIST SENTIMENT IN SUCH COUNTRIES?

Underlying fears about American business are germinating strong potential support for discriminatory measures. The Opinion Research Corporation survey showed:

That 91 percent of the French would favor forcing foreign companies to invest a major part of their profits made in France in government housing programs and similar public welfare projects. In Germany, 77 percent would support the same requirement.

That 71 percent of the French and 66 percent of the Germans would make foreign companies pay a special tax on profits or dividends taken out of their countries.

That 77 percent of the French and 73 percent of the Germans would insist that foreign subsidiaries in their countries be at least half owned by local capital.

The same apprehension and bias concerning U.S. business exists, in even more pronounced form, in Canada—our next-door neighbor and largest trading partner. Sizable American investment in major Canadian industries has caused serious public concern about control of the Canadian economy passing into U.S. hands. This is a public opinion problem of real magnitude—for the issue of "U.S. economic domination" has been aired, often acrimoniously, in the Canadian press for the past decade; studied by a Royal Commission and several Canada-U.S. business groups; debated in Parliament; featured in Canadian election campaigns; and invoked in official representations by the Canadian Government to the U.S. Government.

All these examples could be multiplied many times, for there is abundant evidence that U.S. business has substantial public opinion problems throughout its foreign operating areas. These problems fall into at least five general categories:

1. The general fear that large and aggressive American companies are displacing and eventually will take over domestic industries.

2. The suspicion that U.S. companies are exploiting the economies of other countries for the benefit of American management and stockholders, rather than for local employees and citizens.

3. The feeling that U.S. companies exert political influence for preserving the *status quo,* and thereby frustrate popular demands for economic and social progress.

4. The resentment about high-pressure U.S. business methods, especially in some forms of consumer advertising and sales promotion, which foreigners fear is vulgarizing popular tastes and "Americanizing" their traditional cultures.

5. The widespread criticism that many U.S. companies and their personnel do not assimilate well with foreign communities—that most Americans sent abroad do not understand or appreciate local customs, do not know or try to learn the language, and remain aloof from the local community.

IS U.S. BUSINESS DEALING EFFECTIVELY WITH THESE PROBLEMS?

Some American companies are obviously doing a good job in dealing with public opinion in their foreign operating areas. But most companies appear to be neglecting the public opinion situation or merely paying lip service to it.

The comparatively few U.S. companies practicing good public relations abroad are mostly experienced international operators. These are companies, such as the major petroleum firms, that have long had substantial stakes in other countries. Even so, some of the big oil companies had to learn the importance of public opinion the hard way—by discriminatory treatment or even expropriation.

But the great majority of American companies still have not learned the importance of public opinion to their overseas interests—either the hard or the easy way. Many of these companies are comparative newcomers to the international scene and are so preoccupied with problems of organization, manufacturing and marketing that their managements simply have not gotten around to the seemingly secondary matter of public relations. And there are other companies, some quite large and long active in international business, that have developed substantial public relations operations in the United States but virtually nothing overseas.

WHAT ARE THE DEFECTS OF MOST U.S. PUBLIC RELATIONS ACTIVITIES ABROAD?

Although many companies may consider that they are giving appropriate attention to foreign public opinion, most American public relations activities abroad suffer from several important defects:

1. Lack of clear public relations policy. A great deal of improvised and chaotic "fire fighting" is going on because most companies have not adequately analyzed their basic public opinion problems and determined what should be done about them and who should do it.

2. Over-reliance upon line management to cope with the intangibles and complexities of public opinion. Nationals in line management usually have little knowledge of public opinion and communications techniques. Americans generally lack sufficient knowledge of the foreign environment, and often fail to adapt U.S. public relations techniques to the different conditions prevailing abroad.

3. Underrating the public relations function. When an American company does employ qualified international public relations assistance, it often inhibits effective performance by burying the operation deep in secondary management. Excessive decentralization compounds this difficulty by breaking the public relations function into isolated national compartments.

4. Over-dependence on marketing techniques, especially product advertising and publicity, to deal with public opinion matters. This confuses two quite different problems—the selling of tangible products to customers; and the explanation of the company itself to the citizenry. The citizenry is interested in, and often worried about, many things besides the company's products—such as the company's impact on the local economy, its policies for developing local managerial talent, and its contributions to the country's economic development and social progress. These are not items that an American company can "sell" to the local citizenry, but questions that are best answered by responsible corporate behavior which is effectively communicated to the public.

5. Talking too much, and not listening enough. Most American companies abroad are using only "one-way" communications, concentrating on information that management wants to get over to the public. But there are often substantial differences between what the company is interested in saying and what the public is interested in hearing. Without "two-way" communications, people grow tired of just being talked at—but not listened to—and simply disregard the company's efforts as propaganda.

SO, WHAT SHOULD AMERICAN BUSINESS DO ABOUT THE SITUATION?

The indispensable first step is for top management to give serious attention to its public opinion situation abroad. This should receive the same kind of organized executive attention as the company's financial, manufacturing and marketing activities. There are several reasons why the public opinion area deserves this kind of top management attention:

1. We know from substantial American experience that favorable public opinion helps sales whereas unfavorable public opinion hurts sales. It is simply common sense for customers to prefer to buy consumer or industrial products from companies they know and regard highly. That is why there is a strong correlation between company recognition and reputation, and sales success. And this is even more pertinent abroad where many U.S. firms are comparatively unknown and must acquire sufficient recognition and reputation to compete effectively with long-established local companies.

2. We know from American experience that favorable public opinion helps attract capable employees and develop managerial talent. On the other hand, unfavorable public opinion is a serious obstacle to recruiting and developing qualified personnel. People naturally prefer to work for companies that have high prestige. This is especially important abroad where U.S. firms must compete for relatively scarce skills and talents with prestigious national companies.

3. We know from American experience that favorable opinion among employees, their families and community neighbors helps improve productivity, product quality and plant safety. Conversely, unfavorable opinion among employees tends to impair labor-management relations, reduce productivity, and increase costs. Workers naturally feel more cooperative toward managements which encourage "two-way" communications and consultation. This is also quite important abroad where many labor unions are more radical, and workers were suspicious of American management than in the United States.

4. We know from American experience that favorable public opinion enables management to function with maximum flexibility and efficiency; whereas unfavorable public opinion invites governmental harassment which hampers efficiency and boosts costs. Government naturally tends to intervene in the economic sector when private enterprise appears to be unresponsive to public opinion. This is extremely important abroad where public opinion is basically skeptical of American business, and public officials are tempted to curry popular favor by cracking down on large U.S. companies.

These and other public opinion factors can, over a period of years, make a considerable difference in the profitability of an enterprise. They can mean the difference between a losing venture and a successful venture. In extreme cases where cumulative grievances beget expropriation, they can even mean the difference between a successful enterprise and no enterprise at all.

THEN, HOW DOES TOP MANAGEMENT TACKLE THE PUBLIC OPINION JOB?

It should begin with an analysis of the company's public opinion situation in its principal operating areas overseas. This analysis requires a clear definition of the various groups that are interested or involved in the company's activities, and whose understanding and support are essential to its success. These groups usually include:

the company's employees and their families
other residents of communities where the company operates
local, regional and national government
the company's shareowners and prospective investors
customers and prospective customers
licensees, dealers and distributors
suppliers
the business and financial community
communications media (press, trade journals, television, radio)

These groups should be precisely defined and ranked in order of importance. This, of course, will vary according to the company's operations in different countries.

Then representative samples of each important group should be interviewed to determine:

what proportion of the group knows of the company
how many of these people know what the company does, what products it makes
what these people think about the company's policies and products
what they consider the company's relative strengths and weaknesses
what they would like to see the company do in the future
where they get their information and impressions about the company

Such an audit is extremely valuable to management, especially in overseas operating areas. It pinpoints public opinion problems and opportunities that otherwise might be overlooked. It enables management to gauge the relative importance of such problems and opportunities, and thereby establish specific objectives for its public relations activities. And it provides management with a bench mark against which to measure the effectiveness of its public relations program by subsequent surveys of the same groups.

WHAT DOES AN AUDIT DISCLOSE ABOUT COMPANY POLICY?

The process also identifies any possible policy deficiencies that the company might need to correct before it can expect to earn public confidence and support. This is extremely important because the best communications program cannot persuade people to like bad policies, any more than the best advertising program can sell bad products. The kinds of policy considerations that are likely to show up in a public opinion audit are:

1. Has the company created an acceptable degree of national participation in the enterprise? This involves such matters as issuance of stock in a foreign subsidiary for local investors, representation of major sectors of public interest on the subsidiary's board, and staffing its top management with nationals. Such considerations may determine whether the American company has developed a local constituency with a sufficient stake in the enterprise to promote and defend the company's interests.

2. Is the company making an adequate contribution to the host country's aspirations? This involves the company's contribution to economic development by doing locally as much manufacturing, purchasing, research and other activity as can be economically justified. It involves encouraging the growth of supplier industries. And it also embraces the company's contribution to social progress by assisting local communities to develop better educational, medical and other public services.

3. Does the company have a satisfactory policy for recruiting, training and promoting nationals? This includes such matters as preferential employment for nationals, well-designed training programs to accelerate the movement of nationals into managerial jobs, and a completely open road to all top management positions for qualified nationals.

4. Does the company have an effective program for selecting and training Americans who are sent abroad? This involves a conscious policy of selecting the best rather than the most expendable Americans from the domestic organization for overseas work. It includes intelligent procedures for determining the adaptability of such Americans and their families to foreign service. It involves advance personnel planning to ensure adequate lead-time to train people for specific areas overseas. And it includes sufficient language and cultural training to equip people to function effectively upon arrival in new foreign posts. Such considerations also extend to company cooperation with overall business organizations which are helping train Americans for overseas work, such as the Business Council for International Understanding.

5. Does the company conduct its relations with host governments with sufficient skill and sophistication? This involves such matters as the extent to which the company can promote its economic self-interests and support broader measures for improving local economic and social conditions, without becoming a partisan target in domestic politics. It embraces the company's communications activities with influential sectors of public opinion on questions of a controversial nature. And, in many countries, it touches the very delicate policy problem of maintaining good relations with the incumbent government while developing adequate contact and relationships with opposition groups that are likely to become the successor government.

6. Does the company cooperate effectively on broad policy matters with other companies, and with U.S. Government agencies? This involves such policy considerations as whether American and other foreign companies in the same industry can or should work together to develop favorable governmental and public opinion toward their activities. It also involves the extent of American companies' cooperation with local business interests in

jointly promoting public support for free enterprise activities, such as the Business Council for International Understanding is doing through bi-national councils in Mexico and other countries. And it includes the extent of private enterprise cooperation with the U.S. Information Agency in helping improve local understanding of overall U.S. economic policies.

SHOULD BUSINESS NECESSARILY CHANGE BECAUSE OF PUBLIC OPINION?

The foregoing policy considerations do not imply that American companies necessarily should do all these things, or even that they should change their present policies just because of public opinion. There are sometimes other considerations of equal or perhaps greater importance to management that might well militate against such policy changes. Certain highly-integrated international companies, for example, might risk some loss of managerial flexibility in pricing, scheduling production, and handling earnings among their national subsidiaries if local interests acquired substantial equities in such subsidiaries.

But it is important that management know the nature and extent of any public dissatisfaction with company policies, and that it carefully weigh this with other considerations in determining whether changes in existing policies and practices are warranted. This process is essential to an effective public relations program.

If, as is not unlikely, management discovers that irritating matters can be modified or adjusted without harming the enterprise, it will be in a stronger position to achieve public understanding and support. If, in other instances, management concludes that the enterprise would be damaged by meeting unreasonable public demands, it will know the importance of devoting substantial effort to helping the public appreciate the company's side of the situation.

HOW IS AN EFFECTIVE PUBLIC RELATIONS PROGRAM DEVELOPED?

Once management has analyzed its public opinion situation and considered the policy factors involved, the next step is to develop a written public relations program. The program needs to be as carefully planned as any other important managerial function. A well planned public relations program usually includes the following elements:

1. A statement of the company's public opinion situation in each country. This defines the environment in which public relations must operate, and highlights the main problems and opportunities that must be dealt with. These may include such matters as inadequate recognition of the company, misconceptions about its role in the local economy, and pressures for discriminatory treatment.

2. Establishment of specific public relations objectives. These spell out exactly what public relations is expected to accomplish. Some public rela-

tions tasks are designed to support operating phases of the business such as marketing, personnel recruitment and labor relations. The public relations objective with respect to marketing, for example, can specify the favorable attitudes that need to be created among customers and prospects—in terms of such corporate attributes as research and engineering as well as product advantages. Other public relations tasks are designed to cope with major political and economic issues that affect the company's ability to operate efficiently. These can also be spelled out in terms of particular legislative and administrative matters, and specific public attitudes toward the company's operations and its contributions to the national welfare.

3. Development of public relations activities. Specific activities can be designed to advance the company's objectives, by deeds as well as words, on matters ranging from marketing to the public interest. Such activities might include trade exhibits, industrial safety programs, scientific conferences, technical training schools, and support of education and culture. An oil or motor company, for example, can appropriately promote projects for improved roads and highway safety. A chemical or agricultural implement company might establish experimental farms. The basic principle of all such activities is that economic development is not only in the public interest; it is also in the company's long-range economic interest.

4. Effective communications to the public. Company policies, information and activities can be communicated effectively to appropriate audience groups through defined channels. The general public can be reached through mass media, especially on matters of general interest. Specialized media such as trade journals can carry more detailed information on company operations with greater frequency directly to specific groups. And the company can also develop its own media, such as magazines, newsletters and booklets, to communicate with important groups that cannot adequately be reached through existing commercial media. Such company publications usually are required for employees, employment recruits, dealers and distributors, customers and prospects, and sometimes for local communities. The subject matter of all the company's communications can also be planned to ensure that it accurately represents corporate policy and activities, meets the editorial requirements of commercial media, and is sufficiently interesting and relevant to the various audience groups.

5. Adequate rsources to carry out the program. The manpower and financial requirements of the public relations program can be spelled out in detail. The composition and responsibilities of the public relations staff can be defined. If appropriate, the company's relationship with a professional public relations firm can be specified. And the entire program can be budgeted to provide management with accurate costs for each activity.

6. Evaluation of the program's effectiveness. Provision can be made for periodic evaluation of public relations activities so management can judge performance against objectives and in relation to costs. Resurveys of original audience samples, for example, can demonstrate changes in the awareness and attitudes of various groups toward the company. Regular evaluation can keep the public relations program adapted to changing circumstances.

All the foregoing steps demonstrate that American companies can develop international public relations programs as systematically and effectively as they have planned manufacturing, marketing and other activities overseas. But the real problem is not a lack of capacity for undertaking such public relations programs. The real problem is that most American managements do not yet recognize the seriousness and importance of public opinion to their own self-interests abroad. Therefore, they fail to see the need for such public relations programs.

WHAT ARE THE CONSEQUENCES OF INADEQUATE PUBLIC RELATIONS?

Further shock therapy of the Castro variety may occur before American businessmen are jolted out of their lethargy and self-complacency about public opinion abroad. For the public opinion problems confronting U.S. business overseas are certain to get worse rather than better, unless they are clearly recognized and intelligently treated.

All the fears, jealousies and resentments against American business will become even more explosive as U.S. business steps up its investment and operations abroad, and as competition intensifies throughout world markets. This combustible mixture, further inflamed by growing nationalistic pressures in many countries, could easily blow up again in the face of American business, especially when there is need for a convenient scapegoat.

This could happen in virtually any underdeveloped country if popular demand for economic betterment is too long frustrated, or if the precarious economic balance is upset by sharp drops in commodity export earnings. It might also happen in industrialized countries if there is a serious recession, or substantial unemployment, or even perhaps the eclipse of a major domestic industry by an American competitor.

Such explosions of public resentment against U.S. business could, in turn, force even the most friendly governments to adopt discriminatory and protectionist measures. And this might produce a serious retrogression to the international pattern of blocked currencies, discriminatory taxes, import and export quotas, compulsory hiring of nationals, and even outright expropriation.

Any such moves would, of course, jeopardize the profitability of American business' operations abroad, and undermine its foreign investments. Moreover, they would seriously damage U.S. foreign policy and the free world alliance.

The best insurance against such occurrences is for American business to give high priority to the development of essential public confidence and support for its operations overseas.

Doing so can yield substantial results, because those American companies with well-planned public relations operations have attained considerably greater public understanding and appreciation overseas than other U.S. business. In fact, a few of these American companies have achieved as good a standing as the most highly regarded domestic companies in some countries. But even this posture is likely to become precarious unless more

American companies follow suit and help improve the overall image of U.S. business abroad.

Thus, it is imperative for enlightened American management to tackle seriously its public opinion problems overseas—not only to maximize the long-range profitability of its own foreign operations, but to contribute to the kind of expanding world economy in which free enterprise can flourish indefinitely because it is adequately understood and broadly supported.

32

INFORMATION SOURCES ON FOREIGN MARKETING *

John C. Abbott

In recent years the number of marketing studies and reports has grown enormously. However, many marketing specialists have been working without access to much of the recorded experience and analysis that would be useful to them, particularly from countries other than their own.

Specialized research and instruction in marketing developed first and most rapidly in the United States. Because of the abundance of American publications,[1] there has been some tendency for workers in marketing to give only cursory attention to other sources. The main obstacle, however, has probably been that of ascertaining what other material there is and where it can be found.

LITERATURE ON MARKETING IN OTHER COUNTRIES

Generous provision of private and public funds has stimulated a steady expansion of the volume of publications on marketing outside of North America. A number of texts on marketing have been published in the United Kingdom, Germany, and other countries. Consumer research and opinion sampling agencies are active in most European countries. There is a European Society for Opinion Surveys and Market Research, and several national professional organizations of which the Associazione Italiana per gli Studi di Mercato is one example. Conferences are held at regular intervals and their proceedings published. There are periodicals devoted specifically to marketing—*Vendre* (Paris), *Det Danske Marked* (Copen-

* From the *Journal of Marketing,* national quarterly publication of the American Marketing Association, XXV (January 1961), 42-46. Reprinted by permission.

[1] See S. H. Britt and I. A. Shapiro, "Where to Find Marketing Facts," *Harvard Business Review* (September-October 1962).

hagen), *Studi dei Mercato* (Rome), to mention a few concerned specifically with marketing research—and many others with a broad economic or specialized interest.

The effectiveness of advertising techniques in different national, regional, and social environments has been subjected to informed analysis. Enterprises offering to undertake socio-psychological studies are now numerous in Europe, and an Institute for Motivational Research has been set up in Paris.

The structure of distribution is another major theme inspiring continuing review and analysis. There is a general awareness of the trend from small-scale retailing narrowly specialized by commodity to larger-scale enterprises operating their own centralized buying departments. Corresponding interest has been evinced in the appraisal of such developments in different countries under varying economic, institutional, and social environments.

Reports on projects such as the establishment of a supermarket in Teheran in association with concepts quite different from those familiar in North America, merit wide attention as a contribution of experience to the planning of similar schemes under parallel conditions elsewhere. Analyses of the feasibility of shifting to self-service retail sales methods in different countries are now common. The series "Self-service: le pour et le contre" which reviewed experience in the Netherlands, Austria, Luxembourg, Norway, Sweden, Italy, and Spain in the July to October issues of *Quincailler Belge* is one example.

Public production, trade, and consumption surveys and other data constitute valuable sources of marketing information. The broadening of the scope of governmental intervention in marketing, calling for detailed legislation, is another source of publication, together with the activities of planning and development agencies. Publicly authorized marketing boards are also becoming more numerous.

Marketing Studies

As the need for systematic study and investigation of marketing organization and procedure is recognized, more and more European universities and research institutes are undertaking marketing work. The European Productivity Agency of the Organization for European Economic Cooperation now allocates a substantial portion of its budget to marketing improvement projects; its activities are only one additional stimulus to European research and teaching institutions to concentrate more specifically on marketing.

Marketing survey and research activities are apparent in many other parts of the world. The Directorate of Marketing and Inspection of the Government of India, for example, has published over seventy reports on the marketing of food and agricultural commodities. Most provide detailed information on supply and utilization patterns; market preparation; storage and transport methods; assembly and distribution channels and practices; weights, measures and grades in common use; and prices at different stages of marketing. Marketing investigations have been going on for some time in the Philippines where studies like "Consumers' preferences and retail purchases of poultry and eggs: 300 households in Naga City" are published. A number of reports on marketing in Japan, such as "Marketing in Japan's Iron and Steel Industry: 1959," prepared by the Iron and Steel Market Research Specialists team, are also being issued in English by the Japan Productivity Center.

Publications on marketing in certain parts of Africa are now forthcoming. A paper on the "Distributive trades of Southern Rhodesia" appeared in the *South African Journal of Economics* in 1953. Access may also be obtained to reports on "African consumers in Nyasaland and Tanganyika" (H.M.S.O. London), and on "Consumption patterns in Tanganyika" (East African Statistical Department, Nairobi). Close contact with current economic and trading conditions in the different African territories may be maintained through regular periodicals such as the *Overseas Review* published by Barclays Bank, London, and the *Statistical and Economic Review* of the United Africa Company.

There is a professorship of marketing at the National University of Caracas, Venezuela; and a number of books and papers on marketing in that country are available for study. Articles on marketing organization and methods, and on pricing procedures, etc., in the East European countries and the U.S.S.R. have also been published both in the national languages and in English translations.

Valuable information on marketing areas and channels, consumer preferences, development activities, and government policies affecting marketing are also to be found in U.S. government publications, such as the World Trade Information Service Economic Reports of the U.S. Department of Commerce.

International Marketing Advisory Services

The extent of direct international marketing advisory activity is not always realized. For example, in 1958 the Food and Agriculture Organization (F.A.O.) of the United Nations had some twenty specialists working directly with government departments and began publication of a series of guides on marketing in the less developed countries. More than thirty-five papers on marketing topics were presented at a meeting of specialists from Asian countries held at Delhi in April-May, 1959, under the sponsorship of FAO and the U.N. Economic Commission for Asia and the Far East. Mimeographed copies may be obtained from F.A.O., Rome. With the activities of the U.S. International Co-operation Administration, the Colombo Plan, the Ford and Rockefeller Foundations, and other agencies, the output of studies and reports on marketing in the economically less advanced parts of the world is substantial.

PROBLEMS IN LOCATING FOREIGN SOURCES

The steady intensification of international marketing activity through commercial enterprise, technical assistance, and educational exchanges means that the subject matter of interest to marketing specialists is not limited to that of the individual country with which a particular worker is concerned. In many cases there may be much more to learn from experience in other areas subject to comparable conditions, opportunities, and problems. However, there are difficulties in ascertaining where such information can be found.

It is the function of bibliographical, abstracting, and reviewing services to help users find information. Unfortunately systematic bibliographies of publications on the broad field of marketing in countries outside the U.S.A. are difficult to find or use. There is nothing comparable to Revzan's *Comprehensive Classified Marketing Bibliography* of American sources.

For marketing related to food and agriculture, the U.S. Department of Agriculture's *Bibliography of Agriculture* affords a comprehensive, continuous coverage of publications in a large number of countries. However, because of its scale and the range of topics covered, it is inconvenient to handle. Its lack of selectivity leaves the reader too large a number of titles from which to choose. He must still rely on his own judgment in selecting from a list that ranges from popular articles in farmers' periodicals to careful academic studies.

Due to the mounting volume of printed material, most marketing men are probably willing to reconcile themselves to an informed selection. Of the selective bibliographies available, that contained in *Market Research Methods in Europe,* published by the European Productivity Agency, gives a convenient coverage of European literature on the "fundamentals, methods and procedure of market and marketing research" up to 1954-1955.

Statistical Sources for Market Research, published by the Market Research Society, London, 1957, is a compact survey of sources of statistical information relating to the economy of the United Kingdom. It includes both general references and special studies on population, the distribution of manpower by occupation, output in the main industries, the distributive and export trades, etc.

Reference can also be made to bibliographies such as the *Bibliographie der Marktforschung,* Hamburg, Hamburgisches Welt-Wirtschafts-Archiv (1953). Here the ability and willingness of the average marketing worker to find his way through a foreign language publication becomes an important consideration. Many more would probably do this if assured that it contained information directly relevant to their interests. Access to a bibliography with English translations of the titles, and notes on the contents and character of the most important works, together with the essential arguments and criticism, would be a great encouragement to North American readers in exploring the literature of other countries. Such a guide would also be appreciated as an aid in deciding whether to order a book or photocopies from a distant library or another country.

Inclusion of the most important recent publications is essential in a bibliography. While older material may reflect the main body of experience and analysis on a subject, an investigator approaching it for the first time is left uncertain as to whether recent work has introduced new ideas and methodologies. This uncertainty is especially disconcerting to those responsible for current advice to operational marketing organizations. The time required to compile information and issue it to readers necessarily entails delay, but marketing bibliographies without supplementation are especially subject to criticism on this ground, since they deal with a subject on which the interaction of commercial practice and informed analysis is continuous.

Periodical Sources

For many marketing workers the reviews, booklists, and notes in professional journals constitute the most effective source of information on recent publications in other countries. The *Journal of Marketing* has done much to promote a greater awareness of marketing work outside the United States both by publishing original papers on marketing in other countries, and by devoting part of the section on Marketing Articles in Review to foreign marketing. Most issues also contain some fairly detailed reviews of marketing books published in other countries.

Marketing publications are also noted in some more general source series. *Economic Abstracts,* for example, published in English in the Netherlands, contains short summaries of publications issued during the previous three months and includes "markets," "market research, persuasion," "trade, commerce, communications," "price and value, costs" among the topics covered.

These services are necessarily limited. Articles in other journals may not be included, for instance; official publications are rarely fully covered, yet constitute an important body of literature. A practical difficulty in ascertaining the material available on a particular country or topic is the need to look through a large number of successive issues. For efficient reference, these notes and reviews must be cut out and classified when they appear.

Specialized bibliographical services which classify and comment on relevant publications, and keep their lists up to date by issuing periodic supplements, probably come nearest to meeting the active worker's requirements. *International Marketing,* published in France, recognizes this need and issues an annual bibliographical supplement. The Bibliography of the Chamber of Commerce, Paris, issues monthly check sheets which note publications received by its library both from French and other sources. A detailed system of classification is used, with headings such as "sales organization" and subheadings such as "purchasing and sales policy, stocks and inventories, market studies, consumer presentation, packaging." Similar listings may be found in some other countries.

The demand for a convenient bibliographical service covering the broad international field has still to be met. The Food and Agriculture Organization receives many requests for details of publications on marketing. The decision of the American Marketing Association in 1956 to establish a Committee to prepare a bibliography of publications in English on marketing in countries other than the United States, Canada, and the United Kingdom, is further recognition of American marketing workers' need for closer contact with the literature on marketing under different social and economic settings.

This bibliography is being compiled by Professor Donald F. Mulvihill, School of Commerce and Business Administration, University of Alabama, with the aid of American scholars and marketing men who have had experience in other countries. So far, some 600 references to books, articles, and statistical sources have been assembled.

INTERNATIONAL MARKETING BIBLIOGRAPHY

A bibliographical service can probably be furnished most easily and at least cost by an agency which can carry this task along with other activities, and obtain the co-operation of interested official bodies in various countries. Because of the lack of a comprehensive but selective bibliography of publications on marketing outside the United States, F.A.O. has made a preliminary attempt at this, as regards the marketing of food and agricultural products. Material relating to marketing in general has been included where it deals with techniques and concepts applicable to those commodities.

This project was made possible by a grant from the Food Fair Stores Foundation, arranged with the assistance of Professor Reavis Cox of the Wharton School of Commerce and Finance. The bibliography can be obtained on request from the Marketing Branch, Economic Analysis Division, F.A.O., Rome.

FAO Marketing Bibliography

In this bibliography marketing is defined as "the movement of goods from the producer to the consumer and the business activities associated with it." The economic aspects of such initial processing as may be needed to enable farm products to reach a market and the preparation of produce for sale in export markets have been included, but not international trade. Publications devoted specifically to demand analysis and forecasting and without particular reference to marketing methods have been assigned to a separate FAO Bibliography on Demand Analysis and Projection. The entries are classified under the following headings:

0. Marketing theory, research methodology, teaching material
1. Marketing organization and procedure by areas or commodities
2. Transport, packing, and initial processing
3. Storage and management of stocks
4. Grading, standardization and quality control
5. Information, extension, advisory and related services
6. Credit
7. Markets and marketing agencies
8. Pricing and sales methods
9. Costs and margins
10. Co-operative and other voluntary group marketing
11. Government participation in, and regulation of, marketing

Material on advertising, for example, can be found under "information," "marketing agencies," or "sales methods," depending on the predominant purpose of the publication in which it is treated. Cross references are given where classification under one heading might be misleading. Geographical, commodity, and author indexes coded to show the year, language of publication, and main subject emphasis are also provided.

No distinction is made between printed books, articles in periodicals, mimeographed reports, and official documents so long as copies might be made available on request. With the exception of unpublished theses no material is excluded because it might be out of print. It is assumed that potential users might borrow from a central lending library or request photocopies.

The basic criterion adopted for the selection of titles is their usefulness to readers in countries other than those of publication. Material of temporary interest, or relating to conditions which no longer prevail, is omitted. Recent work is preferred unless there are specific reasons why an earlier treatment is still of interest. However, for some countries material is listed that might not have been if more publications were available.

The geographical and language coverage is circumscribed for the time being by the funds available. Attention is limited to publications relating to countries other than the U.S.A. and Canada, because of the greater need for a co-ordinated bibliographical service for this material. Coverage is also limited to publications in the languages most easily read by the majority of workers in the marketing field.

Maintenance of an Effective Service

To minimize printing delays, keep costs down, and permit addition of the periodic supplements needed to keep the bibliography up to date, an experiment has been made with mimeographed sheets in an adjustable cover. The supplementary sheets and new index pages are sent automatically to holders of the original bibliography.

The correction of discrepancies and omissions and inclusion of new work in these supplements can be done only with the co-operation of marketing specialists in the countries concerned. Extension of coverage beyond national boundaries calls for a more than corresponding improvement in the bibliographical service. Not only must it cover work in different languages, but must also take account of varying professional usage and terminology. It is essential that lists and comments be prepared by specialists in the literature of the countries concerned.

It would seem feasible to establish a chain of marketing bibliographical correspondents with common standards, who would "feed" the international service and at the same time draw upon it for dissemination of marketing information.

Cases

INTRODUCTION

In the Preface to this book we have pointed out that skills of management cannot be acquired merely by taking courses, attending seminars, participating in workshops, listening to lectures, watching educational television, or even selectively reading books and articles. To become a decision maker one simply has to make decisions.

The objective of this section of the book is to provide the student with a wide selection of cases on which he can practice decision making. Each case transfers to the classroom a piece of life from the day of an executive engaged in the management of international business. The cases cover a gamut of topics: market entry and expansion; export policies, procedures, and problems; international human relations; development of marketing programs abroad; and establishment and operation of international companies.

We have included five cases on Industrias Kaiser Argentina, which give the student an unusual opportunity to explore in depth the operations of a large and highly diversified American firm. This intensive exposure is a good supplement to the shorter cases dealing with different countries and companies.

The student studying these cases will find that sound managerial principles do retain validity, no matter what the location of the enterprise. Yet the degree of applicability varies. After all, every business decision is a product of diverse economic, political, and cultural forces that have, consciously or subconsciously, shaped the executive. The significant environmental differences must therefore be duly recognized. This adaptation is still more of an art than a science.

The case method—properly administered—requires each participant to first define the problems and then prescribe appropriate remedial actions. Unlike mathematics or engineering, the "solutions" do not become self-evident even after the administrator has discovered the appropriate formula or principle. There is no one completely "right" or "wrong" answer. The same rule applies to the international management game. When it is over, the participating groups can analyze each other's strategies to see which was most successful. These post-mortems will again bring home the disconcerting point that there is no one correct answer. In a game, as in life, there are always several more or less profitable ways of skinning the cat. By the same token, there are no right or wrong sources of information. The readings and the references merely serve as points of departure. A list of cases and the readings that are related to them appears following this introduction.

Several of the cases have appendixes which carry some of the necessary background information. But for comprehensive descriptions of specific practices, laws, and regulation, the participants should go outside to such standard texts as Horn and Gomez, *International Trade* (Prentice-Hall, 1960). These should be supplemented by such classic manuals as the latest edition of the *Foreign Commerce Handbook* issued by the U.S. Chamber of Commerce, and the U.S. Department of Commerce *Directory of Foreign Development Organizations for Trade and Investment.*

The job of searching for pertinent supporting material can, of course, be divided among several individuals. After all, business administration is a cooperative effort. In the real world it is perfectly all right to ask one's colleagues for advice. However, responsibility for the final decision and development of a plan for implementation rests on the shoulders of the individual student.

CASES AND RELATED READINGS

1. Clean-Away Corporation: Readings 11, 12, 22.
2. The Okinawa Campaign (I): 14, 15.
3. Thornton Machine & Manufacturing, Inc.: 12, 15.
4. Wellbabe Products, Inc.: 30, 32.
5. Renown Products Company (I): 13, 15, 16.
6. Renown Products Company (II): 15, 16, 17.
7. Renown Products Company (III): 15, 16, 17.
8. Reliance Hardware Manufacturing Company: 16, 17.
9. Smithers Paint Company (I): 16.
10. Household Products, Inc. (I): 22.
11. Household Products, Inc. (II): 22.
12. Burroughes Welcome Daraprim: 22.
13. The Okinawa Campaign (III): 12.
14. Far East Representatives, Inc.: 14.
15. Smithers Paint Company (II): 12.
16. Albert Edirsinghe & Co., Ltd.: 15.
17. Federal Cash Registers: 13.
18. New Zealand Appliances, Ltd.: 31.
19. Renown Products Company (IV): 19, 20.
20. The Okinawa Campaign (II): 19, 20.
21. Paragon Plumbing Equipment (I): 30, 31.
22. Paragon Plumbing Equipment (II): 19, 20.
23. Coproducts Corporation: 18, 19, 20.
24. Automotive Exports, Inc.: 19.
25. Stewart Sutherland: 30.
26. Wilbur Armitage: 30.
27. Swift Motors, S.A.: 10, 30.
28. Foster Birkett: 30, 31.
29. American Trading Corporation, Inc.: 27, 30.
30. Captain George Patrios: 30.
31. Richard Conklin: 31.
32. Industrias Kaiser Argentina, S.A. (IV): 17, 32.
33. Packer, Inc.: 23, 24, 25, 26, 27.
34. The Ceylon Plywood Company: 23, 24, 26, 28, 29.
35. Robert Thompson: 23, 24.
36. Holiday in Chittagong: 23.
37. Moosajees, Ltd.: 25, 28, 29.
38. Mr. Walter Murray: 12.
39. Francis X. O'Shea: 11.
40. Hewlett-Packard Company: 12, 13, 14, 15.
41. General Tire and Incatecu, S.A. (I): 30, 31.
42. General Tire and Incatecu, S.A. (II): 19, 20, 30, 31.
43. General Tire and Incatecu, S.A. (III): 19, 20.
44. Kaiser Motors Corporation: 10, 13, 18, 32.

45. Industrias Kaiser Argentina, S.A. (I): 10, 12, 19, 31.
46. Industrias Kaiser Argentina, S.A. (II): 10, 11, 19, 20.
47. Industrias Kaiser Argentina, S.A. (III): 11, 31.
48. Industrias Kaiser Argentina, S.A. (V): 10, 30, 31.
49. Esso Standard Eastern, Inc. (Ceylon): 10, 11, 20, 30, 31.
50. Thomas Randall Knitting Mills: 14, 15, 22, 32.
51. Sony Corporation: 14, 15, 32.

SECTION ONE

International Market Entry and Expansion

1

CLEAN-AWAY CORPORATION

Factors Affecting the Decision to Enter World Business

The Clean-Away Corporation, located in Cincinnati, Ohio, manufactured dishwashers and garbage pulverators for domestic use, and electric and gas cooking equipment and commercial pulverators for restaurants. A relatively young company, Clean-Away had begun manufacturing for sale in the Middle West and, as it prospered there, had expanded into the rest of the United States. In 1962 it was one of the largest manufacturers of its product line, which was fairly widely advertised and in particular favor among house contractors. Frequently these bought Clean-Away equipment for installation in speculative homes; the company's reputation for quality construction and for after-installation service had helped to broaden this particular market.

Competition, particularly in the field of domestic dishwashers and garbage pulverators, was intense and Clean-Away was to some extent handicapped (although in other ways helped) by the fact that it did not produce a full line of domestic appliances. Partly because of growing competition and partly because of a tradition of market expansion, as well as because of the impact of business talk about such aspects of overseas trade as the European Common Market, the company in 1962 was considering the possibility of going into foreign trade.

No particular progress had been made, however, when in March, 1962, the staff assistant to the president, Mr. Donald Gibson, attended a dinner of business executives from various firms in the Cincinnati area. The speaker was a professor from a school of business in Chicago, talking on the subject "Neglected Opportunities for American Marketing in Under-Developed Countries." His thesis ran to the effect that, for U.S. firms which had not entered international business but were giving thought to its possibilities, there might be greater possibilities in the developing countries than in such areas as Europe, Canada, and Australia where competition from local and well-established American companies might be too difficult to meet. While the underdeveloped countries clearly did not present anything like the immediate potential offered by the European Common Market, they might provide newcomers to export trade or overseas operations a chance to get in on the ground floor and grow with the host nation.

To Mr. Gibson the thesis made considerable sense from Clean-Away's standpoint. He thought over what the speaker had proposed and was particularly impressed with some forecasts on growth in Latin America which had been offered. These assumed the expenditures of large amounts in Latin America through the "Alliance for Progress" as well as the inevitable growth which seemed bound to intensify. While the speaker had stipulated that not all countries in Latin America would industrialize at anything like the same rate, he had prophesied that for some, notably Mexico and Brazil, the rate of growth would in a relatively short time exceed that of the United States.

Mr. Gibson accordingly sent the following memorandum to the Clean-Away marketing research department:

March 22, 1962

To: Charles Johnson, Marketing Research

From: Donald Gibson, staff assistant to the president

Subject: Possible Export or Overseas Business

A couple of days ago I attended a meeting of the Executives' Dinner Club and heard a talk by a professor from Chicago on "Neglected Opportunities for American Marketing in Under-Developed Countries." I was very impressed by this since, as you know, we have been thinking about ways in which we could secure some foreign sales.

This speaker was enthusiastic, particularly about the possibilities for growth in Latin America, notably under the Alliance for Progress. In addition, I understand that some of those countries have done a lot of house and apartment building and I wonder if we could not merchandise our dishwashers and pulverators effectively in those areas. It is my understanding that Chile is doing some extensive apartment house building and, of course, Brazil has recently built an entirely new capital city, Brasilia.

To begin with, could you give me any type of information concerning plumbing and sewerage conditions in the Latin American countries? While I am thinking primarily of our domestic appliances, dishwashers and pulverators, there might also be opportunities to sell our commercial electric and gas cooking equipment and our restaurant-type pulverators. In addition to plumbing and sewerage conditions, we should have data on gas and electricity supply.

I shall be glad to have this information as soon as you can supply it. If you have any other ideas on what we should take into consideration in this connection, be sure to include them.

QUESTIONS

1. Where should the marketing research department look for information on sewerage, plumbing, gas and electricity supply in Latin America?
2. What additional information might the department supply Mr. Gibson to help him reach a decision about seeking markets in Latin America?
3. What factors should Clean-Away consider before attempting overseas business?

THE OKINAWA CAMPAIGN (I)

Consideration of Entry into a New Foreign Market

On the morning of March 24, 1954, Mr. Raymond Dekker, General Manager of Automotive Exports, Inc., received a letter from the Ryukyu Trading Company of Okinawa (Exhibit 1, at end of this case). Later in the same day, Mr. Dekker got a telephone call from the Sales Manager of the West Coast Tire Company in Vallejo, California. It developed that the West Coast Tire Company had received an identical letter from the Ryukyu Trading Company. Since AEI was the export agent for the West Coast Tire Company, the Sales Manager told Mr. Dekker that he would forward the letter to him for whatever action AEI might wish to take.

Automotive Exports, Inc. was established in Oakland, California, in 1936. From its inception the company had specialized in exporting automotive replacement parts to the Far East, but had never entered the Okinawa market. The company had experienced a steady growth over the years since 1936, except during World War II when all operations were suspended. In addition to the main office in Oakland, AEI had small branch offices in Seattle, Washington, and Long Beach, California.

AEI had various types of marketing relationships with a number of manufacturers, but operated usually in the role of a manufacturer's export agent.

It might be explained here that the business of the manufacturers' agent is entirely separate and independent of that of his principals; that

> he usually assumes all the exporting responsibilities and risks but occasionally not the credit risk; and that his remuneration is generally in the form of a discount from list price with no retainer fee or commission. The combination export manager, on the other hand, manages the export departments of two or more concerns; his relationship with his principals is more that of an employee subject to their control. All exporting responsibilities and risks are assumed by his respective principals, and the remuneration of the combination export manager is usually in the form of a retainer fee plus a commission on sales. In other words, the manufacturers' export agent employs his own personnel and operates his own business as export representative of perhaps as many as a score or more principals, whereas the combination export manager merely *manages* the export operations of his principals, usually not more than several, and utilizes their business personnel necessary for exporting purposes. The combination export manager may or may not maintain his own private office and small staff, depending upon circumstances. The distinctions, largely technical, may be of no great importance as in the trade the terms "manufacturers' export agent" and "combination export manager" are frequently used interchangeably.[1]

The relationship of AEI to two of its clients who might be considered typical was as follows: The West Coast Tire Company enjoyed a considerable domestic sales volume, using its own marketing organization. However, shortly after AEI was established in 1936, it took over all export activities for the West Coast Tire Company in both the Far Eastern and South American markets. However, after several unfortunate post-war credit experiences in South America, AEI's selling activities there had been terminated. Since 1948, AEI had concentrated on the Far Eastern market.

Another typical supplier was the General Battery Company. General batteries were manufactured in San Jose, California and were exported to European, South American and Far Eastern markets. AEI was the Company's export agent for the Far Eastern market. Two other agents handled the General Battery Company's South American and European export business respectively.

At the time the letter was received from the Ryukyu Trading Company, Mr. Dekker reviewed what knowledge he had of the Okinawa market. This knowledge had been acquired from current foreign trade publications, discussions with other men in the import-export business, and some information supplied by the companies for which he was an agent.

His knowledge of the Okinawa market was as follows:

1. There were about 2,650 American manufactured cars and trucks on the island.

2. This number of cars represented an annual market of approximately $200,000 in replacement parts, excluding tires and batteries, and about $250,000 in tires and batteries. (Note: these figures are derived from what might be termed a standard formula per 1,000 cars and trucks. This formula took account of the fact that the number of trucks and busses, per

[1] Horn, *International Trade Principles & Practices,* 3rd ed. (Englewood Cliffs: Prentice-Hall, Inc., 1951), p. 516.

thousand vehicles was appreciably higher in foreign markets than in the United States, due to lack of other types of for hire transport. It also allowed for the usual foreign practice of repairing and operating vehicles for many years after they ordinarily would have been junked in the United States.)

3. In order to do business in the area it would be necessary to offer a complete line of automobile replacement parts. This was necessary to meet the actual and potential competition.

4. The marketing setup for automotive parts on Okinawa included:

a. The American Post Exchanges (PX's) did little of the business. They could be considered negligible except for minor accessories.

b. Chevrolet and Ford dealers sold both new cars and replacement parts. They tended to concentrate on the sale of new cars and did not fight very aggressively for a share of the parts market.

c. Service stations purchased from the local wholesalers.

d. Big garages (differing in degree from the small service stations) also purchased from local wholesalers.

e. Fleet accounts (these included taxi fleets, bus companies and trucking companies) also purchased from the wholesalers.

5. Automotive parts wholesalers (there were about a dozen on the island) purchased from companies in the United States and Japan. They obtained from Japan only tires and batteries, not parts. These wholesalers placed their orders through indent agents located on Okinawa.

A number of difficulties were anticipated if the company attempted to enter the Okinawa market. The first, and in some ways the most important, of these difficulties was the dollar shortage in the Far East. It would be necessary to obtain import permits and to arrange for dollar financing through Okinawa banks. Mr. Dekker was not certain of the current dollar situation in Okinawa. However, past experience indicated that some difficulty was likely to arise in this regard since practically no country in the Far East had enough dollars to carry on the amount of trade it wanted. Offsetting this difficulty was the fact that automotive parts were often considered to be essential imports by these countries since they lacked other forms of transportation in many areas.

Competition was the second major problem the General Manager expected to encounter. He thought this would take two forms: first, competition on the part of other American exporters to the Far East and, second, competition from manufacturers in Japan. Other American exporters to the Far East would be able to compete with AEI in all lines of automotive replacement parts. The Japanese manufacturers, however, would compete only in tires and batteries. These were comparatively easy to manufacture compared to complex, machined automotive parts. The Japanese manufacturers also had the advantage of easy access to natural rubber markets in the Far East, lower freight rates, and cheap labor. However, the lower cost of labor was offset to some extent by less efficient methods of production in Japanese factories.

The third major difficulty in entering this market concerned the reliability of the agent selected. At the time Mr. Dekker received the letter from

Ryukyu Trading Company, he had no knowledge whatsoever about the reliability, financial reserves, or general reputation of this company. On the basis of past experience, Mr. Dekker believed that of all considerations affecting entry into a foreign market, perhaps the most critical was the reliability of the agent selected. A good agent could help the exporter overcome practically any local market difficulty. On the other hand, a dishonest or unqualified agent would be more of a hindrance than a help, and any relationship with an agent of poor reputation would injure the company's prestige to such an extent that successful entry into the market might never be possible in the future.

The fourth difficulty which Mr. Dekker felt his company would face concerned the differences between foreign and domestic markets, especially differences in customer attitudes. First, the Far East customers had been subjected to a barrage of advertising like American buyers. Many of them felt that if a part were not a so-called "genuine part" it should not be installed in a vehicle for which "genuine parts" were available. Such customers might have to be educated to the fact that it was not the brand name of the part, but its size, specifications, and price that counted. Another inherent difference between domestic and foreign customers was the clannishness of Far East buyers. They were known to stick very closely together and if an exporter made a mistake in dealing with any of them—for instance, being too soft or too hard, attempting to trick or to cheat them, or to use any business practice to which they objected—then that exporter could expect to be frozen out of the market. For this reason, Mr. Dekker felt that if AEI entered this market upon the invitation of the Ryukyu Trading Company, he would have to watch his step and avoid alienating any of his potential customers.

The fifth difficulty which occurred to Mr. Dekker was the danger of an American withdrawal which would eliminate two-thirds of his potential market. This figure was based on the estimated percentage of American-owned-and-operated vehicles versus Japanese-owned-and-operated vehicles on the island of Okinawa. Of course, if the American forces withdrew, it was probable that many of their automobiles would remain on the island. The owners could sell them in Okinawa for far more than their value on the American domestic used-car market. However, Mr. Dekker did not think it likely that more than 50% of the present market would continue to exist in the event of an American withdrawal. Whether or not American military forces would leave Okinawa was unknown. Any answer to it would necessarily require a political and military forecast of the future. Some of Mr. Dekker's business associates believed that U.S. forces would be in Okinawa for many years; others felt that current occupation policies and attitudes toward the government of Japan indicated we would recall as many of our troops as possible and leave Japan to home rule.

Prodded by the letter from the Ryukyu Trading Company, and considering his company's natural desire to expand its markets if possible, Mr. Dekker felt he had to make up his mind quickly. Was this the time, if ever, for AEI to attempt to enter this market? If so, how should the company go about it?

Ryukyu Trading Company [2]

21-Ming, Kohagula-Ku, Mawashi City, Okinawa

Ryukyu Islands

March 19, 1954

Automotive Exports Incorporated
824 Adeline Street
Oakland, California

Dear Sir:

My company has been in the Importing and Exporting business here in Okinawa for the past four years.

Now we are expanding and enlargeing [sic] our sales staff, so we would like new source of buying many items we sell, also information about becoming an Agent for your Company here in the Ryukyu Islands.

Hoping to hear from you very soon.

Very truly yours,

WILLIAM R. SHREEVE
Sales Manager

SUPPLEMENTARY DATA

Mr. Dekker felt that immediate action of some kind would have to be taken in this case. Rapid but discreet inquiry among his business associates in the export trade indicated that the Ryukyu Company had sent similar letters to a number of West Coast export houses as well as to several automotive parts manufacturers who were known to deal extensively in the Far East export market. Mr. Dekker felt that this would arouse considerable interest about the Okinawa market in general, and about the Ryukyu Trading Company as an agent, in particular. Having taken these considerations into account, analyzed the market, and estimated difficulties expected to be encountered, Mr. Dekker determined to enter the Okinawa market at this time and use the Ryukyu Trading Company as an indent agent. This decision, of course, would be subject to working out satisfactory arrangements with the Ryukyu Company and his own domestic suppliers. Mr. Dekker had no knowledge whatsoever of the reliability of the Ryukyu Trading Company. However, he believed that if he took time to make a thorough check on the Ryukyu Company, it was quite likely that someone else would get the business. In addition, Mr. Dekker felt that some risk was justified in entering a new market.

In replying to the Ryukyu Company, Mr. Dekker prepared a large airmail package. This package contained several catalogs of lines of automotive parts which AEI handled. In addition, there was a cover letter which quoted specific prices on certain items which Mr. Dekker advised the

[2] The body of the letter is an exact copy of the original. The letter was signed by an Occidental.

Ryukyu Trading Company he had available for immediate export. These quotations included tires and batteries because Mr. Dekker realized that any competition from Japanese firms would probably arise on those items. Therefore, he wanted to establish a toe-hold with the tires and batteries as soon as possible, with the other parts of his automotive replacement line to follow later. A second reason for quoting tire and battery prices was that Mr. Dekker had available, within ten miles of his office, supplies of these tires and batteries packed for export. Thus, upon receipt of an order, he could make immediate shipment to the Far East. This, he felt, would establish his reputation among the Okinawa buyers as an exporter who gave very fast service. Considering the time ordinarily consumed in shipping goods from the United States to the Far East, any extra speed which he could demonstrate would be to his advantage in future dealings, especially when competing with other American exporters. Also, to increase the probability of receiving orders from the Ryukyu Company, Mr. Dekker reduced his commission on these quoted items from the customary 10% to a very low margin of 7½%. The cost of the airmail package was $50.00 in airmail charges alone. This package was dispatched the day after the letter from the Ryukyu Company was received. Ten days later an order for batteries was received by airmail from the Ryukyu Trading Company.

3

THORNTON MACHINE & MANUFACTURING, INC.

Consideration of Request for Foreign Licensing and World Sales Rights

Thornton Machine & Manufacturing, Inc. is a small machine shop in Seattle. Its primary business, since its founding 10 years ago, has been the design and construction of plywood manufacturing equipment. To supplement this main line, it has also done job shop machine work. At the present time, it employs 26 machinists, 3 engineers and 4 designers.

Charles Thornton, president of the company, had begun the business and for several years operated it as a sole proprietorship. Three years ago he became friendly with the inventor of the Fulchurch Leader-Pull Principle and, in exchange for rights to the principle and cash, incorporated his company, with the shares held largely by himself, the inventor, and a third investor. The inventor and the third investor were primarily interested in capital gains; Thornton depended on the company for a living but also hoped that sometime, perhaps in 10 years, he and his associates would be able to sell out all or part to a larger firm for a substantial gain.

For the past three years, after incorporation, Thornton had been busy developing boring, mining, and tunneling equipment around the principle.

The company's major product seemed likely to be a portable concrete drill, electric-powered, which would cut from three to 14 inch diameter holes with diamond core bits. The drill had advantages over other drills selling from $600 to $1200 in that it could be set up in about five minutes to the ordinary drill's hour or so, and it did not have to be braced or held. In addition, it was cheaper to use, since it produced a straighter, truer bore which reduced diamond wear. International patent protection was extensive.

Sales rose over the three years to about $500,000, and this year the company expected to make a profit. In prior years all available funds had been plowed back into development and this, with the state of the plywood industry, had left the company with a deficit in each year. Lack of working capital continued to be a problem.

The company was interested in selling rights to the principle to manufacturers in other countries, since it could not see how it could sell directly in overseas markets because of its lack of capital. If it could find a single manufacturer who appeared able to distribute on a world-wide basis, Thornton was quite willing to entertain a licensing agreement for all markets, existing and potential. Alternately, if no single licensee could be found, it would be necessary to look for licensees in single countries or market areas.

An article by the inventor on the application of the principle to large equipment, a coal miner costing about $150,000, appeared in a technical journal. As a result of this, Sydney, Limited, of Melbourne, Australia, wrote to Thornton expressing interest in the company's products. One of Sydney's directors, Mr. Oser, an old employee of the firm but a man with limited technical background, was in Canada on a business trip. When Thornton wrote back indicating a willingness to discuss possible business arrangements, Oser was cabled by his company to go to Seattle, which he did.

He was shown the drill and was told something of Thornton's plans for its development of other equipment. On his return to Melbourne, Oser apparently reported favorably to the company. Shortly after, the following letter was received by Thornton.

SYDNEY LIMITED

Manufacturers of Drilling Equipment and Diamond Bits

October 10, 19—

Thornton Machine & Manufacturing, Inc.
6800 Ninth Avenue North
Seattle 7, Washington
U.S.A.

Attention: Mr. Charles Thornton

Dear Sir:

We thank you for your letter of the 1st instant and advise that Mr. J. Oser, on his return, commented favorably on the Fulchurch Pilot Pull Principle although he unfortunately was not able to inspect a machine in operation.

From previous correspondence with you, we understand

that several machines have been made and are in use by interested parties.

We are wondering therefore if it is possible for you to ship one of these out to us on completion of current operations to permit us also to assess the potentiality of the machine under several types of field applications.

In the meantime, we would be pleased to receive for consideration, your proposal regarding manufacturing under license and as in our opinion a limited market exists for such a machine, suggest that you might consider granting us world manufacturing rights or alternatively world rights excluding the U.S.A. market.

Awaiting your further advices with interest. We are,

Yours faithfully,
SYDNEY LIMITED

(T. O. Jones)
SALES EXECUTIVE

Thornton's knowledge of Sydney was very limited. It knew that, in addition to making drilling equipment and diamond bits for sale in Australia, the company operated a contract drilling department. A check by Thornton through its bank indicated that Sydney had a good credit rating and carried substantial bank balances. An American oil-drilling-equipment manufacturer, represented by Sydney in Australia, recommended the company as a competent distributor for its products and stated that the two firms had enjoyed satisfactory relationships for several years.

QUESTIONS

1. What action should Mr. Thornton take in response to Sydney's letter?
2. What reply should he make to the letter while he is deciding what to do?
3. What should Thornton look for in a licensee?
4. Should the company try to find a distributor for the world or look for regional licensees?
5. What other kinds of distribution might it consider, in addition to licensing?

SECTION TWO

International Operating Policies, Procedures, and Problems

4

WELLBABE PRODUCTS, INC. *

Problems of Marketing Research in a Foreign Market

Developing market information in foreign countries is not always the relatively straightforward matter it is in the United States. Such, at least, was the conclusion reached by officials of Wellbabe Products, Inc., makers of proprietary medicines for children. The company was seeking to explore sales potentials in French Canada but had not evolved satisfactory procedures.

WELLBABE PRODUCTS, INC.

Wellbabe Products, Inc., had been founded in 1892 to produce a soothing syrup for babies and young children. The product was extremely successful and for years was the leader in its field. From time to time the company had added new items to its line; these were all proprietary or patent medicines and no attempt was made to market them as ethical drug products.[1]

Cost of ingredients and production for the company's preparations

* Fictitious name.

[1] Ethical drug products are not advertised to the public, but are promoted to physicians, usually with the aid of "detail men" whose job is to keep the medical profession informed about them.

was not high. The bulk of its operating expenses went into advertising, sales promotion, and commissions to salesmen. The company marketed only in the U.S. and sold to druggists, general stores, and other outlets through its own sales force. In addition to responsibility for sales, salesmen were expected to aid dealers in building displays and to keep the general sales manager informed on conditions in their territories and particularly on the activities of competitors.

Advertising was placed through an advertising agency, which had offices in several American cities. Various media were used from time to time. These had included national magazines, farm papers, newspapers, radio, television, and occasional use of outdoor advertising. The company had also offered premiums in exchange for carton flaps, and it sometimes distributed booklets on child care, feeding, and household hints.

In recent years Wellbabe had made increasing use of foreign language publications in various areas, of radio stations offering programs in such languages as Spanish and Italian, and of media aimed at Negro readers or listeners. The general sales manager believed that Wellbabe products were particularly popular among certain ethnic groups and that these could be reached best through media which focused directly on them.

The company made little use of marketing research organizations. Its advertising agency would, on demand, make limited surveys for it free of additional charge, such as checking to see whether salesmen were actually building displays or trying to supplement information from the field. The general sales manager, however, felt that his own records provided most of the data he needed and he kept careful track of sales patterns.

Information he utilized included sales by product and by territory, reports from salesmen on competitive activity—sales promotion efforts, unusual dealer support, deals and price cuts and the like—and reports on competitor advertising which the agency provided. With this, the general sales manager could tell fairly quickly how a particular product was selling and where.

SALES SINCE WORLD WAR II

Overall sales for most of the company's products had declined since the end of World War II and it was this decline which had led the management to consider marketing abroad. Although no specific research had been conducted to determine the reasons for the decline, the company's officials believed they knew pretty well what these were, and the sales figures supported their belief.

In general, American mothers had tended to rely more and more on physicians, pediatricians or general practitioners, when their children became ill. The emergence of antibiotics and a number of other drugs which had significant cure records but could only be secured through physicians' prescriptions was one of the reasons. Another was an increase in the education level which was making many women skeptical of patent medicines and their efficacy. The management group, only half humorously, laid some of the responsibility for their problems at the doorstep of Dr. Benjamin Spock who, in his best-selling book on infant care,[2] emphasized the importance of the physician in the care of the child.

However, in certain areas sales were not only holding up well but were increasing. These areas were rural parts of the U.S., notably in the Deep South, where traditional habits tended to be harder to break. Groups where the family as a unit was important, particularly where there was a grandmother who had used Wellbabe products on her children, seemed to regard them as old friends which should be kept in use. In such markets as the Puerto Rican sections of New York and Mexican-inhabited parts of the Southwest, factors such as cost of medical care, suspicion of doctors, and, again, tradition helped to keep Wellbabe in high favor. It was for these markets that the company used foreign language media, as well as sales promotion material prepared in the appropriate language.

CONSIDERATION OF FOREIGN MARKETS

Wellbabe's management was inclined to feel that, in the long run, the tendency of women to use their products would decline still more. Large-scale immigration into the U.S. was pretty much a thing of the past and the pattern for migrants is, as they acquire education and income, to seek to adopt American habits. This would, the company was sure, extend to use of doctors, and this would be helped by exposure to social service agencies who would certainly recommend modern medical methods.

The company had concluded that one way to hold its own would be to sell its products to foreign markets where the population characteristics in terms of attitudes and education resembled those parts of the U.S. where it was still doing well. It had never sought export sales and was uncertain how to proceed. However, the simplicity of production methods, the almost universal availability of raw materials, and the existence of advertising agents and media in most countries meant that overseas subsidiary operation should not be difficult. Alternatively, and probably preferably at first, it might arrange with a foreign drug maker to produce Wellbabe products and either market them on a royalty basis, or turn them over to local distributors or to a Wellbabe sales force if the company chose to set one up. Customs duties would probably make direct export impractical, although the company did feel that it might ship overseas in bulk for local packaging.

Within easy range of the U.S. were two markets which seemed to merit investigation. One of these was Mexico and the other Canada. Mexico, after some thought, was ruled out. Wellbabe's general sales manager spoke no Spanish, the company's advertising agency had no connections in the country, and the relatively low per capita income and sparse population within easy range of the U.S. border seemed to add up to a fairly costly exploration. Moreover, although this also applied to Canada, the company had no idea where to find a marketing research agency which could operate overseas nor how it would know if any names it turned up were good or bad.

The general sales manager believed that Canada might be easier to in-

[2] *Baby and Child Care,* rev. ed. by Dr. Benjamin Spock (New York: Pocket Books, Inc.).

vestigate. English was widely spoken as one of the two official languages, although the part of Canada which probably was the best bet was French-speaking. This might not be too difficult, Wellbabe thought, since it could at least hope to find an English Canadian agency which might be able to carry on work in both languages.

THE CANADIAN MARKET

Before commissioning a study of any kind, the general sales manager did some preliminary reading on the Canadian market. He learned that more than 30% of all Canadian consumers were French-speaking, a percentage that jumps to about 80% in metropolitan Montreal. Moreover, the proportion of French-speaking consumers was increasing at a higher rate than was that of English Canadians.

The French-Canadian was described [3] as "practical, logical, thrifty, somewhat dubious, and sometimes suspicious . . . Fundamentally he is a religious man, and deeply religious. He does not change in thoughts or habits easily. . . . He is set in his morals. He frowns on risqué art in advertising."

While most of the French were located in the province of Quebec, sizeable groups were also to be found in eastern Ontario, Manitoba, and the Maritime Provinces. Wherever they were, the French clung tenaciously to their language and their religion.

The general sales manager believed that Montreal, while it presented a significant concentration of population, might not be as easy a market to penetrate as would be other parts of Quebec. It seemed to him that the small towns and villages and the surrounding farm areas of rural Quebec would offer more to Wellbabe. Retail outlets still were of the general store variety, doctors were fewer than in cities, and the innate conservatism of the peasant helped to make mothers more apt to treat their children themselves.

It seemed that the Church played a particularly important role in the French villages. The curé or parish priest was considered to be the most influential man in the community, with the mayor or the largest farmer next in status. The population was almost entirely Roman Catholic, as were the people of Puerto Rico and Mexico, and the general sales manager, while he did not associate this with the sale of his products, knew that Roman Catholics did have large families and that the families were of great interest to the Church.

MARKETING RESEARCH PROBLEMS

The very qualities which made the French-Canadians possible customers for Wellbabe—conservatism and traditional—also stood in the way of evaluating their market potential. One of the general sales manager's

[3] *Advertising Age* (Jan. 15, 1963), p. 232.

sources said, about the French, "he looks upon anyone who does not speak French like a French-Canadian as *un Anglais*—an Englishman. For the French-Canadian, an American is always *un Americain* . . . You might think the French-Canadian likes the Irish, because the Irish are Catholics. It is quite the opposite, since he is convinced that a Catholic who does not speak French is a pretty bad buy, indeed. Perhaps you imagine that he looks kindly upon a Frenchman from France. There again you're wrong. He dislikes him thoroughly, and usually refers to him as *un importe* or plainly *un maudit français*." [4]

While the Wellbabe management accepted that Americans were generally well conditioned to the idea of marketing research, thanks to A. C. Nielsen, the Gallup Poll and the general cultural pattern, the general sales manager was inclined to doubt that this would be true of French-Canadians. He was not at all sure that mail questionnaires, interviewers or other devices enquiring into what they might consider their personal business would turn up anything useful in the way of information. However, before Wellbabe did go into the French-Canadian market, it plainly needed considerable data. The general sales manager wondered how this could be secured, whether through somebody in his own organization, through an American research agency, the advertising agency, or help from Canadian practitioners.

QUESTIONS

1. How can the Wellbabe general sales manager find out about marketing research organizations in foreign markets?
2. What method should the company employ to develop data on the rural French-Canadian market?
3. What information should it seek on which to base a decision?

5

RENOWN PRODUCTS COMPANY (I)

Organization for Export Marketing

The Renown Products Company, located in Kirksville, Missouri, manufactured compressors for use in refrigerators, freezers, and air conditioning equipment.

Apart from sales to original equipment manufacturers, the Renown Products Company had an extensive system of distributors ensuring the availability of both parts and service for the compressors throughout the

[4] *Advertising Age* (Jan. 15, 1963), p. 233.

United States. In addition, the Renown dealers actively sought sales of Renown compressors as replacements for other brands of compressors which became worn out through years of service.

It was difficult to become established as a supplier to original equipment manufacturers, because they generally did not favor using a brand of compressor in their refrigerators and air-conditioning equipment unless the compressor manufacturer had a well organized system of distributors and dealers; and it was hard to organize such a system without the products first being used by the original equipment manufacturers. However, Renown was gradually overcoming this handicap. In 1946 the company bought a war-surplus factory for about 10¢ on the dollar. This advantageous purchase, together with aggressive management, resulted in a rapid growth of domestic sales.

The concern's major competitor was the Exeter Machine Company, which was long established in the field, and sold compressors to many of the major original equipment manufacturers. These customers generally used Exeter compressors to the exclusion of all other brands. By mid-1952 Exeter and Renown together accounted for about 90% of the compressors produced by independent manufacturers in the United States, with Exeter outselling Renown about 3 to 1.

Renown's main problem was to get its compressors used by the older and more conservative original equipment manufacturers. Renown's yearly sales were about $12,000,000 per year against about $36,000,000 for Exeter. Moreover, Exeter was doing about $4,800,000 per year in export business against Renown's $150,000. Exeter had a long-established built-in export department which had been headed for over 25 years by the same man. The export manager reported to the executive vice-president in charge of sales and was on a par with the domestic sales manager who also reported to the executive vice-president in charge of sales, Over this long period, Exeter had built up a well established system of dealers throughout the world.

Renown, on the other hand, had no overseas distributors; therefore it had been unable to get its compressors used for any of the export orders obtained by United States original equipment manufacturers. Many of the latter did a large overseas business.

The $150,000 in export sales which Renown obtained during the entire year of 1951 came without any solicitation on the company's part. The president and other executives of Renown were too heavily occupied with the problems resulting from the company's rapid growth to give any attention to establishing overseas distribution. By 1952, however, the President of Renown decided it was absolutely necessary for the firm to have an export program and to attempt to get its share of this business.

In 1946 Mr. James McKenna had joined the Renown Products Company as a sales trainee straight out of high school. He progressed very rapidly in the sales department, for, in addition to his natural talents, he had achieved a good understanding of the mechanical and engineering problems faced by the management of Renown. He was experienced in sales both to the original equipment manufacturers and to Renown's domestic distributors and dealers. Since he had also more or less "grown" with the company, he was familiar with all the company's problems, policies, and personnel.

The president of Renown was thinking about appointing Mr. McKenna as a special assistant to the general sales manager. However since the president was also concerned about the company's lack of an export program, he decided to talk with Mr. McKenna informally to see if he might be interested in taking over this particular branch of the company's business. The president had not come to any decision on this matter but was just taking preliminary sounding. When Mr. McKenna was first approached by the president on this subject, he evinced great enthusiasm in regard to the possibility of his taking over and developing the company's export trade. The president then clearly told Mr. McKenna that he had not yet made any decision on this matter, and asked him which position he would choose if he had the chance of becoming either the export manager or an assistant to the general sales manager, provided that both jobs paid the same salary. Mr. McKenna declared his overwhelming preference was to be the export manager.

Mr. McKenna was 24 years old. He spoke no foreign languages and had never travelled in any foreign country. He had no prior experience or background in export business.

QUESTIONS

1. Should the president appoint Mr. James McKenna as the company's export manager? Explain.
2. In addition to his problem regarding the selection of an export manager, the president was concerned over whether his company's export department should be located at some major trading and seaport city such as San Francisco, or New York, or whether it should be located at the factory in Kirksville, Missouri. What location should have been chosen? Explain.

6

RENOWN PRODUCTS COMPANY (II)

Export Policies

In mid-1952 the president of Renown appointed James McKenna as his new export manager.

The president asked the new export manager to make a study for one to two months on the question of how the new department should be set up, and to submit his recommendation to the president.

QUESTIONS

1. If you were the new export manager what would be your recommendations to the president regarding the organization of the new export department?
2. What steps would you take and what policies would you adopt in relation to the establishment of business with overseas countries?

7

RENOWN PRODUCTS COMPANY (III)

Channels of Distribution Overseas: Combination Export Managers and Independent Exporters

Mr. James McKenna spent two months investigating export operations in various companies and how these might best be modified or adapted to Renown.[1] The result of his studies and conversations with the company's president and general sales manager had led to the establishment of a built-in export department. Its staff consisted of McKenna, a clerk-assistant with experience in foreign trade documentation and correspondence, and a typist.

Renown's new export manager began with an analysis of the few orders the company had received in the past few years, coupled with a survey of Department of Commerce and other figures on overseas markets for Renown's products. As quickly as possible, McKenna made trips to those areas where he figured business could be most readily secured. He recognized, however, that sheer physical limitations of time and space made it impossible for him to cover the world single-handed. Accordingly, the company used other sources of overseas sales in addition to McKenna's department.

By mid-1954 Renown's export sales were running at the rate of about $1,500,000 yearly. The export manager had found the most successful type of overseas distribution to be through having one large distributor (or more in larger countries) invest in a sizeable stock of Renown compressors and parts. These were made available to dealers set up by the distributor throughout his territory.

McKenna, in his own opinion, had established satisfactory distributorships in only one-third of the markets that actively imported compressors from the United States. Since labor cost in compressors was only about 15% of the factory selling price, both Exeter's (Renown's major American competitor) and Renown's export prices were approximately 20% under

[1] For the events leading up to this case, see Renown Products Company (I) and (II).

any British, German, or Japanese competition. Renown's domestic sales had increased 50% between 1952 and mid-1954. It was enjoying the benefits of mass production in its Kirksville, Missouri plant and was building about 4,800 compressors daily.

Through the services of an independent export broker, Renown was selling about $250,000 worth of compressors per year to a Japanese manufacturer and to a Japanese distributor. This independent export broker had been told by the export manager that he was temporarily free to solicit business from any of the other Far Eastern countries.

Renown had not been able to secure any business from the Philippines which, according to U.S. Government figures, was annually importing about $300,000 worth of compressors. McKenna believed that all this business, or the significant part of it, had been going to Exeter.

Twice during the preceding two years, Renown had sent one of its own factory salesmen on a trip through the Far East, including the Philippines. While this man had had no particular training in export marketing—and McKenna had recognized the danger in using him—he had been successful in obtaining good distributors in several areas. In the Philippines, however, he had been unable to secure representation for the company. Similarly, the independent export broker who had been so successful in Japan had not been able to obtain satisfactory orders from the Philippines.

A Seattle exporter who specialized in the shipment of parts for freezing, refrigerating, and air conditioning equipment to the Far East approached the Renown company and asked to be given, over a period of one year, the exclusive sales representation for Renown in the Philippines. This exporter asked the company to quote him the lowest possible costs to which he would add his own mark-up so as to cover profit and selling expenses.

When McKenna had independent exporters attempt to set up distributors for Renown in foreign markets, he had very little success. He had been most successful when he, or one of the factory's own salesmen, set up distributors directly or through a local selling agent, whom he selected to represent the firm. However, the independent Seattle exporter pointed out that each year he shipped over $1,200,000 worth of parts for freezing, refrigerating, and air conditioning equipment to the Philippines, that he maintained five native salesmen of his own in Manila, and that he was well known in the import trade in that country.

Investigation by McKenna indicated the truth of the exporter's claims. However, McKenna was uncertain whether long-run policy objectives of Renown, which essentially were toward maintaining its own export department for operation in as many markets as possible, would be met by using the Seattle exporter. Since this man was buying for his own account, control of his operations by Renown would be difficult. Giving him territorial representation in the Philippines, even for so short a period as one year, might make it hard for Renown to enter that market on its own at some future date.

On the other hand, McKenna had to be aware of the limitations imposed on him by the nature of the organization. He had increased the size of his department somewhat since its formation, and he had gradually added salesmen with export training, taking over some of Renown's domestic salesmen who were keen on overseas marketing. This still did not give him international coverage in as much depth as he would have wished. He wondered if, for some markets, he might seek to use the services of a combination export manager, rather than an independent exporter such as the man in Seattle or the broker who had sold to Japan. If he were to use such a representative, it would only be until sales expanded to the point in the particular market where Renown could take them over directly.

QUESTIONS

1. What decision should Mr. McKenna have made regarding the request received from the Seattle exporter to represent Renown exclusively for one year in the Philippines?
2. Where the export manager worked with independent exporters (as in the sales to Japan), how should he have supported their activities?
3. What are the pros and cons of the use of combination export managers for Mr. McKenna?
4. What should McKenna seek to have included in any agreement for the use of combination export managers, in the event that he decides to use them?

8

RELIANCE HARDWARE MANUFACTURING COMPANY

Appointment of Overseas Agents

The Reliance Hardware Manufacturing Company was an old established firm with factory and main offices located in Cincinnati, Ohio. It was the leading American manufacturer in its particular field, which consisted of specialized hardware items. These were distributed through warehouses located in 12 major cities throughout the United States.

The factory branch warehouses supplied its distributors, who in turn supplied the retailers. Each factory branch warehouse had a large inventory on hand for immediate shipment of distributors' orders. The branch warehouses were supplied by periodic carload shipments from Cincinnati. Each warehouse employed from two to four salesmen who called on the distributors and did missionary work among the retailers.

The factory branch managers were on a guaranteed salary-plus-bonus basis and therefore were most careful of the costs incurred by their respective branch operations as, the more "profit" their branch made, the greater was their year-end bonus.

The Los Angeles branch manager supplied the territory of southern California, southern Nevada, and Arizona. For over 35 years, the New York branch supplied the states of New York and Connecticut, plus most of the export shipments. The export business was handled by four different export commission houses located in New York City. One export commission house handled Central and South America, another Europe, another Africa, and another the Middle and Far East. Alaska was handled by the factory's Seattle branch, Hawaii by its San Francisco branch, Mexico by its Dallas branch, and Canada by its subsidiary Canadian company.

The four export commission houses in New York City were invoiced by the Reliance New York Branch at the domestic distributor's prices less a 10% discount. The commission houses in turn invoiced their overseas distributors at the domestic distributor prices and retained the 10% as their profit for financing and selling the order. In addition, these four export commission houses handled other non-competing hardware items which gave their respective overseas distributors a rather large line of hardware items from which to choose. In the smaller countries these New York export commission houses worked through local commission agents. In the larger countries they maintained their own sales offices with their salesmen on a guaranteed salary and commission basis.

Reliance had an executive vice president in charge of all domestic and export sales. One of his assistants was in direct charge of all the factory branch warehouses. Therefore, company export policy was determined by the executive vice president, by his assistant in charge of the factory branches, and by the New York branch manager in consultation with the four New York export commission houses.

For years the Los Angeles branch manager had tried to get the factory to add the Far Eastern countries to his territory, but since this would have meant taking territory away from the New York branch manager, the Los Angeles manager had never been successful in his attempts. Also, it would have been awkward for the Los Angeles branch to service a New York exporter's orders intended for shipment to the Far East.

The Los Angeles branch manager was approached by a Los Angeles export commission house which specialized in the exportation of hardware items to Far Eastern countries. This Los Angeles exporter explained the following:

(1) Shipments from Los Angeles to the Far East generally took 3 weeks time, as contrasted with 5 weeks time from New York to the Far East.

(2) The Los Angeles exporter sold only hardware items, while the New York commission house presently handling Reliance's line in the Far East sold textiles, liquors, clothing, etc., plus acting as a large scale importer of raw materials from the Orient.

(3) The Los Angeles exporter himself made yearly trips to the Far East, visited all the hardware importers, as well as his salesmen, etc., and by his concentrating only on hardware items had built up a fair sized business since he formed his company in 1946.

The Los Angeles manager explained to the Los Angeles exporter about his desire to have the Far East added to his territory but of his inability to achieve this goal in the past. The Los Angeles exporter also had approached the New York branch manager several times during the past few years asking that his company be appointed dual export agent for the Far East along with the New York commission house. The New York branch manager turned down this request. He had been the branch manager for 35 years and was certain that his four New York export commission houses were obtaining the maximum business from their markets for Reliance.

The Los Angeles exporter was convinced that he could increase Reliance's present business in the Far East by at least $200,000 per year. He soon convinced the Los Angeles manager of this fact, as the latter checked with several of the Los Angeles exporter's other domestic hardware suppliers, and learned that he had done an outstanding sales job for them in the Orient.

QUESTION

As Reliance's Los Angeles Branch Manager, how would you analyze this problem? What would you do, and why?

9

SMITHERS PAINT COMPANY (I)

A Foreign Distributor's Request for Representation

The Smithers Paint Company was a manufacturer and distributor of paints and related products, with gross sales of $80,000,000 annually and export sales of $1,000,000. Smithers followed a policy of concentrating its export market in the Far East and Latin America. General breakdown of annual export sales figures was: Far East $500,000; Latin America $300,000; Miscellaneous (South Pacific) $200,000.

A wholly-owned sales corporation located in the Colon Free Zone of Panama solicited orders in Latin America and billed customers directly. The orders so received were relayed to the home export office in San Francisco, and shipment of goods was made directly to the customers. In Mexico and the Philippines, factories were licensed to manufacture Smithers products and distribution was accomplished through local agents. These plants had been set up to enable continued operations in these markets which were closed off to Smithers by prohibitive import restrictions. The home office was concerned only with supplying raw materials and technical advice to these factories. In Guam, Korea, and Okinawa, exclusive agents had agreements to distribute Smithers products. Some other areas of the Far East had multiple, non-exclusive agents. These agents made orders directly on the export department of the home office, paid for and received goods on their own accounts, and distributed them to retailers in their local areas. Occasionally Smithers products were shipped to other parts of the world, particularly to India and Pakistan, mainly as a result of bids awarded for government construction contracts.

Terms of sale to regular established distributors were 2% cash (letter of credit) or 30 day sight draft. For new or unproven accounts, terms of sale were United States dollars irrevocable confirmed letter of credit without recourse. Smithers used the Wells Fargo Bank or the Bank of America for its overseas transactions.

Organizationally, the export department at the San Francisco home office contained the export manager, a specialist for Latin American accounts, his assistant, a specialist for Far Eastern accounts, his assistant, a documentation specialist, a secretary, and an export packer. The department's function was mainly to service orders. Invoicing, credit, accounting, shipping and manufacturing were handled through regular domestic departments.

Smithers was satisfied with its specialization of market area and with its distributive setup. There were no plans at the moment for expansion into other areas of the world. However, one day the export manager received an unsolicited request from a firm in Beirut, Lebanon, which desired to distribute Smithers products. This letter was especially surprising as Smithers had not considered that there was a Middle East demand for paints at the present time.

ARAB KHMAN
COMMERCE—COMMISSION—REPRESENTATIONS
BEIRUT, LEBANON

Smithers Paint Company
San Francisco
California

Dear Sirs:

We are very pleased to inform you that we are looking for a good manufacturer that will be able to supply us with our requirements for a variety of paints (enamel, lacquer, primer surfacers, etc.) and shall certainly be glad to enter into business relation with your esteemed firm.

We wish to establish sound and lasting business relations with you and feel confident that an interesting amount of business will soon be secured to our reciprocal advantage.

In case you are interested in our inquiry, we would like you to send us by return, catalog, samples, last quotations, discount arrangements, together with any useful information you think we need for a start.

We are very anxious to hear from you soon favourably and trust that we could be able to enter into very pleasant business relations with your esteemed firm for mutual benefit.

Looking forward to hearing from you soon, we beg to remain

Yours faithfully,

(Signed) Arab Khman

Since price sheets, discount arrangements, and samples were not released indiscriminately, this letter of inquiry was answered as follows:

SMITHERS PAINT COMPANY
PAINT PRODUCTS—WALLPAPER—MIRRORS—WHITE LEAD
SAN FRANCISCO, CALIFORNIA

Mr. Arab Khman
Beirut, Lebanon

Dear Mr. Khman:

Thank you for your letter of ______, in which you express your interest in Smithers paints. We find your proposal very interesting and would appreciate further information regarding your firm and the kind of business in which you are engaged. Do you now handle a line of paints?

In order to make an intelligent approach to a market area new to us, we also need additional information regarding the market itself. What quantities of paint are being imported into Lebanon now? From what countries? What brands of U.S.-manufactured paints, if any, are being imported? What are their quality and approximate selling prices? What particular types of finish do you feel there is a market for in Lebanon—house paints, interior and exterior; varnish, enamel, etc; aircraft finishes, marine finishes, industrial finishes, maintenance finishes? In what manner do you think you can best handle the distribution of Smithers paints? Approximately what quantities do you estimate you can sell the first year?

Information of the type indicated above is of the greatest importance to us if we are to provide you with intelligent assistance, such as prices and descriptive material. Any other information or observation you may care to make regarding the potential market for paints in Lebanon will be very much appreciated. Also, please provide us a list of your usual banking and commercial references.

Thank you very much for your interest in Smithers paints. We are enclosing, for your information, a booklet on "How Smithers Paints are Made."

We look forward to hearing from you further.

Very truly yours,

____
Export Manager

EM/as

This in turn was answered as follows:

Smithers Paint Company
San Francisco, California

Gentlemen:

We thank you for your letter of ______, and have the pleasure to enclose, herewith, a list of well-known brands.

In our market, there are two different retailers, the first one purchases and sells only: house paint, interior and exterior; varnish, etc., selling price 350-450 Lebanese piasters per quart (1 U.S. $ = 320-325 L. P.). Customs duty: 35% to protect national factories. Customers request high quality with a large choice of colors ready to apply.

The second one purchases and sells exclusively lacquer, primer, surfacers, and all kinds of car paint. Selling price: 700-900 L. P. per quart. Customs duty: 25% (here no national factories producing this article). In this line retailers require the highest quality possible and do not pay too much attention to colors because they are in a position to reproduce with a few color bases (black, white, red, etc.) the required color.

The most important brands are: SLIK-UP, SIPES, ARMSTRONG, ACME, ARCO. These firms are represented by commission agents and retailers are aware of factory prices. For this reason, we are unable to import for our account and think that it will be better to handle on a commission basis in Lebanon and other parts of the Middle East where we have customers and good relations. We hope you understand our position.

Please note that Lebanon imports approximately 100-tons from all over the world, and particularly from the United States.

Now it is not easy to determine the quantities we can sell. As we have experience in this line, we are in a position to introduce your brand in the Middle East markets in a successful way and to realize an important turnover for our reciprocal advantage.

Concerning our firm we are pleased to inform you that we represent:

Jones Oil and Grease Co., Inc.
Oklahoma City, Oklahoma

Société Française des Freins
Hydrauliques
Saint Ouen, France

and for banking references you can contact: Banque de Syrie & Du Liban, Beirut; Banque Joseph Latit & Fils, Beirut.

Hoping to hear from you at your earliest convenience, we are

Yours very truly,

(Signed) Arab Khman

The Smithers Company up to the time of receipt of these letters had made no sales to the Middle East either to miscellaneous accounts or on government contracts. No studies had been made by Smithers on the potential market in the Middle East for its products. In recent months a salesman had made a good-will tour of Smithers' regular Far Eastern customers, and a consulting firm was employed at the time on a retainer basis to develop contacts for distributors in the Far East. The only information the Smithers Company had on the market in the Middle East and on the inquiring company is contained in the two letters, which are quoted verbatim except for disguised names.

QUESTION

What recommendations would you give for further action by the Smithers Company with regard to the Lebanese inquiry?

10

HOUSEHOLD PRODUCTS, INC. (I) *

Selection of an Advertising Agency for Europe

The potential growth of the European Common Market and the development of a considerable consumer goods market in both Common Market and European Free Trade Area countries, had aroused interest on the part of Household Products' management. The company, a medium-sized maker of food and household items in the U.S.A., had finally decided to manufacture and market some of its products in several European countries. Its only previous experience in Europe had been some sales through importers or brokers in the U.S., so Household had no significant knowledge of how to proceed.

Household did not intend, at least initially, to attempt sales of all its food and non-food lines in Europe. Investigation by the company's executives, its marketing-research department, and outside research consultants indicated that the best potential appeared to lie in three areas: frozen foods, packaged cake and other related mixes, and an all-purpose household liquid cleaner with which it had had great success in the United States. No final decisions had been made as to such things as the production of frozen meals as well as frozen fruits and vegetables, cake flavors, and the like.

A major question for resolution had to do with the selection of an advertising agency. Most of Household's products were sold at retail to consumers and the institutional market was not significant in its operations. The company relied heavily on the use of all types of advertising media, coupled with extensive in-store merchandising support. Marketing management worked closely with the advertising agencies employed, relied on them for many services, and thought of them as almost an extension of the company. However, management did not know what it should or could look for in a European agency, or whether it should seek to use an American, a European, or a combination agency.

* Fictitious name.

HOUSEHOLD PRODUCTS, INC.

Household Products, Inc. had been formed in 1927 as a merger of several smaller companies. These had been producers of packaged food items but, as time went on, Household had added some non-food items, such as cleaners.

Sales in 1962 were $322,780,126. Advertising expenditures were about $20,000,000 during that year. In terms of media employed, the company's expenses for advertising broke down as follows:

Newspapers	30.6%
Magazines	8.1
Radio	5.9
Television	16.8
Sampling, couponing, etc.	12.6
Outdoor	1.5
Trade papers	4.9
Other	19.6
Total	100.0%

The company's marketing organization was on a brand-manager basis. The food items were divided into two divisions and the non-food products made a third; each of these had a general manager. Under each general manager was a brand manager for a single product or, in some cases, for a group of products. The brand manager was responsible for overall marketing management for his brand or brands. He was given considerable latitude for determination of marketing strategy, sales policies, advertising and sales promotion and so forth, within the limits of policy established by corporate management. Each brand manager was directly responsible to the divisional general manager who, in turn, reported to and was also part of the corporate management group.

ADVERTISING AND SALES POLICIES AND PROCEDURES

Some of the Household brands were in actual competition with each other. To some extent, therefore, brand managers' performances were based not only on results in relation to competitors outside the Household company but also within. Corporate management set sales targets for each brand on an annual basis and a brand manager was judged on the way in which he met his targets. For some food items, targets had been at an average required level of a 10% increase in sales each year.

The company employed four advertising agencies, each of which had offices in several American cities and one of which had a Canadian operation, with offices in Montreal and Toronto. Advertising for those brands whose appropriations were handled by American agencies without Canadian offices was either placed directly in Canadian media or, in the case of some where Canadian sales were substantially above other Household products, through Canadian agencies in association with the U.S. firms.

Canadian advertising programs, whether placed through U.S. or Canadian agencies, tended to resemble American programs closely. The company's marketing management firmly believed that differences between the two markets were merely of degree. With intelligent adaptation, an advertisement which would move goods in New York would do so in Los Angeles, Chicago, Montreal, or Winnipeg. Since much of the Canadian population was located close to the international border, U.S. media, particularly radio and television stations, were widely accepted in Canada. In the case of network radio and television shows, which Household from time to time sponsored, the only change required usually was the substituting of Canadian-originated commercials if promotional details for retail stores were different in Canada.

Management did accept that, to reach the French-Canadian market, French-language advertisements had to be used. These, however, were translations of others which were designed to be used in English-language media. In order to be sure that the French copy would be acceptable, French-Canadian translators were employed by a Canadian advertising agency.

PROPOSED EUROPEAN MARKETING PROGRAMS

A number of factors had combined to encourage Household to enter the European consumer market. The European Common Market was one of these, although developments in early 1963 had aroused some apprehension on the part of the company as to the future trend of the ECM. It felt, however, that, regardless of the trend of the Common Market, consumer incomes and living standards in much of Europe would continue to improve.

Household Products had been quick to accept the importance of self-service retailing in the U.S., and its product-research groups had been particularly effective in the development of products and packages particularly suited to self-service stores and supermarkets. Self-service retailing in Europe, after a relatively slow start, especially in England, France, and Italy, had made considerable progress and seemed likely to make more. For this reason, the company reckoned that it might have some advantages over many European producers of competitive products who had not, it felt sure, adapted fully to what was something of a retail revolution.

Another factor encouraging Household to market in Europe was the increased use of television. Some countries did not permit commercial television, but the company's management believed that the increasing cost of television programming would, in time, result in some kind of commercial television in almost all countries. In addition to cost, some countries, such as Denmark and Sweden, were exposed to commercial television from neighboring countries and there was some likelihood that this kind of pressure would help to speed up the spread of commercial telecasting. Even in countries where commercial programs were forbidden, much of the program content was American and this, Household felt sure, would facilitate the sale of products with an American association.

Television was only one of a number of media used by Household and did not rank as its major medium in terms of costs. However, the company had been successful in sponsoring several shows which had secured extremely high ratings and had come to regard itself as a skilled employer of the medium. It believed that this know-how, combined with its experience in self-service stores, would help it obtain product recognition and acceptance fairly quickly.

Household did not intend trying to market in all of the Western European countries immediately. In England it proposed manufacturing through an English producer of non-competitive products which would give it time to develop plants of its own as it appraised the market. It planned to build a factory in The Netherlands to serve the Common Market countries and would export from England to the EFTA nations.

Brands sold in the United States numbered around two dozen, although the number fluctuated from time to time as old lines were dropped and new ones added. The company had not decided how many of these it would try to sell in Europe, but it did not anticipate marketing them all. It was also uncertain as to whether European tastes would prove sufficiently different from those of American consumers to warrant developing new products for particular parts of Europe.

SELECTION OF AN ADVERTISING AGENCY

Some disagreement had developed among the general managers as to the course to follow in finding an advertising agency in Europe. There was general agreement that a single agency would probably be best, at least until business grew to warrant sale of a large number of products on a heavy-volume basis. From this agency, the company would expect marketing assistance. This would include research, either directly or through specialized agencies. The agency would be expected to protect the company against ignorance of the laws governing advertising, packaging, and merchandising, which differed from country to country. Media familiarity would be an important requirement since Household had learned that, in many cases, European media do not provide accurate circulation information and this information might have to be secured indirectly by the agency and supported by judgment.

The company was not entirely certain about its general product philosophy. It knew that consumers in some parts of Canada and the U.S. differed in tastes from those in other parts—those in the western U.S., for example, drink more ground coffee than do Easterners, who are more apt to use instant coffee. Some of Household's management felt that taste differences would be much more widespread in Europe but others argued that the consumer-market development had worked for much homogenization of taste and only adaptation would be required. The advertising agency should be knowledgeable in this field also.

There appeared to be several paths which the company could follow in choosing an agency. The general manager of the prepared-foods division strongly argued that the company should approach one of its four American agencies to see if the firm would be interested in opening a service office in Europe to handle the Household account there. While billings would probably not be enough initially to support a large organization, several American agencies had gone into Europe on this basis and had then grown substantially, with other American accounts and with European clients. In the opinion of the general manager, use of an American agency with which the company was presently doing business meant understanding of its procedures, policies, and products, familiarity with its objectives, and mutual agreement between agency and client as to how Household's advertising, sales promotion, and marketing should be handled.

The general manager of the non-cooked-foods division differed with this view. He agreed that the American agency would have knowledge of Household's domestic operations but he felt that this would be outweighed by its ignorance of Europe. Such knowledge, he believed, could be obtained in one of two ways. The company could invite solicitation of its European business from any of the well-regarded American agencies which had several offices in Europe; these included McCann-Erickson, Young and Rubicam, BBDO, and others, and all were well-versed in European marketing. Alternatively, the company might look at an agency such as Grant, which emphasized international marketing particularly, unlike the others, which were primarily American-oriented. An international agency of this sort should not take too long to familiarize itself with Household, and it knew Europe. It might be that some of the Household domestic appropriation could be transferred to it, to ensure better work in Europe and perhaps in the U.S.

A third view was advanced by the general manager of the non-food division. He believed that the company should pick a European agency, and it had two possible choices open. It could select an agency with branches in various countries, or it could choose an agency which was a member of a larger group. CAMA (Continental Advertising and Marketing Agencies), for example, had members in Belgium, Denmark, Finland, France, Western Germany, Great Britain, Holland, Ireland, Italy, Norway, Sweden, Switzerland, and a New York office, and this was greater coverage than any other agency, either American or Continental, could provide. In either case, the European agencies claimed that they could provide the detailed, intimate knowledge of each European market which was necessary for success.

These agencies maintained that Europe could not be regarded as a common, relatively homogeneous market. Rather, they insisted, entering Europe to sell was to enter many markets and an American company needed the benefit of an over-all service of experts familiar with local conditions, with international training, and who could ensure that each advertising program in each country or city was properly suited to its peculiar market objectives. Only they could support the advertising program with the right kind of marketing guidance.

While these were the apparent choices open to Household, corporate management suggested to the division general managers that another possibility might develop. The company could divide its European advertising into two parts, giving one appropriation to a European agency and the other to an American-owned international agency. Then, presumably, the company could measure sales performance in each case and draw some conclusions as to which agency could do the better job.

Playing one agency against another was fairly common in the food-and-household-products industry, and was aided by the internal competition for brand success. Sales in Europe, however, did not in the immediate future warrant the same kind of brand-management organization. The company believed that it would utilize a general manager with overall marketing responsibility, that some trial and error in product introduction would be inevitable, and that its primary objective was to develop a marketing team. Most of the marketing positions would be staffed, initially at least, by Americans, and there seemed no doubt that these would have enough problems of adjustment, both to living conditions and to business, without throwing in internal competition. The marketing group might, as part of its job of entering a new and probably difficult market, be able to achieve objectives more quickly with only one advertising agency.

QUESTIONS

1. What factors should Household Products consider in selecting an advertising agency for Europe?
2. Which kind of agency should the company select? Why?
3. What should an American company marketing in Europe expect from an advertising agency? How should it ensure that it gets it?
4. Do you believe that "if it'll sell in New York, it'll sell in Paris?"

11

HOUSEHOLD PRODUCTS, INC. (II) *

Advertising, Sales Promotion, and Marketing Factors to Be Considered before Entering Europe

After serious consideration of the factors in the selection of an advertising agency for Europe, the management of Household Products, Inc. decided to pick an agency which was based in New York but had offices in London, Frankfort, Paris, and Rome. The agency had not been previously used by Household, since the company's agencies for its U.S. and Canadian business were all American, without international offices other than in Canada.

* Corporate and personal names fictitious. See Household Products, Inc. (I).

To some extent the choice of an agency might have been considered premature, for Household had not fully thought through its plans for marketing in Europe. It intended to manufacture in the United Kingdom through an existing manufacturer and it had planned to build a factory in The Netherlands to serve the Common Market. However, the difficulties imposed on the Common Market by General De Gaulle's rejection of the British bid for membership except on his own terms in early 1963 suggested that perhaps another look should be taken at the whole situation.

In the U.S., when the company proposed to bring out a new product, it had developed a specific procedure. Corporate management would be presented with a plan of attack, involving in considerable detail the reasons for believing that a market existed, the size of the potential market, the cost of securing it in terms of advertising, sales, and production expense, the advertising and sales promotion methods to be followed, and the plans for test marketing. Funds would then be allotted if the corporate management accepted the plan, or it would ask to have more information or to have changes made.

The company was not certain about the wisdom of this approach in Europe. It had decided to enter the market with three lines, frozen foods, packaged cake and related mixes, and an all-purpose liquid household cleaner, but it had not reduced its thinking to such specifics as the kinds and range of frozen foods to offer, the flavors for its mixes, or even the specific countries in which to sell these and the cleaner. In addition, it wanted to anticipate the possibility of expanding sales for all or as many of its American products as possible as time went on. A further complication in the mind of the company executive who was to head the European operation was that of the amount of modification or adaptation of Household products which would be required for the varied European consumer tastes.

To help clarify his thinking and aid in his presentation to corporate management, the executive turned to the advertising agency. He wrote to the account executive with whom he would be working as follows:

HOUSEHOLD PRODUCTS, INC.

Corporate Headquarters
Chicago, Illinois
March 27, 1963

Mr. Charles Montgomery
Barton, Young and Thompson, Inc.
222 Madison Avenue
New York 17, New York

Dear Mr. Montgomery:

Since we decided to go into European marketing and picked you as advertising agency for our operations there, things have changed somewhat and we are particularly concerned about what is likely to happen in the Common Market. However, we still feel that a big market for our products, food and non-food, exists, but, frankly, we are uncertain how to proceed. As you will recall, our agreement with you is based somewhat on potential, in that we are not yet in a position to determine an advertising appropriation for Europe and our use of your services will be on a fee basis. Essentially, we regard you as a marketing consultant and it is our plan to pick your brains to the ultimate possible.

To help me get things going, I would appreciate it if you would let me have your thoughts on how we might consider proceeding. Particularly, I need to know something about the possible approaches we might take, the kinds of markets which exist, and the ways in which to approach them. Please let me have a letter or memorandum about this as soon as you can.

Sincerely yours,

Walter Thornton

Within a fairly short time, Mr. Thornton received the following memorandum from Mr. Montgomery. Somewhat abridged, it read thus:

1. Market Entry

Essentially, there are two ways of entering a European market:

(i) A cosmetic client of ours did it by *saturation,* and, through the sheer weight of the offensive and follow-up support, has been extremely successful. This involved sewing up a near fool-proof distribution and sales force, swamping every available media relevant to the products, backing up advertising with elaborate display material, merchandising the product right through to the retail outlet, and, at least in the first six months, completely out-advertising and out-selling the competition. If a manufacturer can afford this kind of build-up, if he plans out and streamlines every detail in the operation—assuming that prior to introduction he has analyzed the market (in this case even lipstick colors were specially made up for the U.K.) and established the demand for the product, and determined the correct appeal to reach both trade and consumer—then there is no question as to the validity of the method for such medium-priced, fast-moving, heavy-demand items as lipsticks, powder, and other daily-use cosmetics, and for many products such as you sell here. It is a costly but fast method of establishing the company and its products quickly, breaching the market, and shearing off a sizeable share of market immediately as a base for long-term growth. Today such an operation would probably cost, at minimum, $200,000 in the U.K., $125,000 in Germany, $100,000 in France, and $25,000 in Belgium, for the initial six-month campaign, and would probably demand two-thirds as much again for the second half of the first year. Up to now there has been an element of gamble as well.

(ii) The alternative approach most favored is the "building-block" method. This is a long-term growth operation by which a segment of the market is tested, distribution built up, and retail demand created. The market is expanded area by area until full national distribution and sales are achieved. The advantages of this method are many but I would single out:

a. The risks involved are considerably reduced;

b. The mistakes made are less costly and can be more easily rectified as you go along;

c. The initial financial commitment is limited;

d. Finally, the commitment is small in the event that a total write-off is necessary, or you have to start over in a different direction.

Either area-by-area within any one country, or country-by-country within a total world market, this geographic growth recommends itself to the majority of U.S. companies. It is also, by comparison with the saturation method, extremely economical in cost. Some companies have started out in one country on as little as $2,000. Many companies which may have started out spending as much as 5%-8% of their sales dollar in advertising and sales promotion, five years later have reduced this to even less than 1%, paralleled by as steep a climb in sales growth.

On average, percentage of advertising costs to sales dollars stands around 2.5%. But you will appreciate the numerous factors that must be taken into account in each individual case to get that figure in its correct and profitable perspective.

I would conclude that, particularly in Europe, we are fast approaching the point where the gamble can be eliminated from the saturation method, and the slowness and conservatism of the building-block method can be replaced by a much surer dynamism.

2. Media and Markets

Just as it is possible to duplicate American campaigns in Canada, so with Europe there are campaigns that can be transported across the Atlantic with little or no change, but the converse is probably more prevalent today. The days are gone when you took an American ad and made it "European" by changing "miles" to "kilometres" and "gas" to "petrol." What many U.S. advertisers do is to lay out the broad dimensions of an advertising theme or campaign and then let the local office or agency in each country fill in the detail as dictated by the characteristics of the individual country. Others want their advertising to originate entirely in that country with certain fixed corporated factors being the only restriction. Attached are two case histories of two international advertisers who operate throughout the world—Philip Morris and Shell—one making extensive use of U.S. material or fairly tight adaptations, while the other goes in the other direction to build advertising campaigns country by country. [Cases not included for the sake of space. See *Advertising Age,* Apr. 16, 1962, pp. 52, 53, 54, 86, 87, 88.]

The following are some very general observations to give some idea of how the countries differ and some possible approaches to advertising that might be used.

U.K.: Probably the richest and most sophisticated market in Europe. Advertising to the trade through the grocery trade journals will be an integral part of the overall plan to build distribution. The change-over to supermarkets and self-service outlets is particularly evident in the U.K. and here point-of-sale plays an important role. But a good percentage of retail grocery store volume is still from independent shops as opposed to chain store volume.

To the consumer, four-color advertising in family magazines is important. Newspaper advertising only becomes truly valid and economical once national distribution is achieved, since the major newspapers are national, and local provincial city newspapers are useful only for local retail-store advertising.

TV is a major selling force in the U.K. and can be bought on a regional basis, but it is expensive. A public relations budget would be almost a must. In addition to usual PR activities, editorial in-print media would be invaluable, especially to introduce the product, and PR would be the best initial use of television, specifically in connection with cooking programs. There is no commercial radio available.

France: The toughest market in Europe. Retailing methods, particularly outside the main cities, are extremely primitive. Wholesalers and salesmen are all-powerful. There is a lot of resistance to new products, and in particular, considerable resistance may be felt against canned foods. There is a strong loyalty to the independent "shop around the corner" so that the problems of distribution are going to be considerable. Supermarkets and chains are making some dent, but nothing like that in England or Germany.

Good trade journals and family and general-consumer illustrated magazines are available. Commercial TV is not available inside France, but external French-language TV covers most of the country. However, it offers no local flexibility and would not be a primary consideration. Commercial radio, also available from outside France, would not deliver an appropriate audience.

The point at which print media (which would be the first consumer media selection) can profitably be used nationally is even more closely tied to the market situation and requirements than in any of the other countries. There is so little brand loyalty and awareness that unless consumer advertising and distribution, plus promotion at point of purchase, are closely coordinated, much of this advertising can be wasted.

The major effort initially will be in establishing some kind of distribution pattern.

Sweden: A very compact market in that the majority of the population is centered in a few large urban areas. A very sophisticated and aggressive country in terms of marketing. Some trade journals and good family magazines are available. There is no commercial TV or radio. Newspapers are not national, but a combination of three or four papers would supply national coverage with built-in regional flexibility.

Denmark: Similarly a very compact market. Trade media is available. There are family magazines. No commercial TV, but commercial radio is available and proves very successful for many consumer products. Like Sweden, Denmark is a very modern-minded nation in terms of the retail food business. The newspaper situation is the same as in Sweden.

Norway: Not quite so modern in retail methods and consumer demands as Denmark or Sweden, but the population pattern is much the same. The media availabilities are similar to Sweden and Denmark, but there is no commercial radio or TV.

Netherlands: Very modern country. The housewife has control of the money. Rising market for new products and new brands. Self-service outlets on the rapid increase. Trade magazines available. Print media are important, but one has to take into account very strict dualities of audience—Catholic and Protestant, socialist and conservative—which demand combination media for both audiences. This applies both to newspapers (city-wide circulations) and magazines (national). No commercial TV or radio available.

Belgium: High standard of living. Female influence very strong. Conservative country. Language is the problem here, involving dual media in all cases. Print media the only possibility—newspapers (city-wide circulations) and magazines (national).

Italy: Tremendous upsurge in family income and demand for new and better goods. Italian housewife rules the roost. American products tend to be well received. A very promotionally-receptive market. Some trade magazines are available. Chain stores and self-service outlets are on the increase. To the consumer, illustrated weekly magazines would be the first choice. Commercial TV is very important, but also very limited in availability. Newspapers would not be a primary medium.

The significant factor in Italy is that the densest population, with the most money, influencing all other areas, is in the industrial northern part of Italy.

Germany: Immense prosperity and very aggressive market methods, much on U.S. lines. The growth of vast combines and cooperatives and the influence of supermarkets and self-service chains are the significant factors in Germany, accounting for the majority volume in grocery sales.

Because of centralization of distribution, it is a fact that 38 successful calls in Germany will give you something like 80-85% distribution throughout 185,000 retail outlets.

Consumer advertising support is essential. Women's magazines and general illustrated weeklies and monthlies are influential and carry high-rated leadership. Newspaper readership is strong, although no national coverage is available. A combination of three or four will give you national coverage. TV is a very significant factor, but restricted availabilities and little flexibility, plus cost, discount TV, except to the largest national advertisers.

I hope this will be helpful in your planning.

QUESTIONS

1. Which of the approaches outlined by the agency executive should Household Products follow in entering European marketing? Why?
2. Assume that you are concerned with product management responsibility for one of the product groups to be marketed—frozen foods, cake and other mixes, all-purpose liquid household cleaner—and that discretion as to countries, advertising appropriations, and media selection, and other related factors are largely assigned to you, subject to top management approval. How would you proceed?

3. What additional information should Household obtain before attempting to make final its European marketing programs?
4. Select one product and one country and discuss the kind of advertising copy and media which you would consider most effective for Household.

12

BURROUGHES WELCOME DARAPRIM

Adapting Advertising Copy for an African Market

Mr. Charles H. F. Cruttenden, director of Albert Pemberton, Ltd., an English advertising agency, was commissioned to develop advertising for Daraprim, an anti-malarial medicine. Burroughes Welcome wanted to market this product in Nigeria, where pidgin-English is widely spoken.

Writing in a magazine about the problems of the campaign, Mr. Cruttenden had this to say:

> The west coast of Africa used to be known as the "white man's grave." It was the grave of many a black man as well. Gradually over the years the situation improved, but even today something like 50 per cent of infant mortality alone is accounted for by malaria.
>
> Our client Burroughes Welcome has made big strides in tropical medicines. In fact, it is in the forefront of this science throughout the world. But the densely populated west coast of Africa presented very special selling and distribution problems, despite the fact that Burroughes Welcome has a product which, if taken regularly, will prevent malaria.
>
> The problems were to market this product, to tell the teeming masses about it, and to get them to take it regularly. "Take it once a week or every seven days" means little to the happy-go-lucky, pidgin-English-speaking African.
>
> These people are simple, unsophisticated, charming, and have short memories. They live in the towns and the bush villages. They are the sort of people whom you ask to "bring some mangoes to my house tomorrow" and they will say "yes, sah." You could also say to them, "Bring me some mangoes yesterday" and the answer, as likely as not, would be "yes, sah."
>
> Daraprim is one of the best anti-malarials—though there are others. However, to be effective it must be taken once a week. To tell these people about Daraprim and to get into their minds the vital necessity of taking it every seven days was the task we faced.

As Mr. Cruttenden pointed out, his agency "needed a memorable, straightforward, simple slogan" that would remind these "unsophisticated, charming people" of the necessity to take the drug regularly. In addition to a slogan, Mr. Cruttenden had to decide on the kind of copy appeal that should be used.

QUESTIONS

1. What kind of copy appeal would you recommend for print media or radio commercials for the sale of Daraprim in Nigeria?
2. Devise a slogan for Daraprim which you think would be effective.
3. What characteristics of the Nigerian market would you think significant or wish to know more about in developing an advertising program?

13

THE OKINAWA CAMPAIGN (III)

Meeting Competition through Advertising and Sales Promotion

The initial order received by Automotive Exports, Inc.* from the Ryukyu Trading Company [1] in Okinawa was followed by others. Accordingly, the company decided to enter the Okinawa market as aggressively as possible, and Raymond Dekker, its general manager, took stock of some of the problems.

A major obstacle to increased business was competition from both American and Japanese products. Factories on the main islands of Japan did not produce machined automotive parts, since they lacked a mass market to support local production and distribution of the many different replacement parts for American-made cars, such as gears and axles. However, the proximity of the Japanese manufacturers to the natural rubber supplies of the Far East enabled them to engage in sharp price competition on tires and batteries.[2]

As a rule, Japanese export prices for tires and batteries, of the same size and specifications as corresponding American products, were about 5 percent below the American export price. This was significant, since a 5 percent price difference at the manufacturers' level was often the equivalent of 15 to 20 percent at the retail level, depending upon the pricing policies, freight charges, and other aspects of business for the manufacturers, wholesalers, and retailers involved.

To compete specifically in the field of tires and batteries, Dekker considered the idea of advertising in the Okinawa market to build up buyers' confidence in the superiority of American tires and batteries. He also gave some thought to cutting prices. However, he preferred not to do this, since

* Names of persons and firms fictitious.

[1] See The Okinawa Campaign (I) and (II).

[2] Tires and batteries accounted for approximately $250,000 of the annual $450,000 volume of sales of automotive parts in the Okinawa market.

Automotive already was operating on a very close margin for tires and batteries. Dekker was sure that, as a result of superior American production methods and materials, tires and batteries sold by his company were of better quality than those of Japanese manufacture.

A second major problem was the strong buyer desire for so-called "genuine parts." This was considered to be a serious problem since Mr. Dekker believed that Okinawa wholesalers, retailers, and consumers thought of "genuine parts" as being inherently superior to any private or lesser known brands. "Genuine parts" were those which formed part of the original equipment of a vehicle in most cases, and were either sold under the vehicle manufacturer's name or under those of well-known American makers of vehicle parts which formed original equipment.

The beliefs of the Okinawa sellers and consumers were not founded on fact. Many private-brand automotive replacement parts were technically equal to genuine parts in every way. Both were made to the same specifications, often from the same dies, and in some cases by the same manufacturer, although sold under different names. The problem, however, was to promote this fact among the Okinawan trade.

Several methods of doing this were considered. Among them were the possibility of advertising to the trade and to consumers; personal visits by Automotive representatives to the offices of the dozen or so wholesalers who purchased through the Ryukyu Company; missionary work by these representatives with dealers of importance in the market. A fourth alternative of interest to the company was to raise the prices of Automotive's private-brand lines to equal those of genuine parts. This, it was thought, might avoid an appearance of cheapness on the part of the lines offered by Automotive.

QUESTIONS

1. How should Mr. Dekker deal with competition from Japanese makers of tires and batteries?
2. What advertising policies should Automotive adopt in this market? What objectives should it have?
3. What distributive and sales promotion policies should the company adopt?
4. Should the company raise prices of its private-brand lines in Okinawa?

14

FAR EAST REPRESENTATIVES, INC.

Policy on Unprofitable Lines

Far East Representatives, Inc. was an automotive parts exporting company [1] located in Los Angeles. It was established in 1946 by Mr. Edward Sinclair. The company sold in a number of Far East markets, including: Japan, the Philippines, Indonesia, Thailand, Singapore, and Hong Kong.

During the scramble for markets in the immediate post-war period, the company undertook to sell products in whatever dollar amount and in whatever market it could reach in the Far East. The management of the company felt that such a policy was justified in view of the strong competition it was facing. In eight years F.E.R. grew to be one of the leading exporters of automotive parts to the Far East. However, during the latter part of 1953 and the first part of 1954, Mr. Sinclair realized that there were several areas of marketing policy which required reexamination in the light of the growth of the company's activities and the change in the nature of its competition. After some examination of the matter, Mr. Sinclair was able to outline what he considered to be four basic problems, in regard to marketing policies, which had arisen since the company's establishment in 1946.

The first of these problems dealt with the matter of *highly competitive items*. Highly competitive items were defined as those lines of parts, or individual parts, in which the company faced very sharp price competition from other exporters in its foreign markets. Obviously, in such a case it was very difficult for F.E.R. to obtain a margin of profit sufficient to cover the cost of the operation.

A specific example of such a situation was the following: A United States domestic manufacturer, the X Company, manufactured and exported to most of F.E.R.'s markets a line of king-bolt assemblies. The domestic price of the X Company for quantity orders of these king-bolt assemblies was \$2.70 each, less small trade cash discounts—usually 2 or 3%; this gave a domestic unit price of at least \$2.60 plus a share of the freight. All such assemblies were sold f.o.b. X Company's plant in St. Louis, Missouri. However, the X Company, in order to achieve certain production economies, had arrived at an export policy whereby its king-bolt assemblies were sold in overseas markets, including the Far East, at a price of \$2.20 plus freight and other charges. The added volume made possible by these overseas sales, added to domestic sales, enabled the X Company to achieve a low per-unit cost of production. The overseas selling

[1] For some domestic companies F.E.R. was the exclusive overseas selling agent, but for other companies F.E.R. was only one of several export agents used.

price of the king-bolt assemblies manufactured by the X Company obviously was much lower than that which could be offered by any other American company dealing either exclusively in foreign markets or with a domestic market which would not provide a volume of business sufficient to match the X Company's per-unit costs.

Naturally, F.E.R. had a hard time meeting this type of competition, by the X Company on king-bolt assemblies, and by some other companies in a number of other parts lines. Nonetheless, the company was faced with the problem of supplying its indent agents and their customers in the Far East with a complete line of automotive replacement parts. The apparently easy solution of simply cutting out such a line was of doubtful value. A customer, unable to obtain a complete line of automotive parts from F.E.R.'s representative would be tempted to deal with another factory representative who could supply him with a complete line of parts. Therefore, it was not thought feasible for the company to drop entirely the carrying of king-bolt assemblies (for example) from its automotive parts line.

F.E.R. was currently charging a price of $2.50 plus appropriate freight charges for king-bolt assemblies. Of this price, 10% represented the profit commission, that is gross margin, to F.E.R.; $2.25 was the price paid to the domestic manufacturer. The management of F.E.R. had contacted the manufacturer several times in an attempt to get him to lower his price. However, the manufacturer's reply was that he did not have as large a domestic market volume as the X Company and therefore had higher per-unit costs and a much tighter profit margin on sales. The X Company was able to make a good profit on domestic sales partly as a result of dumping overseas.[2] F.E.R.'s supplier did not feel that dumping would increase volume enough to develop significant production economies.

The second problem area in regard to unprofitable lines concerned the matter of *genuine parts*. There were about 700 basic automobile parts manufactured in the United States. One company may manufacture pistons exclusively, another may specialize on engine bearings, and so forth. Many of these basic parts manufacturers sold their products to General Motors, Ford, and Chrysler Corporation. In turn, Ford, G.M., and Chrysler packaged them under their own labels, and sold them to their domestic dealers as "genuine parts."

Overseas, the export departments of the Big Three sold these genuine parts at a higher than net domestic price to their franchised dealers; and usually in a small country like the Philippines, Ford, G.M., or Chrysler each had only one or two dealers. These are the only ones in that market who can buy their so-called genuine parts direct from the basic manufacturers' export department. However, the Big Three distributed their genuine parts throughout the United States through their own car dealers, and the domestic car dealers had many incentive and volume rebates on these genuine parts that were not customarily enjoyed by the overseas distributors. As a result, to increase their parts volume, it was quite common for

[2] Such "dumping practice" ordinarily was not objected to by foreign countries, which, in most cases, had no domestic competing manufacturers to protect and hence had no anti-dumping laws affecting automotive parts.

Big Three car dealers in seaport cities such as New York, New Orleans, and San Francisco, to cultivate business for such parts among exporters. These genuine parts were usually sold by the car dealers on a cost plus basis to a domestic exporter who would then sell them overseas with as much profit as possible. These parts were actually in competition with the parts sold under the brand of the basic parts manufacturer, but because the "genuine parts" had passed through more hands, their prices were considerably higher. There were numerous domestic car dealers selling these genuine parts; there were numerous exporters buying them; and each exporter had various overseas representatives or sales agents offering them for his account. As a result, there was a great deal of competition in the export market in "genuine parts." There was no such thing as a market price on such parts, and prices varied according to the market, the customer, and the size of the order.

The third major problem which faced the company in regard to unprofitable lines was that of *non-exclusive lines.* This was a bit different from the problems posed by highly competitive items and genuine parts.

Non-exclusive lines in auto parts sold overseas were usually purchased from small to medium-sized factories that used the shotgun approach to overseas distribution and would take on a number of representatives in order to raise their sales volume. These smaller factories ordinarily had established export prices from which they allowed domestic exporters a commission of 10 to 15%. The exporters were requested to quote these prices to their overseas customers. The problem that arose in the sale of non-exclusive lines was that, as sales increased, the successful exporter was subjected to more and more competition from rivals who also had these product lines available to them. This made it very difficult to build up business by concentrating on the promotion of non-exclusive lines, and was a temptation to sharp price-cutting or secret rebates. The crux of the problem, however, was that such lines often represented F.E.R.'s best source of supply from the standpoint of quality or price or both.

The fourth marketing problem confronting F.E.R. was that of unprofitable *small orders,* often referred to by the staff as "those —— —— small orders!" It was almost as costly for F.E.R. to handle the assembly and documentation of a $20 order as it was for a $200 or $20,000 order. Each separate order required licenses, purchase orders to the supplier, receipt of the shipment from the supplier, booking of steamer space, export documentation, financing arrangements, bill of lading, insurance policy, etc. Mr. Sinclair realized that it was not just low-value, or low-volume, or small-size items that accounted for this situation. It was the combination of all three of these factors over and over again in separate orders that caused the problem.

It was common for the Company to receive small orders when it was just getting established in a new market because the customers had never dealt with F.E.R. before; also, it was common to get small orders on a brand which was being introduced for the first time in either an old or a new market. These two types of small orders were not considered to be problems because the Company knew that such orders would only be small for the first time or two; after that they would rise to normal size. Thus the

Appendix

Solutions *	Highly Competitive Items	Genuine Parts	Non-Exclusive Lines	Small Order Problem
Raise Price				
Lower Price				
Stand Pat				
Drop Line				
o				
t				
h				
e				
r				

Suggested Box Entries

B	Best
Pr	Practicable
Po	Possible
N.A.	Not applicable, impossible, etc.

* This list of solutions is not all-inclusive. Other solutions, perhaps better ones, may occur to the student for any or all of the problems listed.

real problem lay with orders which were habitually small by their very nature.

It was Mr. Sinclair's opinion that the small-order problem could not be handled satisfactorily simply by refusing to take orders for and ship such items to F.E.R.'s independent agents, and Company salesmen overseas. But some solution had to be found, as a high proportion of these orders were both troublesome and profitless. In many cases filling them resulted in a cost to the Company greater than the total invoice figure of the order itself.

Mr. Sinclair felt there were a number of possible solutions to the various problems facing the Company. Among these possibilities were: raise prices, lower prices, stand pat, drop the line or item, etc.

However, Mr. Sinclair felt that before any policy could be adopted it would be necessary to consider its probable effect on the sales volume and profits of the firm, and the effect of it on the sales force overseas, both indent agents and direct representatives of the Company. It also would be necessary to consider effects on overseas customers and on the Company's domestic suppliers.

Mr. Sinclair decided that the best method of analysis for the problem would be to decide first what solutions were possible for each of these problems; from these, to pick what solutions were practicable for each problem; and, finally, to determine which of the practicable solutions would be the best for each problem. In his consideration of the matter, Mr. Sinclair arranged his notes in a form indicated in the Appendix, page 375 and at the same time informed several members of his staff that he would like to have them in his office the next morning for a conference on this matter.

15

SMITHERS PAINT COMPANY (II)

Dealing with Foreign Salesmen's Reports and Requests

The export manager of the Smithers Paint Company was looking over a report by one of his salesmen who had made a good-will trip visiting customers in the Far East. He was particularly concerned over some problems which were uncovered:

"As a special service to one of the Japanese container manufacturers, will you contact the San Francisco representatives of an industrial oven manufacturer regarding ovens which will bake cans for beer and grape juice. The container manufacturer has requested information regarding these ovens for some time through his distributor, which is British, but he has not been able to receive any information and believes that possibly the oven manufacturer does not have much confidence in the British firm. Would it be possible for the oven manufacturer to authorize a subsidiary of the Japanese container manufacturer to handle the sale of these ovens so that the container manufacturer could get some action? Indirectly, this would of course help the sale of Smithers beer-can coatings, but they cannot be used until receipt of these ovens. Anything we can do on this will be appreciated.

"A bid made by us to the Purchasing and Contracting Office of the Army on Okinawa was awarded to a local Okinawan firm which quoted Hong Kong paints. Correspondence since from the Smithers distributor on Okinawa states, 'Without protesting, the P & C Office making the award called us in, advising he tried to persuade this outfit to withdraw their bid as he was convinced that they could not meet the specifications. The successful bidder insisted that they could meet specifications and as they were low bidder, insisted they be given the award. (Award made on all items was $6,000, while our bid was $8,000 for the same items at our lowest possible margin.) The P & C Officer went on to say when the paint arrives they will subject it to every possible test to prove the paint does not meet the specifications so that P & C will be able to default the bid, buying from someone who can meet specifications, or someone whose products are known to be equal or superior to those specified.' Too bad we didn't get the business but after the default (it's almost certain there will be one), we may be able to participate.

"Although our paints for the Philippine market are manufactured by a Smithers subsidiary factory near Manila, they are distributed in the Philippine market by a British firm which is also heavily engaged in importing and exporting. According to a new Philippine law only Filipino and American citizens will be allowed to engage in importing and exporting after 1964. I was not able to determine what the British firm intends to do about this. At present they are also acting as agents in the importation of our raw materials.

"I visited with the Chinese manager of a very important dealer for Smithers products in the Philippines. He has the reputation of being very difficult to keep satisfied. We spent about two hours with him and when I left I felt as though everything I had ever learned about the paint business had been extracted. However, the effort was worthwhile as I learned later that the visit had made a tremendous impression on him. It seems that he was under the impression that a representative of Smithers had made a trip to his town just to call on him. He is now one of Smithers' most loyal fans and tells all of his associates of the 'personal' visit from the Smithers representative. To the Chinese this is apparently a matter of pride.

"I had a visit with an American-owned firm in the Philippines which deals in construction materials. The purpose of the visit was to try to interest him in taking on our line of metal window frames. He was most pessimistic about conditions in the Philippines and went into a long discourse on how his firm had refrained from buying Import Licenses, etc., though their integrity had almost cost them their business. As you know, while 'buying licenses' might be considered unethical by our standards, it is common practice in the Philippines. The manager did agree to go over the window-frame catalog to determine whether or not it would be worthwhile to take on this line. I tried to convince him that the window-frame line would be a natural for them as they are in a building-products business (although now principally the manufacturing of cement blocks). In other words, the manager feels that he would have to buy a license if they do decide to go into this business. This is something which needs alternative suggestions.

"Our Philippine distributor is quite concerned with the fact that one of the local companies is selling a cheap line of paints under the name 'Smothers' and have copied Smithers labels, etc., to a point where it is difficult to distinguish one from the other. I still think that Smithers should have their products copyrighted in the Philippines, with the idea in mind that something could possibly be done to keep the 'Smothers Company' from taking advantage of the Smithers label and advertising. There are many in the Philippines who would not consider it unscrupulous to take advantage of the Smithers name and advertising, if they had the opportunity.

"I called on Mr. Stuart, the acting general manager at Manila (and executive vice president, New York) of a well-known British firm. This firm is one of the oldest and best established import-export companies, with branches throughout the Orient. I would estimate that they employ between 40 and 50 people in their Manila offices alone. Mr. Stuart was very cognizant of our company and its operations in the Philippines. As they act as distributors of a number of well-known products (especially American food products) in Bangkok, Kuala Lumpur, Singapore, etc., I approached them with the possibility of their acting as distributors of Smithers products. Mr. Stuart called in his assistant manager and while they both seemed to think there was a good possibility of their firm's handling our products to mutual advantage, they said it would be up to the discretion of their various branch managers. Due to the fact that theirs was such an old, reliable firm, there would be many advantages in having them as distributors. However, on the negative side, they have only once handled a line of paint (that British—about 10 years ago) and would be only acting as distributor and not buying for their own use. Mr. Stuart thought that I should call on their various branches in Southeast Asia and discuss the matter with their managers personally. I told him, however, that my time did not allow for traveling in that area on this particular trip. Instead I can write to the managers involved if you think it would be to our advantage to have them as distributors in those markets in which we are not at present represented.

"I called on the main offices of a trading company which we deal with in Hong Kong. I must say that I received a very cool reception when I mentioned the name of Smithers. The manager had not received an answer to a letter and follow-up cable that he had sent to our home office regarding samples of construction materials which we had promised to send. It took about one half hour of all of the diplomacy I could muster to get the manager 'cooled off.' As you know, I sent a cable from his office and immediate action was taken by our export department in sending the required samples as well as complete pricing information and other data in your cable to him of that same day, followed by detail letter and enclosures. Fortunately, my arrival in Hong Kong was very timely as far as the manager was concerned. According to him, he had just about made up his mind to forget any relationship he might have formed with Smithers.

"Our subsidiary manufacturing company in the Philippines owes the U.S. home office about $40,000 in dividends. However, direct payment is impossible because the Central Bank has blocked exchange allocations for the payment of these dividends. The Central Bank not only has complete control over exchange allocations but also has a shortage of dollars. Because internationally there is little faith in the Philippine peso, all the Philippine imports from any country must be paid for in dollars. As a consequence, the Philippine government requires that all exports be paid for in dollars, also, but in the past there has still been a deficit. Therefore, the Central Bank has limited dollar exchange to use for imports only, and only to those imports which it considers most beneficial to the country as a whole. Our factory has been allocated some dollar exchange for raw materials, although the allocation has always been less than requested and less than that required to utilize the full capacity of the factory. However, dollar exchange has been definitely refused for the payment of dividends."

16

ALBERT EDIRSINGHE & CO., LTD.

Difficulties over Agency Representation

Mr. Albert Edirsinghe was the managing director and major stockholder of Albert Edirsinghe & Co. Ltd., Colombo, Ceylon. An optometrist by training, Mr. Edirsinghe had bought an Australian-established factory for the manufacture of optical goods in the early 1950s. In addition to his factory, which employed about 50 people, Mr. Edirsinghe acted as agent for the import of optical products from various countries.

In 1960 the Ceylon government took over most of the private schools in the country and merged them with the public school system. Purchases of scientific equipment were largely centralized in the Ministry of Education, and among these were microscopes for science classes. Bausch & Lomb, which Mr. Edirsinghe represented, was unable to quote prices which the Ministry of Education could accept, so Mr. Edirsinghe decided to look for alternative sources of supply.

He wrote to a number of optical manufacturers in Japan and, after receiving catalogs from several, selected one, Federal Optical, for solicitation. In June, 1961, Mr. Edirsinghe wrote as follows:

26 June 1961

The Federal Optical Co. Ltd.
15, 2-chome
Shimura-cho
Itahashi-ku
Tokyo, Japan

Dear Sirs:

I thank you for your catalog which was received in my office today. I perused the contents thereof with interest, and we feel it would be possible to introduce and boost your products successfully in this market.

Could you, therefore, please send us your price list, and if they should prove satisfactory, we will request you to consider our appointment as Sole Agents for your products in Ceylon. We shall be obliged, therefore, if you will also send us your terms and conditions for such an Agency along with your price list.

On July 7 he received the following reply from Toyo Corporation of Tokyo:

Thank you very much for your letter of June 26 addressed to the Federal Optical Co. which has been passed over to us since we act as sole agent for exporting to your territory. We would like sincerely to enter business relations with your excellent firm on a permanent basis.

Enclosed we are sending the price list regarding the Federal Microscopes. We shall thank you for kind attention to our offer and be favored with your prompt comment at your earliest convenience.

Yours faithfully,

Toyo Corporation

H. Ito, Manager

Encl: Price list in U.S. dollars

On July 15, Mr. Edirsinghe answered:

We thank you for your letter of the 7th instant, the contents of which we are pleased to note.

As most of our dealings with regard to your instruments will be with the Government of Ceylon, who have recently taken over the entire educational system of the country, we would very much wish to advertise the products in our schools. We would, therefore, request you to send us all available literature for this purpose. We anticipate that such a publicity campaign will result in orders being sent to you direct by the school heads.

We are prepared to take up your offer of Sole Agency provided you give us a discount of 33⅓% on the prices you have sent us. If there are any other terms, please advise us.

Mr. Ito acknowledged this letter and went on to say, on August 18:

Under separate cover, we are sending our literatures covering Federal school microscopes for your advertising use.

We will much appreciate if you promote to sell our microscopes excessively in your schools. However, as a general rule it is our policy to determine a sole agency in foreign countries considering possibilities to attain the target amount agreed upon between both of us in a lasting and close relationship. We therefore would like to talk about this matter after having several business between us.

Regarding the prices in our price list, we are unable to give you the more discounts since the quotations are the best net prices on our microscopes.

Besides the microscopes and alike, our handling covers wide variety of optical products locally manufactured, and we would welcome your kind inquiries of the kind.

In the hope to develop our business together to the profit of both sides, we remain,

Mr. Edirsinghe's reply to this, dated September 8, read:

> You will appreciate that in the process of contacting schools here we will be advertising your products and there is nothing to prevent these schools and also the Government from placing orders directly with you without referring to us, thus depriving us of our legitimate commission on these orders and with no reward for our efforts. This eventuality can only be obviated by my Firm acting as your Sole Agents so that I will receive my commission even on direct orders. I have already an order for a few pieces from a University here, and I shall thank you to send me a pro-forma for the following:
>
> Binocular Microscope Model UD
> Laboratory Microscope Model UKD
>
> Please also send me a separate pro-forma invoice for one Microtone used for dissecting.

This letter was acknowledged by Toyo on September 18. After expressing pleasure over the orders, Mr. Ito went on to say:

> Our delivery is within 60 days to be shipped here after receipt of your confirmed order accompanied with a remittance check or a sight draft Irrevocable Letter of Credit.
>
> Regarding to your concerns for direct order from your schools and also the Government to us, we will promise you never to offer directly to those customers in your territory unless through your firm. We should like to talk the matter with you case by case.

On November 6 the firm orders were sent by Colombo, payment to be made by letter of credit through the Bank of Ceylon. The order was for British £89.13.-5d. Shipment was made from Japan on December 29.

In the meantime, Mr. Edirsinghe wrote on November 23rd to say that the Ceylon Government was calling for tenders for 150 school microscopes. He asked Toyo to quote for this order and on November 24 he followed up to say:

> I have sent you under separate cover yesterday a copy of the tender form of our Government. They are in need of 150 microscopes for the present. They may need more if our supplies are satisfactory. I have shown them the leaflet of your Model UB 900x. You will see that all the details as asked for in the tender are not available in this leaflet. Considering the importance of the tender, can you send us immediately a proforma invoice on the model which you suggest for 150 pieces. In case you have more than one model in view to suit the requirements of the tender, you may send us one set of proforma for each additional model so that we may have an opportunity of submitting many models for their consideration. I have submitted your price list and I leave it to you to give a

> competitive rate so that the Government will place the order direct with you. You may keep 5% as my commission.
>
> As I informed you earlier, this is only an initial order. As all the schools on the Island are now being run by the Government and since it is the policy of the Government to teach science subjects in almost all the schools here, we expect to receive very large orders from them, and it is, therefore, most essential that you submit to us very competitive rates to ensure that we receive these orders from them. Please give this matter your most urgent attention and let us have the information and pro-forma immediately.

On December 4, 1961, Mr. Ito sent two sets of pro forma invoices to Mr. Edirsinghe. Each called for 150 school miscroscopes with spare parts, and the amounts quoted were U.S. $5,880.50 and U.S. $8,139.00. in each case, a commission of 5% was specified for Mr. Edirsinghe, who was referred to as "our representative."

Mr. Edirsinghe submitted the low quotation to the Ministry of Education, but the bid was too late in the year to be accepted. He did no further work on the Toyo Corporation's account. In June, 1962, he learned from a friend in the Ministry of Education that Toyo had quoted directly to the Government for 200 microscopes and that their bid had been accepted. This was likely to be the first of such orders on an annual basis.

No mention had been received from Toyo of commission for this order by early August. Mr. Edirsinghe wondered what action he should take about it, in view of Mr. Ito's earlier letters. While he had not placed the order, he had bought the small shipment for his own account and had sold the goods. In addition, he had circularized Ceylon schools and the Ministry of Education about the Toyo Corporation's products and felt that failure to pay the commission would be a breach of contract. He did not wish to take any action which would jeopardize future relationships since the products seemed to have a definite potential market in Ceylon.

QUESTIONS

1. What action should Mr. Edirsinghe take? Give reasons for the action you suggest.
2. What consequences may follow?
3. Evaluate Mr. Edirsinghe's action in this case.
4. What might he have done differently?

17

FEDERAL CASH REGISTERS *

Price Competition Overseas

SUPERMERCADOS MUNDIALES, S.A.

1, Avenida Bolivar,
Caracas, Venezuela,
May 17

Señor Donald Fraser,
Presidente,
Federal Cash Registers de Venezuela, S.A.
247 Calle Libertad,
Caracas, Venezuela

Dear Donald:

It is with great regret that I have to inform you of our decision to equip our new supermarket with cash registers from the Swiss firm of Strasser[1]Ag. As I told you over the telephone yesterday, I cannot wait until you make another trip to Chicago to see if your head office will give a lower price; I have given my word to the Strasser sales manager and there is no likelihood, if you will forgive my saying so, that you could ever come close enough to their prices to secure our business in future stores.

At least not as matters now stand. I am, however, concerned about your inability to compete, for, as you know, I have friendly feelings toward Federal and personally I and my brothers have benefitted greatly from our attendance at your seminars in Chicago. We have also found the training you offer here to our checkers to be most useful and I think you will admit that in our earlier stores we showed our gratitude tangibly by installing your machines. However, that was before Strasser began to market here and during a time when you had things pretty much your own way.

But, not only am I disturbed about your apparent inability to compete but also about the way in which other American firms are being underpriced. We here have good feelings toward the United States, except for some foolish ones, and we know that you buy most of our oil, so we should buy from you in return. But, leaving apart any difficulties over oil quotas and restrictions, how can we buy from you when other countries, with whom we are also friendly, can outsell you and, I conclude, still make profits? I have certainly not rushed into this purchase of Strasser registers, as you must admit, for I have waited a long time for your counter-offers. It is only when your offers are still above the Swiss one by a substantial margin that I have decided I must act.

* Fictitious name.

Let me review the history of the situation with you, and perhaps you can draw from it some help for the future. I assure you that we will always give you the chance to offer for the business and I hope you will be able to persuade Chicago to support you.

As you know, when I called for the bid on the registers, your original price was well above the Swiss price, by an outlandish figure. You took it up with Chicago and succeeded in getting a reduction which reduced the difference but not sufficiently to be interesting. You went back again for help and this time the suggestion was that you send in German registers from your factory there (which I must say I found a curious thing), but even then, though the difference was reduced from $30,000 for the American machines to $19,000 for the German ones, you were still way over the other price.

You asked me yesterday what the competitor's edge was. I can tell you now that his price is better than yours by $9,000, and I think you must agree that that amount is too much to be sacrificed to sentiment. How he does it, I don't know, nor do I much care. So we have gone ahead and placed the order.

You brought up the question of parts and service, particularly in wartime. To the first, I must in all logic point out that the kind of war which seems likely will make the problem of parts an academic one, but in any event, the chances of our getting parts from a neutral Switzerland are as good as they are of getting them from a U.S. which is sure to be at war.

As to service, I have this to say. We keep open on Saturdays and Sundays in many departments, as you know. We have had occasion, in other stores, to call your company on Friday afternoons for service, to be told that you work the "American weekend" and nobody will be available until Monday. You explain this as being because of labor restrictions and the like. To this I don't care. I do care that Strasser, called on Friday, or any time, will come on Saturday, Sunday, or in the middle of the night. The general sales manager himself will come and work on the register, and it is this that we want, no excuses about "American weekends." If you want our business, you must be prepared to work for it.

So this is the story. If you want to discuss it with me further, I shall be happy at any time to see you. I hope we can remain friends but I am not sure that we can remain in the position of doing business with each other.

My warm regards to your esteemed señora.

With great cordiality,

Jaime Aragon, Presidente

QUESTIONS

1. What action should Donald Fraser take with regard to this letter: (a) Should he take the matter up with Jaime Aragon again? (b) Should he send the letter on to his Chicago headquarters?

2. What bases for action with regard to new business are suggested by the letter?
3. What is the significance of this letter in terms of U.S. business operating abroad?

18

NEW ZEALAND APPLIANCES, LTD. *

Selection and Training of Personnel for Temporary Assignments Abroad

Mr. Charles McDougall is a professor of international business management in a well-known school of administration in a Canadian university. Born and raised in Canada, Mr. McDougall had spent many years in the Province of Quebec with a consequent exposure to the two cultures of that province. This, together with a pre-World War II trip to Europe, overseas military service, and extensive travel in the United States had given him a strong interest in other cultures and countries and the desire to work abroad for at least some years.

Upon completion of the course leading to his master's degree in business, Mr. McDougall taught for some years in various American institutions, utilizing his vacations to visit as much of the country as he could, as well as Mexico and Central America. He returned to graduate school for a doctorate in business, and then secured a year's appointment to a new school of administration in France. This was followed by another year in a college of advanced management in the United Kingdom, at which point he returned to Canada. In the next few years he was able to go abroad again on several occasions, but, apart from a brief visit to North Africa, spent his time in Europe.

In order to develop his knowledge of other parts of the world, Mr. McDougall in 1959 applied for and received a grant and a year's leave of absence to study management in Australia and New Zealand. A temporary post with a large research organization in Australia provided him with effective introductions to senior executives in that country, and he spent some months visiting the major cities and working with companies of various sizes on management problems. During his visits, he noticed marked friendliness toward Americans on the part of Australians although it was also noticeable that the warmth of their welcome to him seemed to increase when they learned of his Canadian citizenship.

New Zealand was also of interest, particularly since its small population, relatively minor industrialization, and comparative isolation from the rest of the world seemed to indicate the existence of an environment in

* Fictitious names.

which management might have developed differently from its counterparts in Canada and the U.S.A. Accordingly, at the end of six months in Australia, he made an arrangement with his research firm to spend some time in their New Zealand offices in Auckland, Wellington, and Christchurch, his work to begin in Auckland.

At the end of one month in Auckland he and his wife went on to Wellington. Shortly after his arrival in that city, he was invited to meet the chairman of the board and the managing director of New Zealand Appliances Limited, who were also the major stockholders of the company. New Zealand Appliances Limited, he learned, had begun operations some years before World War II as an import house, and had secured representation for a number of well-known American, British, and European manufacturers, mainly of consumer goods in the domestic appliance field. Import restrictions and exchange controls after the war had caused the company itself to turn to manufacture, and by 1959 it was producing such diverse products as electric shavers, steam irons, refrigerators, vacuum cleaners, and stoves. Its list of products included many world-famous and well-regarded names.

Mr. McDougall spent some time with Mr. Charles Carpenter and Mr. Fox Tyler, the company's chairman and managing director respectively, and made a number of visits to their plants. To his interest he found that, while some of the dies used were imported from the principals and represented out-moded models in the countries of origins, in a great many other instances New Zealand Appliances produced the items almost entirely, with some sub-contracting. The diversity of products sold made long runs impossible, a situation which the small New Zealand market did little to help, but Mr. McDougall learned that the company was extremely successful and that it could turn out products to sell at little more than their landed price including duty would have been on a wholly-imported basis. Accordingly, consumers and the New Zealand government appeared happy with the situation.

Some weeks after his arrival in Wellington, Mr. McDougall was invited to a cocktail party and dinner with Mr. Carpenter and Mr. Tyler, and was asked to bring his wife. The cocktail party took place in the company's boardroom, which was handsomely furnished, well and tastefully lighted, and with obviously expensive furniture. The room was apparently much used for entertaining, containing a bar and a small kitchen, and Mr. McDougall was particularly struck by the paintings on the walls, some of which were by well-known English artists and were obviously genuine. All in all, he reflected, the board room could hold its own with any in Canada, and some of its features would probably not be found in too many board rooms or executive offices in the United States.

Present at the party, in addition to Mr. and Mrs. Carpenter and Mr. and Mrs. Tyler, were the managing director of an Australian firm whose products New Zealand Appliances made in New Zealand: Mr. and Mrs. McDougall had become friendly with him in Australia and were glad to see him again. In addition, there was a Mr. Knut Hamsen, who was introduced as the retired general sales manager of Dryden, an American manufacturer of major appliances. Since Mr. McDougall knew that Dryden did an extensive overseas trade and had a large international division, he was not particularly surprised at finding a representative of that company present and assumed that Mr. Hamsen was probably making a pleasure trip around Australia after his retirement.

Mr. Hamsen hailed the McDougalls as compatriots and with great cordiality, and Mr. McDougall assumed that his delight in seeing North Americans had led him to ignore their different nationality; certainly the Carpenters and the Tylers were well aware that he was Canadian, although his wife was American. When we found that Mr. Hamsen had been in New Zealand for some four months and was rather tired of it, the reason for the cordiality became apparent: Mr. Hamsen was homesick.

During the cocktail hour Mr. McDougall and Mr. Hamsen talked together at some length and Mr. McDougall appraised Mr. Hamsen as a somewhat extroverted, old-school high-pressure salesman, who had spent his life in the Middle West. He had not, in fact, been general sales manager of Dryden, but of Clark-Johnson, a small maker of stoves which Dryden had taken over during the past year and which had exported only through American-based middlemen or on direct order from abroad. The company had never had an export sales manager and Mr. Hamsen had never travelled outside the United States other than to Canada, which he appeared to regard as a kind of fifty-first state. He said that he had taken an early retirement to develop some property in northern Minnesota as a fishing and hunting resort and had been called back to go to New Zealand to negotiate an agreement with New Zealand Appliances for the manufacture and sale of the Clark-Johnson line of appliances. He indicated that only a substantial financial reward would have led him to New Zealand or anywhere else and that he was eager to get back to Minnesota.

Mr. Hamsen had been in New Zealand for some months and Mr. McDougall felt that negotiations had not gone too smoothly. There was some jocular reference on the part of Mr. Carpenter to a $1400 cable Mr. Hamsen had received from Dryden on some points in the contract, and at one point Mr. Hamsen had gone to Australia to observe the Dryden operations there. Mr. McDougall formed the impression that the Australian trip was also partly to give Mr. Hamsen a change of scenery, and this impression was reinforced by critical references to the standard of New Zealand hotel-keeping which Mr. Hamsen made clear was not up to that of the Hilton or Statler chains.

Mr. McDougall was somewhat puzzled at the delay in completing the agreement between Dryden and New Zealand Appliances, since he knew that Dryden was well experienced internationally, that New Zealand Appliances was certainly familiar with local operations (and with foreign representatives) and already made some Dryden items, and he assumed such negotiations were not new to Mr. Hamsen. However, he gathered that the deal was about to be completed and that Mr. Hamsen was already making plans for his imminent return home.

After cocktails, of which Mr. Hamsen had at least as many as anyone else, the party moved on to a pleasant and, Mr. McDougall knew, expensive club for dinner, where Mr. Carpenter spent some time conferring with the wine waiter and ordered two excellent wines. These were followed by liqueurs. During dinner Mr. Hamsen became quite strident and equally critical of the local scene, springing spiritedly to the defense of the U.S. when Mrs. McDougall, in a discussion of education, said she felt that Australian and New Zealand education was superior to that which she had received in California. However, the hosts tactfully ignored his contentiousness and the evening passed pleasantly.

Mr. and Mrs. McDougall was driven back to their hotel by the Tylers. Mr. McDougall had sat next to Mrs. Tyler at dinner and had found her a charming, cultured person, widely travelled and, he judged, as much at home in the world as with her large family. He learned that the Tylers lived some distance outside Auckland and that young children and a big house, with domestic help hard to get, kept her at times very busy and confined.

On the way to the hotel, after some discussion of plans for a trip the Tylers had proposed for the McDougalls the next day, Mr. Tyler suddenly asked Mr. McDougall what he thought of Mr. Hamsen. McDougall made a non-committal remark, but Mr. Tyler seemed reluctant to let the matter drop. He again asked the question, with greater seriousness, and then Mrs. Tyler entered the conversation.

"Mr. McDougall," she said, "let me tell you how I feel about that man. I haven't seen much of him since he has been here, because, as I told you at dinner, I have been tied up at home this summer with the children and other things. However, I have met him a few times, and I know the Carpenters have done a lot of entertaining of him, because they felt he was unhappy here and homesick. His wife wouldn't come down, you know, even though the Dryden company were quite willing to pay her way, but she didn't think it was worth the long trip. Anyway, a couple of weeks ago we had a visitor from France, the managing director of a company we represent here, although we don't make their products. Fox was away, but Charles Carpenter was here and he and his wife asked me to join them in giving a dinner for Monsieur Marchant. We asked Mr. Hamsen, thinking he might like to meet Monsieur Marchant, even though they make different kinds of products, and we had some other guests, some of them our executives and some outsiders. When the time came to sit down to dinner—it was in our board room—I had Mr. Hamsen on my right and Monsieur Marchant on my left. I had noticed that Mr. Hamsen had been drinking a fair amount but I didn't think much about it—after all, lots of people drink heavily here—until, just as we were sitting down, he remarked in a loud voice, 'I hate those —— —— Frenchmen—I don't know why they don't all stay home!'

"I know Monsieur Marchant didn't speak much English but he didn't have to to understand that; yet there was nothing I could do or say, except to want to die of shame. It got even worse before the night was over, and two of our men finally had to take Mr. Hamsen aside and make him behave himself. It was just horrible and I think he is a horrible man. We have tried to be nice to him because we have been so well looked after when we have been in the United States and Canada, and because we felt sorry for him, but . . ."

"Mr. McDougall," Mr. Tyler broke in, "what kind of people do Americans think we are down here? Why would a company like Dryden send a man like that on this negotiation anyway? They need us; we don't need them, we're doing all the business we really want anyway, and *they* asked *us* to consider taking on the Clark-Johnson line. You know Americans, you've lived in the States and Mrs. McDougall here is a Yankee. Why *would* they send Hamsen down? Furthermore, do you think I ought to tell the Dryden people the way Hamsen behaved at that dinner? We aren't going to see much more of him and the deal is ready to sign, and I guess he'll go back to that ranch of his, or whatever it is, but I just don't know if I ought to let the matter drop or not. You came down here to study our management methods—*you* tell me what you would do if you were me. Here's the hotel; if you're not too tired, let's go in and have a drink and discuss it, and the ladies can work out plans for tomorrow."

QUESTIONS

1. What should Mr. McDougall say to Mr. Tyler?
2. Comment on the situation set forth in this case in terms of any broader implications for international management that seem suggested to you.

19

RENOWN PRODUCTS COMPANY (IV)

Financial Arrangements in Export Marketing

Fairly soon after his appointment as export manager of Renown Products Company [1] of Kirksville, Missouri, James McKenna had been approached by an independent Seattle export house which wished to represent Renown in the Philippines.[2] McKenna had been unable to secure a local firm to distribute Renown's refrigerator and air-conditioner compressors in that market, and attempts by another exporter who had been particularly successful in obtaining business for Renown in Japan had come to nothing in the Philippines.

The Seattle exporter lived up to his original undertaking. Accordingly, in the summer of 1955 Renown had allowed the firm to represent it exclusively in the Philippines market. The Seattle exporter and the son of one of his largest Manila customers had decided to invest equally in a new company formed to distribute Renown compressors in the Philippines through dealers in various centers.

During its first six months of operation, the Philippines company had

[1] Names of persons and firms fictitious.
[2] See Renown Products Company (I), (II), and (III).

been ordering at the rate of about $6,000 per month. Orders had been erratic until it had become familiar with the more popular compressors models and other details of Renown's line. A big problem also had been slow shipments from the factory. These had been taking from 60 to 90 days after receipt of the order, plus another three weeks shipping time from Seattle to Manila.

The Philippine distributing company had been ordering about five different models, not all of which were manufactured by the factory at the same time. The less-than-carload (LCL) freight rate from the plant in Kirksville to Seattle amounted to about 7½ per cent of the FOB factory selling price, because the plant sold its compressors "in export offered FOB factory." If $20,000 worth of compressors were ordered at one time for a single carload shipment, the inland freight from the plant to Seattle docks would be reduced to about 2½ per cent of the FOB factory selling price, by means of a through-ocean bill-of-lading rate.

The factory's terms to the Seattle exporter were 2%/10 days, net 30. The exporter would have liked to buy in carload quantities so as to lower his landed Manila costs per shipment. The factory would have preferred also to make carload shipments because of the greater ease in handling, paper work, and production scheduling. The Renown factory had been invoicing the Seattle exporter who, in turn, invoiced the Philippine distributor at his cost, a system decided upon by the two parties who had concluded that it would mean better control and faster shipments than if the order were sent direct from the Philippines to the plant for factory shipment to Manila.

While the Seattle exporter would have liked carload quantities, he did not want to pay for more compressors than were ordered each time by the Philippine distributing company. Previously, if he had received a $6,000 order from Manila, it would have been accompanied by a letter of credit in his favor. He would then have placed the order with the factory, and, by the time the compressors were shipped, would have collected his $6,000 per the terms of the letter of credit in time to pay the factory within 10 days and so qualify for the 2 per cent cash discount.

At this time, the government of the Philippines was operating a tight system of import controls. Sight draft terms were not allowed by the Philippine Central Bank; only letter of credit terms were permitted. The Central Bank had a minimum margin requirement of 50 per cent on all letters of credit at the time they were opened.

QUESTIONS

1. As the export manager of Renown, how would you analyze this problem?
2. Would you make any changes in your past methods of doing business with the Seattle exporter and the Philippine distributing company?
3. What additional information would you desire, if any, before coming to a final decision in this matter?

20

THE OKINAWA CAMPAIGN (II)

Export Financing and Shipping Arrangements

Once Automotive Exports, Inc.[1] had decided to enter the Okinawa market,[2] Raymond Dekker, the general manager, turned his attention initially to specific arrangements for finance and shipment.

Automotive's intention originally was to have the customers of its Okinawa agent, the Ryukyu Trading Company, finance shipments by letters of credit. On the first order received from Ryukyu, the letter of credit was delayed. Dekker had wanted to make prompt shipment to show the Ryukyu organization and its customers the fast service and deliveries they could expect from Automotive. For this reason, he did not wait for the technicalities involved with the letter-of-credit delay to be resolved but proceeded with the shipment, using a "to order" bill of lading [3] to retain title and control of the merchandise.

As matters turned out, the shipment arrived in Okinawa before the letter of credit was received in the United States. When it did arrive, Automotive presented it and the shipping documents to the United States bank involved. The bank promptly made payments in dollars and airmailed the documents and clearances to its correspondent bank in Okinawa, where they were relayed to the customer.

Dekker had quoted the lowest export prices possible on the order and had advised the Ryukyu Trading Company of its commission percentages as agent, and the terms of sale: letter of credit from the local customer. Since Dekker had discovered that Ryukyu's customers would buy only on a delivered-price basis, Automotive had to give its new agent a fairly accurate basis for estimating c.i.f.[4] charges on each of the lines. On some of the early quotations following the first order, the Ryukyu company's c.i.f. estimates were too low, and its customer's letter of credit did not cover all costs. In these cases, the Ryukyu company's account was charged for the balance. Conversely, when the estimate from Ryukyu was too liberal for c.i.f. charges, the difference was credited to its account. By trial and error, the Ryukyu company improved its c.i.f. quotations and, after several shipments, they corresponded closely to the exact shipping charges.

[1] Names of persons and firms fictitious.

[2] See The Okinawa Campaign (I).

[3] A "to order" bill of lading is a negotiable instrument, a bill of lading payable to the order of the shipper, who endorses it either in blank or to a named person. Goods cannot be secured without his endorsement by the consignee.

[4] C.i.f.—cost, insurance, freight delivered to Okinawa.

The method of freight forwarding from Automotive's American suppliers was found to be critical in the Okinawa shipping arrangements for two reasons: first, to minimize handling charges in order to meet or beat competitive prices and, second, to obtain the advantage of unbroken shipments versus LCL loadings.[5] Generally, it was arranged that the goods would be packed for export at the factory, shipped to a West Coast port, and go forward in one lot to the Far Eastern destination.[6]

Over the years, joint rate arrangements had been established between rail and water carriers on various through routes. Two of these arrangements operated thus: the combined rail and water rate for goods shipped Chicago-New York-Okinawa was the same as for Chicago-San Francisco-Okinawa, despite the fact that ocean shipping rates from New York to Okinawa and from San Francisco to Okinawa were the same. In effect, this was a concession on export rail rates to San Francisco. Because of the joint rate arrangements, it was possible for a West Coast exporter, whose Chicago supplier was 2,000 miles away, to match the freight charges of a New York exporter only 1,000 miles from Chicago.

It was obviously much quicker to ship by rail from Chicago to San Francisco and thence by water than it was to ship by rail from Chicago to New York and then through the Panama Canal to Okinawa. This time advantage was so great that Automotive found it possible practically to disregard New York export competition in the Far Eastern market. This did not, however, enable the company to disregard its West Coast competitors.

After a series of orders had been received from the Ryukyu Company, the financial delays showed clearly that wholesalers on the Island of Okinawa were having considerable trouble getting letters of credit. The reason was that the importer had to make a full deposit of the amount with the local banks before they would open letters of credit. Since a period of about 90 days was required—after the credit was opened and the order placed—before the goods were received in Okinawa, a severe strain was being placed on the working capital of the auto-parts importers.

In view of this, Dekker believed that, if practical, other financial arrangements should be made to replace the particular letter-of-credit procedure being used. The delays in opening letters of credit might have to be accepted as a necessary evil—a condition of doing business in Okinawa. On the other hand, it might be possible to effect other terms of payment.

QUESTIONS

1. Why should Mr. Dekker seek to change the terms of payment, since letters of credit relieve Automotive from any credit risk?
2. What other methods of financing might he explore and what criteria would you apply to each?

[5] Less-than-carload loadings, which incur higher freight rates than do carloads.

[6] In order to do this, two kinds of shipment, full-carload and less-than-carload lots, had to be consolidated into carload shipments by a Chicago consolidator.

21

PARAGON PLUMBING EQUIPMENT (I) *

Decisions on Local Participation in a Manufacturing Subsidiary in Mexico

Paragon Plumbing Equipment, Inc., was a large American manufacturer of bathroom and other plumbing supplies. In addition to several factories in the U.S.A., the company operated subsidiary manufacturing facilities in Canada, the United Kingdom, France, and Australia. Its policy was to supply overseas markets from whichever of its domestic or foreign plants was best able to fill orders.

Paragon had carried on business in Mexico for some years prior to World War II as a sales subsidiary, drawing on American factories for supplies. In 1946 Max Campbell,* president of the Mexican company and an American with 20 years of experience in Latin America, offered to buy the Mexican operation. He proposed to set up his own distributing business and to sell not only Paragon Plumbing Products but also those of other, non-competing manufacturers.

Before moving to Mexico, Campbell had worked in several of Paragon's plants and offices in the U.S. and was well known and regarded by senior management. He knew the company and its policies thoroughly and his conduct of the Mexican subsidiary had met with Paragon's complete satisfaction. While, therefore, it would have been content to continue the status quo in Mexico, Campbell's offer meant funds which the company felt it might more profitably employ in other markets, freedom from responsibility for a subsidiary, and, under the terms of the agreement, no decline in carnings from Mexican sales. For his part, Campbell believed that the plumbing business would not greatly expand and, in addition, he proposed to remain in Mexico permanently and wanted a business into which his sons could come and which they could take over after his retirement.

The company asked its marketing-research department to appraise prospects for plumbing-equipment sales in Mexico. The department's findings were in accord with Campbell's, about which it had not known: that the growth in demand in the foreseeable future would not be great, since Mexico's development had a long way to go before a sizable middle class emerged. Accordingly, Paragon accepted Campbell's offer and he began his own company, Campbell, S.A., in Mexico City.

To the surprise of both Campbell and Paragon, industrialization and a rising standard of living combined with both tourism and a consequent expansion of private dwelling and hotel and motel construction to produce a much higher demand for plumbing fixtures and equipment than either had

* Fictitious name.

anticipated. The company's exports to Mexico grew considerably each year. When, therefore, in 1961, Mr. Campbell approached Paragon's management to propose a manufacturing subsidiary of which he would be president and which would, he stated, be more profitable than others of the company abroad, management was greatly interested.

Campbell, then about 53 and aggressive and energetic, explained his reasons. He intended to turn conduct of his own firm over to his two sons, although he planned to retain a substantial stock interest in Campbell, S.A., then with a net worth of about $300,000. He felt that the company had reached a suitable point for this to be done, that it did not now provide an adequate challenge to him, and that the growth of Mexico made the time right for Paragon to set up manufacturing operations.

Because Campbell was under no illusions about the problems that would be involved in establishing a plant, he suggested that Campbell, S.A. continue to act as distributors for Paragon. There would be an interim period in which not all the product needs could be met from local manufacture and some importation would be necessary. He felt that his sons, with a thorough knowledge of Paragon products and the Mexican market could, under his general supervision, distribute the company's goods more effectively than could a sales branch, either under the factory—which would take time from its development—or separately. In addition, there were advantages to marketing Paragon products in conjunction with Campbell, S.A.'s other lines. At the same time, he recognized that it might be necessary in time to extend operations to include marketing, in which event his own firm would become one among many distributors.

Hector Farnsworth, Paragon's president, had no objection to Campbell's proposals as they affected Campbell and Campbell's firm. He was not as sure about the soundness of Mr. Campbell's ideas for ownership of the Mexican subsidiary, and this had caused him to delay the final decision into 1962.

Mr. Campbell felt strongly that the subsidiary should be entirely owned by Paragon. The only non-Paragon shares issued would be those necessary to qualify the directors of the Mexican subsidiary and even those would be assigned to the company so that no diminution of control existed. While he proposed a stock-option arrangement for himself, in addition to his salary, and perhaps for other executives, the shares concerned would be in Paragon Plumbing Equipment, Inc., and not in Paragon Plumbing Equipment de Mexico, S.A.

It was Mr. Campbell's deep conviction that joint ventures were unreliable and complicated, that they exposed the majority holder to argument and contention, and that the new company would be more efficiently managed if ownership were restricted to one stockholder. He recognized that the stock option logically should be involved with the company on which he and his associates could make the greatest impact, which would be the Mexican subsidiary. However, the market for such shares would have to be limited to the parent company, which presented problems of price establishment; but, if they were to be sold in Mexico, his ownership aims would not be met.

Farnsworth had no desire to dilute his company's equity in its subsidiaries and, in fact, it operated on a wholly-owned basis in other countries. However, the reason for this was largely historical, and the pattern of U.S. investment abroad had changed since the end of World War II. He could see arguments in favor of Mexican participation. There was, to be sure, no legal barrier to full ownership of the Mexican subsidiary; plumbing equipment did not fall into the category of businesses restricted entirely to Mexican ownership nor was it required to admit some Mexican shareholders. On the other hand, certain aspects of business and political life in Mexico in 1961 suggested the wisdom of not relying too heavily on the law as a guide.

Farnsworth knew, for example, that both DuPont and Union Carbide had recently entered Mexico on a joint-venture formula, and he had high respect for the managements of those two companies. He knew also that feelings in many countries, including Canada and Australia, against too heavy ownership of local business by American firms were running high. In these countries and elsewhere, proposals to compel wholly foreign-owned companies to admit nationals to ownership had been put forth.

In Mexico, Mr. Farnsworth was also aware, one of the senior government ministers concerned with interest had indicated on many occasions his conviction that any companies entering Mexico should offer participation to Mexicans, although he had not specified what this participation should be, at least in public. When the issue was raised with Mr. Campbell, the latter had tended to decry the significance of the minister's attitude and had assured Farnsworth that his own influence was sufficient in the right quarters to procure incorporation of Paragon de Mexico without undue delay or difficulty. Campbell insisted that one hundred percent ownership was the only sound basis for Paragon's Mexican operation, no matter what others might say or do.

What was troubling Mr. Farnsworth most was a report of a conversation an American friend had had with a leading Mexican businessman. This man, head of several Mexican companies in which considerable American capital was invested, agreed emphatically with the idea of involving Mexicans in part ownership of new American-stimulated companies. Not only, he said, was there the attitude of the government to consider in both the short and long run, but also the advantage of local know-how and advice.

The Mexican had attended a party a short time before, at which were several politicians, all of whom had held or were holding ministerial rank in the government. The talk had turned to the question of local participation in industry and all agreed, said this man, that this was essential. One even gave as his opinion that 30 percent was about the optimum amount to be allowed to foreigners and indicated his conviction that eventually this would be a legal requirement. Only in this way could Mexico control its industrial destiny and see that Mexican managerial and financial abilities were given just opportunity in their country.

While, therefore, Mr. Farnsworth knew that Mr. Campbell was probably right in assuring Paragon of his ability to secure incorporation of a wholly-owned subsidiary, the Paragon executive wondered about the wisdom of this course. It was true, as Campbell had pointed out, that there were no legal obstacles to such a course; if bureaucratic red tape held it up, Campbell could apply pressure in the right quarters to cut through this and ensure the new company's formation. At the same time, if his appraisal of Mexican attitudes was correct, and if Paragon really intended to enter Mexico for the long pull, was it wise to run the risk of alienation of feelings now and possible unpleasant action later?

Farnsworth did not particularly fear expropriation. Mexico's history, apart from seizure of foreign oil company properties in 1938 and some takeover of large land holdings, had been generally good. In any event, insurance was available against expropriation and other risks of doing business abroad. However, there were other ways in which difficulties might be caused: over-zealous application of rules against the new concern, problems of labor, taxes, import permits, perhaps the stirring up of public opinion which might affect sales.

If, after weighing all the factors as best it could, Paragon decided to invite Mexican participation, there were the questions of "how much," "to whom," and "how" to be answered. The investment proposed by Campbell as his estimate of the costs involved was about $4,000,000 for plant and $6,000,000 for working and other capital requirements. Farnsworth had to admit that his board of directors might very well look with favor on the prospect of obtaining a sizable proportion of this $10,000,000 in Mexico.

One of the points which would have to be considered was clearly that of how much of the necessary funds would be secured there. Paragon would want majority control, and there was no prospect of accepting only 30% interest, the maximum felt to be desirable by one Mexican politician. Majority control, however, was a somewhat loose term and Farnsworth believed that a bare majority, or 51%, would be unacceptable. He was inclined to think that 30% would be the most which could be offered to Mexican associates or to the investing public.

He was not at all sure whether shares in Paragon de Mexico would be attractive to Mexican investors or, for that matter, whether any significant body of potential shareholders existed as in the U.S.A. and Canada. It might be necessary to seek local participation in other ways, to offer an interest to an individual or to a small group, and this possible alternative obviously raised some issues. Campbell's advice would be important in this case but, in the light of his attitude, he might have a certain amount of bias.

In addition to equity financing, Farnsworth felt that other sources of funds in Mexico should be explored, since banks and large institutions might be interested in the proposed factory and their participation should prove acceptable to the country. He asked his financial vice-president to assemble data on the Mexican money markets. In due course the following memorandum was received from the treasurer:

Financial Institutions and Money Markets in Mexico

In Mexico the financial markets are divided into two segments: the organized and unorganized. The organized market consists of the total transactions of the institutions that serve as intermediaries for borrowers and lenders, i.e., those institutions that accumulate savings in some form and make them available to persons or organizations in need of funds. The unorganized market, on the other hand, consists of all lending or investment activities that take place outside the organized market, such as individuals lending directly to or investing directly in a business.

Very little is known of the unorganized market in Mexico, although it is estimated to be substantially larger than the organized market.

The organized money market has grown dramatically in the last decade. An absolute measure of this growth is the increase in the loans and investments of financial institutions. Another is the value of bonds in circulation.

Another measure of the growth is the relationship of checking accounts to total money supply. This indicates a gradual increase in the acceptability of the financial institutions as depositories for funds.

In Mexico, most of the activities conducted through the organized financial markets are for a short term.

1. *Credit is predominantly short term but tending to lengthen.* Mexican law requires that the bulk of credit extended by commercial banks be for a period not exceeding 180 days with the right of only one renewal. The banking loans for more than one year consist of 2-year loans for working capital and 5-year loans for industrial and agricultural purposes.

Even though the lending activities of the private banks are short term from the point of view of the bank, borrowers employ these loans to provide permanent working capital. To accomplish this feat the business manager borrows for brief periods from other sources using various assets as credit, or reduces working capital needs temporarily in order to pay off the bank loans. He then obtains another loan from the same bank. Yet another method is to shift his loan from one bank to another and thus maintain the same amount of borrowing with a revolving group of banks each providing the loans for a one-year term.

National institutions, other than the Banco de Mexico, provide the bulk of credit for terms exceeding one year (10 billion of the 17 billion pesos in this category). The loans of the Nacional Financiera (The National Development Bank) are reflected in this substantial activity.

The other major institutions for long-term lending are the private financieras. In providing term loans the financieras serve the function for which they were specifically created, i.e., economic development.

Term lending comprises the great majority of the credit activities conducted by the mortgage and capitalization banks. Their term loans, however, are relatively small when compared to the total market.

2. *Most of the bonds issued in Mexico are effectively short-term instruments.* The issuing institutions (including government organizations as well as the private institutions) stand ready to pay par value for their bonds at any time. Even though these guarantees are not stated as a contract the institutions have always purchased bonds offered them and have gained public confidence in this policy. With an assured market for bonds at par value these have become very liquid investments. Some investors have even

turned to bonds rather than demand deposits to employ their short term funds.

An exception to this repurchase policy exists with the Mexican corporations. Some business enterprises have been able to sell true long-term bonds. Most of these are mortgage bonds relying on the traditional Mexican preference for real estate security. In addition, a large portion of these bonds are purchased by banks in accordance with the reserve requirements of the Banco de Mexico.

3. *There are few issues of stock offered publicly in Mexico.* One of the reasons for this limited amount of stock has been the concentration of business ownership. In Mexico a few large financial groups own the major share of private enterprise although there are no statistics as to the exact concentration. Accordingly, most business capital additions are derived from retained earnings or privately placed stock issues.

A second reason for the lack of publicly offered stock has been the relatively low effective-interest rates. As indicated earlier, the rate of inflation in Mexico has been controlled, but still increased at an average annual rate of about 6 percent in the past decade. During this same period interest rates on loans ranged from 9% to 18%. Thus businesses paid real interest at times as low as 3%.

A third reason for the lack of publicly offered stock in Mexico is the predominance of small, little known business units and a consequent difficulty in issuing stock for general subscription.

Finally, in view of the limited activity on the security exchanges, potential investors recognizing the illiquidity of stock investments are hesitant to commit their funds to equity securities.

As far as Mr. Farnsworth could determine from this, the market for stocks in Mexico did not appear significant, banks tended not to be interested in long-term indebtedness, but perhaps some individuals might be, and placement of shares in the new company might be difficult if a public offering were made. On the other hand, if Campbell or some other source did turn up a private investor or group of investors able to participate, there was potential friction in such an arrangement if their objectives and those of Paragon did not coincide. This, of course, was one of the reasons Mr. Campbell had argued so strongly for 100% Paragon ownership. Despite this, Farnsworth believed, or thought he did, that some effort should be put forth to involve Mexican capital in the venture.

QUESTIONS

1. Would you support the stand of Mr. Campbell or that of Mr. Farnsworth? Why?
2. In the light of what you might assume to be reasonable objectives for American and Mexican associates in this venture, what areas of difficulty can you foresee between the two groups? How would you seek to minimize these?
3. If Paragon seeks Mexican participation, how much should this be? Why?

4. How should the company attempt to secure Mexican financing?
5. Could Paragon secure Mexican associates in any other way than by entering the money markets or looking for private investors?

22

PARAGON PLUMBING EQUIPMENT (II)

Policies to Minimize the Impact of Inflation Abroad

The issues which faced Paragon Plumbing Equipment, Inc. in deciding how it should set up a Mexican subsidiary were, in the opinion of the president, Hector Farnsworth,* largely concerned with whether or not to involve local ownership.[1] Max Campbell,* head of the company distributing Paragon products there and probably to be president of the new subsidiary, was opposed to anything but 100% ownership for Paragon, since he believed that this was the only basis for successful operation. Farnsworth, on the other hand, was inclined to feel that nationalism in the country would work to affect adversely those foreign firms which did not offer Mexicans a chance to participate directly in investment.

While, then, to some extent the Mexican question revolved primarily about ownership, additional important issues were raised in Farnsworth's mind in connection with Paragon's international development. The company's other factories, in Canada, the United Kingdom, France, and Australia had been established before World War II, under conditions very different from those which existed in 1962. These countries were characterized generally by fiscal responsibility and developed economies which had helped to keep inflation relatively low. On the other hand, many of the nations into which Paragon might venture on the basis of a projected market potential had shown no such stability and their currencies had suffered accordingly.

Even Mexico had devalued the peso several times since the end of World War II and American investment had felt this. However, Mexico's inflation was nothing compared with that in other Latin American countries, such as Chile, Brazil, or Bolivia. It was Mr. Farnsworth's belief that rising standards of living in many countries might warrant serious consideration of investment by Paragon, but he did not relish the prospect of putting money in at one level and then, in a few years, being faced with colossal declines in the value of the assets or with profit repatriation at inflated rates of exchange which affected the dollar value adversely.

Mr. Farnsworth concluded that it would be desirable for the company to establish policies to govern the financing of its foreign operations. He

* Fictitious name.
[1] See Paragon Plumbing Equipment (I).

wanted these policies available to help Campbell keep the Mexican company on the soundest possible fiscal basis. He also wanted them to aid in determining how the company should proceed in other countries. Particularly, he wanted the parent company to be able to provide the greatest amount of help to overseas management to minimize the impact of inflation.

He asked Paragon's financial vice president to prepare a brief memorandum in which would be set forth some of the considerations involved. Particularly, Farnsworth asked for suggestions which might become policy in foreign investment, and for specific ways in which inflation abroad might be countered.

QUESTIONS

1. What policies might Paragon establish for financing foreign subsidiaries in (a) countries with stable currencies and (b) countries which have experienced devaluation or excessive inflation, or have strict exchange controls?
2. How might a company seek to minimize the effect of inflation in countries such as Argentina, Brazil or Chile?

23

COPRODUCTS CORPORATION

Problems of Securing Finance for an Overseas Investment

In 1962 the Coproducts Corporation of San Francisco was seeking funds for the establishment of the first commercial Hiller coconut processing plant in the Philippines. The plant would convert fresh coconut meat into an edible oil and meal by a new process. Local currency and ownership/management participation, a factory site, and adequate raw material were assured. The major remaining problem for the company was to locate an American investor, or group of investors, prepared to advance about $140,000 of risk capital. This sum was required to purchase some of the machinery for the factory and for other American dollar expenditures. If the first plant was as successful as management anticipated, a sizable market for other plants should develop.

Prior to the development of the New Hiller Process, coconut oil has been the primary product of the coconut. It has been made from copra, the dried meat of the coconut. Copra making is a tedious and time consuming operation requiring approximately 30 days and spoils the coconut meat for human consumption. The oil from copra, however, can be refined, bleached, deodorized and made edible. The residue meal can be used only for animal feed. Most of the copra is not processed in the country of origin but is shipped to other countries for the extraction of oil. This requires another 30 to 60 days before the copra is manufactured into finished products.

The Hiller Process takes the specially developed machinery to the source of the coconuts and processes the nut as it is picked from the tree into edible oil and flour in one half hour.

This has taken some seven years of research and development and the process has become available at a time when there is increasing pressure to relocate the process plants in the country of origin rather than the country of use. This process will increase the value of the product, improve the economy of newly emerging nations, into which category most coconut countries fall, and eliminate or reduce nationalistic resentment of foreign exploitation of natural resources. Since the Hiller Process is designed to handle fresh coconuts and is therefore capable of producing products of higher value and greater quality, the company officials believed the entire coconut industry could benefit from adoption of it.

The Coconut Industry [1]

Coconuts are an important source of income in many tropical areas. Major growing countries in terms of production volume are the Philippines, Indonesia, India, Pakistan, Ceylon, Malaya, and Mexico.

Copra is the single most valuable coconut product. This is the dried meat, made by removing the husk, cracking the shell, extracting, and finally drying, the meat, in the sun, over charcoal fires or in kilns to stop decay. In 1961 3,390,000 metric tons of copra were produced, with a value of approximately $500,000,000. Copra is converted into a crude oil and a meal cake by passing it through expellers or by the use of solvent extraction. The oil is further processed and refined for the manufacture of soaps and detergents, margarine, shortening, and other products. The cake or meal is used for cattle feed.

Other coconut products are relatively minor in significance. The next most important is desiccated coconut of which, in 1961, 100,000 metric tons worth about $16,000,000, were exported to all parts of the world from Ceylon and the Philippines. These two countries produce most of the desiccated coconut and export the major share of production. Desiccated coconut, the familiar coconut used in confectionery and bakery products, is meat which has been dried, and ground or shredded under controlled factory conditions without oil removal.

Some coconuts are taken directly from the tree for local consumption or for sale abroad as whole nuts. Their number accounts for a small percentage of total coconut production.

Two major by-products are secured after removal of the coconut meat. The husk or outer fibrous protective coating is used for coir, woven

[1] Food and Agricultural Organization of the United Nations, "Coconut Situation" (June 1962). Quantitative data in this section is based on derivations from statistical charts and tabulations recorded in subject publication. In some cases it has been necessary to combine data from several charts to arrive at the values stated herein.

into mats, rugs, brushes, and similar items. The hard protective shell inside the husk and around the meat is burned to produce charcoal or to fire the boilers of process plants or copra kilns.

History and Development of the Hiller Process

In 1956, at the invitation of President Magsaysay, Stanley Hiller, a California inventor with many patents in various forms of food processing, shipped to and set up in the Philippines a plant to make fresh coconuts into edible oil and meal. The plant operated successfully and produced edible oil and meal, but the equipment had two defects. Coconut meat lodged in the dryer and enzyme action raised the free fatty acid content of the oil to a value higher than desirable. The mechanical energy of the oil press was imparted into the press cake and scorched it slightly, giving the meal a light brown color instead of pure white.

Hiller returned to the United States to redesign the plant to overcome these difficulties. Just before the second plant was completed, President Magsaysay was killed in an airplane accident in March, 1957, and progress on the process was delayed indefinitely in the Philippines.

However, the inventor continued work in the United States. To remove the trouble of spoilage in the drying process, he conceived the idea of drying coconut meat while suspended in hot coconut oil.

The oil press was altered to remove the scorching effect of the press cake. Mr. Hiller was not able to run a full-scale coconut test because of the difficulty of supplying it with large quantities of dried fresh coconut meat. However, he performed tests with materials that approximate the consistency of coconut meat (a mixture of animal meal scraps and chicken and turkey parts) until he was convinced the scorching problem was overcome.

In October 1959, Herbert Rogers, a San Francisco consulting engineer, heard of Hiller's work and saw possibilities of developing the process into a profitable machinery sales and engineering business. A laboratory scale plant was constructed and the feasibility of drying the coconut meats in oil was proved. Large or small batches of meat could be dried down to 5% moisture in less than one half hour.

Having proved the feasibility of the process to his own satisfaction, Rogers formed the Coproducts Corporation, to take over all of Hiller's American and foreign patents applicable to the process and to sell complete plants throughout the world. Hiller joined the company as vice president and technical adviser. The process was called the Hiller Process in honor of the inventor.

Description of the Process

Ripe coconuts are brought to the processing plant usually with husks removed by the grower. In most countries the nuts are opened and meat removed by hand labor, paid on a per 1,000 nuts basis. In countries where labor costs are high, in excess of $2 per day, machine nut opening and meat extraction would be more economical. Coproducts had techniques for machine cracking and meat extraction.

Meat is first passed over an inspection belt where small bits of shell or husk fibers are removed by inspectors. The meat is then ground in coconut oil and the mixture or slurry, pumped into a storage tank to be heated in preparation for drying.

To keep the process simple, drying is done in batches, taking about 30 minutes per batch. Batches are pumped out of the storage tank into the batch dryer, where drying takes place under a vacuum.

Each batch of oil and dried meat is pumped into a tank, from which a conveyor feeds the meat at a uniform rate into the continuous oil press. This expels oil from the dried coconut meat and discharges the press cake. The cake is cooled, ground to a fine meal, and conveyed to a bin for storage and eventual bagging.

The oil produced by the continuous oil, together with excess oil drained from each batch, is pumped to a crude coconut oil tank. Small amounts of meat in suspension, known as "foots" are there removed by filtration. The filtered oil is run to a filtered oil tank and the foots returned to the expeller.

Coconut oil produced from fresh coconut has a very low free fatty acid content, less than 0.5% compared to 5% or more in oil made from copra. The free fatty acid of copra oil is removed by caustic treatment and the oil requires further treating to produce an edible product free of coconut flavor and satisfactory in color. Oil from fresh coconuts, in contrast, requires only deodorizing. After deodorizing, the oil is pumped to a finished oil tank and then to tank trucks or other containers for shipment.

The plant is designed for an input capacity of about 100,000 pounds of raw coconut meat in a 24-hour day (or 100,000 coconuts if the meat averages 1 pound per coconut). The output would be about 30,000 pounds of oil and 20,000 pounds of meal a day. The company believed that, after a few plants had been built and operated, it could determine the size of smaller capacity plants which could be economically produced.

Products Obtained from Processing

Coconut Oil

Refined oil produced by the Hiller Process is immediately suitable for human consumption. This high quality edible oil is produced simply by taking advantage of the natural purity of the fresh nut. Mr. Hiller had conducted tests which indicated that the oil that comes directly from a fresh coconut is completely asterile or neutral. By taking oil from fresh coconuts this advantage is retained. Fresh coconut oil can be used for cooking oil, for the production of margarine, shortening, and candy. Other uses of coconut oil include the manufacture of cosmetics, soaps, detergents, synthetic resins, insecticides, germicides, and special lubricants.

Coconut Meal

In the opinion of the Coproducts Corporation management, production of edible meal was the most significant factor in the process. The meal had a high protein content of approximately 18% to 20% and should have value in underdeveloped countries to increase nutrition standards. Since it was somewhat fibrous, its use in bread would appear to be in mixture with wheat flour, in proportions of approximately 25% meal to 75% flour, which would produce a palatable and nutritious flour. In addition, since the coconut countries do not ordinarily grow wheat, some saving of exchange on purchase of this seemed to be possible. The meal could also be micronized for use as a fortifier with the protein content raised to possibly 35% or 40%.

Other Coconut Products

The company believed that some plants might purchase whole nuts, so that husks and shells would be available for sale. One Hiller plant would make available nearly 6,000,000 pounds of fiber annually and a considerable world market for fiber existed. Management felt that a coconut fiber processing plant might be operated in conjunction with each Hiller plant, depending on the economies of the processing area.

Each plant would have approximately 14,000,000 pounds of waste shell also available for sale each year. The company had determined that plants exist to take such shell and process it into acetic acid, tar, and high-grade charcoal. As with fiber, there appeared to be some basis for operating a shell processing plant in conjunction with the coconut processing plant, again dependent upon circumstances.

Market for Coproducts Process Plants

The Philippines plant for which the Coproducts Corporation sought funds in 1962 was, the company hoped, merely to be the first of many. If this plant was as successful as management anticipated, Mr. Rogers and his associates believed that demand for similar plants, larger or smaller dependent upon local conditions, would be considerable. The basic need was to get one full-scale plant into production so that those who had expressed interest—and the company and Mr. Hiller had received numerous inquiries since news of the process was first made public—would have some tangible basis on which to proceed.

In order to develop some idea of the market for the Coproducts Process, the company used statistics of copra production which were obtained from published sources. It was apparent that the competitive impact of the new process would be felt mainly in the copra industry.

In 1961 world copra production was reported to be approximately 3,390,000 metric tons. This gross figure, company investigation showed, required adjustment to take into account the following factors:

> The basic 4,000 pounds/per hour Hiller machine required about 30 million pounds of fresh coconut meat per year. Many growing areas could not produce the required quantity of coconuts and it was uneconomical to ship whole fresh coconuts over very great distances.
>
> Many countries would continue to demand copra for existing processing equipment.

Custom and market preference would retard acceptance of the new process in some areas; traditional methods were deeply implanted and agricultural operations are usually slow to change.

While Coproducts possessed effective American and foreign patent protection, some competition might develop other fresh coconut processes.

For those reasons, it was estimated that only about 15% of the world copra production would be replaced by the Hiller Process within 10 years. Based on 1961 copra production statistics, the market potential for plant sales would be 80 plants located throughout the coconut growing countries.

The Philippines Operation

Since 40% of the world's coconut production was in the Philippines, Coproducts Corporation preferred to establish the initial plant in that country. A very active interest existed among members of government and industry in improving both coconut product quality and processing techniques which would provide maximum benefits to the local coconut industry.

In addition, the company had an associate who owned a large plantation and was a recognized leader in the industry. He had agreed to participate with Coproducts in a joint venture to establish the first Hiller coconut processing plant on his plantation. He stood ready to provide 50% of the $350,000 capital required to establish the first increment of the first plant. The Coproducts Corporation participation in the first plant required that an additional $140,000 cash be available to the Coproducts Corporation.

Under the agreement between the Corporation and the Philippine partner, a plant with a capacity of 4,000 pounds of fresh coconut meat per hour was to be built in two stages so that initial capital requirements would be minimized; the first stage would provide a plant of 50% capacity. After successful operation at 2000 per hour capacity the second stage would be constructed to increase the plant to its full 4,000 pounds per hour capacity. The Philippine associate undertook to provide fresh coconuts and the company was to retain full management of plant operations under a management contract.

Estimates of contribution and participation by Coproducts and their associate in the Philippine plant were as shown in the table for the half-capacity plant:

	Coproducts Corp. Contribution	Philippines Contribution	Total Project
(1) Equipment and facilities presently available (Estimated Value)	$ 40,000.00	$ 40,000.00	$ 80,000.00
(2) Equipment, facilities and erection costs	135,000.00	85,000.00	220,000.00
(3) Working capital	5,000.00	45,000.00	50,000.00
TOTALS	$180,000.00	$170,000.00	$350,000.00

PROJECTED CASH FLOW
PHILLIPINES COPRODUCTS PLANT
10 YEAR PERIOD

	Description	1	2	3	4	5	6	7
	Receipts							
1	Oil Revenue (11¼¢/lb)	$526,500	$ 972,000	$ 972,000	$ 972,000	$ 972,000	$ 972,000	$ 972,000
2	Meal Revenue (5¢/lb)	132,000	288,000	288,000	288,000	288,000	288,000	288,000
3	Loan—6%-5 years (Expansion)	200,000						
4	Working Capital Contribution	50,000						
5	Total Receipts	$908,500	$1,260,000	$1,260,000	$1,260,000	$1,260,000	$1,260,000	$1,260,000
	Expenditures							
6	Raw Materials	406,000	811,000	811,000	811,000	811,000	811,000	811,000
7	Plant Labor	37,700	55,800	55,800	55,800	55,800	55,800	55,800
8	Operating Overhead (Less Depr.)	17,600	24,300	24,300	24,300	24,300	24,300	24,300
9	Selling & Distribution Expense	36,300	57,200	57,200	57,200	57,200	57,200	57,200
10	Administration & Clerical	19,200	19,500	19,500	19,500	19,500	19,500	19,500
11	Management Services	24,000	17,000	10,000	10,000	10,000	10,000	10,000
12	Subtotal	$540,800	$ 984,800	$ 977,800	$ 977,800	$ 977,800	$ 977,800	$ 977,800
13	Expansion to 4,000#/hr.	200,000						
14	Amortization & Interest 6% Loan		26,000	24,800	23,600	22,400	21,200	
15	Amortization & Interest (Raw Mtl. Loan)		7,200	47,200	44,800	42,400		
16	Total Expenditures Before Taxes	$740,800	$1,018,000	$1,049,800	$1,046,200	$1,042,600	$ 999,000	$ 977,800
17	Taxes (30% Taxable Income)	25,000	63,000	53,000	54,000	55,000	68,000	75,000
18	Total Expenditures	$765,800	$1,081,000	$1,102,800	$1,100,200	$1,097,600	$1,067,000	$1,052,800
19	Net Cash Available (Receipts-Expend.)	$142,700	$ 179,000	$ 159,200	$ 159,800	$ 162,400	$ 193,000	$ 207,200
20	Dividends (60% after 1st year)	$ 50,000	$ 108,000	$ 96,000	$ 96,000	$ 98,000	$ 116,000	$ 124,000

Coproducts Corporation would receive approximately 50% ownership of the Philippines venture. Item No. 1 in the table represented estimated value of equipment, buildings, and facilities which had been constructed and were available for use. The Coproducts contribution of $40,000 represented process equipment on hand. The Philippines contribution of $40,000 represented existing buildings, roads, facilities, and utilities which had been constructed on the plantation.

Construction of the Philippines plant was to be undertaken under a joint-venture agreement between the two parties. Upon completion, the plant was to be transferred to a Philippine corporation and parties in the joint venture would be issued stock in this corporation on the basis of actual contributions as established at the time the plant was placed in operation. It was planned that the new company would also act as agent for the sale of subsequent Hiller process plants in the Philippines.

Coproducts Corporation had prepared a cash-flow projection for the benefit of proposed investors. During the initial year, Philippine operations were estimated at about two-thirds capacity to allow for startup period adjustments. After the first year the plant was scheduled to operate 300 days annually. Operating cost in the projection, including labor and supplies, were based on industry experience.

Revenue projections from oil and meal shown in the projection were based on market estimates for sales in the Philippines. Coproducts estimated that payments for oil sales would be made within 30 to 40 days of production and that, therefore, the Philippines plant would be essentially a cash operation.

Coconut costs would be related to current copra prices which were subject to some fluctuations. Such fluctuations, however, would be reflected in corresponding increases or decreases in the prices of coconut products.

As a 50% owner of the Philippine plant Coproducts Corporation was to receive approximately 50% of any dividends declared by the Philippines operation. The projection assumed that 60% of the cash available annually would be distributed to stockholders after the first year.

Product Sales

Oil

To keep distribution and inventory costs to a minimum, Coproducts planned to sell the edible oil produced from the initial plant to oil processor-distributors in Manila, using a figure of 11¼¢ per pound which industry sources regarded as reasonable. Preliminary investigation indicated the possibility of contracting with processors to take the total output at a premium of approximately ½¢ per pound above copra oil prices and this premium was included in the company's income projections. Sales for oil for future plants would be dictated by local conditions. However, the company believed that its refining-cost savings over copra oil would have the effect of a premium over such oil equal to or greater than that envisaged for the Philippines.

Meal

Since an edible meal free of significant discoloration was a new product, no established market price existed for this product. The company calculated that a price of 5¢ per pound might be obtained, based upon discussions with potential users and the market price for related commodities. Some indication of demand is contained in the following examples:

> A food broker operating in the U.S. and Europe had a client who had been seeking a supply of edible coconut meal for use in specialty bakery products. The initial requirement was for an estimated million pounds annually at a price in the range of 7¢ to 8¢ in Manila.
>
> The management of a large bakery chain in the U.S. had stated a desire to market a bread containing coconut meal when a guaranteed supply of the meal was available. Coconut meal in this case would replace up to approximately 20% wheat flour, at current costs of about 7¢ per pound. Desiccated coconut prices were in the range of 13¢ to 15¢ in Manila, and about 110,000 metric tons of desiccated coconut was produced in 1961.
>
> Coproducts meal appeared to have some possibility of sale as a replacement in part for desiccated coconut. A meal made from corn was being promoted for use as an extender of the coconut content in confectionery products at a price of 8¢ to 10¢ per pound.

Other possibilities included use as an extender in meat products, as a replacement for wheat, thus saving foreign exchange, particularly important in coconut-producing areas, as a breakfast food, and if necessary to prevent inventory buildups during early marketing stages at a premium over copra cake, as cattle food. Copra cake is rancid and burnt during pressing and Coproducts meal was believed to be sufficiently more desirable to be able to secure at least 10% premium over the Manila price for copra cake of about 2.9¢ per pound.

Plant Sales after Philippines Plant Operation

Coproducts Corporation anticipated that expansion of plant sales after demonstration of the success of the initial Philippines operation would be rapid and profitable; a ten year corporate income projection is shown as Appendix 3. The company's optimism was based on potential client contacts in a number of countries and investigations of sites in the Philippines, in Mexico, Malaya, Pakistan, India, Thailand, Guam, South Vietnam, and British Honduras. As a result of a few articles by Mr. Hiller, 45 potential clients actively engaged in the coconut business had indicated considerable interest in the potential of the Hiller Process. It felt that in many cases the interest would lead to negotiations and sale once the initial plant was a demonstrated economic and technical success.

Sales of plants following that in the Philippines were expected to be made on a participation basis. The company felt that, after proof of the Hiller Process, considerable financial aid would be available for investment in coconut-producing countries from international government lending agencies. Considerable private capital in the countries might be expected also to become available for investment in local industries which have a demonstrated operating capability and attractive profit potential. Finally, after the 5th or 6th year of Coproducts operation, the company anticipated that earnings available to Coproducts Corporation would be substantial enough to permit the Corporation itself to help customer-clients in financing new plants.

QUESTIONS

1. How would you classify the investment potential offered by Coproducts Corporation?
2. How should the company go about securing the necessary investment?
3. If you were to invest in this proposal, what safeguards would you seek to establish? What changes in operations or other aspects of the undertaking would you try to have made?
4. Do you consider the Philippines the best choice for an initial plant, if a local associate were available in other coconut-producing countries?

APPENDIXES

1. Financial Statements, Coproducts Corporation, as of September 30, 1962.
2. Patent Data.
3. Income Projection, Coproducts Corporation, 10 Year Period.
4. Coproducts Capitalization after New Investment.

APPENDIX 1

BALANCE SHEET
COPRODUCTS CORPORATION
September 30, 1962

ASSETS

Current Assets—Cash in Bank		$ 189.38
Equipment & Patents		
Equipment & Patents	$ 69,812.00	
Equipment Engineering (Incurred Costs)	54,411.84	
Patents (Incurred Costs)	7,600.16	
Total Equipment & Patents		131,824.00
Organization Expenses (less amortization)		872.24
Deferred Equipment & Patent Payments (Payable to S. Hiller, payments based on a percentage of future plant sales)		40,000.00
Total		$172,885.62

LIABILITIES

Current Liabilities		
Advances Payable Rogers Engineering Co., Inc.	$ 40,008.72	
Total Current Liabilities		$ 40,008.72
Deferred Equipment & Patent Payments (Payable to S. Hiller, payments based on a percentage of future plant sales)		40,000.00
Total		$ 80,008.72
Capital & Surplus (Deficit)		
Common Stock, Par Value $10/share: Authorized 50,000 shares; reserved for promotional services 5,000 shares; issued and outstanding 15,286 shares (H. Rogers, Jr. 7,786 shares; Stanley Hiller 7,500 shares)	152,860.00	
Preferred Stock, Par Value $10/share: Authorized 20,000; issued and outstanding	None	
Surplus (Deficit)	(59,983.10)	
Stockholders Equity		92,876.90
Total		$172,885.62

REVENUES AND EXPENSES
COPRODUCTS CORPORATION

Total to date, revenue and expenses for the period beginning May 1, 1960, and ending September 30, 1962

REVENUE		$12,000.00
EXPENSES:		
Business Promotion	$ 1,857.64	
Car Expense	23.98	
Insurance	547.40	
Office Rent & Utilities	3,826.22	
Office Supplies	2,912.98	
Office Services	10,249.27	
Printing & Reproductions	145.96	
Services—General Manager	18,205.22	
Services—Engineer	11,933.67	
Travel Expense	2,731.49	
Transportation	4,370.32	
Legal Expenses	783.79	
Telephone & Cable	962.75	
Miscellaneous Technical Services	11,412.92	
Amortization & Organization Expenses	436.16	
Taxes—Payroll	881.18	
Taxes—Other	702.15	
TOTAL EXPENSE		71,983.10
DEFICIT		$59,983.10

Appendix 2

Notes on Patents

The Coproducts Corporation possesses a patent on the process in the United States. The protection is granted specifically for the processing of fresh coconut meat into an edible oil and an edible meal. In the major coconut growing countries similar protection has already been granted or is pending final approval by the foreign patent office.

On the press, which is a key factor in the success of the process, the U.S. Patent Office has granted protection on fourteen specific claims relating to detailed design. Likewise similar protection has been granted, or is pending, in the major coconut growing countries. In general it has been found that the foreign patent offices follow the lead of the U.S. Patent Office in accepting or rejecting a particular patent application.

Coproducts Corporation has patents and/or applications on several integral items of process equipment which give the process additional protection.

Appendix 3

Projected Income
Coproducts Corporation
10 Year Period

Item	Description	Development Period 5/60-8/62	Initial Plant Constr. Period	1	2	3	4	5	6	7	8	9	10
1	Number of Plants Sold	0	0	1	2	6	7	10	10	11	11	11	11
2	Cumulative Plants Sold	0	0	1	3	9	16	26	36	47	58	69	80
3	Income (Sales Margin & Plant Operations Participation)		0	$25,000	$270,000	$728,000	$932,000	$1,369,000	$1,538,000	$1,810,000	$1,986,000	$2,162,000	$2,338,000
4	Expenses (Net Operating)		$12,000	31,000	123,000	233,000	262,000	283,000	283,000	290,000	290,000	290,000	290,000
5	Net Profit (Before Tax)		(12,000)	(6,000)	147,000	495,000	670,000	1,086,000	1,255,000	1,520,000	1,696,000	1,872,000	2,048,000
6	Taxes (50% Estimated)				35,000	248,000	335,000	543,000	628,000	760,000	848,000	936,000	1,024,000
7	Net Profit After Tax	($60,000)	(12,000)	(6,000)	112,000	247,000	335,000	543,000	627,000	760,000	848,000	936,000	1,024,000
8	Annual Return Earned on Orig. Inv. (Note 1)				32%	70%	96%	155%	180%	217%	242%	267%	292%
9	Earnings Per Share (Note 2)				$3.20	$7.00	$9.60	$15.50	$18.00	$21.70	$24.20	$26.70	$29.20

NOTES

1. Coproducts Capitalization at End of Initial Plant Construction Period—$350,000 (Rounded)
2. Shares Issued at End of Initial Plant Construction Period — 35,000 (Rounded)
3. Year One is Same as First Year of Initial Plant Operations

APPENDIX 4

COPRODUCTS CORPORATION
(AFTER NEW INVESTMENT)

Possible Forms of Capitalization

At the time of completion of the Basilan Coproducts Plant, the total capitalization of Coproducts would be as follows if common stock were issued for the new capital required.

Stock Issued as of 8/31/62	15,286 Shares	$152,860	45%
Promotional Shares Authorized	5,000 Shares	50,000	15%
New Investment—Basilan	14,000 Shares	140,000	40%
	34,286 Shares		
TOTAL CAPITAL		$342,860	100%

The preceding distribution of capital stocks has been presented for illustrative purposes to give an indication of the approximate equity ownership in Coproducts Corporation for an investment up to $140,000.

The final form of capital structure would depend on the method agreeable to the Corporation and the subscribers. Depending on the investors requirements, possible alternatives to the above are many, such as: issuance of preferred stock; corporate notes with common stock shares attached; serial notes given to the manufacturers for process equipment, or stock issued for equipment, materials, or services in kind.

24

AUTOMOTIVE EXPORTS, INC. *

Use of a Stand-by Letter of Credit to Acquire Overseas Equity

As the business of Automotive Exports, Inc. expanded in the Far East, the company gave some thought to the acquisition of stock interest in distributorships in some of the major markets, on products not in competition with customers to whom they sold on an indent basis. Such an interest would benefit Automotive in several ways. If the distributorships prospered, the profit for Automotive would be more than the commission they were receiving on the sale of goods. The company could exercise some measure of control over the distribution of its products in these markets. It would be better able to plan advertising and sales promotion and see that effective action was taken along these lines. Finally, it would be able to offer more effective representation to its principals and, as a consequence, attract more good accounts.

* Fictitious name. See The Okinawa Campaign cases (cases 2, 13, and 20).

There were, however, some drawbacks to buying into overseas firms. Most of the Far Eastern countries in which Automotive was active were under some measure of foreign exchange control. While the nature of the control varied from country to country, it made repatriation of capital invested uncertain, it sometimes placed restrictions on the payment of dividends, and, in some instances, the official rate of exchange set by the local foreign exchange control authorities varied significantly from the free or black-market rate. The latter mirrored more realistically the opinion held by international traders of the true value of the controlled currency. However realistic this opinion might be, though, companies doing business in such countries were usually required to carry on their affairs at the official rate although the desire to hedge against inflation and currency devaluation provided a temptation to seek other channels.

For some firms expanding abroad, the situation was not too difficult. If they were entering manufacturing or local production, they could often secure special consideration from government officials in the form of tax exemptions, free buildings and sites, or more favorable exchange rates. While restrictions on repatriation might be onerous, some companies were glad to use earnings for local expansion in the hope that, eventually, return to the U.S. of investments and profits would be permitted. In the meantime, the local value position was continually improving.

Other companies might engage in the purchase of products grown or made in the countries where they had their investments. Through one means or another, the sale abroad of these products would provide some return of capital or earnings. Some managers were reluctant to involve their companies in activities of this sort for, apart from questions of legality which might exist, the skills required were often foreign to the regular business of the concerns.

Automotive Exports was in a somewhat special position. Any investment it made in a foreign distributorship would be largely in a company with limited tangible assets and, to a considerable extent, would be for good-will, market familiarity, know-how, and local acceptance. Opportunities to plow back earnings were restricted in comparison with manufacturing organizations and Automotive did not want to become involved in the purchase of products for sale in the U.S. or elsewhere. While the relative investments concerned were likely to be small from the standpoint of an American manufacturer, for Automotive they were of much greater importance.

The company's management had reached no definite conclusions as to what, if anything, it should do about acquiring equity in overseas distributorships when a sudden opportunity forced a decision. The exclusive Philippines distributor of products not sold nor handled by Automotive's other Philippine customers offered Automotive a half interest in his organization for $27,500. Everything about the distributor was favorable. The Philippines were expanding rapidly as a market, and the situation seemed to provide all the advantages felt by Automotive as possibly existing for it in such an ownership prospect.

There were also the disadvantages of exchange control to be evaluated. The Philippine peso was officially controlled at the rate of two per

U.S. dollar. Free market rates, however, were four to the dollar and Automotive knew that a great many illegal deals were being carried out to make sure that this rate was secured. The company had already decided against taking part in this activity. Nor did it want to put money into the country with government sanction at the official rate, only to lose on its investment when, as seemed certain sooner or later, the government altered its restrictions or the peso was turned loose to find its own level.

Essentially, Automotive's problem seemed to be one of how it could acquire equity in the Manila distributorship and also minimize the risks and uncertainties of the Philippines exchange system. Equally, the objectives of the Manila distributor had to be met; not only did he want association with Automotive for long term reasons, but he had particular and immediate need for working capital. Of the $27,500 he had asked for the equity, $25,000 was earmarked for that purpose.

One day, while talking on the telephone to his banker, Automotive's president raised the subject. He explained that he was reluctant to put more than was absolutely necessary in dollar commitments into the Philippines investment, even though he was convinced that the Manila distributor would be successful and grow substantially. However, under the exchange control problems, $2,500 seemed about as much as Automotive ought to consider. He wondered if any alternative existed which would minimize the actual dollar outlay and still secure the equity under conditions acceptable to both parties.

"Yes, I think there might be," said the banker. "You might see whether he would accept a stand-by letter of credit availability in lieu of a direct investment. Take it up with him and let me know, and I think we would be glad to make it possible."

The president of Automotive put down the phone, only to realize that the banker had assumed that he knew what a stand-by letter of credit was and how it might be used. He hated to call the banker back, since it sounded like something he should be familiar with, but he was interested in the banker's belief that it might solve his difficulty.

QUESTIONS

1. What is a stand-by letter of credit as it might be meant here?
2. How might it be used by Automotive Exports in this situation?
3. What are the advantages and risks involved?

SECTION THREE

International Human Relations

25

STEWART SUTHERLAND

Income Tax Avoidance by Officers of a Canadian Company

Stewart Sutherland had joined a chemical manufacturing company upon graduation from engineering school and had had a successful career with that concern. His work had taken him into new areas of expansion for the company and, after about ten years of field supervisory experience, he found himself back in the company's headquarters office on a middle management level. At this point he recognized that future promotions might not come as quickly as they had in the past, since there were relatively few positions in the organization which offered what he felt to be sufficient potential for someone with his background.

His long-run objective was a business of his own but he had not amassed sufficient capital to make this possible, nor did he have specific fields in mind. An acceptable substitute, he had thought from time to time, would be a chief executive's job in some medium or small company, where the decisions would be his to make and the results something he could affect.

When, therefore, he was suddenly approached by the management of Broast-Bounder, Inc., makers of food products widely distributed through grocery stores, about possibly going to Canada to manage their operations there, he was interested enough to pursue the matter further. He pointed out to the grocery maker that he had no background in consumer-goods marketing nor, for that matter, in general management, since his experience had been essentially either as a production executive or a staff man in the chemical industry. These did not seem to be considered major handicaps, and Sutherland formed the impression that Broast-Bounder were interested less in formal qualifications than in potential. The company's president indicated that he was interested in Sutherland because of the latter's possession of the qualities essential for successful direction of the Canadian subsidiary.

After some months of discussion and negotiation, Sutherland agreed to accept the job. He resigned from the chemical company and went to Vancouver, where Broast-Bounder's head office was located. He found himself head of an organization with two Canadian factories, marketing to grocery and related stores across Canada through some eighty salesmen. The senior management group of the company consisted of three Americans and four Canadians.

Upon arrival in Vancouver, Sutherland learned that a large and expensive car was one of the perquisites of his office. In addition, the company provided cars for the senior management group and for the salesmen. Individuals were free to use these for personal purposes and the cars bore no company identification. To all intents and purposes, they were or seemed to be the personal property of the men who were assigned them. Each man, in theory, paid for his own gasoline and oil, but maintenance, greasing, washing, and so forth were done in the company garage. In addition, it was inevitable that some gasoline was paid for by the company, since the rationalization could often be made that, on some occasions, company business was being done, at least indirectly.

Sutherland found that his executive group was cordial and that no apparent American/Canadian friction existed. He also discovered a considerable jealousy of the perquisites granted by the organization. The previous president had been generous in offering such privileges as the cars, for which in many cases there was no real justification in terms of the company's advantage—although this was not true of the salesmen. In addition, Sutherland found himself in a difficult position when he failed to follow previous annual, almost automatic, salary increases.

Toward the end of his first year as president of Broast-Bounder (Canada) Limited, Sutherland found himself working on his income tax. As a Canadian resident he was liable for Canadian tax, but some of the provisions differed from those in the United States. Since he had not had a company-provided car before, the issue raised in the following section of the Canadian tax code bothered Sutherland. Under the heading "Taxable Benefits," the Canadian law stipulates that "taxable benefits are benefits in kind, including generally free board and lodging and the benefit derived from the personal use of automobiles or from accommodation supplied by your employer without charge or at less than reasonable rental."

Upon calculating, Sutherland determined that the value of the use of the company car for personal reasons to him would amount to about $600.00 a year and probably incur a tax liability of some $270.00. Conversations with his executive group had indicated that these men had overlooked this particular requirement of the tax authorities and, moreover, the sales force also did not include use of the company car in making out personal tax returns.

Sutherland was under the impression that the Canadian Tax Department did not seek to enforce this aspect of tax collection rigidly, but he was uncertain as to whether this was really the case. Even if the Internal Revenue people had ignored the use of company cars in the past, it was not certain that they would continue to do so, particularly since Canadian tax tendencies seemed to be toward more severe treatment of business expenses. Even more important to Sutherland was the question of his personal conduct as the responsible head of a large company. He felt strongly that he should report this as income regardless of the apparent leniency of the tax authorities.

However, if he reported it, should he then emphasize to his executive group and his sales force that they were also expected to do the same? If he did this, what effect would it have on the members of the organization to whom the additional tax was probably more significant than to someone with his income? If he reported it and said nothing, what were the chances of returns being cross-checked by the income tax collectors and penalties being assessed against the men concerned, with possible difficulties for his company? Did his responsibility as a taxpayer go beyond his personal situation into his responsibilities as chief executive of the company?

26

WILBUR ARMITAGE

Request for a Bribe by a Customs Officer

When Wilbur Armitage had agreed to move to Mexico City as Latin-American service manager for Thomas-Universal Motors, he and his family drove to the Mexican capital and took up residence in a hotel until they had found a satisfactory house. This was accomplished a few weeks after their arrival and they notified the moving company in Oshkosh, Wisconsin, to ship their household goods to Mexico. Some weeks later Armitage received word that they had arrived at Nogales, Arizona, and the customs broker used by the mover asked him to come to Nogales to facilitate clearance.

He arrived at Nogales one morning, called on the broker, and the two men went across to the Mexican customs office. They exchanged greetings with an inspector, who obviously knew Armitage's broker well, and the trio entered the customs warehouse. Some examination of the Armitage goods was made and then the inspector indicated that they should go into his office to talk. They did this, and the inspector closed the door.

"Señor Armitage," he said, "I find that you have a number of new items in your possession such as a television set, a refrigerator, a freezer and a washing machine on which duty must be paid."

"That is nonsense," was Armitage's rejoinder, "the things you mention are at least a year old. I have the original invoices here, showing just when they were bought and what was paid for them."

"To me, Señor, invoices mean nothing," the inspector answered. "I can see for myself that these are new, and who should know better than a customs officer that invoices can be forged? It is my duty to charge you duty, and I estimate that this will amount to some seven hundred dollars."

Armitage was stunned at this, for his statement about the age of the appliances had been true. He did know that there were some articles in the shipment which were new, such as a couple of cases of whisky and some cases of canned soups, but he felt equally that the duty on these could never amount to seven hundred dollars. At the same time, he was not as certain that he could persuade the inspector of this. Nevertheless he decided to protest and did so vigorously, while the customs broker indicated that he also felt the charge of seven hundred dollars would be high.

"Perhaps it would be somewhat excessive," the inspector said at last. "How would it be if I cut it to three hundred and fifty dollars? This would seem to me to be equitable. Suppose I leave you here with our friend to discuss it."

He left the office, and Armitage at once demanded to know from the customs broker exactly what the situation was. He said he was convinced that there was no basis for even the charge of three hundred and fifty dollars and what, he asked, did the broker have to say about it? Was this or was it not a case of a mordida?

After further debate the broker admitted that it undoubtedly was a mordida request, but he pointed out that the inspector after all had others to pay off (and Armitage thought to himself that among those was probably the broker). It was his advice that Armitage pay the sum and forget the incident.

This infuriated Armitage. "I will do no such thing, blast it! You can ship that stuff back to Oshkosh, and we'll just get along without it. Go tell him to have it sent back to the U.S. side, and I'll make the arrangements. I've never bribed a public official yet, and I'm not starting now! And there'll be no fee for you."

To this the broker hurriedly interrupted to try to calm Armitage down. "If you will go back to your hotel and remain there, I will see what I can do. Be in your room tomorrow morning until I call, and then I will let you know the situation exactly. I am hopeful that I can help you out."

Armitage returned to his hotel and spent a somewhat restless night. He had breakfast sent up to his room and waited for the broker's call. About nine-thirty it came; from the background noise, Armitage judged he was calling from some crowded office, and from the man's tone, he judged it would be difficult for him to be too specific.

"Señor Armitage," the broker said, "about that shipment we discussed yesterday afternoon. Would two hundred dollars seem about right to you to get it moving?"

QUESTIONS

1. What should Armitage tell the customs broker?
2. What are the implications of this case in terms of (a) Armitage (b) his company (c) American business abroad and (d) the host country?

27

SWIFT MOTORS, S.A.

Influence of Overseas Personnel on Public and Government Relations

For a number of years the Swift Motor Company of Gary, Indiana, had operated successfully in Latinia, a South American country. At first the company had exported cars on a fully assembled basis; then it had shipped them in semi-knocked-down form. Fully knocked-down was the next stage, and this concluded with the establishment of an assembling plant, a concession to Latinia's progress toward industrial self-sufficiency.

During most of Swift's operations, once these had passed the stage of simple importation of complete vehicles, the company's Latinian subsidiary, Swift Motors, S.A., had been managed by a veteran salesman, Henry Charles. Charles, American by birth and upbringing, had quickly adapted to life in Latinia. He learned to speak fluent Spanish, he showed an ability to identify with the Latinian business and government community, and he became, as a Swift headquarters man put it, "More Latinian than the Latinians." Swift's activities were characterized by a lack of difficulty with government offices, by increasing sales to a comfortable market position, and by an overall smoothness.

As a consequence of this, the Swift management in Gary had tended to leave Swift Motors S.A. pretty much alone. The subsidiary earned what the management considered to be an adequate return on invested capital, it financed much expansion from earnings, and Mr. Charles made few demands on Gary or Gary on him. During periodic visits to Nueva Latinia, Latinia's capital, Gary officials were amused by the way Charles had adopted Latinian ways and occasionally teased him about his siesta, his reluctance to talk business at meals, and other habits they found somewhat eccentric.

When Charles retired to live in a country resort some miles from Nueva Latinia, he was succeeded by Peter O'Brien. O'Brien was sent down from Gary since management felt that things in the world of business had changed and that nobody in Swift Motors, S.A. was sufficiently in touch with modern management to do the job that the future would require. O'Brien was a young man, a graduate of a school of business, and one of a group sometimes known, in imitation of a similar group in a competitive company, as the Whiz Kids. The Whiz Kids were strong figure men—advocates of control through figures—and O'Brien was determined to introduce similar concepts into Swift Motors, S.A. He was also known to have remarked, "None of that mañana stuff for me. It might have been good enough for old Henry Charles, but I'm going to move that company into tomorrow's world."

Since the habit of leaving Swift Motors, S.A. alone had been fairly well developed in Gary, senior management in the Swift head office assumed that things were going well, in the absence of evidence to the contrary. Certainly sales held up, labor difficulties increased only slightly and were ascribed to the changing tempo of Latinia, and O'Brien appeared to be doing a good job. Abundant returns made their way from Nueva Latinia to Gary.

After O'Brien had been in Latinia for some eighteen months, something happened to disturb the Gary management group. Before Charles retired, he had been working on plans for the establishment of another assembly plant in a city about five hundred miles from Nueva Latinia. Negotiations with the government had dragged on, but this, as Charles pointed out, was not surprising. He was confident that his successor would be able to carry the thing through.

O'Brien did try to work out the proposal but reported to Gary that he was not getting the cooperation from government and other quarters that the plan demanded. After all, this was to be a big new plant, automated to the highest possible degree, carefully designed, and a fine addition to Latinia's industrial growth. Yet, he informed his Gary principals, this did not seem to impress the Latinian people as it should. Finally, after the eighteen months had passed, he wrote to say that agreement to the proposal had been reached, but on such terms and with such conditions that most of the value for Swift had gone.

The Gary management group, disturbed by the result, decided to send a man down to go over the ground with O'Brien and try to find out what had gone wrong and how it could be put right. William Thompson, a man with much overseas experience and with some contacts in Latinia, was chosen, and Thompson arrived in Latinia, was met by O'Brien, and started on a round of meetings with government officials. All the officials were cordial enough, but at the end of a week he was no wiser than he had been when he started. There seemed to be no single reason for the difficulties and no way in which they could be gotten around. O'Brien vigorously blamed it on "those stupid Latinians, they just don't know what's good for them. That's true of so many people down here. I had a lot of trouble just introducing decent control machinery in the plant and the offices, and most of the men I know think I'm crazy." Charles, unfortunately, was away on an extended trip and, therefore, could not help.

One evening, on his return to his hotel, Thompson ran into an old acquaintance, a Latinian whom he had known in several countries, and with whom, at one time, he had been friendly. They were still friends, he supposed, but chance had kept them from much contact; nevertheless, they were glad enough to see each other to exchange an *abrazo* [1] and, at Thompson's suggestion, went into the hotel bar for a drink.

Fairly soon the men were back on the same old footing, and Thompson found himself telling his friend about his difficulties. "You know," he said, "I can't understand it and neither can O'Brien, and Pete's a pretty smart boy. Top management think the world of him; if he can't put it over, we don't know who can."

[1] Literally "embrace," and exchanged by male friends as indicating more cordiality and more intimate friendship than is shown by a handshake.

There was a moment's silence. Then the other spoke. "William," he slowly remarked, "I don't know if I should tell you this, but I think I must. The fault is not with us, with my country, or with your company. Or rather, it is with part of your company. I know a lot about its activities here, and I was a good friend of Henry Charles. I know he is unhappy about things, but I also know he has determined not to do or say anything which would make it hard for people.

"But he was the reason you have done so well down here, and the reason you are now in difficulty is his successor. Charles knew how to think as we do, to act as we do, and we accepted him as one of us. O'Brien, poor fellow, thinks like an American, and that is his trouble. In eighteen months he has lost you the goodwill that Charles built up for you in twenty years, and I don't know how you will get it back. Now, if you will excuse me, I must go, and I apologize for speaking so frankly, but I thought somebody should. Good night."

QUESTIONS

1. What action should William Thompson take and why?
2. How can he evaluate the truth of the Latinian's statements?
3. How should Swift have protected itself against this possibility?
4. How would you screen a candidate for an overseas position of high responsibility?

28

FOSTER BIRKETT *

American-National Relationships under Mutual-Assistance Contracts

Foster Birkett, in his many years of foreign engineering experience, had prided himself on his skill in dealing with people. In no sense a conniver, he had developed a feeling for relationships, particularly with nationals of the countries in which he found himself. Much of his work was as liaison between government officials and American firms, and he felt that he was usually able to operate effectively. Now, however, he was in a situation where friction was present. There were implications for the success of his company's contract, and there were problems involving Americans and Thainesians. He was, he admitted to himself, uncertain how to proceed.

Birkett was the foreign field vice-president of Montana Engineering

* Fictitious name.

Associates, a company engaged in engineering projects in the U.S.A. and abroad. Birkett had been a founder of the company, coming to it after years of experience in the direction of construction in various countries. His work had taken him for extended periods of time to Egypt, China, Lebanon, Thailand, and Rhodesia. He and his family had always adjusted without difficulty to life in these countries and preferred it to that in the U.S.

Montana Engineering acted as both prime and sub-contractor in major construction projects. Since its incorporation in 1951, most of its foreign work had been on government contracts, usually U.S.-financed and sponsored. As foreign field vice-president Birkett was ordinarily concerned with contract negotiations only in their final stages. He would participate in closing discussions, usually held in Washington. Often Birkett could contribute valuable special knowledge of problems and conditions in a particular sphere of operations.

Since Montana usually did not have more than one or two overseas jobs at any time, Birkett also assumed direct responsibility for particular projects as well as overall supervisory authority for Montana's foreign assignments. One such direct job was on a large highway construction program in the southeastern Asian country of Thainesia. There Montana was a sub-contractor concerned with bridge design and erection.

The prime contractor was the Kelly-McDonald Company of Ohio, with a vice-president, Stephen Jackson, in charge in Thainesia. The Thainesian Ministry of Roads was the administering authority, working with the U.S. Agency for International Development which had executed the contract. Thainesian labor was, of course, employed to the maximum degree possible, and many of the engineers working for both Montana and Kelly-McDonald were Thainesians who had been trained in the U.S.

These Thainesians were extremely sensitive about having themselves accepted as the equals of the American engineers working on the contract. In addition, the Thainesian government had displayed some sensitivity about U.S. aid and had, at one stage, refused to accept it, on the grounds of wanting to maintain strict neutrality in the Cold War. For its own policy reasons, the U.S. State Department wanted Thainesia to accept aid.

Jackson had not been out of the United States to any great extent, and the Thainesian project was the first in which he had been required to live abroad. He and his family did not like Thainesia very much, finding the sultry climate oppressive and the people strange. Birkett, on the other hand, was used to the climate, liked the people, and had little use for the American colony of diplomats and businessmen with whom the Jacksons spent their time. He and his wife much preferred to study the country and know the people, and they had many Thainesian friends. Among these were Thainesian government officials, particularly in the Ministry of Roads, and engineers from the project.

From time to time Birkett had been made aware that his preference for Thainesians did not endear him to Jackson. He also believed that, to Jackson, the only reason for being in Thainesia at all was to secure further business for Kelly-McDonald. Jackson was determined to have the contract completed on schedule with which Birkett agreed entirely. However, he did not agree that Jackson's methods, which were a curious combination of intrigue and forthright commanding, were likely to achieve the objective. The Thainesian officials, particularly, seemed to be reaching the point where they were obstructing merely for the sake of frustrating Jackson.

One aspect of the situation which worried Birkett was that Jackson showed no reluctance to discredit Birkett and Montana Engineering, if he could. While some of this was attributable to Jackson's dislike of Thainesia and, by extension, of anybody who liked the country, it was more apt to be due to a wish to hit Kelly-McDonald competition. In some areas Montana and the prime contractor were seeking bids for the same job, and anything Jackson could do which would hurt Montana's reputation in Washington might help Kelly-McDonald.

Jackson was on excellent terms with the AID officials in Thainesia who administered the funds, in conjunction with the Ministry of Roads. These officials were fairly well liked by the Thainesians but, like many Americans, preferred to live to themselves or with other Americans, and Birkett's attitudes had meant that he and his wife saw relatively little of the AID people outside working hours. Even then, Birkett lacked direct access to the AID Agency, having to go through Jackson on anything having to do with finance.

Since Jackson was determined to maintain his reputation as an administrator, any problems of expenditures were interpreted within the strict letter of the law and Birkett suspected that on occasion these interpretations were unnecessarily zealous. When Jackson had refused to authorize extra transport which he had needed, he had been able to work it out through friends in the Ministry of Roads and had not pressed the issue. Other difficulties had generally been resolved in one way or another, often through Birkett's local connections.

A more serious problem, however, was the employment of an additional engineer. It had become obvious to Birkett that, if Montana's part of the job was to be done on time, he would require additional supervisory help. He knew that a competent Thainesian engineer was available and willing to work on the project. He knew that the man's employment by his company would be supported by the Ministry of Roads. Accordingly, he made a request to Jackson to have the man hired and the request was refused. The reason given was that the table of organization for the sub-contractor did not warrant employment of an additional engineer.

In an interview with Jackson, the Kelly-McDonald man had pulled from his desk drawer a document which he did not show Birkett, but which he said was the table of organization. He appeared to read from this, used it to deny the request, and returned the document to the drawer. Birkett left the office furious.

His rage was aggravated by the fact that he had seen the table of organization in Washington and was convinced there *was* a vacancy for an additional engineer on it. For some reason, the table had not been given to him, apparently for reasons having to do with the relationships between the AID Mission and the Thainesian Government, and all matters dealing with it had been left with Jackson. However, Birkett knew that Montana's main office had a copy, and he was debating whether or not to cable them about the engineer.

Even if he did cable, the Montana office would have to go through Kelly-McDonald and AID-Washington, and he was not sure that word of the position would ever pass Jackson to him. While he was pondering what to do, he met an official from the Ministry of Roads with whom he was friendly. Almost inadvertently, Birkett asked the man if he knew where a copy of the table of organization was. "Certainly," his friend replied, "the Minister has one. Why do you ask? If you want to see it, I am sure I can arrange it. But what do you want to have a look at it for, anyway? And why don't you ask Mr. Jackson to show it to you?"

QUESTIONS

1. What answer should Birkett give to the Thainesian official?
2. Should he ask to see the table of organization?
3. If there is a vacancy for an additional engineer, what should he do about it?
4. What are the implications of the situation in terms of the relationships involved, not only between Birkett and Jackson, but also between the governments concerned?

29

AMERICAN TRADING CORPORATION, INC.

The Conflict between Old and New Cultures

Fairly soon after the partition of India into two countries, India and Pakistan, American Trading Corporation began operating in Karachi. At first the company's operations were on a small scale, but business increased at a satisfactory rate. The company's American staff, which had been only one at the beginning of business, rose in ten years to five. More local staff was also employed to handle the increased volume of business but the total salary paid to local personnel never exceeded the total salary paid to the American managerial group.

Edward Bennison, the general manager at the time of this case, had joined the company 10 years before as a junior executive in training. He had gone to American Trading immediately after graduation in liberal arts from a small Indiana college. His rise had been consistent and, prior to his move to Karachi, he had headed a large section in the company's home office. Karachi was his first overseas assignment.

Charles Patterson, a high school graduate, had been a canteen supervisor at one of American's U.S. locations before being assigned to Pakistan. His job in Karachi was that of manager of the small hotel the company ran in connection with its transportation activities.

Henry Langley, the chief accountant in Karachi, had been an assistant accountant in an American division. He had been with American 10 years before he was assigned to Pakistan.

Wesley Sundee, in charge of freight and traffic functions, was a man of about 60 years of age. Unlike the other Americans, he had had long service with American Trading, having worked in Tokyo, Hong Kong, and Delhi before being sent to Pakistan three years before. The other American, Walt Cooksen, was a 30-year-old engineer, a bachelor unlike the others, with just over a year in Karachi.

As far as a relatively impartial observer could tell, only Sundee of the American group had any appreciation of social, cultural, religious, and economic conditions in Pakistan. None of the others displayed much interest in trying to develop such understanding, particularly of the rather difficult interrelationships upon which Pakistan rested. Evidence of this, at least in the eyes of local people, was American's preference for Goanese employees. The Goanese minority in Pakistan, Roman Catholic in religion and, therefore, a minority in a Muslim country, came from the then Portuguese enclave of Goa on the Indian West Coast. To the Pakistanis, the Goanese seemed to have a marked superiority complex, to keep themselves isolated from the Pakistanis, and very pointedly not to mix with the rest of the population. While members of the Pakistani community might feel that American's personnel had no interest in them, Edward Bennison would not have understood their viewpoint. When he took over as general manager, he felt the need for informal gatherings of local managers of all levels to create a more friendly atmosphere in and outside the office. In addition, he wanted to invite high government officials and management men from large industries and commercial firms to these gatherings. In this way, he reckoned, he could foster better relations with the local community, generate business, and create high level contact with the government.

As a policy, therefore, Bennison began asking local managers, their wives, and local dignitaries to cocktail parties. The occasions for these parties were usually American holidays such as New Year's Eve, Christmas Eve, and the like. Muslim religious holidays were not celebrated in this way. Bennison particularly gave such parties whenever a senior executive from American's headquarters or from one of its overseas division visited Karachi. In addition, American personnel who might be travelling through were also usually asked; there were frequent visitors en route to and from the other foreign operations or from the United States.

One of the local employees, a Pakistani named Marghoob Khan, had joined American soon after graduation from the University of Karachi. Mr. Bennison, who had hired him, had indicated that American's policy was to advance a man on the basis of merit and regardless of racial background, religion, or anything else. Since Khan was well educated and, apparently, intelligent, Bennison assured him that his future with the company should be a bright one. Pakistan was growing and progressing, and it was American Trading's policy to grow along with it.

Khan was a devout Muslim, neither drinking alcoholic beverages nor smoking tobacco. He was a bachelor, but his mother and his sisters observed the veil, although his sisters who attended university did adopt modified Western dress for their sessions there. At home, however, they veiled themselves in the presence of men, and Khan was accustomed to this on the part of the sisters, wives, and mothers of his friends. At the same time, he had known girls at university who did not follow the practice, and he accepted that modern ideas had their place in Pakistani society.

A fairly short while after joining American Trading, Khan was invited to one of Bennison's office parties. This one was in honor of the vice-president in charge of Eastern and Far Eastern operations and was attended by several other American Trading people from various branches. The party was held in one of Karachi's best hotels and the management group was invited, with wives.

A local management man, Mr. Sayyed, was sitting with his wife and a visiting American Trading man; the visitor had had several drinks before coming to the party. He said to Mrs. Sayyed, who was sitting next to him, "What would you like to drink?" When Mrs. Sayyed replied that she had ordered a soft drink and did not drink alcohol, the visitor somewhat insistently said, "You are at a party. It shouldn't make any difference to you if you take a few drinks in honor of our visiting vice-president. I am sure your husband won't mind. He can't afford to."

This was Mrs. Sayyed's first such party, and this kind of insistence, particularly from someone she had never met before, confused, irritated, and embarrassed her. Mr. Kahn, who had happened on the scene shortly before, helped her by saying in Urdu, "Ignore him and don't pay any attention." The visitor failed to make any further issue of the matter and left to join another group.

A somewhat similar scene occurred at another table where the company doctor, Dr. Hameed, and his wife were sitting with Mr. Cooksen, who had come alone. By ten p.m. Mr. Cooksen had clearly drunk considerably. He said to Mrs. Hameed, apparently under the influence of the drinks, "What a wonderful night! I suggest you don't go home with your husband tonight, and I'll take you home with me. You know the doctor is getting old and living on pills for his potency. I can't see you spoiling such a wonderful night with him. And don't think I'm drunk either. I can still drive you to my house."

Mr. Khan, observing this with some confusion, noticed that Dr. Hameed himself was drinking heavily and did not appear to be disturbed by the conversation. Nor was he disturbed when Mr. Cooksen received an emergency call from the company offices but refused to leave unless Mrs. Hameed went with him. With some difficulty others persuaded him to go without her and the woman, clearly embarrassed by the situation, managed to get her husband to go home.

Elsewhere in the party, Mr. Bennison was paying court to the wife of another manager and the vice-president was dancing consistently with one of the company secretaries. Neither paid any attention to what was going on elsewhere, other than to urge the Pakistani employees and the Americans to drink and eat heartily.

The episodes at the party disturbed Mr. Khan. As soon as he could on the following day, he sought out one of the senior Pakistani employees and explained that he was upset by the party and wondered what it meant in terms of American Trading and its attitudes. The other man thought for some time and, at length, replied:

"These parties are organized by the management to encourage the local managers to bring their wives and become culturally modernized in the Western sense of the term. Mr. Bennison probably feels that the old local traditional way of living so that sexes do not mix together but remain separate is or should be a thing of the past. One has to be modern in order to make progress.

"To promote this modernization, the management has adopted a few methods. One seems to be that, if other things are equal, such as experience, qualifications, and so forth, those who are sociable as Westerners see it and bring their wives to such parties stand about a 25 per cent better chance for promotion over those who are equally competent but are still traditionalist. If these so-called socially advanced and modern people can also supply 'call girls' to their bosses, their chances of promotion are further advanced by 25 per cent.

"Let me give you an example. I am a university graduate and have been with the company for the last 12 years. I have earned my promotions the slow, hard, and gradual way. But I know a local manager who joined the company only six years ago as a senior clerk. He is now the manager of a department. He is below average in efficiency, productivity, and managerial skill, and he is only a high-school graduate. His subordinates know his job better than he does but still he is one of Mr. Bennison's favorites. The reason—because he is successful at supplying girls to Mr. Bennison.

"As for me, although I have generated more business than anybody else in the office, I know I am not in Mr. Bennison's good books. Mr. Sundee has been fighting my case for further promotion for the last two years, but it seems that Mr. Bennison does not agree. I think I am not sociable according to his definition, for I keep my wife in the veil and do not bring her to these parties. I am afraid that my present position is the end of the line for me in this company, and I should be seeking a position elsewhere where I stand a better chance for progress. I can compete with others in all respects but not in dishonorable practices."

The other man continued. "You know it is immodest to smoke, take tea or eat publicly in the month of Ramadan. But all these American officers except Mr. Sundee smoke and take tea in the office without any hesitation. It seems they have no regard for our feelings.

"This type of behavior, favoritism, corruption, and behind-the-scenes activities is not only destroying my morale and impairing my efficiency, but it is having the same effect on others who hold our old cultural traditions dear to their hearts. After seeing those in the company who are after the so-called Western type of modernization, either because they follow the crowd or on their own initiative, and who prosper by doing so, we who still believe in the old ways of living are placed on the horns of a dilemma. You had better be thinking about how you will decide."

QUESTIONS

1. What course of action should Marghoob Khan follow?
2. Should he make any attempt to pass on his fellow-employee's feelings to others in the company? If so, to whom? How?
3. What sort of attitude should American Trading's home office management take toward this situation?
4. What might it have done to prevent it?

30

CAPTAIN GEORGE PATRIOS

Misunderstanding of Local Feelings in Turkey

George Patrios,* a captain in the U.S. infantry, was sent to Ankara to be a liaison officer in the North Atlantic Treaty Organization (NATO) with Turkish forces. His counterpart was a captain in the Turkish army and Patrios liked the man immediately. He found him tough, able, and rather American in his outlook on life, or so he seemed.

Patrios also liked Turkey and was at some pains to say so. For his first few months he saw little but Ankara; after he had developed some knowledge of the job, he had an opportunity to travel outside the capital. One of his trips was with the Turkish officer, who guided Patrios' car off the main road and into a small city where the Turk had friends.

The streets of much of the city were unpaved, dusty, and dirty. As they were driving along, Patrios remarked to his colleague, "Gosh, what filthy streets! Don't they ever pave them, or at least sprinkle to keep down the dust?"

The Turk did not make a particular reply to this ejaculation, but Patrios found in the next few days that relationships had cooled on the former's part. In fact, it was difficult to get the man to talk and, as far as he could, he dealt with Patrios through intermediaries.

This situation continued for about two weeks and was becoming, if anything, worse. Recognizing that his liaison duties could not be carried out effectively under such conditions, Patrios determined to find out the trouble. He went into the Turk's office one afternoon and said, "I think things have gone far enough between us. Obviously you're mad at me about something and I don't know what it is. Whatever it is, I'd like to find out what, and do something about it."

"You don't know what it is!" the Turkish officer rejoined. "You insulted my country, that is the trouble!"

* Fictitious name.

"Insulted your country?" Patrios said. "I like your country and I've told you so. I think it's great. What do you mean, I insulted it?"

"I mean just this," said his associate. "You said our roads were dirty, that we were too poor to pave them and too stupid to spray them. That, to me, is an insult to my country."

QUESTIONS

1. What should Patrios do or say now?
2. What might he have done to avoid this kind of situation?

31

RICHARD CONKLIN *

Problems of Courtship and Chaperonage in Brazil

Richard Conklin was a young bachelor employed in the Rio de Janeiro subsidiary of a well-known American corporation. Thoroughly competent, Conklin had done excellent work in the United States and during his Latin American stay, and this had led to a senior engineer's position, even though he was under thirty.

Conklin was fluent in Portuguese before he arrived in Brazil and, as a result, had no barrier to effective communications. He had been readily accepted in local society and had experienced no difficulty in finding Brazilian girls to take out. One of the prettiest and most attractive was Maria Garcia del Pino * daughter of a well-respected Rio businessman, and Conklin soon concentrated his attention on her. After six months, during which they saw each other often, the couple felt that they were in love.

During his engagement with Miss del Pino, Conklin had followed the strict Latin American custom of being chaperoned. Either Maria's younger brother or her cousin accompanied them on all occasions.

Just prior to a trip back to the United States, which meant at least a six-months' absence from Brazil, Richard had proposed a drive through the countryside to Maria. Desperately wanting complete privacy for the drive, Maria suddenly suggested to Conklin that her younger brother could be bribed to go to the movies. Then they could take the drive by themselves. Maria said she was certain no one would see them alone together off in the country.

Maria's suggestion caught Conklin completely by surprise. He had always appreciated the Latin American sensitivity to proper chaperoning

* Fictitious name.

and Maria in particular had said that this was a traditional custom that should not be violated. However, he was as unhappy as was she about their impending separation and tempted to accede to her proposal.

QUESTION

What action should Conklin take and why?

32

INDUSTRIAS KAISER ARGENTINA, S.A. (IV) *

Compensation Policies for Expatriate Employees

In the fall of 1955 Mr. William Simmons of the personnel department of Kaiser Motors Corporation was asked by top management to prepare a compensation policy for U.S. personnel assigned to the Argentine manufacturing subsidiary, Industrias Kaiser Argentina. At this time approximately 80 North American personnel of Kaiser Motors had been assigned to IKA on a long-term basis, in addition to those sent over on temporary assignments. The positions held by the U.S. personnel were either managerial or technical, ranging from general manager to first line foremen. A few selected examples of the types of positions held by the U.S. personnel in the IKA organization and the salary schedule for similar positions in the parent company are presented in Exhibit 1, at the end of this case.

Although it was the intention of the management to replace most of the U.S. personnel, except for a few key managerial positions, with local employees as soon as feasible, the change-over was expected to take at least several years. In the meantime the positions would have to be filled by U.S. personnel. These men had responsibility not only for carrying out specific functions they had been assigned to in Argentina, but also for training local personnel to replace them.

Typically, those who had been sent to Argentina had no previous experience in foreign operations, and few of them had any knowledge of either Spanish or local customs. They were selected strictly on the basis of technical competence demonstrated in the United States and their willingness to go overseas. Since the Kaiser Motors Corporation was in the process of discontinuing its passenger-car production in the United States, some of the personnel preferred to stay on with the Kaiser organization by going to Argentina rather than look for employment elsewhere.

Mr. Simmons believed the prime objective of the compensation policy to be that of providing uniform and suitable employment standards for U.S. personnel assigned to IKA. Inasmuch as this was Kaiser Motors' first at-

* Prepared by Dr. Michael Yoshino while a doctoral candidate in the Graduate School of Business, Stanford University.

tempt to prepare a detailed compensation policy for overseas personnel, Mr. Simmons relied heavily on practices of other leading companies in the United States with a considerable amount of experience in international operations. In the course of his preliminary study he had sought advice from personnel managers of several companies. He also found the report by the National Industrial Conference Board, "Compensating Expatriates for the Cost of Living Abroad," helpful in giving him a guide line. After studying practices of the various companies described in the report with a great deal of care, Mr. Simmons noted that there were three major areas—overseas bonus, cost of living allowances, and contingency reserve funds—which required special attention.

OVERSEAS BONUS

According to the study conducted by the National Industrial Conference Board, more than 65% of the participating companies reported that they raised the base salary or provided an overseas bonus for American employees who had been given an overseas assignment. This step was taken to make foreign assignments more attractive and to enable U.S. personnel to meet expenses which they would not encounter in the United States. Although a few companies reported that they provided a standard bonus ranging from $50 to $150 a month to all their overseas personnel, regardless of salary level, the most common overseas bonus was reported to be an increase of between 21 and 25% in the base salary as indicated in Exhibit 2.

The selected comments on representing opinions of various companies are found in Exhibit 3, page 436.

Mr. Simmons learned in his research that the following factors peculiar to foreign operations were usually considered in determining the amount of overseas bonus.

I. Job-Associated Factors:
   a. Handling government and personnel relations.
   b. Training activities dealing with a foreign language.
   c. Ingenuity in solving technical problems without help from the home office.
   d. Isolation from professional resources or contacts.

II. Cultural Factors:
   a. Giving up native land.
   b. Separation of school-age children.
   c. Language problems.
   d. Social adjustments.
   e. Climate.
   f. Health standards.
   g. Types and amounts of food.

III. Social Factors:
   a. Cultural shock.
   b. Limited and different recreational and leisure-time facilities.
   c. A new political and legal environment.
   d. Fears of a politically unstable area.

Some of the personnel managers that Simmons consulted indicated they were in the process of re-examining the advisability of giving a bonus to overseas personnel. They questioned also the necessity of using a substantial overseas bonus to attract competent individuals to international operations. They contended moreover that quite frequently an overseas bonus was based solely on undesirable factors connected with foreign assignments to the complete exclusion of many compensating advantages which were found only in foreign assignments. In many cases, according to these personnel managers, bonuses had underwritten a standard of living considerably higher than that which the employee would enjoy at home. They further maintained that an excessive bonus tended to aggravate the already existing status gap, due to the huge difference in base salary, between U.S. personnel and local employees.

In view of the divergent views expressed, Mr. Simmons was wondering what policy he should recommend to the management in regard to an overseas bonus for the U.S. personnel assigned to IKA. Specifically, he had to decide whether Kaiser Motors should pay the overseas bonus to their U.S. personnel and, if so, what criteria the company should use in establishing the amount to be paid.

COST OF LIVING ALLOWANCES

The study made by the NICB revealed that the cost-of-living allowance was the most common method employed by American companies to help their overseas personnel meet their living costs overseas. The purpose of the allowance, according to the study, was to make it easier for the overseas personnel working in the areas where costs of living were higher than in the United States to maintain, as nearly as possible, the same standard of living they would have in the United States. The NICB study reported that in 60 out of 87 countries studied living costs were higher than in the United States. The opinions expressed by the participating companies on living costs abroad in certain countries are reported in Exhibit 4.

Eighty-four out of 103 participating companies reported that they gave their U.S. personnel cost-of-living allowances of one type or another in those areas where they believed that the cost of living was higher. Although in a few instances, the same allowances were given to each employee, the more common practice was to provide allowances on a sliding scale. According to the NICB study, a number of different methods were employed to measure the differences in cost of living as summarized in Exhibit 5. Selected comments made by various participating companies on the methods they employed in computing the difference in cost-of-living were also reported in Exhibit 6.

Although the State Department local index was used most frequently in measuring the difference in cost of living, Mr. Simmons was advised that indiscriminate application of the index to managerial positions of private industries resulted in excessive allowances for several reasons. First, there were some doubts as to whether the package of goods and services used in calculating the index was an accurate reflection of the employee's consumption behavior overseas. Secondly, since the cost-of-living index was established for a certain income level (annual income $6,500) and family size (2), it would be difficult to apply to other income levels and family sizes. In so doing, it had to be assumed that the incremental expense for every employee in a high cost of living area was the same as that of the employee on which the index was based. Or, in other words, it had to be assumed that current consumption as a function of income followed the same slope abroad as in the United States. For employees of the State Department, this assumption might be reasonable, but when used to determine allowances for American managerial personnel abroad, this approach would often result in excessive allowances.

This difference, Mr. Simmons learned, stemmed from the different living pattern abroad. In the United States, executives as a rule did not level out their consumption expenditure until they reached a fairly high income level. However, the American managerial personnel overseas tended to have an expenditure curve that was significantly flatter than that in the United States, because most American managerial personnel overseas, particularly outside of Western Europe, tended to live and function socially as a group, regardless of income level, to a greater degree than they would in the United States. Moreover, social pressures from the local community and the lack of availability of luxurious items and extravagant social and recreational facilities tended to make their consumption pattern significantly different from that found in the United States.

Another weakness of the State Department index was that it was already out of date when published, and this was particularly true in a country like Argentina where inflationary pressure was high.

In spite of these difficulties, the proponents of the State Department index claimed that it had the advantages of convenience, ease of accessibility and application, and an air of authority. The difficulty of developing a suitable alternative method was an important factor in its favor. After having studied these factors, Mr. Simmons was wondering if he should use the State Department index as a base for computing the cost-of-living adjustment, or if he should develop an alternative method which would be tailored to the needs of the company. If he should decide to take the latter course, he would have to provide a suitable plan for IKA.

CONTINGENCY RESERVE FUND

Another major decision which Mr. Simmons had to make concerned establishment of a so-called contingency reserve fund. The purpose of the contingency reserve fund, as described by personnel directors of the several companies using the plan, was to accrue funds to ensure return transportation to the United States for an employee and his family in the event that he should resign or be discharged before completing a predetermined length of service overseas. Typically, the companies requested each employee to authorize them to withhold each month from his earnings a certain amount, ranging from $50 to $75, until enough reserve was built up to cover the return transportation expenses for himself and his family. The fund would be retained by the company until the employee satisfactorily completed the required term of service, usually ranging from 2 to 3 years, or employment was terminated for the convenience of the company. The executives of the companies using this system believed that the fund would not only serve as an automatic screening process to discourage tourist-type employees from going overseas at the expense of the company but would also provide each employee assigned overseas with an extra incentive to adjust himself to the foreign environment.

Although Mr. Simmons was well aware of these advantages, he was not sure what effect this might have upon the morale of those sent overseas and was fearful of the possibility that this might force maladjusted employees to serve the required term. This would undoubtedly have damaging effects upon the individuals involved as well as the company itself.

Weighing these factors, he was wondering if he should include a similar plan as a part of the compensation policy for the IKA organization.

Exhibit 1

Selected Positions Held by U.S. Personnel in the IKA Organization and the Salary Range for Similar Positions in the U.S. Parent Company

POSITIONS	SALARY RANGE
Works Manager	$17,000—27,000
Chief Engineer	"
Director of Finance	"
Director of Sales	"
Director of Procurement	15,000—23,000
Production Manager	"
Work Engineer	13,700—20,000
Master Mechanic	"
Gen. Superintendent, Machining	12,000—17,400
Gen. Superintendent, Assembly	"

Source: Company Records.

Exhibit 2

Companies with a Higher Base Salary Overseas

OVERSEAS PREMIUM	NUMBER OF COMPANIES
10%-20% of base salary	9
21%-25%	13
Over 25%	4
Unspecified	41 *
Total	67

* Three companies raise base salaries $50 to $150 per month. No information was supplied on the percentage increase given to personnel going overseas.

Source: "Compensating Expatriates for the Cost of Living Abroad." *Studies in Labor Statistics,* No. 14, 1955. Washington, D.C.: National Industrial Conference Board.

Exhibit 3

Comments on Higher Base Salary Than in the United States *

"The size of our foreign subsidiaries or branches and job responsibility are the main factors used in establishing salary rates. While we do not employ an expatriation premium as such, our salary rates abroad are somewhat higher than similar domestic positions."

"Executive and managerial personnel generally are paid a higher salary than in the United States for the same position.

"Technical personnel are usually recruited from the ranks in our United States plant and although generally receiving a 20%-25% salary increase and given titles corresponding to those for similar functions in the United States, their foreign base salary—due to the much smaller scope of operations—doesn't always equal the base salary paid in the United States for the same position. For example, the factory manager of a foreign plant will not necessarily receive the same base salary as the factory manager in our United States factory."

"We endeavor to have the base salary comparable and make allowances in excess of salary by liberal living and entertainment expense accounts."

"Our policy is to augment foreign pay by adding 25% over the base pay for similar jobs in the United States. This is not considered a part of the base pay for the purpose of computing company benefits and is eliminated when the employee returns to the United States."

"Employees are given overseas assignments at base rates for the same job where it exists in the United States. In actual practice, however, jobs in foreign countries by their very nature tend to have no direct counter in the United States. As a result, a foreign sales manager's job, for example, might be rated considerably higher for pay purposes than the same general job were it located within the United States. This higher rating would be due entirely to unique working conditions."

"The base salary is based on individual consideration. Salaries are comparable to those for similar positions in the United States."

"Higher base salaries are maintained for equivalent domestic positions not so much to take care of higher living costs as to provide an incentive to employees who are spending their entire careers in foreign employment. This policy applies to all foreign-assigned employees regardless of location."

"Executive personnel are not paid higher salaries for assignments abroad than they would receive for a comparable job in this country. The

* Source: "Compensating Expatriates for the Cost of Living Abroad." *Studies in Labor Statistics,* No. 14, 1955. Washington, D.C.: National Industrial Conference Board.

reason for this is that these men, as managers of subsidiary companies, or managers of large branches, receive, in most cases, a salary plus commission on all sales in the branch or subsidiary. Thus their remuneration is flexible, and depends to a great extent on the individual's executive ability.

"Managerial personnel who are for the most part service managers, responsible to the subsidiary manager for the proper operation of the service department in a particular country, receive their remuneration in the form of salary. The salary ranges for these jobs are about 25% above those for similar jobs in this country. The purpose is to provide a bonus or incentive to the men to accept employment outside the United States.

"The higher base salary paid to Americans in managerial positions abroad is based on approximately 125% of the salary range for a similar job in the United States."

EXHIBIT 4

COMPANY OPINION ON LIVING COSTS ABROAD, BY COUNTRY, MID-1954

	NO. COS. WITH		% OF COS. WITH
	HIGHER	SAME OR LOWER	HIGHER
South America			
Venezuela	43	0	100
Colombia	26	3	90
Brazil	37	7	84
Argentina	15	5	75
Uruguay	8	4	67
Peru	13	7	65
Chile	4	6	40
Other Latin America			
Dominican Republic	5	0	100
Guatemala	4	0	100
Puerto Rico	8	1	89
El Salvador	3	1	75
Cuba	11	5	69
Panama	9	4	69
Trinidad	3	2	60
Mexico	11	33	25
Jamaica	1	4	20
Africa			
Morocco	5	1	83
Gold Coast	3	1	75
Egypt	6	3	67
Union of South Africa	7	13	35
Australia	3	10	23
Asia			
Middle East			
Saudi Arabia	4	0	100
Lebanon	12	1	92
Turkey	6	1	86

Exhibit 4 (Cont.)

Company Opinion on Living Costs Abroad, by Country, Mid-1954

	NO. COS. WITH		% OF COS. WITH
	HIGHER	SAME OR LOWER	HIGHER
Far East			
Philippines	26	0	100
Pakistan	5	0	100
Japan	24	2	92
Singapore	8	1	89
Indonesia	3	1	75
Thailand	3	1	75
India	9	4	69
Hong Kong	4	2	67
Europe			
France	27	3	90
Sweden	7	2	78
Germany (West)	14	4	78
Italy	17	5	77
Belgium	9	3	75
Switzerland	10	4	71
Spain	6	3	66
Portugal	6	4	60
England	15	14	52
Denmark	2	5	29
Greece	1	6	14
Netherlands	1	6	14

Note: For a country to be listed in this table, at least four companies must have expressed an opinion on living costs. See appendix for additional countries.

Source: "Compensating Expatriates for the Cost of Living Abroad." *Studies in Labor Statistics,* No. 14, 1955. National Industrial Conference Board.

Exhibit 5

Methods Used to Determine Living Cost Differences

TYPES OF METHODS	NO. COMPANIES USING
a. State Department indexes	43
b. Their own cost-of-living research	28
c. General information on cost of living [1]	22
d. Comparison with policies of other companies	17
e. Comparison with research of other companies	13
f. Individual treatment or review	11
g. Executive recommendations and observations	8
h. No method stated	5
i. United Nations index	3
j. Other [2]	7
Total	157 [a]

[1] Includes company knowledge of costs and conditions in foreign areas, and indexes and information from banks and foreign governments.

[2] Includes Heller budget, city worker's family budget, complete expense account, a flat dollar amount or a higher base salary to cover any differences in the cost of living.

[a] Total comes to more than number of companies reporting because some companies use more than one method.

Source: "Compensating Expatriates for the Cost of Living Abroad." *Studies in Labor Statistics,* No. 14, 1955. National Industrial Conference Board.

EXHIBIT 6

COMMENTS ON MEASURING COST-OF-LIVING DIFFERENCES *

"The amount of allowance is determined by using the State Department's index as a base. This base figure is then adjusted to meet our own company situation and in accordance with reports we receive from our own overseas branch offices."

"Cost-of-living allowances, ranging from $60 to $250 a month over and above the basic salaries, are granted employees residing in countries where the cost of living is above that in the States.

"The 'Indexes of Living Costs Abroad (Excluding Quarters)' distributed several times a year by the National Foreign Trade Council, are used as a basis for determining allowances. These statistical data are supplemented by similar information from banks with broad overseas coverage, by practices of other companies operating in the same countries, and by the personal observations of the various executives of the company when in foreign countries.

"Our general objective is to keep a man 'whole' in relationship to his comparable position in the States.

"In addition to the basic salaries shown, all overseas managers and salesmen operate on a quota sales bonus. Bonuses range from nothing to 100% of a man's basic salary. They average about 40% of the basic salaries."

"We have followed the precedents established by the Federal Government and other business concerns that have operated in Latin America for a number of years.

"Allowances have been determined by studying the data prepared by the Department of State and by securing from our employees in each of these countries information concerning their actual expenses for living accommodations."

"The difference is determined by obtaining prices of selected foods, commodities, clothing, etc., in the United States home base and comparing them with the same or closely similar items at the foreign post. Variation in 'usage' is a factor to be considered, as this variation might be very great; viz., an overcoat might cost the same amount in New York City as in Naples, Italy, but this amount would be spent less frequently in Naples than in New York City. Cost of living quarters (housing) is considered separately but is prepared in the same manner as above."

"The cost-of-living adjustment is determined individually by comparing living costs in the particular foreign location with those where the employee normally worked in the United States. This takes into account the employee's individual circumstances, such as size of family, as well as

* Source: "Compensating Expatriates for the Cost of Living Abroad." *Studies in Labor Statistics,* No. 14, 1955. Washington, D.C.: National Industrial Conference Board.

such factors as rent, school costs, food, fuel, clothing, income tax, etc. This specific information is supplied to the company by the employee.

"While outside of the United States, the employee's base salary will not be adjusted as the result of cost-of-living allowances made by the company for people working inside the United States. When the employee returns to the United States on a permanent basis, he loses the foreign service and foreign cost-of-living allowances, and his base salary is adjusted to the extent of any cost-of-living adjustment made in this country during the period of his foreign service."

"Representative employees submit cost-of-living budgets showing amounts of local expenditure necessary to maintain an American standard of living in each foreign country. These amounts are then compared with the amounts of local currency available to these employees through payment in the foreign countries of dollar salaries converted at our standard salary exchange rates, which may or may not be the latest free exchange rates. Cost-of-living allowances, when necessary, are established on the basis of deficits so computed.

"Department of State indexes of living costs are used as a check on the results of these cost-of-living budget comparisons."

"First, we match the average cost-of-living allowances paid by competitive companies. Second, spot cost-of-living studies are made in areas where no sound data are available and where we have sufficient employees to justify the cost of such studies. Third, in areas of no sound data and few employees, we request the highest-paid employee to estimate the percentage by which foreign cost of living exceeds the United States by categories (food, clothing, etc.). This is checked by judgment and an equitable allowance paid.

"Flat-amount cost-of-living allowances are applied where appropriate and competitive with other companies. Percentage allowances appear appropriate where living costs are proportionate to income."

"Annually, each of our American employees on foreign assignment submits a cost-of-living report, which covers average monthly expenditures expressed in local currency. Since we do not place any specific limitations on expenditures reported, these individually prepared reports are reviewed for reasonableness and may be adjusted either up or down. After the reported cost-of-living report has been reviewed, we calculate the 'indicated post allowance' in accordance with a special formula.

"The 'indicated post allowance' is compared with the cost-of-living data reported in the Department of State *Standard Regulations* (*Government Civilians, Foreign Areas*). If the indicated post allowance compares favorably with the data compiled by the State Department, it is then authorized and paid to the employee in local currency. Once authorized, post allowances are not reviewed during the current year unless unforeseen circumstances (such as sudden devaluation of currency, etc.) arise before the time of the next annual review.

"Company has statistical organizations that do research on the cost of living."

"For a cost-of-living allowance, a specific amount is determined by taking the average of three months' actual costs and applying against it 75% of the individual's salary. In each case, actual costs are supported as far as possible with receipted bills, such as rent receipts, paid utility bills, etc. Per diems are established by taking the cost of hotel accommodations for a room with bath in a first class hotel and adding to it the cost of meals, plus service charges and taxis, if any, as well as out-of-pocket tips and a reasonable allowance for daily use of taxis.

"For those whose salaries are $10,000 per year or more, we use a different method from the one stated above to arrive at a cost-of-living allowance. In these cases we apply their actual costs in the foreign post with what they would have been were they living in the United States. If total foreign costs are higher, the difference between these costs and those in New York are paid as a living allowance. If the costs abroad are lower than they would be in New York, no allowance is paid."

"It is usually determined through actual knowledge of conditions in the individual country as a result of previous residence of our employees or of repeated visits by home office personnel. Otherwise, through a comparative study of the allowances granted by the Department of State."

"Up until 1950 we used United States base salary, plus percentages for cost of living and for what we termed isolation pay. Since 1950, we have established individual salaries on the basis of observation of local economics and information secured from other companies having personnel domiciled in the particular country."

APPENDIX

THE STATE DEPARTMENT INTERCOUNTRY INDEXES *

The United States Department of State compiles two intercountry indexes—the *Effective Index* and the *Local Index*. The two indexes are identical, with one exception. The effective index, which is used as a measure of intercountry differences in living costs for Americans employed abroad by the United States Government, takes into consideration prices in government commissaries, post exchanges, etc. The local index which is used by a number of American companies as a measure of intercountry differences in living costs for their American expatriates takes into consideration only the prices in the local market.

These indexes are two of the very few intercountry measures of cost of living applying to Americans working and living abroad. Indexes are computed for almost all major foreign cities. No other intercountry index for Americans has such extensive coverage.

* Source: "Compensating Expatriates for the Cost of Living Abroad." *Studies in Labor Statistics,* No. 14, 1955. Washington, D.C.: National Industrial Conference Board.

The Local Index

The local index is used as an intercountry measure by a number of American companies and is a variation of the State Department's effective index. The indexes are computed in the same manner, but the prices used in the computations differ. Every price used in the computation of the local index is collected in the local market in each foreign city, while the effective index usually uses commissary or post-exchange prices, as well as local prices.

If available, imports from the United States and other countries, where necessary or where savings can be effected, are also used. (See *The Effective Index,* page 443.)

Taxes

There are many characteristics of the local index which should be given due consideration by all companies using or contemplating using it.

An American national employed abroad by our government pays income tax to the United States Government on his basic salary but not on his cost-of-living or quarters allowance. Since the tax rate of United States Government employees is the same whether they work at home or in a foreign country, no tax differential exists. On the other hand, an American national employed abroad by a private company must pay a foreign income tax, if the country of his residence levies such a tax. Since the foreign tax rate is usually different from the United States tax rate, a tax differential does exist. The local index does not measure the tax differential although a number of American companies do consider the tax difference between areas.

Pricing

All prices used in computing the local index are collected in the local market. If an item is not sold in the local market, similar items are priced instead. The substitute items are selected by the government employees who live at the post and prepare the price report. For example: fresh milk is sold in quantity in the United States and is one of the items used in the index, but fresh milk is not available in all foreign countries. In such a situation, an equal amount (as regards calories, volume, etc.) of other forms of milk such as condensed milk, evaporated milk, or powdered milk would be priced for the local index as representative of the price of milk in the foreign city.

Stores Priced

Three local outlets are priced in each foreign city—a high-priced store, a medium-priced store and a low-priced store. The outlets included must be suitable for use by American government employees.

Number of Prices

Three prices are taken in each of three outlets—a high price, an average price, and a low price. The price which is used as representative in the foreign city is the median price of the nine quotations obtained in the three stores. In certain cases, the median price is obtained from the prices of a group of items rather than of an individual item. For instance, the median price obtained for all meats—beef, pork, lamb, and chicken—may be used as the price of all meats.

The Weighting Pattern

The weighting pattern of the local index is exactly the same as that for the effective index. The basic weights were derived from a Washington survey of two-person families. The basic weights, however, have been revised in a number of foreign cities by including additional expenditure. These additional weights, known as "use factors," reflect servant help, health and sanitation at the post, climate and availability of restaurants. (See Effective Index.)

Cost Differentials Not Computed

There are certain major expenditures which are not taken into consideration in the local index. Housing, including fuel, light and gas, is a major expenditure not measured by the local index. The United States Government provides a special housing allowance to their employees. (See Housing Allowance.) There are also a few other expenditures peculiar to employment outside the United States which are not measured in the local index, such as the cost of education. (See *The Effective Index* below for components measured.)

The Effective Index

The effective index is the official measure used to compute the cost-of-living allowances, if any, paid to all United States citizen civilians employed abroad by the government. It compares the cost of living for government employees in foreign locations with that of government employees in Washington, D.C. This index does not measure the difference in housing costs. A special allowance is provided for housing. Procedures followed in the computation of the effective and local indexes are identical except that in the former the median prices at the post include prices from those sources available only to government employees, as well as prices in the local markets.

Prices used in computing the indexes are collected annually or semiannually in the foreign cities, and quarterly in Washington. The indexes may be computed more often, however, if there are any drastic changes in the cost of living or in exchange rates which affect the amount of the allowances. The methodology used in computing total expenditures is identical in Washington, D.C. and the foreign cities. Changes in prices in Washington are taken into consideration, as are any changes in the foreign cities.

The basic weighting patterns of the two indexes are identical, both being determined from a Washington budget. The final weighting pattern for a post, however, will differ from the Washington pattern in a great many respects. The total cost of the Washington budget is compared with the total cost of the same budget in a foreign city by computing the weighted average ratio of prices at the post to prices in Washington. The actual budgets, in dollars and cents, are not calculated as the ratios and weights provide the necessary indexes, with Washington equal to 100.0.

The basic weights used in calculating the index were developed from an expenditure survey made in 1940 by the Bureau of Labor Statistics. Only government employees with two-person families were surveyed. The consumption pattern of government employees in Washington was used as the measure of the level which government employees abroad should maintain. The basic weights used are as follows:

Component	*Weight*
Food	22.7
Clothing	11.5
Household service	5.6
Other household operation	3.1
Furnishings and equipment	7.5
Transportation	9.7
Medical care	7.7
Personal care	2.6
Food away from home	7.9
Recreation	5.0
Tobacco	1.8
Miscellaneous	14.9
Total	100.0

Key items were then chosen to represent all the items which the average government employee's two-person family consumed. These key items make up the "market basket," which is priced in Washington and at each foreign post. The cost of this weighted market basket in Washington is compared with the cost of the same weighted market basket for each foreign post.

The market basket has not always fitted the way of life of the American Government employee in a foreign city. This fact has brought about a revision of the basic weights used for some of the city indexes. The expenditure items that were added are known as "use factors," and are based upon such things as servant help, health and sanitation at the post, climate, and the availability of restaurants.

For example, in many foreign countries, a servant or servants are considered to be a definite necessity by the United States Government for American Government employees. In such cases, the weighting factor for household service is adjusted upwards to include the volume of additional servant help. The type and number of servants allowed depend upon the actual number and type being used by the medium-grade State Department employees in the city. When an allowance is made for servants, additional weight is given for food and clothing for servants, the amount and kind more or less determined by the consumption patterns of the country.

RATE SCALE USED TO DETERMINE LIVING ALLOWANCES FOR GOVERNMENT EMPLOYEES

COST-OF-LIVING INDEX AT POST (WASHINGTON EQUALS 100)	POST CLASSIFICATION	% APPLIED TO SPENDABLE INCOME IN DETERMINING ALLOWANCE
102.5–107.4	1	5
107.5–112.4	2	10
112.5–117.4	3	15
117.5–122.4	4	20
122.5–127.4	5	25
127.5–132.4	6	30
132.5–137.4	7	35
137.5–144.9	8	41.2
145.0–154.9	9	50
155.0–164.9	10	60
165.0–174.9	11	70
175.0–184.9	12	80
185.0–194.9	13	90
195.0–204.9	14	100
205.0–214.9	15	110

The pricing abroad is done by State Department employees, usually a member of the administrative or economic staff. The pricing in Washington is done by the Bureau of Labor Statistics. In overseas stations, prices are collected not only in the local market but also in commissaries, post exchanges, etc.

Since prices must be collected from the stores where government employees actually trade, prices from post exchanges, commissaries, etc., must be taken into consideration in the effective index. The government employee may also have the privilege of importing many items duty free, and these prices are also taken into consideration. While government employees have the use of these special facilities, they must still purchase a number of goods and services from local outlets.

To determine whether to use the local store prices or commissary prices the government employee is asked to fill out a questionnaire listing the stores where he usually buys. The results of these questionnaires determine where the pricing should be done. It may happen that prices are collected from both sources for the effective index. If so, the price used for the market basket is a weighted price. For example: item A cost $1 in the commissary and $2 in the local market. If the questionnaire showed that employees purchase item A in the commissary 80% of the time, the weighted price of item A used in the effective index would be $1.20.

$$\begin{aligned} \$1 \times .80 &= \$\ .80 \\ \$2 \times .20 &= \underline{\ \ \ .40} \\ &\ \ \ \$1.20 \end{aligned}$$

Before obtaining the one local price for each item, a number of prices are collected in the local stores. Prices are collected in the local market for every item, but only those items actually purchased by government employees in the local market are used in the computations of the effective index. Three outlets in the city are chosen from which prices are obtained. Their selection depends upon their suitability for American patronage and their price levels. The three stores chosen represent a high-priced store, a medium-priced store and a low-priced store.

Prices vary from store to store and also within a store. Every item in a store usually has a range in price from high to low. Where a range exists, three prices are obtained—a high price, a medium price, and a low one. Nine prices in all are collected for every item priced in the local market. The local price used in the computations of the index is the median price of the nine local prices. The median price is used because it is not as influenced by extremes as is a simple arithmetic average. Assume the following prices:

PRICES	HIGH-PRICED STORE	MEDIUM-PRICED STORE	LOW-PRICED STORE
High price	$1.50	$1.25	$1.10
Medium price	1.25	1.10	.95
Low price	1.00	.90	.80

When the nine prices are arrayed, the median price is taken as the local price to be used in the computation of the index: $0.80–.90–.95–1.00–1.10–1.10–1.25–1.25–1.50. The median price of $1.10 is the local price.

The effective index is computed at least once a year in each foreign city where our government has American citizen civilians stationed. No attempt is made directly to match by specification all items in Washington and the foreign cities. Every item, or its assumed equivalent, is priced in the foreign cities, and the comparison with Washington is based on medians for each item, except in the food component where subgroup comparisons are made for meats, fruits and vegetables (fresh and canned) and milk. In all other groups, the ratio of medians for each article at each post to the Washington medians for similar articles are combined into a group ratio by use of relative weights for each item.

The foregoing describes how a median price is obtained for one item. The same procedure is followed in obtaining the median price of a number of items in the same group. Four meats—beef, pork, lamb and chicken—are priced if they are available in the local market. Nine prices are obtained for each type of meat. (See previous example of three prices in three stores.) Since four types of meat are priced, thirty-six prices would be obtained. The median price is then used to represent the price of meat, a subgroup for food, in the foreign city.

Prices in Washington are collected on the same form and following the same principles and procedures as at the foreign posts. The medians are determined and used in the same way, but there is only one Washington median which is used for both indexes. Uusually there are two medians—one for each index for a foreign post.

In order for an item to be included in the index, it must be sold in the local market. If an item is not available in the local market, the price of the item may be taken if the item is out of stock only temporarily. If the item is out for stock for a long period, the price would not be taken and a substitute would be obtained.

Pricing a seasonal item depends upon whether it is available in the local market. The only consideration is whether it can be purchased. Some fresh fruits and vegetables may be in short supply when the pricing survey is undertaken; yet, as long as the items are being sold in the market, they would be priced for the index along with the in-season items. There are, however, adjustments for significant seasonal variations in price to eliminate the seasonal factor. Clothing being sold in the market may also depend upon the season.

Only one index number exists for each foreign post, but the government has set up a scale so that the amount of the allowance is in proportion to salaries. The higher the salary the higher is the allowance for the cost of living. The allowance depends not only on salary but also on the family status of the employee; that is, whether he has dependents or not. A person with dependents receives more than an employee with none.

The scale of allowances for an employee with dependents is developed from the expenditure survey made by the Bureau of Labor Statistics. The amount of money which Washington families spent on goods and services varied from income level to income level, and the allowance tables are based on the amount of "spendable income" by salary brackets. The government, in this instance, defines spendable income as the average amount remaining from base salary after deducting for Federal income tax, retirement and savings (including life insurance).

33

PACKER, INC. *

Personnel Policies for Japanese Employees

In the summer of 1962, Thomas Peterson,[1] manager of the Japanese branch of Packer, Inc. was wondering what course of action he should take in establishing a salary policy for prospective Japanese plant employees in view of radically different management concepts prevailing in Japan.

Packer, Inc. was a large cosmetics manufacturer in the United States, with its home office in New York City. The firm was established by Mr. James Packer, father of the present president of the company, around the turn of the century. The company had grown to the point where it was rec-

* Prepared by Dr. Michael Yoshino in Tokyo, under the direction of Professor J. S. Ewing.

[1] Fictitious names throughout.

ognized as a major producer of cosmetics in the United States. In 1961 it recorded sales of over $45 million. The company manufactured medium-priced lines of make-up, perfume, colognes, men's toiletries, and pharmaceuticals to appeal to a broad segment of the middle-class market. Though the major share of the sales came from its domestic operations, the company exported its products to Europe, the Far East and some Latin American countries. It operated small facilities in Canada and Mexico.

The company's business in Japan began in 1928 with the exporting of limited lines of Packer cosmetics. From 1928 until the outbreak of World War II, the company, though the market was limited, established a favorable quality image in the minds of Japanese consumers. Due to tight exchange restrictions after the war, Packer was unable to resume its exports to Japan until 1952, when import-export licenses for a few basic lines were granted by tne Japanese government. These products met with initial success primarily for two reasons. Packer cosmetics, being American, enjoyed a built-in prestige. Moreover, the Japanese cosmetics industry had not yet fully recovered from the wartime damages. Packer products enjoyed, in fact, higher prestige in Japan than they did in the United States. They were favorably received by Japanese movie stars and society women.

The company exported its products through the Kano Trading Co., Ltd., its prewar franchise distributor for Japan, which in turn sold to a number of Japanese wholesalers and retailers. The Kano Trading Company relied on selective distribution, with tight control over its products and distributors, particularly in the area of price maintenance. Mr. Robert Jenkins, assistant export manager of the Packer home office, supervised the Japanese operations and made frequent trips to Japan to provide necessary aid and stimulation.

With increasing business in Japan and apparently bright future prospects, the company established, in 1957, a small but permanent sales liaison office in Tokyo. The specific purpose was to help Japanese distributors in any way possible to develop the market for Packer products. It gave Japanese distributors active support and assistance in such areas as advertising, sales promotion, point-of-sale display, sales-force training and supervision, dealer development and public relations. Sales in Japan had increased appreciably since the opening of the office.

The office force consisted of Mr. Jenkins as the manager, two American-born Japanese with an excellent knowledge of the language who served as assistant managers, and two American-educated Japanese girls recruited in Japan.

In 1960 Packer's U.S. management came to the conclusion that the Japanese market was substantial and different enough to warrant the establishment of local manufacturing facilities. It felt that this action was essential if it was to achieve a significant share of the Japanese market. It also believed that local production would cut down unit costs as well as make it possible to manufacture products particularly suited to the Japanese market.

Mr. Alan Warnick, executive vice president of the company, made a trip to Japan to survey the market and to make on-the-spot contacts with both U.S. and Japanese business leaders and government officials. Originally, the company was interested in establishing a joint operation with a prominent Japanese company. However, upon investigation, Mr. Warnick learned that none of the major companies was at that time interested in such a relationship with a foreign firm. Those which showed interest were either weak financially or incapable of projecting the quality image Packer had built in Japan.

On this trip, however, Mr. Warnick was impressed with the tremendous industrial recovery of Japan and its future potential. Upon his return to the United States, he recommended that the company establish branch manufacturing operations in Japan. The Board of Directors gave its formal approval on the matter in early 1961.

At this time, Mr. Jenkins was called home to replace the export manager who was retiring. To fill the vacancy, management chose Mr. Thomas Peterson, assistant manager of Canadian operations. Mr. Peterson, senior executives felt, had an ideal background, having had both production and export experience. Upon arrival in Japan, Mr. Peterson became busily involved in establishing manufacturing facilities. First, he and his assistants, through the aid of a competent Japanese lawyer, took care of the legal matters necessary for plant establishment. After a considerable search, they located a plant site in Tokyo. Shortly thereafter, building commenced on the site, with the aid of technical personnel sent from the home office.

Mr. Peterson then set out to establish a personnel policy for prospective Japanese employees. The plant would require around 150 to 200 Japanese, mostly young girls, and some supervisory staff. Until then, the branch had not set employment policies for Japanese nationals, since only two had been locally hired. Peterson knew, however, that soon he would begin to recruit supervisory personnel to be trained in Parker's production methods as well as administrative procedures. These, in turn, would be expected to train the locally-hired plant workers.

From a number of discussions Peterson had with both American and Japanese businessmen in Tokyo, he learned that personnel policy was particularly important to Japanese workers because of their basic concepts of work and employment. In addition, recruiting young girls had become increasingly difficult as the demand for them outweighed the supply. Generally, they were attracted to larger firms where they enjoyed higher salary and better fringe benefits. Moreover, production work was looked down on by many young people who preferred "clean" office work. These factors convinced him of the importance of working out a satisfactory employee relations policy if the company were to attract and keep young plant employees. Among the various phases of personnel relations, particularly baffling to him were the salary policies and practices prevalent among Japanese companies.

Following a tradition originating in feudal days, Japanese employers have paternalistic attitudes toward their employees. They were, he had learned from a series of conversations with Japanese businessmen and his assistants, held to be, and considered themselves to be, responsible for the employee's well-being, including his food, clothing, and shelter. The employer took direct responsibility for providing these things, along with such items as medical care and the education of the employee's children.

The Japanese system of rewards, it seemed, was based upon an employee's age, length of service and education. Relatively little emphasis was placed upon ability or job performance. An examination of the basis for the system of rewards and incentives in Japanese firms revealed an important difference in the kind of behavior rewarded in comparison with the industrial systems of the West. Reflecting the paternalistic philosophy, forms of compensation were more varied and less direct.

In order to clarify further his thinking on the matter, Peterson consulted with a number of American managers in Japan to learn their practices. To his disappointment, he learned that the majority of American firms in Japan took the form of joint operations with prominent Japanese firms. In these cases, newly formed subsidiaries drew their personnel primarily from the Japanese parent concerns and thus automatically followed the Japanese salary practices. In consequence, Japanese employees of the joint operations were usually granted the same privileges as those of the parent company in receiving various types of welfare payments and services. They also shared the welfare facilities provided by the Japanese parent company, so that American companies had no major problem as far as the compensation policy was concerned.

He further learned that only a very limited number of firms were operating as branches. These included small liaison offices, airlines, and banks. In the case of small offices where only a handful of personnel were required, there was usually no difficulty in implementing U.S. salary practices. However, the manager of a large foreign airline with over three hundred Japanese personnel, ranging from janitors to assistant general manager, told Mr. Peterson of the difficulty the company had experienced in its initial attempt to use foreign salary practices and payment systems. The company found it necessary to modify its policies substantially by allowing employees various types of welfare payments, bonuses, and retirement allowances. The company had also built a small dormitory for single male employees. It was still facing constant pressure from its employees to increase fringe benefits.

At this time, Mr. Warnick made another trip to Japan to inspect the progress of the operations and to confer with Mr. Peterson on various problems connected with initiating manufacturing operations. He discussed with Mr. Warnick salary policies and practices for prospective Japanese plant employees. Mr. Peterson reviewed the basic difference in Japanese concepts of work and management, and salary policy and practices compared with selected American firms operating in Japan.

It was Mr. Warnick's opinion that employees should be given a fair cash reward for the services they performed for the company, and that responsibility for living and health standards was an individual problem for each worker. The company, he felt, should not meddle in the employee's personal affairs to the extent practiced by Japanese employers. He also voiced strong opposition to the Japanese way of compensating workers in terms of age, length of service, and education. He felt that payment should be based on factors directly relating to the position an individual occupied and the extent to which he or she effectively fulfilled the demands of the position.

He also pointed out that the company could ill afford to undertake to provide the type of welfare given by a typical Japanese firm, particularly during the initial period of its operations. More basically, however, he found it distasteful to be so paternalistic and patronizing to employees. He suggested that Packer should pay wages in cash, basing the rate-of-pay as much as possible on the relationship of the rate of production to the prevailing one in the industry.

He further maintained that young Japanese workers might be won over to the American concept of salary administration easier than it might appear on the surface. Japanese youth were known to be susceptible to new ideas, as evidenced by their quick adoption of such foreign customs as dating and rock-and-roll music, and their fondness for Western dress. He observed that many aspects of traditional Japanese life were not as firmly tied to cultural patterns as many had previously thought, and it might well be that their perception of the role of an employer could easily be changed.

Though Mr. Peterson essentially agreed with Mr. Warnick on these points, he was not sure whether the program suggested by Mr. Warnick would work in Japan, in view of the discouraging comments he had heard from others. In making this decision, he was disturbed by a number of factors. First, he was not sure how deep-rooted the traditional concept of wage payment was among young people, nor was he sure how he could find this out without experimentation which might have a disastrous effect. Secondly, if he were to adopt some phases of the Japanese system, he was wondering how far he should go in this direction and how he could find out which phases to adopt and which to disregard. He also wondered if the company should adopt those practices which top management, including himself, found emotionally difficult to accept. Finally, if he were to work out a compromise plan, he was not sure how he could present it to Mr. Warnick, whose final approval was necessary.

QUESTIONS

1. What factors should Mr. Peterson consider in establishing salary policy for Japanese employees?
2. Should he adopt any phases of the Japanese philosophy and practices? What criteria should he use in selecting which phases to be adopted?
3. Should he adopt those practices which the top management, including himself, find it difficult to accept?
4. If he were to work out a compromise plan, how should he seek Mr. Warnick's approval?

Exhibit 1

No. of Job Applications & Job-Demands of Public Employment Security Offices

Year	Job Applications (A)	Job Demands (B)	A/B
1956	1,199,000	458,000	2.6
1957	1,180,000	572,000	2.1
1958	1,407,000	547,000	2.6
1959	1,341,000	680,000	2.0
1960	1,191,000	881,000	1.4
1961	1,353,000	1,140,000	1.2
1962	1,281,000	1,457,000	0.7

Source: Department of Labor, Japan.

Exhibit 2

Employment Security Bureau
Dept. of Labor, Japan
No. of Job Applications & Job Demands for Graduates of Junior and Senior High Schools

	Junior High School			High School		
Year	Job (A) Applications	Job (B) Demands	B/A	Job (A) Applications	Job (B) Demands	B/A
1956	513,000	511,000	1.0	457,000	360,000	0.8
1957	572,000	680,000	1.2	458,000	491,000	1.1
1958	545,000	677,000	1.2	514,000	547,000	1.1
1959	554,000	668,000	1.2	574,000	641,000	1.1
1960	507,000	949,000	1.9	616,000	897,000	1.5
1961	389,000	1,000,000	1.9	632,000	1,290,000	2.0

Source: Department of Labor, Japan.

34

THE CEYLON PLYWOOD COMPANY

Communication with Employees in a Developing Country

Since it secured independence from Great Britain in 1948, Ceylon has been trying to develop an industrial base. Dependent for foreign exchange and export earnings on three primary products, tea, rubber, and coconuts, all of which are in competition with similar products grown in other countries, the country has tried to reduce its dependence and to minimize a need for foreign exchange by utilizing other island commodities which lend themselves to fabrication within the country and thereby displace imports.

Ceylon has substantial forests which appeared to present some manufacturing opportunities and, after research by the Ceylon Scientific and Industrial Research Organization, a plywood factory to utilize local timber was established about sixty miles southeast of Colombo, the capital. The factory was situated in a small town, on the sea, connected with Colombo by rail and on a river which would permit some movement of logs by water during part of the year. For the remainder of the factory's needs, forests were close enough to keep haulage fairly easy and inexpensive.

As the factory town could not provide an adequate supply of workers for the new factory, the Ceylon Plywood Company found it necessary to recruit employees from neighbouring villages, some of them on the main highway from Colombo to Galle and some of them small agricultural communities a few miles back. In each case, the villages were peopled by easy-going, unsophisticated men and women who for generations had lived with little more effort than that required by mild farming and fishing. Although Ceylon has a literacy rate of about 85 percent in one or the other of the two main languages, Sinhalese and Tamil, education had generally not been concerned with technology.

In the home of the average worker in these villages, there was no electricity, running water, nor anything more elaborate mechanically than, occasionally, a battery-powered radio, a treadle-operated sewing-machine, or a bicycle. Clothing for men was usually a sarong and for women a sari; some of the men might wear a Western-style shirt and the younger men and women might also have a suit or dress of Western design.

Despite the lack of contact with mechanization or technology, workers from the villages displayed considerable ability in learning skills necessary for performing the plywood factory's job. Where possible, these were fragmented so as to simplify training, and training itself was confined to the essentials necessary to get on with the job. If the officials of the factory concerned with production believed that a man had the potential necessary to perform a task, he was trained by a foreman and put to work.

A very simple job was that of firing the boiler which provided steam for the ply-bonding operations and for forming. The boiler was located in a shed some distance from the main factory, where the wood which was burned for fuel could be made available. A village man, Siva Rajana, was hired as fireman, shown what to do, and told that he was to throw wood into the firebox to the degree necessary to keep a needle on the pressure gauge at 150, which was the number of pounds per square inch necessary to keep the factory in operation. If the needle fell below that figure, he was to throw in more wood; if it went above, he could stop firing until the needle showed signs of falling under the 150 figure.

In the humid, hot climate of coastal Ceylon, firing a wood furnace by hand is warm, unpleasant work. However, for a few weeks Rajana performed satisfactorily, and the mill always had adequate pressure. One Wednesday morning, however, the factory operatives discovered there was no pressure at all; a check of the boiler indicated that the fire was out and the fireman asleep beside the furnace. Roused from his sleep somewhat urgently and pressed for an explanation, he pointed to the gauge. This, a foreman found, had had the needle set, presumably by a pair of pliers, at 150 and Rajana indicated that he had done it.

After the steam had been gotten up again, the management met to consider what should be done. Most of the management group agreed that summary dismissal was indicated, but the personnel manager differed. He gave as his opinion, without being able to support it, that the action was an effect, not a cause, of something in the company's labor relations. He asked for an opportunity to talk the whole thing over with Rajana, saying that if he could not establish that something more than malingering or deceit was involved, he would accept the idea of dismissal.

QUESTIONS

1. What explanation can you advance for the fireman's action?
2. How should the personnel manager seek to establish the facts in the case?
3. What action should he take with regard to Rajana?
4. What implications does this have for the Ceylon Plywood Company's labor-relations program?

35

ROBERT THOMPSON *

Inefficiency in Lebanon versus the American Way

After a few years of work in the engineering offices of a large American oil company, Robert Thompson was sent to the company's Lebanon subsidiary. In Beirut, Thompson found himself responsible for the operation of a small design office. Several Lebanese engineers and draftsmen worked under him.

Shortly after his arrival, it became necessary to move the office to another part of the building. On the Saturday afternoon that had been picked for the move, the Lebanese porters who had been brought in to do the moving job arrived to begin work. In Thompson's judgment, the porters were confused about how to move some of the equipment, and they seemed to be working at a rather leisurely pace. Two Lebanese engineers in the office ignored the whole operation.

Thompson was anxious to get the job over and go home. He wondered whether he should step in and give the porters a hand. The thought

* Fictitious name.

also occurred to him that there was a good chance to show how helpful Americans are, how they didn't mind doing manual labor when it would be useful in speeding things up.

QUESTION

What should Bob Thompson do?

36

HOLIDAY IN CHITTAGONG

Lack of Appreciation of Pakistani Religious Customs

Walter Carlson was an oil company refinery engineer. His work, after graduation from engineering school, had taken him to refinery operations in various parts of the United States, to Canada, and to Latin America, and, by the time he was 45, he had developed a reputation as a hard-driving, tough, able executive. He set high standards of performance for himself and for his subordinates.

After many years of plant work, he was transferred to the head office of Inter-Global Oil, an American company with operations in many parts of the world. In response to a request from the government of Pakistan, Inter-Global was building a refinery at Chittagong, in East Pakistan, and Carlson's job was to work on the planning of this refinery. Although he was not in direct charge of the project, he took an active part in the planning and design of the refinery, and in making the necessary arrangements in the U.S. Actual construction, however, was the job of a company specializing in refinery building.

Shortly before the refinery was to go on stream, one of the Americans who had been sent out to manage it took ill, and Carlson, on short notice, was asked to go to Chittagong to take the man's place. He arrived there at about the time operations were to begin and found himself under considerable pressure. Most of the management group were relatively new to Pakistan and to each other, and the problems of developing an effective team spirit were considerable, although the plant general manager was, in Carlson's view, able, and so were the other executives.

Carlson's assistant, a Pakistani engineer, had received training in petroleum engineering in the U.S. and seemed to Carlson to be technically qualified; Carlson had not had time, under the circumstances, to form much of an opinion otherwise, but the man appeared reasonably capable.

Late one afternoon a rush order came through for Carlson's action, and the assistant was involved. When Carlson told the man that he would have to be in the office early the next morning, the Pakistani said "I am sorry, Mr. Carlson, but tomorrow is Eid.[1] It will not be possible for me to be here until late in the afternoon. I thought you knew about the day."

To this Carlson reacted violently: "I don't give a damn if it's Christmas tomorrow! You damn well better be here early and no nonsense." He stepped into his office and slammed the door shut, leaving the Pakistani standing, somewhat nonplussed, in the outer office. Other native employees in the office had heard the exchange, and word about it circulated quickly.

An hour later the telephone in Carlson's office rang. It was the general manager of the refinery, saying "Carlson, the plant's shutting down on a walk-out. The men say, as far as I can find out, that you insulted their religion and they won't go back until we fire you. What the hell did you do and what the hell can we do now?"

QUESTIONS

1. What action should the general manager take?
2. What action should Walter Carlson take?
3. How might this incident have been avoided?

[1] Eid-al-Fiter is celebrated after Ramadan as a Thanksgiving after the Fasting-of-one-month. It is considered as the most important of all the Muslim festivals. Slightly lesser in degree is Eid-al-Bagar, sacrificing animals, which is approximately 2 months and 10 days after Eid-al-Fiter. These religious holidays are government-approved paid holidays, and every employer is expected to exempt workers for prayers which start between 9 and 10 A.M., take from 30 to 45 minutes, and usually are held in a community congregation outside the town. By the time a participant returns it is about noon.

37

MOOSAJEES, LTD.

Motivating Workers for Greater Productivity in a Developing Country

The management group of Moosajees, Limited of Ceylon was concerned with increasing the company's production of combed or hackled coconut fiber for export. A major problem, as the company saw it, was not to increase the number of employees, for space limitations prevented this. Rather, the management believed, ways should be devised to secure increased productivity from individual workers. However, the attitude of Ceylonese employees raised certain difficulties and conventional methods of stimulating productivity had not proved successful.

Coconuts are stripped of their husks, split, and dried into copra, which is shipped abroad to be processed into oil, and this export is one of Ceylon's major foreign-exchange sources. In recent years other coconut products such as fibers have found expanding markets. Increased demand for fibers had led to Moosajees' concern with worker productivity.

Moosajees, Limited was one of Ceylon's major exporters of fiber. The company had a processing plant in Colombo, the country's capital. Recovery of fiber from the husks of coconuts was done at various mills, mainly situated to the north and northeast of Colombo in the coconut-producing areas. The fiber was delivered to Moosajees who, as shippers, stored, sorted, graded, baled, and exported the commodity. The company received two kinds of fibers: mattress and bristle. The latter type, distinguished by its longer staple, could be further processed by combing or hackling. It was then tied into bundles and was used in the production of fiber brushes.

For the purpose of combing or hackling brush fiber it had been customary in Ceylon to use women. Moosajees employed more than 300 women for this purpose. The women were paid on a piece rate, on the basis of a hundredweight (112 pounds) of fiber hackled. Rates varied according to the quality hackled but had risen in recent years from Rupees [1] 5/50 to Rupees 8/25 per hundredweight for the upper quality limit.

As payment was on a piece-rate basis and because of local customs and attitudes, Moosajees had never kept a strict check on attendance or on the exact number of hours worked each day by women employees. Many women living in the neighborhood of the warehouse came to work in their spare time. They worked as long as they felt like it, returning home to prepare meals and attend to their children, or when they were bored with the rather unpleasant and tiring hackling process.

Under the demand situation which prevailed for a long period, the company had been content to accept these conditions of work for its female operatives. While production could not be effectively organized, this had not been particularly significant. Hackling was a hand operation not involving machinery. Normal daylight was adequate for the combers and hacklers, weather conditions in Colombo required little more than a roof on the hackling building, and the irregular output of the women actually made checking their production fairly simple, since it combined to produce a fairly steady, if limited, yield. No timekeeping records were necessary; normal security precautions for the entire warehouse were sufficient; and everybody seemed satisfied.

However, two things occurred which made increased production important. The first of these was an increase in foreign demand for hackled fibers which Moosajees were anxious to meet since the company's management was considerably more profit-oriented than were its women employees. The second was a continuing decline in Ceylon's foreign-exchange position, which had concerned the government and led it to encourage those companies in the export trade to do what they could to expand sales abroad. Moosajees, Limited had, therefore, both economic and patriotic reasons for producing more hackled fiber.

[1] $1 = 4.70 rupees, approx.

The most obvious way to increase output was to hire more employees. Since Ceylon has a chronic unemployment problem, it was not difficult to find women who were willing to work. However, limitations of space prevented any significant expansion in the company's labor force. Moreover, the country's labor laws prohibited the use of female workers in a night shift, so that two- or three-shift operation was impossible. If, as an alternative, the company displaced old but less productive workers in favor of new ones who might be more productive, the result was likely to be difficulties with the government department of labor or with labor organizers. Since the company had never developed production norms which it could enforce, dismissal of an employee for what Moosajees might consider low production would not necessarily be accepted as adequate cause.

The company recognized that one solution might be to work toward the development of production standards, and that this should be prefaced by enforcement of attendance and of working hours. However, an attempt to do this merely led to strong resentment and expressions of annoyance. Any effort to attract women outside normal working hours seemed also destined to fail, since most of the female work force was married and occupied with home duties at those times.

The next step taken was to increase payment for fiber hackled, in the hope that this would lead to greater output. Somewhat to the surprise of the Moosajees management, however, the result was not increased production but poor attendance. Apparently, while Moosajees had not established production norms or tasks for the workers, they themselves had developed earnings objectives of their own. When this objective was reached, the employee merely failed to report for work. If an increase in the piece rate made it possible to secure the objective in less time, then the employee saw little reason to put in more time to earn more than she wanted.

Moosajees' management was considering what it might do. Better enforcement of hours and attendance records was a long-run objective and pretty clearly one which could not be implemented at this time. As the consumption level of Ceylonese rose, it seemed reasonable to assume that increased consumer-goods wants would be developed and that the desire to meet these wants would lead to an interest in higher earnings, but this, too, was in the future. Appeals to produce more goods because of the country's need for export sales was suggested. However, the management doubted that the typical female worker would be moved by patriotic appeals. Ceylon had been independent only since 1948, and national fervor was strongest among intellectuals and government employees. Workers such as Moosajees employed were concerned with little more than food, shelter, clothing, and some relatively simple pleasures.

SECTION FOUR

The New World of International Business Management: Policies and Problems

38

MR. WALTER MURRAY

Developing Suppliers in Italy for an American Variety Chain

Mr. Walter Murray was the resident buyer in Italy for an American variety chain. His primary responsibility was to seek out products made in Italy which might prove profitable items in the stores of his company. The general pattern was for Mr. Murray to send an item which seemed to have possibilities to the buying office of the chain in New York. There it would be reviewed by skilled purchasers who would work out estimates about the quantities of the item which could be sold at varying prices. These estimates would be sent back to Mr. Murray, if the product appeared worth further investigation. Mr. Murray would then return to the manufacturer to see if a price to the chain could be developed which would make sale of the product profitable in the U.S. As a general rule of thumb, the maker's selling price in Italy would have to be about one-fifth of the price at retail in the U.S., to allow for transportation, customs, and normal mark-ups.

The variety chain was interested in articles which were clearly of Italian or foreign origin and which might therefore be expected to sell on that basis. In addition, it sought staple products which were in regular demand and which were not necessarily associated in the customer's mind with foreign goods. Many of the imported products had relatively short counter life since they sold as novelties, but this was to some extent compensated for by higher-than-average markups. It was very difficult for the chain's customers to assign expected prices to novelty items, particularly if these were exclusive to the stores.

In addition to seeking to develop prices which would be profitable to his principal, Mr. Murray had to be sure that quality would be up to the level of the sample and that adequate quantities could be obtained. The variety chain was not the largest in the U.S., but its stores numbered more than one hundred, and it had to be able to offer an item to each store's manager. European manufacturers, particularly those who made many of the goods sold in variety chains, were not used to high volume levels. At least up until World War II, many producers had preferred to shelter behind high-price/low-volume situations which minimized risk.

Sometimes the New York buyers would conclude that a product had sales potential if modifications or changes could be made which would make it more acceptable to American purchasers. The company did not make advances to manufacturers and it would not provide capital for any purpose, particularly for plant expansion. Mr. Murray, however, was quite willing to work with suppliers to see if improvements in their operations to provide lower costs or greater output could be made. As an engineer, he was experienced in production, and he would also attempt to help in other aspects of the Italian maker's activity.

Because of the need for high volume and because of the intense competition for space in the chain's stores, the company could not guarantee orders beyond a relatively short period. On occasion, a trial order would be placed; if this was successful, larger orders would follow. These would be for specific quantities, however, and the supplier had no assurance that similar orders would succeed the first or second, because Mr. Murray was purely an intermediary, all firm orders being placed on instructions from New York.

One product which came to Mr. Murray's attention and which interested him was a plastic, toy building block. A system of projections and indentations on the blocks permitted a remarkably sturdy structure. Building was easy for fairly small children while the range of models possible, the detailing, and the finish made the blocks attractive to older children and, perhaps, to adults as a hobby. The system had been developed by a pair of architects for building models of proposed buildings for display to clients, and the blocks were carefully constructed to scale.

A manufacturer had secured the right to make the blocks from the architects. In addition to sales to other architects, he had been quite successful in securing distribution in many Italian toy shops. Mr. Murray believed that the prices charged by the stores, which were set by the manufacturer, placed the blocks beyond the reach of most Italians and, he was afraid, of many Americans. He knew, however, that Italians tended to spend proportionately more of their incomes on their children than Americans, and the high price had apparently not inhibited shops from stocking them.

A set of blocks was forwarded to New York. Mr. Murray was informed in due course that the company would be interested in a fairly substantial initial order but not at the prices which had been quoted. Mr. Murray went back to the manufacturer and was able to demonstrate that the purchase of additional molding equipment and some changes in the small factory should permit a greatly increased output. This, in turn, would result in prices low enough to interest his variety chain. The manufacturer, however, refused to make the investment or the changes. He stated, in explanation, that to lower the price of the blocks would also lower their prestige with architects, whom he apparently regarded as his most important market.

QUESTIONS

1. What action should Mr. Murray take?
2. How do you explain the attitude of the manufacturer?

39

FRANCIS X. O'SHEA

Violations of International Agreements by Non-U.S. Concerns

One morning, as he sat in his office in Dar-es-Aviv, capital of the small Middle-Eastern country of Omar, Francis X. O'Shea pondered a letter from the New York head office of Nomad Airlines, for which he was Omar's regional sales manager. The letter drew Mr. O'Shea's attention to a report he had recently submitted on passenger traffic originated by his office compared with passengers travelling on other airlines, and commented somewhat acidly on the fact that Mr. O'Shea's performance left something to be desired—at least by New York. There was a strong suggestion that Mr. O'Shea had better improve his showing, and Mr. O'Shea was thinking about how this could be done.

Mr. O'Shea knew that his line was the equal, if not the superior, of competing lines in terms of aircraft and schedules, since it converted early to pure-jet planes. Cabin service, he felt, was not up to the standards of some European lines and was the occasion for constant training of cabin crews in the hope of improving it; however, it was his belief that most, or at least many, of the Omar passengers preferred to fly an American line because of a strong pro-American bias. For that reason, he doubted if the fall in sales could be attributed to any internal cause, and he was fairly sure he knew where the difficulty lay.

It lay, Mr. O'Shea believed, in rate cutting on the part of other airlines. Despite the rigid rules of the International Air Transport Association, or IATA, Mr. O'Shea was sure that some lines were willing to take a chance on the heavy fine which IATA would levy on rate-cutters if it caught them, if this could secure more business. Or rather, he thought, it was perhaps not the lines themselves but the travel agencies with which they dealt that were at fault. Some of these agencies, he knew, would reduce commissions to get business, and he strongly suspected that the lines involved were working with the agencies to make this possible.

Omar is an old country and has for at least two thousand years been a trading nation. Bargaining is a national characteristic, or so Mr. O'Shea had concluded, and it was perfectly natural for an Omarite who contemplated a flight anywhere to see if he could better the published fare. Nomad Airlines had firmly refused to attract business on this basis, and Mr. O'Shea's superior in New York had indicated with no uncertainty the consequences to any Nomad employee who was caught rate-cutting or committing any other breach of IATA regulations. At the same time, Nomad was intensely competitive, and its president disliked nothing more than losing revenue passengers to other carriers.

Mr. O'Shea knew that one of the worst offenders in the matter of rate cutting was a large Dar-es-Aviv travel agency, owned by Omarites. The agency, although it was of local ownership, was associated with important agencies in other countries and it consequently was a firm which could not be treated lightly. In addition, its freight and express department originated a good deal of air cargo traffic and Nomad had secured a considerable amount of business from the agency. Some days before Mr. O'Shea had received the New York letter, some information had come into his hands which, he thought, would enable him to prove to the satisfaction of IATA that the agency and a large European airline were actually cooperating to cut fares, and this information had given Mr. O'Shea cause for thought.

If he could make the charges stick, the agency would probably lose its recognition by the airlines, and perhaps by other travel services, such as steamships and hotels. The airline would also be fined, or so Mr. O'Shea believed. However, the main difficulty in determining a course of action arose from Mr. O'Shea's lack of knowledge about the extent to which other lines and other travel agencies were lowering fares. He knew that his own line, which had frequently taken a somewhat righteous tone in seeking to enforce such IATA agreements as limiting meals for economy passengers to sandwiches, and then limiting the size and constitution of the sandwiches, was not popular with its competitors. If enough of these other lines were involved in the rate cutting, Mr. O'Shea felt that pressure might be brought on IATA to go lightly on the offenders, to let them off with a warning.

If this happened, Mr. O'Shea knew what to expect. The travel agency, if it continued in business, would certainly do everything in its power to take business away from Nomad, and its power was considerable. It would certainly be helped in its action by the competing carriers, and Mr. O'Shea also was apprehensive that other travel agencies would support their injured colleague, since they could see nothing ethically wrong with rate cutting, and since they might easily resent anyone who sought to have one of their number punished. On the other hand, it might be possible to enlist their support first, in the hope that their desire to improve their competitive standing would lead them to help try to eliminate a large agency.

Mr. O'Shea also considered the possibility of persuading New York to blink its eyes at the Omar situation. He doubted that this would be likely, and he was afraid that any request to New York would be met with the adjuration to "get out there and sell the right way." On the other hand, he did not know if the rate-cutting situation was peculiar to Omar or was going on in other Middle Eastern countries; for that matter, it might be happening more widely than that, since airline competition was growing tremendously with the introduction of jet and turbo-jet planes.

QUESTION

What course of action should Mr. O'Shea follow in dealing with the loss of sales apparently caused by rate cutting?

40

HEWLETT-PACKARD COMPANY *

Considerations of Operation in the European Common Market

In view of the establishment of the European Common Market, the management of the Hewlett-Packard Company, manufacturer of electronic instruments in Palo Alto, California, was considering the possibility of manufacturing some of the company's products in countries that were within this growing European market. This decision had been reached on the basis of their assessment of the potential growth of the European market and the several inducements offered by the Common Market to encourage U.S. firms to manufacture their products abroad.

In the spring of 1959, Mr. William R. Hewlett, Executive Vice-President of the company, had been asked by the executive committee to make preliminary recommendations concerning which form of overseas operations would be best suited to the needs of the Hewlett-Packard Company and in which of the six Common Market member nations its operations could be most effectively based.

Mr. Hewlett knew that the company had two alternative methods of manufacturing overseas—licensing or establishing their own subsidiary—and decided to investigate the advantages and disadvantages of each.

Licensing, he found out through reading and talking to his acquaintances experienced in foreign operations, had several advantages. By li-

* Prepared by Dr. Michael Yoshino while a student in the Graduate School of Business, Stanford University, under the direction of Professor J. S. Ewing.

censing manufacturing and marketing rights to overseas firms, Hewlett-Packard management would be dealing with going concerns that had market contacts, experienced management, and established organizations. The extent of Hewlett-Packard's participation would be the provision of technical know-how and some special equipment. Licensing would thus eliminate the tedious job of surveying the market, buying land, constructing plant facilities, selecting personnel, and performing many other tasks which were required when a company established a manufacturing subsidiary overseas. Since licensing made it possible to combine U.S. technical know-how with the experience and skill of the local manufacturer, the adjustment of the product characteristics to local needs was made easier. Moreover, this form of operation was much more flexible because licensing agreements could be reviewed periodically and, if they proved unsatisfactory, the agreements could be terminated by the company much more easily than it could discontinue a manufacturing organization. Thus, Hewlett-Packard's management believed that licensing was particularly attractive to a company like theirs which was relatively inexperienced in the field of foreign operations. Besides, they knew that a number of European manufacturers were quite anxious to enter into a licensing arrangement with a U.S. firm like Hewlett-Packard.

On the other hand, Mr. Hewlett had learned that licensing did have some serious limitations which had to be considered in making this decision. Lack of control over quality of products, distribution, and manufacturing policies often had in the past presented serious problems to U.S. licensors. There were also difficulties which could arise from misunderstandings due to differences in language, philosophy of business management, and commercial customs. The relationship between licensor and licensee was such that the attempts to iron out these problems were often difficult and demanded undue time and attention of already overworked executives of the licensor.

Mr. Hewlett also had noticed the following experience of one American licensor cited in an article appearing in the *Harvard Business Review:* [1]

> A large chemical company licensed a firm to manufacture and sell its products in a European country. The licensee pushed the parent company's name, brand and products and quickly built a substantial volume of business. But the United States company soon discovered that it was receiving only a negligible royalty for its participation in what had become a major market for its products, whereas the licensee was realizing tremendous profits. In order to retrieve control of the market which its own product and name had developed, the licensor was forced to buy a majority interest in the licensee's enlarged and prosperous company.

Most of these problems inherent to licensing would be avoided if a firm established its own manufacturing subsidiary. This form of operation had several attractive advantages. Primarily, the parent company retained tight control over the policies of its foreign subsidiary, particularly if the

[1] "How to research the overseas market by licensing," by Charles Henry Lee, *Harvard Business Review* (January-February 1958).

latter was wholly owned. It could set its own manufacturing as well as distribution policies and quality standard without being bound to the traditional ways of doing things which were frequently found in a foreign company, and most important of all, it could control its own destiny and reap maximum benefits from growth of the market. Establishing a manufacturing subsidiary also had its problems, however. It would be necessary to make long-term financial, managerial, and organizational commitments. Moreover, the parent company had to be prepared to make a large initial outlay for establishing the subsidiary and then sustaining its losses until the subsidiary became self-supporting. Risk factors also had to be considered inasmuch as there was always a possibility that the European Common Market, composed of the six independent nations, might collapse or its progress be seriously retarded. In addition, the parent company had to assume entirely new managerial responsibilities connected with operating a foreign subsidiary. Although Hewlett-Packard had had substantial experience in export operations, its management believed that the nature and magnitude of the problems of management on an international scale were quite different.

Mr. Hewlett planned to take a fact-finding trip to Europe accompanied by his assistant and a lawyer in May, 1960. Prior to this trip, he hoped to reach a tentative decision on which of the two alternative methods of operation would be best suited to the company. He also was anxious to know what factors his group must consider in arriving at the recommendation of which of the six countries should be the center of Hewlett-Packard's European operations.

Background of the Company

The origin of the Hewlett-Packard Company dates back to the undergraduate college days of Bill Hewlett and Dave Packard. In their course of studies at Stanford University they became impressed with the opportunities in the field of electronic instrumentation. Following their graduation in 1934, the two spent several years gaining business experience and continuing their education. Mr. Hewlett, while engaged in graduate study, perfected a new type of audio oscillator. The first instruments were sold to acquaintances in the industry. Immediately, users enthusiastically compared this equipment with the cumbersome and expensive instruments offered by competitors. Mr. Hewlett presented the new oscillator at the 1938 Institute of Radio Engineers meeting in Portland. As a result of this presentation the chief sound engineer for Walt Disney Studios bought nine oscillators for the stereophonic sound presentation of "Fantasia."

Hewlett-Packard was officially organized as a partnership in 1939 with assets of $538. Production was started in Mr. Packard's garage. Initially, profit was ploughed back into the business, and the two partners concentrated on developing new instruments to broaden the base of their operation. Soon the need for more space became apparent, and the business was moved to a concrete-block building near its original site. In 1941 Hewlett-Packard obtained its first government contract from the Army for six signal generators. As the United States became increasingly involved in the war, the company shifted its efforts to filling defense orders.

By 1943, one hundred people were working two shifts a day and sales reached $1,000,000. The volume of business reached a peak in 1944 when sales totaled $1.5 million and about a dozen different instruments were in regular production. The period immediately after the war was one of adjustment for the company's operations.

The firm incorporated in 1947 and sales again reached the 1944 level of $1.5 million. Operating as a corporation the company was able to meet the increasing needs for capital with a minimum of borrowing. During the same year the second major plant building was begun.

In the early 1950's the company introduced about 20 new products a year. With the advent of the Korean conflict the company again became involved in defense work. By 1952 about one half of the company's sales were of equipment that had been developed within the preceding three years. Although the company's increased level of business was not heavily dependent on direct sales to the government, the defense effort stepped-up the over-all demand.

To provide needed working space, another major construction program which more than doubled the total area of the building, was undertaken in 1953. Employment increased from about 300 people in 1951 to about 700 in 1954. In 1957, the company completed construction on two large, ultra-modern buildings on the 40 acre site adjoining the Stanford University campus. Sales reached $27,000,000 and 1,500 people were employed in the organization.

Sales in 1958 went over $30 million, employment jumped to 1,700, and 12 new instruments were introduced. The product line then totaled 373 items. Complete financial statements for 1958, and a 10-year review of earnings are presented as Exhibits 1 through 4.

While the company in the past had not used acquisition of other companies to enhance its growth, it acquired in 1958, through an exchange of Hewlett-Packard stock, 80% of the outstanding stock of the F.L. Moseley Company of Pasadena, California. The F.L. Moseley Company had in recent years enjoyed sales of about $1,500,000 from a line of X-Y recorders and related electronic instruments compatible with the Hewlett-Packard line.

Products Manufactured by Hewlett-Packard

Since its founding, the company's activities had been devoted to the design and manufacture of precision electronic measuring instruments. Although the firm manufactured close to 400 different types of instruments, the products fell into two broad categories. One category, which represented a fairly sophisticated engineering design, was basically an assembly type of operation from standard component parts. The other was equally complicated in design and required a great many special and precision parts, for which expensive tooling was required. The principal types of instruments include oscillators, voltmeters, signal generators, wave form analyzers, frequency-measuring equipment, microwave and waveguide test instruments, and oscilloscopes.

Export Operations

During the company's early stages its exports were handled by a local export house. This house, in turn, had representatives in various countries throughout the world. As the company grew, this method of distribution became unsatisfactory, and by agreement with the export house, the company took over the export operation by establishing an export department. Most of the overseas representatives were retained.

Hewlett-Packard's export market traditionally had run somewhere between 10% and 11% of their total sales. Due to the nature of the products, export sales were almost entirely to the more advanced countries. The company in 1959 had qualified sales representatives in 21 foreign countries. At that time, 60% of its foreign sales came from Europe, about 20% from Canada, and about 10% were divided between Australia and Japan. The remaining 10% was spread throughout the world.

Exhibit 1

HEWLETT-PACKARD COMPANY
BALANCE SHEET
OCTOBER 31, 1958 AND 1957

	October 31	
ASSETS	1958	1957
Current Assets:		
Cash	$ 644,880.43	$ 268,899.16
Notes and accounts receivable less provision for losses in collection: 1958—$8,734.62, 1957—$9,897.70	4,734,143.20	3,475,258.44
Inventories:		
Finished goods and work in process, at approximate cost	3,833,566.42	4,001,993.87
Raw materials, at lower of cost or market	1,518,101.36	1,769,394.14
Deposits and prepaid expenses	95,438.41	76,659.83
Total Current Assets	$10,826,129.82	$ 9,592,205.44
Property, Plant, and Equipment, at cost, less accumulated depreciation and amortization: 1958—$2,083,533.00, 1957—$1,480,128.94	$ 4,883,724.92	$ 4,983,916.51
Other Assets:		
Securities, at cost (1957—$37,800.00 pledged to secure long-term note)	$ 47,800.00	$ 47,800.00
Deferred patent expense	33,622.02	33,622.02
Organization expense	3,960.05	3,960.05
Total Other Assets	$ 85,382.07	$ 85,382.07
Total	$15,795,236.81	$14,661,504.02

EXHIBIT 1 (Cont.)

LIABILITIES	October 31 1958	1957
Current Liabilities:		
Short-term notes payable	$	$ 1,100,000.00
Long-term debt maturing within one year	44,206.81	154,948.92
Accounts payable and accruals	2,428,221.24	1,885,211.90
Provision for federal taxes on income	1,757,872.91	1,768,042.78
Total Current Liabilities	$ 4,230,300.96	$ 4,908,203.60
Long-Term Debt:		
Mortgage payable, 4½% due 1963	$ 375,383.42	$ 419,591.11
Leasehold, 4½% due 1961		300,000.00
Other (1957—$24,154.20 secured)		56,654.20
Total Long-Term Debt	$ 375,383.42	$ 776,245.31
Reserve:		
Capital Stock bonus payable		$ 885,968.00
Capital Stock and Surplus:		
Common stock, par value $1.00 a share Authorized 5,000,000 shares; reserved for stock options 45,461 shares at October 31, 1958, 45,527 shares at October 31, 1957; issued and outstanding, 1958—3,055,373 shares, 1957—3,000,000 shares	$ 3,055,373.00	$ 3,000,000.00
Paid-in Surplus	830,595.00	
Earned Surplus	7,303,584.43	5,091,087.11
Total Capital Stock and Surplus	$11,189,552.43	$ 8,091,087.11
Total	$15,795,236.81	$14,661,504.02

EXHIBIT 2

HEWLETT-PACKARD COMPANY
STATEMENT OF INCOME
YEARS ENDED OCTOBER 31, 1958 AND 1957

	1958	1957
Sales, net	$30,296,647.33	$27,948,789.65
Cost of goods sold	19,247,549.13	17,245,450.01
Gross profit on sales	$11,049,098.20	$10,703,339.64
Selling, administrative and general expense	6,562,678.56	5,738,327.93
Net profit from operations	$ 4,486,419.64	$ 4,965,011.71
Other Income	178,117.50	143,511.04
Total	$ 4,554,537.14	$ 5,108,522.75
Other deductions	83,610.65	110,074.57
Net income before provision for federal taxes on income	$ 4,580,926.49	$ 4,998,448.18
Provision for federal taxes on income	2,368,429.17	2,595,890.91
Net income before special charge	$ 2,212,497.32	$ 2,402,557.27
Special charge, net:		
Capital stock bonus to employees less federal taxes on income attributable thereto		425,264.64
Net income	$ 2,212,497.32	$ 1,977,292.63

EXHIBIT 3

HEWLETT-PACKARD COMPANY
STATEMENT OF SURPLUS
YEAR ENDED OCTOBER 31, 1958

	Paid-in	Earned
Balance, November 1, 1957		$5,091,087.11
Net income for the year		2,212,497.32
Excess of market value over par value of 55,373 shares of capital stock issued to officers and employees as a bonus	$830,595.00	
Balance, October 31, 1958	$830,595.00	$7,303,584.43

EXHIBIT 4

YEAR REVIEW OF EARNINGS
(Years Ended October 31)

	1958	1957	1956	1955	1954
Sales	$30,296,647	$27,948,790	$20,161,621	$15,338,179	$12,599,096
Other Income	178,117	143,511	109,403	74,349	59,914
Total	$30,474,764	$28,092,301	$20,271,024	$15,412,528	$12,659,010
Cost of Goods Sold	$19,247,764	$17,245,450	$11,990,207	$ 9,298,670	$ 8,516,446
Selling, Administrative and General Expense	6,646,289	5,848,403	4,541,827	3,203,014	2,577,405
Other Charges including Renegotiation Refund	—	—	—	36,787	73,375
Federal Taxes on Income	2,368,429	2,595,891	1,935,724	1,557,821	851,014
Total	$28,262,267	$25,689,744	$18,467,758	$14,096,292	$12,018,240
Net Income	$ 2,212,497	$ 2,402,557*	$ 1,803,266	$ 1,316,236	$ 640,770
Dividends Paid	—	$ 6,359	$ 250,000	$ 200,000	$ 150,000
Net Income per Share of Capital Stock**	$.724	$.786	$.590	$.431	$.210
Number of Employees	1749	1507	1169	765	700

	1953	1952	1951	1950	1949
Sales	$12,839,406	$10,952,980	$ 5,538,889	$ 2,301,744	$ 2,230,634
Other Income	43,361	41,441	24,802	11,841	9,682
Total	$12,887,767	$10,994,421	$ 5,563,691	$ 2,313,585	$ 2,240,316
Cost of Goods Sold	$ 7,996,778	$ 6,377,823	$ 4,075,280	$ 1,294,650	$ 1,238,849
Selling, Administrative and General Expense	2,290,537	2,278,643	363,548	658,553	570,153
Other Charges including Renegotiation Refund	20,908	—	—	—	—
Federal Taxes on Income	1,813,678	1,632,116	733,996	143,761	163,899
Total	$12,121,901	$10,288,582	$ 5,172,824	$ 2,096,964	$ 1,972,901
Net Income	$ 765,866	$ 705,839	$ 390,867	$ 216,621	$ 267,415
Dividends Paid	—	$ 60,000	$ 60,000	—	—
Net Income per Share of Capital Stock**	$.251	$.231	$.128	$.071	$.088
Number of Employees	622	573	491	195	145

* Before special charge, net of $425,264.64.
** Computed on the basis of 3,055,373 shares.

Exhibit 5

Selected Economic Indicators of the EEC Nations and the United States

Country	Population mid-1958 (millions)	Labor Force mid-1957	G.N.P. mid-1958	Industrial Growth rate 1948-58 (%)	Average Hourly wage 1957*
W. Germany	51.1	25.3	$ 72.4	13.0	$ .74
Italy	48.6	20.4	$ 39.4	9.0	.59
France	44.6	18.9	$ 60.6	6.2	.89
Netherlands	11.2	4.2	$ 14.3	3.2	.60
Belgium	9.1	3.6	$ 11.2	n.a.	.81
Luxemburg	.3	.2	$ .4	n.a.	n.a.
Common Market	164.9	72.6	$198.3	—	—
U.S.A.	174.1	70.7	$441.7	3.3	2.35

* Male employees in manufacturing including social charges.

Source: *European Common Market and Free Trade Area,* prepared by Rogers, Slade, and Hill, Consultant Marketing Management problems.

Exhibit 6

Gross Domestic Fixed Capital Formation as Percent of Gross National Product

Country	Average Capital formation 1950-53	Average Capital formation 1954-57	Capital formation 1958
Belgium	15	16	16
France	16	18	18
Germany	19	23	22
Italy	19	21	21
Netherlands	20	23	23

Source: *Europe Today,* The First National City Bank of New York.

Exhibit 7

Ownership of Consumer Durables Number of Units per 1,000 Population 1957

Country	Belgium	France	West Germany	Italy	Nether-lands	U.S.A.
Passenger cars	54	70	36	18	25	315
Motor cycles	23	41	48	43	16	3
Bicycles	325	190	315	145	450	143
Radio sets	249	233	277	131	264	890
Television	28	16	23	14	22	274
Refrigerators	53	49	39	20	10	265
Washing machines	151	56	45	6	104	235

Source: *Europe Today,* The First National City Bank of New York.

Exhibit 8

Electronic Component Exports to European Common Market Nations

1954	Electron Tube	Electron Tube Parts	Inductors	Crystal Diodes Transistors	Capacitors	Resistors
Netherlands	$ 68,046	$ 29,481	$ 23,107	$ 16,076	$ 60,852	$ 17,173
Belgium	236,291	5,886	27,911	38,052	53,719	33,244
France	502,854	40,147	74,145	58,932	112,622	224,539
W. Germany	174,815	64,078	14,463	23,740	32,012	10,856
Italy	287,798	77,784	61,721	6,669	39,995	42,619
	$1,329,804	$ 217,376	$201,347	$ 143,469	$299,200	$328,431
$2,519,627						
1957						
Netherlands	$ 74,610	$ 28,992	$ 15,429	$ 154,834	$ 76,388	$ 42,644
Belgium	184,045	1,077	128,049	194,806	142,258	51,699
France	446,523	250,248	163,569	723,866	156,391	244,658
W. Germany	321,908	78,307	20,402	153,694	70,361	80,398
Italy	818,928	202,427	547,594	413,104	79,154	152,834
	$1,846,014	$ 561,051	$875,043	$1,640,304	$531,552	$572,233
$6,026,167						
1958						
Netherlands	$ 40,810	$ 205,582	$ 16,310	$ 672,372	$ 21,547	$105,122
Belgium	162,793	6,964	37,252	77,609	87,431	64,469
France	359,598	249,709	170,316	1,207,073	203,625	248,179
W. Germany	989,190	128,188	57,508	168,043	37,952	87,421
Italy	298,280	444,610	623,783	708,761	102,361	190,174
	$1,850,671	$1,035,053	$905,169	$2,833,858	$452,916	$695,365
$7,773,032						

Figures not available on Luxemburg.

Source: *Electronics* (May 8, 1959).

Exhibit 9

Government Expenditure and Defense Expenditure of the Selected European Nations as % of National Income 1957

	Belgium	Denmark	France	Germany	Italy	Netherlands	Sweden	U.K.
National Income	100%	100%	100%	100%	100%	100%	100%	100%
Government Expenditure	26.6	19.4	30.4	17.4	24.7	25.8	24.5	32.4
Defense Expenditure	4.9	3.3	7.7	4.6	4.1	5.9	5.1	8.7

Per cents computed by the case writer. The original information was obtained from *Statistical Yearbook,* 1958, 10th Issue. New York: Statistical Office of the U.N., 1958.

EXHIBIT 10

PATTERNS OF U.S. INVESTMENT IN THE COMMON MARKET (MILLIONS OF DOLLARS)

Types of Investment	Manufacturing			Petroleum		
Country	1950	1958	% increase	1950	1958	% increase
Belgium-Luxemburg	35	89	154	17	47	176
France	114	270	137	75	179	139
W. Germany	123	315	156	38	164	332
Italy	19	91	379	37	110	197
Netherlands	23	48	109	43	126	193
Total	314	813	159	210	626	198

	All Others			Total Investment			
	1950	1958	% increase	1950	1958	% increase	As % of G.N.P.
Belgium-Luxemburg	13	27	108	65	163	159	1.4%
France	28	78	179	217	527	143	.9%
W. Germany	43	95	121	204	574	164	1.1%
Italy	7	63	800	63	204	319	1.0%
Netherlands	18	51	168	84	225	168	2.4%
Total	109	314	185	633	1,753	177	—

Source: *Europe Today,* The First National City Bank of New York.

EXHIBIT 11

RETURN ON U.S. DIRECT INVESTMENT IN THE EUROPEAN COMMON MARKET 1956-58 (Earnings as percent of total investment)

Country	Manufacturing	Oil	Others	Total
Belgium-Luxemburg	12	9	20	12
France	10	11	11	11
Germany	17	4	19	13
Italy	15	5	11	10
Netherlands	7	6	26	8
Total EEC	13	7	16	11

Source: *Europe Today,* The First National City Bank of New York.

BACKGROUND INFORMATION ON GUATEMALA *

Guatemala is situated about midway between the Equator and the Tropic of Cancer. It is bounded on the south by the Pacific Ocean, on the north and west by Mexico, and on the east by British Honduras, the Atlantic Ocean, Honduras, and El Salvador.

With an area of 42,364 square miles, about the size of Tennessee, Guatemala is the third largest of the Central American Republics after Nicaragua and Honduras.

The temperature of Guatemala ranges from 58° to 83° F., depending on the elevation. There are two main seasons—the rainy or so-called winter season, extending from May to October, and the dry summer season, from November to April.

The population of Guatemala as of June, 1957 was 3,429,000 inhabitants of predominantly Indian blood. Guatemala City ranks first in size (population 293,998) with Quetzaltenango second (population 36,-209).

Guatemala is a republic with 22 departments. The present Constitution entered into effect on March 1, 1956. The executive power is vested in the President who is elected by direct vote, for a non-extendable period of six years and cannot be re-elected for two terms following this term in office.

The legislative branch is the National Congress composed of deputies elected for four-year terms.

STRUCTURE OF THE ECONOMY

The economy of Guatemala is predominantly agricultural although manufacturing is of some importance. The table below indicates Guatemala's gross national product for the fiscal year 1949-50.

Source	Value (in millions of dollars)	Percent of Total
Agriculture, forestry, fishing	$203.2	45.5
Manufacturing	91.4	20.5
Transportation, communications, utilities	64.0	14.3
Wholesale and retail trade	37.9	8.5
Public administration & defense	31.9	7.1
Mining	2.8	.6
Construction	1.5	.3
Others	14.1	3.2
	$446.8	100.0

* Prepared by Ronald H. Chilcote while a student in the Graduate School of Business, Stanford University.

EVENTS OF 1958

Guatemala began the new year in a general atmosphere of uncertainty and political tension which had prevailed since the assassination of President Castillo Armas in July, 1957. Diplomatic ties were strained as a congressional committee recommended that Guatemala break relations with the Dominican Republic in view of the alleged interference by Dominican diplomats in internal affairs of the country. Although there was no rupture in diplomatic relations, the Guatemalan government continued to gather data implicating the Dominican Republic in the slaying of Castillo Armas and in plotting against the government.

During the year clerical and anti-Ydígoras (Ydígoras Fuentes—successor to Castillo Armas) forces renewed claims of Communist activity in Guatemala. In connection with this, the fourth anti-Communist Congress met in Antigua during October. The Congress recommended that the Free World should fight Communism by means of social justice and that the Western World should band together in order to curb Communist infiltration at all levels.

Guatemala has a small airforce and no navy. During the administration of President Ydígoras Fuentes, the position of the Armed Forces had not been clearly defined. The Army had been ambiguous in its backing of the President, for it was not anti-Ydígoras, but neither was it completely behind the President's policy.

President Ydígoras Fuentes signed 17 agreements with the United States International Cooperation Administration (ICA) involving a $9 million expenditure for development projects in public health, education, housing, agriculture, industrial developments, and security. The Guatemalan government gave impetus to development of the El Peten area, which amounts to 1/3 of the total area of Guatemala. A number of private oil companies, primarily North American, began exploring the area for possible oil reserves. The United States and British investors made plans to establish the first oil refinery in Guatemala. More than $4 million were to be invested by Shell Oil Company and Breaux Bridge Co. of Louisiana for the completion of the project. The refinery was to be located near Puerto Barrios, Guatemala's main sea port.

Increase of imports over exports resulted in a $25 million trade deficit and threatened the long-standing stability of the quetzal. Because of the increase in imports the government had to protect its foreign exchange reserves by limiting imports. The import of most items were at 50% to 75% of the 1957 imports. In the case of automobiles with a factory price of more than $2,200, only 25% of the 1957 volume could be imported. The value of exports in 1957 was FOB 108,839,100 quetzales (Q1 = $1) and the total value of import products was CIF 147,354,300 quetzales.

President Ydígoras Fuentes allocated most of the government's budget to the public works program in the hope of completing the Pan American Highway which had been hit by slides in the area of El Tapon Canyon. The government expected that the newly opened highway would give impetus to the ever-increasing tourist trade in Guatemala and other Central American states.

The Minister of Education announced a plan for spending $39 million for school construction throughout the nation. Illiteracy was estimated to be 73% in 1957—the highest in the Central-American Republics. Only 12% of the Budget was allocated for education purposes. The 1957-58 Budget balanced revenue and expenditure at $98,251,980.

PROCESS AND MANUFACTURE OF TIRES

The raw material for the manufacture of tires is a plastic material, that is, it is mouldable and sticky. It absorbs water and is soluble in many organic solvents. Manufacture is based on the fact that the properties of crude rubber change when it is mixed with sulphur and heated. Plasticity becomes elasticity, that is, the material returns to its original shape after being distorted. Processed rubber becomes water repellant and insoluble in many solvents. This process is called vulcanization.

Apart from sulphur and sulphur compounds, many other materials are used in the vulcanization process to produce specific properties, and accelerate vulcanization time.

Tire manufacture involves the following operations and processes: 1. mechanical grinding of the rubber in the mills; 2. mechanical addition of ingredients in the mill; 3. impregnation of cords with the rubber compound in a calendar press; 4. combining the impregnated material with other rubber materials in the rough shape of a tire, in tire-building machines; and 5. vulcanization under heat and pressure.

In manufacturing inner tubes, the rubber compound is shaped into tubes by extrusion. The endless tube is cut into sections; the ends are sealed together and the valve is fitted. They are then vulcanized in the same way as tires. Modern tire manufacture is mainly automatic, and tire-shaping and grinding, as well as mixing, cutting, and many other operations are controlled by instruments. It is not considered necessary to invest additional capital in automation under Central-American conditions.

When tire manufacturing has begun, the factory can use its facilities to produce other rubber goods, such as transmission belts, garden hose and all kinds of rubber sheeting and floor coverings. It did not seem advisable, however, to go in for this kind of production from the very beginning.

Cost production in Mexico's rubber industry in 1949 was approximately as follows: [1]

Raw materials	63.3%
Wages and salaries	18.3%
Miscellaneous costs	18.4%
	100.0%

[1] Mexican figures are given because conditions in Mexico approximate those in Central America.

GUATEMALAN RUBBER INDUSTRY

A law passed in January 1899 offered grants of land for rubber plantings and the maintenance of land for four years. Despite this government effort to stimulate rubber production, rubber exports declined from 239 tons in 1900 to 2 tons in 1923. The areas most suitable for hévea production are parts of Peten and the Motagua Valley. Because of its concentrated population, topography, soils, and climate, the west coast region has been thought to be favorable to hévea production. The basic problem in this area is deficient rainfall, but some small segments between the 500 and 2,500 ft. elevation level are considered to be satisfactory. In the region below the 500 ft. level along the coast, stretching from El Salvador to the Mexican border, the season is too dry; above the 2,500 ft. level the temperatures are too low for commercial production. In 1942 Guatemala developed a 72-acre plantation, Hacienda Tropiohe Grande, located south of Guyotenango; in 1947 there was an additional development of 47 acres. By the end of 1944 it was estimated that there were 1,315 acres of rubber plantings on 16 farms ranging in size from 5 to 704 acres.

The small farm program is sponsored by the Instituto Agropecuario Nacional in Guatemala City. In 1953 total rubber plantings were distributed among eleven large landowners holding 1,895 acres and 35 small farms totaling 137 acres.

During the period from 1949 to 1954 the Firestone Plantations Company established a 210 acre farm in Madre de Diós. In July 1957 Goodyear Rubber Plantations Company began plans to invest $2 million in an attempt to produce 4 million pounds of rubber in the Guatemalan Pacific Coast slopes.

GINSA began production of rubber trees and tubes in July 1958 and efforts have been made with La Hulera, the experimental station maintained jointly by the United States, Guatemala, and the Servicio Cooperativo Interamericano de Agricultura and located on the Pacific Coast, to increase rubber production from the 173,000 pounds produced in 1955 to GINSA's 1960 needs of 2 million pounds per year.

GUATEMALA—BLOOD AND CORRUPTION [2]

Guatemala City shook with violence last week. Store windows were smashed. Battle-dressed soldiers patrolled streets littered with burned, overturned cars. Twenty people were dead, and 500 others had been wounded, in a week of rioting against autocratic President Miguel Ydígoras Fuentes, 66. It was the worst crisis in Ydígoras' four years in office.

Crying Castro. The trouble started when students launched a one-hour strike against the announced returns of last December's congressional election, in which Ydígoras handily improved his majority. As is his habit, Ydígoras called the whole shooting match a "Castro-Communist" plot. No

[2] Reprinted by permission from *Time* (March 23, 1962), p. 35. Courtesy TIME; copyright Time, Inc., 1962.

doubt the Communists would like to overthrow the man who let Guatemala be used as a base for last year's Cuban invasion. But the Reds are by no means the only ones fed up with Ydígoras. Because of organized graft that flourishes like a fungus, the majority of Guatemala's business and professional community has long been bitterly disgusted. Corruption chokes the inflow of capital to a trickle. Anyone wanting to invest in Guatemala faces a maze of red tape that, in many cases, can be cut only by a mordida, or bribe.

An American concern, the Breaux Bridge Oil Refining Co., recently learned what an Alliance for Progress amounts to in Guatemala. Organized by a Houston group with the backing of Shell interests, Breaux Bridge received a concession in 1958 to set up a $5,000,000 refinery—Central America's first—on Guatemala's Caribbean coast. Not long after construction began, Ydígoras personally issued an order that, in effect, forbade all Guatemalan consulates abroad to approve any shipping documents for Breaux. Breaux appealed to the Supreme Court, a tribunal capable of independence, and won an injunction. When the company began laying pipeline to the docks of Puerto Barrios three miles away, the President showed up at the construction site, delivered a threat against the company, and relented only when Breaux agreed to lay its pipeline to a new port he is promoting three miles in the opposite direction.

Chance to Escape. Breaux officials were offered a way out of their troubles. Last May, company representatives claim, one of Ydígoras' relatives dropped into Breaux Bridge's Houston offices and asked for $1,000,000. "Otherwise," he is quoted as saying, "Breaux Bridge will never be able to operate." The firm refused. Last December port authorities announced they had a presidential order to stop pipeline construction. Company officials say they were offered another chance to escape trouble. This time the emissary was a high official in the government. His price, according to Breaux officers: $350,000, "or your troubles will continue." Again the company men said no. Buttressed by another Supreme Court injunction, Breaux Bridge drove ahead.

Now, says a Breaux official, "Our plant is finished, our pipeline is laid. We intend to begin importing crude—knowing full well that it probably will be stopped at the port."

REFERENCES

Arévalo, Juan José, *The Shark and the Sardines.* New York: Lyle Stuart, Publisher, 1961. A nationalist and anti-United States viewpoint.

Flores, Paul S., "Basic Data on the Economy of Guatemala," *World Trade Information Service,* Part 1, No. 56-46. Washington, D.C.: U.S. Department of Commerce, 1956.

Gomez Robles, Julio, *A Statement of the Laws of Guatemala on Matters Affecting Business* (2nd ed.). Washington, D.C.: Pan American Union, 1961.

International Bank for Reconstruction and Development, *The Economic Development of Guatemala.* Baltimore: Johns Hopkins Press, 1952.

Kelsey, Vera, and Lily de Jongh Osborne, *Four Keys to Guatemala* (rev. ed.). New York: Funk and Wagnalls Co., 1961.

Male, P. J. E., *Guatemala*. London: Overseas Economic Surveys (Board of Trade, Commercial Relations and Exports Department), 1956.

Martz, J. D., *Communist Infiltration in Guatemala*. New York: Vantage Press, Inc., 1956.

May, Stacy, and Galo Plaza, *The United Fruit Company in Latin America*. New York: National Planning Association, 1956.

Silvert, K. H., *A Study in Government: Guatemala*. New Orleans: Middle American Research Institute, Tulane University, Publication No. 21, 1954.

Taylor, Philip B., Jr., "The Guatemalan Affair; A Critique of United States Foreign Policy," *The American Political Science Review,* Vol. I, No. 2 (September, 1956), pp. 787-806.

U.S. Committee on Foreign Affairs, *Report of the Special Study Mission to Guatemala*. Washington, D.C.: House of Representatives, Report No. 207, 85th Congress, 1st session, March 19, 1957.

U.S. Department of State, *A Case History of Communist Penetration*. Washington, D.C.: Department of State Publication No. 6465, Inter-American Series 52 (April 1957).

41

GENERAL TIRE AND INCATECU, S.A. (I) *

Political Considerations Affecting the Sale of Common Stock in Guatemala

Mr. George Plihal, a Czechoslovakian, had migrated to Guatemala in the 1930's to make rubber-soled shoes. His company, called Compañía Guatemalteca Incatecu, proved successful in the rubber shoe business and Mr. Plihal then branched into tire retreading. No tires were manufactured in Central America before 1958, and all new tires had to be imported, largely from the United States.

In 1954 the growing demand for motor vehicles and, consequently, for tires, together with the possibility of development of a Central American Common Market, led Mr. Plihal to conclude that his next industrial step should be the organization of a company to manufacture tires in Guatemala. Accordingly, in 1956 he joined with the General Tire and Rubber Company of Akron, Ohio, to establish such an organization. The new

* Prepared by Ronald H. Chilcote while a student in the Graduate School of Business, Stanford University.

company was to be called General Tire and Incatecu, S.A., ordinarily known as GINSA.

General Tire's major contribution was to be the provision of technical assistance for a period of 10 years. This assistance was not to be limited to tires and tubes but was to extend to the development of other products as well. Production and the technical supervision of the factory were to be in charge of General Tire technicians, who were to train Guatemalans to run the operation efficiently. In order to guarantee quality, General Tire was to supervise the purchase of all materials and machinery.

CAPITALIZATION

The initial capital authorized was 1 million quetzales (Q1 = U.S. $1) divided into 100,000 shares at Q10 each. Besides the stock, there was provision for the sale of one billion quetzales bonds, of 10-year maturity, to yield 8% interest. These were guaranteed by the Guatemalan Institute of Production and Development (Instituto de Fomento y de la Producción or INFOP). Pro forma financial statements are shown in Exhibits 1, 2, and 3.

General Tire acquired for its assistance 10% of the common stock and representation by one member on the board of directors. Guatemalan investors were to be offered 50% of the common stock; the rest was allocated for sales in other Central-American countries. Under an agreement with the Organization of the Central-American States or Organización de Estados Centroamericanos (ODECA), 40,000 shares were to be marketed in El Salvador, Honduras, Nicaragua, and Costa Rica.

PLANT

The GINSA factory was to be situated in a future industrial zone, eight kilometers from Guatemala City. The plant was designed by General Tire engineers to produce 120,000 tires per year. Its enclosed area was 80,000 square feet.

Location of the plant was conveniently close to surfaced highways and within a short distance of the Pan-American Highway, which connects Central America with Mexico and the United States.[1] Also close by was the International Railway connecting Guatemala City with both Pacific and Atlantic Ocean ports.

PRINCIPAL RAW MATERIALS

Local rubber production was to provide 1 million pounds annually by the year 1960. The cost was to be one-half million quetzales. Sixty percent

[1] The Pan-American Highway was not finished by the end of 1958. A short stretch linking Guatemala and Mexico needed completion. Vehicles could be shipped by train over this portion.

of GINSA's 1960 raw material requirements was to be provided by 340,-000 rubber trees from more than 33 Guatemalan plantations. Imports, preferably from other Central American countries, were to provide the remaining requirements of approximately 1 million pounds. It was also estimated that by the 1960's another 1.5 million pounds of rubber would be needed for other products as well as numerous articles of latex and sponge. Studies and surveys indicated that by 1964, GINSA's total rubber requirements could be met by local production.

GINSA's hope was that Guatemalan and Central American rubber plantations would be stimulated to increase production since, under the present limited supply, rubber was bought at a premium of $.029 per pound.

An experimental station in Cuyotenango, Retalhuleu, was established by the United States to help increase rubber production. In March 1957 the Goodyear Rubber Plantations of Akron, Ohio, made plans to start a $2 million rubber plantation in southwestern Guatemala.

It was expected that GINSA's production would have a stimulating effect upon the industrialization of Central American sulfur, pine tar, and other products related to the fabrication of tires. Paper and carton industries would benefit by the packaging needs of the tire plant. Rayon and nylon cords, comprising 43% of the cost of a tire, would also be in great demand.

GOVERNMENT CONCESSIONS

George Plihal's shoe factory, Guatemalteca Incatecu, S.A. had been classified by the Ministry of Economy of Guatemala in 1954 as "new integrated industry," under the Industrial Development Law. When GINSA was formed, the Ministry transferred the classification to that company. The following concessions were made under the agreement:

1. Free importation of all kinds of machinery, equipment, and construction materials for the plant.
2. Free importation of raw materials if these could not be obtained within the country at the end of 10 years, including necessary quantities of rubber.
3. Elimination of the following taxes:
   a. no taxes for the first two years.
   b. 75% elimination of taxes for the following two years.
   c. 50% elimination for the fifth and sixth years.
   d. 25% elimination for the seventh and eighth years.

BILATERAL TREATIES

Guatemalan treaties of free trade had been established with El Salvador, Honduras, and Costa Rica. The sale of tires and tubes had been included in the treaties.

In his four-year efforts to find the needed capital to build GINSA, Mr. Plihal had encountered many problems. One large problem was finding an agreement which would provide technical assistance as well as a limited amount of capital for the enterprise and at the same time satisfy the people of Guatemala and other Central American countries; General Tire's contract met these demands. Dealing with and obtaining concessions from the Guatemalan Government posed even greater problems as Guatemalan politics became inevitably linked with Mr. Plihal's plans. On July 25, 1957, the Guatemalan President, Colonel Carlos Castillo Armas, was assassinated, and Mr. Plihal found himself confronted with his greatest problem to date.

President Castillo Armas had remained a controversial figure since his military coup of 1954. Apparently he had been supported by the U.S. in his mysterious overthrow of Communist-backed President Jacobo Arbenz Guzman.[2] In the famous "Palace Intrigue," U.S. Ambassador Peurifoy had suggested to the members of the Guatemalan Congress that the Arbenz administration to be driven out of office. This was unsuccessful, so Peurifoy had arranged a conference with Castillo Armas in El Salvador where Castillo Armas pledged to wipe out the Communists and establish a five-man junta. He had raised an army and had launched attacks along the Honduran border on June 18, 1954. Castillo Armas subsequently took command of the country. He was confirmed President in a plebiscite on October 10, 1954, in which he received 99% of a record vote. One writer stated: "Armas was 'elected' by a farcical YES and NO plebiscite in the Nazi-Communist tradition; less than 10% of the population voted."[3] Nevertheless, American aid started to flow into Guatemala and Guatemala's economy began to prosper. Castillo Armas initiated a vigorous program of land reform, yet in the process 234,000 acres of land expropriated by the Arbenz government were returned to the United Fruit Company.

Castillo Armas had ruled Guatemala for nearly three years within a propering economy. Money became plentiful and businessmen more confident. Yet it seemed obvious to some that United States diplomacy had not succeeded. One writer summed up the situation:

> Guatemalans remember the Liberation as a violent, American-engineered overthrow of a legal government, and today they see American businessmen and advisors sticking out all over . . . the majority see only a foreign "occupation" as they call it, and ignore or forget the good we have done.[4]

One of this "majority," Marroquín Rojas, the editor of the Guatemalan newspaper *La Hora* attacked the United States:

> There are none more enslaved than the people of the United States . . . Not content with their own organized anarchy, so mechanical and

[2] An article in *The Nation* went so far as to state: "Calling the Arbenz regime Communist-controlled was pure McCarthyism." "Cloak and Dagger Politics" (November 9, 1957), p. 314.

[3] D. L. Grahm in *The New Republic* (September 16, 1957), p. 7.

[4] D. L. Grahm, "Has Intervention in Guatemala Paid Off?" in *The New Republic* (September 16, 1957), p. 9.

> deadly, the North Americans are now attempting to foist this unwanted anarchy on all those countries which, though disease-ridden and often poor and troubled, have been, and still are, more happy and free in spirit than those poor gringos, who fancy themselves the most fortunate beings on earth.

It was in the midst of this prosperous but politically uncertain business situation that GINSA offered to sell its 100,000 shares of stock and its billion quetzales of bonds. One day after offering its issue of stock to the public, President Castillo Armas was assassinated. Politically and economically Guatemala was in a state of turmoil and the investing public had lost its confidence.

QUESTIONS

1. What action should Mr. Plihal take in order to sell the stock?
2. What implications do you foresee after he makes his decision?

Exhibit 1

1958-59
Pro Forma Statement of Sources and Uses

Uses		
Machinery and equipment	$1,004,400	
Freight charges	40,000	
Cement and installations	120,000	
Wells and pumps	14,510	
High-tension lines	41,300	
Other equipment, trucks, etc.	55,700	$1,275,910
Organization expenditures	20,000	
Salaries of General Tire technicians	101,800	
Inventories	309,000	
Interest	102,000	
Receivables	240,000	
Other expenses	25,000	797,800
Estimated Capital Needed		$2,073,710
Sources		
100,000 shares at par 10 quetzales	$1,000,000	
10 year bonds	1,000,000	
Trade credits	73,710	
Total		$2,073,710

EXHIBIT 2

GENERAL TIRE AND INCATECU, S.A.
BALANCE SHEET—1958
(PRO-FORMA)

Assets			
Current Assets			
Cash		$943,755	
Inventories		508,680m	$1,452,435
Fixed Assets			
Erection of offices	$ 95,650		
Less depreciation—3%	7,175	88,475	
Machinery and equipment	1,044,400		
Less depreciation—7½%	189,298	855,102	
Installation expenses	120,000		
Less 10% amortization	29,000	91,000	
Lunchroom and Rest-rooms	55,700		
Less depreciation—10%	12,997	42,703	
Other installations	55,810		
Less depreciation—10%	14,202	41,598	
Vehicles	16,000		
Less depreciation	5,912	10,088	1,128,966
Deferred Assets			111,273
Total Assets			$2,692,674
Liabilities			
Current Liabilities			$1,054,886
Net Worth			
Authorized capital	1,500,000		
Less capital not subscribed	408,000		
Subscribed capital			1,092,000
Reserve for Amortization of bonds			200,000
Other Liabilities			345,788
Total of Liabilities and Net Worth			$2,692,674

EXHIBIT 3

GENERAL TIRE AND INCATECU, S.A.
INCOME STATEMENT—1958
(PRO-FORMA)

Net Sales		$3,110,000	
Costs of sales	$1,727,640		
Factory expenses	300,630	2,028,270	
		1,081,818	
General and administrative expenses		469,253	
		612,565	
Interest on bonds		102,000	
		510,565	
Tax on $219,543 profits		54,886	
Net profits in operation		$ 455,679	(approximately 15% on net sales)

42

GENERAL TIRE AND INCATECU, S.A. (II) *

Foreign Antagonism toward U.S. Investment in Guatemala

After a successful 20-year career as a manufacturer of rubber shoes and operator of a tire-retreading business in Guatemala, Mr. George Plihal, a Czechoslovakian immigrant, organized General Tire and Incatecu, S.A., commonly known as GINSA, to produce tires and tubes for sale in Guatemala and other Central-American countries. Ten percent of the common stock of 100,000 shares and one seat on GINSA's board of directors were held by the General Tire and Rubber Company, of Akron, Ohio, in exchange for the provision of technical assistance, development of a labor force, and supervision or purchases over a 10-year period.

The remainder of the common stock was owned throughout Central America. Guatemalans, including Mr. Plihal, subscribed to 50% and 40% had been offered for sale in El Salvador, Honduras, Costa Rica, and Nicaragua. In addition, the company had a bond issue totalling one billion quetzales guaranteed by the Guatemalan government. Par value of the common stock was one quetzal (Q1=U.S.$1) per share.

After the uncertainty caused by the assassination of President Castillo Armas in 1957 had been overcome and the common stock successfully sold,[1] GINSA made rapid progress. In June, 1958, the plant was officially opened by President Miguel Ydígoras Fuentes who proclaimed it "The first industry of our common Central-American market." At the same time that he made his proclamation, the first automobile tire was being molded at the new plant outside Guatemala City.

In his remarks President Ydígoras Fuentes had this to say about the new factory and the company behind it:

> We have now opened the frontiers of five countries of Central America . . . the first of our industries will be GINSA . . . We are going to give guarantees, not for six years but forever in order that there might be opportunity for foreign investment in Guatemala . . . We want to forget the past and begin a new Guatemala, with the best political guarantees . . . to protect industry (and GINSA).
>
> The protection that we give to this industry will become the norm for all other industries that will be established in the country in the manner of GINSA, which is not only a tire factory. GINSA is a symbol for the future industry of the Republic of Guatemala, united with the brotherly nations of Central America.

* Prepared by Ronald H. Chilcote while a student in the Graduate School of Business, Stanford University.

[1] See General Tire and Incatecu, S.A. (I), p. 478.

At the same inaugural ceremony, Mr. George Plihal, founder and president of GINSA, gave his views on the significance of the enterprise:

> The industrial life of Guatemala is marked by the beginning of an accelerated industrialization in Central America . . . there will grow a new active economic population which will bring with it the incorporation of masses of population within the economic and social life of the country. The prosperity of the five republics of the isthmus will bring the economic integration of Central America . . . New regions of national territory will be converted to the active economy, regions which before lived in a primitive stage.
>
> We have ended our task, we have fulfilled our duty. GINSA is a fact. Beginning next Monday tires will come out of this factory made with Guatemalan and Central-American rubber, the greater part of which is superior to synthetic rubber found in today's imported tire. Our tires will be made with the help of the most modern machines and with the most advanced technical assistance. Consequently our tires will be as good or better than imported tires.
>
> GINSA is yours. To you Guatemalans and Central Americans of good faith remains the task of conserving it, stimulating it, and promoting it.

On Monday, the first official production day, a letter appeared in the Guatemalan newspaper, *Prensa Libre,* which indicated that GINSA's agreements with the Guatemalan Government were not in accord with the Industrial Development Law. The letter is reprinted in Exhibit 1 and the Industrial Development Law of Guatemala may be referred to in Exhibit 2. Realizing that the backing of Guatemalans and the government was most important to the continuation of his enterprise, Mr. Plihal was faced with a difficult situation.

QUESTIONS

1. Analyze GINSA's relationship to the Guatemalan Industrial Development Law and evaluate the criticism and recommendations of the newspaper letter.
2. If the recommendations of the editorial seemed likely to interfere with GINSA's plans, what action might be taken?

Exhibit 1

"Ginsa Is Not an Integrated Industry"

Minister of Public Affairs:

1. The Ministry of Economy on August 25, 1954, authorized the Compañía Guatemalteca Incatecu as a "new integrated industry" (stated in the Industrial Development Law No. 459).

The Minister of Economy authorized the following rights and benefits:

a. Right of free importation of machinery for a period of ten years.

b. Importation of semi-manufactured products and primary products specifically forbidden in the Industrial Development Law.

2. The principal objective of Compañía Guatemalteca Incatecu was the installation of a rubber tire and tube factory.

3. The Minister of Economy knows that the fabrication of tires and tubes requires the following materials:

Material	Percentage
Rubber (natural or synthetic)	53.0%
Rayon or nylon fiber	11.0%
Cotton cloth	1.0%
Carbon black	21.0%
Miscellaneous pigments	4.0%
Oils (wax)	4.7%
Wire (for tire tubes)	3.0%
Sulphur	1.3%
Stearic	1.0%
	100.0%

These percentages are subject to variations, but in order to examine the use of raw material, they may be considered approximate.

The above analysis points out the first legal violation by the Ministry of Economy:

Article II (1) of the Industrial Development Law states:

> *Integrated industries, which are those devoted to the manufacture, elaboration or preparation of necessary products through the technical and exclusive use of natural resources available within the territory of the republic. These are subdivided into:*
>
> (a) *Basic industries: those which are of vital importance to human existence, i.e., food, health, clothing, shelter, and protection; and*
>
> (b) *Useful industries: all other industries which, although not vital, nevertheless contribute to comfort, convenience, and luxury.*

The Ministry of Economy ought to classify the Compañía Guatemalteca Incatecu as an Industry of Manufacturing; Article II (2) of the Industrial Development Law says:

> *Manufacturing industries which are those devoted to the manufacture, elaboration, or preparation of products through the combined use of natural resources available in the country with those of foreign origin: or utilizing imported raw materials exclusively, provided machinery and human labor are also employed in the manufacturing process. . . .*

What we point out is confirmed by the fact that of all the materials used in the fabrication of tires and tubes, only rubber will be able to be produced in Guatemala in the future.

The other materials are not produced in the country.

The Minister also has made the concession of semi-manufactured materials with which the Industrial Development Law offers no benefits.

The said agreements indicated that because GINSA has to import raw materials for a period of ten years, it will be in a period of Manufacturing and not Integration.

We also accuse GINSA of a violation of Article IV (1) of Law 459, issued by the Congress of the Republic, which concedes exemptions for the importation of raw and semi-manufactured materials for a period that exceeds the ten years fixed as limit. This violation, because the original date was August 25, 1954, authorized exemptions for a maximum period of three years, but afterwards by means of the agreement of March 15, 1956, the exemptions were increased ten more years.

Before that modification of the original plans, the new Ministry of Economy reconciled the circumstances and, violating Articles XII and IV of Law 459, issued the agreement of March 25, 1956, in which, unlawfully it declared General Tire and Incatecu, S.A. (GINSA) possessor of all benefits primarily acquired by Compañía Guatemalteca Incatecu.

In the agreement to which we refer, aside from not previously fulfilling the requirements of Articles XII and XV of Law 459 of the Congress, there is the illegal situation of the machinery and raw or semi-manufactured raw materials imported by the Compañía Guatemalteca Incatecu, which has changed its name and property to General Tire and Incatecu, Sociedad Anónima (GINSA) thus violating Article 18 of the Industrial Law which states:

> *If the beneficiaries of the exemptions or reductions granted under this law should alienate in any way any articles imported under such exemptions, without prior authorization from the ministry of finance, they shall be required immediately to pay the duties which would have applied, plus a fine of ten times the amount of such duties. The ministry of finance may declare, likewise, the suspension or cancellations of the exemptions already granted.*

Thus the Compañía Guatemalteca Incatecu has been made liable to penalties indicated by the law.

Article XII of Law 459, establishes the legal percentage of foreign capital participation in several types of industries that are able to benefit by this law, and encharges the Ministry of Economy to watch a certain supply of foreign capital participation, this an obligation of the protected company. Nevertheless, the Compañía General Tire and Incatecu is established with stockholders, and since it is impossible for the Ministry of Economy to watch the fulfilling of this obligation, it is possible to dishonor the principle and philosophy that motivate this requisite.

We desire to remain firm in the accusation of the violation committed in accordance with the Industrial Development Law; we do not want to impair the economy of Guatemala, but we only aspire to uphold and respect the laws of the Constitution of the Republic in all their dimensions, without allowing determined enterprises rights which exceed those benefits considered by law.

We ask the Attorney General to make the following provisions:

Petitions

1. Revision of the qualifications which the Ministry of Economy has made to the Compañía Guatemalteca Incatecu, and thereafter General Tire and Incatecu, Sociedad Anónima (GINSA) in accordance with the Industrial Development Law and not exceeding the provisions that Law 459 of the Congress of the Republic concedes, and knowing it as an Industry of Manufacturing, that it not be classified as a *new integrated industry*.

2. Once rectifying the qualifications of the Compañía Guatemalteca Incatecu and GINSA that the Minister of Housing and Public Credit order the recovery of all those taxes and tariff rates of which the Compañía Guatemalteca Incatecu has been allowed to omit payment, since GINSA does not correspond to these qualifications.

3. To declare that GINSA has not fulfilled the requirements stipulated by Articles XII and XV of Law 459 of the Congress of the Republic . . . and that the Ministry of Economy is not able to transfer nor recognize the transferral of the rights of the Compañía Guatemalteca Incatecu to GINSA.

4. To communicate to the Minister of Housing and Public Credit all those articles or machinery or raw materials or semi-manufactured materials that might have been imported by the Compañía Incatecu and transferred to GINSA—a violation of Article XVIII of the Industrial Development Law.

5. To declare that GINSA has violated the stipulated requirements of Article XII of the Industrial Development Law: and to ask the Minister of Economy to take the necessary measures in order to demand that GINSA transfer its actual stock to the registered stockholders, in order to conform with the article and to be able to verify the nature of foreign capital of the said enterprise.

Charles H. Rogers
Jaime Tabarini
Guatemala, June 27, 1958

Exhibit 2

Industrial Development of Guatemala

Article I

The establishment and development of industries which facilitate the more effective utilization of the country's resources and which offer possibilities of economically marketing their products internally or abroad are declared to be a matter of national urgency.

Article II

For the purposes of this law, industries are classified as follows:

1. Integrated industries, which are those devoted to the manufacture, elaboration, or preparation of necessary products, through the tech-

nical and exclusive use of natural resources available within the territory of the Republic. These are, in turn, subdivided into:

a. Basic industries: Those which are of vital importance to human existence, i.e., food, health, clothing, shelter, and protection; and

b. Useful industries: All other industries which, although not vital, nevertheless contribute to comfort, convenience, and luxury.

2. Manufacturing industries, which are those devoted to the manufacture, elaboration, or preparation of products through the combined use of natural resources available in the country with those of foreign origin, or utilizing imported raw materials exclusively, provided machinery and human labor are also employed in the manufacturing process. Excluded are those which involve merely the packaging, assembling, or presentation of product. Manufacturing industries are classified as new or existing.

The Ministry of Economy and Labor will determine, in the respective regulations, the industries which should be included in each category.

Article III

Integrated industries are divided into new and existing industries. New industries shall be understood to comprise those which propose to produce articles which are not manufactured in the country or which are produced in quantities obviously insufficient to supply the country's internal requirements. Existing industries are those already established and which have reached the maximum stage of development in accordance with their capital.

Article IV

New integrated industries will enjoy:

1. Exemption from payment of all taxes, duties, fees, and surcharges on the importation of the following articles.

a. Construction materials of primary importance and of high cost which are necessary for their initial plant and its enlargements;

b. Machinery, equipment, and accessories required for the respective industry;

c. Raw materials needed for the manufacturing process. Such exemptions shall be granted for a period of not more than 10 years, and only if proof is furnished that such articles cannot be advantageously produced in the country or are not produced in sufficient quantities to satisfy the requirements of the internal market.

2. Exemptions from, or reductions of, the following internal taxes:

a. From the tax on business profits (impuesto sobre utilidades de empresas lucratives) or from any tax on income which may be decreed in the future, in a gradually decreasing form and up to the following maximum limits; Total exemption from the tax for the first 2 years; 75% reduction for the following 2 years; 50% reduction for the following 2 years; and 25% for another 2 years. After a maximum period of 8 years, the companies must pay the entire tax.

b. From the real property tax for a period of up to 5 years.

Article V

Basic integrated industries, whether established or to be established, may enjoy the benefits enumerated in sections a, b, and c of numeral 1 of the previous article, in accordance with the respective regulations.

Article VI

Manufacturing industries will be classified according to the percentage of domestic or foreign raw material which they utilize:

a. Those that use more than 80% of domestic raw materials in the manufacture of their products.
b. Those in which the use of domestic raw materials does not assume important proportions but which are capable of providing employment for a considerable number of workers;
c. Those which utilize between 40 and 80% of domestic raw materials;
d. Those which use less than 40% of domestic raw materials.

Article VII

New manufacturing industries embraced in sections a and b of the previous article may enjoy, for a period of up to 8 years, the import duty exemptions or reductions provided for in sections a and b of numeral 1 of Article IV, which shall be granted in accordance with the respective regulations.

They may also enjoy the exemptions or reductions from the business profits tax and the property tax up to the limits contemplated in numeral 2 of the same Article IV.

Article VIII

New manufacturing industries, embraced in section c of Article VI, which utilize between 40 and 80% of domestic raw materials, may enjoy for a period of up to 5 years the reductions or exemptions described in sections a and b of numeral 1, Article IV, which are granted in accordance with the respective regulations.

They may also enjoy reductions in the business profits tax up to the following limits: A reduction of 75% for the first 2 years; of 50% for the following 2 years; and 25% for 1 year more. Companies must pay the entire tax after a period of 5 years, in all cases.

The exemption or reduction on the property tax may be for a period of up to 3 years.

Article IX

New manufacturing industries, which will use less than 40% of domestic raw materials, to which reference is made in section d of Article VI, may enjoy, for one time only, the reductions or exemptions referred to in sections a and b of numeral 1 of Article IV.

Similarly, the executive power may, through the respective ministry, grant reductions on the business profits tax up to a limit of 50% for the first 2 years and up to 25% for the following year.

Article X

Existing manufacturing industries, whether established enterprises or enterprises to be established, may enjoy the import duty exemptions or reductions which would correspond to new manufacturing industries of the same class in accordance with Article VI, provided that in the judgment of the Ministry of Economy said industries should require it in order to better serve the objectives outlined in Article I.

Article XI

Assembly plants are considered as manufacturing industries if they are capable of providing employment to a considerable number of workers.

Article XII

Enterprises to be established, whether integrated or manufacturing industries, must comply with the following requirements before they can enjoy the benefits of this law:

1. Those which elaborate, fabricate, or manufacture products principally to satisfy the domestic market, which do not require a highly developed technique for their better economic development, must be constituted with predominantly Guatemalan capital;

2. Those whose production is destined for the local market but which require a highly developed technique for their better economic development, must preferably have a minimum participation of 33% Guatemalan capital; but if it is fully confirmed before the Ministry of Economy that Guatemalan capital has not made use, within a reasonable period, of the invitation to participate in the respective enterprise, such industries may then be constituted by up to 70% foreign capital.

However, in order to enjoy the benefits of this law, such enterprises must be ready to sell to Guatemalan capital at any time and at a fair market price, the equivalent of 33% of the firm's capital. The Ministry of Economy is charged with enforcing this requirement.

3. Enterprises, whose economic development depends principally on the placing of their products in foreign markets, may be constituted with up to 100% foreign capital.

4. A prior requirement to the authorization of industries devoted to the processing of alcoholic and fermented beverages such as aguardientes, beers and wines, as well as those processing tobacco products such as cigars and cigarettes, whether or not they utilize the benefits of this law is that they must be constituted with at least 70% Guatemalan capital.

Industries operating on the date of the present law are exempt for the requirements of the preceding paragraph.

Article XIII

For the purpose of this law, Guatemalan capital is considered to be that belonging to individual Guatemalan persons or to non-Guatemalan individuals who have their principal business and reside permanently in Guatemala or to Guatemalan juridical persons who invest not less than 60% of their annual profits in Guatemala. Guatemalan capital, for the purposes of section 4 of Article XII, is considered to be that belonging to individual Guatemalan persons or to Guatemalan juridical persons, within which at least 70% of the capital is in the hands of Guatemalans.

Article XIV

Enterprises already established are not obligated to modify their capital structure; but in order to enjoy the benefits of this law, it is required that:

a. Those embraced in numeral 1 of article XII and which are more than 50% foreign-owned must obligate themselves to permit Guatemalan capital to participate to the extent of at least 50% in any future expansion; and

b. Those embraced in numeral 2 of article XII must agree to permit Guatemalan capital to participate, to the extent of at least 33% in future expansion.

Article XV

Those interested in obtaining the benefits authorized by this law must submit an application to the Ministry of Economy containing the following information:

1. A detailed description of the proposed industry;
2. The amount of capital, manner of financing specifying the amounts contributed by Guatemalan and foreign capital, and investment plans;
3. A list of the raw materials to be needed by the industry, with an estimate of annual requirements, separating those of national origin from those of foreign origin;
4. Analysis of the market for the preceding 5-year period, with an indication of the wholesale and retail prices of the goods to be produced or of similar products and substitutes;
5. The export price of such products in the country of origin if imported, the C.I.F. value of Guatemalan ports, and the amount of applicable import duties;
6. The initial productive capacity;
7. Estimate of the unit costs of production, with the following specifications

a. Labor;
b. Raw materials;
c. Light, power, and fuel;
d. Administration expenses in general including wholesale selling expenses;
e. Other manufacturing expenses; and
f. Estimated profits

Established industries interested in obtaining the benefits granted by this law must furnish, to the Ministry of Economy, any data and information which the latter may request.

The above Ministry is required to assist small industries in complying with the requirements referred to in this article.

Article XVI

The Ministry of Economy will consider the application and, if it is approved, will announce the classification of the new industry and will declare the benefits which are to be granted. This decision will be communicated to the Ministry of Finance and Public Credit for execution.

In its respective resolution, the Ministry of Economy will determine the kinds and quantities of construction materials, machinery, equipment, and kinds of raw materials or foreign semi-processed articles to be required by the approved enterprise.

Article XVII

The import duty exemptions will expire, totally or gradually, whenever the Ministry of Economy confirms and resolves that the exempted articles are or can be produced advantageously in the country. The Ministry of Economy will communicate said resolution to the Ministry of Finance for any corresponding effects.

Article XVIII

If the beneficiaries of the exemptions or reductions granted under this law should alienate in any way any articles imported under such exemptions, without prior authorization from the Ministry of Finance, they shall be required immediately to pay the duties which would have applied, plus a fine of 10 times the amount of the duties. The Ministry of Finance may declare, likewise, the suspension or cancellation of the exemptions already granted.

Article XIX

Enterprises which currently enjoy some protection or privilege by virtue of other legal or contractual provisions, may obtain the benefits of this law only by renouncing, before hand, the privileges previously granted.

Article XX

Jointly with the Ministry of Education, the Ministry of Economy will endeavor to establish schools of arts and crafts for the purpose of improving individual productive capacity, and to organize a system of scholarships to foreign countries in order to bring about the formation of skilled groups in industrial technology.

Article XXI

Mining and petroleum industries will be governed by special legislation.

Article XXII

Integrated industries will not be subject to any limitations except those contained in this law. The executive power will regulate this law.

Source: U.S. Department of Commerce. World Trade Information Service, *Economic Reports,* Part 1, No. 56-1.

43

GENERAL TIRE AND INCATECU, S.A. (III) *

Assessing Opportunities and Risks in the Central American Common Market

Mr. George Plihal, a Czechoslovakian, had migrated to Guatemala in the 1920's to manufacture rubber shoes. Successful in this venture, he had then turned to tire retreading, and in 1954, he conceived the idea of a rubber tire and tube factory. This would be built in Guatemala but would serve not only the expanding needs of that country's vehicle population but also the rest of Central America—El Salvador, Honduras, Nicaragua, and Costa Rica.

Mr. Plihal was successful in securing the technical assistance of the General Tire and Rubber Company of Akron, Ohio, in exchange for 10% of the new company's capital stock and one seat on its board of directors. General Tire and Incatecu, S.A., or GINSA as it was ordinarily known, was also able to secure adequate capital through the sale of stocks and bonds, built a plant under General Tire's supervision, and began production in 1958. At the official opening in June, 1958, Guatemalan President Miguel Ydígoras Fuentes hailed the company as "the first industry of our common Central-American market."

ORGANIZATION OF CENTRAL AMERICAN STATES (ODECA)

However enthusiastic President Ydígoras Fuentes might be, the success of the Central American Common Market and, in turn, that of GINSA, was not a certainty. Nevertheless, progress toward the realization of the concept had been made; the difficulty for many was to determine what, in fact, the Central American Common Market did and would present in terms of business and industrial opportunity.

In October 1951, the economic integration of the Central-American countries was begun with the creation of the Organization of Central American States (Organización de Estados Centroamericanos or ODECA) under the Charter of San Salvador, named for the meeting at San Salvador, capital of El Salvador. The purpose of this organization was to seek a solution for a wide variety of mutual economic and social problems with a view to eventual consolidation of Central-American economic activities, and possibly political unification.

* Prepared by Ronald H. Chilcote while a student in the Graduate School of Business, Stanford University.

The foreign ministers of the Central-American countries met a second time at Tegucigalpa, Honduras, in August, 1952, and there specified fields of development to be used in their regional common market:

transportation
industrial technology
cattle raising, dairy products, and preparation of meats, hides, shoes, etc.
cotton and cotton textiles
forestry, lumbering, woodpulp, and paper plants
rubber products, including tires and tubes
oilseeds, fats, and oils
fishing industry
matches
technical and administrative training

The Economic Cooperation Committee established by the countries met at San Jose, Costa Rica, and, again, in a special session at San Salvador, El Salvador, in May, 1955. Another meeting in January, 1956, at Managua, Nicaragua, declared development of the following industries to be of general Central American interest: petroleum derivatives, fertilizers, insecticides, fungicides, veterinary products, biologicals, and injection vials, tires and tubes, paints, varnishes and inks, ceramics, glass, plastics, metal containers, cellulose and paper, fish products, welded pipes, and absorbent cotton.

In June, 1958, the Tegucigalpa Treaty was signed, creating the Central American Common Market. This was followed in September, at San Jose, Costa Rica, by the Central American Treaty on equalization of customs tariffs and a protocol on tariff preferences.

El Salvador, Guatemala, and Honduras signed a Treaty of Economic Association in February, 1960, establishing a free trade area among the three countries. In October, El Salvador, Guatemala, Honduras, and Nicaragua signed the Treaty of Central American Economic Integration. These countries also agreed to establish a Central American Economic Integration Bank. Costa Rica, which had participated in the initial and some subsequent discussions, declined to associate itself at this point for internal reasons. These had to do with politics and what Costa Rica felt was a position which might be weakened rather than strengthened by the common-market approach.

TUBES AND TIRES IN THE COMMON MARKET

Central American imports of all kinds of tires and inner tubes expanded from 520 tons in 1937 to approximately 4,000 tons in 1955, the value of the latter being about $6 million. These figures were approximately equivalent to 20,000 units in 1937 and 154,000 in 1955.

Apparent tire consumption in individual countries and the corresponding trends are shown in Exhibit 1. In terms of volume, Guatemala was the main consumer of tires for passenger cars and trucks (26.7% of total imports in 1950-55) followed by El Salvador, Costa Rica, Nicaragua, and Honduras.

Exhibit 2 indicates the aggregate number of motor vehicles in each country. A comparison of the totals during the period 1950-55 reveals an estimated figure for apparent consumption in terms of tire units of 2.6 tires per vehicle per year. In view of the present condition of the roads in Guatemala, this figure seems reasonable when compared with a utilization factor of 1.5 to 1.8 in the United States and 2.3 to 2.4 in Mexico.

Consumption of tires in Central America was low, not only because of the small number of vehicles but also because of high price. Below are comparative prices of truck tires: [1]

	(price per unit)
El Salvador	\$120
Honduras	\$125
Nicaragua	\$160
Mexico	\$92 (rough figure)
United States	\$106

It was likely that Central America's consumption of tires would expand in the future because:

1. There would be commercial and industrial growth and an increasing use of transport.
2. The establishment of a regional petroleum refinery would reduce the price of petrol.
3. Intensive road building and the Pan American Highway would be stimulated by U.S. financing.

A trend indicated that consumption of tires and tubes would increase from 209,000 units in 1957 to about 400,000 to 600,000 units by 1965. Because of many different types of tires demanded in Central America and because GINSA had to concentrate on some of the main kinds, the total demand could not be satisfied. Another problem was that new vehicles were usually imported with tires. It was therefore to be assumed that one-half of total requirements would be covered by imports, which would leave from 198,000 to 307,000 tires to be supplied from regional production.

GINSA, a factory of minimum economic size, equipped to produce a reasonable range of tire sizes and types, was to manufacture 400 units in three daily shifts. This was equivalent to about 80,000 to 120,000 tires annually.

If would be difficult to manufacture any kind of tire for which requirements were less than 500 units annually. Production would be economic only if the total volume were manufactured in one run and if, apart from the vulcanization die, factory facilities could handle the size and type in question.

Mr. Plihal, GINSA's president, thus found himself in a rather favorable position in 1958. Being the sole tire- and tube-manufacturing plant

[1] Tire size is 8.25 x 20 x 12. Tire prices are inflated by high shipping and railway-freight charges which in some cases account for 35% of the price. Average per capita income in Central America was less than \$200 in 1958.

in Central America, GINSA had only to meet a favorable demand and entrench itself into the Organization of Central American States. However, as has been stated, GINSA's success rested primarily upon the Central American Common Market:

> GINSA is likely to prove a good example of the much needed industrialization that Central American nations can support jointly but not singly.[2]
>
> Importers of foreign-made tires were yelling "monopoly" before the first tire was made—and the term was technically correct. Under laws to encourage industrialization, GINSA imports all machinery and raw materials duty-free for ten years. Tire importers have to pay an ad valorem duty of 22%, which Plihal is trying to have doubled. His stockholders are counting on fat dividends. But GINSA is plowing some of the money back into the country by buying local rubber at a premium of $0.29 per pound.[3]
>
> GINSA will not survive unless the Central American states form a multi-lateral agreement because roads are poor, there are not enough cars, competition cannot be met from the mass-producing American companies, and the market is small.[4]

Thus unification of the common market, at least in the area of rubber products, appeared to be the solution to eliminate the competition of rubber companies outside of Central America who could produce cheaply, meet the high customs duties, and still sell at lower prices than GINSA. However, it was noted that one President of a Central-American country held exclusive rights of a certain foreign company for the importation of the tires as well as a substantial investment in that company. Furthermore, this president was fully entrenched as the political leader for many years to come.

QUESTIONS

1. Analyze GINSA's role in the Central American Common Market. What is the importance of such a common market for GINSA?
2. What might be done to appease the unnamed President of one of the Central-American countries in order that GINSA might assume its position in the market?

[2] American Embassy, Economic Section in San Salvador.
[3] *Time,* Latin American Edition, July 14, 1958.
[4] American Embassy, Economic Section in Managua, Nicaragua.

44

KAISER MOTORS CORPORATION *

Investigation of Investment Opportunities in Argentina

In the mid-1950's, Mr. Henry J. Kaiser, well-known industrialist and chairman of the Board of Kaiser Motors Corporation, was considering the possibility of participating in the establishment of an automobile manufacturing venture in Argentina.

Since 1914 when the Henry J. Kaiser Co. Ltd. was founded in Vancouver, Canada, the Kaiser organization had continued to expand until it included a number of operating companies such as Henry J. Kaiser Company, Kaiser Motors Corporation, Kaiser Aluminum and Chemical Corporation, Kaiser Steel Corporation, Kaiser Gypsum Company and Kaiser Community Homes.

KAISER'S AUTOMOTIVE VENTURE

In July 1945, Mr. Joseph W. Frazer, Chairman of the Board of Graham-Paige Corporation, met with Mr. Henry J. Kaiser in San Francisco to explore the mutual advantages that might accrue from the formation of a new automobile-manufacturing company which would pool the executive, engineering and managerial talents available in both organizations. Subsequently, formal negotiations were initiated and, on July 25, announcements were made of the formation of the Kaiser-Frazer Corporation.

With the termination of the war on August 14, the corporation took immediate steps to enter the automobile-manufacturing field. In the interest of early production and because of greater accessibility to part suppliers, it was deemed desirable to locate the initial manufacturing facilities in the Detroit area. Accordingly, a large bomber plant in Willow Run, Michigan was leased from the Reconstruction Finance Corporation (RFC).

During 1946 many problems of getting into production were encountered. Kaiser-Frazer Corporation was a new customer without existing suppliers in the industry. Raw materials, automotive parts, machine tools, etc. were all in short supply, and there were frequently delays in obtaining requirements. In spite of these initial difficulties, the first automobile came off the production line at the Willow Run Plant in June, 1946, and commercial production began in the last quarter of the same year.

In 1953 a shift in production and sales emphasis from passenger cars to commercial and utility vehicles marked the beginning of a major effort to return the company to a profitable basis. These vehicles included "jeeps,"

* This and other cases on Kaiser Motors Corporation and Industrias Kaiser Argentina prepared by Dr. Michael Yoshino while a doctoral candidate in the Graduate School of Business, Stanford University.

two-and-four-wheel-drive station wagons, four-wheel-drive one-ton trucks, two-and-four-wheel-drive sedan delivery trucks, and such specialized vehicles as cargo and personnel carriers, ambulances and fire engines. In spite of these efforts, the loss of over $27 million was incurred in 1953 (see Exhibit 1 at the end of this case). At the end of 1953 the company's accumulated net loss amounted to over $78 million. (See Exhibit 2.)

The company, through its subsidiary, Willys Motors, Inc., acquired in 1953 the business and physical properties, inventories, and certain other operating assets of Willys-Overland Motors, Inc. at an aggregate purchase price of over $60 million. The automotive business of Willys-Overland Motors, Inc. had been established in 1903, and the company had been engaged in the manufacture of passenger cars, trucks, and other automotive products. At the time of its acquisition by Willys Motors, Inc. the business consisted primarily of the production of military and civilian personnel and cargo vehicles marketed under the trade-mark "jeep." Later in the same year, the name of the company was changed to Kaiser Motors Corporation.

As a part of the Kaiser Motors' efforts to increase its sales of utility vehicles, it had turned to foreign markets where the demand for them was believed to be high. In 1953 the company achieved third place position among U.S. automobile firms by selling over 45,000 vehicles to the foreign markets. At this time, however, many highly promising potential foreign markets were closed to U.S. automobile manufacturers because of foreign-exchange difficulties.

Kaiser's first venture overseas was the establishment of Nederlandse Kaiser-Frazer Fabrieken, N.F., a Netherlands corporation, in 1948. Kaiser obtained a minority interest and agreed to provide knocked-down Kaiser-Frazer automobiles to Nederlandse Kaiser-Frazer, who had contracted to set up facilities to assemble these vehicles. In addition, Kaiser granted the company rights to distribute the products in the Netherlands under Kaiser's trademark.

In April 1952, the company also entered the Brazilian market by establishing Willys-Overland do Brasil, a Brazilian corporation, to assemble and distribute jeeps in Brazil.

ARGENTINE AUTOMOBILE MARKET

Kaiser Motors (then known as Kaiser-Frazer Corporation) began exporting to Argentina in 1947 when it sold 900 vehicles. The company was unable, however, to obtain import permits again until 1951 when it exported 800 vehicles. Thereafter an embargo had been placed on U.S. passenger cars except for a few hundred units purchased by the Argentine government.

Argentina was at this time experiencing a tremendous shortage of automobiles of all kinds. As a result, the automobile prices were extremely high, as indicated in Exhibit 4. There were approximately 483,000 units of motor vehicles in 1953, consisting of 317,000 passenger cars (including taxis), 151,000 trucks, and 15,000 buses. There was one unit of vehicle per 40 inhabitants in comparison with 34, 25, 24, 11, and 4.3 for Cuba, Uruguay, Venezuela, the South African Union, and Australia respectively. 75% of passenger cars and 70% of trucks were at least 10 years old and nearly one-half of these vehicles were reported to be over 20 years old. The Argentine Government estimated that Argentina would require approximately 70,000 new vehicles per year; however, because of foreign exchange problems and lack of a domestic automobile industry, Argentina's annual replacement was only a fraction of the normal rate. The breakdown of Argentine imports of cars and trucks from 1945 to 1954 is presented in Exhibit 3. This continuing shortage, coupled with a substantial increase in population and real buying power, had created an enormous cumulative demand for motor vehicles in Argentina.

There were no automobile manufacturing plants in Argentina in the mid 1950's except for comparatively small government-owned facilities. The Argentine Government was quite anxious to see establishment of integrated automobile-manufacturing facilities, which would eventually produce automobiles with 100% locally manufactured components. The establishment of such a facility would not only save further drain on its foreign exchange, but would enhance its national prestige as a rapidly developing nation.

Mr. Kaiser learned at this time that a group of Argentine industrialists were interested in establishing an integrated automobile manufacturing firm. Subsequently the group approached Kaiser Motors to see if it would consider participating in the new venture. Mr. Kaiser, who had been impressed with the great potentials of Latin America, particularly that of Argentina and Brazil, became interested in the project and instructed his staff to look into the possibility of Kaiser participation in the Argentine venture.

In the course of preliminary negotiations, two alternative methods of participation were made available to Kaiser Motors. The first alternative was essentially a licensing agreement for technical know-how and use of Kaiser trade-marks with the following stipulations:

1. An Argentine company will agree to buy every nine months for three years 10,000 knocked down vehicles or a total of 40,000 vehicles over the period. These vehicles will be Henry J. passenger cars and jeeps. The percentage of the U.S. content will be reduced as follows:

End of the 1st 9 months	70% U.S. content [1]
End of the 2nd 9 months	50% U.S. content
End of the 3rd 9 months	30% U.S. content
End of the 4th 9 months	30% U.S. content

2. The Argentine Government is to issue import licenses, and guarantee the availability of dollar funds for the purchase of all of these vehicles, which is estimated to be around $22,000,000.

3. The Argentine Company is to enter into a royalty agreement under which it receives a royalty of $100 and $50 per vehicle respectively on all "jeep" and passenger cars manufactured by it with wholly Argentine content. To the extent that U.S. content purchased from

[1] U.S. content—value of imported components from the U.S.

Kaiser Motors is included in the vehicle, the royalty is to be reduced proportionately.

The second alternative had all of the features of the first and, in addition, required equity participation on the part of Kaiser Motors. The summary of the second alternative is presented below:

> Kaiser Motors, through its subsidiary Willys Motors Corporation is to supply to the Argentine Company six machine tools having a purchase price of $250,000 and one triple-action and two single-action Hamilton presses, available in the Willow Run Plant, which are valued at $336,500. In addition, Kaiser Motors is to make available the Henry J. body tooling. In consideration for making available these toolings, Kaiser Motors is to receive $5,000,000 of 8% preferred stock of the Argentine Company.

QUESTIONS

1. Should Kaiser Motors Corporation participate in the Argentine venture in view of the prevailing investment climate in Argentina?
2. If Kaiser Motors should decide to participate in the new venture, which alternative would you recommend and why?

EXHIBIT 1

KAISER MOTORS CORPORATION AND SUBSIDIARIES
(Including Willys Motors, Inc., and its Subsidiaries)
Consolidated Results of Operations
Year ended December 31, 1953 *

Income:		
Sales, including $216,527,926 under defense contracts of Willys Motors, Inc., and Subsidiaries		$358,994,064
Net gain from sale of property, plant, and equipment after provision for anticipated losses on disposal of excess facilities		6,201,850
Miscellaneous		470,315
		$365,666,229
Costs and expenses:		
Cost of products sold	$360,247,813	
Selling and administrative	26,960,573	
Interest:		
Long-term debt	3,049,046	
Other	1,540,859	
Dividends paid by Willys Motors, Inc., on its Class A and Class B Preferred Stocks	709,823	
Excess of redemption price over stated amount of 13,978 shares of Class A Preferred Stock of Willys Motors, Inc., redeemed and cancelled	209,670	392,717,784
Consolidated Net Loss		$ 27,051,555

Costs and expenses include depreciation of buildings, machinery, and equipment and amortization of leasehold improvements in the amount of $4,802,901.

* Source: Kaiser Motors Corporation *Annual Report,* 1953.

EXHIBIT 2

KAISER MOTORS CORPORATION AND SUBSIDIARIES
(Including Willys Motors, Inc., and its Subsidiaries)
Consolidated Balance Sheet—December 31, 1953 *

Assets

Current assets:			
Cash			$ 13,354,799
Cash and United States Treasury obligations held in escrow for payment of liabilities assumed from Willys-Overland Motors, Inc.			777,094
Trade accounts receivable		$11,717,977	
Less provision for doubtful accounts		433,126	11,284,851
Recoverable amounts applicable to defense contracts, less partial payments received of $12,545,146			45,675,997
Automotive inventories:			
Finished automobiles		$14,560,069	
All other		28,387,163	42,947,232
Prepaid insurance, taxes, and other expenses			1,259,011
Total current assets			$115,298,984
Investments and other assets:			
Investments in companies manufacturing automobiles in The Netherlands and Israel—at cost		$ 750,821	
Westwillow Housing Development; Land and improvements—at cost	$ 410,181		
Land contracts receivable for houses sold	93,326	503,507	
Miscellaneous		552,160	1,806,488
Property, plant, and equipment—at cost, less accumulated depreciation and amortization:			
Land		$ 967,675	
Buildings	$14,827,168		
Machinery, equipment, and leasehold improvements	35,326,225		
	$50,153,393		
Less accumulated depreciation and amortization	17,579,236	32,574,157	
Special automotive tools, less amortization		6,990,334	40,532,166
Deferred charges:			
Cost of acquiring steel capacity rights to assure a long-term supply of steel, being written off over a period ending in 1954			255,000
			$157,892,638

* Source: Kaiser Motors Corporation *Annual Report,* 1953.

Liabilities and Capital

Current liabilities:		
Notes payable and payments aggregating $7,472,818 due within one year on long-term debt		$ 37,296,372
Trade accounts payable		16,307,078
Payrolls, payroll taxes, and contributions to employees' social security funds and retirement plans		5,241,553
Property, excise, and other taxes		1,789,218
Sundry accrued liabilities		8,468,454
Total current liabilities		$ 69,102,675
Long-term debt:		
To bank	$23,250,000	
To Reconstruction Finance Corporation	18,082,954	
To Henry J. Kaiser Company	22,000,000	
To Graham-Paige Corporation for principal payments on 4% Convertible Debentures	5,497,000	
To Graham-Paige Corporation for debentures retired	2,375,000	
Miscellaneous notes and mortgages payable	1,528,664	72,733,618
Preferred stocks of Willys Motors, Inc.—a subsidiary:		
Class A Preferred Stock, without par value, authorized and outstanding 150,000 shares	$15,000,000	
Class B Preferred Stock, without par value, authorized and outstanding 126,000 shares	12,600,000	27,600,000
Common stock of Kaiser Motors Corporation:		
Par value $1.00 a share:		
Authorized 16,000,000 shares		
Issued 6,811,855 shares		
In treasury 186,200 shares		
Outstanding 6,625,655 shares	$ 6,625,655	
Additional paid-in capital	60,172,059	
	$66,797,714	
Less net loss since organization	78,341,369	
Deficit		11,543,655
		$157,892,638

EXHIBIT 3

ARGENTINE IMPORTS OF CARS AND TRUCKS *

	Total U.S.A.			Total Europe			
	Cars	Trucks	Total	Cars	Trucks	Total	Grand Total
1945	22	1	23	13	156	169	192
1946	6,286	9,155	15,439	2,636	2,959	5,593	21,032
1947	27,723	38,090	65,813	7,567	11,018	18,018	84,398
1948	4,289	6,174	10,463	1,216	3,248	4,462	14,925
1949	1,548	488	2,036	384	1,165	1,549	3,585
1950	728	203	931	587	972	1,559	2,490
1951	9,752	1,714	11,466	4,805	1,190	5,995	17,461
1952	405	1,430	1,835	1,204	3,482	4,686	6,521
1953	1,321	1,421	2,742	2,688	2,617	5,302	8,044
	52,072	58,676	110,748	21,093	26,807	47,900	158,648

EXHIBIT 4

PREVAILING PRICE OF SELECTED TYPES OF AUTOMOBILES IN ARGENTINA—1954 *

Cadillac	$15,000
Chrysler	11,000
Kaiser	9,000
Willys	4,500
Mercedes-Benz	4,500
Mercedes-Benz (No. 200)	9,000

*Source: Company records.

45

INDUSTRIAS KAISER ARGENTINA, S.A. (I) *

Local Participation in a U.S. Overseas Operation

After reviewing the two alternatives presented to him, Mr. Kaiser decided on the second. He believed that the equity participation would assure Kaiser Motors Corporation long-term benefits from the growing Argentine market. Moreover, this arrangement offered the possibility of

* Prepared by Dr. Michael Yoshino while a doctoral candidate in the Graduate School of Business, Stanford University.

profitable and constructive uses of the idle facilities in the United States which had resulted from disappointing sales of Kaiser vehicles.

Representatives of Kaiser Motors and local industrialists next drew up an investment proposal which later was approved by Mr. San Martin, Argentine Minister for Air and Director of Government Industries. Subsequently a meeting was held among the President, the Minister of Foreign Affairs, the Minister for Air, and the Minister for Economics, at which the Minister for Air, Mr. San Martin, outlined in detail to the President the terms and conditions of the proposal. The President granted his approval of the proposal and directed the Economic Council to work out the details. Accordingly the President's Economic Council considered the proposal and, after long deliberations, the Council disapproved it on the ground that dollar funds were not available. They proposed an alternative contract under which Kaiser Motors investment in the Argentina operation would be greatly increased.

When Mr. Kaiser learned of this development, he decided to make major capital and managerial commitments in Argentina. He was drawn not only by the great profit opportunities but also by the challenge involved in assisting Argentina to develop her first integrated automobile plants.

At this time, the Argentine government expressed its interest in participating in the automobile venture through Industrias Aeronáuticas y Mecánicas del Estado, an Argentine government enterprise, with Kaiser Motors and Argentine private investors. Upon learning this, Mr. Kaiser flew to Argentina to initiate formal negotiations with the Government officials. The summary of the trip as reported by Mr. Kaiser is included in the Appendix along with the minutes of a conference held with the Argentine leaders including the President.

After a series of conferences, Industrias Aeronáuticas y Mecánicas del Estado (I.A.M.E., an Argentine government enterprise) and Kaiser Motors Corporation agreed to the general principles on which Kaiser Motors would present to I.A.M.E. a specific proposal relating to the establishment of an automotive plant in Argentina. This proposal, a summary of which is presented in Appendix B, was subsequently submitted. Within 60 days it was to be superseded by a formal agreement which would contain detailed provisions based on the principles agreed to, provided that the following conditions had been satisfied.

(a) The granting of repatriation rights with respect to the contribution of capital to be made by Kaiser Motors and the granting of total exemption from customs duties in Argentina for the assets which constitute the capital contributed by Kaiser Motors.

(b) Approval of the agreement by the proper officials of the I.A.M.E. and by the Board of Directors, stockholders, and financing institutions of Kaiser Motors, to the extent required for full validity of the agreement.

Since the date of agreement to the proposal, negotiations had continued and arrangements had been made for completing all detailed planning so that the final agreement might be signed in the near future.

QUESTIONS

1. Should Kaiser Motors Corporation have made the major financial and managerial commitments in Argentina to the extent described in the proposal in view of the prevailing investment climate? What benefits could the company expect from the proposed Argentine investment? What kinds of risks must the company be prepared to take in undertaking the investment?
2. What are the advantages and possible problem areas in going into partnership with government as in the case of Kaiser Motors?
3. Appraise the manner in which Mr. Kaiser conducted his initial negotiation with the Government leaders.

Appendix 1

Brief Summary of Incidents in Argentina *

1. The Mayor of Buenos Aires, *Sabata,* entertained our party, together with about one hundred and fifty important personages, at a remarkable banquet, at which an orchestra played until 2 a.m.

2. Our first official activity was to spend two hours on the morning after our arrival in conference with the important Minister of Economics, *Gomez Morales.* He impressed us as a very able, astute authority on finance and industry. He showed great perception of the industrial needs of Argentina. We did not go into sufficient detail to discuss any proposals that we might make.

3. On Sunday, President *Peron* invited our entire party to have luncheon with him at his country home. He showed great interest in our presence in Argentina. We spent three and one-half hours with him. El Presidente personally walked with us for two hours completely around his estate, which was alive with activities. He gave a sumptuous luncheon for our party in his home. Upon our arrival at the hotel, we found the President had sent Mrs. Kaiser candy and flowers with his personal card. This hospitality certainly more than continued at his home.

4. On Monday at 8 a.m. we met the President with his three top Ministers—Foreign Affairs, Remorino; Economics, Gomez Morales; Aeronautics, General San Martin—and, representing private industry, Jorge Antonio. He appointed these four to act with himself as a committee to work with us. The President instructed Mr. Antonio, who is president of Mercedes-Benz in Argentina, to take us personally to all the Mercedes-Benz operations around Buenos Aires. This took most of the afternoon. In fact we were right in the midst of a luncheon being given us by the top industrialists and businessmen in Argentina, when word was flashed that President Peron requested us to go to these plants; he sent word he would put his Presidential plane at our disposal following the visits to the Mer-

* Source: Company records.

cedes-Benz plants. At the same time he instructed the Minister of Air, General San Martin, to accompany us to the huge Government-owned plants at Córdoba. The Minister of Air had his own plane escort us to Córdoba. After we had seen the plants with him, he had our Willys distributor accompany us in the President's personal plane to Montevideo, Uruguay. The Mayor of Buenos Aires, Jorge Sabata, issued a proclamation naming me the honor guest of the city, and President Peron declared that upon my return he would make me the guest of Argentina, and that he would assign a plane to take our survey party anywhere in Argentina.

Other reports are attached covering our discussions about automobiles, steel, aluminum, hydro-electric power; also possibilities for the organization of a parent automobile company which would own the Mercedes-Benz operations under one company, with another company owning and operating the manufacture of Kaiser-Willys products. I am satisfied that President Peron, when he sent us to Córdoba suddenly with the Air Minister, had in mind that some of the 200 buildings there, together with some $20,000,000 worth of good equipment, would be turned over to our operations. It was talked that we would establish "the General Motors of Argentina" with the thousand or more vendors already in existence supplying parts for the ultimate 100 percent manufacture of motor vehicles in Argentina. There is plenty of evidence that if such a corporation is created, it would receive national protection.

HENRY J. KAISER—PRESIDENT PERON CONFERENCE

Buenos Aires, President's Office

Present
Argentine Party:
- President Peron
- Minister of Foreign Affairs, Remorino
- Minister of Economics, Gomez Morales
- Minister of Aeronautics, San Martin, who also heads Government Industries
- Jorge Antonio, who the President stated was participating as representative of private industry. He is President of Mercedes-Benz in Argentina and also has 25 Antonio-managed companies operating in a number of fields.
- Intendente (Mayor) Jorge Sabata of Buenos Aires
- Chief of Protocol, Margairat—President's Assistant, who made notes.
- Interpreters

Kaiser Party:
- Henry J. Kaiser
- Mayor Morrison (Mayor of New Orleans and a long-time friend of Mr. Kaiser)
- William Weintraub
- Robert C. Elliott
- Mario Bermudez

Economics Minister: Argentina has less than half the motor vehicles we need. We have as of 1951:

350,000 passenger cars—half our needs
250,000 trucks and station wagons—half our needs
600,000—or only half our needs

We have the purchasing power to buy motor vehicles. We need so many thousands more of cars than are found here now. *Our requirements are estimated at 80,000 to 90,000 vehicles annually,* just for domestic markets, not allowing any for export.

Mr. Antonio: Your representatives here must have told you the tremendous possibilities for selling cars. My figures are much more than these official estimates.

Henry Kaiser: You are an optimist, not a pessimist like the President . . . (Mr. Kaiser poked at Peron) . . . My sights are set on 200,000 a year.

President Peron: No one is a pessimist here. We are manufacturing in Argentina now 40 to 50 per cent of spare parts.

Mr. Kaiser: What is the proper way to start? I'd like to send in a team to make a really serious survey—do it at once. I would hope to be back the end of September to complete it.

Mr. Antonio: Then you should stay here two years and have a rest.

Pres. Peron: After you are here 20 days, I will give you Argentine citizenship so you can do as you please.

Mr. Kaiser: Could a corporation be formed here that would be like a "General Motors of Argentina"? It might produce the Mercedes-Benz vehicles, station wagons, Jeeps—anything else that could be manufactured in Argentina. Then all the cars could be made at low cost. The ownership interests could be worked out. I have no desire to have priority. The objective would be lowering costs of production.

Pres. Peron: (Nodding affirmatively in understanding and indicating agreement) Muy bien! (Very good.) I see your idea clearly. You are pointing out what the General Motors combination accomplished in the United States. And why not start right away like that here?

Mr. Kaiser: We should try to get 2,000 to 3,000 vendors so that we would have two or three different sources for every automotive part. In that way, we would have a competitive set up.

Air Minister: That's our policy. We're doing it on a small scale now.

Mr. Kaiser: We have made a study and from looking at it I would say there must be 1,500 vendors available now.

Mr. Antonio: No doubt there is a sizeable number of vendors.

Air Minister: Our Government-owned plant at Córdoba alone has 380 vendors.

Mr. Kaiser: Apparently the quantity of production is not adequate, however, to achieve low cost. That is what must be achieved.

Pres. Peron: Muy Claro! Muy Bien! (Very clear. Very good.) The cost must be gotten down. I feel exactly the same way about it. We must try to lower costs, then we will be able to export cars. We have cheap manpower that offers a great advantage.

Mr. Antonio: Fifty per cent or sixty per cent of the car should be made by the company itself. We already have vendors making parts of tractors, etc., who could make parts for Argentine automobiles.

Pres. Peron: If you have the time to spare, Mr. Kaiser, I would like you to see the Mercedes-Benz plants—how they are organized.

Mr. Kaiser: We can go right after lunch. (This was agreed.) To make as perfect a plant as possible—to make everything we can in one plant, would there be any problem of getting Mercedes-Benz to join?

Mr. Antonio: We would have to consult the Germans. We could collaborate. We could start by helping each other.

Mercedes-Benz is developing diesel-engine manufacturing that could be a separate company.

Mr. Kaiser: Financially, we could consider having one corporation to get all the advantages that General Motors has in its organization.

Mr. Antonio: You don't need to copy anyone.

Pres. Peron: If we copy you, Mr. Kaiser, we will do all right.

Mr. Kaiser: I've gotten this entirely different idea since being here.

Mr. Antonio: That's what happens to all industrialists who come here. They change their minds. You will be surprised to see all we have already achieved here in a small way.

There is room for more than one or two automobile corporations in Argentina. But the ones who start first will do very well. As to financial structure, I can see one big corporation—*the two corporations working under that block.*

Mr. Kaiser: In the United States the independent auto manufacturers are down to about 4 per cent of the nation's sales. They cannot exist on 4%, and I see no reason for duplicating the mistakes made in the United States here in Argentina.

Pres. Peron: Claro! (That's clear)

Mr. Antonio: The situation is different in the states. Here everything is new and just starting. You have a consumption capacity to draw on for twenty years.

Mr. Kaiser and Mr. Antonio joined in pointing up the proposal before the conference—namely, that one big financial entity or corporation be formed, yet there still would be two companies within such a framework, operating competitively. They pointed out that in this way costs could be so lowered that Argentina might do a real export job in automobiles.

Pres. Peron: You can start right away—immediately. Everything is ready.

Mr. Kaiser: How quickly can we talk to Mercedes-Benz?

Mr. Antonio: Right away, here or wherever you want.

Mr. Kaiser: I don't want to minimize the big task of getting 2,000 to 3,000 vendors in order to obtain low costs so that Argentina can export.

Mr. Antonio: That is very important. Vendors are just being educated in automotive production. Mercedes-Benz pays to send them to Europe to learn. They must be helped.

Mr. Kaiser: I visualize automobile manufacturing being very important to Argentina's industrialization, especially when you consider that in the United States the motor vehicle industry is so important that it employs directly or indirectly one out of every seven employed persons.

Pres. Peron: You face no difficulties. It is up to you to make the decisions and we will put every help at your disposal for you to go ahead.

Air Minister: Between the vendors and plants, we already have 28,000 workers engaged in the automotive industry, and yet that is only a small beginning. Our only shortage is in making automotive bodies in big quantities, but it is easy to get a solution to that.

Mr. Kaiser: You merely need a press plant, dies and the tooling. Nothing is impossible, as President Peron indicated.

Mr. Antonio: You have the good will of Argentina to go ahead. For the material part, Mercedes-Benz has seen the need and has started building up the auto industry here two years ago. We don't have the hundreds of millions of dollars needed to make a big automotive industry ourselves right away. If the Germans were able to take their plants out of Germany, they would all be here now. If the Germans were allowed to, they would move their plants here—they're so anxious to come here.

Pres. Peron: You won't find any difficulties.

Mr. Kaiser: There will be no problems if we have a meeting of the minds. After what I saw yesterday, I think anything is possible to be worked out.

Pres. Peron: Si, si. For you with your organization's know-how it is easy.

Mr. Kaiser: I must bring a team of technicians here.

Pres. Peron: We will give the team all the data needed.

Mr. Kaiser: Will you appoint a group to work with us?

Pres. Peron: Yes, our group will be Mr. Antonio, representing private industry in the group, our Minister of Economics, Gomez Morales, and our Minister of Aeronautics and Industry, General San Martin, who not only heads the Aeronautics industry, but also heads the government corporation that operates government-owned industries.

We have a plant at Córdoba that costs us 80,000,000 pesos a year to operate. It has 8,000 workers on the production of automobiles. We can put that plant at your disposal. All this operation should be absorbed into the private automobile company.

Mr. Antonio: What is your idea, in general, Mr. Kaiser, of the first move?

Mr. Kaiser: To send our team here to talk and to make plans.

Mr. Antonio: Would you want someone sent from Germany, or do you want to go to Germany?

Mr. Kaiser: I would leave that to your judgment.

Mr. Antonio: That is very easy. Could you go to Germany?

Mr. Kaiser: If necessary, I could do anything. I could go to Germany or the President of Mercedes-Benz could come here or we could meet in the United States.

Pres. Peron: It would be very nice to have Mr. Kaiser and the President of Mercedes-Benz here together with us in Argentina.

Mr. Kaiser: On September 17, I am scheduled to be in the Northwest, in Seattle, then I should spend five days in New York and go to Washington to discuss financial matters, so I would like to be back here between September 25 to 30.

Mr. Antonio: When you discuss financing, will you include us in the discussions?

Mr. Kaiser: Oh yes, definitely.

Pres. Peron: Your timing is perfect. When will your team come? When your team comes we will put a plane at their disposal and they can go all around the country anywhere they need to make their studies.

Mr. Kaiser: I don't know what obligations our men have. We have a thousand to 1,500 engineers in Kaiser Engineers. The chief of Kaiser Engineers has been with me twenty years. He speaks Spanish fluently. I would like him to come here.

Pres. Peron: Very good! Magnífico!

Mr. Kaiser: Now as to your foreign exchange problem—your problem of getting United States dollars. I'm convinced the automobile engine of the future will have an aluminum die-cast block. We have participated in building the largest aluminum die-cast press in the world at a cost of a quarter of a million dollars. Probably two million dollars has already been spent in developing the aluminum die-cast block for the engine. I am visualizing that in two or three years the aluminum engine will be ready. Not too much labor is involved in die casting. I have been thinking that the aluminum engine could be produced in Venezuela and a trade arrangement could be worked out whereby Argentina would sell wheat or cattle to Venezuela in order to buy back aluminum engines.

Mr. Antonio: Venezuela only has 5,000,000 people and is full of cars.

Mr. Kaiser: Is it practical that Venezuela might make aluminum die-cast blocks to exchange them for Argentine wheat? Venezuela has ample United States dollars with which to buy aluminum from the United States.

Mr. Antonio: I don't see how such a triangular operation would be feasible. Argentina already has markets for its wheat and meat. Perhaps later it could sell for dollars elsewhere. Venezuela might be interrupted as a source for engines for Argentina's automotive industry.

Mr. Kaiser: I'm just trying to explore how you could get away from your dollar shortage. There is plenty of bauxite to make aluminum anywhere. We have a huge source of bauxite in Jamaica and an aluminum plant might be erected here, but it would cost a vast number of millions of dollars to build an aluminum pig plant.

Air Minister: We use 20,000 tons of aluminum in Argentina a year.

Mr. Kaiser: I don't know whether the Venezuela idea is any good, and if it isn't we can drop it. (Mr. Kaiser showed the Argentine officials copies of the Kaiser Aluminum brochures, suggesting five different types of aluminum fabricating plants that might be built in South American countries, namely:

1. Extrusions
2. Foil
3. Electrical conductor
4. Irrigation pipe
5. Aluminum bodies for motor vehicles.

The Economics Minister agreed that production of more K.W. was most important to the country and that an electrical conductor plant would be a very interesting development. The group also expressed great interest in the making of irrigation pipe and declared that one of the greatest opportunities of all would be making aluminum bodies and motor vehicles since that would reduce the deadweight of trucks a great deal.)

Pres Peron: Claro! Extraordinary! (The President remarked about the different aluminum possibilities presented by Mr. Kaiser.)

Air Minister: Sixty-thousand tons of aluminum is needed yearly here.

(Mr. Kaiser presented to the group, Kaiser Steel's brochure entitled "Steel in Action," and stressed the opportunity of starting a steel-pipe mill that would make square columns for construction. Mr. Kaiser presented the Aluminum and Steel brochures to President Peron.)

Pres. Peron: Thank you very much. It means the future of the world to bring greater industrialization and productivity to South America.

Mr. Kaiser: Here are types of plants that can be started in Argentina.

Pres. Peron: Si, si.

Minister of Economics: We're trying to do the production of tin plate here in Argentina.

(Mr. Kaiser recounted the Kaiser Steel tin plate work and also the development work with American Can to bring out all-aluminum cans.)

Air Minister: Alcoa is very happy with your work.

Mr. Kaiser: Aluminum is the new material of a new age. Aluminum is the metal for use in transportation equipment. Small manufacturers can produce aluminum bodies right here . . . Should we work on the exchange problem? That is the only reason I had Venezuela in mind.

Morrison: The shortage of dollars appears to be a big problem. Venezuela is not essential in the picture. Mr. Kaiser just threw that out as an idea.

Pres. Peron: On the question of getting dollars, Economics Minister Morales will be our expert on foreign exchange to work with you. It is a matter of endeavoring to find equilibrium.

Econ. Min.: As a practical matter, it would be very difficult to work out a three-way arrangement. Venezuela has a free market in dollars. It would require arriving at compensating treaties between Venezuela and Argentina. But take aluminum. There would be no problem. You could ship aluminum pig here first.

Pres. Peron: Today we have much more conversion of money.

Mr. Kaiser: My only thought is to be helpful. My mind is completely open on the question.

Econ. Min.: The Venezuela idea could only be handled if it were placed in private hands. The Government doesn't enter into barter arrangements.

Mr. Kaiser: Is there anything further I can do to be of help?

Pres. Peron: The future developments are incalculable. At the moment, what you have outlined is good. The future is full of possibilities. The thing to do is to start now.

Mr. Antonio: (To Mr. Kaiser) You won't have any problems in dollars? If you bring in a large investment and put Mercedes-Benz into it, the investment probably could be repaid very fast.

Mr. Kaiser: The problems that we must work out are only "opportunities in work clothes."

Pres. Peron: Exacto! (Exactly)

Mr. Antonio: You won't find any better opportunities than right here.

Morrison: Mr. Kaiser's main objectives can be summed up in this way—Mr. Kaiser is saying that not only is he willing to bring Kaiser resources and know-how into the development of a basic automobile industry in Argentina, but he is also ready to assist in other developments, such as in aluminum and steel.

Pres. Peron: Exacto!

(The President at this point expanded the Argentina group to work with the Kaiser group to include the Minister of Foreign Affairs, Remorino, with the President himself cooperating. The meeting broke up, with the President presenting his personally autographed picture inscribed "Al amigo con gran afecto" and all of the Argentina group pledged their fullest co-operation.)

Appendix 2

Proposal of Kaiser Motors Corporation to Join with I.A.M.E. in Establishing an Automotive Manufacturing Company in Argentina *

SUMMARY

I. It is proposed that Kaiser Motors Corporation [1] and I.A.M.E. will form a corporation under the laws of Argentina to manufacture motor vehicles and other related products. The suggested name of the company is Industrias Kaiser de Argentina (IKA)—(Kaiser Industries of Argentina).

II. Products and Capacity

The company will manufacture in Argentina the Kaiser passenger car, the Jeep, the Jeep station wagon, and the Jeep pick-up truck. The capacity will be 40,000 units per year on a one-shift basis. The first vehicles will contain a substantial proportion of components manufactured in the U.S. but when the plant reaches maximum production, 100% of the required components will be manufactured in Argentina.

The company's facilities in Argentina will enable it to manufacture essentially the same components of the finished vehicles that Kaiser now manufactures in its own operations in the United States. The company will acquire from subcontractors and vendors in Argentina essentially the same components which Kaiser now purchases from vendors in the U.S. In order to accomplish this result, the new company will carry on an in-

* The information contained in Appendix 2 has been summarized by the case writer from the original proposal.

[1] References to Kaiser Motors Corporation include its subsidiary, Willys Motors, Inc.

tensive vendor-assistance program in Argentina. Accomplishment of this program will not only enable the new company to carry on a United States-type of automotive manufacturing operation, but will also enable these vendors to manufacture similar components for other Argentine industries, thus greatly strengthening the Argentine economy.

The proposed production schedule and the estimated Argentine content of the vehicles at each stage are shown in the following table.

PROPOSED PRODUCTION SCHEDULE AND ARGENTINE CONTENT

PRODUCTION SCHEDULE

	Jeep	Kaiser	Station Wagon	Truck	Total	Yearly Total
			(construction of facilities)			
1956	10				10	
	75				75	
	200				200	
	400	5			405	
	575	37			602	
	800	100			900	
	1050	200			1250	
	1250	285			1535	
	1400	400			1800	
	1550	525			2075	
	1600	625			2225	
						11,087
1957	1600	700			2300	
	1600	775			2375	
	1600	800			2400	
	1600	800			2400	
	1600	800			2400	
	1600	800			2400	
	1600	800			2400	
	1600	800			2400	
	1600	800			2400	
	1600	800	5	5	2410	
	1600	800	25	25	2450	
	1600	800	200	200	2800	
						29,135
1958	1600	800	300	300	3000	
	1600	800	400	400	3200	

ARGENTINE CONTENT
(As Percentage of Unit Cost)

Jeep	Kaiser	Station Wagon	Truck
57.5%	77%		
86.5%	98%	87%	86%
100.0%	100%	100%	100%

III. Capital

The initial capital will consist of:

A. Machinery, equipment tools, dies, jigs, and fixtures furnished by Kaiser and I.A.M.E.

B. Peso financing in Argentina raised by sale of stock and loans.

C. Profit on sale in Argentina of 1000 Kaiser passenger cars to be purchased from Kaiser.

A preliminary estimate of the capital required is as follows:

Machinery and Equipment	138,706,000 pesos
Buildings and Installation	135,924,000 pesos
Tools, Dies, Jigs, and Fixtures	156,253,000 pesos
Sub-Total	430,883,000 pesos
	160,000,000 pesos
Sub-Total	590,883,000 pesos
Less: Anticipated Profit from Sale of 1000 Kaiser automobiles	111,000,000 pesos
Net Capital Required	479,883,000 pesos

A summary and detailed break-down of the above facilities showing the items to be furnished from the U.S. and the items to be obtained, manufactured or constructed in Argentina, is attached.

IV. Capital to Be Furnished by Kaiser

The capital to be furnished by Kaiser, partly as an investment and partly as a sale for dollars, has an estimated value of $15,121,500 broken down as follows:

Machinery and Equipment	$ 4,814,100
Tools, Dies, Jigs, and Fixtures	8,362,400
1000 Kaiser cars	1,945,000
Total	$15,121,500

It is proposed that of this $15,121,500 worth of assets to be furnished by Kaiser, $10,121,500 worth be furnished as a capital investment and $5,000,000 worth be sold for dollars to the new company. This would be accomplished as follows:

Capital Investment			
Tools, Dies, Jigs, and Fixtures	$ 8,362,400	or	117,074,000 pesos
Machinery and Equipment	1,759,100	or	24,627,000 pesos
Total	$10,121,500	or	141,701,000 pesos
Sales for Dollars			
Machinery and Equipment	$3,055,000	or	42,770,000 pesos
1000 Kaiser cars at 1945 ea.	1,945,000	or	27,230,000 pesos
Total	$5,000,000	or	70,000,000 pesos

V. Capital to Be Furnished by I.A.M.E.

It is proposed that I.A.M.E. furnish machinery and equipment now owned by I.A.M.E., or on order, with an estimated value of $3,120,200 or 43,683,000 pesos. I.A.M.E. might also make further capital contribution as shown in the following paragraph.

VI. Remaining Capital Requirements

The capital investments of Kaiser (141,701,000 pesos) and I.A.M.E. (43,683,000 pesos), as shown above, total 185,384,000 pesos. An additional 294,499,000 pesos will have to be provided in order to furnish the total capital required, or 479,883,000 pesos. The additional pesos may be obtained by any one, or a combination, of the following means:

A. Contribution of additional facilities or tools, jigs, dies, and fixtures by I.A.M.E., either in physical form or as a cash investment,
B. Sale of stock to private investors in Argentina, and
C. Loans from Argentine lending institutions.

VII. Resulting Capital Structure

The final capital structure would depend on the above methods actually employed to raise the necessary proposed capital. A feasible capital structure if satisfactory to I.A.M.E., might be as follows:

A. *Assumptions*

1. Kaiser invests machinery, dies, jigs, and fixtures having a value of	141,701,000 pesos
2. I.A.M.E. invests machinery and equipment having a value of	43,683,000
And so that I.A.M.E.'s share in the new company will be substantial as originally contemplated, it is proposed that I.A.M.E. invest additional facilities, tools, jigs, dies and fixtures, either in physical form or in cash, thus increasing its total investment to	80,000,000
3. Common or preferred stock is sold to private Argentine investors for a total amount of	150,000,000
4. Argentine lending institutions make a loan to the new company of	108,182,000
Total	479,883,000

B. *Resulting Capital Structure*

1. *Stock*		
a. Kaiser	141,701,000	pesos or 38.2%
b. I.A.M.E.	80,000,000	pesos or 21.6%
c. Private Argentine Investors	150,000,000	pesos or 49.2%
Sub-Total	371,701,000	
2. *Loan*	108,182,000	pesos
Total	479,883,000	pesos

VIII. Methods of Valuing and Capitalizing Machinery and Equipment and Tools, Jigs, Dies, and Fixtures

All machinery and equipment and tools, jigs, dies, and fixtures, whether furnished by Kaiser or by I.A.M.E., and whether furnished as a sale for dollars or as a capital investment, shall be valued on the following basis:

A. *Base Value*

1. For new machinery and equipment, 100% of the present cost of equivalent new equipment in the United States.
2. For machinery and equipment manufactured after January 1, 1948, 95% of the present cost of equivalent new equipment in the U.S.
3. For machinery and equipment manufactured between January 1, 1936 and January 1, 1948, 90% of the present cost of equivalent new equipment in the United States.

   Note: The method of valuation set forth in paragraphs 2 and 3 above is the method used by the United States Office of Price Stabilization in establishing ceiling prices for sales of used machinery and equipment during the period 1950-1953.
4. For tools, jigs, dies, and fixtures which are unique and do not have a readily determinable market value, the original cost to Kaiser or I.A.M.E. as the case may be.

   Note: The tools, dies, jigs, and fixtures to be furnished by Kaiser have been currently in use and are in the same condition as when new. The present cost of replacing these items (all made on a custom basis) would be at least 20% higher than their original cost.

B. *Additions to Base Value*

1. In the case of Kaiser-furnished machinery and equipment, tools, dies, jigs, and fixtures, there shall be added to this base value Kaiser's actual cost of dismantling, shipping to United States port and loading on board the vessel.
2. In the case of I.A.M.E.-furnished machinery and equipment, tools, dies, jigs, and fixtures, there shall be added the estimated cost of freight, handling, and any other normal export charges from the plant of the equivalent United States manufacturer to Argentina.
3. The remaining cost of transporting the machinery, equipment, tools, dies, jigs, and fixtures to the plant location (ocean and inland freight and insurance in the case of Kaiser-furnished equipment, and dismantling, inland freight and insurance to the plant location in the case of I.A.M.E.-furnished equipment) shall be paid in pesos by the new company out of its initial capital.
4. All such machinery, equipment, tools, dies, jigs, and fixtures shall be capitalized on the books of the new company at the price in cash or value in stock paid to Kaiser or I.A.M.E., as the case may be, plus the peso cost to the new company of shipping these items to the plant location. Any Argentine customs duties and other taxes would also be paid in pesos

by the new company and included in the capitalization of the equipment.

Note: It is intended to request a customs exemption on the machinery, equipment, tools, dies, jigs, and fixtures to be invested by Kaiser, under the provision of the Investment Law No. 14222.

C. *Rate of Exchange*
For purposes of the above, computations in United States dollars shall be converted into pesos at the official free-market rate published by the Argentine Central Bank, presently, approximately 14 to 1.

IX. Patent Licensing, Engineering and Technical Assistance

Kaiser would license the new company under all existing patents and trademarks under its control required to produce the products to be manufactured by the new company. Royalties would be computed in dollars on the following basis:

A. $40.00 per vehicle on the first 10,000 vehicles produced in any year.
$25.00 per vehicle on the second 10,000 vehicles produced in any year.
$20.00 per vehicle on the third 10,000 vehicles produced in any year.
$15.00 per vehicle on the fourth 10,000 vehicles produced in any year.

B. One-half of this royalty would be payable to Kaiser in pesos, and the remaining one-half of this royalty would be paid in dollars at the official free-market rate of exchange established by the Argentine Central Bank.

C. The above royalty shall be reduced with respect to any vehicle, engine or spare part represented by components obtained from United States sources.

The new company will purchase temporary engineering services and technical assistance from Kaiser under arrangements whereby the dollar cost to Kaiser of furnishing such services, including salaries of United States personnel employed in the United States and the dollar portion of the salaries (in excess of peso living expenses) of United States personnel temporarily in Argentina, would be paid in dollars.

X. Dollar Requirements

The estimated dollar requirements would be as follows:

1955

1. Purchase of machinery and equipment from Kaiser	$3,055,000
2. Purchase of 1000 Kaiser cars	1,945,000
3. Dollar costs of engineering and technical assistance	759,000
Total	$5,759,000

1956	
1. Purchase of component parts and supply through Kaiser from U.S. manufacturers to produce approximately 11,000 vehicles in 1956	$5,458,000
2. Dollar costs of patent royalties, engineering and technical assistance	667,000
Total	$6,125,000
1957	
1. Purchase of component parts and supply through Kaiser from U.S. manufacturers to produce approximately 29,000 vehicles in 1957	$2,931,000
2. Dollar costs of patent royalties, engineering and technical assistance	720,000
Total	$3,651,000
1958	
1. Purchase of component parts and supply through Kaiser from U.S. manufacturers to produce approximately 38,000 vehicles in 1958	$ 495,000
2. Dollar costs of patent royalties, engineering and technical assistance	692,000
Total	$1,187,000
1959 and Thereafter	
1. Purchase of component parts and supply through U.S. manufacturers to produce vehicles in 1959 and thereafter (per year)	$ 300,000
2. Dollar costs of patent royalties, engineering and technical assistance	550,000

Note: Kaiser proposes to furnish the necessary technical assistance so that the I.A.M.E.-Kaiser partnership can carry out a vigorous vendor-assistance program, with the objective of enabling Argentine parts manufacturers to produce all of the required components for the vehicles. These techniques should be developed within the Argentine economy to the maximum extent practicable, so that both the new company and the entire Argentine economy will be supported by a firm base of manufacturing skills. In carrying out this vendor-assistance program, the I.A.M.E.-Kaiser partnership may find that the Argentine parts manufacturers will be unable to obtain from Argentine sources all of the machine tools and materials required to make certain of the more complicated parts. The amounts and types of foreign exchange that may be needed for this purpose have not been included in the above estimate, pending further study by the I.A.M.E.-Kaiser partnership as to the availability of the required machine tools and materials in Argentina or from non-dollar sources in Europe, and the feasibility of redesigning the vehicles so as to eliminate the need for such machine tools and materials.

XI. Management

Documents establishing the new company would provide that Kaiser will have sole responsibility for the management and technical operations of the company, subject to general policies prescribed by the board of directors and stockholders. Representation on the board of directors would in general conform to the respective stock interest of Kaiser, I.A.M.E., and private Argentine investors in the new company.

XII. Other Commitments of Kaiser

Kaiser would unconditionally guarantee that the machinery, equipment, tools, dies, jigs, and fixtures to be furnished to the new company, whether by sale or investment, are in good operating condition and that the facilities of the new company will be engineered, installed and operated in an efficient manner in accordance with practices prevailing in the United States automotive industry, with such adaptations as are required to meet local conditions in Argentina.

XIII. Required Actions of the Argentine Government

The above proposal contemplates that the Argentine government would take the following steps in the form of appropriate government decrees or equivalent binding governmental action:

A. Approve the proposed Kaiser investment as a qualified investment under Law No. 14222, with the right to repatriate capital after ten years in five equal annual installments of 20%.

B. As part of this approval, exempt the physical goods forming the Kaiser investment from Argentine customs duties.

C. Reduce the applicable duty on the new company's imports of components, raw materials, spare parts, and finished or semi knocked-down vehicles for a period of five years.

D. Authorize the purchase of the $5,000,000 of foreign exchange required, at a rate no higher than the official free-market rate published by the Argentine Central Bank, to cover the initial dollar purchases of machinery and vehicles as listed in Para. IV.

E. Agree in principle to authorize the purchase of the foreign exchange required in the first few years of operation as listed in Para. X.

F. Furnish without charge to the new company the land on which the new installations will be constructed.

XIV. General Description of Proposed Facilities

The proposed facilities will consist of all required buildings, utilities, machinery, and equipment to produce 40,000 vehicles annually. The basic layout will provide for the manufacture and assembly of 6-cylinder and 4-cylinder engines, press plant, and complete assembly facilities for the production of stampings and assembling four different kinds of vehicles divided approximately into the following proportions:

20,000 "Jeeps" annually
10,000 Kaisers annually
5,000 pick-ups
5,000 station wagons annually

Survey of the available vendor facilities indicates that reliance can be placed on obtaining the required castings and forgings from vendors who will be supplied with some of the necessary special toolings for the production requirements.

An area of approximately 74 acres is required and the principal facilities consist of the following buildings:

Assembly building
Engine machining building
Stamping plant
Administration building
Service building
Power house
Substation

Estimated Cost of Vehicles

A preliminary estimate of the cost of the vehicles was prepared. This represents the best judgment available at this time. The estimate of cost is predicated upon the assumption that the company's facilities will manufacture essentially the same components of the finished vehicles that Kaiser now manufactures in its own operations in the United States. The company will obtain from subcontractors in Argentina essentially the same components which Kaiser now purchases from vendors in the United States. A study made indicates that by the time the facilities of the new company will be placed in operation some 60 per cent of the total purchased components can be obtained from Argentine vendors, as a result of an intensive vendor-assistance program which would be put in effect during the period of the construction of the facilities.

During the third year of operation practically all such components would be procured in Argentina.

A tabulation follows setting forth the estimated weights of the Kaiser 4-door Sedan and the C. J. 3 B "jeep."

A summary is included indicating the estimated cost of producing the "jeep" and the Kaiser during the first and third years of operation of the new facilities.

The estimates of cost of the materials to be procured from sub-contractors in Argentina represent the best judgment available at this time on the basis of similar cost elements in existence today. As sub-contractors develop mass-production techniques, it is anticipated that their costs and prices will be reduced.

The depreciation of the plant and equipment has been assumed on the straight-line basis over a period of 15 years. All other cost elements are estimated in accordance with prevailing U.S. practice.

The summary of the estimated costs for the first and third years of operation is as follows:

	1956	1958
"Jeeps"	47,631 pesos	45,436 pesos
Kaisers	98,762 pesos	64,439 pesos
Station wagons		52,997 pesos
Trucks		49,554 pesos

ESTIMATED COST OF "JEEP"
(In Pesos)

	1956	1958
Estimated production, units	8,910	19,200
Materials		
Purchased in the U.S.	5,018	409
Freight	901	247
Purchased in Argentina	22,273	39,272
Sub-total	28,192	39,928
Labor and burden	7,057	2,671
Tool amortization	1,161	1,161
Depreciation of plant and equipment	1,351	347
Royalty	540	357
Commercial expense		
General and Administrative	870	223
Engineering	866	222
Sales	1,417	365
Sub-total	3,153	810
Technical assistance	1,219	162
Starting up cost in 1955	4,958	
Total estimated cost per vehicle	47,631	45,436

ESTIMATED COST OF KAISER
(In Pesos)

	1956	1958
Estimated production, units	2,177	9,600
Materials		
Purchased in the U.S.	4,294	216
Freight	2,517	792
Purchased in Argentina	36,961	49,895
Sub-Total	43,772	50,903
Labor and burden	20,313	6,553
Tool amortization	3,394	3,391
Depreciation of plant and equipment	3,888	851
Royalties	540	357
Commercial expense		
General and Administrative	2,503	548
Engineering	2,492	546
Sales	4,079	892
Sub-Total	9,074	1,986
Technical assistance	3,510	398
Starting-up cost in 1955	14,271	
Total estimated cost per vehicle	98,762	64,439

Estimated Prices of Vehicles

For the purposes of this study the following sales prices have been assumed for the vehicles to be produced in Argentina by the new company:

	1956	1957	1958
"Jeep"	100,000	62,000	55,000
Kaiser	150,000	110,000	80,000
Station Wagon		80,000	71,000
Truck		71,000	63,000

The above prices represent an estimated return to the automobile-manufacturing company per unit. The sales prices to the public would be the above amounts, plus an appropriate dealer commission, plus sales tax.

The above estimated prices are used in the Cash Forecast. The estimated prices decrease in each succeeding year on the assumptions that (1) production costs will decrease and (2) as the present pent-up demand begins to be satisfied and the backlog of orders tapers off, sales prices will have to be decreased in order to attract new buyers and insure continued volume production.

Sale of 1000 Kaiser Cars

It is planned that Kaiser will sell to the new company 1000 semi-knocked-down 1954 model Kaiser sedans. This would result in a substantial initial profit to the new company, and would help to provide the necessary initial capital to construct the new facilities and commence operations.

The profit to the new company is estimated as follows:

1.	Selling price from Kaiser to the new company (standard export price including U.S. freight)	$1,945 each
2.	Cost in pesos to new company, including sales and assembly expense (at free-market rate of approximately 14 to 1)	42,000 pesos
3.	Estimated selling price from new company to dealers and distributors	200,000 pesos
4.	Profit before taxes	156,000 pesos
5.	Profit after taxes (if applicable)	111,000 pesos
6.	Multiplied by 1000 cars, the aggregate profit would be	111,000,000 pesos

The semi-knocked-down Kaiser cars will be shipped from Kaiser's Toledo factory against irrevocable letters of credit. A vehicle will be delivered to an assembly plant in Argentina approximately nine weeks later. Allowing one month to assemble and distribute the car for sale in Argentina, and, assuming a rate of 20 vehicles per day, 1000 cars can be sold in a period of six months from the date of initial shipment, thus providing 111,000,000 pesos of the new company's required additional capital in time to be used for the construction of facilities and preparation for the beginning of manufacturing operations.

Vendors

The various surveys of Argentine industry conducted by Kaiser and Willys personnel disclose a potential source for every part needed to manufacture automobiles and trucks in quantity. Existing suppliers of automotive-type parts indicated a strong desire to obtain high-volume manufacture, and expressed an intention to expand as rapidly as such business developed. They have already attained a high degree of mechanical skill and need only technical assistance in mass-production techniques to augment their output.

In view of this favorable situation, virtually all of the components and assemblies currently furnished by vendors in the United States appear to be obtainable from existing private suppliers. I.A.M.E., with its diversification of equipment, skilled personnel, and engineering knowledge, will also become a major supplier of components to the extent that its facilities are available. I.A.M.E. should also be able to supply cutting tools, dies, jigs, and fixtures for the new company and its suppliers throughout the nation.

The ultimate goal of a vehicle containing substantially 100% Argentine components can be attained more rapidly by developing a broad industrial base of suppliers for automotive manufacturing in Argentina—through resulting decentralization of technical problems and utilization of existing skilled engineers and plant capacities—than by attempting to manufacture all vehicle components directly in the facilities of the new company.

It is therefore contemplated that the new company will acquire the facilities, equipment, tools, jigs, dies, and fixtures to manufacture in Argentina essentially the same components of the finished vehicles that Kaiser now manufactures in its own operations in the United States.

The company would acquire from sub-contractors and vendors in Argentina essentially the same components which Kaiser now purchases from vendors in the United States. This program will enable the new company's vendors to manufacture similar components for other Argentine industries, thus greatly strengthening the Argentine economy.

Since many types of parts similar to the required components are already being produced in Argentina, it is expected that a substantial proportion of Argentine content can be achieved by the time the facilities of the new company are ready for operation. During the construction and equipment-installation period, the selected suppliers will be preparing to meet the production schedule. Many suppliers will find it necessary to rearrange their equipment, provide new tools, equipment and plant, locate sources of materials, and develop methods which will assure strict control of product quality. The tools, jigs, dies, and fixtures which Kaiser will furnish to the new company include items which Kaiser has furnished to its parts suppliers and other vendors in the United States, and which will also be suitable for use by the parts suppliers and other vendors of the new company in Argentina. The availability of these items should be of substantial assistance to the Argentine vendors in preparing to produce parts for the new company. In addition, Kaiser will provide the technical assistance necessary so that the new company can carry on a vigorous vendor-assistance program.

Appendix 3

The Profile of Henry J. Kaiser *

The following excerpts on Henry J. Kaiser and his organization are taken from two articles in *Fortune* magazine. The accuracy of these descriptions has been confirmed by the case writer through a series of interviews with men who have worked with him closely over a period of time.

* "Arrival of Henry J. Kaiser," *Fortune,* July 1951. "Henry J. Kaiser," *Fortune,* October 1943. Reprinted by Special Permission. © 1943, 1951 Time Inc.

Modest Beginning

"Henry J. Kaiser was born in 1882 in Canajoharie, an upstate New York village of 2,500. His German-born father, Frank John Kaiser, was a custom shoemaker. The only boy of the four Kaiser children, Henry cared nothing for making shoes. Always building things, he kept the house littered with tools and materials. He also had a flair for photography, and was determined to get ahead in the world. When he was fourteen he got a job as a delivery boy in a Utica department store. Showing some artistic ability in his photographic hobby, he was promoted to the drapery department. Four or five years later he hired himself out to a photographer in the nearby resort town of Lake Placid. 'At the end of the first year,' he says, 'I had a half interest in the business. At the end of three years I owned it in full.'

"Next the growing photographer set up shop in the resort town of Daytona Beach, Florida. He made enough money to put up two small buildings there. As business increased, he added a store in Palm Beach and a counter in a St. Augustine store. The Kaiser photographic stores acted as agents for Eastman Kodak.

"To get into a fundamental industrial line, he sold his photographic business. After some cogitation, he picked the hardware business and went to Spokane, Washington. With a continent's span between him and his past, Kaiser set about realizing his ambition. He applied at a large hardware firm called McGowan Bros. and remembers 'hounding one man so steadily that he nearly threw me out.' He was with the store two years, becoming an assistant buyer in sporting goods, then city sales manager.

"In Spokane he changed jobs to go to work with the Hawkeye Sand & Gravel Co., buying a little stock and arranging to pay for more out of his earnings as a salesman. Not long afterward a Chicago construction firm named J. F. Hill landed a contract in the city of Spokane. Kaiser called on the company to sell his line of aggregates and left with a job to build and manage their sand and gravel plant. Hill sent Kaiser to Vancouver in 1913 to put up another sand and gravel plant. While in British Columbia he saw a chance to get into the construction business on his own. With money borrowed from a Vancouver bank, he bought some secondhand wheelbarrows, concrete mixers and a couple of teams. With these he successfully bid a $250,000 paving contract in Nanaimo.

"Out of this chance salesman's bid for an operator's profits came the Henry J. Kaiser Co. Ltd., one predecessor of the Henry J. Kaiser Company. The new firm stayed in Vancouver only a little while, then moved to Victoria, then to Seattle, then to California. 'We paved 1,000 miles of highway in British Columbia, California, and Washington,' says its founder, 'and besides that we built fifteen sand and gravel plants.'

Colorful Personality

"Henry J. Kaiser's most obvious characteristic is his tendency to go the whole hog, to carry things almost to the point of excess. It manifests itself in practically everything he does. The headquarters of his empire is in Oakland, California, where he maintains an office that seems less appropriate for a contractor than for a cosmetics manufacturer. Kaiser spends about half of his time on the other side of the continent, alternating between a suite in Washington, a suite at the Waldorf-Astoria and a set of offices in Rockefeller Center in New York. Since only a fraction of the actual production job is done on the East Coast, Kaiser is inclined to run the main show by remote control. His executives commute back and forth and half of Kaiser's working day seems to be given to telephone talks with men thousands of miles away.

"Kaiser's friends have always worried that he will work himself to death, and if not himself then his unprotesting young men. Feliz Kahn says, 'He is untiring—he pounds you.' Apparently he has always been that way. Clay Bedford tells a story of a business trip to Cuba he made with Kaiser fifteen years ago, when he was a mere freshman in the old Kaiser Paving Co.: 'We shared a stateroom together and it seemed to me Mr. Kaiser never slept. He lay on the bed thinking and tossing. Just when I'd be ready to doze off he'd whisper, "Clay! Clay! Are you awake?" Then he'd be off on some ideas he'd just thought of.' When hard pressed or thwarted Henry Kaiser is intensely unsentimental. Among his intimates his rages and threats are as famous as his appetite. The cord swells in his neck; his round body shakes all over, the words are flung out with triple hammer speed. Men who have been bawled out over the telephone say they could hear him pounding the table a continent's span away. Kaiser, aroused often over something relatively insignificant, is extremely violent. Taunting, goading, brushing aside all argument, he seems bent upon luring the other person into a fight. In recent years he has been involved in several episodes of lapel seizing and shoulder spinning, one involving a three-star general, another a federal investigator.

"The secret—or the least understood fact—of his success is that he has chosen and built up a group of managers who as a group probably have no peer anywhere. It is not that any one of them is a genius. It is that under Henry they consistently outperform themselves. Kaiser's great talent is his ability to choose good men and get them to work twice as hard, twice as long, and twice as effectively as they would for anyone else. And what is more, he has had the sense and tact to use their talents to compensate for his own deficiencies.

"Kaiser has done this simply by letting as many men as possible in on making the important decisions and thenceforth giving them almost complete responsibility. This management system developed naturally enough. As a contractor who pooled his talents with other contractors in bidding on jobs, Kaiser early acquired the habit of talking through a problem and coming to a joint decision. He continued to do so in his own company.

"Probably because they have to think constantly in terms of new things, Kaiser's top management have developed a remarkable versatility. New assignments for them have often meant a change of function as well as location. So there it is—a kind of inspired resourcefulness combined with extremely hard work and thoroughgoing day to day operations. In his audacious, bumbling, but highly intuitive way, Henry Kaiser has built up a management group that provides the perfect foil for his excesses."

46

INDUSTRIAS KAISER ARGENTINA, S.A. (II) *

Conflict in a Joint Venture over Capital Equipment Valuation

Industrias Aeronáuticas y Mecánicas del Estado (IAME), an Argentine Government enterprise, and Kaiser Motors Corporation agreed in the mid 1950's upon a specific Kaiser proposal relating to the establishment of an automotive plant in Argentina. It was agreed that Kaiser Motors Corporation would contribute specified assets to establish an integrated automotive industry in Argentina, and that the company would receive in return a payment of $5,000,000, together with common stock in the new Argentine automotive company for the remainder of their contribution. The proposal contained a detailed list of items and a specific method of valuation, resulting in an estimated dollar value of approximately $15,000,000 (including 1,000 automobiles worth $2,000,000 to be exported for immediate distribution). Apart from the 1,000 automobiles, the understanding was that the company would contribute specified machinery, equipment, tools, dies, etc. with a value of approximately $13,000,000 and would receive in return a payment of $3,000,000 in cash and common stock with a par value equivalent to $10,000,000 at the rate of exchange applicable under law No. 14,222.

It was upon the basis of this understanding that Kaiser Motors agreed, at the request of Dr. Gomez Morales, Minister of Finance, to eliminate from a preliminary proposal the payment of annual royalties in dollars for the use of inventions, technical information, know-how and trademarks, involving an estimated payment of approximately $500,000 per year. Although it was the company's standard practice to charge such royalties to all other companies manufacturing or assembling Kaiser and Willys products abroad, the company agreed to waive the payment of royalties in dollars in the case of Argentina, largely in reliance on the expectation of receiving common stock with a dollar value of approximately $10,000,000 under Law No. 14,222 on which the Kaiser Motors would be entitled to convert dividends into dollars up to 8% of the dollar investment, or $800,000 per year.

The agreement provided that the value of the machinery, equipment,

* Prepared by Dr. Michael Yoshino while a doctoral candidate in the Graduate School of Business, Stanford University.

tools, dies, etc. to be contributed by Kaiser Motors Corporation, estimated at $13,000,000, would be finally determined by the parties after receiving the report of a Mixed Valuation Commission to be appointed by both parties. The agreement provided that the commission would prepare its report:

> —on the basis that the valuation shall be computed as the replacement value in the country of origin less wear and tear due to use of assets under consideration, and pursuant to the instructions that IAME and Kaiser shall deliver to it on detail—[1]

At the same time as the agreement was made, the members of the Mixed Valuation Commission were named by both Kaiser Motors Corporation and IAME. Representing the Kaiser group were Messrs. George Burpee, senior partner of an engineering firm, Coverdale & Colpitts, James Drum and James McCloud, employees of Kaiser Motors Corporation. The three members of the Mixed Commission appointed by IAME were as follows:

> Ing. Jaime Barcezat, an engineer on the staff of IAME;
> Ing. Ernesto Gaudioso, proposed by the Secretary of Economic Affairs as the joint representative of the Ministry of Finance and Minister of Industry;
> Ing. Cesar Rubin, proposed by the Secretary of Economic Affairs as the representative of private investors in the new company.

The Mixed Valuation Commission convened for its first meeting a week later at the office of Minister of Aeronautics, Brigadier Mayor Juan I. San Martin who was also President of IAME.

At this meeting IAME and Kaiser formally transmitted their detailed instructions to the Commission, in both Spanish and English text. The English text is included in Exhibit 2.

The Mixed Valuation Commission arrived in the United States shortly thereafter and immediately started their valuation task both at the Toledo and Shadyside plants. The valuation studies, including physical inspections, examination of Kaiser cost records and consultations with machinery manufacturers, continued for about a month and a half. Instead of the minor differences of engineering opinion which had been expected, the Argentine and United States members of the Commission came up with final values more than $5,000,000 apart. The United States group headed by George Burpee arrived at a final value of $14,547,410. The Argentine members arrived at a final value of $9,422,920. Both of these figures included estimated costs of preparation for shipment and freight to the United States port, totaling $949,420 on which the United States and Argentine members were in agreement. Eliminating preparation for shipment and freight, the final valuation found by the United States members was $13,597,990, and by the Argentine members $8,473,500, a difference of $5,124,490. Exhibit 3 indicates the differences in valuation by items.

[1] Excerpt from Article 12 of the Agreement—the entire text of Article 12 is included in Exhibit 1.

At the same time, the Argentine and United States members were in agreement on the replacement value of the Kaiser assets, namely $14,-589,841. The major part of the $5,124,490 difference was in the deduction for wear and tear due to use for a single category of items, namely the body dies, fixtures and special tools for the Kaiser automobiles.

On this point, the management of Kaiser Motors Corporation believed that the Argentine members had departed from the detailed instructions given to the Commission, and the provisions of Article 12 of the Agreement. Instead of computing the deduction for wear and tear due to use, they computed a deduction based upon a business judgment as to the probable date when the useful life of the tools and dies would be terminated by a basic model change. The parties did not instruct the Valuation Commission to make this business judgment. Instead they instructed the Valuation Commission to calculate replacement values less wear and tear due to use. Moreover, the Kaiser Management maintained that it could be readily demonstrated that the facts did not support the business judgment which the Argentine members reached. They contended that in the European automotive industry, which was far more comparable to the Argentine situation than the U.S. automobile industry, the basic model changes requiring the manufacture of new major body dies occurred at very infrequent intervals. There were many European instances in which the same basic body dies had been used for more than a decade, and in some of these cases, the dies had been imported from the United States after several years of use. The management believed that the annual production volume of 40,000 vehicles just would not support frequent model changes and as a matter of fact this would be contrary to the desire of the Argentine government to supply much-desired automobiles at a minimum cost.

On the basis of the final value found by the Argentine members, the Kaiser stock investment in the new Argentine company would be reduced from $10,000,000 to less than $6,500,000 and the annual dividends which Kaiser would have the right to convert into dollars under Law No. 14,222 would be reduced from $8,000,000 to approximately $5,000,000. A reduction of this magnitude in the stock interest and earnings the company might hope to convert into dollars constituted a major change in their basic understanding during the previous negotiations and raised major doubts in the minds of the Kaiser management as to whether the venture should go forward under this term. Baffled with the possible causes for this recent development in spite of the seemingly clear agreements the members of the Kaiser top management were wondering what courses of action they should take inasmuch as the Argentine members of the Valuation Commission were scheduled to return to Argentina in a few days.

QUESTIONS

1. What do you think are the basic reasons for the difference of opinion? How could this have been prevented?
2. What action should the Kaiser management take to correct the situation? Should it work with the members of the Valuation Commission

who were still in the United States at this time or should it work directly with the Argentine Government officials?

3. Should Kaiser Motors still proceed with the Argentine investment on the basis proposed by the Argentine members of the Commission?

Exhibit 1

Article 12 of the Agreement

The value of the machinery, equipment, tools, jigs, dies and other assets to be included by Kaiser and IAME in the new company in accordance with the provisions of Article 2 and the value and purchase price of the items to be sold by Kaiser to the new company in accordance with Article 4 shall be definitely established between Kaiser and IAME taking into consideration the opinion of a Mixed Commission to be appointed by them. This Mixed Valuation Commission shall prepare its report on the basis that the valuation shall be computed as the replacement value in the country of origin less wear and tear due to use of the assets under consideration and pursuant to the instructions that IAME and Kaiser shall deliver to it in detail, within the next five days. The report of the Commission shall be delivered within thirty days thereafter, and if necessary, the parties hereto shall mutually agree to extend this period.

Exhibit 2

Instructions for the Mixed Valuation Commission Constituted by I.A.M.E. and Kaiser in Accordance with Article 12 of the Document

I

All the machinery and equipment that IAME and Kaiser supply to the new Company whether those in the nature of capital contributions or those that Kaiser sells to the new Company in accordance with Article 4 of the document, shall be valued by the Mixed Commission, following the formulas set out below:

1. For new machinery and equipment, the value will be the purchase price in the country of origin.
2. For used machinery and equipment, the value shall be taken as the replacement value in the country of origin, less wear and tear due to use.
3. In connection with machinery and equipment the replacement value of which is estimated at $6,000 United States dollars or more, such items shall be examined individually.
4. In connection with machinery and equipment of a replacement value below $6,000 United States dollars, the Commission shall proceed to appraise by lots, carrying out a sufficient number of individual analyses to establish their value.

5. Without prejudice to the preceding provisions, the Commissions may amplify or limit the procedures above indicated in order to arrive firmly and quickly at true valuations.

II

For tools, dies, jigs and fixtures, in determining their value, the following shall apply.

1. Replacement value less wear and tear due to use.
2. When the tools, dies, jigs and fixtures have an individual replacement value exceeding $6,000 dollars, they shall be examined individually.
3. When the tools, dies, jigs and fixtures have an individual replacement value of less than $6,000 dollars, they shall be appraised by lots making a sufficient number of individual analyses to determine their value as a group.

To the values thus established, for machinery and equipment as well as for tools, dies, jigs and fixtures, there shall be added the estimated or actual cost of packing and transportation to the port of embarkation, expressly excluding any dismantling expense.

It is understood that transportation expenses to be computed for items located in the United States shall be the expenses to be incurred in the transportation of same from the present location to the port of embarkation, and that in connection with items in the Argentine Republic, there shall be added to the determined values the cost of transportation of same from the place of origin to Argentina and the cost of transportation to the place where the plant is to be built. The expenses to be incurred for packing and transportation, if in foreign currency, shall be calculated in foreign currency and then converted into United States dollars, in accordance with the exchange rates set out below.

The expenses to be incurred in Argentine currency for the foregoing reasons, shall be calculated in said currency.

The valuation of machinery, equipment, tools, dies, jigs, and fixtures shall be computed in United States dollars, and if the items originate in other countries, the following exchange rates shall apply:

Lire	625.00
Pounds	0.357
Swiss Fr.	4.316
French Fr.	350.0
Marks	4.20

1 Dollar

The Commission shall bear in mind that its mission is of an advisory character.

The opinion of the Commission as to the valuation it may make shall represent, as approximately as possible, the real value of the entire group examined, considered as a whole.

The report of the Commission shall serve as a sound basis for the final establishment by IAME and Kaiser of the values they shall transfer into the new Company.

EXHIBIT 3

SUMMARY OF VALUATION OF EQUIPMENT AND SPECIAL TOOLS PROPOSED BY KAISER MOTORS CORPORATION TO ESTABLISH AN AUTOMOTIVE MANUFACTURING COMPANY IN ARGENTINA

Section	Asset Items	Replacement Cost U$S	Valuation after Deduction for Wear and Tear Due to Use: Per Kaiser Appointees		Per IAME Appointees	
			Per Cent Reduction for Wear and Tear	Net Values U$S	Per Cent Reduction for Wear and Tear	Net Values U$S
I	Eng. Plant Mach. & Equip.	2,022,287	12.5	1,770,210	34.7	1,319,825
II	Press Plant Facilities	1,554,619	9.4	1,408,091	30.9	1,073,703
III	Assembly Plant Facilities	716,634	10.8	639,529	30.8	496,215
IV	Maintenance & Material Handling Facilities	348,764	23.2	267,840	34.5	228,592
	Total Sec. I to IV	4,642,304	12.0	4,085,670	32.8	3,118,335
	Special Tools, Dies, Jigs, & Fixtures					
V	Engine, Plant Special Tools	696,555	4.7	664,088	30.7	483,021
VI	Special Tools & Fixtures for Use on IAME Machines & for Receiving Inspection	53,074	10.8	47,342	33.6	35,239
VII	Foundry, Patterns, Cores etc. for Engine Parts	292,504	7.1	271,704	53.0	138,347
VIII	Foundry Patterns, Cores, etc. for Steering Gear Parts	14,052	4.9	13,367	38.1	8,695
IX	Foreign Dies for Engine Parts	3,375	10.0	3,038	30.0	2,363
X	Miscellaneous Special Tools & Dies for Other Engine Parts	110,203	5.2	104,425	40.3	65,746
XI	Body Dies, Fixtures, & Special Tools	8,491,007	4.2	8,136,579	47.2	4,481,317
XII	Dies, Models, & Checking Fixtures	286,767	5.3	271,777	51.0	140,435
	Total Section V to XII	9,947,537	4.4	9,512,320	46.2	5,355,165
	Total Section I to XII	14,589,841	6.8	13,597,990	41.9	8,473,500
	Estimated Preparation for Shipment, Including Packing			760,445		760,445
	Est. Freight to U.S. Port			188,975		188,975
	GRAND TOTAL			14,547,410		9,422,920

47

INDUSTRIAS KAISER ARGENTINA, S.A. (III) *

Personnel Problems under Sensitive Political Conditions

In July, 1955, the management of Industrias Kaiser Argentina, S.A., a subsidiary of Kaiser Motors Corporation, was faced with the problem of dealing with a competent Argentine engineering supervisor who had denounced the policies of the Peron Government.

Industrias Kaiser Argentina, S.A., an Argentine corporation popularly known as IKA, was formed on January 18, 1955, under a contract with the Argentine government in response to its request to assist in starting an automotive-manufacturing industry in Argentina.

Approximately half of the 3,600,000 shares of ordinary stock having a par value of 100 pesos per share were sold to more than 8,000 individual Argentine investors in an over-subscribed public offering. The Argentine government through Industrias Aeronáuticas y Mecánas del Estado (IAME), an Argentine government enterprise, subscribed to 23% of the stock.

Kaiser Motors Corporation invested machinery, equipment, tools and other related items necessary for manufacturing vehicles and granted an exclusive license to manufacture and sell in Argentina the passenger cars and "jeeps" under the trade names owned by Kaiser. For these contributions Kaiser Motors Corporation received 31% in the equity of the new company. On February 8, 1955, Córdoba was chosen as the plant site and in April of the same year construction began under the direction of Kaiser Engineering International.[1]

POLITICAL CONDITIONS IN ARGENTINA—JULY 1955 [2]

During the first few months of 1955 political conditions in Argentina had been volatile. The revolt of June 16, 1955 lasted less than half a day, but it was the most serious threat Peron had faced since he emerged as the political leader of Argentina in 1945.

* Prepared by Dr. Michael Yoshino while a doctoral candidate in the Graduate School of Business, Stanford University.

[1] Kaiser Engineering International was formed as a subsidiary of Kaiser Engineering Co. for the express purpose of undertaking construction of the Argentine automobile plant.

[2] The information presented in this section is based on Arthur P. Whitaker, *Argentine Upheaval,* The Foreign Policy Research Institute Series. Foreign Policy Research Institute, University of Pennsylvania.

Elected President of Argentina in February, 1946 and re-elected five years later, Peron established and maintained a nationalistic and authoritarian regime. From the start, the oppressive character of the regime provoked strong opposition in various sectors of Argentine society. Prior to June, 1955 this found its most serious expression in a revolt in September, 1951 by a part of the Army, many of whose officers had never been reconciled to the alliance of the armed forces with the Peron government. Poor timing and teamwork among their leaders was said to have cost them the support of other elements among the armed forces as well as among the civilian population and the revolt was suppressed quickly and almost bloodlessly.

The circumstances of the June, 1955 revolt were quite different, for at first the rebels had complete control of the air and they struck only a few hours after the public announcement that Peron had been excommunicated for expelling two Roman Catholic prelates from Argentina, which had a very serious impact throughout the Republic. Under the Argentine Constitution the Catholic Church had been state-supported for more than a hundred years and the overwhelming majority of Argentines were Roman Catholics. The excommunication came as the climax of a seven-months controversy of mounting intensity between Peron's government and the Catholic Church.

In the early years of his first administration, Peron had sought to work with the Catholic Church and had met with considerable success in the effort, but a rift began to appear between the two around 1950. This rift widened gradually in the next four years and developed into a bitter and violent controversy from November, 1954 to June, 1955.

At first the Church leaders' displeasure was concentrated on certain Peron measures such as legalization of divorce and secularization of education. However, in the early months of 1955, other issues were brought into the dispute, and a large number of Catholic priests and lay leaders were arrested by Peron's police. On May 1 Peron's followers formally initiated a movement to separate Church and State through a constitutional amendment. The following weeks were marked by even more violent demonstrations and by counter-demonstrations and clashes between the rival demonstrators.

The breaking point came when the Church authorities failed to obey a government order forbidding a Corpus Christi procession and a riot ensued. Peron retaliated with the expulsion of the two Catholic prelates from Argentina on June 14; and on June 16 Peron's excommunication was announced. A few hours later the revolt began.

There is no evidence that the Catholic hierarchy supported the revolt. It appeared that the naval officers had been planning to rebel for two or three years past, quite independently of the Church-State controversy. Nevertheless, there was little question that the conspirators sought to take advantage of the situation created by that controversy. Though the revolt was put down in a few hours, it was followed by much unrest and violence through the month of July.

PERSONNEL PROBLEMS FACING THE IKA MANAGEMENT—JULY 1955

In spite of the political instability, construction of building and installation of facilities at Córdoba progressed rapidly. The engineers, a group composed of both U.S. citizens and Argentine nationals, had developed good working relationships.

Shortly after the June revolt, the management of IKA learned that one of the Argentine engineering supervisors, Ricardo Antonio, had often denounced the policies of the National government in private conversation with his friends.

Antonio had joined the company in March, 1955 to assist Kaiser engineers from the United States in constructing the new plants in Córdoba. He had been graduated from the University of Buenos Aires in engineering and, prior to joining IKA, had worked for a small engineering firm in Buenos Aires for nearly ten years. There he held both technical and supervisory positions.

His former employer was extremely reluctant to let him go; however, he had finally consented on the condition that Antonio would return to the firm if he should become dissatisfied with IKA. His performance at IKA had been very satisfactory and in a short time he had gained the respect and confidence of the men he was working with. Antonio himself had been quite satisfied with his new position and had frequently expressed to his friends that he felt a deep professional pride and challenge in being a part of the IKA program and hoped to stay with the company permanently.

Since the June revolt, Antonio had frequently denounced the Peron government privately to his close friends. Although he disagreed on a wide range of the Peron policies, the increasingly deteriorating relationship between Church and State was of particular concern to him, for he had always been a devout Catholic and had once aspired to become a priest. Most of his close friends agreed with him, partly because of their objective appraisal of the prevailing conditions and partly out of sympathy for him. They had recently discovered that Antonio's uncle, a Naval officer, to whom he had been quite close, had been a participant in the last revolt and had been killed by the Peron forces.

The management of IKA took no action inasmuch as Antonio's opposition had been limited to vocal expressions of his opinions to a few intimate friends. Recently, however, a major local stockholder had approached the IKA management with a request that Antonio be dismissed immediately. The stockholder would not reveal how he happened to find out Antonio's feelings on the matter, but contended that although IKA was a private enterprise and free to make business decisions that it deemed advisable, in his judgment a company in which the government through IAME had a substantial share of its capital stock, should take into consideration the extremely sensitive existing political conditions. He also insisted that future appointments of any importance should be made only after thorough investigation into the political background of the applicants and consultation with IAME.

IKA's management was reluctant to dismiss Antonio on this ground inasmuch as he had proved himself competent and had demonstrated potential for future development. It was also aware of the difficulty of recruiting well-qualified supervisors with technical background. Yet the management did not wish to antagonize the important local stockholder and the Argentine government since so much of the future progress of IKA would depend upon their support.

The decision was further complicated by the fact that Kaiser Motors Corporation, a U.S. concern, held the controlling interest in the company. Thus any action the management might take could conceivably have broader political implications, particularly in U.S.-Argentine relations.

QUESTIONS

1. What action should the IKA management take in regard to Ricardo Antonio and the stockholder?
2. Should the company investigate the political background of prospective employees for supervisory positions?
3. What kind of corporate image should IKA create in Argentina? To what extent should it identify itself with the local government?

48

INDUSTRIAS KAISER ARGENTINA, S.A. (V) *

Relationships with a Foreign Government in Transition

In December, 1955, the management of Kaiser Motors Corporation was faced with a series of extremely critical problems with its Argentine subsidiary, Industrias Kaiser Argentina (IKA), in view of recent political developments in the country.

Industrias Kaiser Argentina, S.A., an Argentine corporation, was organized on January 18, 1955 with an authorized capitalization of 3,600,-000 shares of ordinary stock having a par value of 100 pesos per share. The primary purpose of the new enterprise was to manufacture and distribute Kaiser passenger cars and the Willys "jeep" line.

Approximately half of the stock was sold to more than 8,000 individual Argentine investors in an over-subscribed public offering and the Argentine government held 23% of the stock.

* Prepared by Dr. Michael Yoshino while a doctoral candidate in the Graduate School of Business, Stanford University.

Kaiser Motors Corporation invested machinery, equipment, tools, and other related items necessary for manufacturing automotive products for which it received shares representing approximately 31% of the equity in the company.

On February 7, 1955, Córdoba was chosen as the plant site and a few weeks later construction began under the direction of Kaiser Engineering International.

During the next eight months, the company made good progress on all parts of the program. One hundred U.S. engineers and a large Argentine staff completed the major part of the initial engineering and procurement work. By December 1955, the M$N [1] 150,000,000 plant in Córdoba was 80% completed and over $7,000,000 worth of equipment had arrived from the United States to be installed in the new plant.

Meantime, a careful study was initiated to select approximately 40 dealers to handle IKA products out of over 600 enthusiastic applicants. More than 7,000 applications were on file for employment at the new plant.

RECENT POLITICAL DEVELOPMENTS IN ARGENTINA

Throughout 1955 the Republic of Argentina saw considerable political unrest and a series of insurrections. Although there were a number of attempts to overthrow the Peron government prior to 1955, all of them had failed. On June 17, 1955, however, a more formidable rebellion broke out, supported by elements of the Army, Navy, and Air Force. Though the revolt was put down in a matter of hours, it was followed by much uneasiness and mob violence.

At dawn on Friday, September 16, another revolt took place at Córdoba under the direction of General Eduardo Lonardi which led to the overthrow of the government. Three days later Peron resigned from the presidency, fled to the Paraguayan embassy, and asked for asylum. A provisional government headed by Lonardi was established on the same day. On September 25, Mr. Edgar Kaiser, President of Kaiser Motors, flew to Argentina to determine the course of action for its Argentine subsidiary in view of the recent political developments. While he was there he met with President Lonardi and other leaders of the Provisional Government to discuss the future of IKA.

President Lonardi opened the meeting by expressing his desire that the new government's relationship with IKA should start in the most harmonious and friendly way. Mr. Kaiser responded to this by stating that the management of Kaiser Motors believed that it was a great opportunity for them to work in Argentina and they seriously intended to build up the Argentine content of vehicles as rapidly as possible by developing the ability of Argentine industry to produce component parts. He further emphasized the role which IKA could play in building the Argentine economy. Then Mr. Kaiser raised a number of specific points relative to IKA's progress that required prompt government action. The President

[1] Argentine pesos or "moneda nacional."

asked him to submit a detailed list of the government actions necessary for further progress of IKA and assured Mr. Kaiser that the new Government would carry out "not only the IKA contract but all other government obligations," and further emphasized that this was a government formed by responsible people, that they intended to comply with all existing commitments, and that they wanted to encourage foreign investment in Argentina. The meeting ended in the most congenial atmosphere.

The IKA board approved of going forward with the program in reliance on these assurances. On October 2, the IKA management submitted to the government a list of items in the original agreement which required immediate government action. The summary of the list is presented in Exhibit 1 at the end of the case.

No government actions were forthcoming through the middle of November when further changes in the new government took place.

FURTHER DEVELOPMENTS IN ARGENTINA

President Lonardi made a good start but then began to fumble under pressure from the ill-matched groups around him who were united only in their opposition to Peron; they ranged from moderate liberals to ultranationalists. President Lonardi had declared after the successful revolt that "there are neither victors nor vanquished" and had made an appeal for unity in the name of all Argentines. This statement aroused the doubts of the strong adversaries of the Peron regime. These elements became increasingly dissatisfied with the President, whom they accused of being too slow in cleaning out all vestiges of the Peron government and putting Argentina on the road to recovery.

A series of Cabinet shuffles were the outward signs of President Lonardi's desperate struggle to balance these forces and cling to the middle of the road. However, the pressure from the dissatisfied groups became so great that on November 10, he was forced to resign from the Presidency and was replaced by 52-year-old Major General Pedro Eugenio Aramburu.

Throughout the months of November and December, the IKA management kept in close contact with the Argentine government and frequently requested from the government actions on the points previously indicated. Although the IKA management was assured repeatedly by the government that actions would be received in a matter of days, by the end of December no actions were yet forthcoming. Further delays would leave IKA no alternative but to suspend operations, inasmuch as the company would exhaust its funds in a few weeks. This would result in a great loss not only to Kaiser Motors and the Argentine government, but also to thousands of private investors.

INTERDICTION DECREE

Further complications developed on December 29, 1955, when IKA was placed on the government interdiction list to be investigated. On December 9, 1955, the government had established a National Council for Recovery of Property, empowered to determine whether certain individuals and corporations had unlawfully acquired assets as a result of dealings with the former government. The decree froze the assets of the individuals and corporations listed, as well as the stock of such corporations. The National Council for Recovery of Property was directed to authorize all the transactions in the ordinary course of business. The individuals and corporations affected and their stockholders were permitted to file proofs with the Council establishing that the assets concerned were legally acquired. If the proof were rejected, the assets were to be transferred to a National Recovery Fund.

IKA was not included in the list of firms attached to the Decree of December 9. However, on December 26 a Supplemental Decree was issued, listing substantially all firms which had entered into contractual arrangements with the government, including IKA.

Interdicted companies were allowed to carry on normal business transactions in limited ways under the supervision of a "veedor" (observer) who would be assigned to the firms under interdiction and who would be empowered to grant approval on behalf of the Council for particular company transactions as being in the ordinary course of business. However, the firms were not allowed to engage in exchange transactions on the free market and they were required to obtain permits from the Central Bank for any such transactions. This would prevent IKA from making free-market remittances to pay its obligations to Kaiser Motors for technical assistance as all other firms were authorized to do under existing exchange regulations.

The IKA management was given no indication by the government as to when the investigations would be completed. Meantime the publicity of the IKA interdiction which was widely circulated throughout the United States, had adverse effects on the entire Kaiser organization.

QUESTION

What action should the management of IKA take at this time?

EXHIBIT 1

PROGRESS OF INDUSTRIAS KAISER ARGENTINA, S.A.*

A. *Plant construction—started March 12, 1955*		
Expended to date:	M$N	58,000,000
Commitments:	M$N	62,000,000
Total expended and committed:	M$N	120,000,000
Per cent Completion—Major Building Structures		—80%
B. *Installation of machinery*		
1. *Machinery invested by Kaiser Motors Corp.*		
Arrived in port of Buenos Aires:	U$S	5,535,735 or 69%
Estimated date of completing shipments from U.S.:		January 6, 1956

* Source: Prepared by the case writer from company records.

EXHIBIT I (*cont.*)

Note: Certain special tools will be retained for U.S. vendor use until vendor selection in Argentina is made. The U$S value of these tools is no more than U$S 500,000.		
2. *Machinery sold by Kaiser Motors Corp. to Industrias Kaiser Argentina*		
Arrived in port of Buenos Aires:	U$S	1,936,603 or 64%
Estimated date of completion of shipments from U.S.:		January 6, 1956
Note: Engine Plant and Press Plant equipment installation proceeding concurrently with receipt of equipment at Plant site and completion of building construction.		
3. *Machinery and equipment to be invested by IAME*		
(a) Foreign origin, total value:	U$S	3,078,166
Delivered to IKA:	U$S	384,250—12%
On order by IAME:	U$S	1,086,199—35%
(b) Procured locally—total value estimated:	M$N	33,305,676
Delivered:	M$N	8,200,000—24%
Remainder is in process of being manufactured.		
C. *Orders placed for production materials*		
1. With Argentine suppliers	M$N	100,000,000
2. With U.S. suppliers	U$S	1,000,000
D. *Cumulative total of expenditures and commitments*		
1. Expenditures	M$N	194,000,000
2. Commitments	M$N	180,000,000
Total expenditures and commitments	M$N	374,000,000
Total capital		
Stock	M$N	360,000,000
Loan	M$N	200,000,000
	M$N	560,000,000
Percent of total capital expended or committed		6%

EXHIBIT 2

THE ITEMS ON WHICH IMMEDIATE GOVERNMENT ACTIONS WERE REQUIRED

A. Issuance of the following authorizations by Central Bank:

1. Exchange permits to IAME for purchase of machinery to fulfill its capital subscription under contract.

2. Exchange permits for purchase of necessary raw materials for 1956 production, as provided in basic contract.

3. Exchange permits for purchase of necessary component production parts for 1956 production, as provided in basic contract.

4. Exchange permits for purchase of necessary production machinery required by Argentine suppliers, as provided in basic contract.

5. Approval of additional U$S 800,000 machinery investment proposed by Kaiser.

B. Authorization to sell the 650 remaining imported cars, at prices sufficient to help defray the company's pre-production expenses, as intended under the basic contract.

C. Granting of the loan from the Industrial Bank committed by the Bank's resolution of March 24, 1955. Under the basic contract, the first M$N 60,000,000 under this loan were due on IKA's request beginning October 1, 1955 and IKA has requested that payment be made on December 1. An additional M$N 75,000,000 is due January 1, 1955.

49

ESSO STANDARD EASTERN, INC. (CEYLON) *

Difficult Financial Relations with the Government of Ceylon

In August, 1962 the managers of the three foreign oil companies operating in Ceylon, Shell, Caltex, and Esso Standard Eastern, met with the Ceylon finance minister, Mr. Felix Dias Bandaranaike. Mr. Bandaranaike had, a short time before, submitted his budget for the forthcoming fiscal year to the Ceylon parliament. He had made it clear that the country's foreign exchange position was bad and that, in addition, revenues were expected to be substantially below estimated expenditures. To cope with the deficit, new taxes were to be imposed and a cut in the subsidized rice ration as well. (The latter proved to be politically unpopular and was later suspended.)

To help in meeting the foreign exchange problem, the minister asked the oil companies for their assistance. Their decision was to be communicated to him within a week. Three choices were given to the companies:

1. An ad valorem rate of duty on imported oil products.
2. A quota system for each company's imports.
3. Purchase from the cheapest possible sources as a means of reducing their c.i.f. prices.

None of these choices was particularly palatable to the oil companies. An increase in duty, if passed on to consumers, would result in some loss of sales, and the companies were already facing a market decline because

* This case is concerned with the Ceylon branch of Esso Standard Eastern, Inc. Ceylon does not form part of the company's corporate name and is used here merely to identify the location of the case and to distinguish this operation from others of the company.

of the advent on the competitive scene of the government-owned Ceylon Petroleum Corporation. A quota system would make it difficult to improve market position and Esso Standard Eastern (and its foreign competitors) had already planned aggressive action to improve market share, despite the new company. Finally, purchase from the cheapest possible sources would be repugnant to the company-owned refineries from which the Ceylon-based corporations bought finished products. Perhaps even more repugnant was the fact that cheapest possible sources were Russia or other Iron Curtain countries and the political and other implications of this on the world scene were considerable. The territory manager of Esso Standard wondered which choice, if any, his company should advocate, both to his competitors—for mutual agreement was desirable—and to his area headquarters in Bombay, India. Alternatively, perhaps other ideas could be proposed to the finance minister which would be less irksome to the foreign companies.

THE 1962 SITUATION

According to the statement released to the press by the finance minister's office [1] 90% of the goods imported to Ceylon paid duty based on the c.i.f. (cost, insurance, and freight) value. Petrol and other oils were among the few products which paid a flat rate of duty based on quantities. The duty for petrol (gasoline) was Rupees two per gallon. ($ U.S. 1 = Rs. 4.75 approx.)

On this basis, when the companies' c.i.f. price was 48 Ceylon cents per gallon on regular petrol, the duty worked out as 417% on petrol. But on that determination, the Ceylon Petroleum Corporation, which imported petrol at a lower price, was paying 550% duty. If this ad valorem rate were applied to the higher price of the foreign companies' products, the result would be a higher duty for them.

The quota system proposed would apply to allocations of foreign exchange and would be based on market share. Since the Ceylon Petroleum Corporation held 50% of the market, it would receive half of the foreign exchange which could be allocated for Ceylon's oil needs. Foreign exchange would be given to the other companies on the basis of their market shares and the c.i.f. costs of petrol imported by the government corporation. Since its c.i.f. costs were lower, this in effect would mean that the companies would be able to import only a smaller quantity than they were presently doing, unless they imported from cheaper sources.

Ceylon Treasury sources estimated that, on the quota system of imports, the government would make a foreign exchange saving of Rs.13 to Rs.15 million. On an ad valorem rate the government would get an additional duty of Rs.20 million. If the companies decided to lower their import costs, the government expected that, in addition to saving Rs.13 to Rs.15 million on foreign exchange, the companies' profits would increase and the government would obtain more revenue from the profits tax.

[1] *Ceylon Daily News* (Colombo, Aug. 8, 1962), p. 1.

Mr. Bandaranaike told the oil companies that the government was facing a severe foreign exchange situation. It had already asked the people to make certain sacrifices in view of the present difficulty. In the same manner, he expected the companies to figure out ways and means of arresting the drain on foreign exchange. If the oil executives could offer additional suggestions as to how they could save exchange, he would welcome their views and any other observations they had to make on his proposals.

HISTORICAL BACKGROUND

For many years oil products were marketed in Ceylon by three foreign companies, Shell, controlled by Royal Dutch-Shell, Caltex, owned by Texaco and Standard Oil Company (California), and Standard-Vacuum, or Stanvac. Standard-Vacuum, a jointly-owned affiliate of Socony Mobil and Standard Oil Company (N.J.), had been dissolved upon mutual agreement of the two principals and its Standard Oil (N.J.) activities were replaced in 1962 by a new affiliate, Esso Standard Eastern, Inc. The manager of the Ceylon operations, an American, reported to the Bombay headquarters of Esso Standard Eastern, Inc., which, in turn, reported to the New York head office of Esso Standard Eastern, Inc.

Kerosene is important in Ceylon for cooking and lighting but the oil companies also marketed gasoline, diesel fuel, bunker fuel, lubricants and other products. Foreign companies drew finished products from refineries in their international organizations.

Ceylon, following its independence from Great Britain in 1948, moved through a brief period of free enterprise into socialism. Many government corporations were established, some in competition with existing private business and others to develop resources or provide employment in situations which private industry had not entered. The oil industry, dominated by foreign capital, had been a frequent target for attacks on the basis of excessive profits, equally excessive high prices to Ceylon consumers, and unnecessary drains on foreign exchange.

The companies had not been indifferent to the charges and, in the mid-1950's, proposals for an industry refinery had been submitted to the government. The market was not large enough to warrant more than one refinery but the companies felt that one plant would enable them to serve Ceylon more economically for all concerned. A change in government policy after the election as prime minister in 1956 of S.W.R.D. Bandaranaike was continued by his widow, Mrs. Sirimo Bandaranaike, who was elected to replace him after his assassination. This led to the alteration of original plans. Other factors were involved, such as the world supply position of petroleum products and, in particular, supply and prices of crude oil. This contributed, in the words of a Ceylon newspaper,[2] "to the weakening of the power of the oil monopolies on which sources Ceylon's supplies are dependent."

Perhaps partly stimulated by the apparent trend of government

[2] *Ceylon Daily News* (Colombo, Aug. 8, 1962), p. 1.

thought, the foreign oil companies began a policy of Ceylonization, replacing overseas employees by qualified nationals as these became available. In 1957 Stanvac had had seven overseas personnel; in early 1962 the number working for Esso Standard Eastern was three. At the same time the companies, fearful of the socialistic policies now evident, submitted a new proposal for a refinery. Two more were put forth by independent American oil finance groups and a fourth was developed by an association of joint Indian-French financiers. Since private ownership of a refinery had by this time been rejected by the government, the only proposal seriously studied was the New Asia Petroleum Refinery plan of the Indian-French group.

In 1959 negotiations on this scheme too broke down, but the idea was examined again in 1961 by the Ceylon Development Division. The division decided to consider the refinery and a fertilizer plant as joint projects. A year later, when the finance minister had confronted the foreign companies with his choices, an announcement was made that plans to set up a refinery before the end of the year were almost ready. In addition to estimated savings of Rs.60 and Rs.65 million in foreign exchange, it was claimed that the refinery would provide employment for 1,000 Ceylonese and that there was some prospect of petro-chemical industrial development in conjunction with it.

THE CEYLON PETROLEUM CORPORATION

Announcement of the proposed refinery was another in a series of difficulties which had confronted the oil industry in Ceylon since 1956. As the finance minister's statement indicated, 50% of their market had been lost to the Ceylon Petroleum Corporation. If a refinery, built and operated by the government, used the cheapest crude available to provide the Corporation with its needs, the result could hardly be to their benefit. Even though the foreign companies might be able to purchase refined products to better advantage within their own associated company groups, their management doubted whether they would be able to continue to do this. It seemed likely that they would be pressed to use the local refinery for the Corporation could not take all of the output which an economically-sized plant could produce.

In December, 1960 a bill had been introduced in the Ceylonese House of Representatives for the establishment of the Ceylon Petroleum Corporation. The bill passed the Senate in May, 1961 and became law in that month. Under the powers granted to it, the government company began taking over property from the foreign companies in July, 1961, and, by the middle of the following year, had absorbed approximately 179 filling and service stations, 98 kerosene agencies, and some bunkering facilities. Market share of retail sales at the time of the Corporation's inception had been approximately 60% Shell, 20% Esso Standard Eastern, and 20% Caltex, and stations were assumed in the same proportion.

The Ceylon Petroleum Corporation began marketing in 1962 and, as has been said, by August had about 50% of the island's market for oil products. However, of this 50%, a considerable proportion came from government and government-controlled business. The foreign companies believed that many consumers would still prefer their products, some from loyalty, some because they felt that the goods were better than those sold by the Petroleum Corporation, or in some cases because of opposition to the government's policies. In consequence, before the finance minister made his demands and before the announcement of the refinery, the foreign companies had decided to continue in business in Ceylon and to compete aggressively for increased shares of the market.

A question which was very much involved with the whole situation was the matter of compensation to be paid for the assets taken over by the government company. The bill which had brought it into existence had provided a mechanism for compensation, based on the depreciated value of the assets. The companies contended that compensation should be related to the assets' present worth in terms of (a) replacement cost, and (b) profit-producing ability or "good will," based on established international principles applied in similar areas.

In July, 1962 the Ceylon Government notified the oil companies that they and the Petroleum Corporation should negotiate and agree on the compensation payable, with the clauses in the act as guiding principles. This would eliminate the lengthy delay that would result if the procedure in the act were strictly followed. The oil companies did not agree to this because of the basic differences of opinion about the value of the assets confiscated.

Esso Standard Eastern had brought to the attention of the U.S. State Department the situation and had engaged the services of an assessor and a legal counsel for arguing its case for compensation. The State Department, in turn, had brought to the attention of the Ceylon Government that any "unfair" compensation (not in keeping with the standard of international law) paid to the American oil companies for assets lost to the Corporation might have repercussions on U.S. Government aid to Ceylon. Under an amendment to the Foreign Aid provision passed by Congress in 1962, aid to countries confiscating assets of Americans without adequate compensation could be cut off.

According to published reports, the oil companies valued the confiscated property at about $9,500,000. Of this amount, Shell's share was estimated to be $5,600,000 and the remainder was divided between Caltex and Esso Standard Eastern.[3] Apart from the remaining assets of the two oil companies, American investment in Ceylon was trivial. British companies, on the other hand, owned tea estates and rubber plantations conservatively valued at $730,000,000, or about half the investment the United States had lost in Cuba. Taxation and other restrictions had handicapped the estate and plantation owners in continuing to develop their properties. There was some feeling that Ceylonese fiscal policies had been shortsighted, since tea and rubber were important foreign exchange earners and,

[3] "Ceylon Pushes to Left in Scrap with U.S.," by Anthony Mann, *The National Observer* (1963), p. 12.

in the opinion at least of the investing companies, funds for plant and other improvement were essential if the country's exchange position were not to deteriorate further.

American aid to Ceylon over the seven years up to 1963 had totaled $84,000,000. It had taken a variety of forms, including work on the elimination of a weed which was damaging rice crops, in public health, road building, airport construction, and education. When the Hickenlooper amendment was finally invoked against Ceylon, aid payments of $4,000,000 were suspended although some of the programs involving public health were continued.

QUESTIONS

1. What choice should the national manager of Esso Standard Eastern make among the foreign minister's alternatives?
2. Are there any other ways in which the oil companies could save foreign exchange for the country which would fall within their policies as you might imagine them to be?
3. Would you recommend that Esso Standard continue operations in Ceylon?
4. What policies might the foreign oil companies have followed which would have prevented the developments outlined in the case?
5. What implications does this case have for American companies elsewhere?

50

THOMAS RANDALL KNITTING MILLS *

An Australian Manufacturer Deliberates an American Offer to Franchise

Thomas Randall Knitting Mills of Sydney, Australia, makers of women's knitted outerwear, had been approached by Mary Jane, Inc.* of New York, which produced comparable products. The American company offered Randall the Australian franchise to produce and sell garments under the Mary Jane label.

The Randall management was uncertain whether to accept the offer

* Fictitious name.

and on what terms. Many aspects of the proposal were attractive. At the same time, the financial commitments for Randall seemed excessive or could become so. In addition, the Australian firm had some reservations about Mary Jane's long-run motives for the Australian market. In an effort to bring the basic issues into focus and to secure advice, Alan Randall, general sales manager of Thomas Randall, asked an American consultant with whom he had become friendly to sit down to discuss the whole idea.

Colin Peterson, the consultant, was at this time in Australia temporarily on other assignments; he and Randall had seen each other on previous visits. Because of client pressures, he did not feel that he could go into the questions raised very thoroughly and told Randall so. The Australian replied that he believed even a short meeting could be helpful, since he felt that an outside, well-qualified viewpoint might serve to bring up points he and his associates might otherwise overlook.

The meeting between the two men was recorded, since Randall wanted to be able to go over the ground again, alone and with his colleagues. The material which follows is condensed from the transcript of their talk.

THOMAS RANDALL KNITTING MILLS

Thomas Randall considered itself to be one of the foremost makers of women's knitted outerwear in Australia. Founded in 1939 and still family owned and managed, the company had after much effort developed a well-regarded name among trade and public for good quality merchandise which sold at a fair price. Its products were not in the highest price and fashion brackets but were felt to be upper middle class merchandise. The company's factory was located in Sydney.

All products were branded with the Randall name, which was nationally advertised and well accepted. Distribution was effected through two wholesalers. One sold in the Australian states of Victoria, Tasmania, South Australia, and West Australia. The other covered New South Wales and Queensland. Annual sales were about $2,240,000 and the company had operated for some years at a satisfactory profit level.

While Randall distributed nationally throughout Australia and promoted on the same basis, about 60% of sales came from New South Wales and Victoria. Naturally enough, some lines sold better in cities than in country markets and the company attempted to anticipate local fashion trends when making production schedules. Winter garments accounted for about seven months of Randall's production and summer items the remainder.

For a number of years knitwear fashions in Australia had been strongly influenced by Europe. However, as conditions improved to permit increased imports from the United States, American fashions showed a market impact which Randall believed would grow. The company watched American market trends closely. The reversal of seasons between the Northern and Southern hemispheres meant that it could offer in the Australian winter or summer lines based on big sellers in the preceding and corresponding U.S. seasons. It did not have access to advance fashions in the United States, that is, it did not know until garments were actually shown what U.S. makers had had in mind for the season.

THE MARY JANE OFFER

Without solicitation or enquiry from Randall, Mary Jane, Inc., through a representative who had visited Australia, offered Randall the franchise to make and sell its lines. The royalty asked would be $12,200 [1] for the first year, $22,400 for the second year, and in succeeding years 10% of sales with a $44,800 minimum. In addition to the use of its brand name, Mary Jane undertook to provide promotional material which had been used in the U.S., although it would not underwrite any Australian advertising costs. It also agreed to supply Randall with two sample ranges each year—a winter and summer weight knitted outerwear range—and production data on all lines.

Mary Jane and Randall products were, in the opinion of Randall, comparable in quantity and style. American firms, however, had access to new fibers and fabrics before Australian companies had, and this was an important factor. Mary Jane was considered to be one of the leaders in ability to produce new designs, new fabrics, and combinations of fabrics. Part of the proposed agreement covered the provision to Randall, in addition to production data and sample ranges, of information on new products which Mary Jane was considering but might not have decided to make: these might or might not be saleable in Australia.

When the offer was made, Mary Jane was not selling in Australia and its name was completely unknown to consumers. Despite this, the American firm's initial suggestion was that Randall should drop its old brand and market all goods under the Mary Jane name. Even if Randall had any intention of doing this—and it had worked too hard and too long to build a brand reputation to give the idea any serious consideration—Mary Jane's refusal to offer financial support for advertising and sales promotion made the suggestion impossible to accept. To introduce a new label would cost a lot of money and take a lot of time.

"What we have in mind, Colin," Alan Randall said, "is to run the Mary Jane products on a competitive basis under their own label. Or we might perhaps move them in a slightly different price range which wouldn't be competing but would be close enough. As I remember you telling me once, in Canada GM, Ford, and Chrysler all have cars which are almost identical but carry different names, and where a slight price differential seems to make the customers confused enough to send some to Ford and some to Monarch, and some to Chevrolet and some to the low-priced Pontiac, and some to Plymouth and some to the low-priced Dodge—well, you know.

"We estimate it would take sales of about $1,120,000 to support the minimum royalty payment. That is about half our present turnover. At this level we would be over the breakeven point and would make some

[1] Australian pounds have been converted to U.S. dollars: A1 = $2.24.

money on the line, but not as much as we make on our own goods. I should point out that there is nothing to stop us from taking one of their ideas and producing it as a Thomas Randall garment. As long as we do turn out sufficient of their stuff a year to give them $44,800 and still make some money out of it, there's no control on their part of what we use and what we don't use.

"I should point out, too, with regard to your question about advertising, that we would have two years in which we would not be obligated to use the Mary Jane name. In other words, in exchange for the royalty they would send us the sample lines, production and promotional data, but we could either produce their lines or ours, if we wished—or, of course, both. After two years, we would be required to bring out Mary Jane garments. Personally, I feel that they should invest a little money in advertising here apart from just their samples and their ideas—I feel they should come good with some cold hard dollars to back it up with. Because we're expected to pay $44,800 a year on royalties for the receipt of these ideas and their name, and the name at the moment means nothing. I think the value to us does not lie in the name but in the ideas they'll give us—and then the question is whether or not the $44,800 is worth it for those.

"To sum it up at this point, they have come to us cold, out of the blue, with this proposal and we have made no approaches to them or to anyone else. If we don't accept the offer, they may take it to another manufacturer. What we would gain, I guess, is the benefit of American research in new fibres and designs, some of which may be saleable here and some of which may not. We may be able to do a lot with their name but, if we do, we might lose our own—in other words, they might turn out to be the tail that wags the dog, if we become known more for making Mary Jane than for Thomas Randall.

"I should tell you some of the other things that occur to us. As far as the ideas go, here's one which may show you what I mean. Dad happened to be in the States five months or so ago, and saw a new fabric in the synthetic class called a plush knit. It's an orlon fabric, knitted fine, and it's brushed, which raises a high pile which is clipped off short, so that the material has a sort of very soft velvet feel. This is a trend which is just hitting the market here in a limited degree, Dad saw it in the U.S. five months ago, but it had been creeping on the American market for 12 months. We could have had a seven month lead on other manufacturers if we had got on to it sooner.

"As it is now, we have about a four or five month lead and we've got to fight pretty keenly to cash in on it, because as soon as the smaller makers get hold of it, they'll start chopping prices and hence the idea is very short lived. We estimate that, by getting the extra lead on a new fabric such as that, we can cash in on it pretty well. We can have a one-season run before the others come in on the same fabric. That is an example of how Mary Jane might help us with new things like this.

"Well, this will give you a rough idea of the background of the company and of this offer. Why don't you, if you will, ask me some questions about things I haven't brought up and then see what you think about it all and what we ought to do."

QUESTIONS

1. What questions should the consultant put to Mr. Randall now?
2. What kinds of answers would you expect or hope to receive to these questions?
3. On the basis of the questions and answers, what action might Mr. Peterson suggest to Mr. Randall?

51

SONY CORPORATION *

Evaluation of the U.S. Market for a Transistorized Television Receiver

In early 1962, the management of the Sony Corporation of Tokyo, Japan was considering introduction of a new product—small, portable, transistorized television sets—in the United States. Mr. Suzuki, manager of the company's International Division had been asked to evaluate the advisability of proceeding to market the unit and to estimate the size of the potential market in the United States.

THE PORTABLE, TRANSISTORIZED TELEVISION SET

After several years of intensive research and development effort, the company had succeeded in making commercially feasible what it called one of the major electronic achievements of the century—the world's first lightweight, compact, direct-view transistorized television set. This was made possible by development of very-high-frequency and powerful transistors.

According to the company's description, the receiver uses about an 8½ inch, direct-view, rectangular tube on which it displays its pictures. The screen utilizes a specially developed aluminized picture tube having automatic focusing and a high efficiency electron gun. Width and height are about 8 inches, the depth is 10 inches without the battery pack that plugs into the rear, and 12 inches with it. A built-in monopole antenna telescopes out of the back. Three push buttons labeled "AC," "DC," and "OFF" establish the various modes of operation when used singly or in combination. The set can be operated from an AC power line, its own battery pack or from a 12 volt car or boat battery. Moreover, batteries can be "trickle charged" while the set is being operated from AC current. Minimum power

* Prepared by Dr. Michael Yoshino in Tokyo under the direction of Professor J. S. Ewing.

consumption is involved because the set uses only one-tenth the power consumed by conventional sets.

User controls at the top rear are for vertical and horizontal synchronization, brightness, and gain. Also on top are the channel-selector switch concentric with the fine-tuning control and the volume control. An oval speaker fires out of the bottom.

On the back are connectors for external AC, external DC (12 volts) and jacks for 75- or 300-ohm antennas. Flanking thc push buttons at the front are two earphone jacks, one of which cuts out the speaker. Included accessories are a zip-on carrying case, an AC cord, a length of 300-ohm line terminating in a plug matched to the receiver input, an earphone, and spare fuses. An optional kit permits operation from the cigarette-lighter socket of any 12-volt automotive system.

Weighing a little over 13 pounds, more than 17 pounds with the power pack added, the set is reasonably portable. The lead-acid storage batteries will run the receiver for three hours. Charging is accomplished by depressing the "AC" and "OFF" buttons simultaneously while the set is plugged into the line.

The November 1961 issue of the magazine *Electronics World* evaluated the performance of the product as follows:

> The manufacturer rates the 8-301 W at 30 microvolts sensitivity for a useable picture. In practice, sensitivity appeared quite commendable. In a medium-fringe area outside New York City, we were able to get useable to fairly good reception on all channels with the built-in monopole. In-city reception left nothing to be desired, with useful results obtained even inside a moving auto.
>
> In fact, not even picture wash out was serious in the shade of the car's interior on a sunny day. However, you can forget about daytime, outdoor use in such places as your favorite bathing beach. Indoor pictures were sharp, clear, bright, and viewable by a number of people at a reasonable distance.
>
> Adjustment was somewhat more critical than on modern tube sets, and some re-setting was required during the warm up period. Set too high, the "Gain" control results in horizontal pulling and other signs of overload; set too low, it lets the picture fall out of sync. Between these points, however, it has a broad range of adjustment that was found to be quite adequate.

SONY CORPORATION

On Oct. 1, 1945, 37-year-old Masaru Ibuka gathered around him several capable engineers, formerly of Nippon Sokuteiki Ltd. (Japan Instruments Corp.), manufacturer of precision instruments. With them he established in the bombed-out Shirokiya Building in downtown Tokyo a small laboratory on funds of $500, for research and manufacture of electronic communications and measuring instruments.

Mr. Ibuka was born in 1908. Early in his boyhood, he manifested an interest in and an ability for mechanics and engineering. While he was an engineering student at Waseda University, he invented a moving neon sign which was exhibited at the International Exposition in Paris in 1937.

Upon graduation from university, he joined the Photo Chemical Laboratory where he developed the first all Japan-made sound recording system for the motion picture. Subsequently, he went to work for Nippon Sokuteiki Ltd. as a research engineer. Later he became the managing director in charge of engineering and research at the age of 33. He continued in that position until the termination of the war when the demand for its products no longer existed, and the company was liquidated. Throughout this time, however, he continued his interest in inventions, and at the time of the organization of the new company, he held over forty domestic as well as foreign patents.

Though the company, called Tokyo Tsushin Kogyo Company, was organized, it had neither capital nor equipment. It initially had to manufacture a variety of simple products such as shortwave convertors to be attached to a regular radio and a primitive form of electric blanket. For the first month or two Mr. Ibuka had to draw upon his own meager savings to meet the payroll.

In spite of initial hardships, the new company began to make simple telecommunication equipment for the Ministry of Transportation and Communication. One of the major difficulties the company encountered was a tremendous shortage of vacuum tubes. These were almost impossible to obtain, and the small amount which were available either were sold at ridiculously high black-market prices or only to those customers who had enjoyed a long established business relationship with suppliers. Since the new company had neither the funds nor the connections, it had to develop an alternative for vacuum tubes. The group combined a carbon microphone and a tuning fork and developed a non-vacuum tube oscillator. Utilizing this, the company started to develop many non-tube communication pieces of equipment and took orders and sold to various government agencies such as the National Railways Corp. and the Japan Telegraph and Telephone Corp. On May 7, 1946, the firm was reorganized under the name of Tokyo Tsushin Kogyo (Tokyo Communications Industrial), with a capital of ¥ 190,000.

About this time "NHK"—the Japanese National Broadcasting System —decided to renew all its broadcasting equipment and introduce a new American concept. NHK chose Mr. Ibuka's company to build the completely new equipment because of its superior technical skill. The reinstallation work was performed speedily and efficiently, in spite of the dire shortage of materials, through the concerted efforts of a highly cohesive engineering group.

In 1948 Mr. Ibuka accidentally saw a wire recorder for the first time in his life. This caught his fancy. Though he knew virtually nothing of its market, he intuitively felt that this was the product that the firm should take on and improve by applying its engineering know-how. During the next year and a half, all the members of the group exerted a strong effort to develop magnetic recording tapes and tape recorders. In 1950, the company released its first tape recorder with the trade name "Tapecorder."

The brand name became a synonym for the magnetic tape recorder in Japan. The sales of tape recorders jumped from 200 units in 1950 to 2,000 units and 4,000 units in 1951 and 1952 respectively. The introduction of tape recorders substantially changed the nature of the company and its relative success solidified its financial foundation.

In March 1952, Mr. Ibuka went to the United States for the first time, with two objectives in mind. The first was to sound out the potential market in the United States for further improved models of tape recorders and the second was to learn as much as possible of a radically new development in electronics—transistors. Upon his return, Ibuka and his group decided to take transistor development as their next aim, because they firmly believed the transistor to be the future of the electronics industry. They felt also that it could be developed only by the close cooperation between scientists and engineers which was the main asset of the company.

At that time, transistor application was limited mostly to audio use in low-frequency equipment. Few even thought of trying it in the radio field. However, Ibuka made a decision to concentrate all the efforts of the group to develop transistors for radio use. In August 1953, the company entered into a transistor technical-aid contract with Western Electric Co. to become Japan's first transistor patent licensee.

In 1955, the company was successful in manufacturing commercially Japan's first domestically-produced transistors. In August of the same year, the company began manufacturing transistors for high-frequency radio use as well as all-transistor, battery-operated radios. In the same month, the trading regulatory committee of the Tokyo Securities Brokers' Association designated the company's stock for over-the-counter trading. Capital at that time was ¥. 100 million.

In April 1957, the world's first pocket-size transistor radio was introduced to the market under the brand name of Sony. It created an entirely new market in radios. The concept of radios as a piece of household furniture was completely changed with the advent of the pocket-size set. A radio became a normal possession for many more people. The new concept caused an explosion in the radio market.

With this radio, the name "Sony" became so well-known throughout the world that the company changed its name from Tokyo Tsushin Kogyo Co. to Sony Corporation on January 1, 1958.

In the field of Semiconductor engineering, Sony scientists and engigeers intensified their efforts to develop new high-frequency transistor and semiconductor devices. In 1957, in the Sony semiconductor laboratory, scientist Dr. Esaki found an entirely new phenomenon and invented a new diode—the Esaki diode.

The tunnel or Esaki diode is a revolutionary semiconductor device. Although it can perform many of the functions of conventional units, its principles of operation are entirely different from the operating principles of other semiconductor devices and vacuum tubes. It is much cheaper and simpler to manufacture than the transistor, and it is free from any effect of nuclear radiation and temperature and can operate at a very high frequency. Its fast switching speed is essential to computers and future electronic devices. The Esaki tunnel diode has been proclaimed as the greatest invention since the transistor in the electronics world.

In 1958 with the successful development of the very-high-frequency transistor, Sony marketed the first all transistor FM/AM radio. Subsequently, further advancement in the very-high-frequency transistor made it possible for Sony to release on the market the first all-transistor direct-view portable TV.

The management of Sony attributed this phenomenal growth to what it called Sony spirit—always pioneer, develop new products and create new work most suitable for the Japanese people. It was widely believed among the Japanese business leaders that this philosophy was mainly responsible for Sony's phenomenal growth and its development of new and unique products. Sony had many firsts both in the Japanese and the world market. Major significant developments were as follows:

First in Japan:		
	Magnetic recording tape	1949
	Tape recorder	1950
	Transistor	1954
	All-transistor radio	1955
First in the world:		
	Pocket-size transistor radio	1957
	All-transistor FM/AM radio	1958
	All-transistorized portable T.V.	1961

In order to cope with rapid expansion of the company, an 8-story, 505,000 square ft. building including a new transistor-T.V. factory and main administration offices was to be completed in March 1962. In Atsugi, 30 miles south of Tokyo, the company had just completed a new transistor mass-production plant and in Yokohama, a Basic Research Institute was also established. The Sendai factory which was built in 1954 was expanded to double its capacity.

Since it had been a very important basic policy of the company from its inception constantly to conduct research in unexplored fields and develop new products, and to avoid being involved in heavy competition with other companies in manufacturing and selling already existing products, the company put increasing emphasis on research and development.

Expenditure for research and development in 1961 amounted to $2.3 million or 4.5% of net sales. In early 1962 it had more than 500 graduate engineers and scientists who were involved in R & D. The research effort was divided into four areas: basic research and development of semiconductors, new product development, and improvement and modification of existing products.

Sony's marketing problem was said to be quite unique in Japan. It was believed that Sony and one or two other new firms brought a new concept of marketing to the Japanese consumer-electronics market and offered a challenge to more conservative giants in the industry.

The Sony marketing program, according to its marketing director, was based upon the philosophy that (1) the products must have superior and unique features which would satisfy either the apparent or latent wants of consumers, (2) the market can be created and developed through active sales promotion. This was contrary to the prevalent belief among the Japanese industrial giants that the market was only of a given and relatively fixed size. (3) In introducing a new product, the company does not push the product itself; rather, it tries to change through sales promotions the existing concept consumers have about the product. Company officials felt that this was the only way a long sustained market for a new product could be created. This concept was well exemplified in the introduction of transistor radios when the company was successful in changing the long held attitude of a radio as largely a household item to that of an individualized accessory.

Sony Trading Co., a wholly owned subsidiary of Sony Corporation, handled the marketing of all Sony products with regional offices in Tokyo, Osaka, Nagoya, Fukuoka, Sapporo, Hiroshima, and Sendai. It had over 10,000 retail outlets and a number of service stations throughout Japan.

SONY'S INTERNATIONAL OPERATIONS

Shortly after the company brought out its transistor radios in Japan, Mr. Morita went to the United States to develop the U.S. market for transistor radios. During this trip, a large U.S. distributor offered to purchase a minimum of 10,000 units a year, providing that it could sell the product under its own brand. Though the offer at that time was extremely attractive to the company, the management decided to market its products under its own brand—Sony—throughout the world. As a result, in early 1962, the Sony trade-mark was registered in 120 countries, and was believed by the company to be the most widely registered trade name in the world.

Export sales were only around $20,000 as late as 1956, but increased steadily. In 1961, the total export sales jumped to over $20,000,000, accounting for over 37% of total sales. The company sold its products virtually throughout the world except to countries in the Communist bloc.

The international division in the parent company was responsible for Sony's entire export sales and manufacturing abroad. It had a sales and service subsidiary in the U.S. and Switzerland to serve the American and European markets respectively. It also maintained a branch office in Hong Kong to serve the market in Southeast Asia. In 1959, the company accepted a favorable offer from the Irish Government as a part of its industrialization program and established its first manufacturing subsidiary in Shannon, Ireland, making it the only Japanese electronics firm with a plant overseas. The Irish plant began as a small plant with a capital of £50,000 and about 100 employees. The company was managed by three personnel from Japan and the rest were local citizens. Operations in early 1962 were limited to the assembling of transistor radios with a monthly capacity of around 5,000 units. The company, however, planned to manufacture in the future transistor radios and tape recorders for the European market.

U.S. OPERATIONS

In 1956 the company began to export its transistor radios to the United States through a large Japanese export house. This sold the radios to American wholesalers, who in turn distributed them to about 1,500 retailers. Coverage was primarily limited to the East- and West-coast markets. Though sales had increased from year to year, the management was not completely satisfied with this arrangement for several reasons. First, because of its very nature, the export house was not well suited to Sony's concept of market development. Moreover, it had no control over either the types of retail outlets handling the product or their selling methods. There were disturbing reports of price cutting and irresponsible action on the part of some retailers.

Management believed that these factors were detrimental to the healthy development of the company in the United States and, in February 1960, it established a sales and service subsidiary, Sony Corporation of America with its home office in New York City. The company was incorporated in the United States as a wholly owned subsidiary of the parent company with Mr. Ibuka as chairman of the board and Mr. Morita as its president. Though the executive vice president and financial manager were Japanese, the rest of the management positions were filled by American citizens. Mr. Morita took special pains to select capable men for the two key positions, marketing manager and sales manager. Both of these men were brought to Sony's home office in Tokyo for an intensive three-week training and orientation on Sony's marketing concept.

The initial objectives of the company were to establish the prestige of Sony products and the quality image of the company as one of the major technological leaders in the electronics industry. The company had to achieve this goal with a relatively small amount of money. First it took a series of advertisements in such national magazines as *Life, Newsweek, Esquire,* and *The New Yorker,* taking the institutional approach of hammering the themes of "Sony means quality" and "research makes the difference."

It also sought to evaluate each of the existing retail outlets in terms of the high quality standard that the company wished to achieve. As a result of this survey, the company discontinued some outlets, particularly discount houses, while others withdrew voluntarily because of the company's strong objection to price cutting. It sought to select those outlets which were helpful in developing the desired image. Though retail outlets were not given exclusive territory, they were provided with strong sales support in the forms of sales aids, sales catalogs, point-of-sales display, display shelves, cooperative advertising, sales training, and national advertising in printed media.

The management also selected salesmen carefully, for it knew that the personal relationship between salesmen and dealers usually played an important role in projecting the right image of the company to ultimate consumers. It selected its salesmen from those with a technical background and some sales experience. They worked on a base salary plus commission and reported to a district sales manager who in turn was responsible to a regional manager.

In early 1962, the company maintained its branch offices in Chicago, Los Angeles, San Francisco, and Dallas. It also had over 80 service stations throughout the country. In late 1961, the company had opened a show room on Fifth Avenue, New York City to display its products. The sales force increased to over 120 salesmen. With the exception of the New York and Chicago markets, where it sold direct to retailers, the company used wholesalers. Margins for wholesalers and retailers were 15% on dealer's cost and 33% on retail price respectively, plus quantity discount. The company had over 10,000 retailers carrying its products in the United States and it still planned to increase the number of outlets.

At the end of the first year's operation as a wholly owned subsidiary, the company recorded total sales of $3.5 million, an over $1 million increase from the 1959 result. In 1961 the sales reached over $6.5 million.

Sales were approximately 40% from the Eastern States, 25% from the 11 Western States, 13% from the Greater Chicago market, 12% from the South and 10% from the Midwestern States. The company was doing better than the national average of consumer electronics products sales on both coasts but failed to measure up to it in the South and Midwest.

Company officials attributed Sony's apparent success in the U.S. market to three factors. First, high-quality products with unique features have frequently sold themselves through word-of-mouth. Moreover the product's unique qualities made promotions more effective per dollar expenditure. Secondly, the brand name Sony was easy to pronounce and remember. Finally, the emphasis upon quality and servicing instead of price had helped to erase much of the American consumer's resistance to the purchase of Japanese products.

Against this background, the company was considering the advisability of introducing its new product to the U.S. market. The television set had been introduced to the Japanese market at a price of ¥65,000 ($178) about a month earlier, and it had stirred up much interest among dealers and the general public. However, one month of experience, though favorable, was believed to be too short to make useful generalizations as to the set's future sales trends. The monthly production capacity had been around 10,000 units, but in the very near future it was to be increased to 30,000 units.

The opinions of the management were sharply divided on this issue. Those who were in favor of immediate introduction pointed out that Sony could easily change the concept of television sets from that of their being a household item to one which regarded them as an individual, portable unit, thus opening up the entire new market as it had done with radios.

Now that the company had had some experience with radios and had established its prestige image in the minds of the American consumers, the job should be easier than that required of radio some years previously. The group also maintained that, since the product was comparatively expensive, the affluent U.S. market offered the best prospect for sustained sales and the company should be the first to skim this rich market. Inasmuch as other Japanese and U.S. firms were in the process of developing a similar product, it was doubtful that the company could maintain its technological leadership indefinitely. Therefore, immediate introduction seemed crucial. Besides, being first again would further reinforce Sony's image as a technological leader of the world electronics industry.

The fact that the sales of transistor radios—the company's major product—were somewhat lagging at this time was another major reason for immediately introducing transistorized television sets. The drop in the sales of transistor radios was primarily due to rigid export restrictions and increasingly keener competition from both U.S. and Japanese firms. The group emphasized that the company should try to boost its sagging sales by taking full advantage of the new product.

Those who were against immediate introduction pointed out the essential difference in the nature of the job required to change the concept of radio and that of television sets. The latter was substantially more expensive, and consumers were hesitant to buy small-screen sets with batteries. The latter point was substantiated by the report from several prominent New York City Sony dealers. They claimed that small-screen sets had never sold well to American consumers, and more than one company looked back with regret to production runs of small-size screen sets which fell far below the most pessimistic sales expectation. One dealer mentioned the experience of one major manufacturer who tried out 8-inch sets and, to his dismay, found that his customers seemed to be largely relatives who were looking for a different present for the graduates who had everything. Sales stopped there and the company soon discontinued its production. Dealers also pointed out that the consumers were fearful of battery-operated sets, because the actual life of batteries often proved to be far less than expected. For these reasons, the group maintained that the promotional job required to sell the television set would be substantially more expensive and difficult than with radios. They were doubtful if the company was prepared to go all out for the necessary expensive sales promotion, and claimed that the company's limited resources could probably be better used to promote transistor radios at this time.

Another factor the company had to consider was that there had been increasing feeling among some leaders of the Japanese electronics industry and government officials that Japan should avoid any protectionist outcry in the U.S. in order to assure healthy long-run growth in the U.S. market. This could be done rapidly by selling components to U.S. corporations rather than by exporting finished products to be resold under the Japanese brand names. Though the prevalence of this opinion was difficult to assess at this time, it was, nevertheless, a factor to be considered in the decision.

Mr. Suzuki, manager of the international division, was asked by the president to evaluate each of the points presented in the light of his knowledge of the U.S. market. In this process, Mr. Suzuki came to the conclusion that the first step was to get some rough idea of the potential U.S. market for the new product. To base his estimate, he had his assistant gather some pertinent data on the consumer-electronics market available from secondary sources in Japan. The data are presented in the appendix.

QUESTIONS

1. What approach should Mr. Suzuki use in evaluating the points expressed by the two groups? What additional information would he need to evaluate them?

2. How should Mr. Suzuki go about estimating the potential market for the product? Does the information presented in Appendix A answer the crucial question?
3. Should the company introduce the product at this time?

APPENDIX

CONSUMER-ELECTRONICS MARKET IN THE U.S.

Growing Market

Consumer electronics is likely to show less increase in the next five years, but these are likely to be less spectacular than other segments of our industry. Last year's total was $2.67 billion. This year's will be about $2.7 billion. By 1965 the consumer market should be $2.9 billion and by 1970 it should grow to $4 billion. In television receivers, radios and phonographs, the shift in emphasis will be towards new developments—color and stereo in radios and phonographs. Black-and-white receivers, which will reach $1,030 million by the end of this year, may decline to $1,000 million by 1965. Filling the gap, however, could be an increase in color TV receivers, with a possible gain of $25 million this year over last year's $75 million, and a climb to perhaps $140 million by 1965. In a-m radio there will be a drop off over the next five years, countered by a rise in the market for f-m receivers, particularly those equipped for stereo. Monaural phonographs should remain constant, while stereo record players will surely show at least moderate increase.

The population explosion and the rise in educational levels are bringing the high levels of purchasing power. Consumer desires are exploited to the point where they are confused with consumer needs, so that what was once considered a luxury item is, or will be, thought of as a necessity. A prime example is the television set, once a status symbol for the privileged few, and now the major source of entertainment.

But where are those increasing consumer dollars going? Television receiver sales, representing 40% of the consumer-electronics market, have presently leveled off at a little over 6 million sets a year. Sales of phonographs and radios, each taking about 20% of the consumer market, declined somewhat last year as compared with 1960. A big surge may come in color TV, now that many set makers are represented in the market. Promising opportunities exist in the non-entertainment home-electronics field, such as in electronic ovens, air purifiers and ionizers, and thermoelectric refrigerators and water coolers.

Black-White Television

Although 88% of U.S. homes have at least one TV set, and this figure may be close to the ultimate saturation percentage, the 1961 TV sales should be over 6.2 million sets, an increase over 1960 (5.9 million), 1959 (5.7 million) and 1958 (5.1 million). Six and four-tenths million receivers should be sold every year for at least the next ten years, despite the approach of saturation.

The future market will be largely replacements and extra sets. In 1959 the percentage of replacement sets to total sets in use exceeded substantially, for the first time, the percentage of sets to new TV homes. Last year replacement sets totaled 3.8 million, or 6.8 percent of the total sets bought, while sets for new TV homes amounted to 1.1 million, or two percent of the 55.6 million sets in use at the beginning of the year.

Optimistic estimates place the yearly TV set sales at 8.5 to 9 million between 1962 and 1970, based on the population increase and 14% replacement rate.

While the 19- and 23-inch picture tubes may dominate the black-and-white TV market in 1962, Admiral is stressing the 24- and 27-inch receivers. Sylvania considers the 23-incher to be an attractive size but says there is a trend toward the larger sizes, particularly the 27-inch.

Although many purchasers stress portability of a TV set when buying one, especially an extra one, the set really doesn't get moved around in the home. Usually it remains in the bedroom which is coming up fast as the most likely location of the second set.

Many U.S. manufacturers feel that battery-powered portable TV sets are impractical at present. Prices are high, and the picture size small for people who have become accustomed to at least a 19-inch screen.

Color Television

A dozen companies are offering color TV sets this winter. RCA, Packard-Bell, Emerson-Dumont, Magnavox, Admiral, Olympic, Sears, and Philco have been joined this winter by Zenith, General Electric, and Sylvania. Westinghouse and Motorola both sold color TV receivers from 1955 through 1957, but neither has revealed plans for reentering the field at present.

Color sets are selling better than last year, and estimates by top industry people for this year's sales range from 250,000 to 500,000 with one guess of 750,000. The 1961 sales are expected to add up to 150,000.

Increased sales this season are partly due to more color programming. In the half-dozen largest U.S. cities, about 20 to 40 hours of color are broadcast weekly.

Prices of many color TV receivers are in the $600 to $700 range. The Sears Roebuck consolette lists for $450.

Hopes were once high for Paramount's single-gun Lawrence tube to lower prices, but a Lawrence-tube set, when and if it is finally perfected, will cost, according to Paramount, about $400 on a mass-production basis of half a million sets a year.

Last fall a Japanese company brought out a $300 color TV set, using two single-gun tubes, and based on the two-color theory developed by Polaroid's Edwing H. Land. The theory was also substantiated mathematically by Huseyin Yilmaz of Sylvania.